D0938618

CALIFORNIA
HOME COOKING

Also by Michele Anna Jordan

CALIFORNIA
HOME COOKING

American Cooking
in the California Style

Michele Anna Jordan

THE HARVARD COMMON PRESS
BOSTON, MASSACHUSETTS

. . . .

THE HARVARD COMMON PRESS
535 Albany Street
Boston, Massachusetts 02118

Copyright © 1997 by Michele Anna Jordan
Illustrations copyright © 1997 by Melissa Sweet

Printed in the United States of America
Printed on acid-free paper

Library of Congress Cataloging-in-Publication Data

Jordan, Michele Anna.
California home cooking : American cooking in the California style / Michele Anna Jordan.
p. cm.
Includes bibliographical references and index.
ISBN 1-55832-118-7 (alk. paper). — ISBN 1-55832-119-5 (pbk.: alk paper)
1. Cookery, American—California style. 2. Cookery—
California.
I. Title.
TX715.3.C34J67 1997   97-31827
641.59794—dc21

Special bulk-order discounts are available on this and other Harvard Common Press books. Companies and organizations may purchase books for premiums or resale, or may arrange a custom edition, by contacting the Marketing Director at the address above.

Cover and text illustrations by Melissa Sweet
Cover and text design by Kathleen Herlihy-Paoli, Inkstone Design

10 9 8 7 6 5 4 3 2 1

For John, Nancy, Annie, and Andrew

For David Browne

and

For Ginny Stanford

CONTENTS

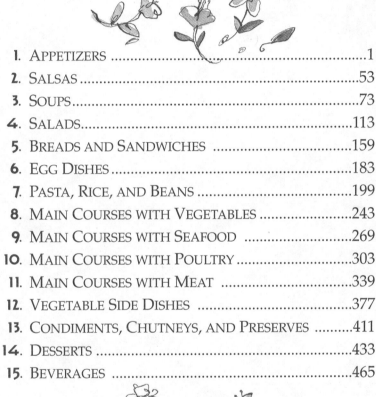

ACKNOWLEDGMENTS

"Well, you have to eat," my friend John Kramer said more times than I can count. "Come on over."

"Please come to dinner. We really want to see you," Annie, a delightful, beautiful, and talented young teenager would urge on my answering machine when I was attempting to hide.

But shouldn't I still be working? No, John was right, I did have to eat. I would force myself, fatigued and guilty, to go.

I'd drag myself away from my computer and away from the manuscript for *California Home Cooking* that grew, in its most unwieldy period, to over a thousand pages. I'd make the short drive to the beautiful Tuscan-style home where John, his wife, Nancy Dobbs, and their two children, Annie and Andrew, welcomed me with just the right amount of sympathy, with endlessly entertaining stories, and with intelligent conversation. Andrew, one of the most amazing young humans I've ever had the pleasure to know, made me tiny clay tacos and charmed me with his adventurous palate. We've peeled a lot of garlic together, this enchanting six year old and I.

Most nights, I would help John in the kitchen as we cooked with garlic, tomatoes, and green beans from their garden, pasta from the pantry, clams from the coast

nearby. Andrew picked little lettuces for salad and strawberries for dessert. John and Nancy were always there with more pinot noir whenever my glass was empty. During the comet Hale-Bopp's appearance, they got out the telescope, and when they abandoned me for a three-week vacation in Portugal—I had to decline their invitation to join them, of course, deadlines being what they are—they returned with a remarkable gift, a rare bottle of that forbidden aperitif, absinthe. That I've made it through the last couple of years has had a great deal to do with their warmth and friendship. This is what California home cooking really is about: the pleasure of sharing it with close friends.

David Browne has played an enormously important role in my life, urging me to take difficult steps, teaching me to be brave, and helping me to achieve distance when necessary and to establish closeness when I'd rather run in the opposite direction. For more years than I can say, he has been a kind and knowledgeable shepherd as I've struggled to grow into myself. Thank you so much, David.

To Ginny Stanford: What a year, eh? Ginny has seen me through each of the nine books I've written so far and has never wavered in her faith and belief in me. She listens to my laments with patience, and reads draft after draft after draft of a single essay. And every time I think I won't make it through some new hell—a pugnacious copyeditor, the latest broken heart, an IRS audit—she'll present a convincing argument not only about why I will but why I'll be glad I did. Her prodigious appetite is a great asset to a food writer, and that she'll gossip about virtually anything at a moment's notice is almost more than I could have hoped for in a best friend. I'm very glad Ginny, who was born in Missouri, heard the siren song of California.

Shortly after I began working on *California Home Cooking*, I got a phone call from my old friend Scott Murray, at the time general manager of KRCB-FM, the new National Public Radio affiliate in Sonoma County. He asked me to do a show about food, wine, and agriculture, and it wasn't long before "Mouthful with Michele Anna Jordan" aired for the first time. That was over two years ago. Several people have been instrumental in making "Mouthful" a reality: Robin Pressman, the station's talented and dedicated program director; my friend Nancy Dobbs, president of the station; Evelyn Anderson, who produced and engineered during the show's first year; and Rob Cole, my perverse musical muse, who provides all manner of assistance and inspiration. More than anyone else, Albert Casselhoff, who loves radio as much as I do, has shared his talent, technical expertise, and inspiration. As engineer, he's worked to give the show the shape and sound I've wanted. He also brings a sensitive palate and intelligent curiosity to the show. Recently, Albert has forced me to overcome my fear of

electronics, so that I now do what I've wanted to do since I was a kid—play music on the radio, proof indeed that dreams do come true. Thank you, Albert.

Doe Coover is a wonderful agent, insightful, intuitive, hard-working, and supportive. Had it not been for a chance meeting between us in Nancy Harmon Jenkins's rental car, I wouldn't have known about this book until I saw it on a store shelf, with someone else's name on the cover. But in our brief conversation, Doe realized quickly that I've longed to explore the culinary traditions and personalities of my home state. Writing this book allowed me to do so and to make invaluable connections for future research. Thank you, Doe. I will be forever grateful.

My editor at the Harvard Common Press, Dan Rosenberg, is smart, talented, and possessed of a delightfully perverse sense of humor. I've learned a tremendous amount working with him.

As I worked on this book, I met wonderful, generous, and fascinating people, too many to thank by name here: farmers, cheesemakers, farmers' market managers, librarians, newspaper food editors, and many wonderful home cooks, who provided information, tips, inspiration, and recipes along the way. I couldn't have written this book without them. I offer a special thank you to Pat Keats of the California Historical Library, who was patient, helpful, and understanding as I plumbed the depths of their archives.

Thank you to Betty Ellsworth, for continuing to interpret my recipes with talent and an intuitive sense of what I want, often realizing it before I do, and for being a good friend during difficult times. To my assistant of many years, Lesa Tanner, thank you for your enthusiasm and unwavering support, your calm efficiency, your good sense, and for that first bottle of absinthe, perhaps the biggest surprise I have ever received.

Finally, thank you to my colleagues, family, and friends, new and old, who are, after all, the point of all this hard work: my lovely daughters, Gina and Nicolle, who never fail to amaze and delight me; my dear friends John Boland and James Carroll; Amy Rennert, my former editor at *San Francisco Focus*, who assigned the story, about Alice Waters and Chez Panisse, for which I won a James Beard Journalism Award; Anne Dickerson, my current editor at *San Francisco* magazine; Ruth Lively of *Kitchen Garden* magazine; Diane Holt and Tim Fish of the Santa Rosa *Press Democrat*; Steve Garner of KSRO-AM, who is very much an on-air role model; Ridgely Evers and Colleen McGlynn; Bonnie Sheerin; Monica Merga; Ana de Shore; Jon, Michel, Griffin, and Jordan Stong; Jerry and Patty Hertz; Peter Cooper and Robin Pressman; Miriam Silver; Sara Peyton; David Siracusa; Mary and Guy Duryee; Gerald and Cameron Hirogoyen; Greil and Jenny Marcus; the handsome and charming Sid Nappi; and Chris Isaak, one of my favorite dinner companions.

INTRODUCTION

"California home cooking," I said to nearly everyone I saw as I was writing this book, "What do you think?"

A farmer from Healdsburg laughed. "You mean take-out pizza, don't you?" he asked, as he served me a lunch of fresh-smoked salmon and sauvignon blanc from a nearby winery.

"There is such a thing?" several friends asked skeptically, as we lingered around my kitchen table over mesclun salads dressed with raspberry vinaigrette and croutons slathered with fresh goat cheese.

"No, there is definitely not such a thing," a colleague insisted adamantly, as we slurped raw oysters topped with pineapple salsa, the waters of Tomales Bay slapping the nearby shore.

Over the last two decades, California cuisine has been heralded as the latest thing, condemned as a precious contrivance, dismissed as out of fashion, and credited with transforming the way we all eat. It's all true. But each declaration is a small part of a complex and continuing conversation. It is a conversation at once about California home cooking—what we Californians do in our eleven million home kitchens—and California cuisine—what is done in our restaurants. It's about what each is, or whether they exist at all,

and it's about who invented them and whether they will survive.

The lines between California cuisine and California home cooking are blurred. Since the gourmet revolution of the 1970s, much of the focus has been on the former, fueled in part by the obsession with celebrity chefs. In fact, each has influenced the other in a continual cross-pollination. Today, you no longer can understand one without the other.

As a California native and a cook by both inclination and profession, I set out to write this book already armed with a strong sense of where my own cooking fit into the larger tradition. As I attempted to sort out what was authentic and enduring from what would vanish as a misguided trend, I relied primarily upon my own instincts, which served me well. California cooking and California cuisine both proved to be very much what I always had thought they were: casual styles of cooking that unite several cuisines—most importantly, Spanish, Mexican, and Italian—and, making abundant use of California's year-round harvest of high-quality produce, transform them into something unique and original. Within this broad definition there is room for every nuance, for tremendous creativity, and for the influences of the dozens of immigrant groups who have left their imprint on California home cooking since the state's earliest days.

This is not to say I did not make new discoveries. I did, and some of them were startling to me. I scoured archives, sorted through boxes of yellowed newspaper clippings from the turn of the century, unearthed early menus, and read the handwritten notes of young brides in the margins of old cookbooks. In these early documents I found recipes that called for chipotles, fresh pasta, raspberry vinegar, polenta, nopales, dried tomatoes, avocados, and every kind of fresh herb. I found sources that called for the use of California and European wine, both in recipes and for the table, in ways we would call knowledgeable and sophisticated today. Certainly, these ingredients were presented in a different context from what we now expect, and many appeared alongside canned mushroom soup, Jell-O, tiny marshmallows, white sauces thick with flour, and similar ingredients from previous eras. Yet it became clear as I read recipe after recipe that many so-called new ingredients are really rediscoveries of foods that have been in California's pantry for a long time.

California home cooking, like California cuisine, is a style of cooking shaped by many overlapping influences, including the land itself, the dearness of water, the early European settlers and the later immigrants from every continent, the rise of the automobile, the growth of corporate agriculture, and, of course, the changing eating habits of Americans. All of these elements have been distilled into a distinctive culinary style that had its genesis in the state's ear-

liest days and continues to evolve.

California home cooking currently is undergoing a period of significant change, as Asian cuisines, long established within the state's ethnic communities, enter the mainstream. Fifteen years ago, a typical home kitchen in California was likely to be stocked with pasta, olive oil, fruit vinegars, hot sauce, dried chiles, goat cheese, dried tomatoes, chutneys, and soy sauce. But if your pantry also included fish sauce, wasabi, sesame oil, oyster sauce, soba noodles, chile paste, and nori seaweed, your friends might be reluctant to invite you to dinner. "Oh, you're such a gourmet," they would say, "I would be so intimidated to cook for you." Thankfully, that's changing. Asian ingredients have taken their rightful place in the California home pantry and now are available in most supermarkets throughout the state.

What is called California cuisine also is not a static tradition. Unlike classical French cuisine, the techniques, conventions, and vocabulary of which were refined and codified long ago, California cuisine is a newer invention and one that is still evolving. It is a contemporary creation, the product of several influences that converged in the early 1970s at a small Berkeley restaurant, Chez Panisse, and soon spread throughout the state and the country. But to look only to this recent period is to miss some of the most important elements in the development of cooking and eating in the Golden State.

Land

The foundation of both formal California cuisine and informal California home cooking is the land itself. The geography of California is immensely diverse, encompassing 155,973 square miles of land and 850 miles of ocean coast. The state passes through ten degrees of latitude. It encompasses the highest point in the contiguous United States, Mt. Whitney, at 14,494 feet, and the lowest, at Badwater in Death Valley, 282 feet below sea level and one of the hottest, driest places on the planet. Along much of the state's eastern border is the Sierra Nevada mountain range, the state's rugged backbone. Active and dormant volcanoes and an infamous network of earthquake faults ring the state.

Stretching north and south for four hundred and fifty miles is California's verdant heart, the great Central Valley, one of the most productive agricultural regions in the world. The valley is sheltered on all sides, by the Klamath Mountains to the north, the southern Cascades to the northeast, the Sierra Nevadas along the east, the Tehachapi Mountains and the Transverse Range to the south, the Southern Coast Range to the south and southwest, and the Coast Range along the western border. The Central Valley's twenty-five thousand square miles encompass the Anderson Valley and Sacramento Valley in the north and the San Joaquin Valley in the south. Enormous farms in the Central Valley grow most of California's major crops, including

barley, beans, tree fruit, nuts, cauliflower, broccoli, melons, carrots, olives, table grapes, sugar beets, and other fruit and vegetables. There is extensive cotton farming, and there are large cattle ranches and poultry and dairy farms. Very few crops—cranberries are one, hazelnuts another—fail to find a welcoming home somewhere in the California landscape. In 1996, cash receipts from farming reached nearly $23.4 billion, for a net farm income of almost $5.5 billion.

The Coast Range and smaller systems like the Mayacamas Mountains, which divide the Sonoma and Napa valleys, shelter fertile inland valleys, many close enough to the ocean to be caressed by fog and sea breezes. In these valleys, rich alluvial soils and hundreds of microclimates support a huge variety of agriculture, from the apples, pears, and marijuana of the north coast to the artichokes, lettuce, and strawberries of the Monterey area and the productive truck farms of southern California. These valleys also contain some of the finest viticultural acreage in the world, as the increasing recognition of the quality of our wines attests. This is where the olive oil renaissance is under way, too, and where you'll find small-scale family farms raising the specialty crops that have become so important in California cooking. Organic dairy farms and cattle ranches, factories for handcrafted cheeses, farms with small flocks of quail, duck, and free-range chicken, orchards of apricots grown for eating fresh rather than for canning and drying, and organically grown heirloom vegetables thrive in these valleys. Many of these small farms and ranches are a short drive from farmers' markets and urban restaurants, the ideal outlets for these carefully tended foods.

There is more to California than its long growing seasons and opulent harvests. Though the land is bathed in sunshine much of the year, there usually is plenty of rain in the winter months. Yet even in a normal year, the dry season might stretch from April to November, and, during a drought cycle, there can be years of little rainfall. The state's reservoirs sink dangerously low. Everything and everyone seems parched and exhausted, stretched thin and brittle.

Droughts in 1862 and again in 1865 killed thousands of cattle. Today, serious agricultural losses from droughts are mitigated by the vast water storage and delivery system built in the twentieth century. But still nearly everyone suffers: Lawns dry up, home gardeners lose their backyard crops, pipes creak and shudder, showers become precious. If it's a long drought, families take to eating their daily meals on paper plates, with dishes, and the washing they require, reserved for special occasions.

Droughts are not the only specter. In spite of California's reputation as an idyllic Eden—the state is named after a fictitious earthly paradise in the sixteenth-century Spanish romance *Las Sergas de Esplandían*—nature is frequently brutal. As blessed as California is with fertile soil and temperate climate, there are omnipresent threats, from droughts to earthquakes, wildfires, mudslides, and floods.

Before Europeans settled in the state, the land needed no human intervention to provide its natural harvest, ready for the taking. When the first settlers arrived in 1769 during the Sacred Expedition, so-called because its purpose was to bring Christianity to Native Americans, they encountered people living well on fish and shellfish from rivers, lakes, and ocean, on small and large game that roamed the land, on birds that nested in the wetlands, and on scores of wild plants, from seaweeds, onions, and mushrooms to grapes, berries, and acorns, that grew everywhere. A few tribes practiced limited farming, such as the Mohave and Yuma Indians, who planted corn and beans in the flood plain of the lower Colorado River, but most native Californians were hunter-gatherers who lived in comfortable harmony with the land.

Europeans

The Spanish missionaries, led by Father Junípero Serra and Father Juan Crespí, brought agriculture. They planted olives, grapes, nuts, wheat, barley, corn, beans, tomatoes, chiles, pomegranates, walnuts, and more. They brought livestock and taught the Native Americans to tend the herds and flocks. The Spanish padres made the state's first wine and pressed its first olive oil.

Twenty-one missions were established during the Spanish period, which lasted for sixty-five years. Eventually the missions were secularized and the land sold, primarily to Mexican aristocrats who operated their vast holdings, called ranchos, like feudal fiefdoms.

Patio living in the California of the 1950s revived the popularity of grilling, but during the days of the ranchos the barbecue already was a common form of celebration. Goat, lamb, and beef were cooked over open fires and in huge pits in the ground, and were served with a sauce, called *sarsa*, of diced tomatoes, chiles, cilantro, and onions. Chiles were grown in the rancho gardens and hung in the sun to dry. In the fall, when the pigs were killed, the rancheros used the dried chiles to make chorizo, a spicy pork sausage. Dried corn was ground to make tortillas and tamales. These ingredients and techniques retain an important place in contemporary California cooking.

After Mexico gained its freedom from the Spanish crown, California came under its rule. From 1822 until the Bear Flag Revolt in the summer of 1846 and the subsequent war with Mexico, California belonged to its southern neighbor. In February of 1848 the war ended and, in the Treaty of Guadalupe Hidalgo, California was ceded to the United States. In 1850, California became the thirty-first state of the Union.

Mexican populations declined until the turn of the twentieth century, with persons of Mexican ancestry encountering tremendous prejudice, a problem that continues to this day. Immigration, both legal and illegal, began in earnest during the Mexican Revolution, 1910 to 1915, and has never slowed. Today, Los Angeles has the second largest Mexican population in the world, second only to Mexico City.

It wasn't until the discovery of gold in 1848 that California's first major agricultural expansion began. Then, the rush was on and immigrants came in fast waves. Most came to build a new life. Some sought their fortune by any means necessary, and the land was overrun by treasure seekers, opportunists, and more than a few outlaws. If the previous period of development had been slow and steady, the next was frenetic. From 1846 to 1860, for example, the population of San Francisco swelled from less than five hundred to nearly sixty thousand, a phenomenon repeated all over the state. New residents needed food, clothing, shelter, furniture, and other provisions, and the miners who had struck it rich would pay any price. For entrepreneurs, there were fortunes to be made.

The Spanish had carefully woven the first threads in the vast tapestry of California. Now, immigrants from all over the world contributed their signature strands.

Beyond Spaniards and Mexicans, perhaps no group of immigrants has had as profound an influence as the Italians, who began arriving in large numbers with the Gold Rush. By 1920, only Mexicans had a greater population in California. Though they arrived with the Gold Rush, many Italian settlers turned to farming and fishing. Today, most Californians take the Italian heritage for granted, forgetting that it was Italians who planted the first artichokes and fennel, who planted grapes for table wine, and who grew tomatoes, zucchini, broccoli, and cauliflower. Many a nineteenth-century *nonna* dried her tomatoes in the California sun. We may not think of Italian food when we eat a fresh artichoke, grate dry jack cheese over our salad, or even toss pasta with garlic and olive oil, but in fact these very California foods have their roots in Italian soil. Italians established the first food processing and distribution industries in the state, crucial contributions to the success of California's agriculture.

French immigrants, too, came in response to the Gold Rush. By the mid-nineteenth century, there were many French settlers in Calaveras County, where they planted orchards of olives trees, mostly of the French variety picholine, that still thrive. For well over a century, French grape varieties have dominated California viticulture, a situation only now beginning to change, and only slightly at that. The French varietals, especially chardonnay, sauvignon blanc, pinot noir, merlot, and cabernet sauvignon, still reign.

Germans had an impact as well. Charles Krug and the Wente brothers were early winemakers; others established breweries. Claus Spreckels launched the sugar-refining industry, and it was a German botanist who first described what would become the California state flower, the golden poppy, now a protected plant that grows wild throughout the state. John Sutter, at whose mill gold was first discovered on January 24, 1848, though born in Switzerland, was of German ancestry.

In the 1880s, Armenians settled near Fresno in the San Joaquin Valley, raising melons, figs, pistachios, and raisins, as they had in their homelands. Spanish Basque immigrants became sheepherders and cheesemakers on the coast north of San Francisco. When they moved inland, some settled around Alturas in Modoc County, in the northeastern corner of the state, while others settled in Kern County, east of Los Angeles. In the mid-twentieth century, French Basques came, settling in San Francisco, Fresno, and the Bakersfield area of Kern County, where many became ranchers and sheep farmers.

Asians

Although thousands of Asians came to California in the mid-nineteenth century, they exercised less influence than Europeans did on the state's developing style of cooking. Chinese were exploited by landowners as cheap laborers in the mines and, later, on the Central Pacific Railroad. When the railroad was completed in 1869, many Chinese returned to their homeland. Others stayed, and turned to fishing and farming. Although they were successful, their success was undercut by rampant prejudice against them, a bias given the weight of law by state and federal legislation that limited Chinese immigration and prevented Asian ownership of land. There were thriving Chinese communities in nineteenth-century California, notably in Sacramento and the Sacramento Delta, San Francisco, Oakland, and Los Angeles, but it wouldn't be until much later that Asian cooking would have a substantial impact on the state's cuisine.

Japanese immigrants encountered similar kinds of discrimination, a fact that eclipsed their substantial talent as farmers and fishermen. In spite of many obstacles, productive farms in both northern and southern California were owned and operated by Japanese immigrants and their children. With the bombing of Pearl Harbor and World War II, the bias approached the flash point. In one of the state's most shameful periods, thousands of Japanese residents, many of them native-born U.S. citizens, were forced to abandon their lives and homes and move to relocation camps. Many, such as the Chino family of southern California, lost everything.

Twenty-one miles north of San Diego and five miles inland from the Pacific, near

the tony addresses of Rancho Santa Fe, is the Vegetable Shop, a tiny roadside stand run by the Chino family, who operate a fifty-six-acre farm here. Today, the farm is run by Tom Haryua Chino, his brothers, Koo and Fumio, and his sister, Kazumi. Their parents, Junzo Chino and Hatsuyo Noda, and their parents' families, had worked in agriculture in southern California since the early 1900s. Junzo and Hatsuyo were married in 1930, started a family, and, by the late 1930s, owned their own farm. When the family was sent to a relocation camp in Parker, Arizona, in 1942, they signed their land over to a trusted friend. Upon their return, they found, as did so many others in similar circumstances, that they had been betrayed. They had nothing. After years of working extremely hard for others, Junzo Chino finally was able to buy land, at first just an acre or two at a time, until he again had his own farm.

The Chinos and their remarkable produce came to play a role in the unfolding of contemporary California cuisine, when, in 1976, Alice Waters discovered them. Thereafter, their produce has set the standard for variety, taste, and quality among a new generation of family farmers. Today, the reputation of the Chinos' produce approaches the mythical. They grow an enormous diversity of produce, and they are obsessive about the quality of every last toothpick-thin green bean, every tiny leaf of Thai basil, every golden beet.

A Spirit of Rebellion

Through the first seven decades of the twentieth century, California was shaped by the same forces as the rest of the country: two world wars; the Great Depression; battles between labor unions and management; the birth of television and the growth of commercial air travel; and, within the home, the small-appliance revolution, including, for a short time, the all-electric kitchen.

More so than any other state did, California threw in its lot with the automobile, building a massive network of freeways, which in turn led to the rise of vast suburbs. The state's famous love affair with the automobile deeply influenced its eating habits. The diners of the 1930s and 1940s, the drive-ins of the 1950s and 1960s, and the fast-food establishments of the 1960s and since all served an increasingly mobile public. Shopping for food changed, too: The first modern supermarket in the U.S. was in Los Angeles, providing a model for one-stop, once-a-week, large-volume shopping, with an emphasis on nonperishable packaged foods.

Convenience foods, from canned and frozen vegetables to TV dinners, were embraced with the same gusto in California as they were elsewhere. Yet even during the lowest point in American cuisine, California was different. We may have eaten TV dinners like everyone else, but we often had a fresh steamed artichoke along-

side. Sandwiches might have been made with airy white bread, but they sometimes included slices of fresh avocado. Tacos were filled with ground beef, iceberg lettuce, and ketchup, but still they were tacos, made with corn tortillas. If you had a grandpa who gardened, tomatoes tasted good and you probably had plenty of fresh garlic, too.

By the middle of the century, family farming had evolved into corporate agribusiness. Farms were growing bigger, and farming practices were becoming more brutal to the land, water, and air. The planting of the same crops in the same acreage year after year was depleting soils. Pesticides and herbicides poisoned not only land and water but also the workers who sprayed the chemicals on or otherwise toiled in the fields.

Then came the Civil Rights Movement, the assassination of President Kennedy, Berkeley's Free Speech Movement, the Vietnam War, the Summer of Love. The forces that shook American society to its roots had a transformative effect on virtually everything, and that included agriculture, food, and cooking in the Golden State. If any single factor is responsible for the birth of California cuisine and the metamorphosis of California home cooking, it is the spirit of rebellion of this period. Everything changed.

The hippies of the era were not known for their culinary sophistication; in fact, closer to the opposite was true. There is a neo-Puritanism among many liberals and progressives, from antiwar protesters of the 1960s to their counterparts today, that scorns sensual pleasure, especially when it comes from good food and wine. On the other hand, by the late 1960s bland American foods were seen as products of the exploitation of, among others, the farmworkers of the Central Valley, represented by the National Farm Workers Association, founded by Cesar Chavez in 1962. To continue to eat as one's parent's had fed you was to embrace an oppressive political and social philosophy.

It was during this period of exuberant rebellion and heady optimism that Chez Panisse opened. When Chavez called for a boycott of iceberg lettuce in the mid-1970s—not, of course, because it lacked taste but because the growing of it oppressed the workers he represented—Alice Waters was right there with little mesclun salads. Something that might easily have been dismissed as a bourgeois indulgence was embraced as a morally superior alternative to corporate agriculture. That it tasted a lot better, too, certainly didn't hurt. Not every young California activist became a customer of Chez Panisse; indeed, most couldn't afford to, even when the prix fixe dinner was $3.95. But they played an important role, nonetheless.

At this time, young people were heading to the country, establishing communes, starting food co-ops, and beginning to garden. More than a few stayed, and those who were able to buy the land they lived on are doing very well twenty-five years later. This back-to-the-earth idealism was a perfect fit with Chez Panisse, and many of the purveyors who knocked on the restaurant's back door, baskets of edible flowers, bouquets of herbs, and hand-crafted cheeses in hand, were a product of this time. Although few talk about it, it is no secret that many of the best boutique farmers in California today perfected their techniques on illegal crops of marijuana.

Chez Panisse is the axis upon which contemporary California cuisine and California home cooking turn. I do not mean to overstate its importance, but the fact remains that much of our current culinary harvest, from our dedicated artisan farmers and the easy access we have to their products to our inspired young chefs and the career possibilities that exist for them, has its roots in Alice Waters's fertile imagination. You don't need to know any of this to cook in the California style; it is important only if you wish to understand its contemporary foundation.

California cooking has transformed not only its own but the nation's pantry. It's easy to forget just a decade or two after the fact that many of the things one expects to find in any supermarket anywhere, like mangos, lemon grass, fresh cilantro, raspberry vinegar, fish sauce, goat cheese, sundried tomatoes, and a wide variety of salsas and extra virgin olive oils, were first widely celebrated in the California cooking of the 1970s and 1980s. Even roasted garlic, a signature of Chez Panisse since its beginning, recently made its way into a canned soup, Campbell's Potato Soup with Roasted Garlic.

Grapes

I live in the Russian River Valley appellation, one of 130 American Viticultural Areas, or AVAs, in the United States, 80 of which are in California. Eleven of them are in Sonoma County, where I make my home. A California native, I ended up in the small town of Sebastopol, in the fog bank nine miles from the coast as the crow flies, for the simple reason that someone who liked my writing offered me a charming cottage at a decent rent. I have stayed for other reasons.

I am not what you would call a typical Californian; I lack certain credentials. I have red hair, not blonde, and the first time I dated a surfer was last year. I have never had a suntan. I prefer the Ramones to the Beach Boys, Puccini to the Grateful Dead. I think New Yorkers are the friendliest people I've ever met, Manhattan the most wonderful city. I am not a California chauvinist. I frequently threaten to move. But every time the possibility arises, I stay put.

Why? The answer has to do with the size of the sky from my deck, the big bowl of stars overhead I have come to love, the golden light of October, the scent of the sea that comes in with the fog, a perverse fascination with earthquakes, the farmer who grows the best white peaches I have ever tasted, and the fact that Olive, my little black cat, loves it here. Yet if I have to name one single reason, it may be this: the wine.

The Russian River Valley has some of the finest viticultural land anywhere, especially for my favorite grape, the hard-to-

tame pinot noir. I simply can't bear the thought of not having some of the best pinot noirs in the world practically outside my back door.

I can, I believe, trace my fondness for this land to a single person, to Joe Rochioli, a man I barely know, a tenacious yet unassuming visionary whose family settled, in the 1930s, as peasant farmers on Westside Road along the Russian River southwest of Healdsburg. In the 1960s, Joe's neighbors boasted about harvesting fifteen tons of grapes per acre, and they urged him to plant the same prolific gamay beaujolais clones they were growing. Was it stubbornness, pride, or true vision that led Joe to search out, instead, a French clone of pinot noir? He's not saying. Joe coddled his fruit before it was fashionable to do so, dropping hundreds of beautiful young clusters to the ground in order to decrease the yield to about two tons per acre, a practice only recently adopted in California (but understood in France for centuries) as essential for premium pinot noir. For years, Joe's attention to quality made little difference. He sold his fruit for less than $200 a ton and watched as the gorgeous grapes were dumped in with inferior fruit to be sold as California Burgundy. Today, Joe Rochioli's pinot noir grapes are among the region's most expensive (more than $2000 a ton) and sought-after fruit.

Russian River Valley resembles a square roughly in the center of Sonoma County. Nearly ten thousand of the ninety-six thousand acres in the valley are planted in grapes. Fog, which in the summer often lingers past noon, keeps temperatures

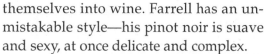

cooler than in valleys farther inland, and the alluvial soils encourage vigorous vine growth. The area's finest wines, from J. Rochioli Vineyards, Lynmar Winery, Williams-Selyem, and Gary Farrell (wine-maker at Davis Bynum Winery and for his own label as well), rarely make it very far; there simply isn't enough of them. Only the spectacular sparkling wines from Iron Horse Vineyards are available in such quantities that the rest of the country can readily enjoy them. How can I even think of leaving?

I confess to having fallen under the spell of Russian River Valley's pinot noirs, particularly those from Gary Farrell, one of a handful of winemakers who buys grapes from the Allen Vineyard, forty acres planted and maintained by Joe Rochioli and one of the best vineyards in the state. Farrell, whose wines regularly win awards, is modest and shy, a winemaker who insists his wines reflect the vineyards rather than his winemaking technique. Certainly, *terroir*, the subtle alchemy among land, climate, and grape, plays a fundamental role. Yet so does the winemaker, who shepherds the grapes as they turn

themselves into wine. Farrell has an un-mistakable style—his pinot noir is suave and sexy, at once delicate and complex.

I sometimes think I overstate the deli-cious magic of Gary Farrell's pinot noirs, and then someone opens a bottle, I take a sip, and I am transported. Gary's pinot noir is the James Dean of wine, sultry and dangerous. Petulant and undaunted, it is Courtney Love in Frances Farmer's wed-ding dress, kissing her new husband Kurt Cobain, trade winds rustling their hair, heartbreak looming ahead. It's Nirvana's "Aneurysm," it's Tim Buckley's "Sweet Surrender," it's Renata Tebaldi singing "Sogno di Doretta" from *La Rondine*. In its finest vintages, pinot noir is Lord Peter Wimsey with Harriet Vane in a wine-red frock. And I have recently begun harbor-ing a secret and probably foolish dream that someday I will have a little patch of land where I can plant a few vines myself.

My fascination with a particular vine-yard, wine, and winemaker may seem narrow, but I have learned a great deal about California as a wine-producing region by limiting my focus to a specific grape varietal in a specific area. Califor-nia is simply too big to get your arms around easily. For me, exploring Russian River Valley pinot noir in detail—learn-ing about grape varieties and grape-growing, about the importance of soil and weather, about trellising techniques and the art of cooperage, about each of the many facets of winemaking—gave me the foundation I needed to understand wines from other viticultural areas, in California and elsewhere.

As California matures as a winemaking region, more and more viticultural areas are developing reputations for signature wines made from varietals that thrive in a particular soil and microclimate. Mendocino County has the Anderson Valley (not to be confused with the other Anderson Valley, in the northern part of the Central Valley), where chardonnay and pinot noir are showing great promise and where the German varietals gewürztraminer and riesling also thrive. High above Napa Valley, Dunn Vineyards Cabernet Sauvignon, Peter Michael Chardonnay, and the wines of Liparita Cellars have put Howell Mountain on the map. The tiny Sky Vineyards, whose bold zinfandels have won a cult following, has made the reputation of Mount Veeder, in the Mayacamas Range. In Santa Barbara County, the Santa Maria Valley produces premium chardonnays and pinot noirs, such as those of Au Bon Climat, Byron, and Foxen Vineyard. The AVA California Shenandoah Valley, in the foothills of the Sierra Nevadas, a region not often associated with wine, has twelve hundred acres of grapes, many of them zinfandel vines planted decades ago by Italian immigrants. The viticultural areas of Dry Creek Valley, Sonoma Valley, and Rutherford (where Francis Ford Coppola has restored Gustave Niebaum's nineteenth-century estate) have all developed excellent reputations for their zinfandels, much from century-old vines.

The AVA system may be new and far from perfect, but it is tremendously helpful in sorting out the wines of California, where, at last count, there were 680 wineries. If you want to understand California wine, my advice is to develop a working understanding of the AVA system and then to trust your own palate. Drink wines you like, not wines you're told you should like. At the same time, be adventurous. Don't rely only on major producers with their huge distribution networks; instead, ferret out wines from among the hundreds of smaller family wineries in the state. There are, of course, excellent books on the subject, including two of my favorites: *California Wine*, by James Laube, and *The Heartbreak Grape: A California Winemaker's Search for the Perfect Pinot Noir*, by Marq de Villiers.

Coda

What is a recipe, really? To my way of thinking it is a story, an invitation to adventure, a road map by a lone explorer. It is not the only route to your destination. It has been only in recent decades that recipe writing has developed the strict conventions that now govern the production of cookbooks. Ingredients listed in order before the instructions, specific measurements in teaspoons, half teaspoons, quarter teaspoons, and pinches, careful descriptions of each cut, crimp, and fold, this is not the way information was passed between our grandmothers and great-grandmothers, our aunts and their friends. They exchanged recipes by word of mouth and in brief written descriptions with few specific measurements or cooking times. People were more comfortable in the kitchen in those days, and not just because they had to spend so much time there.

Because most of us do not have the luxury of spending all day in the kitchen, many of us have not developed the intuitive sense that would guide us through the kind of casual recipes that for generations were the foundation of home cooking. We like exact details in our recipes. I have tried, in *California Home Cooking*, to translate casual recipes into easy-to-follow instructions guaranteed to work. Still, there are questions you must consider with these as with any recipes: Is my medium heat the same as your medium heat? What if my salt is saltier than your salt? Is a medium onion in my kitchen a small onion, or a large one, in yours? These inevitable variations mean you must get to know your ingredients and develop an intuitive relationship with the foods you cook, so that you can tell when

an artichoke is cooked through, when chicken should be pulled off the grill, when a flat sauce will perk right up with a little salt. These are things a written recipe cannot teach, but they are lessons you will learn if you pay attention as you cook.

I read cookbooks as I read novels, curled up in bed at night, exploring some new culinary adventure. The recipes I read serve as inspirations, ideas that linger for months or years and finally emerge when I find myself alone in the kitchen with time on my hands. I hope you will do the same with *California Home Cooking*. Certainly, cook with it. But also, let it inspire your own style, your own recipes. In this book, I give you my California, the place I have called home since birth, sometimes happily, sometimes reluctantly, but always with an appetite that is deliciously satisfied time after time. I hope you will make California, and California home cooking, your own.

Chapter 1

APPETIZERS

APPETIZERS

Radishes with Butter and
Coarse Salt • 5

Bagna Cauda • 6

Roasted Red Peppers • 7

Malvi Doshi's Spicy Stuffed
Bananas • 8

Fresh Tomato Aspic • 9

Avocado Mousse • 10

Spicy Hummus • 11

Grilled Bread with Garlic and
Olive Oil • 12

Mexican Sopes • 14

Carrot Fritters • 15

Pumpkin Empanadas • 17

Cucumbers with Cream Cheese
and Pepper Jam • 18

Walnut Grapes • 18

Whole Roasted Garlics • 21

Eggplant Rolls with Roasted
Peppers • 22

Stuffed Zucchini Blossoms • 22

Marinated Chèvre with
Olives • 23

Chèvre with Dried Tomato
Relish • 24

Chèvre Gratin • 26

Brie, Pear, and Prosciutto
Pizza • 28

Oysters on the Half Shell • 29

Spicy Grilled Oysters • 32

Grilled Sardines • 32

Sardines in Garlic Butter • 33

Grilled Prawns with
Strawberries and Fennel • 34

Crispy Shrimp-and-Crab
Toast • 35

New Potatoes with Golden
Caviar • 37

Fresh Spring Rolls • 37

Mahogany Chicken Wings • 39

Chipotle Chicken Wings • 40

Foie Gras with Sautéed
Apples • 41

Terrine of Foie Gras • 43

Spicy Steak Tartare • 43

Spicy Beef Strips and Rice
Balls • 44

Roasted Garlic Meatballs • 45

Thai Meatballs with Coconut-
Peanut Sauce • 47

Thai Lamb in Romaine
Leaves • 48

Minced Lamb Dolmas • 50

Grilled BLT Kebabs • 51

RADISHES WITH BUTTER AND COARSE SALT

*N*othing could be simpler than crisp radishes served with butter and salt alongside. For the best results, get your radishes from your garden or your local farmers' market. If you have a goat cheese maker near where you live, ask if they have goat butter, which is surprisingly delicate and flavorful.

SERVES 4 TO 6

2 dozen radishes, preferably Easter
     Egg or French Breakfast, trimmed
     with a few leaves attached
¼ cup unsalted butter
Kosher salt

Arrange the radishes on a serving platter. Put the butter in a small ramekin and the salt in a salt cellar or small dish. Serve immediately. Spread a little butter on a radish, then sprinkle it with salt.

Flavor's Midwife

• • • • • • • • • • • • • • • • • • • •

Nearly all of the recipes in this book were tested using kosher salt, one of the better culinary salts available. If you cook with standard table salt, some adjustment may be necessary wherever kosher salt is called for. Because table salt is denser and less flaky than kosher salt, you might need less. As more varieties of sea salt become available, I find myself using them more and more frequently to finish dishes. A sprinkling of a condiment salt such as the delicately flavored *fleur de sel* from Brittany, or silky Hawaiian red salt, which contains a small amount of natural clay, contributes a wonderful taste and texture to many dishes. Salt is an essential seasoning that heightens the taste of nearly all foods and completes the taste of many, actually bringing the flavors to the palate. And, because it melts slowly on the tongue, salt brings together all of the elements of a dish to create a harmonious, lingering finish.

BAGNA CAUDA

*V*ariations abound of this classic Italian dish, the name of which means, literally, hot bath—in this instance, a hot bath of garlicky butter, olive oil, and anchovies. Many Californians find it an ideal way to feature the abundant fresh produce of the state.

SERVES 4 TO 6

5 or 6 different seasonal vegetables for dipping (suggestions are given at the end of the recipe)
1 loaf of rustic-style French or Italian bread, cut into chunks
½ pound butter
1 large head of garlic, cloves separated, peeled, and minced
2 to 4 anchovy fillets, rinsed and minced
1 cup extra virgin olive oil
Kosher salt
Black pepper in a mill

Have the seasonal vegetables ready. Heat the bread chunks in a 325°F oven.

In a small heavy saucepan, heat the butter until it is bubbly. Add the garlic, reduce the heat, and simmer over low heat until the garlic is soft, about 5 minutes. Stir in the anchovies, and simmer for 3 or 4 minutes more. Add the olive oil, heat through, remove from the heat, and season with salt and pepper. Pour the sauce into a heatproof container and set it on a stand over a warming candle.

Arrange the vegetables on a platter with the bread and serve at once, with the sauce alongside. Guests dip pieces of vegetables and chunks of bread into the sauce.

Variation:

Add two or three dozen grilled small oysters to your selection of bread and vegetables. Spoon a little sauce over each oyster.

Seasonal Vegetables for Bagna Cauda

YEAR-ROUND
Lettuce leaves (a selection of several types)
Spinach leaves
Radishes, trimmed
Large carrots, cut into diagonal slices, or baby carrots, trimmed
New potatoes, cut in half and roasted with a little olive oil

SPRING
Roasted Asparagus (page 383)
Sugar snap peas
Artichokes, boiled, steamed, or braised (see pages 381–83)
Grilled Spring Onions (page 395)
Young fava beans, shelled
Fennel bulb, cut into wide strips

SUMMER AND FALL
Tomatoes, cut into wedges
Cherry tomatoes
Green beans, blanched
Beet greens

Golden beets, roasted and cut into
wedges
Cardoons, strings removed, parboiled
Fresh corn, shucked and cut into
2-inch lengths

WINTER
Broccoli florets, blanched
Cauliflower florets, blanched
Broccoli rabe, blanched
Belgian endive, spears separated
Radicchio, leaves separated
Beets, roasted and cut into wedges

ROASTED RED PEPPERS

In the early fall, farmers' markets throughout California offer a rainbow of sweet and hot peppers—plump red and meaty orange bells; purple bells that turn green when cooked; and chile peppers of every sort, including tiny habaneros whose delicate orange flesh belies their searing heat. At the Ferry Plaza Farm Market in San Francisco, Larry Tiller of Warm Springs Farm in Healdsburg roasts peppers on the spot in a large basket roaster fueled with propane, filling the air with their aroma as he cooks them. Although these peppers are exceptionally easy to prepare at home, Larry can't roast them fast enough; there is always a line when peppers are in season.

SERVES 4 TO 6

4 large or 6 small red bell peppers,
roasted, peeled, and seeded
6 garlic cloves, very thinly sliced
3 tablespoons extra virgin olive oil
Black pepper in a mill
10 anchovy fillets

Cut the peppers into medium julienne strips and place them in a medium serving bowl or on a platter. Add the garlic, olive oil, and several turns of pepper, and toss together lightly. Cut the anchovies in half crosswise, add them to the peppers, and toss again lightly. Serve the peppers alongside warm slices of country-style bread.

Variation:

Dice 4 to 6 ounces of feta cheese into small (⅓-inch) squares, and toss with the pepper strips.

MALVI DOSHI'S SPICY STUFFED BANANAS

These spicy, succulent bananas are served at The Ganges, a small Indian restaurant in San Francisco. Very easy to prepare at home, they make an excellent appetizer or an addition to other curries or to rice.

SERVES 4

2 ripe but slightly firm bananas
¼ cup coconut powder (available in Asian markets) or ¼ cup finely grated unsweetened coconut

¼ teaspoon kosher salt, or to taste
2 or 3 serrano or jalapeño chiles, minced
1 1-inch piece of fresh ginger, peeled and finely grated
2 teaspoons fresh lemon juice
¾ cup minced cilantro leaves
1 tablespoon peanut oil
Sprigs of cilantro, for garnish
Chapati or whole wheat tortillas

Wash and trim the bananas on both ends. Cut each banana into 2½-inch rounds, leaving the skin intact. Make 2 deep cuts on one end of each piece of banana, making an X that extends about half-way into the banana.

In a small bowl, combine the coconut, salt, chiles, ginger, lemon juice, and

Onions and Garlic Are Good for You

Malvi Doshi and her husband settled in San Francisco in the 1970s and opened their restaurant, The Ganges, in 1986. More than a decade later, the restaurant remains one of San Francisco's better kept culinary secrets, a tiny jewel of a place tucked away in a restored Victorian in the Upper Haight, near the University of San Francisco. The casual restaurant, with its traditional Indian decor and seating, is home to scores of students who appreciate Malvi's inexpensive vegetarian fare.

Malvi translates the foods of her homeland with passion and finesse. Raised in a strictly vegetarian Vashnavite household in Surat, on the coast north of Bombay, Malvi credits her mother with shaping her unique style of cooking. Vashnavs traditionally do not eat onions or garlic, but her mother believed they were good for you—and her father eventually relaxed his rigid enforcement of tradition—and so Malvi's cooking possesses a depth of flavor absent in most traditional fare from this region. Of all the morsels I've savored at The Ganges, from spicy pickled carrots to pineapple chutney to Malvi's delicately flavored Gujarati-style curries and fiery green-chile fritters, my favorite remains her stuffed bananas. The Ganges is also the best place in the Bay Area to find the traditional drink chai, as hot, sweet, and spicy as it should be.

chopped cilantro. Press the mixture deep into the cut of each piece of banana. Set the pieces aside.

In a skillet just big enough to hold all the banana pieces, heat the oil. Add the bananas, skins down, and cook the pieces, turning them when the skin has darkened, about 2 minutes. Continue until the skin has darkened on all sides. Remove the bananas from the heat.

Place the cilantro sprigs on a serving platter, set the bananas on top, and serve immediately, with chapati or tortillas on the side.

FRESH TOMATO
ASPIC

As I browse through California cookbooks from the fifties, forties, and earlier, I invariably encounter recipes for tomato aspic. It was served on California tables even at the turn of the century, the little *San Rafael Cook Book* (First Presbyterian Church, 1906) reveals. Unlike so many dishes that have become dated, tomato aspic should not be discarded as hopelessly retro. In its season and with the proper accompaniments, it can be an appealing and festive addition to many meals.

SERVES 6 TO 10
(OR 4 TO 6 AS A
MAIN COURSE)

4 cups Tomato Concassé (page 98)
1 teaspoon kosher salt
3 tablespoons fresh lemon juice
1 small red onion, diced
8 garlic cloves, peeled
1 bay leaf
2 to 3 sprigs each of thyme and basil
2 celery ribs, leaves attached
2 tablespoons (2 packages)
    unflavored gelatin
½ cup cold water
Tabasco sauce

Combine the tomatoes, salt, lemon juice, onion, garlic, bay leaf, thyme, basil, and celery in a large nonreactive pan, and bring the mixture to a boil. Reduce the heat, and simmer for 20 minutes. Remove the pan from the heat, and discard the bay leaf, thyme, basil, and celery. Puree the tomato mixture with an immersion blender or in a conventional blender. Strain the puree and discard the solids.

Soak the gelatin in the cold water for 5 minutes, then add it to the hot tomato juice, stirring until it is completely dissolved. Add water to make 4 cups, and season with Tabasco to taste.

Pour the liquid into a 4-cup decorative mold. Refrigerate the mold until the aspic is firmly set, at least 3 hours. Dip the mold quickly and carefully into hot water (in the kitchen sink or a large bowl), then quickly wipe the mold dry. Place a serving platter over the top, and invert the mold so that the aspic drops onto the platter. Serve the aspic immediately, or refrigerate it until you are ready to serve.

Variations:

WITH PRAWNS AND AÏOLI: Make the aspic in a ring mold. On the serving platter, surround the aspic with cooked and chilled prawns and fill the center of the ring with Aïoli (page 417).

WITH SCALLOP CEVICHE AND AVOCADO SAUCE: Make the aspic in a ring mold. Before serving, fill the center of the ring with Scallop Ceviche (page 139) and drizzle the aspic and ceviche with Avocado Sauce (page 63).

WITH GUACAMOLE: Make the aspic in a ring mold. On the serving platter, fill the center of the ring with Guacamole (page 65) and surround the aspic with tortilla chips.

WITH BAY SHRIMP AND CUCUMBER: Use a 6-cup mold to make the aspic. Refrigerate the aspic until it is about half set, about 45 minutes, then fold 1 pound of cooked and chilled bay shrimp into the aspic. Continue chilling the aspic until it is firm. Peel and thinly slice 1 or 2 cucumbers, and arrange them around the outside of the aspic on the serving platter. Serve with Aïoli (page 417), Avocado Sauce (page 63), or Spicy Lime Dressing (page 139).

AVOCADO MOUSSE

Avocado mousse is elegant and unique to California, where the first Hass avocado—now the dominant commercial variety in the United States—was discovered among an orchard of other varieties (see page 64). Make this mousse when there is an abundance of avocados.

SERVES 6 TO 8

1 tablespoon (1 package) unflavored gelatin
2 tablespoons cold water
½ cup boiling water
¼ cup fresh lemon or lime juice
1 cup pureed avocado (from 2 medium avocados)
½ teaspoon ground cumin
1 teaspoon kosher salt
1 teaspoon Tabasco sauce
½ cup crème fraîche (or substitute; see Note, page 37) or sour cream

In a small bowl, soak the gelatin in the cold water for 10 minutes. Add the boiling water, and stir until dissolved. Set the bowl aside to cool slightly.

In a medium bowl, combine the lemon or lime juice, avocado puree, cumin, salt, Tabasco, and crème fraîche or sour cream. Stir in the gelatin. Pour the mixture into a small mold, and refrigerate the mold until the mousse is completely set, at least 3 hours.

When the mousse is set, dip the mold quickly and carefully into hot water (in the kitchen sink or a large bowl), then quickly wipe the mold dry. Place a serving platter over the top, and invert the mold so that the mousse drops onto the platter. Serve the mousse immediately, or refrigerate it until you are ready to serve.

SPICY HUMMUS

*H*ummus is excellent as a dip for crudités and as a sandwich spread. The smoky chipotles add an irresistible element that blends beautifully with the chickpeas.

MAKES ABOUT 3 CUPS

2 cups cooked or canned chickpeas
½ cup cooking or canning liquid from the chickpeas or water
8 garlic cloves
2 canned chipotles in adobo sauce
¾ cup raw sesame tahini
Juice of 1 lemon, or more to taste
1 tablespoon cumin seeds, toasted and ground, or 2 teaspoons ground cumin
3 tablespoons extra virgin olive oil
2 teaspoons kosher salt, or more to taste
2 tablespoons minced Italian parsley

In a food processor fitted with a metal blade, combine the chickpeas, ¼ cup of the chickpea liquid or water, the garlic, and the chipotles. Pulse until you have a fairly smooth puree. Add the tahini and lemon juice, and pulse again until the tahini has been incorporated into the chickpeas.

Transfer the mixture to a medium bowl. Stir in the cumin, olive oil, salt, and parsley. Taste the hummus, and adjust the seasoning if necessary with additional salt and lemon juice. If the hummus seems too thick, stir in more canning liquid or

water to loosen it slightly. Transfer the hummus to a serving bowl, cover, and refrigerate for at least 1 hour before serving. Hummus will keep, tightly covered, in the refrigerator for about 7 days.

California Crudités

*P*latters of vegetables have always been a popular appetizer, and with the abundance of beautiful vegetables now available at farmers' markets, it's easier than ever to find your favorites among the best of the season. Refer to the seasonal market guide (page 118). Then, pair the vegetables with an appropriate sauce. Leafy greens—which do make excellent crudité selections, popular in California if not elsewhere—are best served with a light sauce such as a vinaigrette. Florets and firmer leaves such as broccoli, cauliflower, and artichokes take best to a creamy dip, such as Aïoli (page 417) or Homemade Mayonnaise (page 416). Crunchy root vegetables and other firm vegetables, such as sliced carrots, radishes, and jicama, or strips of raw bell peppers, or cooked beets, can stand up to denser purees, like Spicy Hummus. Keep in mind that the quality of the vegetables, regardless of their type, is the most important element.

GRILLED BREAD WITH GARLIC AND OLIVE OIL

*C*all it whatever you like—toast, fettunta, bruschetta—good bread toasted over any sort of grill is enormously popular, as it should be. Certainly, Californians, with their propensity to cook out of doors, can be found tossing slices of San Francisco sourdough on the Weber year-round. And you find apartment dwellers with stovetop grills, as well as devotees of Tuscan grills, which fit into nearly any fireplace, making grilled bread. Do you heat with a wood stove? No problem; most can accommodate a few slices of bread on top. The classic version is simple—just good bread, garlic, olive oil, and salt and pepper. But there are dozens of variations, limited only by the seasons and what is at hand. My favorite ones are listed at the end of the recipe.

SERVES 4

1 loaf crusty country bread, cut into
   ¾-inch slices
4 large garlic cloves, cut in half but
   not peeled

California Olive Oil

*O*live oil is not a new industry in California. Mission olive trees, by far the most common variety in the state, were planted more than two hundred years ago by Franciscan padres at their first mission, San Diego de Alcalá, to provide cooking oil and table fruit for the new settlements.

California's first commercial olive oil was probably produced in 1871, at Camulos Mills in Ventura County. At about the same time, new groves were planted around the state with cuttings from existing trees and with saplings from imported Italian and French varieties, more suitable for oil, introduced by recent immigrants. It wasn't long before the olive oil produced in the New World rivaled that of Europe. In 1900, a California olive oil took a gold medal at the world's fair in Paris.

International recognition did not usher in a new era. California's oils could not compete with less expensive European oils, and farmers found growing table olives more lucrative than growing olives for oil. That economic reality remains today: Olives sold to canners can bring as much as eight hundred dollars per ton; olives for oil bring half that or less. For much of the twentieth century, new plantings were mainly of the Mission, Manzanilla, and Sevillano varieties—best as table olives but not so great for oil. Many groves of olive trees suitable for premium oil were ripped out as farmers sought other uses for their land; some orchards were abandoned and neglected for decades.

Until the 1990s, most of the state's olive oil was made from fruit rejected (general-

½ cup extra virgin olive oil

Kosher salt

Black pepper in a mill

Prepare a charcoal fire or heat a stove-top grill. Grill the bread slices until they are well browned on both sides. Transfer the bread to a platter, rub each piece on one side with the cut garlic, and drizzle with olive oil. Sprinkle with a little salt and pepper and serve immediately.

Variations:

CATALAN STYLE: Cut several small to medium ripe tomatoes in half (through the equator). Rub the toast with garlic, then rub with a tomato half, pushing firmly so that the pulp disappears into the bread. Drizzle with olive oil, season with salt and pepper, and serve immediately.

WITH TOMATO CONCASSÉ: Rub the toast with garlic, then spoon a little Tomato Concassé (page 98) on top. Add the olive oil and salt and pepper.

WITH CHERRY TOMATOES: Cut 1 pint of cherry tomatoes into quarters, toss them with a tablespoon of snipped chives, and season them with salt and pepper. Rub the toast with garlic, spoon the tomatoes over the bread, then drizzle with olive oil.

WITH BEANS: Mash 1½ cups of warm

ly, for size) by the canners. However, in California as elsewhere, as more people have come to demand bolder and more flavorful high-quality olive oils, and as the health benefits of olive oil have become widely known, the oil market has steadily expanded. California's producers, including an ever-increasing number of newcomers, now vie for a share of it.

Most experts agree that, to compete in the world market for first-class condiment olive oil, the state's producers must turn to olive varieties more suitable for oil-making. Ridgely Evers, whose DaVero olive oil may be the best yet produced in California, was the first person in this century to import Italian varieties ideal for oil. His oil is made from Leccino, Frantoio, Maurino, and Pendolino olives, from trees grown from cuttings taken at Fattoria Mansi Bernardini in the Luccese village of Segromigno-in-Monte.

After the olives are picked by hand, they are trucked from Evers's Dry Creek Valley farm to Frantoio, a restaurant and olive oil factory in Mill Valley. There the oil is made in the traditional fashion. The olives are crushed under huge granite wheels. The resulting paste is layered on nylon mats, which are stacked in a hydraulic press. The oil is slowly squeezed out and sent through a centrifuge to separate it from the vegetable water. Although the new oil is delicious, it must settle for several weeks if it is to have a shelf life of more than 2 or 3 months. After settling, it is bottled in dark glass so that light does not alter its flavor. The oil is rich and round, pleasantly bitter, and has a slightly spicy finish. When Evers is asked why he calls his oil DaVero, he says, "There's an Italian expression, *davvero*, that means 'indeed' or 'really.' It is used to say, 'This is the best,' or 'This is the real thing.'"

cooked cannellini beans with several cloves of finely minced garlic, 2 teaspoons of minced fresh sage, 3 to 4 tablespoons of extra virgin olive oil, and salt and pepper. Spread the mash over the grilled bread, and serve.

WITH BEANS AND GREENS: In olive oil, sauté either spinach leaves or Swiss chard (stems removed, leaves sliced crosswise) with some minced garlic and lemon zest until the greens are just limp. Spread the grilled bread with mashed cannellini beans (see above), top with the sautéed greens, season with salt and pepper, and serve immediately.

WITH TOMATO, BASIL, AND FRESH MOZZARELLA: Grill the bread on 1 side, and rub the toasted side with garlic. Place a thin slice of fresh mozzarella on the same side. Return the bread to the grill and toast the other side. Transfer the bread to a plate, and top each piece with a basil leaf and a slice of tomato. Drizzle with olive oil, season with salt and pepper, and serve immediately.

WITH ANCHOVIES: After adding tomatoes to the bread (by any method), drape an anchovy fillet over the top of each slice before serving.

WITH MUSHROOMS: Put 4 tablespoons of olive oil in a large skillet over medium heat. Add 1 large shallot, minced, 2 garlic cloves, minced, and 2 tablespoons minced Italian parsley. Sauté until the shallot and garlic are soft and fragrant, about 8 minutes. Add ¾ pound mushrooms (use a mix of available mushrooms, such as chanterelles, shiitakes, cremini, and oysters), diced, and sauté until the mushrooms are limp, about 10 minutes. Season with salt and pepper, and add 2 to 3 tablespoons of the sauté to each slice of grilled bread.

Making Oil from Olives

"**C**ut the olives from the tree when they are quite ripe; keep them for three or four weeks in the dark; mill them; put the paste in sacks, strong but porous; press them and you have oil of the best quality. To have a second grade of oil, put the pressed paste in hot water, and press again. This water mixed with oil should be put in jars, and when the oil floats to the surface it can be taken off, filtered, and put in bottles. If you add a little salt before the filtering, you will be repaid for the trouble."

Mrs. Juan Foster, *How We Cook in Los Angeles* (1894)

MEXICAN SOPES

*T*hese rounds of dough, which vaguely resemble hollowed-out English muffins, are made, as tortillas are, with masa harina. Yet unlike tortillas, they are easy to shape and cook without the practice necessary for making good corn tortillas. Sopes are a common snack in Mexican homes throughout California. Fill sopes with beans, shredded meat, crumbled cheese, or seafood, and top them with minced red onion, salsa, shredded cheese, guacamole, cilantro, or sliced radishes. Choose the filling(s) and topping(s) you like, aiming for an appealing combination of flavors, textures, and temperatures. Two fillings I like are Border Town Chipotle Pork (page 373) and the egg and chorizo filling for Breakfast Burritos (page 188).

MAKES 8 SOPES

¼ cup lard

2 teaspoons kosher salt

2 cups masa harina

1¼ cups warm water, plus more if needed

Put the lard in a medium mixing bowl and beat it with a wooden spoon until it is light and fluffy. Add the salt and ¼ cup of the masa harina, and mix well. Add, in alternating ¼-cup measures of each, the rest of the masa harina and warm water, mixing well after each addition. If the finished dough is not pliable enough, work in a little more warm water.

Divide the dough in half, and divide each half into 4 equal pieces. Wet your hands with water, and roll each of the 8 pieces into a ball about the size of a lime. On a work surface, pat down each ball into a circle about 3 inches in diameter.

Lightly oil a heavy skillet or, if you have one, a Mexican comal, and place it over medium-high heat. When the oil is hot, cook the sopes on 1 side for 3 minutes, turn them, and cook them for 2 minutes more; they should take on just a bit of color on each side. Remove the sopes from the pan and use your fingers to pinch up a rim about ⅜ inch high around the edge. Return the sopes to the pan, rim side up, and cook them for 2 minutes more.

Fill and top the sopes as you like, and serve immediately.

CARROT FRITTERS

I have never found a better carrot recipe—these sweet and savory fritters are utterly irresistible. Serve them as an appetizer, as an accompaniment to roast chicken, or even as a main course.

SERVES 4 TO 6

Peanut oil for deep-frying

4 cups grated peeled carrots

¼ cup minced cilantro leaves

1 teaspoon grated fresh ginger

2 teaspoon cumin seed, toasted and crushed

1 tablespoon white mustard seeds

4 tablespoons all-purpose flour

2 teaspoons baking powder

1 teaspoon salt

1 teaspoon fresh-ground black pepper

4 eggs, lightly beaten

1 large bunch cilantro, broken into sprigs

Honey-Ginger Mustard (page 421)

In a deep-frying pan, heat about 2 inches of peanut oil to 350°F. While the oil is heating, quickly mix the fritter batter. In a large mixing bowl, toss together the carrots, minced cilantro, and ginger. In a small bowl, combine the cumin, mustard seeds, flour, baking powder, salt, and pepper. Add the mixture to the carrots, and toss together lightly. Pour the beaten eggs over the carrot mixture and toss quickly with a fork.

The Carrot Capital

Due east of San Diego and just north of the Mexican border lies the small town of Holtville, population 5,575. To the north are the Salton Sea, Joshua Tree National Park, and the great Mojave Desert, a California far removed from the densely populated areas of the coastal and central valleys.

Decades ago, Holtville proclaimed itself the Carrot Capital of the World and in 1948 set out to prove it with its first Carrot Carnival. A Carrot Queen (Charlotte Von Flue, who went on to marry farmer Gene Johnston) was chosen, and seventeen floats joined the parade, which included a local businessman dressed as Bugs Bunny. At the time, one in three carrots in the United States came from the Holtville area, which shipped ten thousand carloads of carrots that year. Today the Carrot Festival, as it has been rechristened, continues, with its Carrot Queen, cooking contests, and carrot-inspired revelry.

Make the fritters: Use a small (1-ounce) ice cream scoop or a soup spoon to shape the fritters, and drop them, one by one, into the hot oil, being careful not to crowd them. Turn the fritters after 1 minute, and fry until they are golden brown, about 1 minute more. Using a slotted spoon, transfer the fritters to absorbent paper to drain. Allowing the oil to return to 350°F after each addition, continue until all the batter has been used.

Spread the cilantro sprigs on a serving platter, place the fritters on top, and serve immediately, with the honey-ginger mustard sauce on the side.

PUMPKIN EMPANADAS

*I*n early California, Spanish and Mexican traditions dominated much of home cooking, as you would expect. Native ingredients like wild game, turkey, corn, and pumpkin were common. Pumpkin and winter squash are still used to fill Mexican-style turnovers.

MAKES ABOUT 30 TURNOVERS

2 tablespoons butter
1 tablespoon minced garlic
1 serrano chile, minced
Pinch of ground cumin
Pinch of cayenne
2 cups mashed cooked sugar
    pumpkin or other winter squash
1 teaspoon kosher salt
1 teaspoon fresh-ground black
    pepper
Pastry for Savory Turnovers (recipe
    follows)
1 cup shelled pumpkin seeds, toasted

In a small saucepan, heat the butter over medium heat until it is foamy. Add the garlic and serrano, and sauté them for 2 minutes. Add the cumin and cayenne, then add the sautéed mixture to the squash. Season with salt and pepper and mix well.

Preheat the oven to 325°F. Lightly oil a baking sheet.

Roll out the pastry dough fairly thin. Cut 3-inch rounds and fill each round with a generous tablespoon of the squash mixture. Fold the edges up and seal them, and place the empanadas on the baking sheet. Bake them for 20 minutes, until golden brown. Remove the empanadas from the oven, set them on a serving platter, and serve them immediately, with the pumpkin seeds alongside or scattered over them.

Pastry for Savory Turnovers

MAKES ENOUGH FOR 30 TURNOVERS

4 ounces old-fashioned (without
    gum) cream cheese or young
    (not aged) chèvre, at room
    temperature
¾ cup unsalted butter, at room
    temperature
¼ teaspoon kosher salt
¼ teaspoon Tabasco sauce
2 tablespoons toasted sesame seeds
¼ cup grated dry jack
1½ cups all-purpose flour

In a medium bowl, cream together the cream cheese and butter. Add the salt, Tabasco, and sesame seeds. Add the grated cheese and flour, and mix the dough with a wooden spoon until smooth. Cover the dough and refrigerate it for 30 minutes before rolling it out.

Cucumbers with Cream Cheese and Pepper Jam

*S*everal small companies produce jalapeño jams and jellies that are at once sweet and hot. My favorite, with lots of body and depth of flavor, is from Happy Haven Ranch, a tiny farm near the southern edge of Sonoma Mountain in northern California.

Try to find old-fashioned cream cheese for this and other recipes in this book. Old-fashioned cream cheese, readily available throughout California, is simply cream cheese without gum or similar additives, which are added to most national brands to make them smoother and denser. Old-fashioned cream cheese is slightly crumbly yet spreads easily and has an excellent flavor.

MAKES 3 TO 4 DOZEN ROUNDS

6 ounces old-fashioned (without gum) cream cheese
4 tablespoons half-and-half
1 serrano chile, minced
1 garlic clove, minced
1 tablespoon minced Italian parsley
2 teaspoons minced cilantro
1 teaspoon minced basil
1 teaspoon minced thyme
2 medium cucumbers, washed thoroughly and cut into ¼-inch rounds
Red and/or green hot pepper jam

Using a wooden spoon or an electric mixer (but not a food processor), beat together the cream cheese and half-and-half until smooth. Add the serrano, garlic, parsley, cilantro, basil, and thyme, and mix together well. Place the mixture in a pastry bag fitted with a large star tip. Arrange the cucumber slices on a work surface and pipe a star of cream cheese onto each one. Top each slice with a small dollop of pepper jam, arrange them on a serving tray, and serve immediately.

Variation:

If you do not have a pastry bag, dry off the cucumber slices to make them less slippery, and use a spoon or knife to put the cream cheese mixture on top of them.

Walnut Grapes

*I*f you can get fresh grape leaves, use some as a garnish for these sweet-and-savory grapes. Smooth several large leaves over a serving platter, and arrange the grapes on top to resemble a plump cluster.

SERVES 6 TO 8

1 pound red seedless table grapes, such as Red Flame
6 ounces Roquefort, Oregon blue, or other blue-veined cheese
½ to ¾ cup heavy cream
1 cup toasted walnuts, finely chopped

Fresh grape leaves, for garnish,
optional

Wash the grapes thoroughly, pluck them from their stems, and dry them thoroughly. Discard any bruised or damaged grapes.

In a food processor fitted with a metal blade, combine the cheese and cream, pulsing quickly until the mixture is smooth. Transfer the mixture to a medium bowl. Place the walnuts in another medium bowl.

Add 3 or 4 grapes at a time to the cheese mixture and use the tip of a spoon to roll each grape around until it is coated with cheese. Carefully transfer each grape to the bowl of toasted walnuts. Shake the bowl so that the grape rolls around in the walnuts and becomes fully coated. Set each covered grape on a wax paper-lined baking sheet. Continue until all the grapes are coated. Refrigerate the grapes for at least 2 hours before serving.

Arrange the grapes on a serving platter, and garnish with fresh grape leaves, if you like. The grapes may also be served as a dessert, accompanied by a tawny port or a late-harvest wine.

Grapes of Wrath

In the 1930s, close to half a million white Protestants left their homes in Oklahoma, Missouri, Texas, and Arkansas and headed west to California. Most settled in California's Central Valley and provided labor for the harvest, a fact that distressed the state's major growers, who feared the Okies would demand better treatment than the Chinese, Japanese, Mexican, and Filipino workers they had exploited for decades. John Steinbeck, who chronicled the dismal conditions in which the Okies struggled to survive in his novel *Grapes of Wrath*, wrote, in *The Harvest Gypsies* (1936), that major growers feared "they would eventually have to give up their methods of repression, starvation wages, jailing, and beating...."

"'Being American citizens [the white transients] are going to demand the so-called American standards of living.... They are going to be the finest pabulum for unionization,'" George Clements, spokesperson for the region's farmers, commented to Steinbeck. Fears proved unfounded; most Okies resisted union appeals and were happy to provide scab labor when immigrant workers protested wage reductions. Treatment of farmworkers, and disputes over both legal and illegal immigrants, continue to cause tremendous controversy in California's agriculture.

Garlic-A-Month Club

Egmont Tripp, who moved to California from his native Germany in the 1970s, began Sunshine Farms, his organic gardens that specialize in garlic varieties from around the world, in 1986. The farm is near the northern end of the Alexander Valley viticultural area. Each year Egmont grows dozens of varieties of garlic, some from single bulbs brought from as far away as Lithuania or the Ukraine. He plants in the fall and harvests in June, and, after he cures the garlic, he begins to sell it in July. In 1996, he began his Garlic-A-Month Club. Members receive a pound of a different variety of garlic each month for six months. He also publishes a newsletter describing in detail the garlics he has available. Among the kinds he grows and sells are:

ASIAN TEMPEST: Very hot, from Korea.

BROWN TEMPEST: Fiery raw taste, with an appealing finish.

CALIFORNIA LATE: Spicy and hot; stores well; good for baking.

CHESNOK RED: Well-rounded flavors, from the Georgian Republic.

CHET'S ITALIAN RED: Very flavorful, from Washington State.

EARLY RED ITALIAN: An early-harvest garlic that stores very well.

GEORGIAN ACHATAMI: Very hot; good for baking.

GEORGIAN CRYSTAL: Very spicy; from the Georgian Republic.

GERMAN RED: From California's old-time German gardeners.

INCHELIUM RED: Big bulbs excellent for baking; first found on an Indian Reservation in Washington State.

PERSIAN STAR: Mild, pleasantly flavored, from Uzbekistan.

POLISH CARPATHIAN: Hot and spicy, from the Carpathian Mountains in southeast Poland.

RED RUSSIAN: Russian immigrants brought this variety to British Columbia.

ROMANIAN RED: From Romania via British Columbia; stores well.

SPANISH ROJA: Moderately spicy; introduced into Oregon around 1900.

YUGOSLAVIAN: Hot and spicy, with a pleasingly warm finish.

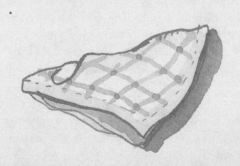

WHOLE ROASTED GARLICS

• •

Alice Waters made whole roasted garlics famous when she prepared them at a press luncheon in New York featuring America's new young chefs. Her meal dazzled critics, who wrote about the little heads of garlic and tiny lettuces she brought, their roots still packed in garden soil, all the way from California. The media attention focused on Chez Panisse specifically and California cuisine in general changed things dramatically. It wasn't long before young salad greens—sometimes mesclun, sometimes a single variety of lettuce—appeared not only in restaurants everywhere, but in retail markets. Today, scores of California farmers make their living growing specialty lettuces and harvesting the leaves when they are very young. Roasted garlic, too, quickly became a staple of restaurant chefs and home cooks throughout the state.

SERVES 4

4 heads of garlic
½ to ¾ cup extra virgin olive oil
2 tablespoons unsalted butter, optional
¼ cup water
Kosher salt
Black pepper in a mill
1 5-ounce log of young (not aged) chèvre, such as chabis

2 tablespoons snipped chives
Baguette slices or croutons

Preheat the oven to 350°F.

Remove the papery outer skin of the garlic, leaving the bulbs intact. If the roots are particularly long or if there is dirt embedded in them, trim the roots. Place the garlic in a small baking dish with a lid. Pour the olive oil over the garlic until it reaches half-way up the side of the bulbs. If you like, press a piece of butter into the top of each bulb. Add the water to the dish, season with a little salt and pepper, and cover the dish. Bake the garlic until it is soft when pressed with your thumb; this will take between 40 and 90 minutes, depending on the size, variety, and age of the garlic. Remove the garlic from the oven, uncover the dish, and let the garlic cool slightly. Lift the bulbs out of the cooking liquid and let them drain on a rack or absorbent paper.

To serve, place a bulb of garlic on each of 4 serving plates. Divide the chèvre among the plates, spoon 1 or 2 tablespoons of the cooking liquid over the chèvre, and scatter the chives over all. Add several baguette slices or croutons to each plate, and serve immediately.

If you like, you can strain the remaining cooking liquid, place it in a container with a lid, and reserve it for another purpose, such as making a vinaigrette or basting chicken or fish during grilling.

EGGPLANT ROLLS WITH ROASTED PEPPERS

Eggplant wrapped around cheese has become an extremely popular appetizer in California. It seems nearly everyone has a variation; some use feta instead of mozzarella, while others use fresh goat cheese mixed with herbs; some serve it with salsa; some bake the rolls until the cheese is melted.

Be sure to cook the eggplant until it is soft and creamy; undercooked, it is tough and bitter. I serve these rolls on a bed of roasted peppers, but you can serve them solo, too.

MAKES 25 TO 30 ROLLS

Olive oil
5 or 6 Japanese eggplants, cut into
    ¼-inch-thick slices
4 ounces semisoft cheese, such as
    fresh mozzarella, asiago, or
    Monterey jack, chilled
2 large red bell peppers, roasted and
    cut into julienne
4 garlic cloves, thinly sliced
4 tablespoons balsamic vinegar
Kosher salt
Black pepper in a mill
2 tablespoons minced Italian parsley

Preheat the oven to 350°F. Pour a thin layer of olive oil on a baking sheet. Arrange the eggplant slices on top, and drizzle each slice with a little more olive oil. Bake the eggplant until it is soft, creamy, and slightly golden, 20 to 25 minutes. Remove the eggplant slices from the oven, transfer them to absorbent paper, and allow them to cool.

Cut the cheese into thin slices, and set a slice on each piece of eggplant. Roll the pieces lengthwise, and set the rolls aside.

In a small bowl, toss together the peppers, garlic, and 3 tablespoons of the vinegar. To serve, place the pepper mixture on a serving platter and arrange the eggplant rolls on top. Season with salt and pepper, scatter the parsley over all, drizzle with the remaining 1 tablespoon vinegar, and serve immediately.

STUFFED ZUCCHINI BLOSSOMS

I developed this recipe to use up some very ripe taupinière goat cheese from Laura Chenel. That day, the farmers' market had beautiful zucchini blossoms, still damp with morning dew. This filling is equally good in poblano chiles that have been roasted and peeled. Serve this dish with your favorite tomato salsa alongside.

SERVES 4

4 ounces soft aged chèvre, such as
    taupinière
4 ounces young (not aged) chèvre,
    such as chabis

⅓ cup Tomato Concassé (page 98)
Kosher salt
Black pepper in a mill
2 tablespoons snipped chives
8 to 10 zucchini blossoms

Mix the cheeses together by hand until they are well blended. Add the concassé and mix until smooth. Add salt and pepper to taste, and mix in the chives. Fill each zucchini blossom with about 2 tablespoons of the mixture, enough to fill it but not so much that the blossom can't be gently

Seeing Stars

In 1976, a friend gave Nancy Gaffney a goat. By the time she moved to a little seaside cottage north of Santa Cruz eight years later, that goat had produced an entire herd. And, if you have goats, it seems you will inevitably make goat cheese, which Nancy began to do after settling into her new location. When she first moved to the edge of the Pacific, she was dazzled by the brilliance of the stars and so christened her fledgling company Sea Stars Goat Cheese. Except during the winter, when the goats are pregnant and milk production plummets, Gaffney's fifty goats produce enough milk for about five hundred pounds of cheese a week—including a remarkably good dry ricotta, and beautiful wheels of chèvre covered with edible organic flower petals—which she sells throughout Santa Cruz and Santa Clara counties.

pushed closed. Refrigerate the stuffed blossoms for at least 1 hour or up to 3 hours before serving.

MARINATED CHÈVRE WITH OLIVES

It seems that chèvre finally has outgrown its trendiness and taken its place among the staple cheeses available in most markets. In California, supermarkets offer several varieties, and good goat cheese now is available nearly everywhere in the country.

SERVES 4 TO 6

1 5-ounce log of young (not aged) chèvre
6 garlic cloves
2 to 3 strips of lemon zest
1 teaspoon black peppercorns
1 small sprig of thyme or rosemary
1 cup olives, such as picholine, niçoise, kalamata, or salt-cured black, drained and pitted
Extra virgin olive oil
Sprigs of thyme or rosemary, for garnish
Baguette slices or croutons

Place the chèvre in a small bowl, and add the garlic, lemon zest, peppercorns, thyme or rosemary, and olives. Pour the olive oil over until it covers everything completely. Let the mixture stand at room temperature for 3 or 4 hours, or in the refrigerator for up to 5 or 6 days. To serve, bring to room temperature, pour off the olive oil, reserving it for another purpose, and arrange the chèvre on a platter. Surround the chèvre with the olives, and garnish with some herb sprigs. Serve with baguette slices or croutons.

CHÈVRE WITH DRIED TOMATO RELISH

*S*ome people might say that goat cheese and sun-dried tomatoes have become two of the most over-used ingredients in recent years. Yet their cliché status cannot eclipse the harmony of their marriage; they go together exceedingly well. In this recipe, the other ingredients and their amounts can be altered to what suits your taste. You might add a little heat with minced jalapeños, use green olives instead of black, or add some capers. It is important to use the best olive oil you can find, and the best garlic, too (the fresher and hotter, the better).

SERVES 12

3 heads of garlic, cloves separated
  and cut into slivers
2 cups extra virgin olive oil
½ cup dried tomato bits or ½ cup
  dried tomatoes in oil, minced

¼ cup minced California black olives
¼ cup minced kalamata olives
¼ cup finely minced Preserved
  Lemons (page 429)
1 tablespoon minced oregano
1 tablespoon minced Italian parsley
Kosher salt
2 8-ounce logs of chèvre
½ cup toasted walnuts, chopped
Baguette slices, croutons, or tortilla
  chips

Place the garlic in a nonreactive saucepan and add enough olive oil to cover the garlic by ¼ inch. Simmer over very low heat for 10 minutes. Remove the pan from the heat, and let the garlic cool to room temperature. Transfer the garlic and olive oil to a large bowl. Add the dried tomatoes, olives, preserved lemons, herbs, and salt, and toss lightly to mix. Taste the relish and add salt if necessary. Add the remaining olive oil.

To serve, place the chèvre on a large serving platter, spoon the relish over, and garnish with the walnuts. Serve immediately, with baguette slices, croutons, or tortilla chips.

Nonna's Dried Tomatoes

Karen Cox is married to a tomato farmer in Stanislaus County. In 1985, after watching dried tomatoes become the latest California food craze, she bought a hundred home dehydrators, set them up in her garage, and launched her company, Just Tomatoes. Her inspiration came from her Italian grandmother, who used an old Sicilian method for preserving tomatoes at the end of the season. "My Nonna cooked down her excess garden tomatoes, poured this sauce on a huge platter and put it out in the sun to thicken to a paste. She stored it covered with olive oil in a crock; never once did she scold any of the grandchildren whose finger marks were left in the paste," Karen writes in her self-published cookbook, *Just Dried Tomatoes!*.

Californians who live where the summers are hot and dry often make their own dried tomatoes. In her book, Cox tells the story of a woman from Marin County who places her tomatoes inside the back window of her car, then drives around as usual. After a week of baking in the hot sun, the tomatoes are ready. A *very* California approach.

The domestic dried tomato industry was launched in 1979, when Healdsburg's resident tomato visionary, Ruth Waltenspiel of Timber Crest Farms, decided to compete with the newly popular but high-priced sun-dried tomatoes imported from Italy. She began with two truckloads of tomatoes. The first truckload proceeded beautifully until about two in the morning, when Ruth turned off the heaters and fans and went to bed. Early the next morning she discovered the tomatoes had not been as dry as she'd thought; they were, in fact, full of green mold. That was the end of the first truckload, which ended up in the orchard as compost. With the second truckload, Ruth had learned from her mistake, and Timber Crest Farms was on its way to creating a domestic dried tomato industry. Today they process hundreds of truckloads each year, drying them in the same enormous dehydrators where they dry organic apricots, peaches, and other fruits. They sell their tomatoes dried in bags, packed in olive oil, as bits (which are convenient for cooking), and processed into chutneys, sauces, and other products.

Since then, other California producers have added dried tomatoes to their lines, and a few focus exclusively on them. George Bonacich, who grows wonderful apricots in the Santa Clara Valley, now markets authentic sun-dried tomatoes (most commercial dried tomatoes are dehydrated rather than dried in the sun, as George does his). One of the best places to find excellent sun-dried tomatoes is at farmers' markets, where many tomato farmers offer their own.

CHÈVRE GRATIN

No American author better reveals the culinary secrets of France than Patricia Wells. When she was in California promoting a new book, I was pleased to have her as a guest on my radio show, "Mouthful." As I leafed through *Patricia Wells at Home in Provence* (Scribner, 1996), I came upon a recipe that made my mouth water instantly. That night, I used the recipe as inspiration for this simple combination of flavors and textures, so suited to California in the fall, when the air is crisp and cool.

SERVES 4

¼ cup extra virgin olive oil
6 garlic cloves, minced
8 ounces young (not aged) chèvre
4 tablespoons minced herbs, such as
  oregano, thyme, basil, or Italian
  parsley, or a combination
2 cups Basic Tomato Sauce (recipe
  follows) or 2 cups chopped fresh
  tomatoes
1 cup oil–cured or salt–cured black
  olives
Sprigs of herbs, for garnish
Baguette slices, croutons, or warm
  country–style bread

In a small saucepan over medium-low heat, heat the olive oil. Add the garlic, and simmer gently for 5 minutes. Remove the pan from the heat.

Preheat an oven broiler. Break the cheese into chunks and divide it among 4 4-ounce ramekins, or spread the chunks over the surface of a large, shallow baking dish. Scatter the minced herbs over the cheese, and spoon the tomato sauce or tomatoes into the ramekins or baking dish. Top each portion with some of the olive oil and garlic, and divide the olives among the portions.

Place the ramekins or baking dish under the broiler until the cheese is melted, about 3 or 4 minutes. Remove the gratin from the oven, and garnish with the herb sprigs. Serve immediately, with baguettes, croutons, or bread.

Basic Tomato Sauce

This is an all-purpose tomato sauce best made near the end of tomato season, when there is an abundance of fruit that must be preserved before the first frost. The sauce can be frozen as well as canned. If canning, add 1 tablespoon fresh lemon juice to each quart of sauce. Use it wherever tomato sauce is needed.

MAKES ABOUT 5 CUPS

5 pounds ripe red tomatoes, peeled,
  seeded, and diced
1 bay leaf
3 tablespoons olive oil
2 yellow onions, minced
2 teaspoons minced garlic
5 basil leaves, minced
2 tablespoons minced Italian parsley
  leaves
Kosher salt
Black pepper in a mill

1 tablespoon sugar, optional

Bring the tomatoes to a boil in a large nonreactive pot over medium heat. Reduce the heat, and simmer for 10 minutes. Transfer the tomatoes to a fine strainer lined with cheesecloth. Let the excess liquid drain for 10 minutes; reserve the liquid for another use. Return the drained tomato pulp to the pot, add the bay leaf, and simmer over low heat until most of the liquid has evaporated.

Meanwhile, heat the olive oil in a heavy skillet over medium heat. Add the onions, and sauté them until they are very soft and fragrant, about 15 minutes. Add the garlic, basil, and parsley, and sauté for 2 minutes more. Remove the bay leaf from the cooked tomato pulp, discard it, and stir the pulp into the onion mixture. Taste the sauce and season with salt and pepper. If the sauce is too acidic or a little flat, add the sugar and return the sauce to the heat for 3 minutes more. For a completely smooth sauce, pass it through a food mill. This sauce will keep, refrigerated, for up to 1 week. It can also be frozen or canned.

Variation:

For golden tomato sauce, use gold or yellow tomatoes in place of red ones. Omit the bay leaf and garlic. Use butter in place of the olive oil, and 1 large shallot, minced, in place of the yellow onion.

Cheese and Fruit

O ne of the easiest and most welcome appetizers—or desserts, for that matter—is a selection of beautiful cheeses and seasonal fruit. When selecting cheeses to serve before a meal, choose a variety of contrasting textures and flavors, perhaps a wedge of dry jack joined by an aged chèvre such as a taupinière, and a lusciously creamy teleme or St. André. I avoid cheddars and similar cheeses that I associate more with the actual meal than with its tempting prelude. Add fruit sparingly, such as a scattering of pomegranate seeds in the fall, sliced kumquats and oranges in the winter, and berries in the spring and summer. Olives make good accompaniments, too. To serve following the meal, add a robust blue-veined cheese, sliced apple, and toasted nuts, such as almonds, pecans, or walnuts.

BRIE, PEAR, AND PROSCIUTTO PIZZA

Once you remove tomato sauce, pizza becomes something very different from what you find in the freezer section of your supermarket. Toppings take center stage, and subtler combinations of flavors become possible. In California, pizza without sauce is very common, in restaurants and in home kitchens. This version makes an excellent appetizer and is best served with a California white wine, such as a sauvignon blanc, or with a true dry rosé.

SERVES 4

4 tablespoons unsalted butter
1 to 2 pears, peeled and cut into
  ¼-inch-thick slices
½ pound young arugula leaves or
  beet greens
1 12-inch pizza shell (page 262)
Cornmeal
3 ounces prosciutto, sliced thin
8 ounces brie, sliced very thin
Black pepper in a mill

Heat 2 tablespoons of the butter in a heavy skillet over medium heat. When the butter is foamy, add several pear slices, and sauté them for about 3 minutes on each side, until they are lightly browned. Transfer the pears to a plate. Continue until all of the pears have been sautéed, using additional butter as necessary. When all of the pears have been sautéed, add the

greens to the skillet. Cook them, covered, until they are just wilted, about 2 minutes, and remove them from the heat. In a

The Original 27 Counties

When Sir Francis Drake, the first European to land in what would become **Marin County**, arrived, he found a large population of Native Americans, the Coast Miwok peoples. Many Miwoks still live here, and their customs and foods can be experienced at a surviving Miwok village, now an educational center, located within the Point Reyes National Seashore. Marin today is the wealthiest county in the state. Although much of the county is suburban, the western portion is densely forested, sparsely populated, and very beautiful. Much of the agriculture here is small-scale, with an emphasis on top-quality products. There is Niman-Shell Beef, which raises natural-fed cattle; there are many vegetable farms that grow out-of-the-ordinary and heirloom varieties; and, at MacEvoy Ranch, near San Antonio Creek at the northern end of the county, there is the state's largest planting of Italian varietal olive trees. Excellent oysters are grown in Tomales Bay. The southern portion of the county includes the haunting Mt. Tamalpais and the spectacular Golden Gate Recreation Area, where Basque sheepherders operated a cheesemaking farm in the nineteenth century.

small saucepan, melt the remaining 2 tablespoons of butter.

Preheat the oven to 500°F. Dust a work surface with cornmeal and set the pizza shell on top. Brush the dough with the melted butter, place the strips of prosciutto on top, and spread the greens on top of the prosciutto. Arrange the cheese over the greens. Scatter the pears on top, and grind black pepper over all. Transfer the pizza to a baking sheet, pizza pan, or pizza stone sprinkled with cornmeal and bake until the crust is lightly golden and the cheese fully melted, about 15 to 20 minutes. Let the pizza rest for 5 minutes, and then cut it into 8 wedges. Serve immediately.

Baked Brie with Honey and Pistachios

Preheat the oven to 475°F. Place an 8-ounce round of brie on a small ovenproof serving plate. Drizzle it with 3 tablespoons of dark honey, and scatter ½ cup of roasted and shelled pistachios over the top. Bake for 5 to 7 minutes, until the brie is quite hot but not completely melted. Serve with apple slices and sweet baguette slices alongside.

OYSTERS ON THE HALF SHELL

There's a knack to opening oysters. It takes a good oyster knife, a strong wrist, knowledge of an oyster's anatomy, and plenty of perseverance. It can be tricky, too, and I still bear scars where an oyster knife plunged into my wrist not once, but twice, on the same occasion. The handiest tool for opening oysters is an experienced shucker, if you're lucky enough to know one.

SERVES 4 TO 6

6 dozen small oysters
Ice
1 lemon
Tabasco sauce

Open the oysters and arrange them on top of the ice. Cut the lemon into thin wedges, and cut the wedges in half. Place the lemon pieces in a small serving bowl, and set the bowl alongside the oysters, with a bottle of Tabasco. Serve immediately, with one or both of the mignonette sauces.

Hog Wash Mignonette

Hog Island Shellfish Company, which grows oysters and other shellfish in Tomales Bay in Marin County, gives this mignonette recipe to oyster bars around the state. It is an utterly wonderful accompaniment to the briny shellfish.

½ cup unseasoned rice vinegar
½ cup seasoned rice vinegar
Juice of 2 limes
1 shallot, minced
1 serrano chile, minced
¼ teaspoon minced fresh ginger
2 tablespoons chopped cilantro leaves
¼ teaspoon kosher salt

Combine all of the ingredients in a

Olympia Oyster Cocktail

At the turn of the last century, oyster bars were popular everywhere shellfish was readily available. San Franscico had dozens; today, only Swan Oyster Depot on Polk Street remains. One of the tales told frequently at the bar's old marble counter is of a dedicated shellfish glutton who dumped dozens of little Olympia oysters into a cup of cocktail sauce, drank it down, and announced he had just made himself an oyster cocktail. Bars all over the city began serving the savory concoction, which quickly became a San Francisco tradition. It's easy to duplicate at home, if you happen to have a hundred or so fresh-shucked Olympia oysters and a cup of ice cold cocktail sauce on hand. If not, put Swan Oyster Depot on your itinerary when you visit San Francisco.

glass bowl. Refrigerate for at least 30 minutes before serving. To serve, transfer the wash to a serving bowl and use a teaspoon to add some to each oyster.

Raspberry Mignonette

Bay Bottom Beds grows their Preston Point Miyagi oysters, some of the finest oysters around, near the mouth of Tomales Bay. This is their signature mignonette sauce, bright, delicate, and perfectly suited to their sweet oysters. For a fuller-bodied version, use black raspberry vinegar instead of red, but be certain that it is a low-acid variety.

1 cup low-acid (4.5 percent) red
    raspberry vinegar
1 shallot, minced
Juice of 1 lemon
Kosher salt
Black pepper in a mill

Combine all of the ingredients in a glass bowl. Refrigerate for at least 30 minutes before serving. To serve, transfer the mignonette to a serving bowl and use a teaspoon to add some to each oyster.

A Glossary of West Coast Oysters

Oysters feed by filtering nutrients from sea water as the tides wash over them. For that reason, the particular bay, inlet, or other body of water in which they live leaves its mark on their taste. The subtle variations among oysters from one source or another are highly prized by oyster lovers. San Francisco Bay once teemed with tiny, sweet Olympia oysters, which virtually disappeared in the early twentieth century. Some blame overharvesting, others the raw sewage that spilled into the bay for years. The real culprit, I was told by Paul Olin, marine advisor for the University of California Cooperative Extension, is the sediment carried into the bay from the surrounding watershed. Oysters do still live in San Francisco Bay, but they have not been harvested commercially for decades.

Oyster nomenclature can be confusing. Some oysters are named for the location in which they live, some for their species, others with a proprietary name trademarked by their producer. Here are the market names for West Coast oysters:

BELON
The highly prized European flat oyster, especially popular in France, now is cultivated at both Tomales Bay and Eureka. Strong, briny metallic flavor and firm flesh.

HOG ISLAND SWEETWATER
A trademarked name for the *Crassostrea gigas* oysters raised by the Hog Island Shellfish Company of Tomales Bay. Sweet and mild, with a deep cup.

KUMAMOTO
A small Japanese native now cultivated along the coast of California and Oregon. Plump and mild, pleasantly creamy, and deep-cupped.

OLYMPIA
The only oyster native to the West Coast, this tiny creature once grew wild throughout coastal Pacific waters. Now most are raised in Puget Sound in Washington. Very sweet, mildly salty, with a vaguely coppery taste.

PRESTON POINT MIYAGI
The Bay Bottom Beds company's Pacific *Crassostrea gigas*, cultivated near the northern end of Tomales Bay. Sweet, firm-fleshed, and clean-tasting, with firm shells that make them easier to open than many others.

TRIPLOID
When temperatures rise, oysters turn sexy; their flesh softens and they release a milky liquid that makes them unsuitable for half-shell eating. Triploids, raised in Tomales Bay, were bred to circumvent this problem: They remain firm, briny, and mildly sweet even during the summer.

SPICY GRILLED OYSTERS

Grilled oysters have several advantages for home cooks, and at a summer backyard party in California it is more common to find grilled oysters than oysters on the half shell. During the summer, when ocean waters are warm, most species of oysters become too soft and milky to be served raw. More important, perhaps, shucking a raw oyster properly is difficult, requiring a combination of strength and skill. When you cook oysters on the grill, however, they pop open when they are done. Oh, yes: They are also quite delicious.

SERVES 4 TO 6

1 cup unsalted butter
10 garlic cloves, minced
2 anchovy fillets, drained
2 tablespoons Tabasco sauce
4 to 6 dozen medium oysters

Prepare a very hot fire in an outdoor grill.

In a small saucepan, melt the butter over medium heat. Add the garlic and anchovies, and sauté them for 2 minutes. Add the Tabasco. Remove the pan from the heat and keep it warm.

Place the oysters on the grill, flat side down, until they just begin to pop open, about 3 to 6 minutes, depending on the heat of the grill. Grill the oysters in batches if necessary. Using tongs to remove the oysters from the grill, set them flat side up on a serving platter. Remove and discard the flat halves of the shells, and spoon a little of the sauce over each cooked oyster. Serve hot.

GRILLED SARDINES

I was sitting at the bar of a seafood restaurant at the coast when a nearby couple struck up a conversation with me. He was a fisherman, he told me, from Stockton. Over deep-fried calamari, he entertained me with fishing tales, and, when I asked him about sardines, he laughed. "Well, they're great for bait," he said, "but I wouldn't eat 'em." That's how most Americans seem to feel about the little fish—a pity, because fresh sardines are utterly delicious, whether grilled and drizzled with olive oil and lemon juice or sautéed in butter and garlic. They are enormously popular throughout the Mediterranean, where they are served as snacks and are eaten whole, heads and all, with the fingers.

SERVES 6 TO 8

2 tablespoons olive oil
2 to 3 dozen fresh sardines, cleaned
   (see Note)
Kosher salt
Black pepper in a mill
1 lemon, cut into wedges

Prepare a very hot fire in a grill.

Pour the olive oil into a medium bowl, add the sardines, and turn them to coat them thoroughly. Rub off any excess oil with your fingers, and place the sardines on the grill. Grill them for 3 minutes. Turn the sardines, and grill them until the skin is crisp and browned, 2 or 3 minutes more. Season with salt and pepper. Transfer the sardines to a serving platter, garnish with lemon wedges, and serve immediately.

NOTE: To clean sardines, rinse them under cool water and, as you do so, rub them to remove their scales. If you are lucky enough to have just-caught sardines, you will first need to pull off the gills located at the side of the head and pull out the innards by running your finger along the lower cavity, grabbing and pulling the innards at the same time.

SARDINES IN GARLIC BUTTER

For just a year or so, there was a charming little restaurant a couple of miles from my home in Sebastopol. I was probably their most devoted customer, and next to the phone they posted a notice with my phone number: "Call Michele when there's fresh sardines," it read. One rainy night, a call came. I jumped into my car, and as I raced out of the driveway I hit a deep mud puddle and became hopelessly stuck. Not to be denied those succulent sardines I

already could taste, I grabbed my umbrella and walked into town.

SERVES 4 TO 6

2 to 3 dozen fresh sardines, cleaned (see Note, to left)
Kosher salt
Black pepper in a mill
4 tablespoons unsalted butter
4 to 5 garlic cloves, minced
2 lemons, 1 cut in half and 1 cut into wedges

Season the sardines with salt and pepper. In a large heavy skillet over medium heat, heat the butter until it is foamy. Add the garlic, and sauté for 2 minutes. Add the sardines, and sauté for 3 or 4 minutes more. Turn them, and sauté until the sardines are slightly golden and cooked through, about 4 minutes. Transfer the sardines to a serving platter.

Raise the heat to high, and squeeze the juice from the lemon halves into the pan. Swirl the juice in the pan, and reduce it by half. Pour the pan juices over the sardines, garnish with lemon wedges, and serve immediately.

Variation:

Sauté the sardines in 4 to 5 tablespoons of olive oil instead of butter. In a small bowl, combine 5 cloves of garlic, chopped, a generous pinch of paprika, 1 tablespoon of kosher salt, and black pepper. After turning the sardines, scatter the garlic mixture over them, and sauté them for another 2 or 3 minutes more. Pour ¼ cup red wine vinegar over the sardines, simmer for 30 seconds, then transfer the sardines to a serving platter. Raise the heat and simmer until the vinegar is reduced by half. Stir in 1 tablespoon of minced Italian parsley, pour the sauce over the sardines, garnish with lemon wedges, and serve immediately.

GRILLED PRAWNS WITH STRAWBERRIES AND FENNEL

*A*t first glance, this combination of flavors might seem unusual. Yet it's evocative of so many traditional Asian dishes, including Chinese sweet-and-sour prawns with chunks of pineapple. In this dish, the sweetness is provided by strawberries, honey, and fennel, while the tartness comes from the acid in the strawberries and from the vinegar. If the use of *prawns* is confusing to you, keep in mind that in California we use *shrimp* to designate smaller crustaceans like bay shrimp and rock shrimp and *prawn* for their larger cousins.

SERVES 6 TO 8

1½ pounds prawns or large shrimp (12 to 15 per pound), peeled and deveined, with tails intact

24 to 30 bamboo skewers, soaked in water for at least 1 hour
30 whole strawberries
1 cup Honey Pepper Vinaigrette (page 157)
2 cups sliced strawberries
1 large or 2 small fennel bulbs, trimmed and sliced thin
1 tablespoon mint leaves, cut into thin julienne
Sprigs of mint

Prepare a very hot fire in a grill.

Thread each skewer with 2 prawns and 1 or 2 whole strawberries. Brush the prawns with a small amount of the vinaigrette, and place them on the grill. Turn the prawns after 2 minutes, brush them again with the vinaigrette, and continue cooking until the prawns turn pink, about 2 to 3 minutes. Do not overcook.

Quickly toss together the sliced strawberries and sliced fennel and spread the mixture over a serving platter. Stir the julienned mint into the remaining vinaigrette. Place the skewers on the bed of fennel and strawberries, spoon the vinaigrette over, garnish with mint sprigs, and serve immediately.

CRISPY SHRIMP-AND-CRAB TOAST

*H*ere is an example of a classic California product—sourdough bread—influencing a traditional dish from another cuisine, in this case Thai. Kasma Loha-Unchit loved the sourdough bread she found when she came to the U.S. from Thailand and began using it in place of the blander bread she had used at home; she was kind enough to share this recipe with me.

SERVES 4 TO 6

25 ¼-inch slices of a sourdough baguette (about ⅔ of a baguette)
¾ pound shrimp, shelled, deveined, and finely chopped
¾ cup cooked crab meat
1 teaspoon white pepper, preferably fresh-ground
4 large garlic cloves, minced
2 to 3 teaspoons minced cilantro roots or bottom stems (not leaves)
½ teaspoon sea salt or kosher salt
1 teaspoon sugar
2 teaspoons fish sauce
1 egg, beaten
2 tablespoons sesame seeds
2 cups peanut oil, or more, for deep-frying
25 cilantro leaves, preferably small ones
3 serrano chiles, seeded and cut into slivers

1 cucumber, sliced thin
2 tablespoons pickled ginger (available in Asian markets)
½ cup Sweet-and-Sour Plum Sauce (recipe follows), or bottled plum sauce

Preheat the oven to 200°F. Spread the bread slices on a baking sheet and toast them in the oven for 10 to 15 minutes, or until they are completely dry. Set them aside.

In a medium bowl, combine the shrimp and crab. Using a mortar and pestle, pulverize the white pepper until it forms a fine powder. Add the garlic and cilantro roots or stems, and pound them together with the pepper to make a fine paste. Add the paste to the shrimp and crab. Add the salt, sugar, fish sauce, and egg, and mix together thoroughly.

Spread some of the shrimp mixture firmly onto each baguette slice, mounding it in the middle and rounding it off at the edges. Scatter each piece with sesame seeds and press the seeds lightly into the shrimp.

Place 2 cups of oil in a wok or medium skillet, and set it over high heat. When the oil is hot, reduce the heat to medium and fry each baguette slice, spread side down, for 1½ to 2 minutes, or until the bread is golden brown. Turn the slices and fry them, bread side down, for just a few seconds more. Transfer the toasts to absorbent paper, then cool them briefly on a wire rack.

Top each toast with a cilantro leaf and a sliver of serrano. Arrange the toasts on a

It Rains Fishes

"We don't have salmon, halibut, or sea bass in Thailand," Kasma Loha-Unchit recalls, "and the crab in Thailand are very small. I love the Dungeness crab here."

Kasma came to California from Thailand in 1972 and settled in Oakland. She found herself inspired not only by the seafood, but also by the produce.

"There are so many chiles—jalapeños, serranos, Fresno peppers. I use them a lot. The flavors of my cooking are still authentically Thai, but I use California vegetables for their good color and good taste. Asparagus is just beginning in Thailand, and it's never as good as it is in California. We don't have so many squashes. The corn here is wonderful. And I love sourdough bread."

Kasma learned to cook in Thailand as a young girl at her mother's side. When she first arrived in the U.S., she found little interest in the cooking of her homeland and there were many ingredients she could not find. Things changed in the 1980s, when Thai cuisine became enormously popular and the ingredients became available. Kasma began teaching cooking classes; some students came looking for a healthier way to eat, and others had been intrigued by the foods in Thai restaurants. She continues to teach today, and she also leads culinary tours to Thailand.

In 1994, Kasma's first cookbook, *It Rains Fishes: Legends, Traditions and the Joys of Thai Cooking*, was published. The book is one of the most delightful and informative books on food I have ever read.

---

serving platter lined with cucumber slices and pickled ginger. Serve while still warm and crispy, with the plum sauce on the side.

Sweet-and-Sour Plum Sauce

MAKES ABOUT ½ CUP

2 red serrano chiles or 2 jalapeños, minced, or 1 teaspoon ground dried red chiles or red chile flakes

2 Chinese salted or pickled plums, pitted (available in Asian markets)

⅓ cup sugar

3 tablespoons distilled white vinegar

If you are using fresh chiles, use a mortar and pestle to grind them to a paste. Add the plums to this paste (or to the dried chiles), and grind more until the plums are incorporated in the paste. Transfer the mixture to a small saucepan, add the sugar and vinegar, set over low heat, and stir until the sugar is melted. Simmer for 1 or 2 minutes, or until the mixture is smooth and thick. Transfer the sauce to a small dish and let it cool before serving.

NEW POTATOES WITH GOLDEN CAVIAR

In the early 1980s, nearly every party one might go to would feature a version of this appetizer, an enticing little morsel that seemed, for a time, synonymous with California Cuisine. You don't see it as often these days, which is too bad; it deserves to be part of any good cook's repertoire.

American golden caviar, harvested from whitefish in the Great Lakes, is much less expensive than sturgeon caviar.

SERVES 4 TO 6

1½ pounds small new red potatoes, scrubbed and cut in half
3 tablespoons butter
Kosher salt
Black pepper in a mill
½ cup crème fraîche (see Note)
2 ounces American golden caviar or other caviar
Handful of chives, cut into 1½-inch lengths

Preheat the oven to 350°F.

Cook the potatoes in boiling salted water until they are just tender, about 10 to 12 minutes. Rinse them under cool water and dry them thoroughly. Using a melon baller, scoop out an indentation from the rounded side of each potato half; reserve the removed potato balls for another purpose.

Put the butter on a baking sheet and place the sheet in the oven until the butter is melted. Remove the sheet from the oven, spread the melted butter evenly over the surface of the sheet, then set the potatoes, flat side down, on the sheet. Season with salt and pepper. Bake the potatoes for 15 to 20 minutes, or until they are lightly browned. Remove them from the oven, and let them cool slightly.

Arrange the potatoes on a serving platter. Place about ½ teaspoon of crème fraîche in the indentation in the top of each potato half, and top with a small spoonful of caviar. Garnish each potato half with a stalk of chive, and serve immediately.

NOTE: If crème fraîche is unavailable, make a substitute: Mix together ⅔ cup sour cream and ⅓ cup heavy cream. Let them sit, unrefrigerated, for 6 hours or overnight. Store in the refrigerator and use as you would true crème fraîche.

FRESH SPRING ROLLS

Asian cooking has been a part of California cooking since the mid-1800s, but it has not been until recently that many of the necessary ingredients have become readily accessible. Cooking classes in Thai, Korean, Japanese, and many styles of Chinese cuisines have made the techniques accessible, too. Home cooks who twenty years ago never would have considered anything more complicated than teriyaki chicken, a dish that came to California from Hawaii, now understand the basic grammar of many Asian cuisines.

SERVES 4 TO 6

4 ounces thin rice noodles
  (vermicelli)
Boiling water
8 spring roll wrappers
2 cups mesclun or red leaf lettuce,
  torn into medium pieces
1½ cups cooked chicken meat, cut into
  small julienne or shredded (see
  Note)
1 small cucumber, peeled, quartered
  lengthwise, seeded, and cut into
  thin julienne
2 tablespoons mint leaves
2 tablespoons cilantro leaves
¾ cup mustard, onion, or bean
  sprouts
¼ cup Thai Chile Lime Sauce (page
  149)
3 tablespoons hoisin sauce
½ teaspoon Thai red curry paste
  (available in Asian markets)
Sprigs of mint and cilantro, for
  garnish

Place the rice noodles in a large bowl, pour boiling water over them, and let them stand for 3 minutes. Rinse them thoroughly, drain completely, and set them aside.

Prepare the wrappers: Fill a large bowl with warm water (about 110°F) and cover a work surface with a damp tea towel. Dip a wrapper in the water, turning it so that it is fully wet. Set it on the tea towel, smooth it out, and fold the tea towel over it to cover it. When the wrapper is completely softened, about 1 minute, place a few pieces of mesclun or lettuce greens in the center of the circle, leaving about a 2-inch border on the bottom. Place some of the noodles on top of the greens, and top the noodles with some of the chicken, followed by the cucumber, mint leaves, cilantro leaves, and sprouts. Drizzle a small spoonful of the lime chile sauce over the filling. To form the roll, fold the bottom part of the wrapper up over the filling and then fold in the two sides. Using both hands, shape what looks like a Mexican-style burrito. Repeat until all 8 of the wrappers have been filled and shaped.

In a small bowl, mix together the hoisin sauce, 2 tablespoons water, and the curry paste. To serve, cut each spring roll into 3 or 4 pieces, arrange on individual plates, and garnish with sprigs of cilantro and mint. Serve with the hoisin mixture as a dipping sauce and with the remaining lime chile sauce alongside.

NOTE: You can use leftover chicken in this recipe, such as Thai-style Grilled Chicken Breast (page 313), Lemon-scented Thai Chicken (page 314), or even simple roasted chicken. You can also substitute shrimp, duck, pork, lamb, or beef for the chicken.

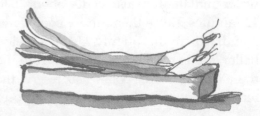

MAHOGANY CHICKEN WINGS

*I*n this version of spicy chicken wings, the wings are cloaked in a syrupy sauce similar but not identical to classic teriyaki sauce; orange juice, orange zest, and hot pepper flakes create a more complex flavor.

SERVES 6 TO 8

1½ cups fresh orange juice
1½ cups soy sauce
1½ cups (packed) brown sugar
6 to 8 garlic cloves, minced
1 1½-inch piece fresh ginger, peeled and minced
Zest of 2 oranges, minced fine
½ teaspoon crushed red chile flakes
40 chicken drummettes, rinsed and dried
4 to 5 scallions, trimmed and cut into small rounds
1 orange, sliced thin

Combine the orange juice, soy sauce, sugar, garlic, ginger, orange zest, and chile flakes in a heavy saucepan over medium heat. Heat the mixture through and stir to dissolve the sugar. Remove the sauce from the heat and let it cool. Place the chicken drummettes in a glass or crockery bowl or baking dish and pour the cooled marinade over them, turning them so they are well coated. Cover the dish and refrigerate it for several hours or overnight.

Chinese Popcorn

In China, the most popular snack in movie theaters is sautéed chicken feet. You find them in California, too, in Chinatowns, in home kitchens, and in family recipe books, where they might be seasoned with soy sauce, rice wine, and ginger. Chickens sold without their feet and heads are as distressing to Asians as is the sight of heads and feet to most Americans who shop in supermarkets, where meats bear little if any resemblance to the original bird or other animal. Even most European markets sell chickens intact; they are essential for achieving full flavor in a stock or stewed bird.

Preheat the oven to 375°F. Remove the wings from the marinade (do not discard the marinade) and arrange them on oiled baking sheets. Bake them, turning them once and basting them with marinade 2 or 3 times, for about 45 minutes, or until they are glossy.

Place the wings on a serving platter, scatter the scallions over the top, and garnish with orange slices. Serve immediately, with plenty of napkins.

Variation:

Use a whole chicken, cut up, in place of the chicken drummettes, and serve as a main course with steamed rice. Bring the remaining marinade to a boil, reduce it by half, and spoon it over the rice. Garnish with scallions and orange slices.

CHIPOTLE CHICKEN WINGS

• •

"*I*f olive oil has a taste as old as water," Jacqueline Higuera McMahan writes in the *Chipotle Chile Cook Book*, "the chipotle chile has a fragrance as old and elusive as smoke." The word *chipotle* comes from Nahuatl, the language of the Aztecs, from *chil*, chile, and *pochilli*, smoke. The Aztecs smoked plump, thick-skinned jalapeños to preserve them (the humidity made it difficult to preserve them by drying); their flavor was a byproduct of the smoking process. Until recently, it was easiest to find chipotles in Latin markets *en adobo*, that is, in a thick sauce of ancho chiles, tomatoes, vinegar, and herbs, packed in cans. Today, dried chipotles are readily available throughout California, thanks in part to Lee and Wayne James, farmers in Healdsburg. They operate Tierra Vegetables, which specializes in a selection of smoked and dried chiles, sold at farmers' markets and by mail order (see Resources).

SERVES 4 TO 6

12 dried chipotles
Boiling water
6 garlic cloves, crushed
¼ cup fresh lime juice (from 2 to 3 limes)
¼ cup canned tomato sauce or Basic Tomato Sauce (page 26)
Kosher salt
Black pepper in a mill
2 pounds (20 to 24) chicken drummettes
¼ cup sour cream
2 tablespoons half-and-half
2 tablespoons minced cilantro leaves
1 serrano chile, minced
Sprigs of cilantro, large stems removed

In a small bowl, cover the chipotles with boiling water. Set the bowl aside for 30 minutes. Drain the chipotles.

Preheat the oven to 325°F. Combine the chipotles, garlic, lime juice, and tomato sauce in a blender or food processor, and blend well. Season with salt and pepper. Arrange the drummettes in a baking dish that will hold them all in a single layer, and pour the chipotle sauce over them. Bake, turning once, for 40 minutes, or until they are golden brown.

Meanwhile, make a cilantro cream: Stir together the sour cream and half-and-half in a small bowl. Stir in the cilantro, serrano, and salt to taste. Set the bowl aside.

Remove the drummettes from the oven and let them rest for 5 minutes. To serve, spread the cilantro sprigs on a serving platter and arrange the drummettes on top. Serve immediately, with the cilantro cream on the side.

Bustelo's

Larry Watson, a mechanical design engineer by trade, fell in love with chile peppers while living in Cholula, halfway between Mexico City and Veracruz in the state of Puebla, where he watched his friend and neighbor Justino make chipotles by smoking ripe jalapeños. Many years later, Larry settled in the wine country of northern California, where, as is inevitable, he encountered the pretensions of wine connoisseurs. When Larry began making a line of hot pepper sauces, called Bustelo's, he mimicked a winemaker's attention to detail. "I use a blend of excellent red, white, and rice vinegars," he would tell his friends. "I blend my chiles to fill the entire mouth, from a chipotle bass to a habanero top note. I use only fresh-peeled garlic. I age Bustelo's in American white oak barrels for a minimum of one year."

When he shared his first pepper sauces with his friends, they loved them, although Larry says it took him two years to realize that their description that "Bustelo has a big nose, full mouth, and long finish" referred to him and not his new product. Now, he makes six hundred cases of Bustelo's a year. What began as a friendly send-up of friends' attitudes has become a successful business. Each bottle of Bustelo's announces that the "pungent capsicum-acetic acid solution is intended for gastric and aphrodisiac stimulation."

Variation:

Replace the chipotle sauce with 3 tablespoons achiote (available at Latin markets and specialty food stores), 3 serrano chiles, minced, 4 garlic cloves, crushed, the juice of 1 lemon, and ⅓ cup warm water, blended well in a blender or food processor. This version is less spicy, but with distinct Mexican flavors.

FOIE GRAS WITH SAUTÉED APPLES

Seared foie gras can be difficult to prepare at home because most home kitchens are not equipped with stoves that generate enough heat to cook it properly. If foie gras is cooked too slowly, it virtually disintegrates. Should you have a commercial range—in California, more and more devoted home cooks do—or simply have a daring personality, just be sure the pan is very hot before adding the foie gras. One-third to one-half of a foie gras will easily serve 6 people or more; reserve the remainder for another recipe, such as Terrine of Foie Gras (page 43). If you cannot get foie gras from a local supplier, you can order it by mail (see Resources).

SERVES 6

2½ cups filtered apple juice
½ cup apple cider vinegar
1 teaspoon fresh-ground pepper
4 tablespoons butter
⅓ to ½ duck foie gras, at room
    temperature, cut into 6 generous
    ½-inch slices
Kosher salt
Black pepper in a mill
1 or 2 firm tart apples, peeled, and cut
    into ¼-inch slices

Make the cider sauce: Pour 1 cup of the apple juice in a small saucepan over medium heat, and simmer until the juice has nearly completely evaporated. Add the remaining apple juice, the vinegar, and the 1 teaspoon pepper, and reduce by two-thirds. Remove the sauce from the heat, and swirl in 1 tablespoon of the butter, a teaspoon at a time, until it is just incorporated. Set the pan aside and keep it warm.

Season the foie gras slices lightly with salt and pepper. In a skillet or sauté pan, heat the remaining 3 tablespoons butter over medium heat until it is foamy. Add half of the apple slices, and sauté them for 3 to 4 minutes, turn them, and sauté them 3 to 4 minutes more, until they are golden. Divide the apples among 6 warmed serving plates, pour any pan juices over the apples, and wipe the pan dry.

Raise the heat under the pan as high as possible. When the pan is very hot, add 3 slices of foie gras. Sear them on 1 side for about 30 seconds, turn them, and sear them on the other side, for 30 seconds more.

Another French Connection

In 1985, Guillermo and Junny Gonzalez and their daughters, Maria and Helena, left their native El Salvador. They studied the production of foie gras in the Périgord in southwestern France, then began to search for a place in the United States to begin their own farm. They were drawn to the temperate climate and fertile soil of northern California, and eventually purchased a farm nestled against the southeastern edge of Sonoma Mountain, in the appellation of Carneros. Today their company, Sonoma Foie Gras, provides foie gras and other Muscovy duck products to chefs and home cooks. Foie gras is the fattened liver of duck and geese; it became a delicacy long ago in Egypt, when geese flying south for the winter were killed for food. Their enlarged livers—the birds eat enormous amounts in preparation for their long flight—became highly valued for their rich taste and voluptuous texture. The Egyptians developed a technique, which the French went on to perfect, of fattening farm-raised geese to produce the same effect. Sonoma Foie Gras is one of two companies in the U.S. producing foie gras.

Transfer the slices to the serving plates, setting 1 slice on top of each portion of apples. Discard any fat that has collected in the pan, and cook the remaining 3 slices in the same way.

Spoon some of the cider sauce over each portion, add salt and pepper, and serve immediately.

TERRINE OF FOIE GRAS

*T*his is a simple yet extraordinary appetizer to prepare for the holidays or a very special occasion. The recipe was developed by Junny Gonzalez of Sonoma Foie Gras.

SERVES 8 TO 10

1 duck foie gras
Kosher salt
White pepper, preferably fresh-
    ground
2 tablespoons Cognac, Armagnac, or
    other brandy, or white wine
Croutons or toasted bread

Let the foie gras rest at room temperature for 30 minutes, and then remove it from its package. Cut the large and small lobes apart and remove any visible fat. Cut part way through the bottom of each lobe, open gently with your fingers, and remove and discard the large vein. If any small pieces break off, tuck them into the larger pieces. Season the foie gras all over with salt and pepper, and press the pieces into a terrine, smooth side up. Sprinkle the liquor over the foie gras, cover with the terrine lid, and refrigerate overnight.

Preheat the oven to 200°F. Remove the foie gras from the refrigerator and let it rest at room temperature for 20 minutes. Set the terrine in a roasting pan filled with hot water that comes half-way up the sides of the terrine, and place the pan on the middle rack of the oven. Cook for 20 minutes. Remove the pan from the oven, and the terrine from its bath, and let the terrine rest until it has cooled slightly. Pour off and save any fat that has melted. Press the foie gras gently into the terrine, using the lid turned upside down, cover the terrine again, and refrigerate for 3 days before serving. (The flavors will develop during this time.) To serve, gently loosen the edges of the terrine with a knife, remove and save the visible fat, and slice the foie gras. Serve with croutons or toast. The terrine will keep, covered, in the refrigerator for up to 10 days and in the freezer for up to 3 months.

SPICY STEAK TARTARE

*M*any people consider raw beef and raw eggs pleasures of the past, too dangerous to be enjoyed today. I feel otherwise. If you know the sources of your products, buy only the best from absolutely reputable purveyors, and practice good sanitation in your preparation, I believe you can enjoy classic dishes such as steak tartare, which was extremely popular in California's early days, and its spicy variation here.

1 baguette, sliced thin
2 pounds steak, such as rib-eye,
  New York strip, or filet mignon
3 egg yolks
1 teaspoon Dijon mustard
1 teaspoon Tabasco sauce
1 serrano chile, minced
4 garlic cloves, minced
Kosher salt
Black pepper in a mill
6 garlic cloves, unpeeled
Extra virgin olive oil
¼ cup minced cilantro leaves

Preheat the oven to 300°F. Spread out the baguette slices on a baking sheet and bake them until they are dry and golden. Remove them from the oven and set them aside.

Trim away any exterior fat from the beef, and cut the beef into chunks. Chop the meat fine, or grind it in a hand-cranked meat grinder fitted with a medium blade. Place the ground meat in a medium bowl, add the egg yolks, mustard, Tabasco, serrano, and minced garlic, and mix well with a fork. Season with salt and pepper and refrigerate, covered, until ready to serve.

Cut the whole cloves of garlic in half lengthwise, and rub each toasted baguette slice with garlic. Arrange the toasts on serving platters and drizzle each with olive oil. Top each slice with a spoonful of the steak tartare. Sprinkle minced cilantro over each piece, and serve immediately.

SPICY BEEF STRIPS AND RICE BALLS

Many Asian cuisines feature strips of meat, poultry, or fish eaten with a small ball of rice, often simply scooped up with your fingers. This recipe builds on the tradition, pressing the rice into balls, wrapping them with marinated steak, and threading them on skewers. If you don't want to make the rice balls, stir-fry the marinated beef and serve it on top of the sticky rice.

1¼ pounds rib-eye steak or other
  boneless cut
½ cup soy sauce
2 tablespoons fish sauce
2 tablespoons sugar
2 teaspoons minced garlic
2 serrano chiles, minced
20 to 24 bamboo skewers
2 cups cooked Sticky Rice (page 218)
Sprigs of cilantro, for garnish
¼ cup Thai Lime Chile Sauce (page
  149)

Cut the steak in ¼-inch-wide crosswise strips and place them in a shallow bowl. In another small bowl, mix together the soy sauce, fish sauce, sugar, garlic, and serranos, and pour the mixture over the beef. Let the beef marinate for about 1 hour in the refrigerator. While the beef marinates, soak the bamboo skewers in water.

Using your hands, press some of the rice into a small ball 1 to 1½ inches in diameter, pressing firmly so that it sticks together well. Continue until you have used all of the rice.

Prepare a stovetop or outdoor grill. Remove the beef from the marinade, a strip at a time, and wrap it around a rice ball. Carefully thread the ball onto a bamboo skewer, pressing the rice firmly if necessary to keep it on the skewer. Continue, putting one beef strip and one rice ball on each skewer, until all the strips and balls have been placed on skewers. Brush the beef-rice balls with the marinade. Grill at a medium-hot temperature until the meat is just rare, about 2 minutes on each side. Set the balls on a platter, garnish with cilantro sprigs, and serve immediately, with the lime chile sauce on the side.

Roasted Garlic Puree

P reheat the oven to 325°F. Clean 2 or 3 heads of garlic, leaving the bulb intact but removing any dirt that may cling to the roots and as much of the dry outer skin as will come off easily. Place the garlic in a small ovenproof dish or pan, add ½ cup olive oil and ¼ cup water, and season with salt and pepper. Cover the dish, and bake for 50 to 60 minutes, until the garlic is quite soft. Remove from the oven, transfer the garlic to absorbent paper, and let it cool. When the garlic is cool enough to handle, place a head on a cutting board, remove the root, and use the heel of your hand to press out the garlic pulp. If necessary, squeeze out the pulp clove by clove. Scrape the pulp off the cutting board, place it in a small bowl, and mash it with a fork until it is smooth. Each bulb will yield about 2 tablespoons of puree. Use immediately or refrigerate, covered, for up to 4 days.

ROASTED GARLIC MEATBALLS

G ilroy, inland from Monterey, is the center of garlic production in California. Thousands of tons of garlic are grown in the area each year, most of it for the processed garlic industry. Much of the garlic grown around Gilroy is of a single white-skinned variety, hot and sharp in taste, known variously as California Early, California Late, California White, and California Silverskin. Elsewhere in the state, farmers and backyard gardeners grow varieties with more complex flavors and textures. All garlic is tamed when roasted until soft. In this recipe, roasted garlic contributes both flavor and texture, resulting in meatballs that are moister than most. For a main course, serve these meatballs with pasta, olive oil, and grated cheese.

SERVES 6 TO 8

2 tablespoons olive oil
2 shallots, minced
10 garlic cloves, minced
1 pound ground beef
1 pound ground pork
½ cup Roasted Garlic Puree (page 45)
2 tablespoons minced Italian parsley
1 teaspoon fresh thyme leaves
1 teaspoon minced oregano leaves
4 ounces (¾ cup) dry jack or Parmigiano-Reggiano, grated
1¼ cups Fresh Bread Crumbs (see box)
Kosher salt
Black pepper in a mill
Flour, for dusting
Sprigs of Italian parsley
½ cup sour cream or crème fraîche (or substitute; see Note, page 37)

Heat the olive oil in a small sauté pan over medium heat. Add the shallots, and sauté them until they are transparent,

about 6 minutes. Add the garlic, and sauté 2 minutes more. Remove the pan from the heat and let it cool.

In a medium bowl, combine the beef, pork, and garlic puree. With a slotted spoon, add the sautéed shallots and garlic. Add the parsley, thyme, oregano, cheese, and bread crumbs. Mix thoroughly. Using the same sauté pan, sauté a small amount of the mixture, taste, and season the entire mixture with salt and pepper.

To form the meatballs, dust your hands with flour and roll about 2 teaspoons of the mixture between your palms. Place the formed meatball on a baking sheet or wax

Fresh Bread Crumbs

To make fresh bread crumbs, cut slices from a loaf of 1- or 2-day-old bread and tear the slices into chunks. Place about 1 cup of chunks in a food processor fitted with a metal blade. Pulse until the chunks have been reduced to crumbs, empty the crumbs into a bowl, and continue until you have made as many bread crumbs as you need. Store them in a sealed container in the refrigerator.

To toast the crumbs, spread them over a baking sheet, place them in a preheated 300°F oven, and toast them for 10 to 15 minutes, or until they are lightly golden. Remove them from the oven, let them cool, and store them in a sealed container in the refrigerator.

paper and continue until all have been made. (The meatballs can be covered tightly with plastic wrap and refrigerated for up to 1 day.)

Preheat the oven to 350°F. To cook, sauté several meatballs at a time in a large heavy sauté pan, until they are evenly browned. Place the cooked meatballs on a baking sheet, and when all of them have been browned, bake them for 15 minutes. Remove them from the oven and let them rest 5 minutes.

To serve, spread the parsley over a serving platter and arrange the meatballs on top. Put the sour cream or crème fraîche in a small bowl and place it on the platter, with plenty of toothpicks alongside. Serve immediately.

THAI MEATBALLS WITH COCONUT- PEANUT SAUCE

*I*f any meatballs are left over, toss them with glass noodles and Thai Lime Chile Sauce (page 149) and serve the Coconut-Peanut Sauce alongside. It is not traditional, but it is delicious.

SERVES 4 TO 6

8 ounces ground pork
4 ounces ground beef
6 garlic cloves, minced
¼ cup minced cilantro leaves
1 teaspoon grated fresh ginger
1 to 2 serrano chiles, minced
1 teaspoon lime zest, minced
2 tablespoons fish sauce
2 eggs, beaten
½ cup all-purpose flour
Peanut oil, for frying
1 to 2 bunches of cilantro, separated into sprigs
2 tablespoons mint leaves, cut into thin ribbons
1¼ cups Coconut-Peanut Sauce (recipe follows)

Combine the pork, beef, garlic, minced cilantro, ginger, serranos, and lime zest in a medium bowl. Add the fish sauce and eggs and mix until well combined.

Put the flour in a bowl and dust your hands with it. Roll 2 teaspoons of meat into a 1-inch ball between your palms. Drop the meatball into the flour, shake the bowl to coat it thoroughly, then transfer it to a baking sheet or wax paper. Continue until all the meatballs have been formed.

Heat about 2 inches of oil in a wok over medium-high heat until it is very hot but not smoking. Add the meatballs, 3 or 4 at a time, and fry them, turning them once, until they are lightly browned. Transfer the meatballs to absorbent paper. Continue until all of the meatballs have been cooked.

To serve, spread the cilantro sprigs on a platter, arrange the meatballs on top, and scatter the mint ribbons over the meatballs. Spoon the Coconut-Peanut Sauce into a small dish and set it on the platter, along with plenty of toothpicks for the meatballs. Serve immediately.

Coconut-Peanut Sauce

Similar recipes suggest peanut butter in place of ground peanuts, but I do not recommend it. This sauce can also be served with grilled or roasted chicken.

MAKES ABOUT 1¼ CUPS

1 tablespoon peanut oil
2 serrano chiles, minced
2 tablespoons minced scallions
4 garlic cloves, minced
2 ounces shelled roasted peanuts, ground
1 cup thick coconut milk
1 or 2 tablespoons coconut cream
2 to 3 tablespoons fish sauce
1 teaspoon lime zest, minced
Juice of 1 lime
1 tablespoon minced cilantro

In a small saucepan or in a wok, heat the peanut oil over medium heat. Add the serranos, scallions, and garlic, and sauté them, stirring constantly, for 3 minutes. Add the peanuts, reduce the heat to low, and stir in the coconut milk, 1 tablespoon of the coconut cream, 2 tablespoons of the fish sauce, the lime zest, and the lime juice. Stir and heat through but do not boil. Taste the sauce and adjust the seasoning with more coconut cream and more fish sauce. Remove from the heat, stir in the cilantro, and serve, or refrigerate until ready to serve. (If you reheat the sauce, do not boil it.)

THAI LAMB IN ROMAINE LEAVES

In this recipe, the evocative and classically Thai combination of ginger, chiles, cilantro, and lime juice highlights ground lamb. If you prefer, you can use ground beef, ground pork, or ground chicken.

SERVES 4

1 head romaine lettuce, leaves separated
1 tablespoon olive oil
3 garlic cloves, minced
1 2-inch piece of ginger, peeled and grated
1 pound ground lamb
¼ teaspoon dried red pepper flakes
1 serrano chile, minced
3 tablespoons fresh lime juice (from 1 to 2 limes)
1 tablespoon fish sauce
¼ cup mint leaves, cut into thin julienne
¼ cup cilantro leaves
2 teaspoons sugar
1 teaspoon sesame seeds, lightly toasted

Cut the larger lettuce leaves in halves or in thirds, so that all leaves are approximately 3 inches by 3 or 4 inches. Heat the olive oil in a skillet over medium-low heat, add the garlic and ginger, and sauté for 2 minutes. Add the lamb and cook it, breaking it up with a fork, until it loses its

color. Stir in the red pepper flakes and remove from the heat.

In a small bowl, mix together the serrano, lime juice, fish sauce, half of the mint, half of the cilantro, and the sugar. Drizzle half of the sauce over the lamb, and toss quickly.

To serve, place the lamb in a serving dish, set the dish on a large platter, and surround the dish with the lettuce leaves. Serve the remaining sauce and the sesame seeds, in bowls, alongside. Guests spoon some of the lamb into a lettuce leaf, add a dab of sauce and a

sprinkling of sesame seeds, roll up the leaf, and eat it in a single bite.

Grape Leaves

· ·

The grapevine is an integral element of the California landscape. From Los Angeles, where there are a few small vineyards in the eastern hills, up to the wine country along the north coast, grapevines are everywhere. In some areas, vast expanses of newly planted vineyards stretch as far as the eye can see; in other places, gnarled old vines serve as reminders of California's long history as America's first viticultural region.

Grape leaves are everywhere, too, and not just in the landscape. They appear on wine labels and posters, on jewelry, on fabrics used for everything from clothing to curtains and tablecloths. Iron is forged into elaborate decorative leaves and vines, and grape leaves are molded into cement and stucco frescoes. Fresh, grape leaves adorn buffet tables and are used as coasters.

Once common as a food only in ethnic communities, such as the Armenian enclaves of the Central Valley, edible grape leaves today are almost as ubiquitous as the California sun. You find them bottled in jars in every grocery store and supermarket.

Grape leaves have many uses. Wrap small circles or squares of cheese in a single leaf, grill it until the cheese melts, and serve with hot bread. Fill the cavity of a rainbow trout with minced herbs, lemon zest, and bread crumbs, brush the outside of the fish with olive oil and lemon and season it with salt and pepper, and wrap the fish in 2 or 3 grape leaves. Brush the leaves with olive oil, and grill or bake until done, about 7 or 8 minutes on each side on a hot grill or 20 minutes in a 375°F oven.

MINCED LAMB DOLMAS

*M*y first taste of a grape leaf came about twenty-five years ago, at a party following the annual Stanford-Berkeley football game, and I have been making these lamb-stuffed leaves ever since. I usually serve them as an appetizer, but occasionally I serve them as a main course, accompanied by Roasted Eggplant Soup (page 86) and rice.

SERVES 6 TO 8

1½ pounds shoulder or leg lamb meat, trimmed of fat
2 tablespoons olive oil
6 garlic cloves, minced
1 tablespoon minced oregano
1 tablespoon minced lemon zest
1 tablespoon fresh-ground black pepper
Kosher salt
1 cup Basic Tomato Sauce (page 26) or canned tomato sauce
¾ cup beef stock
Juice of 2 lemons
¼ cup extra virgin olive oil
30 to 40 bottled grape leaves

Cut the lamb meat into cubes, and, using a very sharp knife, mince the cubes fine. Heat the 2 tablespoons olive oil in a heavy frying pan over medium heat. Add the minced lamb and cook it, using a fork to break it up, until it is almost done but

still slightly pink. Add the garlic, oregano, and 2 teaspoons of the lemon zest, and sauté for 2 two minutes more. Remove from the heat, and add 1 teaspoon of the black pepper and salt to taste. Let the mixture cool to room temperature.

Make the sauce: In a small saucepan, combine the tomato sauce, stock, lemon juice, ¼ cup olive oil, the remaining lemon zest, and the remaining black pepper. Add salt to taste. Bring to a boil, reduce the heat, and simmer for 5 minutes. Remove from the heat and set aside.

The Original 27 Counties

Colusa County lies due north of Napa and Yolo counties in north-central California. It is a sparsely populated, mostly agricultural area, bounded on the east by the Sacramento River. Long a center of wheat production (the northern part of the original county eventually became Glenn County, named for Hugh Glenn, known in his day as the Wheat King), today it is also known for rice farming. The Colusa Rice and Waterfowl Festival is held each year in November—the only celebration in the country, as far as I know, to celebrate rice and ducks in tandem—and the county is also home to the annual California State Duck Calling Championship. Sugar beets are another important crop, and there is livestock and dairy farming as well.

Preheat the oven to 325°F. Line a shallow baking dish with the grape leaves. Place a leaf, dull side up, on your work surface, and place 1½ to 2 teaspoons of filling in the center. Fold up the stem end of the leaf over the filling, fold in the 2 sides, and roll the bundle towards the tip of the leaf. Place the leaf, seam side down, in the baking dish. When all of the grape leaves have been filled and rolled, pour the sauce over them. Bake them for 40 minutes, or until the leaves are very tender and the sauce is bubbly hot. Remove the dolmas from the oven and let them cool for 10 minutes before serving.

GRILLED BLT KEBABS

Californians have been to known to grill virtually everything, from apricots to burritos and pizzas to whole stuffed turkeys. For this appetizer, I have retooled the classic BLT ingredients to fit onto skewers.

SERVES 4 TO 8

32 1½-inch cubes of sourdough bread
⅓ cup extra virgin olive oil

Kosher salt
Black pepper in a mill
8 12-inch-long wooden skewers, soaked in water for 1 hour
8 ounces of lean bacon, fried until not quite crisp and cut into 2-inch pieces
24 cherry tomatoes
4 cups salad greens, such as mesclun, romaine lettuce, or red leaf lettuce
½ cup Aïoli (page 417)

Preheat an outdoor or stovetop grill.

Place the bread squares in a medium bowl, drizzle the olive oil over them, and toss until the bread absorbs the oil. Season with salt and pepper, and toss again.

Thread a bread square onto a skewer, followed by a piece of bacon, a cherry tomato, and another piece of bacon. Repeat until the skewer has 4 pieces of bread and 3 cherry tomatoes. Continue until all the skewers have been filled.

Grill the kebabs, turning them so that the bread is golden on each side. Arrange the salad greens on a large serving platter, set the kebabs on the greens, and serve immediately, with the Aïoli on the side.

Chapter 2

SALSAS

SALSAS

Salsa Mexicana • 57

Salsa Cruda • 57

Cherry Tomato Salsa • 58

Gilroy Garlic Salsa • 58

Roasted Tomato Salsa • 59

Desperation Salsa • 60

Salvador's Smoked Tomatillo
    Salsa • 61

Smoky Corn Salsa • 62

Avocado Sauce • 63

Avocado Salsa • 64

Guacamole • 65

Roasted Pepper Salsa • 65

Zucchini Salsa • 67

Cranberry Salsa • 67

Strawberry Salsa • 68

Bing Cherry Salsa • 68

Mango Salsa • 69

Grilled Pineapple–Chipotle
    Salsa • 70

California Nachos • 70

SALSA MEXICANA

Chips and salsa are everywhere in California, as appetizers and as afternoon snacks. Casual Mexican restaurants often feature salsa bars, with a selection of salsas from mild to spicy and smooth to chunky. Pico de gallo, as this salsa is often called, is probably the most common of the traditional Mexican salsas. It is ideal whenever you want a savory condiment to serve alongside tacos and quesadillas and with all types of grilled seafood. Plum tomatoes are not the best choice for this salsa because they are not particularly juicy; if they are all you have, you may need to add a little water or tomato juice for the right consistency.

MAKES ABOUT 2½ TO 3 CUPS

4 large ripe red tomatoes, cored and
  chopped
1 white onion, diced
3 serrano or jalapeño chiles, minced
½ cup minced cilantro leaves
½ teaspoon kosher salt

Toss together the tomatoes, onion, chiles, and cilantro in a medium bowl. Add the salt, taste, and adjust the seasoning. Let the salsa rest at room temperature for at least 30 minutes before serving. Refrigerate, covered, for up to 3 days.

SALSA CRUDA

Salsa Cruda has a greater depth of flavor and more texture than Salsa Mexicana. It is one of the best choices for classic chips and salsa, and it should be a part of every summer salsa bar. It is also excellent spooned over steamed rice or served as a condiment with grilled scallions.

MAKES ABOUT 2 CUPS

4 ripe red tomatoes, peeled, seeded,
  and coarsely chopped
1 white onion, diced
4 garlic cloves, minced
3 serrano or jalapeño chiles, minced
Juice of ½ lime
2 tablespoons red wine vinegar
¼ cup extra virgin olive oil
½ cup minced cilantro leaves
1 tablespoon minced oregano
Kosher salt
Black pepper in a mill

Place the chopped tomatoes in a strainer lined with cheesecloth, and let them drain for 20 minutes. (Reserve the liquid for another purpose, or discard it.) In a medium bowl, combine the drained tomatoes with the onion, garlic, chiles, lime, vinegar, and olive oil. Toss to blend well. Stir in the cilantro and oregano. Taste, and add salt and pepper. Let the salsa rest at room temperature for at least 30 minutes before serving. Refrigerate, covered, for up to 3 days.

CHERRY TOMATO SALSA

*M*ake this salsa when you have plenty of excellent cherry tomatoes. They need not be of as many varieties as are called for in this recipe. If different colors are available, by all means use them; but freshness and flavor are what count the most. This salsa is a bit too chunky to use with chips. It is better as a condiment, with poached chicken, grilled seafood, or with simple rice and bean dishes. It is also excellent tossed with pasta.

MAKES ABOUT 4 CUPS

1 cup yellow currant or small yellow cherry tomatoes
1 cup small orange cherry tomatoes, such as Sungolds
1 cup red currant or small cherry tomatoes, such as Sweet 100s
1 to 2 jalapeños, seeded and minced
1 small red onion, diced
2 tablespoons fresh lime juice (from 1 to 2 limes)
¼ cup extra virgin olive oil
1 tablespoon minced basil leaves
1 tablespoon minced cilantro leaves
Kosher salt
Black pepper in a mill

Cut the currant tomatoes in half and the cherry tomatoes into quarters. Toss the tomatoes in a medium bowl. Add the jalapeño, using 2 for more heat, and the onion, lime juice, olive oil, basil, and cilantro, and toss again. Taste, and add salt and pepper. Let the salsa rest at room temperature for at least 30 minutes before serving. Refrigerate, covered, for up to 2 days.

GILROY GARLIC SALSA

*T*he Gilroy Garlic Festival is one of the most famous food celebrations in the country. The July air is saturated with the aroma of raw and cooked garlic as thousands of garlic lovers flock to the small town where ninety percent of the nation's garlic crop is raised. Most of Gilroy's garlic is California Late, a large-cloved garlic with considerable heat. Because garlic plays a central role in this salsa, it is an excellent place to use a less common variety of garlic (see page 20) such as Spanish Rojo or Persian Star.

MAKES ABOUT 2 CUPS

4 ripe red tomatoes, peeled, cored, and cut in half
1 small red onion, chopped
½ medium cucumber, peeled, seeded, and chopped
8 garlic cloves, minced
2 to 3 serrano chiles, minced
2 tablespoons tomato puree
Juice of 1 lemon
¼ cup extra virgin olive oil

¼ cup snipped chives
2 tablespoons minced cilantro leaves
Kosher salt
Black pepper in a mill

Gently squeeze out the seeds and excess liquid from the tomato halves. Chop them coarse, and put them in a medium bowl. Add the onion, cucumber, garlic, and serranos, using 3 for more heat, and toss. In a small bowl, mix together the tomato puree, lemon juice, and olive oil. Pour the mixture over the vegetables, and toss to blend well. Add the chives and cilantro, and toss again. Taste, and add salt and pepper. Refrigerate the salsa for 1 hour before serving. Store, covered, in the refrigerator for up to 2 days.

ROASTED TOMATO SALSA

Roasting the vegetables before making the salsa concentrates their flavors, which are then accented by a bold splash of good tequila. Serve with chips as part of a salsa buffet, with quesadillas (pages 251 and 307), and as a condiment with Spanish Rice (page 221).

MAKES ABOUT 2½ CUPS

1½ pounds ripe red tomatoes,
    preferably Romas
1 yellow onion, unpeeled, quartered

3 to 4 jalapeños
6 garlic cloves, unpeeled
1 tablespoon olive oil
2 tablespoons aged tequila
Juice of 1 lime
2 tablespoons minced cilantro leaves
Kosher salt
Black pepper in a mill

Preheat the oven to 350°F. Put the tomatoes, onion, jalapeños, and garlic in a baking dish, drizzle the olive oil over them, and roast until all are tender, 35 to 40 minutes. Remove them from the oven and let them cool until they are easy to handle. Pour the roasting juices into a bowl, and set the bowl aside.

Peel, core, and seed the tomatoes. Squeeze the pulp out of the garlic cloves. Pass the tomatoes and garlic through a food mill, or chop them very fine with a knife, and put them in a medium bowl. Peel and dice the onion, and add it to the tomatoes and garlic. Seed and mince the jalapeños, and add them to the bowl. Toss to blend well, add the tequila and lime juice, and toss again. If the mixture is too thick, add the reserved roasting juices. Add the cilantro, taste, and season with salt and pepper. Refrigerate for at least 1 hour before serving. Store, covered, in the refrigerator for up to 3 days.

To Peel a Tomato

Plunging a tomato into a pot of boiling water for 30 to 60 seconds is the most commonly recommended technique for peeling a tomato but not the best one. Left in its bath for more than 15 seconds, a tomato will become mushy. Five to 10 seconds are better; occasionally, but only rarely, a stubborn one will need 15 seconds.

Better yet: Hold the tomato with the tines of a large fork, set the tomato over a gas flame, and, rotating the fork constantly so that the flesh doesn't cook, scorch the skin. You will need 5 to 15 seconds, depending on the tomato's size.

The water-bath method dilutes the tomato's flavor slightly; flame, on the other hand, intensifies it. With either method, set the tomato aside until it is cool enough to handle, and the skins will pull away easily. Do not put the tomato in cold water, which will only dilute the flavor more.

You may need neither water nor flame. The skin of a fresh-from-garden tomato should come off easily when pulled by the blade of a very sharp knife, although the process can be slow. To encourage the skin to loosen, first rub the tomato with the dull edge of the knife, and then peel it with the sharp edge. You may also peel firm-fleshed tomatoes, such as Romas, using a standard vegetable peeler.

DESPERATION SALSA

When tomatoes are no longer in season, use good canned tomatoes rather than hard, mealy winter tomatoes. Muir Glen, a company based in Sacramento, produces excellent canned organic tomatoes, including diced tomatoes ideal for salsa. Muir Glen tomatoes are packed in porcelain-lined cans, which eliminates the metallic taste other canned tomatoes have. Muir Glen tomatoes are widely distributed; many supermarkets and most natural foods stores carry them.

MAKES ABOUT 3 CUPS

1 shallot, unpeeled
4 garlic cloves, unpeeled
2 dried chipotles
1 16-ounce can of diced tomatoes
6 scallions, cut into thin rounds
2 tablespoons extra virgin olive oil
Juice of 1 lime
2 tablespoons red wine vinegar
2 tablespoons minced cilantro leaves
Kosher salt
Black pepper in a mill

Place a small heavy frying pan over medium-high heat. When the pan is very hot, add the shallot, garlic, and chipotles. Cook until the shallot and garlic are toasted and the chipotles plump with steam, about 7 to 10 minutes. Remove them from the heat and transfer them to a work surface. When they are cool enough to handle, peel the shallot and garlic.

Put the shallot, garlic, and chipotles in an electric spice grinder with 2 tablespoons of the tomatoes, and pulse until a smooth paste is formed. In a medium bowl, combine the paste with the remaining tomatoes and the scallions, olive oil, lime juice, vinegar, and cilantro. Taste, and season with salt and pepper. Let the salsa rest at room temperature for 30 minutes before serving. Refrigerate, covered, for up to 4 days.

SALVADOR'S SMOKED TOMATILLO SALSA

This is Salvador Ceja's prize-winning salsa, and a very different sauce from the fresh salsas most Americans know. In Mexico, Salvador's homeland, *salsa* refers to any sauce. This salsa is best used as a sauce for grilled meats, such as Grilled Pork Chops with Salvador's Salsa (page 368). (If you own a home smoker, you can use it instead of a charcoal grill.)

MAKES ABOUT 5 CUPS

4 cups hickory chips or other wood chips, soaked in water for at least 1 hour, for smoking
3 pounds tomatillos, husks removed
¼ cup pumpkin seeds

12 dried chiles de arbol
1 large guajillo chile
6 large garlic cloves, chopped coarse
1 teaspoon minced garlic
1½ cups hot water
Kosher salt

At least 1½ hours before you smoke the tomatillos, prepare a fire in a charcoal grill. When the fire has cooled and the coals are completely covered with thick white ash, scatter the soaked chips over the coals. There should be plenty of smoke; add more moistened chips if there is not. Oil the grill rack lightly, and set the tomatillos on the rack. Cover the grill, and smoke the tomatillos for 15 minutes. Remove the tomatillos from the heat.

In a dry skillet over medium heat, lightly toast the pumpkin seeds; do not let them burn. Remove the seeds and set them aside. Add the chile de arbol and the guajillo chile to the skillet, and roast them, on both sides, until they are golden brown, 3 to 4 minutes per side; do not let them burn. Remove the chiles and set them aside.

Add the chopped garlic to the skillet, and roast the garlic, for 3 to 4 minutes, or until it is until golden brown. Put ⅓ of the tomatillos, the pumpkin seeds, the chile de arbol, the guajillo chile, the roasted garlic, and the minced garlic in a blender, and blend until the pumpkin seeds are well ground. Add the remaining tomatillos, and blend until the salsa is smooth. Transfer to a medium bowl and stir in 1 cup of the hot water. Stir in as much of the remaining ½ cup as necessary to achieve the consistency you like. Taste, and add salt. Serve immediately, or store, covered, in the refrigerator for up to 1 week.

Salvador Ceja Moves North

Salvador Ceja came to California from his native Michoacán, in Mexico, in 1980, bringing with him a love of cooking, a knowledge of traditional techniques, and the fiery-hot recipes he learned from his mother. I met Salvador when I judged a salsa contest sponsored by KSRO radio, the biggest AM station in Sonoma County. The top prize went to Salvador's Smoky Tomatillo Salsa, a sensational brew of enticing flavors with an intriguing complexity that bespoke Salvador's heritage. Today, Salvador works in a wine-country bakery and cooks at home for his wife and five children, who love hot foods, he says. In addition to pork chops grilled and topped with his salsa (page 368), one of Salvador's favorite recipes is chicken mole tamales rich with the dark flavors of ancho and pasilla chiles, chocolate, cinnamon, garlic, and cloves.

SMOKY CORN SALSA

*U*nrefined corn oil is full of the aroma and flavor of fresh corn. If you have some, use it in this recipe, where it will contribute another layer of corn flavor. Spectrum Naturals, a northern California company that produces oils, vinegars, and condiments from organically grown ingredients, makes a very good unrefined corn oil that is widely distributed nationally. If you can't find unrefined corn oil, use a good mild olive oil rather than a refined corn oil, which has virtually no taste.

MAKES ABOUT 2 CUPS

3 ears of fresh corn
1 small red onion, minced
2 serrano or jalepeño chiles, minced
1 red bell pepper, minced
2 teaspoons pureed canned chipotles in adobo
Juice of 2 limes
⅓ cup unrefined corn oil or extra virgin olive oil
¼ cup minced cilantro leaves
Kosher salt
Black pepper in a mill

Prepare an outdoor or stovetop grill. Remove the husks and silk from the corn. Grill the ears quickly, turning them so they cook and color evenly, for about 5 minutes, until they have darkened slightly but have not blackened. Remove the ears from the grill, and set them aside to cool. When they are cool enough to handle, cut the kernels from the ears, and put the kernels in a medium bowl. Add the onion, chiles, bell pepper, and chipotles, and toss together. Add the lime juice, corn oil, and cilantro, and toss again. Season with salt and pepper. Let the salsa rest at room temperature for 30 minutes before serving. Serve immediately, or store, covered, in the refrigerator for up to 3 days.

Variation:

Instead of grilling the ears of corn, boil them for 1 or 2 minutes, drain them, and let them cool. Remove the kernels from the ears. Omit the chipotles, and add in their place 1 large or 2 medium ripe red tomatoes, peeled, seeded, and minced, and 1 yellow or orange bell pepper, diced.

AVOCADO SAUCE

Among the best things I have ever tasted were the pork tacos I had one day, at seven in the morning, outside the Baja California town of La Paz. A friend and I had just dropped off a car for repairs when a young boy not more than twelve years old wheeled a handcart up to where we stood. On the cart, fragrant pork turned on a vertical spit; next to the spit were a container of minced white onions and another of minced cilantro. There was a plastic pitcher, too, such as you might find filled with maple syrup in a diner, but this one was filled with avocado sauce. A griddle stood hot and ready for the small corn tortillas stacked next to it. After slapping several tortillas onto the grill, the boy used a huge knife to shave off slices of pork, which he minced and, when the tortillas were hot, scooped onto them. Then he set the whole affair on a square of wax paper. After topping the meat with onions and cilantro, he poured avocado sauce over it all and handed it to me. I will never forget that first bite. I ate seven of those tacos before the car was ready. As we drove off, I looked back at the boy standing there in the rising heat of the day, and my only regret was that I hadn't gotten one more taco for the drive back into town.

MAKES ABOUT 1 CUP

1 large ripe avocado, pitted and
   coarsely chopped
1 to 3 serrano chiles, chopped
3 tablespoons fresh lime juice (from 1
   to 2 limes)
1 teaspoon kosher salt

Place the avocado in a blender or food processor. Add the serranos, using more or less depending on the heat you want, the lime juice, the salt, and ¼ cup water, and blend or pulse until smooth. Thin with more water, if you like. Refrigerate until ready to serve. The sauce will keep, covered, in the refrigerator for 1 day.

The Mother Avocado Tree

The Avocado Growers Exchange was formed in 1924, by which time California growers were shipping nineteen different varieties of avocado around the world. With plans to develop his own two-acre orchard, Rudolph Hass, a postal worker, purchased seedlings from a nurseryman in Whittier in the latter part of the same decade.

The years passed and Hass's trees grew. Hass's children were the first to notice that one tree was different, with unusual dark green, nubbly skinned fruit. They preferred it to the fruit from the other trees, and eventually they got their father to take notice. In 1935 Hass patented the tree and entered into an agreement with the nurseryman to share the income from the sale of the tree's offspring. Today, Hass avocados account for eighty-five percent of California production. Fuerte avocados, once the dominant variety, fill in during the few months when Hass trees do not bear.

No other source for this variety of avocado has ever been found. Whenever you buy a Hass avocado, you are purchasing a descendant of that one tree, which still grows where it was planted. Originally the area was full of avocado orchards; housing developments since have taken over and the tree, marked only by a small bronze plaque, stands in the front yard of a modest home on West Road in La Habra Heights. No one knows how much longer it will live, but it has survived droughts, floods, hard freezes, and earthquakes and continues to produce its luscious fruit.

AVOCADO SALSA

Do not confuse this salsa with guacamole, which happens sometimes when I serve it. It is another thing entirely, with textures and flavors inappropriate in a true guacamole. The radishes add a particularly refreshing element. Serve the salsa with chips or as a condiment with tacos or quesadillas.

MAKES ABOUT 2 CUPS

15 small radishes, minced
1 small red onion, minced
3 serrano chiles, seeded and minced

2 ripe avocados, pitted and cut into chunks
¼ cup fresh lime juice (from 2 to 3 limes)
3 tablespoons extra virgin olive oil
⅓ cup minced cilantro leaves
Kosher salt
Black pepper in a mill

Combine the radishes, onion, and serranos in a small bowl, and toss well. Set the bowl aside. In a blender or food processor, blend the avocado chunks and the lime juice to a smooth puree, stopping, if necessary, to push down the avocado. Transfer the puree to a bowl, add the radish mixture, and fold together quickly. Stir in the olive oil and cilantro. Taste, and season with salt and pepper. Serve immediately, or refrigerate, covered, for up to 1 day.

GUACAMOLE

There must be as many versions of guacamole as there are counties in California—maybe more. This one remains close to its Mexican roots, without the addition of cream cheese or any of the other things Californians add with abandon. A *molcajete* is a Mexican mortar and pestle, made of granite or volcanic stone. Its rough surface and heavy weight make it ideal for crushing tough-skinned chiles and for reducing garlic and onions to a paste quickly. If you do not have a molcajete, use a knife to mince the onion, garlic, serranos, and cilantro together with the salt until they nearly form a paste. Use a food processor only in a pinch.

SERVES 4

½ medium white onion, minced
2 garlic cloves, peeled
3 serrano chiles, minced
1 teaspoon kosher salt
¼ cup minced cilantro leaves
3 large Hass avocados
1 medium ripe red tomato, minced

Put a third of the onion in a small bowl, and set the bowl aside. Put the rest of the onion and the garlic in the base of a molcajete, if you are using one. Add the serranos and the salt, and pound the mixture into a paste. Add 2 tablespoons of the cilantro, and crush it into the paste. Add the remaining cilantro to the reserved onion.

Cut the avocados in half, remove the pits, and scoop out the flesh into a medium bowl. Use a fork to mash the avocado, then add it to the molcajete, using the fork to fold the onion-garlic paste into the avocado. Set aside 2 tablespoons of the minced tomato, and add the rest to the avocado-onion mixture. Mix together lightly, then scatter the reserved onion-cilantro mixture and the reserved tomato over the top. Serve immediately.

ROASTED PEPPER SALSA

Serve this smoky salsa on quesadillas (pages 251 and 307) or Black Bean Tamales (page 241), with grilled seafood, or simply with chips.

MAKES ABOUT 1¼ CUPS

3 dried chipotles
2 tablespoons olive oil
1 yellow onion, minced
4 garlic cloves, minced
3 large red bell peppers, roasted, seeded, and diced
1 cup Tomato Concassé (page 98) or 2 large tomatoes, cored and diced

3 to 4 tablespoons fresh lime juice
   (from 2 to 3 limes)
Kosher salt

Put the chipotles in a small bowl and cover them with boiling water. Set them aside for at least 20 minutes to soften.

Meanwhile, heat the olive oil in a skillet over medium heat. Add the onion, and sauté it until it is very soft and fragrant, about 15 minutes. Add the garlic and half of the roasted peppers, and sauté for 2 minutes more. Remove the skillet from the heat.

Drain the chipotles and reserve the soaking water. Chop the chipotles coarse and place them in a molcajete or a mortar. Add a tablespoon of the sautéed onion mixture and grind it into a smooth paste with the chipotles. Add and grind the rest of the onion mixture, 1 tablespoon at a time. Transfer to a medium bowl, fold in the remaining roasted peppers, the tomato concassé or diced tomatoes, and 3 tablespoons of the lime juice. Taste, add the remaining lime juice if you like, and season with salt. If the salsa is a little too thick, add some of the soaking water until it reaches the consistency you want. Serve immediately, or store, covered, in the refrigerator for up to 7 days.

NOTE: In place of dried chipotles, you can use 2 to 3 canned chipotles in adobo sauce. Puree them rather than chop them.

Shopping with Cupid

When Soviet Premier Nikita Khrushchev visited California in the late 1950s, his visits to two locations were highly publicized. The rotund ruler asked to be taken to Disneyland, where he displayed great delight during his visit. His northern California itinerary included the Marina Safeway in San Francisco, a flagship store heralded not only for its perfection of the capitalist vision but for its romantic possibilities—for decades its aisles were considered a prime location for finding romance.

Nowadays, Cupid seems to prefer open-air farmers' markets. Julie Levinson and Bret Jeremy met while shopping at San Francisco's Ferry Plaza Market in May of 1994. By November, both had quit their jobs, she as a dress designer and he as a caterer, and they had launched a line of fire-roasted salsas sold under the name Native Kjalii Foods. A year later, the two were married. Since then, sales have skyrocketed and their salsas are found in retail stores in an ever-widening area. Yet, for sentimental reasons, they continue to sell them each Saturday at the Ferry Plaza Market.

ZUCCHINI SALSA

*I*s it possible to have too many zucchini recipes? By the end of summer, there's bound to be an abundance, even if you don't have a vegetable garden. It is best to use zucchini before they grow too large; with big ones you get a smaller ratio of skin to flesh, and therefore less flavor. This salsa is excellent spooned over sliced tomatoes and as a condiment with grilled polenta triangles. My favorite way to serve it is to cut plum tomatoes in half lengthwise, scoop out the seeds, ribs, and gel, fill them with the salsa, and top them with Chipotle Mayonnaise (page 418).

MAKES ABOUT 2 CUPS

1 medium green zucchini, cut into
    ¼-inch dice
1 medium yellow zucchini or
    1 additional green zucchini, cut
    into ¼-inch dice
1 small red onion, minced
2 garlic cloves, minced
1 serrano or jalapeño chile, minced
½ cup Tomato Concassé (page 98)
    or 1 large tomato, cored and diced
1 teaspoon minced basil leaves
1 teaspoon minced Italian parsley
Juice of ½ lemon
2 tablespoons extra virgin olive oil
1 teaspoon kosher salt
Black pepper in a mill

Put the zucchini, onion, garlic, and chile in a medium bowl, and toss to combine. Add the tomato concassé or diced tomato, basil, parsley, lemon juice, olive oil, and salt, and toss again. Taste, and season with black pepper. Let the salsa rest at room temperature for 30 minutes before serving. Serve immediately, or store, covered, in the refrigerator for up to 4 days.

CRANBERRY SALSA

*C*ranberry salsa has become very popular in California in recent years, although many versions more closely resemble the traditional cranberry-orange relish served with Thanksgiving dinner than they do a true salsa. There's no orange juice in this one, and chile peppers and cilantro bring it closer to salsa. Make it in the fall when cranberries are in season. Serve it with turkey tacos, turkey quesadillas, or turkey tamales that you make on the days following Thanksgiving.

MAKES ABOUT 3 CUPS

1 package (12 ounces) cranberries
4 serrano or jalapeño chiles, minced
1 small red onion, diced
¼ cup sugar
2 tablespoons cranberry vinegar,
    raspberry vinegar, or red wine
    vinegar
¼ cup extra virgin olive oil
1 tablespoon minced cilantro leaves
2 teaspoons minced sage leaves

Kosher salt
Black pepper in a mill

Put the cranberries in a food processor and pulse until they are minced fine. Transfer them to a medium bowl, add the chiles and onion, and toss well. Add the sugar, vinegar, olive oil, cilantro, and sage, and toss again. Taste, and season with salt and pepper. Let the salsa rest at room temperature for at least 30 minutes before serving. Store, covered, in the refrigerator for up to 2 days.

STRAWBERRY SALSA

Fruit salsas have become quite familiar in California. Often, several fruits are mixed together, sometimes combined with more traditional ingredients like tomatoes. I prefer to keep things simple and highlight the flavor of a single fruit. This salsa makes an excellent topping for plain yogurt, and it is wonderful with grilled prawns or poached chicken.

MAKES ABOUT 2 CUPS

1 pint strawberries, stemmed and diced
2 tablespoons sugar
1 to 2 serrano chiles, minced
½ red onion, minced

3 tablespoons strawberry or red raspberry vinegar, preferably, or 3 tablespoons red wine vinegar
2 tablespoons minced cilantro leaves
Kosher salt
Black pepper in a mill

Place the strawberries and the sugar in a medium bowl, and toss lightly. Cover, and refrigerate for at least 1 hour.

Remove the bowl from the refrigerator. Add the serrano, onion, vinegar, and cilantro, and toss together lightly. Season with salt and pepper. Let the salsa rest at room temperature for least 20 minutes before serving. Store, covered, in the refrigerator for up to 2 days.

BING CHERRY SALSA

In early May California's bing cherries come into season, a full month or more before they do in Oregon, Washington, and Michigan. If the weather cooperates—if there have been no late rains or early heat waves—their brief season overlaps with the year's first corn, and that's when I like to make this salsa. In years when the weather does not provide the opportunity, I simply omit the corn and make cherry salsa. The salsa is an excellent accompaniment for grilled or poached wild salmon, which is usually available at this time, as well as for gravlax and smoked salmon.

2 ears of fresh corn, shucked
1 pound ripe Bing cherries, pitted and
  cut into quarters
2 small shallots, minced
1 small jalapeño or serrano chile,
  minced
2 teaspoons minced spearmint or
  peppermint
1 teaspoon minced thyme
3 tablespoons unrefined corn oil,
  preferably, or 3 tablespoons olive oil
2 tablespoons cherry, raspberry, or
  sherry vinegar
½ teaspoon kosher salt

Place the corn in a large pot of cold water, and set the pot over high heat. When the water comes to a boil, use tongs to remove the corn and plunge it briefly into a bowl of cold water. Drain the corn on absorbent paper, and cut the kernels from the ears.

Toss together the corn and cherries in a medium bowl. Add the shallots, chile, mint, thyme, oil, and vinegar, and toss well. Taste, and correct the seasoning, adding more vinegar if the salsa is too sweet and a pinch more salt if you like. Let the salsa rest for 30 minutes before serving. Store, covered, in the refrigerator for up to 3 days.

MANGO SALSA

· ·

*I*f you can find a jalapeño or serrano that is red, its color will brighten up the already beautiful golden-orange of the mangos. Serve this salsa on seafood, especially grilled salmon or chilled smoked salmon, or on poached chicken. It is also an ideal accompaniment for Channa Dal (page 259), Chicken Curry (page 310), and all Indian curries.

2 large or 3 small ripe mangos
1 small red onion, diced
1 serrano chile, preferably red, seeded
  and minced
1 jalapeño, preferably red, seeded and
  minced
¼ cup minced cilantro
Juice of 1 lime
3 to 4 tablespoons rice vinegar
2 tablespoons extra virgin olive oil
Pinch of kosher salt
Pinch of cayenne

With a very sharp knife, peel the mango and cut the fruit from the seed. Cut the mango flesh into ¼-inch cubes, being sure to use any flesh that has clung to the mango seeds. Put the mango in a medium bowl, and add the onion, serrano, jalapeño, cilantro, lime juice, vinegar, and olive oil, and toss together. Taste, and add a pinch of salt and a pinch of cayenne. Correct the seasonings with more lime juice, vinegar, or salt, if necessary. Let the salsa rest for 30 minutes before serving. Store, covered, in the refrigerator for up to 3 days.

GRILLED PINEAPPLE-CHIPOTLE SALSA

I first made this salsa to go with some seafood tacos I was making. I loved the combination and now use it with any seafood, especially grilled shrimp, salmon, shark, or halibut.

MAKES ABOUT 2½ CUPS

½ of a fresh pineapple, peeled, cored, and sliced (to yield about 2½ cups)
4 tomatillos, husks removed, chopped
2 canned chipotles in adobo sauce
1 to 2 tablespoons tequila
1 garlic clove, minced
½ cup minced cilantro leaves
½ red onion, minced
Kosher salt

Prepare an outdoor or stovetop grill. Grill the pineapple slices until they just begin to color slightly, about 3 to 4 minutes on each side. Remove them from the heat, and set them aside to cool. When the pineapple is cool enough to handle, dice it.

Put the tomatillos, chipotles, tequila, and garlic in a food processor or blender, and pulse or blend until smooth. Add 1 cup of the pineapple, and pulse or blend briefly;

the puree should not be too smooth. Transfer to a medium bowl, and fold in the remaining pineapple, the cilantro, and the onion. Taste, and season with salt. Let the salsa rest for 30 minutes before serving. Store, covered, in the refrigerator for up to 3 days.

CALIFORNIA NACHOS

As I pursued the story of home cooking in California, I came across a recipe called Texas Dish for Two in *The New California Cook Book* (1955) by Genevieve Callahan. The recipe calls for a bag of corn chips spread over the bottom of a pie pan. The chips are topped with a can of chili con carne, sliced scallions, sliced tomatoes, and cheese, and baked until the cheese melts. This recipe is the closest I've come to an early version of nachos, a dish popularized in California in the early 1980s and now found, needless to say, throughout the country. The secret to making good nachos is simple: Use excellent ingredients. I think people have forgotten how inviting a dish this can be, especially in hot weather with Agua Fresca (page 472), margaritas, or cold beer served alongside.

SERVES 4 TO 6

1 tablespoon olive oil
3 to 4 serrano chiles, minced
½ cup sour cream

¼ cup minced cilantro leaves
½ teaspoon kosher salt
Black pepper in a mill
8 ounces tortilla chips
2 cups cooked and seasoned black
   beans (see pages 235–36) or
   good-quality canned cooked
   black beans
6 ounces grated St. George or
   Monterey jack
1½ cups Smoky Corn Salsa (page 62)

Preheat the oven to 325°F.

In a small sauté pan, heat the olive oil, and add the serranos. Sauté them until they are just soft, 3 to 4 minutes. Remove them from the heat and let them cool.

In a blender or food processor, make a cilantro cream: Combine the sour cream, half of the cilantro leaves, 1 teaspoon of the sautéed serranos, the salt, and 2 or 3 turns of black pepper. Pulse or blend until the mixture is smooth, and transfer to a small serving bowl.

On a large ovenproof serving platter, spread out half of the tortilla chips. Spoon half of the beans over the chips, sprinkle half of the remaining serranos over the beans, scatter half of the cheese over all,

St. George Cheese

• •

Joe and Mary Matos came to Sonoma County from the island of St. George in the Azores. On a small piece of land at the western edge of Santa Rosa, they produce a single type of cheese from a herd of cows that grazes across from the driveway to their factory. The calves are fed the whey that remains after the cheese is made. The Matoses' St. George cheese is semihard, slightly sharp, and full-flavored. It melts beautifully, making it ideal for cooking. Most of the cheese is sold by mail order (see Resources); the rest is sold at the small shop next to the factory's aging room.

and top with half of the corn salsa. Repeat with chips, beans, serranos, and cheese. Bake the nachos until the cheese is just melted, about 7 minutes. Remove from the oven, spoon the remaining corn salsa on top, and serve with with cilantro cream on the side.

Chapter 3

SOUPS

SOUPS

STRAWBERRY SOUP

Because of a climate ideally suited to the strawberry, California leads the nation in production. The season is long, extending from mid-February or early March through November. In the last several decades, yields from commercial berry farms have soared from about 5 tons per acre to more than 20. At the same time, however, taste has declined. Today's commercial berries are not as sweet or flavorful as those you can grow yourself or find at farmers' markets.

The year's first strawberries usually come from Oxnard, where nearly a quarter of the state's crop is grown. The state celebrates its strawberry with at least three festivals, including the long-running Garden Grove Strawberry Festival, founded in 1958. Oxnard, dubbed the Strawberry Capital of the World, launched a festival in 1983, the same year the Arroyo Grande Strawberry Festival was founded.

SERVES 4

3 pints strawberries, stems removed
¼ cup sugar, or more to taste, plus 1
   tablespoon sugar
Pinch of ground cardamom
2 cups white wine, such as sauvignon
   blanc, or 2 cups dry rosé, plus more
   for thinning
Black pepper in a mill

2 tablespoons sliced mint leaves

Set aside 2 cups of the strawberries. Coarsely chop the remaining strawberries, and place them in a blender. Add the ¼ cup sugar, the cardamom, and 2 cups of the wine, and blend the mixture until it is smooth. Transfer the puree to a soup tureen or other large container, taste, and add more sugar if you like. Thin with additional white wine to achieve a proper soup consistency. Season with pepper, and stir. Refrigerate the soup until it is well chilled, about 2 hours.

Meanwhile, slice the reserved strawberries, sprinkle them with the 1 tablespoon sugar, and refrigerate them.

To serve, divide the sliced strawberries among individual soup bowls and ladle the chilled soup over them. Grind black pepper over each bowl and sprinkle with mint. Serve immediately.

PLUM SOUP

For many years, my friend A.J. lived in a beautiful, remote area of Sonoma County, where he grew succulent tomatoes and crisp, sweet peppers, which he canned with vinegar and garlic, as his mother, a native of Sicily, had done when he was a child. Fat, nearly black concord grapes hung over his patio, and he had a tree that every year yielded a crop of dense, sweet plums, which I occasionally transformed into this intensely flavored soup, a perfect prelude to a main course of pork, duck, or game.

SERVES 4 TO 6

2 pounds Santa Rosa plums,
    unpeeled, cut into chunks
3 cloves
5 cardamom seeds
2 cups medium-dry white wine
⅓ to ⅔ cup sugar
2 tablespoons butter
¼ cup crème fraîche (or substitute;
    see Note, page 37)

Place the chunks of plum in a heavy nonreactive saucepan, and add the cloves, cardamom, wine, and 1¾ cups water. Over medium heat, simmer, covered, until the plums are tender, about 15 minutes. Remove the pan from the heat, and remove and discard the cloves. Using a slotted spoon, transfer the plums to a food processor or blender; do not discard the cooking liquid you leave behind in the saucepan. Process or blend the plums until they form a very smooth puree.

Return the saucepan with the cooking liquid to the heat, add sugar to taste, depending on the sweetness of the fruit, and cook over high heat until the mixture is reduced by one-third. Reduce the heat to low, add the plum puree, and stir well. Stir in the butter 1 tablespoon at a time, waiting until the first has melted before adding the second. If necessary, thin the soup with more white wine until you have a proper soup consistency. Heat the soup through thoroughly.

To serve, ladle the soup into individual soup bowls and top each portion with crème fraîche. Serve immediately.

Variation:

Refrigerate the soup and serve it chilled.

PEACH SOUP

*D*essert soups are common in Chinese cuisine. They are served to "fill in the cracks," a concept that makes more sense when you see someone pat her belly as she explains. You can serve this soup following a meal or as the first course of a light lunch in the summer, when peaches are at their peak. If you are lucky enough to have white peaches, set aside a few for this dish.

SERVES 4 TO 6

3½ pounds ripe peaches
Juice of 1 lemon
3 cups white wine
1 1-inch cinnamon stick
2 cloves
3 cardamom seeds
1 tablespoon mint leaves, cut into
    ribbons

Peel and slice two of the peaches, put them in a shallow bowl, and drizzle with the lemon juice. Cover the peaches with plastic wrap, and refrigerate them until ready to use.

Cut the remaining peaches in half; remove their pits but do not peel them. Place the peach halves in a large nonreactive saucepan or kettle, and add the wine, cinnamon, cloves, and cardamom. Add water until the peaches are completely immersed in liquid. Simmer, partially covered, over medium-low heat until the peaches are completely tender, 20 to 30 minutes. Remove from the heat and let the peaches cool in the liquid. When they are cool enough to handle, use a slotted spoon to remove the peaches from their liquid; do not discard the liquid. Puree the peaches in a food mill or by pushing them through a sieve. Bring the cooking liquid to a boil, reduce the heat, and simmer until it is reduced by one-half.

Place the peach puree in a serving bowl, strain the cooking liquid, and add enough to the peach puree to achieve a proper soup consistency. Refrigerate the soup until it is thoroughly chilled, at least 2 hours. To serve, ladle into individual soup bowls, and garnish with the reserved peach slices and the mint ribbons.

MELON GAZPACHO

*U*se this recipe as a basic guideline for melon soup, but vary the amount of liquid according to the melons you use. A puree of a dense melon such as cantaloupe, for example, may need to be thinned with additional liquid. Watermelon, with its high percentage of water, on the other hand will produce a very thin puree that is really more of a juice; although it may seem too thin for a soup, it is utterly refreshing in hot weather. For increased body, add more diced melon. This is an outstanding accompaniment to spicy food, especially Mexican fare.

SERVES 4 TO 6

4 cups melon puree, from about 2
    pounds melon, such as crenshaw,
    casaba, cantaloupe, Charentais,
    honeydew, or watermelon
1 cup Champagne
1 to 2 serrano chiles, minced
4 cups diced melon
2 tablespoons sliced mint leaves
2 tablespoons minced cilantro leaves

Make the melon puree: Use a sharp knife to remove the pulp from the melon. Remove and discard any seeds, and chop the pulp coarse. Place the pulp in a bowl with high sides, and puree using an immersion blender. For a smoother puree, pass the pulp through a sieve.

Combine the puree with the other

ingredients in a soup tureen and refrigerate until well chilled, at least 3 hours. Served in chilled soup bowls.

CRANBERRY SOUP WITH ORANGE ZEST PASTA

I developed this recipe shortly after an election the results of which disappointed me. With Thanksgiving just a few weeks away, I vowed not to have a traditional feast until a future election reversed the results. That year, I served my guests steamed clams, pumpkin risotto, pan-roasted duck, braised radicchio with pancetta and chèvre, and, for dessert, this ruby-red soup with its pale orange pasta. Everyone loved the meal, but as Dylan, the five-year-old nephew of a close friend, left, I heard him say, "Mama, when are we going to have Thanksgiving?"

This special-occasion soup really is best with fresh-made pasta, which this recipe calls for. To make the soup with commercial pasta, cook 6 ounces of fettuccine and toss the cooked and drained noodles with 2 tablespoons minced orange zest.

SERVES 4 TO 6

12 ounces (1 package) fresh
    cranberries
¾ cup sugar
2 cloves
2 allspice berries, or 2 additional
    cloves
1 1-inch cinnamon stick
2 cups Beaujolais
1 cup fresh orange juice
Orange Zest Pasta (recipe follows)
1 tablespoon julienned orange zest
Crème fraîche (or substitute; see
    Note, page 37), optional

Combine the cranberries, sugar, cloves, allspice berries, cinnamon, and 2 cups water in a heavy pot, and bring to a boil, stirring constantly until the sugar is dissolved. Lower the heat, and simmer until the cranberries are very soft, 10 to 15 minutes. Remove the mixture from the heat, discard the cloves, allspice berries, and cinnamon stick, and puree with an immersion blender or in a blender or food processor. Strain the puree and return it to the pot. Stir in the wine and the orange juice, and simmer for 10 minutes more.

Cook the pasta until it is al dente, rinse it and drain it well, and divide it among individual shallow soup bowls. Ladle the soup over the pasta and garnish each serving with orange zest and a dollop of crème fraîche, if you like. Serve immediately.

Variation:

Make the soup in advance and chill it. Shortly before serving, cook the pasta, rinse it in cool water for several minutes, and continue as in the main recipe, serving the dish cold instead of hot.

Holy Water

"**I**t is easy to forget that the only natural force over which we have any control out here is water, and that only recently. In my memory California summers were characterized by the coughing in the pipes that meant the well was dry, and California winters by all-night watches on rivers about to crest, by sandbagging, by dynamite on the levees and flooding on the first floor. Even now the place is not all that hospitable to extensive settlement. As I write a fire has been burning out of control for two weeks in the ranges behind the Big Sur coast. Flash floods last night wiped out all major roads into Imperial County. I noticed this morning a hairline crack in a living-room tile from last week's earthquake, a 4.4 I never felt. In the part of California where I now live aridity is the single most prominent feature of the climate, and I am not pleased to see, this year, cactus spreading wild to the sea. There will be days this winter when the humidity will drop to ten, seven, four. Tumbleweed will blow against my house and the sound of the rattlesnake will be duplicated a hundred times a day by dried bougainvillea drifting in my driveway. The apparent ease of California life is an illusion, and those who believe the illusion real live here in only the most temporary way. I know as well as the next person that there is considerable transcendent value in a river running wild and undammed, a river running free over granite, but I have also lived beneath such a river when it was running in flood, and gone without showers when it was running dry."

Joan Didion, from "Holy Water," in *The White Album* (Simon and Schuster, 1979)

Orange Zest Pasta

For the best results, roll the pasta as thin as possible before cutting it with a decorative blade.

SERVES 4 TO 6

1⅓ cups unbleached all-purpose flour
⅓ cup powdered sugar, sifted
½ teaspoon kosher salt
3 tablespoons minced orange zest
2 large eggs

Combine the flour, sugar, salt, orange zest, and 1 egg in a food processor, and pulse until the mixture is well combined. Add the second egg, and pulse again until the dough is uniformly moist and crumbly. Turn the dough out onto a floured work surface, gather it together, and knead it until it is smooth, about 7 to 10 minutes. Let the dough rest, covered, for 45 minutes.

To roll out the dough, cut it into 4 or 5 pieces. Use your hands to shape 1 piece into a thick rectangle. With the rollers of the pasta machine set as far apart as possible, crank the rectangle of dough through the machine. Fold the dough in thirds and repeat the process on the widest setting 4 to 6 times, until the dough becomes very smooth and very elastic. If the dough gets too sticky, dust it with a little flour. Continue, advancing the setting to the next narrowest width, through setting number 4. Repeat with each piece of dough. Finally, roll each piece through the final 2 settings. After the last pass through the machine, cut the sheet in half and either hang the dough on a pasta drying rack or over the back of a chair. Let the pasta rest for 15 minutes before cutting it.

If you have a cutting attachment on your pasta machine, use it to cut the pasta into ½-inch-wide fettuccine. If not, return the sheet of dough to your work surface and sprinkle it lightly with flour. Roll up the dough lengthwise, and, using a very sharp knife, cut through the roll at intervals of ½ inch. Unravel the pasta pinwheels carefully. Sprinkle them with flour or fine cornmeal and let them rest, covered with a towel, for up to 1 hour.

CHILLED AVOCADO SOUP

There are many versions of avocado soup in California, some served chilled, some hot. Some include cream, which I find eclipses the flavor of the avocado. To my palate, this creamy but creamless version, bright, tangy, and mild-ly spicy, with that edge of sweetness that avocados have, is the best.

SERVES 4 TO 6

2 tablespoons olive oil
1 small yellow or white onion, minced
3 serrano chiles, minced
2 garlic cloves, minced
3 ripe Hass avocados
3½ cups chicken stock
2 tablespoons fresh lime juice
3 tablespoons minced cilantro leaves
Kosher salt
Black pepper in a mill

Heat the olive oil in a small skillet over medium heat, add the onions, and sauté them until they are limp and fragrant, about 10 minutes. Add the serranos, sauté 5 minutes, then add the garlic and sauté 2 minutes more. Remove from the heat and let cool slightly.

Cut the avocados in half and remove the pits. Scoop out the flesh and place it in a blender or food processor. Add half of the stock and the onion mixture, and puree. Transfer to a large container, stir in the remaining stock, and refrigerate until the soup is well chilled, at least 3 hours.

To serve, stir in the lime juice and half of the cilantro, season with salt and pepper, and ladle into chilled soup bowls. Sprinkle the remaining cilantro over each portion, and serve immediately.

Variations:

WITH CHERRY TOMATO SALSA: Cut 1 cup cherry tomatoes into quarters, and toss them with 2 tablespoons minced onion, 1 minced serrano chile, the juice of half a lime, and kosher salt and black pepper to taste. Spoon a little of the salsa over each portion of soup.

WITH BAY SHRIMP: Toss 8 ounces cooked bay shrimp with the juice of 1 lime and 1 tablespoon minced onion. Divide among the chilled soup bowls and ladle the soup on top.

WITH BACON AND BLUE CHEESE: Fry 4 strips of bacon until they are crisp, drain them on absorbent paper, then crumble the bacon and scatter some over each serving of soup. Crumble 2 ounces of blue cheese and scatter it over the soup.

CHILLED CUCUMBER SOUP

Chilled cucumber soup is a time-honored classic that appeared on tables as early as California's first decades as a state, and well into this century, too. Today, you don't see it as often as you once did, but it remains one of the most refreshing soups around.

SERVES 6

3 cucumbers, peeled, seeded, and chopped coarse

½ red onion, diced
Sprig of thyme
¼ cup all-purpose flour
2½ cups chicken stock
White pepper, preferably fresh-ground
½ teaspoon kosher salt
1 cup plain low-fat (not non-fat) yogurt
1 tablespoon grated lemon zest
1 tablespoon snipped chives

In a medium saucepan over low heat, combine the cucumbers, onion, thyme, and 1½ cups water. Simmer, covered, until the cucumbers are tender, about 20 minutes. Remove the pan from the heat, and remove and discard the thyme. Let the mixture cool slightly, then puree it in a food mill, a blender, or a food processor, or with an immersion blender.

In a clean saucepan, combine the flour with a ½ cup of the chicken stock, stirring constantly until the flour is smooth. Stir in the remaining stock, ½ cup at a time, then stir in the cucumber puree. Season with white pepper and salt, bring to a boil, reduce the heat to low, and simmer for 3 minutes. Remove the pan from the heat, and strain the soup. Refrigerate it until it is well chilled, at least 2 hours.

When the mixture is fully chilled, stir in the yogurt and the lemon zest. Taste, adjust the seasoning, and ladle into chilled soup bowls. Garnish each portion with chives, and serve immediately.

RED GAZPACHO

*M*ention gazpacho and many of us think of a chunky liquid salad with a bounty of diced uncooked vegetables. Yet gazpacho began in Andalusia as something much different, a combination of stale bread and bread crumbs—ingredients that peasants could not afford to waste—with vinegar, water, olive oil, and garlic, served at room temperature. This gazpacho omits many of the vegetables common today in favor of a streamlined version in the spirit of its ancestor. Be sure to mince the tomatoes nearly to a pulp before combining them with the other ingredients.

SERVES 4 TO 6

8 to 10 large ripe red tomatoes, peeled, seeded, and minced
4 cups chicken stock
2 to 3 serrano chiles, minced
6 garlic cloves, minced
1 small red onion, minced
2 tablespoons red wine vinegar
¼ cup minced herbs, such as Italian parsley, basil, oregano, cilantro, or a combination
Kosher salt
Black pepper in a mill
¼ cup extra virgin olive oil
1 cup fresh bread crumbs (see page 46)

Put the tomatoes in a large bowl and pour the chicken stock over them. Add the serranos, using 3 if you want more heat, and the garlic, onion, vinegar, and herbs. Taste, and season with salt and pepper. Refrigerate the soup, covered, for at least 1 hour before serving.

Meanwhile, heat 2 tablespoons of the olive oil in a skillet over medium-high heat. Add the bread crumbs, and sauté them, stirring constantly, until they are golden brown. Remove them from the heat and set them aside to let them cool to room temperature.

To serve, ladle the soup into chilled soup bowls, scatter bread crumbs over each portion, drizzle with the remaining olive oil, and serve immediately.

CREAMY GAZPACHO WITH GOLDEN TOMATOES

*T*his gazpacho use avocados to create a creamy soup that highlights the rich, satiny textures of golden tomatoes. Certainly, you can make this soup with any ripe tomatoes, but it is best and most beautiful when golden tomatoes are available. The tomatoes should be minced so fine that they nearly blend into the avocado puree; they should not stand out as chunks.

SERVES 4 TO 6

4 lemon cucumbers or 2 medium
   green cucumbers, peeled, seeded,
   and diced (to yield about 1½ cups)
2 teaspoons kosher salt
1 ripe avocado, diced
Juice of 1 lime
1 cup chicken stock
6 to 8 medium golden and yellow
   tomatoes, preferably, or 6 to 8 ripe
   red tomatoes, peeled, seeded, and
   minced (to yield about 2 cups)
2 jalapeños, minced
4 garlic cloves, minced
2 tablespoons minced cilantro
Kosher salt
Black pepper in a mill
Best-quality extra virgin olive oil
1 cup yellow currant tomatoes,
   halved, or 1 cup yellow or red
   cherry tomatoes, quartered

In a small bowl, toss together the cucumber and the 2 teaspoons of salt. Transfer to a strainer, and let the cucumbers drain for 30 minutes.

Put the avocado, lime juice, stock, and 1 cup of water in a blender, and puree until very smooth. Transfer the puree to a medium bowl, and stir in the golden or yellow tomatoes and the jalapeños, garlic, and cilantro. Gently squeeze out as much moisture as possible from the cucumbers, and stir them into the gazpacho. Taste, and season with salt and pepper. Refrigerate the gazpacho for at least 1 hour before serving.

To serve, ladle the gazpacho into chilled soup bowls and top each serving with a scatter of the small tomatoes, a drizzle of

olive oil, and a grind or two of pepper. Serve immediately.

TOMATO-CILANTRO SOUP

This soup couldn't be simpler to make, yet its bright, refreshing taste keeps everyone coming back for more; I once served gallons of it every week in a small restaurant I operated in Sonoma County. If you are one of those people who don't like cilantro, substitute Italian parsley, fresh basil, chives, or a combination. When tomatoes are out of season, you can make a pretty good version using good canned tomatoes.

SERVES 6

4 pounds ripe red, orange, or yellow
   slicing tomatoes, peeled, seeded,
   and chopped
¼ cup olive oil
1 yellow onion, chopped
8 garlic cloves, minced
2 cups chicken stock
1 tablespoon Madeira
½ cup minced cilantro leaves
Kosher salt
Black pepper in a mill
½ cup Cilantro Sauce (page 285)

Place the tomatoes in a strainer lined with cheesecloth, and let them drain for 20 minutes. Reserve the strained liquid for another purpose, or discard it.

Heat the olive oil in a large nonreactive stockpot over low heat. Add the onion, and sauté it until it is very soft and very fragrant and has just begun to caramelize, 20 to 25 minutes. Add the garlic, and sauté for 2 minutes more. Stir in the stock and the tomatoes, and increase the heat to bring the soup to a boil. Reduce the heat, and simmer the soup for 15 minutes. Add the Madeira, and simmer for 5 minutes more. Stir in the minced cilantro, taste, and season with salt and pepper. Ladle into warmed soup bowls, top each portion with a generous spoonful of Cilantro Sauce, and serve immediately.

Variation:

For a smoother soup, puree with an immersion blender at the end of the simmering time.

Roasted Eggplant Soup with Tapenade

Eggplant makes sensational soup, acting as a canvas for other flavors; here they come from the sweetness of roasted peppers and the tangy acidity of a tapenade.

SERVES 4

2 large eggplants (about 1¾ pounds total)
¼ cup olive oil
1 red onion, diced
8 garlic cloves, minced
3 cups chicken stock or vegetable stock
2 teaspoons kosher salt
1 teaspoon fresh-ground black pepper
¼ cup minced Italian parsley
¼ cup Olive Tapenade (page 422)
1 large or 2 small red bell peppers, roasted, peeled, seeded, and cut into julienne

Preheat the oven to 325°F. Cut the eggplants in half lengthwise. Brush the cut side of each piece with olive oil, place the halves cut side up on a baking sheet, and roast them in the oven until tender, about 45 minutes. Remove them from the oven, let them cool, peel them, and cut them into medium dice.

In a heavy pot or deep skillet over medium heat, heat the remaining olive oil. Add the onions, and sauté them until they are limp and fragrant, about 10 minutes. Add the garlic, and sauté for 2 minutes more. Add the diced eggplant, reduce the heat to low, and cook until all the vegetables are very soft, about 20 minutes. Add the stock, bring to a simmer, and cook, covered, for 15 minutes. Remove from the heat, cool slightly, and puree in a food mill or with an immersion blender. Return the soup to the pot, if necessary, add the salt, pepper, and half of the parsley, and heat through. Add some water if the soup is too thick, and heat through again.

Ladle the soup into warmed soup bowls. Add a tablespoon of tapenade to each serving and run a knife through it to swirl it into the soup. Top the servings with the remaining parsley and the red pepper julienne. Serve immediately.

GREEN GARLIC SOUP

*G*arlic is planted in the fall, and by spring the young shoots are tender and flavorful, similar to leeks and onions but more delicate. It may take several dozen plants to make a pound of green garlic, and the best place to find them, if not in your own garden, is at a farmers' market, where they are available in March and early April.

SERVES 4 TO 6

1 pound green garlics, cleaned and
  roots trimmed
8 cups chicken stock
4 tablespoons butter
1 large or 2 medium shallots, minced
1 pound new potatoes, such as Yellow
  Finn, scrubbed
1 teaspoon white pepper, preferably
  fresh-ground
2 teaspoons kosher salt
¼ cup sour cream or crème fraîche
  (or substitute; see Note, page 37)
3 tablespoons half-and-half

3 tablespoons snipped chives

Cut the stems from the green garlics, leaving about 2 inches of green attached to the white part. Cut the stems into 1- to 2-inch-long pieces, put them in a large pot with the chicken stock, and set the pot over high heat. Bring to a boil, reduce the heat, and simmer, uncovered, for 15 minutes. Remove from the heat, cover, and let steep for 30 minutes. Strain the liquid, discard the cooked stems, and reserve the broth.

Meanwhile, cut the white part and the attached green part crosswise into rounds. Place a stockpot over medium heat, and add the butter. When the butter is melted and foamy, add the shallots, and cook them until they are limp and fragrant, 5 to 6 minutes. Add the green garlic rounds and cook them until they are limp, about 10 minutes, stirring frequently. Do not brown them. Slice the potatoes, add them to the pot, stir, and cook for 4 to 5 minutes more. Add the reserved broth, bring the soup to a boil, reduce the heat, and simmer, partially covered, until the potatoes are tender, 15 to 20 minutes. Puree the soup using an immersion blender. Add ¾ teaspoon of the pepper and 1½ teaspoons of the salt, taste, and adjust the seasoning.

While the soup is cooking, make the chive cream: In a small bowl, combine the sour cream or crème fraîche with the half-and-half, the remaining ¼ teaspoon of the pepper, the remaining ½ teaspoon of the salt, and the chives. Mix until the cream is smooth, and set it aside.

To serve, ladle the soup into warmed soup bowls, top each portion with about

1 tablespoon of the chive cream, and serve immediately.

The Birth of the Farmers' Market

"In the very beginning the Farmers Market [in Hollywood] was a cluster of farm stalls tenanted by small-time growers who sold direct to the consumer. The main appeal was the extra freshness of vegetables still damp from the morning soil, of fruits ripened on the tree rather than picked hard and green so that they would ship better.

"And of course the farmers' wives brought in their homemade jams and jellies, their pickles, their relish ... and alongside the new-laid eggs and the plump, fresh-dressed chickens, there were cookies baked in the farm kitchens, and homemade bread and big, wonderful chocolate layer cakes."

Neill and Fred Beck, *Farmers Market Cook Book* (Holt, 1951)

SPRING CHARD SOUP WITH SMOKED CHILES

In this recipe, green garlic becomes a supporting player in a soup that combines the bright taste of chard with the deep, haunting flavor of smoked chiles, ideal when spring has begun yet the chill is not quite gone from the air. If you can't find green garlic, you may use leeks instead.

SERVES 4 TO 6

¾ pound green garlic, trimmed of roots and all but 3 inches of green stems, preferably, or 3 medium leeks, white parts only
3 tablespoons olive oil
1 small white onion, minced
1 large bunch Swiss chard, trimmed and chopped
1 pound new potatoes, such as Yellow Finn, scrubbed and cut into 1-inch cubes
2 cups chicken stock
2 dried smoked chiles, such as chipotle or ancho, snipped or cut into strips, or 1 teaspoon crushed dried red chile flakes
2 teaspoons kosher salt
Black pepper in a mill

Cut the green garlic crosswise into small rounds. In a large stockpot over medium heat, heat the olive oil. Add the onion, and sauté it for 7 to 8 minutes. Add the green garlic, and sauté it until it wilts, 6 to 7 minutes, stirring frequently so that it does not brown. Add the chard, cover the pot, and cook until the chard wilts, about 5 minutes. Add the potatoes, stock, chiles, and 6 cups water. Bring the soup to a boil, reduce the heat, and simmer until the potatoes are tender, 20 to 30 minutes. Season with salt and pepper, and serve immediately.

SATAN'S LILY SOUP

I devised this soup, obviously inspired by the classic French onion soup, during a huge storm in northern California. Not long into the storm, we lost power, as often happens when there is wind and rain, of which we have plenty almost every winter. I had all of these ingredients on hand, so I lost myself in the preparation of this savory soup, oblivious to the inconveniences at hand. As far as the name goes, onions once were called Satan's lilies, but what seemed really devilish was the lack of electricity—and, therefore, water, too—which continued for five days.

SERVES 4 TO 6

3 tablespoons butter
3 tablespoons olive oil
3 yellow onions, sliced thin
2 red onions, sliced thin

1 leek, white part only, cleaned and sliced thin
1 head of garlic, cloves separated, peeled, and sliced thin
8 to 10 scallions, trimmed and cut into small rounds
¼ cup brandy
1 cup red wine
4 cups beef stock
Kosher salt
Black pepper in a mill
4 to 6 slices of good bread (2-day-old bread is ideal)
4 to 6 ounces cheese, such as asiago, fontina, gruyère, or Monterey jack, grated

In a large, heavy soup kettle, heat the butter and olive oil until the butter is foamy. Add the yellow onions, red onion, and leek, and sauté them over medium heat until they are very limp and fragrant, and completely tender, about 30 minutes. Add the garlic and scallions, and sauté another 5 minutes. Turn the heat to high, add the brandy, shake the pan, and cook rapidly until the brandy has evaporated. Add the wine, stock, and 2 cups water, bring to a boil, reduce to a simmer, lower the heat, and cook for about 20 minutes. Taste the soup and season it with salt and several turns of black pepper.

To serve, ladle the soup into several deep soup bowls and set a piece of bread on top of each serving. Divide the cheese among the servings and carefully place the soup in a 375°F oven for about 7 minutes, until the cheese is melted. Remove the soup from the oven, place each bowl on a saucer, and serve it immediately.

Variation:

To simplify matters and to make a more traditional version of this soup, omit the leeks, shallots, and scallions, use just a few cloves of garlic, and increase the onions—all red or all yellow—to 6 or 7.

AUNTIE ELLEN'S LOTUS ROOT SOUP

*Y*ou might find this soup simmering on the back burner of a friend's stove—if your friend happened to have an Auntie Ellen from Canton overseeing the kitchen. I discovered this soup in *Jang Food: An Inherited Taste*, a collection of family recipes copied and bound by the Jang family of southern California, originally from the province of Canton. The collection is an eclectic mix of favorite recipes, from Irish soda bread to Italian gnocchi to classic Cantonese dishes, such as this soup. Lisa Jang, Auntie Ellen's niece, and her husband, Jorge Rebagliati, own Bay Bottom Beds, one of the oyster farms that leases a portion of Tomales Bay. Their Preston Point oysters, named for the jut of land near their farm, are among the finest in California. This soup is strictly Cantonese and you will need to visit an Asian market for many of the ingredients.

SERVES 6 TO 8

1 dried cuttlefish (*mark yee*), soaked overnight and washed clean
2 pounds pork neck bones
6 large dried Chinese black mushrooms, soaked in water for 2 hours and drained
2 to 3 dried red dates (*jujube*, or *hung jo*), soaked in water for 3 hours and drained
2 pounds fresh lotus root
Salt
1 scallion, green and white parts, cut into thin rounds

Peel off and remove the bone of the cuttlefish and cut the fish into small chunks. Place the cuttlefish, pork, black mushrooms, red dates, and 4 to 5 quarts water in a large stockpot. Bring to a boil, reduce the heat, and simmer, partially covered, for 2 hours.

Wash the lotus root, cut each root in half lengthwise, and cut into thin slices. Add the lotus root to the soup, and simmer, partially covered, for 3 hours more. Taste the soup, season with salt, and serve, garnished with scallion.

North Coast Borscht

True to its roots as a hearty main-course soup, this borscht will warm your bones as it pleases your palate. Be sure to give it its full cooking time, so that the various flavors mingle.

SERVES 8

5 tablespoons olive oil
2 yellow onions, diced
2 carrots, minced
6 garlic cloves, minced
1 tablespoon caraway seeds
4 medium potatoes (about 2½ pounds), peeled and sliced
6 red beets, trimmed, peeled, and quartered
1 14-ounce can whole tomatoes
1 head of cabbage, cored and shredded
8 cups beef stock
¼ cup red wine vinegar
Kosher salt
Black pepper in a mill
2 teaspoons minced dill
½ cup sour cream

In a large stockpot, heat the olive oil over medium heat. Add the onions, and sauté them until they are limp and fragrant, about 15 minutes. Add the carrots, and sauté for 7 to 8 minutes more. Add the garlic and caraway seeds, and sauté for 2 minutes more. Add the potatoes, beets, tomatoes, and cabbage, and pour the stock and vinegar over the vegetables. Bring to a boil, reduce the heat, and simmer, partially covered, until the vegetables are very, very tender, about 1½ hours. Taste the soup, season with salt and pepper, and stir in the dill. Ladle into soup bowls, add 1 tablespoon of sour cream to each portion, and serve immediately. Toasted rye bread is a good accompaniment.

Pumpkin and Roasted Garlic Soup

Some people like to hollow out a jack-o'-lantern pumpkin to use as a tureen. To do so, choose a Halloween pumpkin, which has a larger cavity, rather than one grown for food. Cut a circle around the stem end, somewhat larger than you might for a jack-o'-lantern, so that it will be easy to ladle out the soup. Do not discard the stem end. Remove as many of the seeds as you can with your fingers, and then use a large spoon to scrape out the remaining seeds and fibers. Rinse the pumpkin and invert it onto a tea towel to drain. Brush the inside with olive oil. Before serving, put it in a 375°F oven for about 15 minutes. Place it on a serving plate, carefully pour the soup into it, cover with the stem end, and bring it to the table, with the croutons or bread crumbs in a basket alongside.

SERVES 4

1 medium to large sugar pumpkin, seeded and cut into large chunks
Olive oil
3 allspice berries, preferably, or 3 cloves
1 2-inch cinnamon stick
2 tablespoons butter
1 yellow onion, minced
1 teaspoon chipotle powder or 1 dried chipotle, minced
¼ cup Roasted Garlic Puree (page 45)
1 teaspoon grated fresh ginger
1½ cups half-and-half
Kosher salt
Black pepper in a mill
Croutons (page 121) or fresh bread crumbs, toasted (see page 46)

Preheat the oven to 375°F. Spread out the pumpkin pieces on a baking sheet and brush each piece with olive oil. Bake for 45 minutes, or until the pumpkin is completely tender. Remove the pumpkin from the oven and let it cool.

When the pumpkin is cool enough to handle, remove the skin from several pieces and place the flesh in a bowl. Reserve the skins. With a fork, mash the flesh into a fine pulp. Continue until you have 2 cups of pulp. Set the pulp aside.

Make a pumpkin stock: Put the remaining pumpkin pieces, the reserved skins, the allspice berries, and the cinnamon in a large heavy stockpot. Add water to cover. Bring to a boil over medium-high heat, reduce the heat, and simmer gently for about 1½ hours, adding more water if necessary, until the broth is fragrant with the aroma of, and tastes like, pumpkin. Remove the stock from the heat, strain it, and return the liquid to the clean pot. Over high heat, reduce the liquid until you have about 3 cups of pumpkin stock. Set the stock aside.

Melt the butter in a large heavy stockpot over medium heat. Add the onion, and sauté it until it is very soft and fragrant, about 15 minutes. Stir in the chipotle, the pumpkin pulp, the pumpkin stock, the roasted garlic puree, and the ginger. Reduce the heat to very low, and simmer for 10 minutes. Add the half-and-half, and heat through but do not bring to a boil again. Taste, and season with salt and pepper.

To serve, ladle into warmed soup bowls and top each portion with 2 croutons or a spoonful of toasted bread crumbs. Serve immediately.

POTATO-CHEDDAR SOUP

This is one of my favorite bone-warming soups. I've occasionally poured some of the soup into a hot thermos and driven to the coast to watch a storm come in from the Pacific; it's the ideal accompaniment to such an adventure, and I've always felt utterly safe and warm as the winds, rains, and waves roared around me.

SERVES 6 TO 8

¼ cup olive oil
2 yellow onions, diced
2 carrots, peeled and diced
10 garlic cloves, minced
4 pounds potatoes, scrubbed and diced
4 cups chicken stock
3 cups (12 ounces) grated cheddar
½ cup minced Italian parsley
Kosher salt
Black pepper in a mill

Heat the olive oil in a large stockpot over low heat. Add the onions, and sauté them until they are soft and fragrant, about 15 minutes. Add the carrots, and sauté for 10 minutes more. Add the garlic, and sauté for 2 minutes more. Add the potatoes, stock, and 3 cups of water. Bring to a boil, reduce the heat to low, and simmer, covered, until the potatoes are tender, about 15 minutes. Remove the soup from the heat. Puree the soup with an immersion blender or in a conventional blender. Return the soup to low heat, and stir in the cheese and parsley. Season with salt and pepper, and serve immediately.

Variation:

Add 4 or 5 dried chipotles to the soup with the potatoes. Reduce the amount of cheese to 2 cups, and replace the parsley with ¼ cup minced cilantro leaves. Add 1 pound of a spicy sausage, cooked and cut into thin rounds, with the cheese and cilantro.

SHIITAKE-CHÈVRE SOUP

Although you can make a fine soup using chicken stock, smoked duck stock adds a richness and a depth of flavor that are unsurpassed, making it worth the extra effort it may take to get smoked duck. Likewise, you can use any young chèvre in this soup, but if you have some ripe and creamy Chenel taupinière, by all means use it.

SERVES 6 TO 8

1 pound shiitake mushrooms
3 tablespoons butter
3 large shallots, minced
¼ cup Madeira
3 cups chicken stock or smoked duck stock

2 cups half-and-half

8 ounces young (not aged) chèvre, crumbled

Black pepper in a mill

Kosher salt

2 tablespoons snipped chives

Remove the stems from the shiitakes, and discard the stems or reserve them for a vegetable stock. Set aside a quarter of the shiitake caps, and chop the remaining caps fine either with a knife or in a food processor.

Melt the butter in a heavy stockpot over medium-low heat. Add the shallots, and sauté them until they are soft and fragrant, 5 to 7 minutes. Reduce the heat to low, add the chopped shiitakes, and sauté them until they are very soft, about 15 minutes. Slice the reserved caps, and add them and the Madeira to the pot. Bring to a boil, reduce the heat, and simmer, covered, until the shiitake slices have wilted, about 5 minutes. Add the stock, and simmer for 10 minutes more. Reduce the heat to low, and stir in the half-and-half and the chèvre. Stir until the cheese is melted and is well incorporated into the soup; do not let the soup

Twenty Goats

Before Chez Panisse Café introduced its signature salad of field greens and chèvre, many Americans were unfamiliar with goat cheese and its hundreds of French variations. Between this simple salad and the little cheeses handcrafted in Sebastopol by Laura Chenel, an entire new industry was launched.

"When I was first making my cheese," Chenel recalls, "I thought it would just go to retail stores. I couldn't imagine a restaurant wanting it. There was a wonderful wine and cheese shop in San Francisco, and the owner told me I *must* take my cheeses to Alice Waters. At the time, I had no idea who she was. So I took my cheeses down to Berkeley. I set them out on a counter and everyone tasted them. Alice got a big smile on her face and said, 'Oh, yeah, I'll take sixty [5 ounces each] of these a week.' That was a huge order at the time and it's never stopped. Now Chez Panisse takes between fifty and a hundred pounds a week." Chenel made her first cheeses with milk from her herd of twenty goats. Today, she has three hundred and fifty goats and produces close to a half-million pounds of cheese a year.

boil. Season with several turns of black pepper, taste, and add salt and more black pepper to taste. Ladle into warmed soup bowls, and top each serving with a sprinkling of chives. Serve immediately.

FORT ROSS RUSSIAN-STYLE VEGETABLE SOUP

*M*any California State Historic Parks feature Living History programs that offer visitors an opportunity to experience community life at the time a settlement was established. Staff dress in period costumes and attempt to portray a typical day in the 1800s, when most California regions were just being settled. Fort Ross, near what is now the northern end of Sonoma County, was the southernmost outpost of the Russian-American Company, a commercial hunting and trading company chartered by the Tsar of Russia. The town was first settled by Ivan Alexandrovich Kuskov, who arrived in March of 1812, accompanied by a party of Russians and native Alaskans. Pomos, a Native American group, lived in the area, but the newcomers soon negotiated a deal to allow construction to begin.

Eventually, Spanish and Mexican settlers came, too, creating a unique cultural diversity at Fort Ross. Today, many of the buildings have been restored, including the chapel, the first Russian Orthodox structure built in North America outside of Alaska. Robin Joy, one of the park's interpreters, develops recipes based on ingredients available to the settlers. I have adapted this hearty Russian vegetable soup from her recipe.

SERVES 8

4 tablespoons butter or olive oil
1 yellow onion, diced
1 leek, white and light green parts only, cleaned and sliced thin
1 medium carrot, minced
4 garlic cloves, minced
1 medium celery root, peeled and sliced thin
2 medium Jerusalem artichokes, scrubbed and sliced thin
2 medium potatoes, peeled and diced
1½ pounds white cabbage, cored and shredded, or 1½ pounds sauerkraut, rinsed and drained
1 bay leaf
1 sprig of oregano or marjoram
8 cups water or vegetable broth
Kosher salt and black pepper in a mill
¼ cup sour cream
1 tablespoon minced dill

In a large stockpot, heat the butter or olive oil over medium heat. Add the onions and leeks, and sauté them until they are limp, about 8 to 10 minutes. Add the carrots, and sauté for 5 to 6 minutes more. Add the garlic, and sauté for 2 minutes more. Add the celery root, Jerusalem artichokes, potatoes, cabbage or sauerkraut, bay leaf, and oregano or marjoram. Pour in the water or stock. Bring to a boil, reduce the heat, and simmer, partially covered, until the vegetables are very tender, about 1 hour. Taste the soup, and season with salt and pepper. Ladle into soup bowls, top each portion with 1 tablespoon of sour cream and a sprinkling of dill, and serve immediately.

Ground Rats

The western pocket gopher plagues gardeners and farmers throughout California. There are as many tales of the gophers' tenacity as there are home remedies for their demise. Among the most enduring stories is that it was the gopher that drove the Russians out of California. In his book *Garlic Is Life* (Ten Speed Press, 1996), Chester Aaron tracks down one of the tales' sources:

"A local paper recently ran a story about a stained diary found in the attic of an old home in Sebastopol, about ten miles from my home in Occidental. The diary contains entries written by one of the Russian soldiers who had traveled south from Alaska in the 1830s. He may have been one of the troopers in the contingent that built Fort Ross on the coast, sixty miles north of Occidental. One translated excerpt from the diary was of great interest to me: '... we could have survived on this land if it weren't for the ground rats.'"

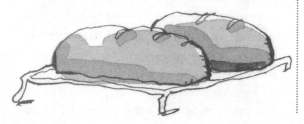

ASIAN NOODLE SOUP

When I was a little girl, my mother used to take me out to dinner every Friday night. Sometimes we went to an Italian restaurant, but my fondest memories are of a tiny Cantonese café with big comfortable booths, wooden tables, and bright green walls. My favorite dish was a huge bowl of steaming noodles in a fragrant broth, topped with sliced smoked pork, scallion rounds, and half a hard-boiled egg. I learned quickly to use chopsticks, and I particularly loved the wide porcelain soup spoons the waiter brought to the table. Now, I suspect I would find that soup I so loved bland, but I thoroughly enjoy this spicier version.

SERVES 4

8 cups chicken stock
3 thin slices of fresh ginger
4 garlic cloves, peeled
3 to 4 serrano or Thai chiles
1 tablespoon fish sauce
2 tablespoons soy sauce
Juice of 1 lime
12 ounces somen noodles or thin rice
    noodles
4 scallions, cut into thin rounds
8 ounces shiitake mushrooms, sliced
    and sautéed, optional

8 ounces cooked chicken, cut into
   medium julienne (see Note)
¼ cup cilantro leaves, torn into small
   pieces

In a large stockpot, combine the stock
with the ginger, garlic, and chiles, and
bring to a boil. Remove the pot from the
heat and let steep, covered, for 30 minutes.
Using a slotted spoon, remove and discard
the ginger, garlic, and chiles. Add the fish
sauce, soy sauce, and lime juice to the stock
and reheat it.

Cook the noodles in boiling salted
water for 2½ minutes, or according to the
package directions, until they are tender.
Drain them, divide them among 4 serving
bowls, and top each portion with scallions and, if you like, shiitakes. Ladle the
seasoned stock over each serving, top with
chicken and cilantro leaves, and serve
immediately.

NOTE: Set aside leftover Thai-style
Grilled Chicken Breast (page 313) to use in
this dish. Refrigerate the cooked chicken,
covered, after cooking, and slice it thin.

Variations:

Add ¼ cup minced lemon grass to the
stock along with the ginger, garlic, and
chiles, and substitute the juice of ½ lemon
for the lime juice.

Use 8 ounces of sliced cooked duck
breast, beef, pork, or lamb in place of the
chicken.

SHEEPHERDER'S SOUP

*W*hen Basque sheepherders led
their seminomadic lives in
the undulating hills along
California's north coast, they needed
hearty fare to sustain them. Beans were
easy to carry, and certain greens—wild
onions and wild leeks, for example—could
be harvested in transit. And, of course,
there was sheep's milk, most of which was
made into cheese but some of which was
used in cooking. In this recipe, I simply call
for cow's milk.

SERVES 6 TO 8

1 pound dried lima beans, soaked
   overnight and drained
3 tablespoons butter
1 yellow onion, diced
2 leeks, white and light green parts
   only, cleaned and sliced thin
2 celery ribs
2 cups Tomato Concassé (recipe
   follows) or 2 cups canned crushed
   tomatoes
2 cups milk
Kernels from 3 to 4 ears of fresh corn
3 tablespoons chopped Italian parsley
Tabasco sauce
Kosher salt
Black pepper in a mill

In a large stockpot over medium-low
heat, cook the lima beans in plenty of water

until they are barely tender, about 40 minutes. As they cook, skim off any foam that forms and any skins that float to the top. When the beans are done, drain them and set them aside.

Return the pot to the heat, melt the butter, and cook the onion, leeks, and celery until they are very soft, about 20 minutes. Add the cooked lima beans, the tomatoes, and 3 cups of water, and simmer, covered, for 20 minutes. Stir in the milk, corn, and parsley, simmer for 5 minutes, and remove from the heat. Taste, and season with Tabasco, salt, and pepper. Serve immediately, with plenty of hot bread alongside.

Tomato Concassé

Tomato concassé is used in many recipes, from salsas and soups to more complex dishes. It can also be tossed with pasta, spooned over grilled fish, or served as a condiment with summer risottos. *Concassé* is French for crushed or ground, but in culinary usage it refers to tomatoes chopped very fine, nearly to a pulp.

MAKES ABOUT 3½ CUPS

3 pounds ripe red tomatoes
Kosher salt to taste

Peel a tomato by placing it on the tines of a long fork and holding it over a gas flame. Rotating the fork constantly so that the flesh doesn't cook, sear the skin. You will need about 5 to 15 seconds, depending on the tomato's size. Repeat until all of the tomatoes have been seared. Set the tomatoes aside to cool. When they are cool enough to handle, remove their skins. Cut them in half horizontally (through the equator), cut out the core, and gently squeeze out the seeds and gel. Chop them fine, and put them in a strainer lined with cheesecloth. Let them drain for at least 20 minutes; reserve the liquid for another use. Transfer the tomatoes to a nonreactive bowl, and season with salt. Use immediately, or store, covered, in the refrigerator for up to 3 days.

Variation:

For golden tomato concassé, prepare 3 pounds ripe golden tomatoes as directed. Add 1 shallot, minced, 2 garlic cloves, minced, 1 tablespoon minced basil leaves, and salt.

FALL MINESTRONE

*M*inestrone made of vegetables fresh from the garden is outstanding. Fall is a great time to make it—the harvest is threatening to overwhelm us and there's a chill in the air that makes our thoughts turn to soup.

SERVES 6 TO 8

½ cup olive oil
1 yellow onion, diced
1 carrot, peeled and diced
2 leeks, white part only, cleaned and
    sliced thin

3 cups Tomato Concassé (page 98)
8 cups beef stock
¼ pound pancetta or bacon, diced
1 head of garlic, cloves separated,
    peeled, and minced
2 tablespoons minced Italian parsley
1 tablespoon chopped oregano
4 small zucchini, sliced
2 cups cooked or canned white beans
2 cups sliced Swiss chard
6 ounces dried small pasta, such as
    orzo, rosemarina, or small shells
Kosher salt
Black pepper in a mill
1 cup (4 ounces) grated dry jack

In a large heavy stockpot over medium heat, heat all but 1 tablespoon of the olive oil. Add the onion, carrot, and leeks, and sauté until the vegetables are very soft, about 20 minutes. Add the tomato concassé and the stock, and simmer for 15 minutes.

In a skillet over medium heat, fry the pancetta or bacon in the remaining 1 tablespoon of olive oil. When the meat begins to brown, add the garlic, and sauté for 2 minutes more. Add the parsley and oregano, remove from the heat, and add the skillet's contents to the soup mixture. Add the zucchini, beans, chard, and pasta. Simmer until the pasta is tender, 7 to 10 minutes, depending on its shape.

Remove the soup from the heat, taste, and season with salt and pepper. Ladle into warmed soup bowls, and garnish each serving with grated cheese. Serve immediately.

Variations:

In early spring, omit the zucchini and use 1 cup fresh shelled peas in its place. In summer, omit the chard and add ¼ pound haricots verts and 2 tablespoons minced basil.

WHITE BEAN AND HAMHOCK SOUP

From petite pink beans, small whites, and baby limas to garbanzos, kidney beans, and large limas, California is a major producer of dried beans and peas. For decades, California bean crops have been limited to the standards, but in recent years some farmers have begun growing heirloom varieties, including varieties of cannellini beans, which can be used in this recipe.

SERVES 4 TO 6

1 pound dried white beans or dried
    lima beans, soaked in water
    overnight and drained
2 yellow onions, cut into chunks
Handful of garlic cloves, peeled
3 hamhocks
1 bay leaf
1 teaspoon black peppercorns
Kosher salt
Black pepper in a mill
Tabasco sauce

99

In a large stockpot, combine the beans, onions, and garlic. Cover them with 8 cups of water, and bring to a boil. Reduce the heat to low, and cook, partially covered, for 1 hour, occasionally skimming off any foam that forms on top. Add the hamhocks, bay leaf, and peppercorns, and simmer until the beans and onions fall apart and the meat is ready to fall off the bone, about 1 hour more. Remove the bones, pull off the meat, and stir it back into the soup. Remove and discard the bay leaf. Taste, season with salt and ground pepper, and thin with water if necessary to reach the proper soup consistency. Serve with Tabasco on the side, along with hot country-style bread or cornbread.

BIG SUR BLACK BEAN SOUP

Big Sur is the sort of damp place where you expect to eat black bean soup. You can generally find it on the menus of the area's casual inns and restaurants, where diners are likely to have spent the day hiking along the beach or in the forest.

SERVES 4 TO 6

3 tablespoons olive oil
1 yellow onion, diced
1 carrot, peeled and minced
2 celery ribs, minced
3 garlic cloves, minced
1 teaspoon cumin seeds
½ teaspoon crushed red pepper flakes
3 cups black beans, soaked in water overnight and drained
1 jalapeño, or 2 for more heat
2 bay leaves
Kosher salt
Black pepper in a mill

In a large heavy stockpot over medium heat, heat the olive oil. Add the onion, carrot, and celery, and cook them until they are tender and fragrant, about 15 minutes. Add the garlic, and sauté for 2 minutes more. Add the cumin and red pepper, and stir for 1 minute. Add the black beans and 6 cups of water. Using a paring knife, make several lengthwise slits in the jalapeño, add it the soup, and add the bay leaves. Bring to a boil, reduce the heat, and simmer the beans until they are completely tender and begin to fall apart, 40 to 90 minutes, depending on the age of the beans. As the beans cook, add more water, if needed, to keep them from becoming too dry.

Remove and discard the jalapeño and the bay leaves. If you like, you can puree half of the beans using an immersion blender, or simply cook them for 15 minutes more, until they nearly dissolve.

Stir the soup, taste, and season with salt and pepper. Ladle into soup bowls and serve immediately. Or refrigerate, and reheat when ready to serve.

Serve the soup with a spoonful of Avocado Sauce (page 63), your favorite salsa (see chapter 2), or some grated cheddar cheese.

Water Is Life

Water is the single most important ingredient in California cooking. If you have plenty of good-tasting water, you might shrug and say, "Of course. So what?" But water in California is a constant problem, a matter of dispute. Those who have it fight with those who want it. "Water is life, don't waste it" is a slogan often posted above kitchen and bathroom spigots. Enormous amounts of water are moved through the state in an elaborate system of dams, aqueducts, siphons, pumps, bays, weirs, and drains. Water is diverted from the Colorado River; it is pumped over the Tehachapi Mountains to quench the immense thirst of Los Angeles. Without this massive transport of water much of California agriculture would vanish. City water can be expensive, and when the state is in the midst of a drought, water is rationed. Well water, on which many Californians rely, often contains iron, sulfur, and other impurities that stain fabric and tarnish porcelain, including human teeth. Everyone in the state, it seems, has a water filter. Often we cook with bottled spring water, particularly in soups, where off-flavors in tap water may be easily detected. An outsider might look at bottled water as an affectation, but in California we know otherwise.

LENTIL SOUP WITH SIEVED EGG

One of the legacies of the 1960s was lentil soup, found on the menu of virtually every health-food restaurant for years thereafter. Most were thick and bland, like a heavy stew, and were seasoned only with soy sauce. In recent years, lentils have been cooked with increasing finesse, in part because of the popularity of French country cuisine and the availability of French-style lentils *de Puy*, which cook fast and don't get mushy.

SERVES 4 TO 6

1½ cups brown lentils or green French
   lentils
3 tablespoons olive oil
1 yellow onion, minced
2 celery ribs, diced
1 medium carrot, diced
1 tablespoon minced garlic
1 cup Tomato Concassé (page 98) or
   canned diced tomatoes
4 cups beef stock
½ teaspoon crushed red pepper flakes
1 teaspoon kosher salt
1 teaspoon fresh-ground black
   pepper
1 tablespoon minced Italian parsley
1 hard-boiled egg, sieved
2 tablespoons minced red onion

Soak the lentils overnight in plenty of water. Drain them and rinse them.

In a heavy stockpot over medium heat, heat the olive oil. Add the onion, and sauté until translucent, 8 to 10 minutes. Add the celery and carrots, and sauté until the vegetables are very soft, about 20 minutes. Add the garlic, and sauté for 2 minutes more. Add the concassé or diced tomatoes, lentils, stock, red pepper, and 4 cups of water. Bring to a boil, reduce the heat, and simmer, partially covered, until the lentils are completely tender, 25 to 60 minutes, depending on the type and age of the lentils.

Taste the soup, season with salt and black pepper, and ladle into warmed soup bowls. Top each portion with some of the minced parsley, sieved egg, and minced red onion, and serve immediately.

CRAB VICHYSSOISE

*V*ichyssoise may be the sexiest of all chilled soups, perhaps because of its name, which rolls off the tongue like a whisper or a kiss. In this version, Dungeness crab adds an elegant and delicious flourish.

SERVES 4 TO 6

3 tablespoons butter
4 leeks, white part only, cleaned and sliced thin
1 small yellow onion, diced
2 pounds (about 4 large) russet potatoes, peeled and sliced thin
3 cups chicken stock

1 cup heavy cream
Kosher salt
White pepper, preferably fresh-ground
1¼ pounds cooked Dungeness crab meat (from 1 small to medium crab), leg meat reserved separately
2 teaspoons minced lemon zest
1 tablespoon snipped chives

In a large stockpot over medium-low heat, melt the butter until it is foamy. Add the leeks, and sauté them until they are wilted, about 7 minutes. Add the onion, and sauté until very soft and fragrant, about 15 minutes. Add the potatoes, and sauté for 2 minutes more. Pour in the stock and 3 cups of water, and increase the heat to bring to a boil. Reduce the heat, and simmer, uncovered, until the potatoes are tender, 15 to 20 minutes. Puree the soup thoroughly, using an immersion blender, a food mill, or a conventional blender, then strain it through a sieve. Add the cream, taste, and season with salt and white pepper. Refrigerate the soup until it is thoroughly chilled, at least 2 hours.

To serve, fold in the crab meat, ladle into chilled soup bowls, set a segment of the reserved crab leg on each serving, and garnish with lemon zest and chives. Serve immediately.

OYSTER CHOWDER

*P*urists may consider this main-dish oyster chowder a travesty—it has ingredients other than oysters and cream. Yet little interferes with the flavor or texture of the oysters. Feel free to omit the butter, onion, pancetta, and parsley if you must. For a devilish flourish, place a whole, unbroken egg yolk in the bottom of each soup bowl and then ladle the chowder over it with such delicate care that the yolk remains whole and is heated by the creamy broth, a suggestion made by M.F.K. Fisher in *Consider the Oyster*.

SERVES 4 TO 6

¼ cup butter
1 small yellow onion, diced fine
3 ounces pancetta or bacon, diced fine
1 cup strained oyster liquor
2 to 3 cups heavy cream
1 quart (about 3 to 4 dozen) fresh-shucked small Pacific oysters
2 tablespoons minced Italian parsley
Black pepper in a mill

In a small heavy skillet, melt the butter over medium heat. Add the onion, and sauté until translucent, 8 to 10 minutes. Add the pancetta or bacon, and sauté for 10 minutes more. Set aside.

In a medium stockpot over medium heat, bring the oyster liquor to a simmer. Skim off any foam, add 2 cups of the cream, and bring back to a simmer. Stir in the onion mixture, add the oysters, and cook until the oysters' edges just curl, 3 to 5 minutes, depending on their size. Do not overcook them. For a thinner soup, stir in the remaining 1 cup of the cream and heat through. Stir in the parsley, grind black pepper over all, and remove from the heat. Serve immediately, with hot sourdough bread.

SAUSALITO CRAB-TOMATO BISQUE

*J*ohn Kramer, a political scientist, is one of the best home cooks I know. In the 1970s, when he lived in Sausalito, there was a restaurant called Soupçon near his home. It was a tiny place, arranged like a railroad car, with an eccentric, homey menu. Every Thursday night, John would call and reserve a bowl of Crab Tomato Bisque. The chef always gave him an enormous portion, perhaps two quarts, and often other guests would glare at him after being told the soup was sold out. Just before the restaurant went out of business, John bought the recipe for a hundred dollars. He hadn't looked at it in years when I asked him about it. When he found it—the ink faded but still legible—he kindly shared it with me. Purists insist that seafood bisque be made with fish stock rather than chicken stock, but this is how Soupçon made theirs. Few home cooks take the time to make fish stock, but should you find yourself having to please a stickler for detail, you are welcome to make your own (see Appendix 1).

SERVES 6 TO 8

4 tablespoons unsalted butter
1 yellow onion, diced
2 celery ribs, diced
1 tablespoon minced Italian parsley
½ teaspoon marjoram
2 teaspoons chopped basil
1 bay leaf
½ teaspoon white pepper, preferably fresh-ground
8 cups chicken stock or fish stock
1 16-ounce can organic diced tomatoes, preferably, or
    1 14-ounce can diced tomatoes
¼ cup sherry
2 tablespoons sugar
2 teaspoons fresh lemon juice
1 to 2 whole Dungeness crabs, cleaned, cracked, and cut into 1-inch pieces
1 cup heavy cream
1 cup half-and-half
Milk, if necessary

Melt the butter in a large stockpot over medium heat. Add the onion and celery, and sauté them until they are soft and fragrant, 8 to 10 minutes. Add the parsley, marjoram, basil, bay leaf, and white pepper, and stir in the stock, diced tomatoes, sherry, sugar, and lemon juice. Bring to a boil over high heat, reduce the heat to low, and simmer, covered, for 20 minutes. Add the crab pieces, cream, and half-and-half, and heat through thoroughly but do not let boil again. If necessary, thin with milk to achieve a proper soup consistency, and heat through again. Serve immediately.

SALMON CHOWDER WITH GINGER AND LEMON GRASS

The Chinook salmon, also called King, Tyee, and Quinnat, has a natural range that stretches from San Diego north to the Bering Sea and west to Japan. They are most abundant from central California northward. Their numbers are carefully monitored and commercial salmon fishing is strictly regulated. Wild salmon has a much better flavor and texture than the increasingly available farm-raised salmon; when you have a choice, buy wild. Salmon is often the first choice for backyard barbecues; if you grill a whole fish, as we often do in California, set aside some of the leftovers for this chowder.

Lemon grass, fresh ginger, and coconut milk contribute delicate Thai elements to this dazzling summer soup, ideal for a special occasion.

SERVES 6

¼ cup olive oil
1 yellow onion, diced
3 garlic cloves, minced
1 serrano chile, minced

1 2-inch piece of ginger, peeled, chopped, and squeezed through a garlic press

4 cups fish stock, hot

2 stalks lemon grass, bruised and cut into 1-inch pieces

Juice of 1 lime

½ cup dry white wine, such as sauvignon blanc

2 medium tomatoes, peeled, seeded, and diced

1 cup (from about 2 ears) fresh corn kernels

1 pound salmon fillet, skinned and cut into 1-inch cubes

¾ cup coconut milk

¼ cup cilantro leaves

Kosher salt

Black pepper in a mill

Heat the olive oil in a heavy stockpot over medium heat. Add the onion, and sauté until very soft and fragrant, about 15 minutes. Add the garlic, and sauté for 2 minutes more. Add the serrano and ginger, stir, and add the hot stock. Add the lemon grass, lower the heat, and simmer, covered, for 15 minutes. Add the lime juice, wine, and tomatoes, and simmer for 15 minutes more. Using tongs, remove and discard the lemon grass. Add the corn and the salmon and simmer gently over low heat for 5 minutes. Stir in the coconut milk and cilantro, and season with salt and pepper. Taste the soup, adjust the seasoning, and ladle into warmed soup bowls. Serve immediately.

ARTICHOKE SOUP WITH CHICKEN AND CHIVES

*I*n "The Social Status of a Vegetable," an essay in her first book, *Serve It Forth*, M.F.K. Fisher tackles vegetable snobbery. In France, leeks once were dismissed as "the asparagus of the poor." Old Mrs. Davidson, Fisher tells us, displayed a pompous distaste for cabbage, because it reminded her of the slums. Fisher's mother, Edith Kennedy, had a horror of turnips, from growing up in an area crowded with Swedish immigrants who seemed to live on them. Fisher's Grandmother Holbrook, raised in the Midwest, had an unusual manner of dismissing someone she saw as a vulgar social climber: "Oh, Mrs. Zubzub is the kind of woman who serves artichokes!" In California, where everyone eats artichokes all the time, the comment would have been meaningless.

SERVES 4 TO 6

6 medium artichokes, boiled until just tender (see page 381)

3 tablespoons olive oil

1 small yellow onion, diced

1 shallot, minced

6 garlic cloves, minced

1 cup Tomato Concassé (page 98)

6 ounces cooked chicken meat, cut into medium julienne

3 cups chicken stock

1 cup cream or half-and-half
2 tablespoons snipped chives
Kosher salt
Black pepper in a mill

Separate the leaves of the artichokes from the hearts, and scoop out and discard the thistle-like chokes in the center. Dice the hearts and set them aside. Cut the meat from the base of each artichoke leaf into thin julienne, and set it aside separately.

Heat the olive oil in a large stockpot over medium-low heat. Add the onion and shallot, and sauté them until they are very soft and fragrant, about 15 minutes. Add the garlic, and sauté for 2 minutes more. Add the tomato concassé, and simmer, stirring constantly, for 3 to 4 minutes to evaporate the excess liquid in the tomatoes. Add the reserved artichoke hearts and the chicken meat, stir in the stock, and bring to a boil. Reduce the heat, and simmer, uncovered, for 15 minutes. Stir in the cream or half-and-half, and heat through but do not boil. Remove the pot from the heat, and stir in the reserved artichoke julienne and the chives. Season with salt and pepper, taste, and adjust the seasoning. Ladle into warmed soup bowls and serve immediately.

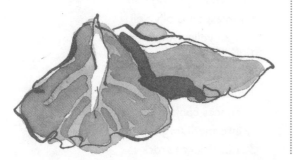

THAI CHICKEN AND RICE SOUP

Galanga is a root, similar in appearance to fresh ginger, that is used in many traditional Thai dishes. As California's Thai population increases and as Thai food becomes more popular among home cooks, fresh galanga has become increasingly available in Asian markets. Some is even grown now in California, and it is also available dried or frozen. If you cannot find galanga, you can use fresh ginger in its place; the dish will be different but still very good. Kaffir lime leaves also can be found in Asian markets. This recipe calls for poached chicken because it is moist and very tender, but you can use any cooked chicken. If you happen to have cooked duck on hand, use it instead of the chicken; duck is outstanding in this soup.

SERVES 4 TO 6

6 skinless chicken thighs or 4 skinless
   chicken breasts
Kosher salt
Black pepper in a mill
4 cups chicken stock, hot
3 tablespoons peanut oil
1 small red onion, diced
6 scallions, green and white parts,
   sliced thin
3 garlic cloves, minced
4 serrano chiles, sliced thin
3 cups coconut milk

2 stalks lemon grass, bruised and cut
   diagonally into 1-inch-long pieces
1 2-inch piece fresh or frozen
   galanga, sliced very thin
4 kaffir lime leaves, cut in slivers, or 1
   teaspoon minced lime zest
Juice of 2 limes
3 tablespoons fish sauce
3 cups cooked Jasmine Rice (page
   218)
¼ cup minced cilantro leaves

Preheat the oven to 350°F. Season the chicken pieces on both sides with salt and pepper, and place them in a shallow baking dish that will hold them all in a single layer. Pour in stock to cover the pieces. Poach the chicken for 20 minutes. Remove the chicken pieces from the oven, and let them cool in the stock.

While the chicken cools, heat the peanut oil in a large heavy stockpot over medium heat. Add the onion, and sauté it until it is soft and transparent, about 7 minutes. Add the scallions, and sauté them until they are limp, 6 to 7 minutes. Add the garlic and serranos, and sauté for 2 minutes more. Add the poaching liquid and any remaining stock, and the coconut milk, lemon grass, galanga, and lime leaves or lime zest. Bring to a boil, reduce the heat, and simmer, covered, for 15 minutes.

Pull the chicken meat from the bones. Slice it, and stir it into the soup along with the lime juice and fish sauce. To serve, divide the jasmine rice among serving bowls and ladle the soup over. Top each portion with some minced cilantro, and serve immediately.

BEEF AND BARLEY SOUP

Twice a year, on the day after Thanksgiving and the day after Christmas, my mother made soup. She would place the turkey carcass in a huge pot filled with water, add leftover dark meat (which she hated), giblets, and gravy, and cook it for hours, until the entire house was filled with the aroma of that simmering turkey. Finally, just a half hour before dinner, she would add the little pearls of barley that I so loved. I would eat that wonderful soup every day, and sometimes twice a day, until it was gone, at which point I would beg her to make more. She never did, and this soup became as much a talisman of the holdays as the glittering tree or my filled stocking on Christmas morning. I developed this version using beef rather than turkey to evoke, if remotely, that well-loved soup of my childhood.

SERVES 4 TO 6

⅓ cup all-purpose flour
2 teaspoons dry mustard, sifted
1 teaspoon kosher salt, plus more to
   taste
2 teaspoons fresh-ground black
   pepper, plus more to taste
1 pound beef stew meat, cut into
   1½-inch cubes and trimmed of
   excess fat
3 tablespoons olive oil
1 yellow onion, diced

1 shallot, minced

1 cup diced peeled carrots

1 pound (about 3 medium) diced red
   new potatoes

20 garlic cloves, peeled

1 14-ounce can of diced tomatoes

4 cups beef stock

¼ teaspoon crushed red pepper
   flakes

5 to 6 juniper berries

2 to 3 allspice berries, preferably,
   or 2 to 3 cloves

2 sprigs of thyme

1 sprig of oregano

1 cup uncooked barley

Combine the flour, dry mustard, 1 teaspoon salt, and 2 teaspoons pepper in a
paper lunch bag or a small plastic bag. Add
the beef to the bag, and shake vigorously
to coat the meat thoroughly. Empty the bag
into a strainer, and shake off excess flour.

Place the olive oil in a large heavy
stockpot over medium heat. Add the beef,
and brown on it on all sides, stirring frequently so that it does not burn. Reduce the
heat to low, add the onion and shallot, and
sauté them, stirring frequently, until they
are fragrant and transparent, about 15 minutes. Stir in the carrots, potatoes, and garlic,
and sauté for 2 minutes more. Add the
tomatoes, stock, crushed red pepper, and 4
cups of water, and increase the heat to
bring to a boil. While the liquid is heating
up, tie up the juniper, allspice, thyme,
and oregano in a small piece of cheesecloth,
and add the spice bag to the soup. Once the
liquid boils, reduce the heat, and simmer,

partially covered, for 30 minutes. Stir in the
barley, and continue to simmer, partially
covered, for 45 minutes more.

Taste the soup and correct the seasoning with more salt and pepper. Remove
from the heat, remove and discard the
spice bag, and let rest for 5 to 10 minutes
before serving. Serve the soup immediately, or refrigerate it and reheat it to serve.

PORTUGUESE KALE SOUP

*W*hen I was growing up, my
grandparents lived around
the corner from a Portuguese
community center in a small town northeast of San Francisco. From the second
story window of their house, I would
watch an annual parade—small but colorful, and full of drums and brassy music—
snake through the street toward the community center, where the music, as well
as enticing aromas from foods I could not
imagine then but now recognize as garlic
and hot peppers, would fill the air long
into the evening. Oh, how I wanted to be
a part of those celebrations!

SERVES 6 TO 8

3 pounds beef short ribs

2 yellow onions, chopped

1 head of garlic, cloves separated and
   peeled

3 bunches of kale, trimmed and
   chopped

3 large russet potatoes, scrubbed and
cubed
2 cups cooked or canned red beans
1 teaspoon crushed red pepper flakes
Kosher salt
Black pepper in a mill

In a large heavy stockpot, combine the short ribs and 8 cups of water, and bring to a boil. Reduce the heat, and simmer, partially covered, for 45 minutes, removing any foam that forms. Add the onions, garlic, kale, potatoes, beans, and red pepper, and simmer until the vegetables are completely tender, about 45 minutes. Taste and season with salt and pepper. Ladle into warmed soup bowls, and serve immediately.

CLOVERDALE MEATBALL SOUP

Whenever I can, I buy my garlic from Sunshine Farms in Cloverdale in northern Sonoma County, where they grow dozens of varieties of garlic, all more complex in flavor than the ubiquitous California White grown in Gilroy. I use Cloverdale garlic when I make this soup, my version of the classic Mexican *sopa de albondigas*, very popular in California's early years. Then the savory meatballs were seasoned with *yerba buena*, a pungent herb that grew wild throughout the area that would become San Francisco.

SERVES 4 TO 6

3 tablespoons olive oil
1 small yellow onion, diced
6 garlic cloves, minced
2 serrano chiles, minced
3 large ripe red tomatoes, peeled,
seeded, and minced, or 1½ cups
Tomato Concassé (page 98)
2 medium carrots, diced
2 medium zucchini, cut into
¼-inch dice
1 recipe Roasted Garlic Meatballs
(page 45)
6 cups chicken stock, duck stock, or
beef stock, hot
2 serrano chiles, slit lengthwise in
several places
3 sprigs of cilantro
Kosher salt
Black pepper in a mill
½ cup minced cilantro leaves

In a large heavy stockpot over medium-low heat, heat the olive oil. Add the onion, and sauté until it is very soft and fragrant, about 15 minutes. Add the garlic and the minced serranos, and sauté for 2 minutes more. Add the tomatoes, increase the heat, and simmer for 5 minutes to reduce the excess liquid in the tomatoes. Add the carrots and zucchini, then add the meatballs, taking care that they do not break apart.

Pour in the hot stock, add the whole serranos and the cilantro sprigs, and bring the soup to a boil. Reduce the heat to very low and simmer, uncovered, for 45 minutes. Taste, and season with salt and pepper. Using tongs, remove the whole serranos and the cilantro sprigs. Ladle the soup into warmed soup bowls, scatter minced cilantro over each portion, and serve immediately.

SPICY SAUSAGE AND BROCCOLI SOUP

Orecchiette, "little ears," are small rounds of pasta. They are thicker than other small shapes, making them ideal in a soup because they do not become too soft or disintegrate, as other pasta shapes sometimes do. This soup was inspired by the classic Italian pairing of orecchiette with broccoli; the addition of sausage and cannellini beans, though not traditional, makes this a hearty main-course soup.

SERVES 4 TO 6

1 pound hot Italian sausage
2 cups dry white wine
3 tablespoons olive oil
1 yellow onion, minced
6 garlic cloves, minced
½ teaspoon crushed red pepper flakes
1 teaspoon minced lemon zest
6 to 8 cups beef stock
1½ cups cooked or canned cannellini beans
8 ounces dried orecchiette pasta

3 cups broccoli florets, larger florets broken into pieces
Kosher salt
Black pepper in a mill
Dry jack or Parmigiano-Reggiano

In a large heavy stockpot over medium heat, arrange the sausages in a single layer. Add the wine, and bring to a boil. Reduce the heat, and simmer the sausages, uncovered, turning them once, until they are almost cooked through, about 15 minutes. Transfer the sausages to a platter and let them cool slightly. Increase the heat and reduce the liquid to about 1 tablespoon.

Cut the sausages into ¼-inch rounds, and set them aside. Add the olive oil and onion to the liquid in the pot, and cook over medium heat until the onion is very soft and fragrant, about 15 minutes. Add the garlic, and sauté for 2 minutes more. Stir in the red pepper, lemon zest, and sliced sausages. Add the stock and cannellini beans, and increase the heat to bring the soup to a boil. Reduce the heat, and simmer, covered, for 15 minutes. Add the orecchiette, and simmer for 8 minutes more, then add the broccoli, and simmer until the pasta is tender, about 5 minutes more. Remove from the heat, taste, and season with salt and pepper. Ladle into warmed soup bowls, grate cheese over each portion, and serve immediately.

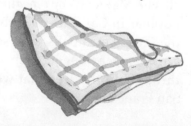

FALL HARVEST SOUP

½ head of cabbage, cored and
  shredded
2 cups chicken stock or duck stock
2 cups cooked or canned chickpeas
Kosher salt
Black pepper in a mill
¼ cup cilantro leaves

This soup illustrates one of the aspects of California I love most—the abundance of fresh seasonal produce and the inspiration that comes with its constant presence. After a long day of work, I often long for soup; many times I have opened the refrigerator and concocted a soup from whatever was at hand. In this instance, I had a large piece of kuri squash, a half head of white cabbage, and some Mexican sausage. I keep several types of stock in my freezer most of the time and they are invaluable in moments like this. A good stock is the best gift you can give your soup; see Appendix 1 for some stock recipes.

SERVES 6 TO 8

3 tablespoons olive oil
1 yellow onion, diced
3 garlic cloves, minced
1 pound Mexican chorizo, casings
  removed
3 cups diced winter squash, such as
  kuri, sugar pumpkin, or butternut
2 medium russet potatoes, scrubbed
  and diced

Heat the olive oil in a large heavy stockpot over medium heat. Add the onion, and sauté until soft and fragrant, about 10 minutes. Add the garlic, and sauté for 2 minutes more. Add the chorizo, breaking it up with a fork as it cooks. When the chorizo is cooked through and appears to have rendered its fat, drain off the excess fat, and return the pot to the heat.

Add the squash and potatoes, and sauté for 3 to 4 minutes, stirring frequently. Add the cabbage, stir until the cabbage wilts, then add the stock, the chickpeas, and 2 cups of water. Increase the heat to bring the soup to a boil, reduce the heat, and simmer, partially covered, for 20 to 30 minutes, or until the squash and potatoes are just tender. Taste the soup, and season with salt and pepper. Ladle into warmed soup bowls, and top each serving with a sprinkling of cilantro leaves. Serve immediately.

Chapter 4

SALADS

SALADS

GREENS WITH WALNUTS AND CHÈVRE

· ·

Greens with chèvre has become ubiquitous in California restaurants and home kitchens. It is a dish that evokes the affinities between the foods of California and France. The version that first made the dish popular was a signature salad of Chez Panisse. In my rendition, walnuts add another dimension.

SERVES 4 TO 6

1 5-ounce log of young (not aged) chèvre, such as chabis
½ cup walnuts, toasted and chopped
⅓ cup walnut oil, preferably, or ⅓ cup extra virgin olive oil
6 cups mixed greens, such as arugula, young lettuces, miner's lettuce, and nasturtium leaves
1 to 2 tablespoons Champagne vinegar, preferably, or 1 to 2 tablespoons red wine vinegar
Kosher salt
Black pepper in a mill
12 Baguette Croutons (recipe follows)

Preheat the oven to 375°F. Cut the chèvre into rounds ½ inch thick, place the walnuts on a small plate, and press both sides of each cheese round into the walnuts until the nuts adhere to the surface. Set the rounds on a baking sheet and place the sheet in the oven until the cheese is heated through but not completely melted, 6 to 7 minutes.

Meanwhile, pour the walnut oil into a large bowl and add the greens, using your hands to turn them in the oil until each leaf is fully coated. Add the vinegar, toss again, and season with salt and pepper. Divide the greens among individual serving plates. Place 1 or 2 rounds of chèvre on top of each serving of greens. Add 2 or 3 croutons, and serve immediately.

Baguette Croutons

MAKES 30 TO 40 CROUTONS

1 baguette
Extra virgin olive oil
Kosher salt
Black pepper in a mill

Preheat the oven to 250°F. Cut the baguette into thin slices, and place the slices on a baking sheet. Brush the top of each slice with olive oil, and sprinkle with salt and pepper. Bake until the croutons are dry and lightly toasted, 15 to 20 minutes. Let the croutons cool, and use them immediately or store them in an airtight container.

A Seasonal Guide to Farmers' Markets

There may be no better place than a farmers' market to gain a visceral sense of the seasons. Today, it is easy to become alienated from the ebb and flow of the land. Supermarkets offer abundant produce all year long, and, though there is something seductive about that, before long the year-round sameness becomes deadening. For many people, it has become impossible to remember what is in season when. A few visits to a local farmers' market will remedy the situation, for a simple reason: the produce is grown by the farmers who sell it. It is not purchased from distributors, imported from the southern hemisphere, or shipped from Mexico. Simply open your eyes, look around, and there you have it: spring's offerings, or summer's, fall's, or winter's. Increasingly, farmers' markets offer seasonal products other than produce, such as fresh-caught fish, backyard eggs, handcrafted cheeses, and organic honeys, and this season-by-season guide includes the most common. Keep in mind that many foods span more than one season; this list includes them when they first appear or when they are at their peak.

SPRING: apricots, artichokes, arugula, asparagus, Bing cherries, first corn, garlic fronds, green garlic, kumquats, baby leeks, loquats, morel mushrooms, new goat cheese, spring onions, Vidalia onions, snow peas, sugar snap peas, new potatoes, radishes, rhubarb, young salad greens, squash blossoms, strawberries, Better Boy and Early Girl tomatoes, turnips.

SUMMER: Gravenstein apples, avocados, beets, berries (blackberries, blueberries, gooseberries, olallieberries, raspberries), cabbage, cardoons, Queen Anne cherries, corn, cucumbers, eggplant, garlic, grape leaves, green beans and haricots verts, herbs and herb flowers, kohlrabi, melons, nasturtium flowers and leaves, okra, sweet onions, Valencia oranges, bell and chile peppers, stone fruit (nectarines, peaches, plums), tomatoes, wild salmon, zucchini and other summer squash.

FALL: almonds, apples, dates, fennel, figs, grapes, fall mushrooms (boletes, chanterelles, hen-of-the-woods), olives, Asian pears, pistachios, pomegranates, prunes, radicchio, green tomatoes, walnuts, winter squash.

WINTER: broccoli, broccoli rabe, brussels sprouts, cabbage, cauliflower, celery root, grapefruit, jerusalem artichokes, kiwi, Meyer lemons, new olive oil, oranges (blood, mandarin, navel), oysters, pears, persimmons, quince, rutabagas, tangerines, turnips.

PARSLEY SALAD

"*He's* like parsley—found in every sauce," an Italian saying goes, referring to those people you seem to run into everywhere. In this salad, cooking's most common herb is featured for its own merits. If you are used to parsley as a garnish or in small quantities as an herb, this salad might seem unusual. In fact, salads made mostly of parsley are common wherever good parsley is found. Five varieties of parsley dominate the market today, the most common being, of course, curly leaf parsley. Its texture is not suited to salad; make this when you find young lacy leaves of Italian parsley (more mature leaves may be too strongly flavored to stand alone). To serve a parsley salad in the winter, omit the tomatoes and add curls of a hard cheese such as dry jack, if you like.

SERVES 4 TO 6

6 cups young Italian parsley
3 tablespoons extra virgin olive oil
2 teaspoons red wine vinegar
Kosher salt
Black pepper in a mill
1 cup cherry tomatoes, halved

Trim away any large stems from the parsley. Pour the olive oil into a large salad bowl, add the parsley, and toss it until it is evenly coated with oil. Sprinkle the vinegar over the parsley, season with salt and pepper, and toss again. Add the cherry tomatoes, toss a final time, and serve immediately.

CAESAR SALAD

Caesar Cardini is nearly a household name. If not his full name, then certainly his first is uttered daily by millions. There are several stories of how the salad was first devised, but it is certain that it was prepared by Cardini himself at his restaurant in Tijuana, just south of San Diego across the California-Mexico border. Most agree on the basic structure of the salad—it should be made at the table with whole leaves of romaine lettuce and good olive oil. A clove of garlic should either scent the oil or be rubbed over the inside of the bowl before the salad is made. Anchovies are essential, the Parmigiano-Reggiano cheese should be fresh-grated, and the lemon juice should be fresh-squeezed. The croutons traditionally are homemade, with stale sourdough bread, and a coddled egg is a must. The original Caesar salad has evolved into many variations, some of which Cardini would find impossible to recognize. Yet even he encouraged what many consider a heinous shortcut, with his own brand of bottled Caesar salad dressing.

SERVES 4 TO 6

2 large or 3 to 4 small heads of
   romaine lettuce
½ cup extra virgin olive oil

3 garlic cloves, pressed or minced

3 anchovy fillets, minced

Juice of 2 lemons

1 to 2 eggs, boiled for just 1 minute

Kosher salt

Black pepper in a mill

3 ounces (¾ cup) fresh-grated
   Parmigiano-Reggiano or dry jack

3 cups Dry Jack Croutons (recipe
   follows; see the Variations)

6 to 8 whole anchovy fillets

Clean the lettuce thoroughly, separating the leaves and discarding the core. Put the leaves in a large bowl, cover with a damp cloth, and refrigerate for at least 30 minutes.

Pour the olive oil into a large shallow bowl, and add the garlic and minced anchovies. Mix thoroughly with a fork. Add the lettuce, a handful at a time, and turn it in the oil until it is thoroughly coated. Add the lemon juice, toss again, and then break in the egg or eggs. Using your hands, continue to turn the lettuce over and over until it is thoroughly coated and the egg has disappeared into the dressing itself. Season with salt and pepper, add the cheese, and toss thoroughly. Add the croutons, and toss again. Divide the salad among individual

Tips for Farmers' Market Shopping

Place your car keys in your pocket or purse before you begin shopping. Market managers have told me that shoppers are always leaving their keys behind in the farmers' booths.

Bring along several strong cloth or string bags.

If you think you will be buying dairy products, poultry, seafood, or strawberries, bring along a cooler with ice. A bucket of water will be useful if you will be buying a lot of flowers.

Go early and walk the market before making your purchases; taste and compare whenever possible.

Don't shop with a list. Look for what is at its peak, then build a meal around it. Having a well-stocked pantry of staples back home makes this a breeze.

Take large or heavy items to your car immediately, or ask the farmer to set them aside for you.

Remember to take small bills and plenty of change. Do guard against pickpockets, an increasing problem as markets become more popular.

Don't barter over small items, only large quantities (lugs of peaches, for example), and only near the end of the market day.

Ask questions even if you think you know the answer—it's often not what you expect. You can learn a lot about your food from the people who grow it.

Remember to bring sunscreen if the weather calls for it.

Relax and try not to hurry. The pleasure of being at the market is nearly as important as what you buy there.

serving plates. Top each portion with an anchovy fillet, and serve immediately.

Variations:

WITH GRILLED CHICKEN BREAST: Brush 3 boneless half breasts of chicken with olive oil, season with salt and pepper, and grill on a stovetop or outdoor grill until cooked through but still slightly moist. Remove from the grill, let rest 2 or 3 minutes, cut in diagonal crosswise slices, and divide among the salads, on top of the lettuce. Serve immediately.

WITH GRILLED SHRIMP OR PRAWNS: Clean and devein 24 medium shrimp or 18 large prawns, but leave them in their shells. Marinate them in olive oil, lemon juice, salt, and pepper for 30 minutes. Sauté or grill them, and divide them among the individual salads. Serve immediately.

Croutons

MAKES 3 CUPS

½ cup extra virgin olive oil
2 garlic cloves, pressed
1 teaspoon kosher salt
Black pepper in a mill
3 cups bread cubes from day-old
  country-style bread

Preheat the oven to 250°F. In a large glass jar or other lidded container, combine the olive oil, garlic, salt, and several turns of pepper. Add the bread cubes, close the container, and shake vigorously until the bread has absorbed all of the oil and the cubes are evenly coated. Spread the bread cubes over a baking sheet, and bake them until they are dry and slightly golden, about 25 minutes. Let the croutons cool, and use them immediately or store them in an airtight container.

Variations:

To make Black Pepper Croutons, use 2 teaspoons black pepper.

To make Dry Jack Croutons, add ¼ cup (1 ounce) finely grated dry jack cheese to the jar after the oil has been absorbed, and close and shake the jar again.

BARIANI'S SPINACH SALAD

"*T*his is the type of food I grew up on," says Emanuele Bariani of Sacramento, where he and his family produce—and market under their family name—an extra virgin olive oil from very old trees. Bariani olive oil is ideal in this salad, created by Emanuele's mother.

SERVES 4

1 pound spinach leaves, torn
5 ounces cremini mushrooms, thinly
  sliced
1 small red onion, sliced thin
2 ounces gorgonzola, crumbled
1 garlic clove, minced
1 teaspoon thyme leaves

Summer Tomato Salads

A recipe for tomato salads is scarcely necessary; all you need are a few rules of thumb. Always use the best tomatoes you can find, and choose a variety appropriate to the style of preparation. Plum tomatoes, with their dense flesh, for example, are not well suited to salads. Medium to large slicing tomatoes are ideal. Choose one large or two medium tomatoes per person, or more if the salad will be the main part of the meal. For making a simple tomato salad, don't bother peeling the tomatoes. For something more elegant to serve at a dinner party, do peel them. Thick-skinned commercial tomatoes, developed for ease of storage and shipping, should be peeled; in fact, they should avoided entirely whenever you can get better quality local varieties.

Slice the tomato through its equator (that is, horizontally), not through its ends or poles (vertically). Make slices, not wedges. Cut the slices ¼ inch thick and parallel with the equator. Discard the stem and blossom ends and arrange the slices on a plate or platter. Then drizzle the slices with extra virgin olive oil and sprinkle them with kosher salt and fresh-ground pepper. Be sure to have plenty of good crusty bread on hand to soak up the juices that gather on the plate. If possible, vary the colors and types of tomatoes on each plate, for a more visually striking effect.

⅓ cup extra virgin olive oil
2 tablespoons red wine vinegar
Kosher salt
Black pepper in a mill

Put the spinach in a large salad bowl, and add the mushrooms, onion, and gorgonzola. In a small bowl, whisk together the garlic, thyme, olive oil, and vinegar, and season with salt and pepper. Pour the dressing over the spinach mixture, and toss gently. Add several more turns of pepper, and serve immediately.

SIMPLE TOMATO SALAD

In most parts of California, the tomato season—from the moment the first backyard tomato ripens until the first frost—runs from middle or late June through October, with more and more varieties coming into season as the months go by. This is the only time, to my mind, to eat fresh tomatoes, in salads or otherwise.

SERVES 4

6 large tomatoes, sliced
4 garlic cloves, minced
3 tablespoons minced Italian parsley
Best-quality extra virgin olive oil
Kosher salt
Black pepper in a mill

Arrange the sliced tomatoes on 1 large or 4 individual plates. Scatter the garlic and parsley over the tomatoes, drizzle with olive oil, and season with salt and pepper. Let the salad rest for at least 10 minutes (but not longer than 1 hour), so that the flavors can mingle.

Variations:

WITH CHEESE: Scatter ½ cup (2 ounces) of a grated hard cheese, such as dry jack, Parmigiano-Reggiano, romano, or aged asiago, over the tomatoes after the olive oil has been added, or use a vegetable peeler to make curls of 2 ounces of cheese, and scatter them over the tomatoes just before serving.

WITH FRESH MOZZARELLA AND BASIL: Slice 6 ounces of fresh mozzarella and place the slices here and there between the tomato slices. Cut 10 to 12 basil leaves lengthwise into very thin strips and scatter them over the top of the salad.

WITH TUNA AND LEMON: Slice 1 lemon very thin and place the slices between the tomato slices. Drain a 6- or 6½-ounce can of good-quality tuna and scatter the tuna over the tomatoes and lemons. If your market has Meyer lemons, use one here.

WITH ANCHOVIES, FETA, AND OLIVES: Soak 6 anchovy fillets in 2 tablespoons red wine vinegar for 20 minutes. Slice a small red onion into ⅛-inch-thick rounds, and place the slices on top of the tomatoes. Use 1 rather than 3 tablespoons minced parsley, and add 1 teaspoon minced oregano with it. Cut 2 ounces of feta cheese into small cubes and scatter the cubes over the tomatoes. Cut the anchovy fillets crosswise in half and drape them over the salad. Scatter ½ cup olives over the top before adding the olive oil, salt, and pepper.

HEIRLOOM TOMATO SALAD

*Y*ou hear a lot about tomato varieties these days. Heirloom tomatoes have become fashionable among backyard gardeners and small farmers, who sell them at farmers' markets throughout the country. If you are lucky enough to have access to an assortment of heirloom tomatoes, this salad will showcase them handsomely. I first made this recipe when a local farmer gave me an array of beautiful tomatoes: tiny yellow and red currant tomatoes not much bigger than pearls; ripe Green Grape tomatoes; Sungold cherry tomatoes as sweet as candy; green and white Zebra Stripe tomatoes; heartshaped, blood-red Brandywines with their thick flesh. I never make this salad the same way twice; I search my garden or the farmers' markets for the best tomatoes, and I add other vegetables—bell peppers of different colors, lemon cucumbers, chile hot peppers—that interest me. Use the best and most interesting tomatoes you can find.

SERVES 6 TO 8

The Electric Editor Has a Green Thumb

Mention the Santa Clara Valley and people think software, computers, and suburban sprawl. It's been known as Silicon Valley for as long as most of us can remember. Yet, as late as the 1960s, the principal products of the region included canned and dried fruits as well as high-tech electronics, an industry then in its infancy. Not so long ago, ranchers raised cattle and poultry there. In the 1920s and 1930s, the area was known as the Valley of Heart's Delight, because of its rich harvest of fruits, vegetables, flowers, and grains. Its apricots were some of the most highly prized in the country.

Farms no longer dominate the landscape, but the valley's agriculture has proven irrepressible, with lush gardens and small farms tucked here and there amid the clutter. Brian Gardiner of Los Gatos exemplifies the area's duality, its juxtaposition of high-tech esoterica and agricultural abundance. By day, Gardiner creates software for his company, Electric Editor. During the evening and on weekends, he farms three plots of land, one third of an acre at his Los Gatos home and two single-acre patches in Willow Glen, a suburb of San Jose.

"I love growing things," Gardiner, a native of Wales, says, "especially if they are edible." One night a few years back, Gardiner's wife complained to a friend about how hard it was getting to keep up with Brian's harvest. The friend called a friend who was a chef and who proved an eager first customer for Gardiner's tomatoes and peppers, then his specialties. A new business, From the Ground, was born. Now, Gardiner grows heirloom tomatoes such as Brandywine and Old Flame, which he picks and delivers, he says, at the exact moment of ripeness when the sugar and acid are in perfect balance, to half a dozen chefs. He also grows eight varieties of peppers, a Provençal salad mix, sweet corn, herbs, lavender, bronze fennel, leeks, kales, cabbages, and more, consulting with his chefs before he plants to find out what they will want.

6 to 8 large slicing tomatoes of various colors, cored and sliced

6 ounces semisoft cheese, such as fresh mozzarella, fresh pecorino, or fresh asiago, sliced thin

1 medium sweet onion, sliced very thin

10 basil leaves

4 peach tomatoes (pale yellow with slightly fuzzy skin), cut into 6 wedges each

4 zebra stripe tomatoes, cut into 6 wedges each

1 cup orange cherry tomatoes, quartered

1 cup red cherry tomatoes, quartered

6 garlic cloves, minced
Kosher salt
Black pepper in a mill
⅓ cup O Olive Oil (see Resources) or other olive oil crushed with lemons (see Note), or best-quality extra virgin olive oil
Sprigs of red and yellow currant tomatoes
1 loaf of country-style bread, hot

Place the sliced tomatoes on a large platter and tuck the cheese, onions, and basil leaves among the slices. Arrange the wedged tomatoes over them, then scatter the cherry tomatoes on top. Scatter the garlic over all, and season generously with salt and pepper. Drizzle olive oil over the entire salad. Garnish with the sprigs of currant tomatoes, and serve immediately, with the hot bread on the side.

NOTE: O Olive Oil, produced in northern California, is made by crushing together ripe organic Mission olives with Meyer lemons. An Italian brand, Agrumato, is produced similarly. If neither is available, use a best-quality extra virgin olive oil. Do not use a flavored olive oil.

BREAD AND CHERRY TOMATO SALAD

In climate, landscape, and agriculture, California is similar in many ways to the southern European countries on the Mediterranean. Not surprisingly, Spanish, Provençal, and Greek cuisines all have had enormous influence on the casual home cooking of California, but it is Italian cooking that has had the greatest impact. Without ever opening a cookbook, many home cooks create meals day after day that would make you swear you were sitting on a veranda overlooking the Ligurian Sea.

SERVES 4 TO 6

⅓ cup red wine vinegar
2 shallots, minced
4 garlic cloves, minced
¾ cup extra virgin olive oil
Juice of 1 lemon
3 tablespoons minced herbs, such as Italian parsley, oregano, marjoram, chives, or a combination
Kosher salt
Black pepper in a mill
4 cups day-old Italian bread, cut into 1-inch cubes
6 ounces fresh mozzarella, cut into small cubes
4 cups cherry tomatoes, preferably a mix of different colors, quartered

½ cup California black, oil–cured
black, or kalamata olives, pitted
and sliced

Put the vinegar, shallots, and garlic in
a medium bowl, and set the bowl aside for
20 minutes. Stir in the olive oil, lemon juice,
and herbs. Taste, and season with salt and
pepper.

In a large bowl, toss together the bread
and mozzarella. Pour two-thirds of the
dressing over, and toss again. Set the bowl
aside for 30 minutes. Add the tomatoes, the
olives, and the remaining dressing, and
toss thoroughly. Taste, season with salt and
pepper, and serve immediately.

Variation:

To make the salad with grilled shrimp:
Omit the mozzarella. Clean and devein 1
pound of medium shrimp, season them
with salt, pepper, and lemon juice, and
set them aside to marinate for 30 minutes.

Don't Chill Tomatoes

Never refrigerate a tomato; it will
become mealy and lose its flavor
at temperatures below 56°F. Use raw
tomatoes within 3 or 4 days of their harvest. Chopped tomatoes, covered with
vinegar and olive oil, can be stored in
the refrigerator for use within 1 day in
sauces, salsas, or vinaigrettes.

Grill them on an outdoor or stovetop grill
until they just turn pink, about 2 minutes
on each side. Set them aside to cool, then
add them to the salad with the tomatoes
and olives. Add ½ cup (2 ounces) grated
dry jack, toss, season with salt and pepper,
and serve.

BLUEBERRY COLESLAW

Berry vinegars are widely
available now. Most are fairly
high in acid, from 6 to 7 percent. Lower-acid vinegars, such as 4.5
percent varieties, allow the taste of the
berries to dominate, which is why I prefer
them for recipes like this one. Blueberry
coleslaw is an excellent accompaniment to
roast duck or to smoked duck sandwiches,
and it is an ideal picnic dish.

SERVES 6 TO 8

1 medium green cabbage, shredded
1 small red onion, minced
¼ cup chopped Italian parsley
2 tablespoons minced orange zest
1 cup Blueberry Mayonnaise (page
    418)
½ cup crème fraîche (or substitute;
    see Note, page 37) or sour cream
¼ cup blueberry vinegar, preferably
    low–acid
3 tablespoons fresh-squeezed orange
    juice

¼ cup sugar
1 teaspoon ground cloves
Kosher salt
Black pepper in a mill
1 pint fresh blueberries
Orange slices, for garnish

In a large bowl, toss together the cabbage, onion, parsley, and orange zest. In a small bowl, whisk together the mayonnaise, crème fraîche or sour cream, vinegar, orange juice, sugar, and cloves. Taste, and season with salt and pepper. Pour the dressing over the cabbage mixture, and toss until well coated. Reserve a few blueberries for garnish, and toss the rest with the coleslaw. Transfer the coleslaw to a serving platter, garnish with the reserved blueberries and the orange slices, and serve.

Variation:

For Raspberry Coleslaw, omit the orange zest, and use Raspberry Mayonnaise (page 418) instead of blueberry, raspberry vinegar instead of blueberry, and 2 tablespoons of lemon juice in place of the orange juice. Replace the cloves with 1 tablespoon ground cumin, and, of course, use whole raspberries instead of blueberries. Garnish the coleslaw with sprigs of Italian parsley.

ASIAN COLESLAW WITH GINGER VINAIGRETTE

Nearly everyone loves coleslaw, which we can make anytime in California because cabbage is practically a year-round crop. Sweet or sour, crunchy or well marinated in its own dressing, it comes in endless variations, including this one, with Asian flavors like ginger, chile, sesame, and lime.

SERVES 4 TO 6

1 small red or green cabbage, shredded
4 medium carrots, grated
1 small red onion, diced

GINGER VINAIGRETTE
2 tablespoons rice vinegar
3 tablespoons lime juice
1 to 2 garlic cloves, pressed
2 serrano chiles or 1 Thai chile, minced
1 tablespoon finely grated fresh ginger
2 tablespoons sugar
2 tablespoons Chinese hot mustard or Dijon mustard
⅓ cup toasted (dark) sesame oil
⅓ cup peanut oil
3 tablespoons minced cilantro leaves
Kosher salt
Black pepper in a mill

2 tablespoons sesame seeds, toasted

Toss together in a large bowl the cabbage, carrots, and onion.

Make the vinaigrette: Whisk together in a small bowl the vinegar, lime juice, garlic, chiles, ginger, sugar, and mustard. Slowly whisk in the 2 oils. Add the cilantro, taste, and season with salt and pepper.

Pour the vinaigrette over the vegetables, and toss until they are well coated. Scatter the sesame seeds over the slaw, and serve immediately or refrigerate until ready to serve.

Asian Cucumber Salad

Peel, cut in half, and slice thin 1 large or 2 medium cucumbers. In a small bowl, combine ¼ cup rice vinegar, the juice of 1 lime, ¼ cup sugar, 1 teaspoon kosher salt, and 1 teaspoon crushed red pepper flakes. Pour the dressing over the cucumbers, and add a few torn mint leaves and a few torn cilantro leaves. Chill for about 20 minutes before serving.

BROCCOLI, CAULIFLOWER, AND OLIVE SALAD WITH MUSTARD VINAIGRETTE

An ideal winter salad, this combination of flavors and textures is both bright and satisfying, in part because the broccoli and cauliflower are cooked, essential for the full development of their flavors. One of the more unfortunate developments in contemporary California cooking has been an overemphasis on raw foods, in turn an understandable overreaction to decades of mushy vegetables. Certain vegetables, however, should be cooked or at least blanched, among them these two, as well as mushrooms, green beans, and, of course, eggplant.

SERVES 4 TO 6

4 cups broccoli florets
4 cups cauliflower florets
6 ounces black olives, pitted and sliced

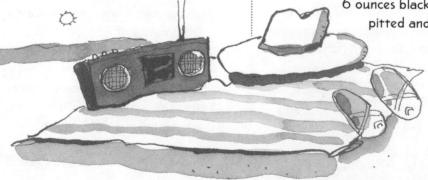

¾ cup Mustard Vinaigrette (page 152)
2 hard-boiled eggs, sieved or grated
Black pepper in a mill

In a large pot of rapidly boiling salted water, parboil the broccoli and cauliflower until they are just tender. Do not overcook. Drain, refresh in ice water, drain again thoroughly, and place in a medium bowl. Add the olives.

Pour the mustard vinaigrette over the vegetables, and toss lightly. Transfer the salad to a serving platter, top with the eggs, season with pepper, and serve immediately.

Variation:

Omit the mustard vinaigrette and sieved egg. Mix 6 ounces plain yogurt with 2½ tablespoons Dijon mustard, 1 teaspoon thyme leaves, 2 tablespoons minced black olives, and 2 teaspoons fresh-ground black pepper. Pour the dressing over the vegetables, and toss together until the vegetables are well coated. Transfer the salad to a serving platter or individual plates, and serve immediately.

FENNEL SALAD WITH DRY JACK

*W*ild fennel is just one of the features the California landscape shares with the Mediterranean region, where the feathery plant is a native. Its aroma permeates the air along country lanes and highways in many regions of the state, and its strong flavor is a welcome addition to dishes such as seafood stews. Cultivated fennel is similar in taste and aroma to wild fennel, but it possesses another quality, too, a plump white bulb that is as delicate in flavor as the leaves are robust. The bulb's texture is crisp and appealing; it makes a lovely salad on its own, dressed simply with olive oil and lemon juice.

SERVES 4

2 large or 3 medium fennel bulbs, trimmed
3 tablespoons extra virgin olive oil
Juice of ½ lemon
Kosher salt
Black pepper in a mill
1 2-ounce piece dry jack or Parmigiano-Reggiano
Sprigs of fennel leaves, for garnish, optional

Cut the fennel crosswise in very thin slivers and place it in a medium bowl. Drizzle the olive oil over the fennel, and toss quickly. Add the lemon juice, toss again, and season with salt and pepper. Divide the salad among individual serving plates. Use a vegetable peeler to cut curls from the cheese, and scatter several curls over each portion. Serve immediately, garnished with fennel leaves, if you like.

POTATO SALAD WITH CHÈVRE MAYONNAISE

*I*f you don't want to make Chèvre Mayonnaise, add 2 tablespoons Dijon mustard and 3 tablespoons minced black olives to ¾ cup of commercial mayonnaise, and continue as directed. The salad won't be quite as rich, and it will be closer to traditional potato salad. Both versions are delicious.

SERVES 6 TO 8

2 pounds russet potatoes, scrubbed
1 tablespoon Dijon mustard
1 shallot, minced
2 garlic cloves, minced
1 tablespoon minced Italian parsley
1 tablespoon Champagne vinegar or
   white wine vinegar
Juice of 1 lemon
⅔ cup extra virgin olive oil
Kosher salt
Black pepper in a mill
8 to 10 scallions, green and white
   parts, cut into thin rounds
3 celery ribs, diced
15 radishes, sliced
6 ounces pitted black olives, sliced
1 pint cherry tomatoes, halved (see
   Note)
3 hard-boiled eggs, sliced
1 cup Chèvre Mayonnaise (page
   420), at room temperature

The Drought Years

"**B**otanical spring. Volunteers everywhere. Popping out of the long-dry soil after the first good rain—wheat, sorghum, sweet alyssum, morning glory, narcissus, daffodil, onions, potatoes, chard, squash—none of them planted by me. Recruits, too—poppies, sweet peas, scabiosas, nasturtiums, clarkia, penstemon, bitter cress, carrots, beets, brussels sprouts, mustard greens, lettuce, roquette, snow peas, and acres of calendulas. Not bad for a gardener with three or four gallons of water a day, total. Not bad for a year of drought. Chancy, to hope too much. If the drought doesn't get me, the sparrows are waiting in line. If I fend off the birds, the gophers are standing by. And there's always the probability of frost up here at 2,600 feet. Slim chance. But what else is there to do but hope."

Judith Goodman, 7 December 1977, in *Recipes for Living in Big Sur* (Big Sur Historical Society, 1981)

Cook the potatoes in a large pot of rapidly boiling water until they are tender but not mushy, about 25 minutes.

While the potatoes cook, make a mustard vinaigrette: Combine the mustard, shallot, garlic, parsley, vinegar, and lemon juice in a small bowl, and whisk in the olive oil. Taste, and season with salt and pepper.

Drain the potatoes thoroughly, let them cool slightly, and slice them thin. Place them in a medium mixing bowl, pour the mustard vinaigrette over them, and toss thoroughly. Set the bowl aside for 30 minutes.

Add the scallions, celery, radishes, olives, and half of the tomatoes to the potatoes, and toss together. Add the eggs, and toss quickly and lightly. Fold in the Chèvre Mayonnaise, add several turns of black pepper, taste, and correct the seasoning with salt and pepper. Scatter the rest of the tomatoes over the top. Serve immediately, or store, covered, in the refrigerator for up to 3 days; bring to room temperature before serving.

NOTE: I prefer a mix of yellow, orange, and gold cherry tomatoes, and I omit them entirely when tomatoes are not in season.

UN–L.A. CHICKPEA SALAD

Food historian Evan Jones writes, in *American Food*, about two dishes, common in early California, that feature chickpeas. One, he says, evolved in Los Angeles from a Louisiana recipe similar to the bean-and-rice dish called Moors and Christians. The Los Angeles version was bland, with sausages, ground beef, cooked chicken, and tomato paste, but no chile peppers. More typical to the state was a salad version, tossed with green chiles, scallions, and green pepper, seasoned, as I have done here, with cumin, oil, and vinegar. The un-L.A. version was served at barbecues as an appetizer, or in lettuce cups as a salad.

SERVES 6 TO 8

4 cups cooked or canned chickpeas
1 small red onion, diced
3 to 4 garlic cloves, minced
3 poblano chiles, roasted, seeded, and diced
1 to 2 serrano chiles, minced
8 to 10 scallions, green and white parts, cut into thin rounds
⅓ cup red wine vinegar
⅔ cup extra virgin olive oil
Juice of 1 lemon
1 teaspoon ground cumin
1 teaspoon kosher salt
Black pepper in a mill
1 teaspoon cumin seeds, toasted

In a large bowl, toss together the chickpeas, onion, garlic, chiles, and scallions. In a small bowl, mix together the vinegar, olive oil, lemon juice, cumin, salt, and pepper. Pour the dressing over the vegetables, toss thoroughly, taste, and correct the seasoning. Scatter the cumin seeds over, and let the salad rest at room temperature for at least 15 minutes before serving.

PERSEPHONE'S SALAD

In California, there is a moment in August when the light changes. The light coming in my windows suddenly has a certain glow; I look outside and everything seems bathed in gold—in an instant, the California fall has arrived. There may be no more beautiful time in the state than when the lush hills and fertile valleys, heavy with the season's harvest, are awash in this intoxicating golden light. I know with certainty that the next time I go to the market, I will find the season's first pomegranates. I have never been wrong, and I developed this recipe many years ago to celebrate the first scarlet jewels of autumn.

SERVES 6

1 cup uncooked white rice, cooked
  and cooled to room temperature
1 cup Lemon Vinaigrette (page 153)
2 cups yellow, orange, and red currant
  tomatoes, halved, or 2 cups small
  cherry tomatoes, quartered
1 small red onion, diced
¾ cup pomegranate seeds
½ cup cranberries, minced in a food
  processor
Kosher salt
Black pepper in a mill
2 tablespoons minced Italian parsley
2 tablespoons snipped chives

Put the cooked rice into a medium bowl. Drizzle ½ cup of the vinaigrette over the rice, and toss the rice with a fork to mix in the dressing. Set the rice aside for 30 minutes. Add the tomatoes, onion, pomegranate seeds, and cranberries, and toss lightly. Pour the remaining ½ cup of vinaigrette over the rice, and toss again.

Sacred Seeds

When Gaspar de Portolá, a native of Catalonia and the first Spanish governor of the Californias, and Father Junípero Serra accepted the assignment of traveling north to Alta California, the journey was christened the Sacred Expedition. Portolá and Serra actually led the second party of the expedition, the first having left on March 24, 1769, with a herd of cattle, horses, and mules and twenty-seven soldiers to drive them. The second group left on May 15. A third convoy traveled by sea with three small ships, the *San Antonio*, the *San Carlos*, and the *San José*. Nearly half of the three hundred men in the expedition died en route. As the survivors built the missions that would extend from San Diego north to Sonoma, they introduced many plants—olives and oranges, for example—essential to California today. Among the seeds and seedlings to make the voyage was the pomegranate, the fruit of Persephone. Plantings were sparse into the early twentieth century; today, California produces nearly all of the domestic crop.

Taste, and season with salt and pepper. Add the parsley and chives, toss, and serve immediately.

Mexican Rice and Bean Salad

*R*ice and beans make a good foundation for a salad, and such a salad can be made at any time of year, using seasonal produce and dressed with just about any vinaigrette. For an Italian-style salad, for example, use Red Wine Vinaigrette (page 152), omit the cumin and chipotles, use Italian parsley and oregano in place of cilantro, and add ½ pound Italian sausage, fried and sliced thin. Be sure to serve all rice and bean salads at room temperature.

SERVES 6 TO 8

2 cups cooked or canned black beans
2 cups cooked long-grain white rice
Kernels from 2 ears of cooked fresh
    corn
1 cup Lime Vinaigrette (a Variation
    on Lemon Vinaigrette, page 152)
2 teaspoons ground cumin
½ teaspoon ground dried chipotles or
    cayenne
3 tablespoons minced cilantro leaves
1 red onion, diced
2 small zucchini, diced
1 red bell pepper, diced
1 gold or orange bell pepper, diced

1 poblano chile, cut into small dice
Kosher salt
Black pepper in a mill

Once they are cooked, let the beans, rice, and corn cool to room temperature. Put the beans, rice, and corn in a large bowl, and toss together lightly.

Make the dressing: In a small bowl, combine the vinaigrette, cumin, chipotles or cayenne, and half of the cilantro. Spoon half of the dressing over the rice mixture, and toss lightly. Put the onion, zucchini, bell peppers, and poblano in a medium bowl, pour the rest of the dressing over, and toss. Let both the rice mixture and the onion mixture rest for 30 minutes. Add the onion mixture to the rice mixture, toss together, and season with salt and pepper. Scatter the rest of the cilantro over the salad, and serve immediately. The salad can be refrigerated, covered, for up to 3 days; bring back to room temperature before serving.

Seed Pasta Salad with Golden Tomatoes

A pasta salad should not resemble a creamy potato salad, yet, alas, many of them do. Here, small seed pasta (*seme di melone*) plays an equal role with other ingredients. As with other salads that include pasta, this one is best served at room temperature. If you must store it in the refrigerator, be sure to remove it 30 minutes before serving.

SERVES 4 TO 6

4 ounces dried seme di melone pasta, or orzo or rosemarina pasta
2 cups small golden cherry tomatoes, halved, or 2 cups pear tomatoes, preferably golden, halved
2 tablespoons minced red onion
3 garlic cloves, minced
1 tablespoon snipped chives
½ cup sliced niçoise olives
¼ cup extra virgin olive oil, plus more as needed
Juice of 1 lemon
Kosher salt
Black pepper in a mill
4 cups mixed salad greens, such as mesclun
2 ounces (about ½ cup) grated tome, dry jack, Parmigiano-Reggiano, or aged asiago

Cook the pasta in a large pot of rapidly boiling salted water until it is just done. Drain, rinse in cool water, and drain again. Transfer the pasta to a medium bowl, and add the tomatoes, onion, garlic, chives, and olives. Toss with 2 tablespoons of the olive oil and half of the lemon juice, and season with salt and pepper. Set the bowl aside.

Place the greens in a mixing bowl, drizzle the remaining olive oil and lemon juice over, and, using your hands, toss lightly and quickly so that the greens are thoroughly coated. Season with salt and

pepper, toss again, and divide the greens among individual serving plates. Spoon some of the pasta mixture over each portion, sprinkle with some of the cheese, and serve immediately.

SUMMER PASTA SALAD

*S*esame oil and rice vinegar join together to create an evocative Asian flavor in this salad. Remember that all pasta salads should be served at room temperature, never chilled, and that they taste best shortly after they are made. You can make this salad with diced red slicing tomatoes, but a variety of smaller tomatoes will make it more interesting and colorful.

SERVES 6 TO 8

12 ounces small pasta, such as small shells, tripolini, or farfellini
3 cups small tomatoes, such as cherry, small pear, or currant, or 3 cups diced slicing tomatoes
Kernels from 3 ears of cooked corn
¼ cup toasted sesame oil
3 tablespoons peanut oil
¼ cup rice vinegar
Juice of 1 lime
½ teaspoon sugar
½ teaspoon grated fresh ginger
Kosher salt
Black pepper in a mill

Pinch of cayenne
1 tablespoon minced basil, preferably
   Thai
1 tablespoon minced cilantro
1 tablespoon sesame seeds, toasted

Cook the pasta in a large pot of boiling salted water until it is just done. Drain, rinse in cool water, drain again, and transfer to a large bowl. If you have cherry tomatoes or small pear tomatoes, cut them in half; if you have currant tomatoes, leave them whole. Add the tomatoes and the corn to the pasta.

In a small bowl, make a vinaigrette: Whisk together the oils, vinegar, lime juice, sugar, and ginger. Taste, and season with salt, pepper, and cayenne.

Pour the vinaigrette over the pasta, toss, add the basil and cilantro, and toss again. Scatter the sesame seeds over the salad, and serve within 1 hour. This salad can be refrigerated; remove it from the refrigerator 30 minutes before serving so that it can come back to room temperature.

Variation:

Sauté 1 pound of medium shrimp in sesame oil, toss with salt, pepper, and cayenne, and arrange over the top of the salad just before serving.

NICOLLE'S PASTA SALAD

*U*ntil my daughter Nicolle used Honey Pepper Vinaigrette (page 157) to make a pasta salad very much like this one, I had used the dressing only with grilled prawns and grilled leg of lamb. Her salad was so good that we now make it whenever there are cherry tomatoes ripe on the vine. For a homey presentation—one that was popular in California in the 1950s—serve the salad in hollowed-out tomatoes set on a bed of salad greens. The Yellow Ruffle tomato, an heirloom variety with minimal flavor, is ideal for stuffing because it is nearly hollow right off the vine.

SERVES 6 TO 8

8 ounces cooked bay shrimp
¾ cup Honey Pepper Vinaigrette
   (page 157)
12 ounces small pasta, such as small
   shells, farfellini, tripolini, or
   pennette
4 cups cherry tomatoes, quartered
1 small red onion, diced
2 tablespoons snipped chives
2 tablespoons minced Italian parsley
2 tablespoons julienned mint leaves
Kosher salt
Sprigs of fresh herbs, such as mint,
   oregano, or Italian parsley, for
   garnish

Place the shrimp in a large bowl and toss them with 2 tablespoons of the vinaigrette. Set the bowl aside.

Cook the pasta in a large pot of boiling salted water until it is just done. Drain, rinse in cool water, and drain again. Add to the shrimp the pasta, tomatoes, and onion, and toss lightly. Add the remaining dressing, and toss again. Add the chives, parsley, and mint, and toss lightly. Taste, and season with salt. Garnish with the herb sprigs, and serve immediately.

ANTONIO'S ORANGE SALAD

This classic Sicilian recipe came to me indirectly from a man who, at the age of ninety-one, was still eating this salad nearly every day. He came to New England from Sicily as a young man, bringing many of his family's traditional recipes with him. His son, in turn, brought along the recipes when he moved to California in the early 1970s. I spent many hours in the son's kitchen as he recreated his parents' rustic fare. This salad is wonderful in the early winter, when newly pressed California olive oil is first available and blood oranges are just ripening.

SERVES 4 TO 6

6 medium oranges, preferably blood oranges
3 to 4 tablespoons extra virgin olive oil
Sea salt or kosher salt
Black pepper in a mill
½ cup sliced pitted green or oil-cured black olives

Peel the oranges, removing all of the pith, cut them into ¼-inch slices, and arrange them in concentric circles on a serving plate or in small circles on individual serving plates. Drizzle olive oil over the oranges, season with a light sprinkling of salt and a generous amount of pepper, and scatter the olives over the oranges. Let the salad rest for 20 minutes or so before serving.

Variation:

Slice thin 5 oranges, peeled, 1 or 2 lemons, peeled, and 1 small red onion. Arrange the oranges, lemons, and onions in circles on individual plates, tucking a slice of lemon or a slice of onion between orange slices. Add the olive oil, salt, pepper, and olives. Using a vegetable peeler, cut 4 or 5 curls of Parmigiano-Reggiano or dry jack cheese to scatter over each plate. Let the salad rest before serving.

My First Orange

Oranges were first introduced into California in 1770; by 1792 they flourished at Mission Buena Ventura near Los Angeles. William Wolfskill, a Kentucky trapper, planted the first commercial grove in 1841, and his success was an inspiration to other farmers. The Orange Growers' Protective Union was formed in 1885. Orange County, home of Disneyland, is named for the vast orchards that once thrived in the area.

Yet, though I had lived in California since birth, I have no memory of eating an orange, or even seeing one, until I was five years old and in kindergarten in a small town on the Napa River. About half-way through the year, our teacher prepared us for a new student who had just arrived from China. Explaining the many cultural differences we would discover in our new classmate, she encouraged us to be friendly and accepting. May Lim arrived the next day, and I recall the rush of envy I felt as I saw her for the first time. School authorities had relaxed the strict dress code and allowed her to wear long pants—under her dress, of course—while the rest of the little girls shivered that winter day in short dresses and ankle socks. May looked so warm and cozy, and as soon as I subdued my jealousy, we became fast friends. When she came to my house to play for the first time, her parents sent lovely gifts of food, including the most beautiful orange—a bright, shimmering talisman—I have ever seen.

AVOCADO– GRAPEFRUIT SALAD WITH POMEGRANATE SEEDS

Citrus fruit is harvested year round in California, the varieties and regions changing with the seasons. Our lemon crop is the largest in the nation, but California is second to Florida in the production of oranges and grapefruit. Two varieties of grapefruit—Marsh, a white-fleshed fruit, and Redblush, with deep-pink flesh—dominate commercial production, which is centered in the low desert valleys in the winter and in the higher valleys of southern California in the summer. The desert orchards produce superior fruit. Use either red or white grapefruit in this salad.

SERVES 4

2 grapefruits
2 ripe avocados, pitted and sliced
   lengthwise
2 tablespoons avocado oil or olive oil
2 teaspoons grapefruit juice
Kosher salt

Black pepper in a mill
Seeds from 1 pomegranate

Peel the grapefruit, cutting through all of the rind so that the sections of fruit are exposed. Cut each section of grapefruit away from the surrounding membrane. Arrange the grapefruit sections on 4 individual serving plates. Arrange the avocado slices on the plates with the grapefruit. Drizzle oil, then grapefruit juice, over each salad. Sprinkle the avocado with salt, grind pepper over each portion, and scatter pomegranate seeds over the top. Serve immediately.

SUMMER MELON SALAD

The Crane family has been growing their famous melon for over a hundred years, since shortly after the first Crane arrived as a pioneer in 1852. The large melon, with its soft orange flesh, resembles a cantaloupe. Some of the melons are sold from the Crane Melon Barn in Santa Rosa—people come from all over to buy them—and others are shipped around the world.

SERVES 4 TO 6

3 small to medium melons, such as Crane, cantaloupe, crenshaw, honeydew, or casaba
1 cup Pineapple Vinaigrette (page 156)
Kosher salt
Black pepper in a mill
4 to 6 cups arugula leaves
¼ pound prosciutto, sliced very thin and cut crosswise into 2-inch-wide strips
½ cup hazelnuts, toasted and skins rubbed off
Sprigs of mint

Cut the melons in half and scoop out and discard the seeds. Cut one half of each melon into wedges about ⅜ inch thick. Place the wedges on a large platter. Using a melon baller, scoop balls out of the remaining halves, and add the balls to the platter. Drizzle half of the vinaigrette over the wedges and balls, season with salt and pepper, and refrigerate for 1 hour.

Divide the arugula among individual serving plates. Arrange the chilled melon wedges in a circle or semicircle on top of the arugula, and place a prosciutto strip on top of each wedge. Spoon chilled melon balls over each portion, and drizzle the salads with the remaining vinaigrette. Scatter hazelnuts over each salad, garnish with mint, and serve immediately.

SCALLOP CEVICHE

Although bay scallops are har-vested along the Atlantic seaboard and not in Califor-nia, they are popular here when we can get them. Calico scallops, smaller and less flavorful than bay scallops, are easier to get and may be used in this recipe. It is common to find scallops sautéed in butter and garlic, and they are often an ingredient in seafood pastas and stews. My favorite way to prepare them is this ceviche, a traditional dish in Latin America that is very popular in California, too. If you have avoided ceviche because you've found it overly fishy-tasting, or have not cared for its texture, try again with this version, a refreshing salad for a hot summer day.

SERVES 4

1 pound bay scallops
1 teaspoon kosher salt
¾ cup fresh lime juice (from about 8 limes)
1 small red onion, diced
1¼ cups Spicy Lime Dressing (recipe follows)
2 ripe Hass avocados
8 to 10 radishes, trimmed and cut into julienne
2 tablespoons minced cilantro leaves

Place the scallops in a nonreactive dish, sprinkle with the salt, and pour the lime juice over. Toss until all the scallops are bathed in the juice. Cover, and refrigerate for at least 6 hours, stirring 2 or 3 times.

Drain the scallops, discarding the liquid. Place them in a clean bowl, add the onion, and toss well. Add 3 tablespoons of the dressing, and toss again.

Cut the avocados in half, peel each half, and place one half on each of 4 serving plates. Divide the ceviche among the servings, spooning it into the cavity of the avocado and allowing it to tumble over onto the plate. Spoon the remaining dressing over the salads, scatter each portion with radishes and cilantro, and serve immediately.

Variation:

Omit the Spicy Lime Dressing and use Avocado Sauce (page 63) in its place. Garnish each portion with ½ cup cherry tomatoes, cut in half.

Spicy Lime Dressing

MAKES ABOUT 1¼ CUPS

⅓ cup fresh lime juice (from about 4 limes)
1 shallot, minced
6 garlic cloves, minced
¾ cup extra virgin olive oil
1 teaspoon cayenne, or less if you like less heat
1 teaspoon kosher salt
Black pepper in a mill

In a small bowl, combine the lime juice with the shallot and garlic. Whisk in the olive oil, cayenne, and salt. Add several turns of black pepper, taste, and adjust the seasonings.

ARTICHOKE AND CRAB SALAD, FOR ANNA

My friend Anna Cherney lived a remarkable life. She was born in Odessa, Russia, in 1902, and came with her family to the U.S. when she was two years old. The child of a poor family, she left school early and worked as a secretary in her hometown of New York. At eighteen, with the love of her life, Charlie Cherney, she left and traveled the country in a Ford flatbed truck on which Charlie had built a tiny, fully equipped house, complete with redwood shingles. Everywhere they went, newspapers published photographs of "The Little House on Wheels." They financed much of their trip by offering tours of the house and selling postcard pictures of it for a nickel. On the first leg of their two-year journey, they arrived in Philadelphia, flat broke. It wasn't long before they'd made a few hundred dollars by driving around town with a huge banner advertising the latest film from Columbia Pictures. In Minnesota, Anna danced with an Indian chief in full regalia, and, when they arrived in Reno, Nevada, they were married. After they reached California, they continued their travels by ship, travel-ing to Anna's homeland. Eventually, they settled in San Francisco, then moved north to Sonoma County, where for years they operated an egg farm high atop a beautiful ridge in Sebastopol.

When I met Anna, she was in her eighties. She had been an activist all her life; the first time I went to her house was to prepare dinner for a benefit for Sonoma County's Peace and Justice Center. Over the years, I cooked for Anna and her guests many times. In her final years, sometimes it was just us and a friend or two. She loved salmon topped with my mango salsa, and she also loved my crab cakes. One day she called me and I could tell from her voice she was feeling a little blue, a little lonely. I knew she loved both crab and artichokes, so I gathered up all of the ingredients for a new recipe I was developing, and headed over. It was a lovely evening.

Anna died in April of 1996. Throughout her life, she was a generous supporter of causes and of people she believed in, including me. It was through Anna's belief in me, and her support, that I was able to make the transition from full-time chef and part-time writer to full-time writer. I am forever indebted to her.

SERVES 4

4 large artichokes, boiled (see page 381)

Meat from 1 large cooked Dungeness crab (or see Note)

¾ cup Louis Dressing (page 142)

1 lemon, cut into wedges

Carefully remove the inner leaves (reserving the edible ones) of each artichoke to form a small basket, with the heart as the bottom and the outer layers of leaves as the sides. Cut out and discard the thistle-like choke, and set each artichoke basket on a salad plate.

In a small bowl, toss the crabmeat with half of the dressing. Divide the dressed crabmeat among the artichokes, placing it in the center of each basket. Add a generous spoonful of the remaining dressing to each serving, on top of the crabmeat, and set the crab legs on top of the dressing. Arrange the reserved artichoke leaves and the lemon wedges around each portion, and serve immediately, with the remaining dressing alongside.

NOTE: You can make this salad with 2 pounds cooked crabmeat, canned or fresh from your fishmonger. Simply omit the step in which you put the legs on top of the salad.

CRAB LOUIS

For a while, simply put, people of taste or conscience did not eat iceberg lettuce. With the rise of California cuisine in the 1970s, combined with ongoing Farm Workers Union strikes that called for its boycott, iceberg became a symbol, for some, of all manner of evil: corporate agribusiness; chemical pesticides and fertilizers; the bland foods of the 1950s; conservative politics; probably even Viet-

nam and Kent State. Iceberg's modest return to favor represents not so much a swing of the social pendulum as an appreciation of the quality it and nothing else possesses: a bright crispness that can be as cooling and refreshing as a plunge into a Los Angeles swimming pool. In a crab or shrimp Louis, it is essential; more flavorful greens with diverse textures would interfere with the pristine flavor of the seafood. The salad itself dates back to turn-of-the-century San Francisco, where several variations were served.

SERVES 4

1 head of iceberg lettuce, outer leaves discarded
Meat from 1 large cooked Dungeness crab (or see Note)
2 medium ripe tomatoes, cut into wedges
4 hard-boiled eggs, cut into wedges
2 cups Louis Dressing (recipe follows)
Cayenne
4 sprigs of Italian parsley
1 lemon, cut into wedges

Cut the lettuce head into quarters, cut the quarters into medium chunks, and divide the chunks among 4 individual salad plates. Divide the crabmeat, excluding the legs, placing it on top of the lettuce in the center of each plate. Arrange tomato wedges and egg wedges around the edge of each plate. Spoon some of the dressing over the crabmeat. Divide the crab legs among the portions, setting them in

the center of the plate on top of the dressing. Garnish each salad with a pinch of
cayenne, a sprig of Italian parsley, and 1 or
2 lemon wedges. Serve immediately, with
the remaining dressing alongside.

NOTE: You can make this salad with 2
pounds cooked crabmeat, canned or fresh
from your fishmonger. Simply omit the
step in which you divide the legs among
the portions.

Variation:

To make a Shrimp Louis, substitute 2
cups cooked bay shrimp for the crab. Or
make a Combination Louis, with 1 cup
each of bay shrimp and crab.

Louis Dressing

MAKES ABOUT 2 CUPS

⅓ cup heavy cream
⅓ cup chili sauce
1 cup mayonnaise, preferably
   homemade (page 416)
6 scallions, white and green parts, cut
   into thin rounds
2 tablespoons minced Italian parsley
Juice of 1 lemon
Kosher salt
Black pepper in a mill
Pinch of cayenne

Whip the cream until soft peaks form.
Using a rubber spatula, fold together the
cream, chili sauce, and mayonnaise in a
small bowl. Mix in the scallions, parsley,

and lemon juice, and season with salt,
pepper, and cayenne. Cover, and refrigerate until ready to use.

OCEANSIDE SEAFOOD SALAD

Oceanside once was a small town an
hour or so north of San Diego; it
was a fishing center and home to
huge avocado groves. It is the place where
I spent the first year of my life. Oceanside
is no longer the isolated place it once was;
now it's part of the long succession of
housing developments and strip malls that
stretches from the Mexican border south of
San Diego nearly all the way north to Santa
Barbara. This recipe, which I discovered in
Neill and Fred Beck's *Farmers Market Cook
Book* (Holt, 1951), and have revised for
today's palate, pays tribute to those earlier
times.

SERVES 4

1 head of butter lettuce, leaves
   separated
2 ripe Hass avocados
Juice of ½ lemon
Kosher salt
Black pepper in a mill
¾ cup mayonnaise, preferably
   homemade (page 416)
2 tablespoons Dijon mustard
6 ounces (about 1 cup) cooked
   crabmeat

6 ounces (about 1 cup) cooked small
   bay shrimp
2 tablespoons capers, rinsed
2 cups cherry tomatoes, cut in half
4 large sections of cooked crab leg,
   shelled, or an additional 6 ounces
   cooked crabmeat
12 medium to large shrimp, cooked
   and shelled, with tails
¼ cup Homemade Tartar Sauce
   (recipe follows)
Paprika
1 lemon, cut into wedges

Arrange the lettuce leaves on 4 individual plates. Cut the avocados in half, remove the pits, and peel them. Brush the avocado halves inside and out with lemon juice, season them with salt and pepper, and place them, cavity side up, on top of the lettuce.

In a small bowl, mix together the mayonnaise and mustard. In a medium bowl, quickly toss together the crabmeat, bay shrimp, and 1 tablespoon of the capers with the mayonnaise mixture. Divide the dressed seafood among the servings, placing it in the cavity of each avocado. Scatter the tomatoes over the salads. Set a crab leg and 3 of the medium to large shrimps on top of each mound of seafood, and top with a generous spoonful of tartar sauce. Dust each portion with paprika, scatter with some of the remaining capers, garnish with a lemon wedge, and serve immediately.

Homemade Tartar Sauce

In a small bowl, combine ½ cup mayonnaise, 2 teaspoons Dijon mustard, 2 teaspoons fresh lemon juice, 2 teaspoons minced gherkins, 2 scallions, sliced thin, and 1 garlic clove, minced. You will have about ¾ cup sauce.

TROUT–FENNEL SALAD

*U*pscale markets and delis often have smoked trout for sale. If you find some, use it in this recipe. If you cannot find any, prepare fresh trout by whatever method you prefer, and chill it before you make the salad.

SERVES 4

½ cup mayonnaise
2 tablespoons minced herbs, such as
   Italian parsley, oregano, marjoram,
   thyme, chives, or a combination
2 medium fennel bulbs, trimmed
3 tablespoons extra virgin olive oil
Juice of ½ lemon
Kosher salt
Black pepper in a mill
2 poached or smoked trout, boned,
   skinned, and broken into chunks,
   chilled
Sprigs of thyme or Italian parsley, for
   garnish

Mix together the mayonnaise and the minced herbs in a small bowl, and set the bowl aside.

Cut the fennel bulbs crosswise into slices, cut the slices into slivers, and place the slivers in a medium bowl. Drizzle the olive oil over the fennel, toss quickly, add the lemon juice, and toss again. Season with salt and pepper. Add the trout, and toss the salad very gently. Divide the salad among individual serving plates, and top each portion with a spoonful of the herbed mayonnaise. Garnish with the herb sprigs, and serve immediately.

GLASS NOODLE SALAD

Glass noodles are made of dried mung bean threads and packaged in tight bundles. In the market, they can be confused with rice noodles, so read the package carefully. When cooked, glass noodles plump up, soften, and become slightly gelatinous. They hold up well in soups, and are commonly served with meats and vegetables, too. In this salad, they are combined in a spicy dressing with squid and ground chicken or pork. Squid leads all other seafood in dollar sales in California, although most of it goes to restaurants and not to home cooks, who until recently have been reluctant to cook it. Most squid today is sold cleaned; it should have a mild, fresh aroma when you buy, and it should not have a fishy smell. The secret to cooking squid successfully is to buy it very fresh and to cook it very quickly.

SERVES 4 TO 6

4 ounces glass (mung bean thread) noodles
4 tablespoons minced garlic
6 serrano chiles, minced
¼ cup fish sauce
6 tablespoons fresh lime juice (from about 4 limes)
1 tablespoon sugar
½ pound squid, cleaned, bodies separated from tentacles
2 tablespoons peanut oil
½ pound ground chicken or ground pork
3 cups fresh salad greens, such as mesclun
2 tablespoons torn cilantro leaves
1 tablespoon torn mint leaves
3 scallions, white and green parts, sliced
4 tablespoons fried shallots (see the Variation, page 395)

Put the noodles in a large bowl, cover them with water, and let them soak for 30 minutes. Drain the noodles, and cook them in boiling water until they are plump and translucent, 5 to 6 minutes. Drain, rinse thoroughly in cool water, and drain again. Place the noodles in a bowl, and place the bowl in the refrigerator.

Make the dressing: In a small bowl, combine 2 tablespoons of the garlic and half of the serranos with the fish sauce, lime juice, and sugar. Set the bowl aside.

Slice the bodies of the squid into narrow rings; leave the tentacles whole. Heat the oil in a wok or frying pan over medium heat, add 1 tablespoon of the garlic and half the remaining serranos, and cook, stirring constantly, for 2 minutes. Do not let the garlic brown. Increase the heat to high, add the squid rings and tentacles, and cook, stirring constantly, until the squid turns firm and white, 2 to 3 minutes. Transfer the squid to a bowl, return the wok to the heat, lower the heat to medium, and add the remaining garlic and serranos. Add the chicken, and cook, stirring constantly and breaking up the chicken or pork with a fork, until it loses its pink color, about 6 minutes. Remove from the heat.

Spread the greens on a platter. In a large bowl, toss together the chilled noodles, the chicken or pork, all of the squid except for 2 or 3 sets of tentacles, the cilantro, the mint, the scallions, and half of the dressing. Place this mixture on top of the greens. Pour the remaining dressing over, scatter with fried shallots, garnish with the reserved tentacles, and serve immediately.

GREEN OLIVE CHICKEN SALAD

The color of an olive does not indicate its variety; instead, it reveals when it was harvested. All olives start out green, turn purple for a time, and, if left on the tree long enough, end up black. Among the hundreds of varieties of olives, you will find many shades of these three colors. A "cracked" olive is just what it says; its flesh has been cracked, usually to allow flavors to penetrate. In California, cracked green olives marinated in herbs are sold in bulk in many markets. If you cannot find cracked green olives, simply use your favorite olive in this recipe. Similarly, if you prefer chicken breasts to thighs, feel free to substitute them; I simply find the darker meat of thighs more flavorful than breast meat.

SERVES 4 TO 6

3 to 4 chicken thigh–leg pieces
Kosher salt
Black pepper in a mill
Olive oil
8 ounces cracked green olives, pitted
1 tablespoon minced Italian parsley
1 teaspoon minced oregano
2 tablespoons extra virgin olive oil
1 fennel bulb, trimmed and sliced thin

Preheat the oven to 375°F. Season the chicken pieces with salt and pepper, place them in a shallow baking pan, and drizzle them with olive oil. Bake for 20 to 25 minutes, until the juices run clear when a joint is pricked with a fork. Transfer the chicken pieces to a rack, and let them cool until they are cool enough to handle.

Remove and discard the skin from the chicken, and pull the meat from the bone. Tear the meat (do not cut it) into medium pieces, and place the pieces in a medium bowl. Add the olives, parsley, and oregano, and toss together with a fork. Drizzle the extra virgin olive oil over the chicken, season with salt and pepper, and toss again.

To serve, spread the fennel slices over a serving platter or individual plates, top with the chicken salad, and serve immediately.

CURRIED CHICKEN SALAD

An Indian-style curry should be served with yogurt, chutney, and nuts, such as roasted peanuts, almonds, or, as we often do in California, pistachios. The complex flavors of curry do not reach their full bloom without the counterpoints provided by an array of tastes and textures. In this salad, chutney and yogurt are garnishes, and nuts are both in the salad and a garnish.

SERVES 4

2 firm ripe pears
Juice of ½ lemon
1 pound cooked chicken meat, diced
½ small yellow onion, minced
1 serrano chile, minced
½ cup golden raisins, soaked for 30 minutes in warm water and drained
½ cup shelled pistachios, toasted
¾ cup Curry Mayonnaise (page 420)
Kosher salt
Black pepper in a mill
½ cup plain yogurt
¼ cup Gren Tomato–Pear Chutney (page 426) or bottled chutney

Peel the pears, core them, and cut them lengthwise into ¼-inch-thick slices. Place the slices in a small bowl, cover them with cold water, and add the lemon juice to keep them from browning. Set the bowl aside.

In a medium bowl, combine the chicken, onion, chile, raisins, and half of the pistachios. Fold in the mayonnaise, taste, and season with salt and pepper.

Place the pear slices on 4 individual serving plates, arranging them like the spokes of a wheel or the 5 points of a star. Divide the chicken mixture among the plates, placing it in the center of each one. Top each salad with 2 tablespoons of yogurt and 1 tablespoon of chutney, garnish with the remaining pistachio nuts, and serve immediately.

AVOCADO AND PEAR SALAD WITH SMOKED CHICKEN

There is scarcely a time in California when pears are not in season. Eight varieties dominate the commercial market, their seasons spread out in such a way that you can find a juicy pear almost any time. Red Bartletts are particularly beautiful, and the comice is one of the sweetest of all pears. Nelis pears, in season from October through April, have a wonderfully creamy texture. There is no need to search for a particular variety of pear for this salad; simply choose what is at its peak.

Like most composed salads, this one can be varied. The fragrant dressing is essential, as is the interplay of sweet and savory tastes and smooth and crunchy textures. But if you don't have smoked chicken, use roasted chicken, or omit the chicken entirely. If you have no arugula, use any type of salad green.

SERVES 4

1 firm ripe pear
Juice of ¼ lemon
1 shallot, minced
1 teaspoon snipped chives
2 tablespoons pear vinegar,
    preferably, or Champagne vinegar
3 tablespoons hazelnut oil
3 tablespoons peanut oil
Kosher salt

Black pepper in a mill
2 cups arugula leaves
1 ripe Hass avocado, pitted and cut
    lengthwise into ⅛-inch slices
4 ounces (about 1 cup) smoked
    chicken meat, cut into medium
    julienne
¼ cup hazelnuts, toasted lightly and
    skinned

Peel the pear, core it, and cut it lengthwise into ⅛-inch-thick slices. Place the slices in a small bowl, cover them with cold water, and add the lemon juice to keep them from browning. Set the bowl aside.

In a small bowl, whisk together the shallot, chives, vinegar, and hazelnut and peanut oils. Taste, and season with salt and pepper. In a separate bowl, toss the arugula with half of the dressing. Place the dressed arugula in the center of each of 4 salad plates. Arrange the pear and avocado slices around the arugula, and divide the chicken among the portions, on top of the arugula. Spoon the remaining dressing over the salads, scatter a few hazelnuts over each one, and serve immediately.

WILD RICE, CRANBERRY, AND SMOKED DUCK SALAD

There is no native wild rice in California. A small amount is grown commercially, in the Upper Lakes area of Lake County and in the major rice-growing counties, Butte and Colusa, from seeds recently imported. Still, we cook a lot with wild rice, using it in soups, salads, and stuffings for poultry. Cranberries do not grow in California, either, but they have long been popular. They are grown on the other side of the Oregon border, around the coastal town of Bandon, where there is a huge celebration each year during their harvest in September. In the nineteenth century, homesteaders on Oregon's Clatsop Plain gathered wild cranberries and shipped them to settlers in California.

This salad makes a lovely fall dish, perfect on a holiday table. In other seasons, omit the cranberries and orange.

SERVES 4 TO 6

1 cup uncooked wild rice
1 cup duck stock or chicken stock
2 teaspoons salt
½ cup extra virgin olive oil
3 tablespoons sherry vinegar or cranberry vinegar
1 tablespoon fresh orange juice
1 teaspoon minced garlic
Kosher salt
Black pepper in a mill
½ cup minced fresh cranberries
½ cup chopped walnuts, toasted
2 teaspoons grated orange zest
2 tablespoons minced Italian parsley
1 tablespoon minced chives
6 ounces smoked duck meat, coarsely chopped
1 orange, peeled and sliced, for garnish

In a large heavy pot over medium heat, combine the wild rice with the stock, 2 teaspoons of salt, and 2 cups of water. Bring to a boil, reduce the heat, and simmer, covered, until all of the liquid has been absorbed and the rice is tender but not mushy, 40 to 50 minutes. Transfer the rice to a large serving bowl, fluff it with a fork, and set it aside to cool.

While the rice cooks, make the dressing: Whisk together the olive oil, vinegar, orange juice, and garlic. Taste, and season with salt and pepper.

When the rice is cool, add to it the cranberries, walnuts, orange zest, half of the parsley, and half of the chives. Pour half of the dressing over, and toss with a fork. Add the duck meat, toss again, taste, and season with more salt and pepper, if necessary. Drizzle the remaining dressing over the salad, scatter the remaining parsley and chives over the top, garnish with orange slices, and serve immediately.

THAI LIME BEEF SALAD

Versions of this salad appear on menus in many Thai restaurants in California, and it is one of the simplest Thai recipes to make at home. The lime chile sauce, a hallmark of Thai cooking, offers the classic and irresistible quartet of sweet, hot, sour, and salty. You can use the sauce as a dressing for other salads and as a dipping sauce for spring rolls.

SERVES 4

1 or 2 good-quality steaks, trimmed of bone and fat, for a total of 10 to 12 ounces meat
Kosher salt
Black pepper in a mill
4 cups salad greens, such as mesclun or another mix of bitter and mild young greens
¼ cup cilantro leaves
2 tablespoons mint leaves
¼ cup Thai Lime Chile Sauce (recipe follows)
4 sprigs of mint
1 lime, quartered

Prepare an outdoor or stovetop grill, or preheat the broiler. Season the steak with salt and pepper, place it on the grill or under the broiler, and cook for about 5 minutes, turn, and cook for 3 to 4 minutes more, or until the meat is cooked rare. Remove the steak from the heat and let it rest briefly.

In a large bowl, toss together the greens, cilantro, and mint leaves. Divide the mixture among 4 individual plates. Cut the meat across the grain into thin slices, and arrange the slices on top of the greens. Spoon one-fourth of the sauce over each portion, garnish with a mint sprig and a lime wedge, and serve immediately.

Thai Lime Chile Sauce

MAKES ABOUT ¼ CUP

5 garlic cloves, minced
5 serrano chiles, minced
1 tablespoon fish sauce
2 tablespoons fresh lime juice (from 1 to 2 limes)
2 teaspoons sugar

In a small bowl, combine all of the ingredients.

POTATO SALAD WITH GRILLED STEAK

Potato salad is an essential element of summer barbecues in California, just as it is elsewhere. In this California recipe, the grill plays an important role. This salad is an excellent way to enjoy red meat in a small quantity, without giving it up entirely.

SERVES 4 TO 6

2 pounds red new potatoes, scrubbed
1 medium or 2 small fennel bulbs,
    trimmed and sliced very thin
16 to 20 radishes, trimmed and sliced
    thin
1 small red onion, sliced thin
6 to 8 ounces green beans, blanched
¾ cup Warm Bacon–Shallot
    Vinaigrette (page 158)
1 or 2 thick good-quality steaks,
    trimmed of bone and fat, for a
    total of about 1 pound meat
Kosher salt
Black pepper in a mill
1 tablespoon minced Italian parsley

Cook the potatoes in a large pot of rapidly boiling water until they are tender but not mushy, 15 to 25 minutes, depending on their size.

Prepare an outdoor or stovetop grill. Drain the potatoes, let them cool slightly, slice them thin, and place them in a large bowl. Add the fennel, radishes, onion, and half of the green beans. Spoon on half of the vinaigrette, and toss lightly but thoroughly. Transfer the vegetables to a large serving platter.

Season the steaks with salt and pepper, and grill them until they are rare or medium-rare, about 4 to 7 minutes per side, depending on their thickness and on the doneness you want. Transfer the steaks to a work surface, let them rest 5 minutes, and cut them across the grain into ⅛-inch slices. Arrange the steak slices over the top of the vegetables. Reheat the remaining vinaigrette, if necessary, and spoon it over

the salad. Scatter the remaining green beans and the parsley over the top. Serve immediately.

MARSHALL HOUSE POTATO SALAD

"I always added the bacon drippings to the potatoes," says Axel Roelz, chef and owner of Santa Rosa's Marshall House restaurant, which, alas, closed on New Year's Eve, 1995. "But I didn't tell my customers because they would get upset." During the restaurant's ten years of operation, Roelz received scores of requests for the recipe. I wanted it, too, but I waited too long—the restaurant closed before I asked. So I tracked down Axel at his Santa Rosa home. He was happy to offer his recipe, yet as he described it, something seemed amiss. "What about the bacon drippings?" I asked, several times. He hedged, I pressed, and finally he made his delicious confession. Roelz's customers boasted that when they would make the salad at home, they would drain off every last droplet of fat before adding the bacon to the potatoes. Yet those flavorful drippings, he insists, are the key ingredient, the element that kept customers coming back for more. And therein lies the secret of a great potato salad: At its best, it's an indulgence, a luxury, a guilty yet irresistible pleasure.

3 pounds potatoes, such as Yukon
    Gold, Yellow Finn, or russet,
    scrubbed
Kosher salt
1 teaspoon caraway seeds
8 ounces bacon
⅓ cup olive oil
¾ cup beef stock
1 medium yellow onion, minced
½ teaspoon white pepper
3 tablespoons minced Italian parsley
½ teaspoon sugar
⅓ to ½ cup distilled vinegar
2 tablespoons coarse-grain mustard
    mixed with 3 tablespoons
    mayonnaise
2 hard-boiled eggs, sliced
Tomato wedges, for garnish
Sprigs of Italian parsley, for garnish

Place the potatoes in a large pot, cover
them with water, add 1 tablespoon of salt
and the caraway seeds, and bring to a boil
over high heat. Cook the potatoes until
they are fork tender, 20 to 25 minutes.
Drain them, and let them stand until they
are cool enough to handle, but still warm.
Peel them and slice them very thin.

Fry the bacon until it is almost crisp,
and remove it with a slotted spoon. Pour
the drippings over the potatoes. Crumble
the bacon. Add the bacon, oil, stock, onion,
2 teaspoons of salt, white pepper, parsley,
sugar, ⅓ cup of the vinegar, and the mus-
tard-mayonnaise mixture to the warm
potatoes, and mix gently but thoroughly.

Taste the salad, add the remaining vinegar
if necessary, and adjust the seasoning with
more salt and pepper to taste. Transfer
the salad to a serving platter, and garnish
with the eggs, tomatoes, and parsley. Serve
immediately.

VINAIGRETTES

WHITE WINE VINAIGRETTE

I prefer vinaigrettes with a touch of
lemon or lime juice in them, but
it is not essential. Increase the
amount of vinegar and eliminate the lemon
juice if it suits your palate.

3 tablespoons white wine vinegar or
    Champagne vinegar
1 tablespoon lemon juice
1 teaspoon dry mustard
1 garlic clove, minced
1 shallot, minced
¾ cup extra virgin olive oil
1 tablespoon minced Italian parsley
1 tablespoon snipped chives

1 teaspoon kosher salt
Black pepper in a mill

In a small bowl, combine the vinegar, lemon juice, mustard, garlic, and shallot. Whisk in the olive oil, add the parsley and chives, and season with salt and pepper. Use immediately, or refrigerate, covered, for up to 1 week; bring to room temperature before using.

RED WINE VINAIGRETTE

I f you prefer mild vinaigrettes, select a vinegar low in acid; for more tartness, choose a high-acid vinegar.

MAKES ABOUT 1 CUP

¼ cup red wine vinegar
1 teaspoon lemon juice
2 garlic cloves, minced
2 tablespoons minced fresh herbs, such as thyme, oregano, Italian parsley, chives, or a combination
1 teaspoon Dijon mustard
¾ cup extra virgin olive oil
1 teaspoon kosher salt
Black pepper in a mill

In a small bowl, combine the vinegar, lemon juice, garlic, herbs, and mustard. Whisk in the olive oil, and season with salt and pepper. Use immediately, or refriger-

Vinegar

W hen you buy vinegar, do check its level of acidity, which will be expressed as a percentage (6 percent, for example), or in grain (60 grain, for example). The higher the number, the more acetic acid the vinegar has and the stronger it is. For vinaigrettes, choose a level of acidity that suits your palate. If you use vinegar for preserving, the acidity must be at least 5 percent.

ate, covered, for up to 1 week; bring to room temperature before using.

MUSTARD VINAIGRETTE

M ustard vinaigrette can be made seconds before you toss it with your favorite greens or pasta, spoon it over a baked potato or roasted asparagus, or slather it on a grilled chicken sandwich. For such uses, it can be a simple mixture of oil, vinegar, prepared mustard, salt, and pepper. For more depth and complexity, add anchovies, honey, garlic, balsamic vinegar, herbs, or spices. This version has a strong jolt of Dijon mustard and a bass note of garlic.

MAKES ABOUT 1½ CUPS

2 tablespoons Dijon mustard

1 shallot, minced

2 garlic cloves, minced

1 teaspoon thyme leaves

1 teaspoon minced Italian parsley

½ teaspoon kosher salt

½ teaspoon fresh-ground black
   pepper

2 teaspoons dry mustard

4 tablespoons fresh lemon juice

1½ cups extra virgin olive oil

Put the Dijon mustard, shallot, garlic, herbs, salt, and pepper in a bowl, and whisk together. In a separate bowl, combine the dry mustard with the lemon juice, then stir this mixture into the Dijon mustard mixture. Slowly whisk in the olive oil, taste, and adjust the seasoning. Use immediately, or refrigerate, covered, for up to 1 week; bring to room temperature before using.

To Store Oils

Most culinary oils, including olive oil, should be stored in tinted (not clear) glass in a cool, dark pantry away from heat and light. Buy oil in quantities you will use in 6 months or less. Do not store olive oil in the refrigerator, where its delicate flavors will be destroyed. Hazelnut oil and walnut oil, on the other hand, are unstable and will go rancid quickly unless they are kept in the refrigerator.

LEMON VINAIGRETTE

Lemon vinaigrette is best when it is first made and all of the flavors are still at their peak. It's a versatile dressing, as good on leaves of butter lettuce as on complex rice salads or grilled chicken sandwiches.

MAKES ABOUT 1¼ CUPS

⅓ cup fresh lemon juice

1 teaspoon Dijon mustard

2 garlic cloves, minced

1 tablespoon minced fresh herbs, such
   as thyme, oregano, Italian parsley,
   chives, or a combination

¾ cup extra virgin olive oil

¾ teaspoon kosher salt

Black pepper in a mill

In a small bowl, whisk together the lemon juice and mustard. Add the garlic and herbs, and whisk in the olive oil. Season with salt and pepper. Use immediately, or refrigerate, covered, for up to 3 to 4 days; bring to room temperature before using.

Variation:

For lime vinaigrette, use ⅓ cup fresh lime juice (from about 4 limes) instead of the lemon juice.

Fruit Vinegars

Preserving California's bounty is one of the delights of living in the midst of it. One of the ways to distill its essence is to make fruit vinegars, best done when a large quantity of fruit is available at a reasonable price. Check your local farmers' market, whether you live in California or not.

To make fruit vinegar, combine 8 cups of whole berries or chopped fruit with 1 quart medium-acid (5 to 6½ percent acidity) vinegar in a large glass jar or crock. The vinegar should just cover the fruit; add more if necessary. Store the mixture, covered, in a cool pantry or in the refrigerator for up to 7 days, tasting now and then to determine when the vinegar is sufficiently infused with the fruit. Strain the mixture through a strainer lined with cheesecloth, then strain it again through a coffee filter. Store the infused vinegar in glass bottles, closed with a cork, in a cool, dark cupboard. Use within 3 months.

The best flavor combinations include: strawberries with red wine vinegar (for strawberries, use a low-acid vinegar); other berries (raspberry, blackberry, boysenberry, blueberry, or cranberry) with white wine or Champagne vinegar; pears, quince, pineapple, and persimmons with Champagne vinegar; and stone fruits (peaches, apricots, nectarines) with apple cider vinegar. Avoid using vinegars that have been aged in oak; their flavors will eclipse the flavors of the fruit.

WALNUT VINAIGRETTE

Try to make this dressing with unrefined walnut oil, which tastes fully like walnuts. Refined walnut oil, for years the only type produced in this country—it is made in California—has almost no walnut flavor. Unrefined walnut oil is quite perishable; it must be stored in the refrigerator, and it should be used within 3 months of purchase.

MAKES ABOUT 1 CUP

2 tablespoons balsamic vinegar
2 tablespoons red wine, such as zinfandel or merlot
1 shallot, minced
2 tablespoons chopped walnuts
1 teaspoon fresh-ground black pepper
⅓ cup unrefined walnut oil
½ cup peanut oil
Kosher salt

Combine the vinegar, wine, shallot, walnuts, and pepper in a small mixing

bowl. Whisk in the walnut oil, followed by the peanut oil. Taste, and season with salt. Use immediately, or store, covered, in the refrigerator for up to 3 days; bring to room temperature before using.

RED RASPBERRY VINAIGRETTE

Here's one of those tired clichés of California cuisine, the sort of thing that makes you want to roll your eyes when the waiter slowly explains it. Although a number of excellent dishes have been overdone in this way, there is no reason to dismiss them entirely. Just use them appropriately, and understand their context. Raspberry vinegar is nothing new, and not native to California. The most common of all fruit vinegars, it has been used in France for centuries. Most French versions are higher in acid than many of those produced in California. Take note of the acidity of a vinegar before making a dressing; the higher the number, the stronger the vinegar. A low-acid vinegar allows its fruit's flavor to show through.

MAKES ABOUT 1 CUP

¼ cup low-acid (about 4.5 percent) red raspberry vinegar
1 small shallot, peeled and minced
¼ teaspoon sugar
2 teaspoons minced Italian parsley

¾ cup mild olive oil
Kosher salt
Black pepper in a mill

In a small bowl, combine the vinegar, shallot, sugar, and parsley. Whisk in the olive oil, and season with salt and pepper. Use immediately, or store, covered, in a cool, dark spot for up to 3 days.

BLACK RASPBERRY VINAIGRETTE

Black raspberry vinegar has more body and more depth of flavor than red raspberry vinegar; it makes a rich vinaigrette that is excellent with poultry and meat salads.

MAKES ABOUT 1 CUP

⅓ cup black raspberry vinegar
¼ teaspoon dry mustard
½ teaspoon sugar
Pinch of ground clove
1 garlic clove, minced
⅔ cup olive oil
Kosher salt
Black pepper in a mill

In a small bowl, whisk together the vinegar, mustard, sugar, and clove. Add the garlic, and whisk in the olive oil. Season with salt and pepper. Use immediately, or refrigerate, covered, for up to 1 week; bring to room temperature before using.

CRANBERRY VINAIGRETTE

se this beautiful dressing for the fall and winter holidays, when cranberries are in season. It is excellent on simple green salads, wild rice salads, or composed salads that call for duck or turkey.

MAKES ABOUT 1 CUP

¼ cup cranberry vinegar (see Fruit Vinegars, page 154)
1 teaspoon very thinly sliced orange zest
Pinch of ground allspice
Pinch of sugar
⅓ cup hazelnut oil
⅓ cup peanut oil
Pinch of kosher salt
¼ teaspoon fresh-ground black pepper

In a small bowl, whisk together the vinegar, orange zest, allspice, and sugar. Add the hazelnut oil, followed by the peanut oil, salt, and pepper. Taste, and correct the seasoning. Use immediately, or refrigerate, covered, for up to 3 to 4 days; bring to room temperature before using.

PINEAPPLE VINAIGRETTE

se this vinaigrette on all types of fruit salads, especially ones with melons, pineapple, grapefruit, or any tropical fruit. It is also excellent with avocado and with seafood salads. If you do not have hazelnut oil, simply replace it with additional olive oil.

MAKES ABOUT 1 CUP

2 tablespoons Champagne vinegar
1 tablespoon pineapple juice
1 teaspoon honey, warmed
2 garlic cloves, crushed
½ teaspoon vanilla extract
1 tablespoon tequila, optional
3 tablespoons hazelnut oil
½ cup mild olive oil
Kosher salt
Black pepper in a mill
6 mint leaves, cut into julienne

In a small bowl, combine the vinegar, pineapple juice, honey, and garlic. Set the bowl aside for 30 minutes. Strain the mixture into a medium bowl and discard the garlic. Add the vanilla and tequila. Slowly whisk in the oils. Taste, and season with salt and pepper. Stir in the mint leaves, and set aside until ready to use.

The Bee in the Glass

California's honeybee industry was launched in 1852 when Christopher Shelton moved twelve colonies to a spot just north of San Jose. Today, the state produces more than nineteen million pounds of honey, a byproduct of the more crucial pollination industry. Commercial beekeepers—there are about two thousand nationwide—follow the bloom, loading huge trucks with hundreds of hives and moving from farm to farm, field to field, and state to state while their bees pollinate the blossoms that rely upon them. Like many essential aspects of agriculture, this operation takes place away from the public eye, as beekeepers move through the southern states in the winter, then northeast to pollinate cranberries, west for Midwest clover, and on to California for the almond bloom. Three weeks out of the year, almond growers in the Central Valley round up a million hives at a cost of $35 each for their almond trees, which are entirely dependent upon bees for pollination.

According to the National Honey Board, about one-third of what we eat is directly or indirectly dependent upon bees.

Think of a glass of milk, the cow that produces it, the alfalfa the cow eats—there you find the bee in the glass. Alfalfa, apples, peaches, apricots, cherries, melons, and cucumbers are among the foods that require the transfer of pollen that comes when a bee nuzzles down into a flower to suckle nectar and emerges with its face full of pollen, which it carries to the next flower, and the next and the next. The yield of crops as well as their prices are all affected by bees. Without them, hundreds of plants would disappear.

The color and flavor of honey is influenced by the nectar the bees drink. In Provence, dark, rich lavender honey is highly prized. Now, with both Sonoma County and Santa Cruz County having vast plantings of lavender, a limited amount of California lavender honey is available. The bulk of the state's honey, however, comes from almonds, alfalfa, clover, eucalyptus, orange blossom, and fireweed. Most commercial honey is a blend of several types. Look for single-flower honeys at farmers' markets and specialty food stores.

HONEY PEPPER VINAIGRETTE

During my twelve years as a chef with my own catering company, this vinaigrette was one of my most requested recipes. I dress simple green salads with it, toss it with pasta and summer tomatoes, and I use it as a marinade for grilled prawns and grilled lamb.

MAKES ABOUT 1¼ CUPS

3 tablespoons sherry vinegar
3 tablespoons balsamic vinegar
¼ cup honey, warmed

1 shallot, minced
3 garlic cloves, minced
2 tablespoons fresh-ground black
  pepper
1 teaspoon kosher salt
¾ to 1 cup mild olive oil

In a medium bowl, mix together the vinegars and the honey. Stir in the shallot, garlic, pepper, and salt. Whisk in ¾ cup of the olive oil. Taste, and add more olive oil if you like. Use immediately.

WARM BACON-SHALLOT VINAIGRETTE

This dressing is splendid with potatoes, whether in a potato salad (see page 150) or simply over sliced boiled potatoes. To dress it up a bit, add sieved hard-boiled egg just before serving.

MAKES ABOUT ¾ CUP

4 slices of bacon
3 shallots, minced
4 garlic cloves, minced
4 tablespoons Champagne vinegar
  or white wine vinegar
Juice of ½ lemon
½ teaspoon sugar
2 tablespoons minced Italian parsley
½ cup olive oil
Kosher salt
Black pepper in a mill

Fry the bacon in a skillet over medium-high heat until thoroughly crisp, then transfer it to absorbent paper. Reduce the heat to medium, add the shallots to the bacon drippings, and simmer them until they are limp and fragrant, about 8 minutes. Add the garlic, and sauté for 2 minutes more. Add the vinegar, lemon juice, sugar, and parsley, and simmer for 1 minute. Add the olive oil and heat it through. Remove the skillet from the heat. Season with salt and pepper, crumble the bacon and stir it in, taste, and correct the seasoning. Use immediately, or store, covered, in the refrigerator for up to 2 days; reheat before serving.

Chapter 5

BREADS
AND
SANDWICHES

BREADS AND SANDWICHES

AEBELSKIVERS (DANISH DOUGH BALLS)

• •

Aebelskivers, which my friend Rikka Rasmussen, from the town of Solvang (see page 372), near Santa Barbara, refers to as "dough bombs," are the classic dish of the California Danish community. Mention the name in the right circles and eyes will light up and people will beg for your recipe. They require a special pan, called a skiver pan, which can be found in better cookware stores. They are served at breakfast or brunch.

MAKES ABOUT 18 TO 20
2 ½-INCH DOUGH BALLS

2 cups all-purpose flour
1 teaspoon baking soda
1 teaspoon baking powder
3 eggs, separated
1 to 2 tablespoons sugar
½ teaspoon salt
2 cups buttermilk
Bacon drippings or mild oil, such as peanut, corn, or safflower, for frying
Powdered sugar
Danish-style raspberry jam (see Note)
Maple syrup

Sift together the flour, baking soda, and baking powder into a small bowl, and set the bowl aside.

In a medium mixing bowl, beat the egg yolks with a whisk until they are pale yellow. Add the sugar, using 2 tablespoons if you want more sweetness, salt, and buttermilk, and whisk to incorporate them thoroughly. Using a wooden spoon, add the flour mixture to the egg mixture, stirring quickly to combine thoroughly. Beat the egg whites until they form stiff but not dry peaks, and fold them quickly into the batter; do not overmix.

Preheat the skiver pan so that it is very hot. Lower the heat to medium, and place a small amount of bacon drippings or cooking oil in each well of the pan. Fill each well two-thirds full with batter. Cook over medium heat until each aebelskiver is bubbly, then turn each one carefully, using an ice pick or a long wooden skewer (or even a knitting needle). Cook the first batch of aebelskivers until they are uniformly golden, then transfer them to an ovenproof serving plate in a warm oven. Continue until all of the batter has been used.

Sift powdered sugar over the aebelskivers, and serve them, with raspberry jam and maple syrup alongside.

NOTE: To make Danish-style raspberry jam, mix 1 cup of raspberry jam with the juice of 1 lemon.

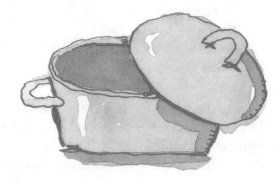

SOURDOUGH WAFFLES WITH BACON

On special occasions—Christmas, birthdays, the Fourth of July—my mother made waffles with bacon, a combination I still love. She did not cook the bacon separately, but instead let half a rasher sizzle in the waffle iron for a few minutes before pouring the batter on top. She would serve the waffle bacon side down, and there was nothing better than finding that savory, salty prize beneath the toasty surface of the waffle with its cloak of sweet maple syrup. Keep in mind that you must begin this recipe the night before.

SERVES 4 TO 6

¼ cup warm water
2 teaspoons (about 1 package) active dry yeast
1 tablespoon sugar
1¼ cups milk, scalded
2 large eggs, beaten
4 tablespoons unsalted butter, melted
1 teaspoon salt
1½ cups all-purpose flour
8 slices of bacon, cut crosswise in half
Maple syrup

Put the warm water and the yeast in a large mixing bowl. Set the bowl aside for 5 minutes, until the yeast swells and becomes creamy (if it doesn't, begin again with new yeast). Stir in the sugar, milk, eggs, butter, and salt, and mix well. Add the flour, and stir until the batter is creamy. Cover the bowl loosely with wax paper and a tea towel, and let the bowl stand at room temperature for 2 hours. Stir the batter, which should be bubbly by this time, cover the bowl tightly with plastic wrap, and refrigerate for at least 12 hours or up to 2 days.

Prepare a waffle iron. When it is hot, add a strip of bacon across the center of each waffle platform. Cook the bacon until it begins to brown slightly, then turn it over. Pour the batter over the bacon, close the waffle iron, and cook until the indicator light shows that the waffle is done or until the lid lifts off easily.

Transfer the cooked waffles to an ovenproof plate in a warm oven. Continue until all of the batter has been used. Serve immediately, with plenty of maple syrup.

SAGE AND DRY JACK SCONES

As an avid tea drinker, I love the little accompaniments that make up a traditional afternoon tea. I am particularly fond of sage, and I developed this recipe to make use of the sage that grows outside my kitchen door.

MAKES 8 TO 12 SCONES

2 cups all-purpose flour
1 tablespoon baking powder

½ teaspoon salt
5 tablespoons unsalted butter,
   chilled, cut into ¼-inch pieces
¾ cup half-and-half
1 egg, beaten
2 tablespoons minced sage leaves
¾ cup grated dry jack
8 to 12 sage leaves
Heavy cream

Preheat the oven to 450°F. Place a baking sheet in the oven, so that the sheet heats up as the oven preheats.

Mix together the flour, baking powder, and salt in a medium mixing bowl. Add the butter, and, using your fingertips or a pastry blender, quickly work the butter into the flour mixture so that it has the consistency of bread crumbs. Pour the half-and-half into a small bowl, and stir the egg and the minced sage into it.

Make a well in the center of the flour mixture, pour the milk mixture into the well, and mix lightly and quickly with a fork until a loose, soft dough forms. Add the cheese, and mix quickly with your fingers. Turn out the dough onto a lightly floured surface. Knead very gently for 30 seconds.

With a rolling pin or the palm of your hand, spread out the dough into a rectangle ¾ inch thick. With a sharp knife, cut the dough into 8 to 12 triangles. Brush the surface of each triangle with cream, and gently press a sage leaf into the center of each scone. Brush with more cream if the extra moistness is necessary to make the leaf stay in place.

Using a spatula, transfer the scones to the hot baking sheet. Bake until they are lightly golden, about 10 minutes. Remove the scones from the oven and transfer them to a cooling rack. Serve the scones warm.

JALAPEÑO CORNBREAD

Perhaps because of the abundance of produce, Californians tend to add ingredients, as if by whim, to traditional recipes. California chili, for example, might include carrots, celery, olives, and other unexpected additions, and it is almost always topped with condiments like diced yellow onion, sliced scallion, minced cilantro, and grated cheddar. We muck around with cornbread, too, as in this recipe with its sautéed jalapeños, chipotle or other chile powder, and cheddar cheese. Serve this cornbread with Beef Chili Colorado (page 359), Red Beans and Rice (page 239), or by itself with butter and a hot pepper jam.

MAKES 1 8-BY-8-INCH BREAD

½ cup butter
2 to 3 jalapeños, minced
2 cups cornmeal, preferably
   stoneground
1 tablespoon sugar
1 teaspoon chipotle powder or other
   dried chile powder, or 1 teaspoon
   crushed dried red chiles

1 teaspoon baking powder
1 cup boiling water
½ cup milk, hot
2 eggs, beaten
1 cup (4 ounces) grated cheddar

Preheat the oven to 425°F.

Melt the butter in a small saucepan over medium heat. Add the jalapeños, using 3 for more heat, and sauté them until they are soft, 4 to 5 minutes. Remove the jalapeños from the heat, and brush the inside of an 8-by-8-inch cake pan with a little butter from the pan. Do not discard the remaining butter.

Combine the cornmeal, sugar, chile powder or crushed chiles, and baking powder in a medium bowl. Add the hot butter from the pan, and stir with a wooden spoon until well blended. Add the boiling water, and stir until smooth. Stir in the milk and eggs, then fold in the cheese. Pour the batter into the cake pan, and bake until the bread is lightly browned on top and firm in the center when pressed lightly, about 30 minutes. Remove the bread from the oven, and let it cool in its pan for 5 minutes. Cut the bread into wedges, and serve immediately.

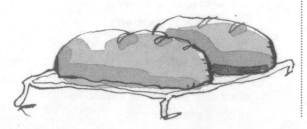

CARROT BREAD

• •

*J*anice Dolphin is a stained-glass artist who moved north from Berkeley to the old coastal town of Gualala, where she trains animals, grooms cats, dogs, and goats, and takes care of wealthy people's pets. She's a perfect example of the sort of ingenuity both possible and necessary for those determined to live in California's more remote areas, far from the easy-to-come-by jobs of the cities. She's also a terrific cook, and the creator of this earthy carrot bread.

MAKES 2 9-INCH LOAVES

3 cups all-purpose flour
2 teaspoons baking powder
1½ teaspoons salt
2 teaspoons ground cinnamon
4 eggs
2 cups brown sugar
1½ cups peanut oil
2 cups finely shredded carrots

Preheat the oven to 350°F. Butter and lightly flour 2 9-by-5-inch loaf pans. Sift together in a medium bowl the flour, baking powder, salt, and cinnamon.

In a large mixing bowl, beat the eggs until they are pale yellow. Add the brown sugar gradually, beating until the mixture is thick. Add the oil and the carrots, and stir thoroughly to incorporate them. Quickly fold in the flour mixture. Pour the batter into the loaf pans, and bake the bread in the center of the oven for 1 hour, or until the centers of the loaves spring back when pressed lightly. Remove from the oven, and let the loaves rest for 5 minutes in their pans. Remove the bread from the pans, and let the loaves cool on racks. Serve at room temperature, with butter or with a flavored butter, such as nasturtium or pistachio (see page 416).

The Baker's Oven

"For a while after we went to Whittier there was one bakery going, run by a German, and usually at Christmas our turkey would be stuffed and taken down to be roasted in his undying oven. I think this happened a few times with large pots of beans, too, which stayed there overnight. The baker left town in 1916 . . . and his brother-in-law took over. The day before his Grand Opening, he sent home with Rex [Kennedy, Fisher's father, who ran the town's newspaper] a great platter of gleaming sweet cakes, called Butter Flies because they made the butter fly, his new ad would say in the paper. We had a special treat that afternoon, and sat around in the dining room and drank pitchers of milk and ate the delicious surprise. Grandmother tasted one, pronounced it good, and then dismissed it scornfully as a bribe."

M.F.K. Fisher, *Among Friends* (Knopf, 1971)

PERSIMMON BREAD

After all the leaves have dropped from a persimmon tree, the fruits remain attached to their branches, hanging like so many winter jewels shimmering in the California fog. Not all of the fruit is harvested, and many persimmons are free for the taking.

MAKES 1 8-BY-11-INCH LOAF

1⅔ cups all-purpose flour
1 teaspoon baking powder
1 teaspoon baking soda
½ teaspoon salt
3 ripe persimmons
½ cup butter, at room temperature
1 cup sugar
2 eggs, beaten
¾ cup toasted pecans or walnuts, chopped fine

Preheat the oven to 325°F. Butter an 8-by-11-inch baking pan. In a small bowl, combine the flour, baking powder, baking soda, and salt.

Cut the persimmons in half, discard the pits, and push and rub the flesh through a sieve; there should be about ¾ cup pulp. In a medium mixing bowl, beat the butter with the sugar until light and fluffy. Stir in the eggs and the persimmon pulp, and continue stirring until the mixture is smooth and creamy.

Quickly fold the flour mixture into

the persimmon mixture, then fold in the nuts. Pour the batter into the buttered pan. Bake for 45 minutes, or until the top springs back when pressed lightly.

Remove the bread from the oven, and let it rest for 5 minutes in its pan. Remove the bread from the pan. Serve the bread warm or at room temperature, with butter or nasturtium butter (page 416).

California's Field Crops

Descriptions of California agriculture frequently refer to field crops, but what exactly are they? Field crops are grains used for food, fiber, and livestock feed. California has several million acres devoted to these crops, which include the smaller grains barley, wheat, and oats, which have been important since the days of the Spanish missions. Other California field crops are corn, cotton, alfalfa seed, hops, hay, dry beans, clover seed, rice, sugar beets, and irrigated pasture grasses.

FOCACCIA

This dough rises most effectively if it rests in a slightly warm area, but do not set it too close to a direct source of heat. My house is frequently quite cold in winter, so I set the dough on a heating pad covered with several layers of towels (to diffuse the heat). In a warm room, it is not necessary to make such special arrangements. Focaccia is best the day it is made, but it can be refrigerated, wrapped tightly in plastic wrap, for up to 2 days; reheat it in the oven before serving.

Long popular in California's Italian communities, focaccia today can be found in virtually every corner bakery and neighborhood coffeehouse in the state. Home cooks buy it ready-baked, for sandwiches, and quite a few make it at home, too.

MAKES 1 12-BY-17-INCH BREAD

2¼ teaspoons (about 1 package)
    active dry yeast
¼ cup warm water
5½ tablespoons extra virgin olive oil
1 cup plus 1 to 2 tablespoons water,
    at room temperature
4¼ cups unbleached all-purpose
    flour
2½ teaspoons kosher salt
1 teaspoon coarse sea salt
Water in a spray bottle

Put the yeast and the ¼ cup warm water in the bowl of a heavy-duty mixer and let stand until the yeast is creamy, about 10 minutes. Add 1½ tablespoons of the olive oil and 1 cup of the room-temperature water, and stir the mixture with the paddle. Add the flour and the kosher salt, and mix on low speed until the dough comes together, adding the additional 1 to 2 tablespoons water if necessary for the dough to come together. Change to the dough hook, and knead on low speed for 2 minutes. Knead on high speed for 2 to 3 minutes more, until the dough is smooth and velvety. Oil a large bowl with olive oil, and transfer the dough to the bowl. Cover tightly with plastic wrap, and place the bowl in a warm but not hot place. Let the dough rise until is doubled in size, about 1½ hours.

Lightly oil a 12-by-17-inch sheet pan. Turn out the dough onto a very lightly floured surface, and shape the dough to fit into the pan. Transfer the dough to the pan, cover the pan with a tea towel, and let the dough rise for 30 minutes. Use your fingertips to make ½-inch dimples over the entire surface of the dough. Cover the pan with a moist tea towel, and let the dough rise until is doubled in size again, 1½ to 2 hours.

Preheat the oven to 400°F. Brush the dough with the remaining 4 tablespoons of olive oil, and sprinkle the top with the sea salt.

Bake the focaccia, spraying it with water every 4 or 5 minutes, for 15 to 20 minutes, or until it is a light golden brown. When the focaccia is done, immediately transfer it to a rack. Let it cool, and serve it, cut into pieces, at room temperature.

Variations:

WITH TOMATO SAUCE: Instead of brushing the dough with 4 tablespoons of olive oil only, brush it with a combination of 2 tablespoons extra virgin olive oil and 6 tablespoons tomato sauce. Grind some black pepper over the dough with the sea salt.

WITH TOMATO SAUCE AND SCALLIONS: Instead of brushing the dough with 4 tablespoons of olive oil only, top it with the tomato sauce and olive oil, as in the variation above, and spread ½ cup sliced scallions, white and green parts, over the focaccia. Grind some black pepper over the dough with the sea salt.

WITH TOMATO CONCASSÉ: Instead of brushing the dough with 4 tablespoons of olive oil only, spread it with a combination of 2 tablespoons extra virgin olive oil and ½ cup Tomato Concassé (page 98). Grind some black pepper over the dough with the sea salt. Before serving, sprinkle with minced fresh herbs, such as basil or oregano.

WITH TAPENADE: Instead of brushing the dough with 4 tablespoons of olive oil only, spread it with 3 to 4 tablespoons of Olive Tapenade (page 422). Before serving, scatter fresh basil leaves, cut into ribbons, over the top.

WITH GORGONZOLA, LEMON, AND ROSEMARY: After brushing the dough with olive oil, dot it with 2 ounces gorgonzola cheese, crumbled, 1 teaspoon minced rosemary, and thin lemon wedges. Grind some black pepper over the dough with the sea salt.

Lou's Sourdough Bread

MAKES ABOUT 1
2-POUND LOAF

o make sourdough bread, you
need a sourdough starter, a spongy
mixture of flour, water, and wild
yeast that can be kept alive indefinitely.
When vintner Lou Preston, of Preston
Vineyards & Winery in Dry Creek Valley,
one of the most passionate bakers I know,
first took a baking class, he was given a
starter begun years earlier at Tassajara

The Bread Revolution

"**D**o they really exist, those mahogany-colored wheels of country bread with creamy interiors, crackly crusted chewy loaves that still taste of the grains of the fields? . . . Today those breads can still be found, but you must look for them. Their existence was severely endangered during the 1950s and 1960s, when mass production and industrialization centralized baking. Fortunately, they have been revived by artisan bakers all over the country, so that their tastes remain part of another generation's patrimony."—Carol Field, *The Italian Baker*

Field's words about Italy might just as well have been written about the United States. Not so long ago good bread was as hard to get as flavorful tomatoes. Nowadays you can get good bread just about anywhere in the country, and a quiet revolution, begun in California in the late 1970s, is a big part of the reason you can.

Steve Sullivan, who started as a busboy at Chez Panisse and went on to bake the restaurant's breads, opened his own Acme Bakery in the early 1980s in a Berkeley building shared with Kermit Lynch Wine Merchant and Alice Waters's Café Fanny. Word of Acme's European-style hearth breads spread like juicy gossip; from the beginning, there was not enough Acme bread to keep up with demand. A major expansion in the late 1980s merely increased the bread's popularity. It wasn't long before Sullivan's success spawned other fine new Bay Area bakeries, such as Il Fornaio in San Francisco, Semifreddi's in Emeryville, and Grace Baking Co. in Oakland.

There were other pioneers. To the south, in Capitola, Gayle and Joe Ortiz's Gayle's Bakery had opened in 1978, and the Ortizes continue to produce some of the finest breads around. After traveling through the U.S. and Europe in search of perfect techniques, Joe published *The Village Baker*, an exhaustive and authoritative bread cookbook geared to the home cook. In southern California, Nancy Silverton of Campanile brought real bread to Los Angeles. By the 1990s, the bread revolution had spread throughout the United States.

Bakery in San Francisco. An adventurous and independent soul, Lou soon decided to make his own.

To make a starter, you need to capture wild yeast; commercial yeast does not produce the sour flavors that wild yeasts do. Because his wines are made using natural fermentation, Lou needed to look no further than one of his own vineyards, a

hundred-year-old zinfandel vineyard, to be exact. He picked three bunches of grapes that had on them a nice bloom, that is, plenty of wild yeast spores. He made a soupy batter of flour and water, pressed the grapes down into it, covered it, and left it at room temperature for three days, stirring it every day. By the end of three days, tiny pin-prick-sized bubbles indicated the yeast

What do I mean by real bread? Pain levain, the classic hearth loaf, combines just three ingredients: water, salt, and organic flour, the quality of which is essential because slow fermentation by wild yeast present in the flour develops the natural flavors of the grain. A highly processed flour, stripped of nutrients, yeast, and nuances of flavor, will have no depth to yield. Pain levain begins with a starter of flour and water; during long hours and days of fermentation yeast produces alcohol and delicately sour flavors. The starter is fed with additional flour and water until a portion of it is combined with more flour, water, and salt to create a final dough, which undergoes at least two more fermentations before it is baked, preferably in a stone or brick hearth oven with a powerful steam injector. True pain levain is shaped by hand and goes through its final fermentation in canvas-lined baskets, which contributes to its unique, rustic appearance. This process cannot be shortened without a noticeable loss of quality; compromises such as commercial yeast and fermentations at higher temperatures yield inferior results. Although the best loaves of traditional pain levain are made with a large percentage of organic whole wheat, Ameri-

cans overwhelmingly prefer white bread and nearly all bakers adjust their formulas to reflect this taste.

Perhaps the most telling signs of the success of America's bread revolution come from the *Coupe du Monde de la Boulangerie,* or World Cup of Baking, in Paris. At the 1996 competition, the U.S. team won first place in traditional breads, a category commonly cornered by Europeans. The winning team included two northern California bakers, Craig Ponsford of Artisan Bakers in Sonoma and Glenn Mitchell of Oakland's Grace Baking Co.

In *The Italian Baker,* Carol Field writes that bread is so integral to life in Italy that it is embedded in the very language. Bread stands for all things simple, honest, and good; a reliable man, for example, is said to be "a piece of bread." To leave behind hard bread is to leave behind hard times. *"Senza il pane tutto diventa organo,"* the Italians say. "Without bread, everyone is an orphan." Although it has come to us slowly, real bread is here at last, as good a harbinger for the millennium as any I can imagine.

was growing active. The activity grew more intense and his starter was on its way. Nearly a decade later, the starter is thriving.

"A starter gets hungry," he explains, "especially when you store it at room temperature. The yeast will exhaust the nutrients, and you don't want a tired starter, which has bad leavening power. When you go on vacation, your starter is just like a pet—you can't leave home and not feed it." You can slow down its appetite, however, by keeping it in the refrigerator.

When Lou is not baking, he keeps about a quart of starter on hand, feeding it every day or so and throwing out half of it with each feeding. When he begins to bake, as he does now every day when he is not traveling, he feeds it twice a day and lets the quantity increase.

With Carol Field's *The Italian Baker* as a guide, Lou's breads got better and better. Limited to just four loaves at a time by the small oven in the winery's kitchen, he decided to build a larger outdoor oven. His in-laws are from in Calaveras County, where there is a long history of baking in outdoor brick and adobe ovens. There are a number of old ovens, including stone ovens shaped like beehives, tucked here and there in Dry Creek Valley, too. With these other ovens as models and inspiration, and with plenty of natural clay on the property of the winery, Lou built an Italian-style wood-fired fournou, crafted from willow saplings cut from Dry Creek and clay dug from a hill next to his zinfandel vines.

When pressed for a recipe, Lou hedges. "I don't use a recipe," he insists. When I

beg, the closest he comes is a narrative explanation.

"You need time to make sourdough bread. You can't make it quickly," he insists. "It requires slow fermentations at cool temperatures. There are a lot of things you must pay attention to. You need good-quality flour but not necessarily high-gluten flour; you need a good brand, but all-purpose is okay.

"And it is very important not to over-knead. If you work a dough too vigorously, it heats up, and the flavor and color are bleached out. It is better to knead by hand [rather than in a mixer or processor]; once the water is fully incorporated, it is easy and fun.

"A good starting point for a novice is to begin with about ½ to ⅔ cup of starter, 1⅔ cups of water, ½ pound of flour, and about 2 teaspoons of salt. This will make a 2-pound loaf. Put the starter in a large bowl, add the water, and mix, breaking up the starter with your fingers if necessary. Add the flour and salt and mix until you get a very wet mass of dough. Keep working it until the water is absorbed and it begins to feel like dough, then put it on a lightly floured surface. Don't add too much flour; instead, use a dough scraper.

"Knead the dough until it springs back when you poke at it. You are looking for a thin, translucent sheet that doesn't tear around the outside of the dough. Put the dough in a large, lightly oiled bowl, cover the bowl, and let it rise for an hour. Carefully dump it out and fold it over itself, as you would fold a letter. Do not punch it down, but stretch it and pull it instead.

California Wheat

From border to border, north to south, wheat grows throughout the entire length of California. Near the Oregon border, the soft winter white varieties suitable for cakes, pastries, noodles, and tortillas and other flatbreads are grown. In the Sacramento and San Joaquin Valleys, Klasic wheat, used in breads, hard rolls, steambreads, and Chinese noodles, is the main variety. The hard durum wheat Desert Durum, essential in the production of pasta, is grown in the Imperial Valley, Palo Verde Valley, and San Joaquin Valley. Several other varieties of wheat are grown throughout the state. One bushel of wheat, weighing about 42 pounds, can produce 73 loaves of bread. California growers produce forty-five million bushels of wheat each year.

Return the dough to the bowl, stretch it again in 1 hour, and once more an hour after that. After 3 rises, form the loaf. The outside surface of the dough should be a web of gluten that you use to let the dough make its own shape. Cover the dough, set it in a cool place, and let the dough rise for several hours or overnight.

"You must bake your bread on some sort of stone, such as unglazed Mexican paver tiles, which are much cheaper than commercial pizza stones. Preheat the oven and the tile thoroughly, to 450°F; it will take at least 45 minutes for the stone to absorb enough heat. Use a knife to slash the top of the uncooked loaf; this will control expansion and put the cracks where you want them. Slashed, your bread will gain more volume. Bake for 50 to 60 minutes."

If you don't have a baker's paddle, use an inverted baking sheet sprinkled with cornmeal to transfer the loaf to the oven. For steam, Lou recommends throwing 3 or 4 small glasses of water directly into the oven during the first 10 minutes, even though manufacturers' instructions caution otherwise. Lou did it this way for years. Now that he has an outdoor oven, he uses a garden hose.

By the mid-1990s, Lou's technique, as well as the reputation of his breads, had grown. He baked enough bread to sell some in the tasting room, and *Gourmet* magazine had even written to ask for a recipe. In 1996, he received approval from the county to build a commercial bakery next to his winery's tasting room. The new bakery, complete with a wood-burning brick oven, opened in the fall of 1997.

BAGELS WITH CHÈVRE AND SPROUTS

The overabundant use of sprouts, especially alfalfa sprouts, is perhaps one of the more unfortunate legacies of the health food movement. Sometime in the early 1970s, they began to appear in virtually everything—from black bean tostadas and shrimp tacos to Caesar salads and sandwiches of every sort, including hamburgers. Otherwise beautiful salads were ruined when they were topped with an enormous mound of stringy sprouts. But when sprouts are used with restraint and in the proper context, they can be utterly refreshing. I like them on toast, or, as they are here, on toasted bagels with cream cheese or chèvre. I do find alfalfa sprouts rather unpleasant, and I prefer the spiciness of onion sprouts, increasingly available in markets, or mustard-seed sprouts, very easy to grow at home.

SERVES 4

4 bagels, split
4 ounces young (not aged) chèvre or old-fashioned (without gum) cream cheese
Hot sauce
Kosher salt
Black pepper in a mill
2 cups alfalfa, onion, or mustard-seed sprouts

Toast the bagels, spread cheese over each cut side, and add a few drops of hot sauce. Season to taste with salt and pepper, and top each bagel half with sprouts. Serve immediately, open faced, or place the 2 halves of each bagel together, cut the sandwiches in half, and wrap them tightly for lunches, picnics, and so on.

ZUCCHINI SANDWICHES WITH AÏOLI

This is one of my favorite summer sandwiches, an ideal way to make use of an excess of zucchini from the garden. A single plant can be dauntingly productive, which fact led to August 8 being officially dubbed "National Sneak Some Zucchini onto Your Neighbors' Porch Night." Be sure to hold back a few for these yummy and very California sandwiches.

SERVES 4

3 cups grated zucchini
1 teaspoon lemon zest
Juice of 1 lemon
8 slices of sourdough bread
2 avocados, pitted and sliced
2 cups (8 ounces) grated jack cheese
¼ cup Aïoli (page 417)

Preheat the oven to 400°F, or preheat the broiler. Toss the zucchini with the lemon zest and lemon juice in a medium bowl. Place 4 slices of bread on a baking sheet, and divide the avocado among the slices. Top the avocado with the zucchini mixture, then top the zucchini with the jack. Place these slices in the oven or under the broiler until the cheese is completely melted but not browned. Meanwhile, toast the remaining 4 slices of bread and spread each with aïoli. Remove the slices from the oven or broiler, and place the toasted slices of bread on top. Cut the sandwiches in half diagonally, and serve immediately.

PORTOBELLO MUSHROOM SANDWICHES

Portobello mushrooms have become enormously popular. Originally from Italy, portobellos are larger, hardier cousins of cremini. With a long growing cycle that gives them a dense texture and deep, meat-like flavors, they are favorites of vegetarians. One reason they are in favor in California is that they are great for grilling—because they are large, they don't fall through the grill as smaller mushrooms do. They are also among the least expensive of the specialty mushrooms.

SERVES 2

3 tablespoons extra virgin olive oil
1 teaspoon balsamic vinegar
2 teaspoons fresh lemon juice
1 to 2 garlic cloves, crushed
1 large (about 8 ounces) portobello
    mushroom, stem removed
Kosher salt
Black pepper in a mill
¼ cup flavored mayonnaise (see
    Note)
2 sourdough rolls, whole wheat
    hamburger rolls, or 4 slices of
    country-style bread
Handful of salad greens, such as
    mesclun

Combine the olive oil, vinegar, lemon juice, and garlic in a medium bowl. Put the mushroom in a shallow bowl, season both sides with salt and pepper, and pour the marinade over it, turning it to coat it thoroughly. Let it marinate for at least 1 hour, or as long as overnight (refrigerated if overnight).

Prepare an outdoor or stovetop grill. When the grill is hot, set the mushroom on the grill, cap side up, and cook for about 7 minutes, giving it a 90° turn once so that it is well marked by the grill. Turn the mushroom over and cook, cap side down, rotating the mushroom once, until it is completely tender, 10 to 15 minutes, depending on the size of the mushroom. Remove the mushroom from the heat and let it rest.

Toast the bread while the mushroom rests. With your knife at a sharp angle, cut the mushroom diagonally into ¼-inch-wide slices. Spread mayonnaise on each slice of bread, arrange half of the mushroom slices on 2 of the slices, season with salt and pepper, top with greens, and place the remaining slices on top. Serve immediately.

NOTE: Nearly any flavored mayonnaise (see page 182) will go beautifully with the grilled mushroom. I also like Chèvre Mayonnaise with Olives (page 420).

OYSTER LOAF

There are many versions of the famous Oyster Loaf, originally made popular in nineteenth-century San Francisco. It was created at the Mayes Oyster House, on California Street, in the 1860s. The traditional technique involves hollowing out a round loaf of sourdough bread so that it forms a basket and lid. Cooked oysters are put inside the loaf. It's not easy to serve this version—when you slice it, the oysters scoot out the sides of the cut bread. In the version here, sourdough rolls make individual servings that are easier to eat.

SERVES 4

4 sourdough rolls, not split
½ cup butter
3 garlic cloves, minced
Tabasco sauce
¼ cup all-purpose flour
Black pepper in a mill
2 eggs, beaten

½ cup fine-ground cornmeal
3 dozen small oysters, shucked
1 lemon, cut into wedges

Preheat the oven to 375°F. Cut each roll lengthwise in two, cutting so that that top "half" is thinner than the bottom and forms a sort of lid. Hollow out the inside of the bottom half of each roll so that it forms a little basket.

Melt the butter in a small saucepan over medium heat. Add the garlic and 3 to 4 dashes of Tabasco. Brush the insides of all of the pieces of roll with butter from the pan; reserve the butter that remains. Toast the rolls in the oven until they are just golden and slightly crisp on the inside. Remove them from the oven and set them aside.

Put the flour in a small bowl and season it with pepper. In another small bowl, combine the eggs with 2 to 3 dashes of Tabasco. Put the cornmeal in a third bowl. Dredge the oysters in the flour, shaking each to remove any excess flour. Dip the oysters in the egg and then in the cornmeal.

Put 2 to 3 tablespoons of the reserved butter in a heavy skillet over medium-high heat. Fry the oysters until they are crisp and golden, 2 to 3 minutes; do not overcook them. Fill the bottom of each roll with fried oysters, pour some of the remaining melted butter over, and cover with the top half of the roll. Serve immediately, with a wedge of lemon alongside. Or wrap each oyster loaf in foil until ready to serve, and reheat in a 325°F oven for 10 minutes before serving.

Manifold Destiny

Life in California is utterly dependent upon the automobile. Public transportation is limited and inefficient and it is the state's elaborate freeway system that unites it. It could have been done differently, but it wasn't, and most Californians consider a car essential, driving as much as two hours each way to work. The price of gas is frequently higher in California than elsewhere, and congestion on both city streets and freeways is a maddening and still increasing problem.

In 1923 *The Motorists Luncheon Book* paid tribute to a different time, when Californians simply took to the open road. It offered culinary tips, recipes, and lists of cooking equipment that would make their journey more pleasant. Perhaps most intriguing is the book's final suggestion: "There are certain makes of machines where the heat from the exhaust manifold can be utilized *en route* for foods hermetically sealed. Canned beans, tamales, chili con carne, chicken and many other substantials can be packed in with the engine and kept hot or heated on the way with no danger of taint from the gasoline."

Tuna Focaccia Sandwiches

These sandwiches make excellent picnic food; just be sure to keep them properly chilled as you transport them. If tomatoes are in season, add a few slices to each sandwich.

SERVES 4

4 small Yukon Gold or Yellow Finn potatoes
1 12-by-17-inch Focaccia (page 168) or bakery-bought focaccia of similar size
1 6- to 6½-ounce can tuna, drained
3 garlic cloves, peeled
¾ cup mayonnaise, homemade (see page 416) or store-bought
3 hard-boiled eggs, sliced
Kosher salt
Black pepper in a mill
2 cups salad greens or thin-sliced purple cabbage

Boil the potatoes in rapidly boiling salted water until they are tender, 15 to 20 minutes. Drain them and set them aside to cool slightly. Slice them thin.

Cut the focaccia into 8 pieces of equal size. Combine the tuna, garlic, and mayonnaise in a food processor, and pulse until the mixture is very smooth. Spread the tuna mayonnaise over the top of each piece of focaccia. For each sandwich, cover one piece of the focaccia with potato slices

and the other piece with egg slices. Season both pieces with salt and pepper. Add greens or cabbage, close the sandwich, and cut it in half. Serve immediately, or wrap tightly in plastic wrap and refrigerate until ready to serve.

CHICKEN, BASIL, AND RASPBERRY SANDWICHES

The marriage of chicken and raspberries is a good one, with many variations. In this very California sandwich, chicken is paired with both fresh raspberries and a mayonnaise made with raspberry vinegar.

SERVES 4

4 sourdough rolls, split
¾ cup Raspberry Mayonnaise (page 418)
12 large basil leaves
1 sweet onion or red onion, sliced thin
1¼ pounds cooked (preferably roasted) chicken meat, sliced
Kosher salt
Black pepper in a mill
2 cups shredded red cabbage
1 cup raspberries

Set the rolls on a work surface and spread each side of each roll with a generous amount of raspberry mayonnaise. Place 3 basil leaves on the bottom half of

each roll, arrange a layer of onion slices on top of the basil, and top with sliced chicken. Season with salt and pepper. Divide the cabbage among the sandwiches, placing it on top of the chicken. Set the sandwiches, open faced, on individual serving plates. Scatter raspberries over each, and serve immediately.

GRILLED CHICKEN SANDWICHES WITH OLIVES

As I was testing recipes for this book, I had some chèvre mayonnaise left over. A chicken breast beckoned from the refrigerator, and the grill was already hot. How could I resist?

SERVES 4

4 full boneless and skinless chicken breasts
Kosher salt
Black pepper in a mill
4 French rolls, split
½ cup Chèvre Mayonnaise with Olives (page 420)
¾ cup pitted black olives, such as California, oil-cured, niçoise, or a combination, sliced
2 cups salad greens, such as arugula or mesclun

Preheat a medium fire on a grill. Season

the chicken breasts with salt and pepper and grill them, turning them once, until they are tender but cooked through, about 7 minutes on each side. Open the rolls on a work surface, spread each side of each roll with mayonnaise, and scatter olives over the mayonnaise. Place a chicken breast on the bottom of each roll, and top with greens. Close the sandwich, cut it in half, and serve immediately.

Variation:

Omit the mayonnaise and olives, and douse the chicken breasts with Mustard Vinaigrette (page 152).

ITALIAN SALAMI SANDWICHES

*N*early as much of a California classic as an Italian one, this simple combination of flavors and textures can't be beat.

SERVES 4

1⅓ cups julienned roasted red bell peppers
4 garlic cloves, sliced thin
2 tablespoons red wine vinegar
Kosher salt
Black pepper in a mill
4 sourdough rolls, split
8 ounces soppressatta or other Italian salami, sliced thin

2 ripe tomatoes, sliced thin
6 ounces fresh mozzarella, sliced thin
Extra virgin olive oil
2 cups arugula leaves

Preheat the oven to 375°F. In a small bowl, toss together the roasted peppers, garlic, and vinegar. Season with salt and pepper, and set the bowl aside.

Set the rolls on a work surface. Divide the soppressatta among the rolls, placing it on the bottom half of each roll. Divide the tomato slices among the sandwiches, placing them on top of the salami. Place ⅓ cup of the marinated peppers on top of the tomatoes on each sandwich, and top the peppers with slices of mozzarella. Set each sandwich, open faced, on a baking sheet, and bake the sandwiches for about 10 minutes, or until the mozzarella is completely melted. Remove from the oven, drizzle olive oil over the sandwich halves, and divide the arugula among the sandwiches. Close the sandwiches, cut them in half, and serve immediately.

Meet Mr. Tomato

Professor Charles Rick eats tomato sandwiches every day when tomatoes are in season. His favorite recipe is simple enough: He toasts heavy bread and adds mayonnaise, tomato slices, a splash of basil vinegar, salt, and pepper. "I eat it all the time and never get tired of it," he says. He grows tomatoes in his backyard, and he makes his own dried tomatoes using a forced-air dehydrator.

Rick, professor emeritus in the Department of Vegetable Crops at the University of California at Davis, has devoted his life to the study of the tomato. Nearly sixty years after beginning his work, he remains an unfettered enthusiast of the willful fruit, which so far has refused to surrender to humankind's efforts to transform it into a year-round plant. Largely because of Rick's efforts, the chromosome maps of the tomato are among the best-known of any flowering plant. Today, Professor Rick, or Mr. Tomato as he is often called, oversees the Tomato Genetics Resource Center, which catalogs and stores the seeds of about three thousand types of tomato plants, including about a thousand wild species, subspecies, and varieties.

MEDITERRANEAN BLT

If the only BLT you've ever had was in a diner or coffee shop, you'll be amazed at how delicious one can be, especially when summer tomatoes are at their peak.

SERVES 4

1 12-by-17-inch Focaccia (page 168) or bakery-bought focaccia of similar size
½ cup Aïoli (page 417) or mayonnaise, homemade (see page 416) or store-bought
6 medium ripe tomatoes, cored and sliced
2 avocados, pitted and sliced
Kosher salt
Black pepper in a mill
12 slices of bacon or pancetta, fried until crisp
2 cups fresh arugula leaves

Cut the focaccia into 8 pieces of equal size, and spread each piece with aïoli or mayonnaise. For each sandwich, top one piece of focaccia with tomato slices and another piece with avocado slices. Season both halves with salt and pepper. Place 1½ pieces of bacon each on top of the tomato and the avocado. Divide the arugala among the sandwiches, close them, and cut them in half. Serve immediately.

PATRICK'S JALAPEÑO BURGERS

· ·

For several years, my friend Patrick Bouquet and I cooked together almost daily, first in a small restaurant I managed and then with my catering company, The Jaded Palate. He's always been an exceptional cook—except for a brief period when, in attempt to impress his wife, he gave up using salt entirely. When he went on to other things, I missed him in the kitchen, in spite of his habit of doing everything at the last possible second. He came up with this recipe one day when he had forgotten to prepare a lunch special, and he has never let me forget that it instantly became one of our most popular dishes. Today, Patrick works in the computer industry in Silicon Valley, cooks on the weekends, and makes tamales every Christmas with his wife, Rachel Cisneros (see page 365).

SERVES 4

8 garlic cloves, minced

3 to 4 jalapeños, minced

1¼ pounds ground chuck, not extra lean

Kosher salt

Black pepper in a mill

4 sourdough rolls, split

1 cup (4 ounces) grated jalapeño jack cheese

The Flowerburgers, Part 4

· ·

Baudelaire opened up a hamburger stand in San Francisco, but he put flowers between the buns. People would come in and say, "Give me a hamburger with plenty of onions on it." Baudelaire would give them a flowerburger instead and the people would say, "What kind of a hamburger stand is this?"

Richard Brautigan, "The Flowerburgers, Part 4," in *The Pill Versus the Springhill Mine Disaster* (Delta, 1968). Brautigan lived for years in or near San Francisco and captured in his poetry, short stories, and novels a lyrical and surrealistic vision of California.

¾ cup Chipotle Mayonnaise (page
    418) or other flavored mayonnaise
    (see box)
½ red onion, sliced
1 avocado, pitted and sliced
    lengthwise
2 tablespoons cilantro leaves

Prepare a medium-high fire in a grill.

In a medium bowl, mix together the garlic, jalapeños, using 4 for more heat, and ground chuck, and season lightly with salt and pepper. Form the meat into 4 thick patties. Grill the burgers for 3 to 4 minutes, turn them, top each with cheese, and cook for 3 to 4 minutes more for rare burgers, or 5 to 6 minutes more for medium-rare.

Meanwhile, lightly toast the rolls on the grill. Remove them and spread both halves of each roll with mayonnaise. Place the burgers on the bottom halves, and top each burger with onion slices, avocado slices, and a sprinkling of cilantro leaves. Serve immediately.

Flavored Mayonnaise

Few things match the voluptuousness of fresh-made mayonnaise, yet we don't always have time to make it. You can add zip to homemade (see page 416) or store-bought mayonnaise by combining it with such flavorings as Tabasco sauce or dried tomatoes. Flavored mayonnaise has the same shelf-life as the original, but, because it is so easy to make, I usually prepare it in quantities I will use immediately.

WITH TABASCO SAUCE: Mix 2 teaspoons Tabasco with ⅓ cup mayonnaise. Serve with seafood sandwiches, fried fish, or cracked crab.

WITH HABANERO HOT SAUCE: Mix 1 teaspoon green habanero hot sauce (such as El Yucateco from Mexico) with ⅓ cup mayonnaise. Serve with crudités, particularly carrots, celery, jicama, and radishes.

WITH WASABI: Stir together 1 tablespoon wasabi powder and 2 teaspoons water. Let the paste sit for 20 minutes. Mix the paste with ⅓ cup mayonnaise, and serve with grilled seafood, especially tuna.

WITH DRIED TOMATOES: Mix 1 tablespoon pureed dried tomatoes with ⅓ cup mayonnaise. Serve with chicken sandwiches, eggplant sandwiches, or portobello sandwiches, with burgers, and with potato salads.

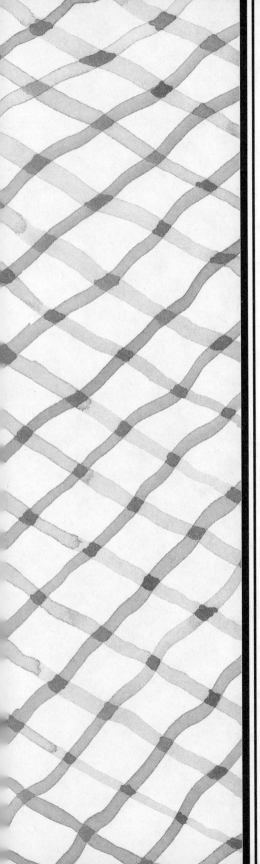

Chapter 6

EGG DISHES

EGG DISHES

FARMERS' MARKET BAKED EGGS

. . . .

I stumbled upon a version of this dish in the infinitely charming *Farmers Market Cook Book* by Neill and Fred Beck, published in 1951 with an introduction by M.F.K. Fisher. The irreverent treatise on the Los Angeles Farmers Market is full of a lot of good spirits and a few good recipes, like the one for baked eggs. This lusty dish really does demand the kind of fresh ingredients you find in a good farmers' market; in fact, I don't think you should bother with it when all you have are standard supermarket goods. Wait until you find real backyard eggs with their rich orange yolks, along with silky garden tomatoes and cream fresh from the farm—that's when this dish is sensational, worth every single forbidden bite of cholesterol, fat, and calories.

SERVES 4

4 slices of tomato

Kosher salt

Black pepper in a mill

4 eggs

½ teaspoon minced marjoram or oregano

¼ cup heavy cream

4 slices of bacon, fried until just crisp

Boiling water

Preheat the oven to 325°F. Butter the inside of 4 small (4-ounce) ramekins. Place a slice of tomato in the bottom of each ramekin and season it with salt and pepper. Break an egg into each ramekin and season the eggs with a pinch of marjoram or oregano and with salt and pepper. Spoon 1 tablespoon of cream over each egg, then crumble one slice of bacon on top.

Place the ramekins in a baking dish and carefully pour boiling water into the dish until it comes half-way up the sides of the ramekins. Bake until the whites are set, 15 to 20 minutes. Remove the dish from the oven, carefully remove the ramekins from the dish, and serve immediately, accompanied by plenty of good toasted bread.

SCRAMBLED EGGS WITH BRAINS

. . . .

In her essay "A Depression Christmas," writer Betty Fussell tells of growing up in Riverside, California, during the Depression. On Christmas Eve, her stepmother prepared this dish as part of the holiday celebration. "In our house," Betty writes, "this was not a sophisticated French dish cloaked with capers and *beurre noir*, but poverty food— cheap and, to most of my friends, disgusting. To me brains were lovely, not only for their creamy softness but because they redeemed the plain scrambled eggs that were our common everyday supper. Little did I dream that eggs fresh from the nest, annealed with nothing but sweet butter, would in my adult years be scarce as hen's teeth and precious as repentance." Brains, too, along with most other organ meats, have become nearly as scarce—and as forbidden by today's dietary admonitions—as fresh eggs themselves.

SERVES 4 TO 6

1 pound calf's brains
Boiling water
1 tablespoon vinegar or lemon juice
8 eggs
⅓ cup milk
Kosher salt
Black pepper to taste
3 tablespoons butter
2 to 3 tablespoons minced Italian
    parsley

Soak the brains in cold water for at least 1 hour. Remove as much of the membrane as you can without tearing the flesh. Place the brains in a saucepan, cover them with boiling water, add the vinegar or lemon juice, and simmer very gently for 15 minutes. Drain the brains, let them cool, and, if possible, remove more of the membrane. Delicately pull the brains apart into small pieces.

Break the eggs into a large bowl, add the milk, salt, and pepper, and beat together. Add the brains.

Melt the butter in a large cast-iron skillet over medium heat. Add the egg mixture, reduce the heat to low, and stir constantly with a spatula or spoon until the eggs form soft curds. Remove from the heat immediately, scatter parsley over the top, and serve.

BREAKFAST BURRITOS

I discovered chorizo when I was ten years old. Occasionally, my mother would indulge my curiosity and allow me to pick out unusual items at the market. When I was seven, I chose tins of smoked oysters; not long after that, smoked salmon piqued my interest. I would devote hours in the kitchen to my dazzling discoveries, arranging them on pretty plates or experimenting with crude recipes. I found chorizo particularly inspiring. I'd creep into the kitchen after my mother was asleep, fry the sausage slowly with onions, and spoon the mixture onto a rose-tinted plate. I'd pour a glass of milk and tiptoe into my bedroom, where I savored the spicy sausage slowly, by candlelight. One night I failed to see the phone cord stretched across the hallway, and down I went. The plate landed upside down and the greasy chorizo soaked into our new white rug, making a stain that was forever after a sponge for every speck of dust and dirt that came near it.

SERVES 4

8 ounces Mexican chorizo, skinned
    and broken into small pieces
1 small yellow onion, minced
4 garlic cloves, minced
4 large flour tortillas
6 eggs, lightly beaten
Kosher salt
Black pepper in a mill

3 tablespoons torn cilantro leaves
1 ripe avocado, pitted and sliced
   lengthwise
Salsa Mexicana (page 57) or Salsa
   Cruda (page 57)

Place the chorizo in a heavy skillet over medium heat. Sauté it, using a fork to break it up further, until it is crumbly and gives up most of its fat, 2 to 3 minutes. Using a slotted spoon, transfer the chorizo to a dish. Pour off and discard all but 2 tablespoons of the fat in the pan, return the pan to the heat, and add the onion. Sauté until the onion is limp and fragrant, about

10 minutes. Add the garlic, and sauté for 2 minutes more.

While the onion and garlic are cooking, heat the tortillas in a steamer or frying pan. When they are warm, wrap them in a tea towel or, if you have one, in a cloth-lined tortilla basket. Set them aside.

Season the eggs with salt and pepper, and pour them into the skillet with the onion and garlic. Cook the eggs, stirring and turning constantly with a fork, for 2 to 3 minutes, or until they are about half done. Add the chorizo, garlic, and onion, mix them in gently, and continue to cook until the eggs are set.

Remove from the heat, and, working

Okie Burritos

"Most of us who worked at the shed were Okies, though there was a sprinkling of Negroes and Mexicans and Filipinos. And most Okies at the shed were second-generation kids like me, whose parents had struggled into California from the Midwest or Southwest during dust bowl days.

"... We truckers ate our lunches on the wooden deck next to the ice house. The syrupy heat of the valley was somewhat less oppressive next to the ice.... Johnny Dominguez brought homemade burritos for lunch every single day. I'd never tasted one, and they looked so tempting that I asked him one day to trade me for my deviled-meat sandwich and he agreed. Inside the burrito were the beans I expected, but

different, all squashed with little hot peppers that tingled more than burned, and meat and cheese; it was the dangest thing I'd ever eaten. 'God, that's good,' I said.

"'Your sandwich would gag a maggot, hey,' Johnny answering, the other men chuckling. 'Who ever heard of ketchup and mustard on deviled meat?'

"'That's a okie burrito,' Wash countered, laughing at the sour-faced Johnny.

"'Gawwd damn. It's no wonder you Okies are so skinny, hey....'" Johnny shook his head in mock despair, but he kept eating.

Gerald Haslam, "Wild Goose: Memories of a Valley Summer," in *Okies: Selected Stories* (Peregrine Smith, 1975) quickly, fill the tortillas: Remove a tortilla from the towel or basket, set it on a work surface, spoon one fourth of the eggs and chorizo down the center, and top with cilantro, avocado, and salsa. Fold the bottom and top edges of the tortilla over the filling and then roll in the sides to form a cylinder. Set aside and keep warm until all of the burritos are made. Serve immediately, with additional salsa on the side.

HUEVOS RANCHEROS

The huevos rancheros tradition extends back to California's earliest days, when large rancheros served as rest stops for travelers. Today, you find a version on the menu of nearly every coffee shop and diner in the state. Often, the dish arrives as greasy fried eggs atop a mound of gummy canned refried beans smothered in tomato sauce, the whole affair slathered in cheese—a filling but not very satisfying dish. Other versions are beautifully done. Many do include beans, often black beans, but the original dish had no beans and I think it works best without them. Plump, tender pinto beans do make a good side dish, though, as does Spanish Rice (page 221) or fried potatoes. Cold beer, Agua Fresca (page 472), or iced hibiscus tea are the best warm-weather accompaniments. In winter months, use canned in-

stead of fresh tomatoes and serve Mexican Hot Chocolate (page 474) alongside.

SERVES 4

4 tablespoons olive oil
1 large yellow onion, sliced thin
2 poblano chiles, seeded and cut into thin julienne
2 serrano chiles, seeded and minced
6 garlic cloves, sliced thin
8 medium ripe tomatoes, peeled, seeded, and chopped fine
2 teaspoons minced oregano
Kosher salt
Black pepper in a mill
8 eggs
8 corn tortillas
¾ cup (3 ounces) grated cheddar or jack cheese
2 tablespoons minced cilantro leaves, optional

Make the sauce: Heat the olive oil in a very large skillet (see Note) over medium-low heat. Add the onion, and sauté it until it is limp, about 7 minutes. Add the chiles, and sauté them until they are tender, about 8 minutes. Add the garlic, and sauté for 2 minutes more. Add the tomatoes and oregano, reduce the heat to low, and simmer for 5 minutes. Season with salt and pepper.

Break the eggs into the sauce, taking care not to break the yolks. Spoon some sauce up and over the eggs, and cover the pan. Cook until the whites of the eggs are just set, about 5 minutes.

While the eggs cook, cook the tortillas on a hot griddle or over a gas flame until they are almost, but not quite, crisp. Place 2 tortillas side by side on each of 4 warmed serving plates.

When the eggs are done, use a large serving spoon and carefully transfer them on top of the tortillas; each plate gets 2 eggs. Spoon sauce over each portion, followed by cheese and cilantro. Serve immediately, accompanied by your favorite hot salsa.

NOTE: Instead of poaching the eggs in the sauce, you can fry the eggs separately or poach them separately. You may need to do this if your skillet is not large enough for the 8 eggs.

Señora Benicia Vallejo

....

On the northeastern edge of the San Francisco Bay, at the entrance of the water system that leads into the Delta, lie two cities, side by side—Benicia and Vallejo—named for General Mariano Vallejo and his wife, Benicia. In his 1914 book, *Bohemian San Francisco: The Elegant Art of Dining*, Clarence E. Edwords traced some of the earlier influences on the cooks of his day; one of the sources he turned to was a collection of recipes from Señora Vallejo, a prominent hostess and cook in the mid-nineteenth century. From her we have an early rendition of beef fajitas. Cut the steak into pieces, her recipe tells us, sprinkle the pieces with flour, and then beat the flour into the steak. Fry it in a pan with olive oil and, in a separate pan, fry three good-sized onions and three green peppers. Add the onions and peppers to the steak, cover with water, simmer a few minutes, and then serve on a hot platter. Señora Vallejo also prepared Spanish eggs of good reputation, Edwords told his readers. Empty a can of tomatoes in a frying pan, she said, and thicken them with bread. Add two or three small green peppers and an onion sliced fine. Add a little butter and salt to taste, let the mixture simmer gently for a while, and then carefully break on top the number of eggs desired. Spoon the simmering tomato mixture over the eggs until they are cooked.

CALIFORNIA EGGS BENEDICT

*E*ggs Benedict is an indulgence, full of wonderful things that we are encouraged to abandon, notably butter and eggs. You wouldn't want to eat this dish often, but an occasional indulgence is good for you. I developed this dish to celebrate the brief season when both asparagus and raspberries are at their peak. The raspberry hollandaise is a richer, denser sauce than a classic hollandaise, with the flavor and aroma of the berries quite pronounced.

SERVES 4 TO 8

16 plump asparagus spears
1 tablespoon olive oil
Kosher salt
Black pepper in a mill
3 egg yolks
2 tablespoons plus ½ teaspoon low-acid (4.5 percent) raspberry vinegar, preferably, or 1 tablespoon plus ¼ teaspoon medium- or high-acid raspberry vinegar
1 teaspoon fresh lemon juice
½ teaspoon kosher salt
Pinch of sugar
Pinch of white pepper
½ cup butter, bubbling hot
8 eggs
8 slices of country-style bread
8 thin slices of prosciutto
1 cup raspberries

Preheat the oven to 500°F. Snap off and discard the tough ends of the asparagus, and place the edible spears on a baking sheet. Drizzle them with the olive oil, and toss them to coat all of the spears. Season with salt and black pepper. Roast them until they are tender, 8 to 15 minutes, depending on the thickness of the spears.

Make the raspberry hollandaise: Place the egg yolks, 2 tablespoons vinegar, lemon juice, ½ teaspoon salt, sugar, and white pepper in a blender or a food processor fitted with a metal blade. Cover and run the machine at top speed for 5 seconds. With the machine still running, remove the lid and add the hot butter in a slow, steady stream. Leave the sauce in the container, and transfer the container to a pot or bowl of hot water.

Bring a medium saucepan of water to a boil. Add the remaining ½ teaspoon of vinegar to the boiling water and poach 2 of the eggs until the whites are set but the yolks still runny, 3 to 4 minutes. Remove the eggs with a slotted spoon and keep them warm. Continue, 2 eggs at a time, until all of the eggs have been poached.

Toast the bread, and place 1 (if you are serving 1 egg to each of 8 people) or 2 (if you are serving 2 eggs to each of 4 people) slices on individual serving plates. Place 2 spears of asparagus on each slice of toast, drape a slice of prosciutto over the asparagus, and place a poached egg on top. Spoon hollandaise over each egg. Divide the raspberries among the portions, scattering them over the top. Grind black pepper over each portion, and serve immediately.

GARLIC OMELET WITH CILANTRO SAUCE

· ·

We always look for the freshest tomatoes, asparagus, and lettuce, but we don't always search out fresh garlic. Garlic should be very firm to the touch and should not have green shoots poking out the top of the bulb. This omelet is particularly good when there's a new crop of garlic, or when you can get one of the less common varieties, such as Creole Red or Spanish Roja.

SERVES 2

4 teaspoons olive oil
8 garlic cloves, minced
6 eggs
2 tablespoons minced chives
Kosher salt
Black pepper in a mill
4 ounces creamy aged chèvre, such
    as taupinière, sliced, preferably, or
    4 ounces other good melting
    cheese, grated or sliced
½ cup Cilantro Sauce (page 285)

Heat 2 teaspoons of the olive oil in an omelet pan over medium heat. Add half of the garlic, and sauté for 2 minutes. Quickly break 3 eggs into a small bowl, add half of the chives, season with salt and pepper, and beat quickly with a fork. Increase the heat to medium-high, and pour the eggs into the omelet pan, swirling the pan to dis-

tribute the eggs evenly and to combine the eggs and garlic. Using a fork, move the cooked egg toward the center of the pan and let the uncooked egg flow out toward the edges. When the eggs are almost set, scatter half of the cheese over them, fold the omelet in half, cook for 30 seconds more, then transfer it to a warmed serving plate. Make the second omelet in the same manner. Spoon a little sauce over each omelet, and serve immediately, with the remaining sauce on the side.

OMELET WITH BACON AND APRICOT PRESERVES

· ·

I find the combination of sweet apricots, creamy eggs, and crunchy, salty bacon in this dish thoroughly appealing—especially on a summer evening during the apricot season, when I serve the omelet with grilled apricots on the side for a casual light supper.

SERVES 2

6 slices of bacon or pancetta
4 teaspoons unsalted butter
6 eggs
Kosher salt
Black pepper in a mill
¼ cup apricot preserves or apricot
    jam

In a heavy skillet over medium heat, fry the bacon or pancetta until it is just crisp. Transfer it to absorbent paper. Crumble 2 slices of the bacon into a small bowl; leave the remaining bacon whole.

Heat 2 teaspoons of the butter in an omelet pan over medium heat. Quickly break 3 eggs into a small bowl, season with salt and pepper, and beat quickly with a fork. When the butter is foamy, pour the eggs into the pan, swirling the pan to distribute the eggs evenly. Using a fork, move the cooked egg toward the center of the pan and let the uncooked egg flow out toward the edges. When the eggs are almost set, place about 1½ tablespoons of the apricot preserves or jam over half of the omelet, and top with 2 slices of bacon, breaking them in half if necessary. Fold the omelet in half, cook for 30 seconds more, then transfer it to a warmed serving plate. Make the second omelet in the same manner. Top each omelet with a teaspoon of the remaining preserves or jam, scatter the crumbled bacon over the top, and serve immediately.

LA HABRA HEIGHTS AVOCADO OMELET

rowing up in California, it is easy to take so many things from the earth for granted, such as the Hass avocados that lend their velvety texture to this simple omelet. Do not substitute another variety of avocado. Fuerte avocados, for example, are too watery and can be too stringy, and they lack the intensity of flavor that makes this omelet so inviting. I've named this recipe after the town in which the original Hass avocado tree still stands (see page 64).

SERVES 2

4 teaspoons unsalted butter
6 eggs
Kosher salt
Black pepper in a mill
½ cup (2 ounces) grated cheese, such
    as Monterey jack, Italian fontina,
    or St. George
1 ripe Hass avocado, pitted and sliced
¾ cup Salsa Cruda (page 57) or
    Avocado Salsa (page 64)

Heat 2 teaspoons of the butter in an omelet pan over medium heat. Quickly break 3 eggs into a small bowl, season with salt and pepper, and beat quickly with a fork. When the butter is foamy, pour the eggs into the pan, swirling the pan to distribute the eggs evenly. Using a fork, move the cooked egg toward the center of the pan and let the uncooked egg flow out toward the edges. When the eggs are almost set, scatter half of the cheese over them, then arrange half of the avocado slices in a single layer over half of the omelet. Fold the omelet in half, cook for 30 seconds more, then transfer it to a warmed serving plate. Make the second omelet in the same manner. Spoon a little of the salsa over each omelet, and serve immediately, with the remaining salsa on the side.

The First Egg

"The day the Farmers Market opened none of the farmers or merchants knew for sure that anybody would come and buy anything.

"The boys made up a little pool—25 cents each. And whoever made the first sale would win the pool.

"The market opened at 9 A.M., July 14, 1934. The first sale was made at 9:03—and it was an egg.

"Eggs have played a big part in the Farmers Market's history, just as eggs play an important role in cooking.

"Du-Par's Farmhouse Restaurant in the Farmers Market is famous for scrambled eggs. Jim Dunn and Ed Parsons know how.

"We do not offer a recipe for scrambled eggs because by now you, dear reader, know how to scramble eggs or else you will never learn."

Neill and Fred Beck, *Farmers Market Cook Book* (Holt and Company, 1951)

MONTEREY JACK SOUFFLÉ

*S*oufflés are easier to make than rumor has it. And all soufflés fall— they are *supposed* to do so. If fear of falling has been holding you back, give this soufflé, which features Monterey jack, California's signature cheese, a try.

SERVES 4

4 tablespoons unsalted butter
2 tablespoons finely grated Parmigiano-Reggiano or dry jack
2 tablespoons all-purpose flour
¾ cup milk, hot
5 eggs, separated
2 cups (8 ounces) coarsely grated Monterey jack mixed with 2 tablespoons grated Parmigiano-Reggiano
1 teaspoon kosher salt
¾ teaspoon white pepper, preferably fresh-ground
⅛ teaspoon cayenne

Preheat the oven to 350°F. Coat the inside of a 2-quart soufflé dish with 2 tablespoons of the butter. Add the finely grated cheese and shake the dish to distribute the cheese evenly over the sides and bottom.

Melt the remaining 2 tablespoons of butter in the top of a double boiler set over simmering water. Add the flour, and stir until smooth. Slowly pour in the hot milk, whisking constantly. Cook, continuing to whisk, about 4 minutes, until the mixture thickens. Remove the top of the double boiler from the heat (leaving the bottom over the heat), and let the mixture cool for 5 minutes. Add to the flour mixture the egg yolks, one at a time, alternating with ¼ cups of the coarsely grated cheese, until all of the cheese and all of the yolks have been incorporated. Place the top of the double boiler back over the bottom, and stir constantly with a wooden spoon until the cheese is completely melted. Stir in the salt, white pepper, and cayenne. Remove from the heat and set aside. Beat the egg whites until they form stiff but not dry peaks. Fold the egg whites, in 2 batches, into the yolk-cheese mixture. Pour into the soufflé dish, and bake until the soufflé is golden on top, 35 to 40 minutes. Serve immediately.

ROASTED GARLIC SOUFFLÉ

Italian fontina is a rich, buttery cheese ideally suited to the nutty flavor of roasted garlic. If it is not available, use emmenthal or another good swiss cheese, or use a combination of emmenthal and Monterey jack.

SERVES 6

BOUQUET GARNI
Sprig of thyme
2 sprigs of Italian parsley
1 bay leaf
1 teaspoon black peppercorns
1 small onion, cut into quarters

1½ cups half-and-half
1¼ cups heavy cream
2 tablespoons finely grated dry jack
½ cup Roasted Garlic Puree (page 45)
5 eggs, separated
1 cup (4 ounces) grated Italian fontina
1 cup (4 ounces) grated dry jack
Kosher salt
Black pepper in a mill
¼ teaspoon cayenne

Make the bouquet garni: Place all of the ingredients on a piece of cheesecloth, pull up the sides of the cloth, and tie the top with string.

Combine the half-and-half and cream in a heavy saucepan, and add the bouquet garni. Bring to a boil, reduce the heat, and simmer gently for 20 to 30 minutes, to reduce the liquid by one third. Remove from the heat and let cool slightly. Remove and discard the bouquet garni.

Preheat the oven to 400°F. Butter a 2-quart soufflé dish and dust it with the 2 tablespoons finely grated dry jack.

Stir the garlic puree into the cream mixture. Beat the egg yolks lightly, and add them to the saucepan. Stir in the 1 cup fontina and 1 cup jack, and season with salt, pepper, and half of the cayenne.

Beat the egg whites until they form stiff but not dry peaks. Fold the egg whites, in 2 batches, into the yolk-cheese mixture. Pour into the soufflé dish, and sprinkle the top with the remaining cayenne. Bake for 10 minutes, reduce the heat to 350°F, and bake for 20 minutes more, until the soufflé is puffy and the top golden brown. Remove from the oven, and serve immediately.

ONION PIE WITH PANCETTA

his contemporary version of onion pie is excellent, but if there's no crème fraîche, no chèvre, and no pancetta, you can still enjoy its sweet and savory flavors by using a cup of sour cream, no cheese, and bacon. Served with a wedge of cheddar alongside, and with a big green salad, it's a perfect dinner for a stormy night.

SERVES 4 TO 6

1 recipe Pastry for Savory Tarts (page 396)

2 tablespoons unsalted butter

2½ pounds red onions or sweet onions, sliced very thin

1 teaspoon minced rosemary

3 eggs, beaten

¾ cup crème fraîche (or substitute; see Note, page 37) or sour cream

1 cup (4 ounces) young (not aged) chèvre, crumbled, or aged chèvre, grated

1 teaspoon kosher salt

Black pepper in a mill

4 ounces pancetta or bacon, fried until just crisp, crumbled

4 to 6 small sprigs of rosemary, for garnish

Line a 9-inch tart pan with the shell, prick the shell with a fork, and refrigerate it.

In a heavy sauté pan over low heat, melt the butter until it is foamy. Add the onions, and sauté them until they are very soft and fragrant, about 15 minutes. Add the rosemary, remove from the heat, and let cool.

Preheat the oven to 450°F.

In a medium bowl, mix together the eggs, crème fraîche or sour cream, and chèvre. Add the salt and pepper.

Spread the onions over the bottom of the shell. Pour the egg-cheese mixture over, and scatter the pancetta or bacon on top. Bake for 10 minutes, reduce the heat to 300°F, and bake for 30 minutes more, or until the top is slightly browned. Remove the pie from the oven, and let it rest for 10 minutes. Cut the pie into wedges, and garnish each slice with a small sprig of rosemary.

Chapter 7

PASTA, RICE, AND BEANS

PASTA, RICE, AND BEANS

FRESH PASTA

*B*y the late 1970s in California, it seemed everyone had a pasta machine, and people took to boasting that they never used dried pasta. Retail stores specializing in fresh pasta proliferated, and several new California companies began producing packaged fresh-dried pasta. There are times when fresh pasta is not suitable—classic spaghetti carbonara, for example, is best made with dried pasta. But it is ideal in certain dishes, particularly when the pasta is dressed with a light sauce that will accent rather than overwhelm its delicate structure. It is also easy to work additional ingredients into fresh pasta, such as spices, herbs, and purees that contribute both color and flavor to the noodles; see the Variations for some examples. Simple fresh pasta tossed with a little unsalted butter or flavored butter (see page 415) and grated dry jack cheese is an excellent side dish or light main course.

MAKES 1 POUND

1⅓ cups semolina flour
⅔ cup unbleached all-purpose flour
½ teaspoon kosher salt
2 eggs, at room temperature

Combine the semolina flour, all-purpose flour, and salt in the container of a food processor. Add 1 egg, and pulse until the egg is evenly distributed. Using a rubber spatula, scrape the sides of the container. Add the remaining egg and 1½ tablespoons water, and pulse until the dough comes together. Turn it out onto a floured surface and knead it until it is smooth and elastic, about 10 minutes. Shape the dough into a ball, cover it with a tea towel, and let it rest for 1 to 2 hours, during which time the dough will soften considerably.

To roll out the dough, cut it into 4 or 5 pieces. Use your hands to shape 1 piece into a thick rectangle. With the rollers of the pasta machine set as far apart as possible, roll the rectangle of dough through the machine. Fold the dough in thirds as you would fold a letter; repeat the process of rolling and folding on the widest setting 4 to 6 times, until the dough becomes very smooth and very elastic. If the dough gets too sticky, dust it with a little flour. Advance the setting to the next narrowest width, roll the dough through 1 time, and continue through setting #4. Repeat the process with each rectangle of dough.

Finally, roll each piece through the narrowest 2 settings. After the last pass through the machine, cut each sheet in half (the sheets should be about 12 to 14 inches long) and hang the dough on a pasta rack or over the back of a chair. Let the sheets rest for 10 minutes, until the dough is dry to the touch but still pliant, before cutting them (see "To Cut Fresh Pasta").

NOTE: To make 1½ pounds of pasta, to serve 6 to 8 as a main course, use 2 cups semolina flour, 1 cup unbleached all-purpose flour, ¾ teaspoon kosher salt, 3 eggs, and 3 tablespoons water.

To Cut Fresh Pasta

After pasta dough has been stretched and allowed to dry briefly, it must be cut immediately, before all of its moisture evaporates. Most pasta machines come with at least one attachment for cutting noodles, and it is simple to crank a sheet of pasta through the blade. Common blades include fettucine (¼ inch wide), linguine (⅛ inch wide), and spaghetti.

To cut pasta by hand: Set a pasta sheet on a lightly floured work surface and roll it into a cylinder. Using a sharp knife, make crosswise cuts of the appropriate width. Pappardelle, for example, are 1¼ inches wide; tagliatelle are ½ inch wide. Pasta for lasagne should be cut to fit the length of the pan. Fresh pasta can also be cut into ½-inch squares, called quadrucci, and used in soups.

Let cut fresh pasta dry for 15 minutes before cooking it. To store fresh pasta, wrap it, airtight, in plastic wrap, and refrigerate it; use within 2 or 3 days.

Variations:

FOR BLACK PEPPER PASTA: Add 1 or 2 teaspoons fresh-ground black pepper to the flour mixture.

FOR GARLIC PASTA: Replace the water with 2 tablespoons fresh garlic puree or Roasted Garlic Puree (page 45).

FOR BEET PASTA: Replace the water with ¼ cup pureed cooked red beets.

FOR PUMPKIN-ROSEMARY PASTA: Omit the water. Add ⅓ cup pumpkin puree and 1 teaspoon minced rosemary to the flour mixture with the second egg.

FOR CARROT-CUMIN PASTA: Omit the water. Add ⅓ cup pureed cooked carrots and ½ teaspoon ground cumin to the flour mixture with the second egg.

FOR OLIVE-BASIL PASTA: Replace the water with 2 tablespoons pureed kalamata olives, and add 2 tablespoons minced basil.

PAPPARDELLE WITH WALNUTS AND DRY JACK

Pappardelle are noodles cut 1¼ inches wide. Although they are available in stores as dried pasta, they are one of the simplest fresh pastas to make because it is easy to cut them by hand, without a pasta machine. Do try to find fresh walnuts for this dish. In California, walnuts are harvested in the fall and appear at farmers' markets for a few weeks beginning in October. For a more substantial fall dish, add sliced sautéed pears and thin slices of prosciutto.

SERVES 4

1 pound fresh pappardelle
(page 203) or ½ pound dried
pappardelle or lasagne

⅓ cup extra virgin olive oil or ¼ cup
  butter, melted
Fresh-grated nutmeg
¾ cup walnuts, toasted and coarsely
  chopped
1 tablespoon minced Italian parsley
Kosher salt
Black pepper in a mill
3 ounces dry jack, in 1 piece
Sprigs of Italian parsley, for garnish

Bring a large pot of salted water to a
boil. Cook the pasta until it is al dente,
about 2 minutes for fresh pasta, 8 to 10
minutes for dried. Drain the pasta, rinse it
quickly in warm water, and drain it again.
Place the pasta in a large bowl, drizzle the
olive oil over it, and add several gratings
of fresh nutmeg. Add the walnuts and
parsley, and toss gently but thoroughly.
Season with salt and pepper, and divide
the pasta among serving plates. Using a
vegetable peeler, make curls of cheese
and scatter several over each portion. Top
each portion with a scant grating of nutmeg and a sprig of parsley, and serve
immediately.

CHESTER'S GARLIC PASTA

· ·

*M*y friend Chester Aaron grows
dozens of varieties of garlic
at his garden in the town of
Occidental, near the coast in Sonoma
County. This recipe is my version of one
that appears in Chester's book *Garlic Is Life*
(Ten Speed Press, 1996).

SERVES 6 TO 8

½ cup plus 1 tablespoon extra virgin
  olive oil
2 cups basil leaves, shredded
15 Roma tomatoes, quartered
  lengthwise
8 Purple Tip or other fresh garlic
  cloves, minced
1 teaspoon kosher salt
Black pepper in a mill
1 pound dried spaghettini or linguine
Hard cheese for grating, such as dry
  jack, tome, asiago, or Parmigiano-
  Reggiano

Pour the ½ cup of olive oil into a large
bowl, and add the basil, tomatoes, garlic,
salt, and several turns of pepper. Let the
mixture sit, stirring it now and then, at
room temperature for 2 to 3 hours.
  Bring a large pot of salted water to a
boil. Cook the pasta until it is al dente.
While the pasta cooks, place the basil mixture in a large saucepan over very low heat,
and warm through.

Drain the pasta, place it in a large serving bowl, and toss with the remaining 1 tablespoon of olive oil. Add the basil mixture, and toss lightly. Serve immediately, garnished with grated cheese.

SPAGHETTINI AL PESTO

*T*am indebted to my California friend and colleague, Viana La Place, for reviving for me the pleasures of pesto. In the 1980s, pesto suddenly was everywhere—and that includes some dishes where it didn't belong. Many versions were overprocessed to the point that the flavors and textures of the ingredients were lost. Then Viana published her delightful book, *The Unplugged Kitchen*, and I noticed her recipe for pesto made with a mortar and pestle (see Note

Absinthe and Pasta

"In North Beach harmless Anarchists sit and drink their forbidden absinthe, and dream their dreams of fire and sword, while they talk in whispers of what they are going to do to the crowned heads of Europe. [Nearby] in a shop on Grant Street you now find yourself surrounded with sausages, from floor to ceiling, from side wall to side wall, and such sausage it is! Strings so thin as to appear about the size of a lady's little finger to individual sausages as large as the thigh of a giant, they hang in festoons, crawl over beams, lie among shelves, decorate counters . . . and invite you to taste them in the slices that lay on the butcher's block. One can well imagine being in a cave of flesh.... [H]ere too are cheeses in wonderful variety . . . from goats' milk, asses' milk,

cows' milk and mares' milk, and also cheeses from Spain, Mexico, Germany, Switzerland, and all the other countries where they make cheese, even including the U.S.... [N]earby is a window full of bread, from long sticks of grissini to great solid loaves; across the street is the Costa Brothers, a big grocery store with canned goods and boxes with peculiar foods you are unaccustomed to. Shelves are filled with wine. Not far away, a pasta factory. You will see raviolis made by the hundreds; tagliarini, tortellini, macaroni, spaghetti, capellini, perciateli, tagliatelli...."

Clarence E. Edwords, *Bohemian San Francisco: The Elegant Art of Dining* (Paul Eder and Company, 1914) below), not in a food processor. I didn't think I'd paid much attention, but as spring evolved into summer I was captured one morning by the aroma of fresh basil. I wanted pesto again, at last. You may never put another leaf of basil into your food processor once you've made your own handmade pesto.

SERVES 4 TO 6

2 cups loosely packed basil leaves, preferably small leaves

6 garlic cloves, crushed

1 teaspoon kosher salt

¼ cup loosely packed Italian parsley, leaves only

½ cup (2 ounces) grated Parmigiano-Reggiano

¼ cup (1 ounce) grated aged asiago

½ cup best-quality extra virgin olive oil

1 pound dried spaghettini or dried linguine

1 piece (3 to 4 ounces) Parmigiano-Reggiano or aged asiago

Do not wash the basil leaves; using a damp tea towel or paper towel, brush off any dust or dirt. Remove any stems or tough central veins.

Place the garlic and salt in a mortar, and begin to grind with the pestle in a circular motion, pounding gently now and then to break up the garlic. When the garlic has been reduced nearly to a paste, add a few basil leaves and parsley leaves, and grind in a circular motion until the leaves are completely broken up. Continue

until all of the basil and parsley has been incorporated.

Add the two grated cheeses, mixing them in thoroughly. If necessary, use a rubber spatula to scrape the pesto from the sides of the mortar. Slowly drizzle in the olive oil, mixing constantly to incorporate it into the pesto. Add salt to taste. Cover the mortar with a plate.

Bring a large pot of salted water to a boil. Cook the pasta until it is al dente. Before draining the pasta, take 2 tablespoons of the cooking water and stir it into the pesto. Drain the pasta, and transfer it to a large serving bowl. Spoon half of the pesto over it, and toss lightly. Serve the pasta, and pass the remaining pesto in the mortar. Pass the cheese, too, with a grater.

NOTE: Use a large marble mortar, or a ceramic mortar with a scored interior that facilitates grinding. You'll get better texture with a wooden pestle than with a marble one.

SPAGHETTI WITH TAPENADE, BASIL, AND TOMATOES

Today there are many brands of tapenade available at groceries and specialty food stores, but the best is still homemade. If you do not have the time to make it but have some store-bought tapenade in the pantry, this recipe offers an excellent way to make good use of its flavors.

SERVES 4 TO 6

1 pound dried spaghetti or linguine
1 cup Olive Tapenade (page 422)
1 cup packed basil leaves
3 tablespoons extra virgin olive oil, or
    more
1 pint ripe cherry tomatoes, cut in half
Basil leaves, for garnish

Bring a large pot of salted water to a boil. Cook the pasta until it is al dente.

While the pasta cooks, make a tapenade sauce: Place half of the tapenade, the 1 cup of basil leaves, and the 3 tablespoons of olive oil in a food processor fitted with a metal blade. Pulse several times until the mixture forms a coarse puree. Transfer the mixture to a small bowl, and stir in the remaining half of the tapenade. Toss together, adding a little more olive oil if necessary to achieve the consistency of a sauce. Transfer the tapenade sauce to a large serving bowl.

When the pasta is done, drain it and add it to the serving bowl. Toss it with the tapenade sauce until the noodles are thoroughly coated. Add the cherry tomatoes and toss again. Divide the pasta among individual plates, garnish each portion with basil leaves, and serve immediately.

LINGUINE WITH CHÈVRE, HERBS, AND TOMATOES

This simple pasta is quick to make and offers a hearty but not heavy meal, ideal when a summer nights turn cool, as they often do throughout much of California.

SERVES 4

¾ pound dried linguine
4 tablespoons extra virgin olive oil
3 garlic cloves
3 cups cherry tomatoes, cut in half, or
    4 medium slicing tomatoes, cut
    into wedges
½ cup chicken stock, preferably
    homemade (see Appendix 1)
½ cup minced herbs, such as basil,
    thyme, oregano, Italian parsley,
    summer savory, or a combination
4 ounces young (not aged) chèvre,
    crumbled
Kosher salt
Black pepper in a mill

Bring a large pot of salted water to a boil. Cook the linguine until it is al dente.

While the linguine cooks, make the sauce: Heat 2 tablespoons of the olive oil in a heavy skillet over medium heat. Add the garlic, and sauté it until it just begins to color. Remove the garlic and discard it. Add the tomatoes, and sauté them for 4 minutes, shaking the pan several times so that they cook evenly. (If you are using slicing tomatoes, turn the wedges once.) Transfer the tomatoes to a serving bowl. Add the stock to the skillet, increase the heat to high, swirl the skillet to loosen any pan juices, and reduce the liquid by one third.

Drain the pasta and put it in the bowl on top of the tomatoes. Scatter the chèvre and the herbs over the pasta, and pour the sauce over all. Add the remaining 2 tablespoons of olive oil, toss gently, season with salt and pepper, and serve immediately. If you like, serve with some additional olive oil at the table for those who want it.

PASTA WITH BLACKEYE PEAS

California produces two peas—about ninety percent of the black-eyes grown in this country, and all of the chickpeas. Nearly all the blackeyes are grown in the San Joaquin Valley; chickpeas and a variety of other beans such as limas are grown in eastern Contra Costa County. Beans and peas have long been the domain of major producers farming with highly mechanized techniques and the full menu of chemicals on which agribusiness has relied since the 1940s. Recently, small-scale growers have begun cultivating beans and peas and it is becoming easier to find ones that have been grown without chemical pesticides,

herbicides, or fertilizers. This dish is adapted from an old California recipe.

SERVES 4 TO 6

8 ounces dried small pasta, such as
   tripolini or small shells
¼ cup olive oil
1 yellow onion, diced
3 celery ribs, sliced thin
1 tablespoon minced garlic
1 bunch (about ¾ pound) Swiss
   chard, trimmed of stems and tough
   ribs, and cut into thin strips
1 tablespoon red wine vinegar
1 teaspoon minced lemon zest
1½ cups cooked or canned blackeye
   peas
Kosher salt
Black pepper in a mill
3 tablespoons extra virgin olive oil

Bring a large pot of salted water to a boil. Cook the pasta until it is al dente.

While the pasta cooks, heat the ¼ cup olive oil in a large sauté pan over medium heat. Add the onion, and sauté for 8 minutes. Add the celery, and sauté until the onion and celery are limp and fragrant, about 8 minutes more. Add the garlic, and sauté for 2 minutes more. Add the Swiss chard and the vinegar, cover the pan, and cook until the chard is limp, 2 to 3 minutes. Add the lemon zest and peas, and toss together.

Drain the pasta, rinse it quickly, and and drain it thoroughly again. Transfer it to a large serving bowl. Add the vegetable mixture to the pasta, season with salt and pepper, toss well, and divide among individual plates. Drizzle extra virgin olive oil over each portion, and serve immediately.

BUSTELO'S PASTA AL ZINFANDEL

*L*arry and Susan Watson, whose company is called Bustelo's Backyard, gave me this recipe, which features one of their infamously hot chile-pepper sauces. In their rendering, you start with two bottles of zinfandel, using ¾ cup for the pasta sauce and saving the rest to drink with dinner.

SERVES 6

1 pound dried spaghetti or linguine
2 tablespoons olive oil
1 pound portobello mushrooms, sliced
10 large garlic cloves, chopped
¾ cup California zinfandel
1 tablespoon Bustelo's Very Hot
    Pepper Sauce (or other hot pepper
    sauce), or more to taste
2 cups tomato sauce
Kosher salt
Black pepper in a mill
2 cups (8 ounces) grated dry jack or
    Parmigiano–Reggiano

Bring a large pot of salted water to a boil. Cook the pasta until it is al dente. Drain the pasta and transfer it to a large serving bowl.

While the pasta cooks, begin making the sauce: Heat the olive oil in a large heavy skillet over medium heat. Add the mushrooms and garlic, and sauté until the mushrooms begin to release their moisture and become limp, about 10 minutes. Add the wine and hot sauce, reduce the heat to low, and simmer, uncovered, for 10 minutes. Add the tomato sauce to the mushroom mixture, and simmer for 5 minutes more. Taste the sauce, and season with salt, pepper, and more hot sauce to taste.

Pour the sauce over the pasta, and toss thoroughly. Scatter some of the cheese over the pasta, and serve immediately, with the remaining cheese on the side.

LINGUINE WITH DUNGENESS CRAB

*D*ungeness crab comes into season in the late fall, and in a good year it is both cheap and plentiful by December. Then, after eating my fill of it simply cooked, chilled, and cracked, I use it in a few recipes that highlight its pristine taste, such as this tangy, spicy pasta.

SERVES 4

1 pound dried linguine
½ cup unsalted butter
2 tablespoons minced garlic
1 tablespoon Tabasco sauce
1 teaspoon kosher salt

Black pepper in a mill
1½ pounds Dungeness crabmeat,
  cooked, legs separate
2 tablespoons minced Italian parsley
Lemon wedges

Bring a large pot of salted water to a boil. Cook the linguine until it is al dente. Drain the linguine, and transfer it to a large bowl.

While the linguine cooks, melt the butter in a small saucepan over medium heat. Add the garlic and Tabasco. Simmer for 2 minutes, remove from the heat, and season with salt and pepper.

When the pasta is done, pour half of the garlic butter over the pasta. Add half of the crabmeat, excluding the legs, and all of the parsley, and toss gently but thoroughly. Divide the pasta among individual plates. Divide the remaining crabmeat, including the legs, among the servings. Drizzle with some of the remaining garlic butter, garnish with lemon wedges, and serve immediately.

LINGUINE WITH ARTICHOKES AND CLAMS

Small artichokes are often referred to as baby artichokes, a misnomer. The size of an artichoke indicates not its age but where it grows on the plant. Large ones grow on the central stalk, small ones on side branches. There's an earthiness to both artichokes and clams that is highlighted when the two are joined together, as they are in this simple dish.

SERVES 4 TO 6

1 pound very small artichokes,
  trimmed of tough outer leaves and
  cut in half
¼ cup unsalted butter
2 shallots, minced
8 garlic cloves, minced
¾ teaspoon crushed red pepper
1 cup dry white wine
Juice of 1 lemon
3 pounds cherrystone, manila, or
  littleneck clams, scrubbed
1 pound dried linguine
Black pepper in a mill
1 lemon, cut into wedges

Place the artichokes in a medium pot, add enough water to cover them, and bring the water to a boil over high heat. Reduce the heat, and simmer, uncovered, until the artichokes are barely tender, about 12

Norma Jean, Artichoke Queen

California is one of the world's lead-ing growers of artichokes. They were introduced into the state by Italian immigrants in the early nineteenth cen-tury, but it wasn't until the end of the century that the succulent thistle be-came an agricultural crop, initially in the area of Half Moon Bay, south of San Francisco. Today, production ex-tends from Monterey south along the coast to Santa Barbara County. The ma-jority of artichokes are grown on the Monterey Peninsula, where the town of Castroville has long proclaimed itself the Artichoke Capital of the World. There's a restaurant shaped like a giant artichoke, and scores of roadside stands sell artichokes. Castroville's most poignant claim to fame is perhaps its 1947 Artichoke Queen, Marilyn Mon-roe, then a struggling young starlet on a publicity tour. According to California writer Patricia Rain, some of today's old-timers, then young men, fondly re-member the kiss she bestowed upon each of them. And, according to the story, she did, in fact, like artichokes.

stirring frequently, until they are soft and fragrant, about 7 minutes. Do not let them brown. Add the red pepper and wine, increase the heat, and reduce the liquid by half. Add the artichokes, lemon juice, and clams, and simmer, covered, until all or nearly all of the clams just open, 3 to 5 minutes; use a slotted spoon to remove and discard any clams that do not open. Re-move from the heat and keep warm.

Meanwhile, cook the linguine: Bring a large pot of salted water to a boil. Cook the linguine until it is al dente. Drain it, rinse it, drain it again, and transfer it to a large shallow serving bowl.

Place the opened clams and the arti-chokes over the top of the pasta, then pour the cooking liquid over all. Season with pepper, garnish with lemon wedges, and serve immediately.

CHICKEN PASTA WITH ROSEMARY

When I have no particular recipe in mind, I mince a little rosemary and garlic, mix in some lemon juice, and start looking for something to marinate or season with the mixture. The trio of flavors has boundless uses. I served this combination—with lamb, not chicken—at my first dinner party and have never tired of the way the flavors play off each other and enhance whatever they touch.

minutes. Drain the artichokes, rinse them, and set them aside.

Melt the butter in a large pot over medium heat. When the butter is foamy, add the shallots and garlic, and sauté,

4 boneless and skinless chicken
  breasts
⅔ cup Rosemary-Lemon Marinade
  (recipe follows)

ROSEMARY BUTTER
½ cup butter, at room temperature
1 tablespoon minced rosemary
1 garlic clove
1 teaspoon lemon zest

1 pound fresh garlic pasta, cut into
  linguine or fettuccine (page 203),
  or ¾ pound dried linguine or
  fettucine
Lemon wedges and sprigs of
  rosemary, for garnish

Cut the chicken into 1-inch strips, place them in a nonreactive bowl, and cover them with the marinade. Marinate the chicken, refrigerated, for 1 to 2 hours. Remove the chicken from the refrigerator 15 minutes before cooking.

Make the rosemary butter: Place the butter, minced rosemary, garlic, and lemon zest in a food processor, and pulse until they are well blended. Or put the ingredients in a small bowl and mix them together with a fork.

Bring a large pot of salted water to a boil. Heat a medium sauté pan or a wok over medium-high heat. Add the chicken and marinade, and sauté until the chicken is just done, 4 to 5 minutes. Before the chicken is done, add the pasta to the boiling water, stir, and cook for 2 to 3 min-

utes, until it is al dente. Drain the pasta, and place it in a large bowl. Toss it with the rosemary butter, and transfer it to a serving platter. Using a slotted spoon, place the chicken on top of the pasta. Garnish with lemon wedges and rosemary sprigs, and serve immediately.

Rosemary-Lemon Marinade

2 garlic cloves, minced
¼ cup fresh lemon juice
1 tablespoon chopped rosemary
¼ teaspoon thyme leaves
¼ teaspoon kosher salt
½ teaspoon fresh-ground black
  pepper
⅓ cup extra virgin olive oil

In a small bowl, mix together all of the ingredients except the olive oil. Slowly whisk in the olive oil.

PASTA WITH CHICKEN, OLIVES, AND DRIED TOMATO CREAM SAUCE

•••••••••••••••••••••••••••••

ried tomato puree is sometimes available in supermarkets or specialty food stores. It comes in small jars or tubes; most brands are very good. If you have some, you can use it instead of pureeing the tomatoes yourself. If you make fresh pasta for this dish, tomato-flavored or olive-and-basil-flavored noodles will work nicely.

SERVES 4

DRIED TOMATO CREAM SAUCE
1½ cups heavy cream
1 sprig of thyme
1 cup chicken stock
12 pieces dried tomatoes packed in oil, pureed, or 3 tablespoons store-bought dried tomato puree
¾ teaspoon thyme leaves
Kosher salt
Black pepper in a mill

1 pound fresh fettucine or ¾ pound dried fettucine
½ cup pitted olives, such as kalamata, niçoise, or California black, sliced
¾ pound cooked chicken meat, cut into strips, warm

4 sprigs of thyme
8 pieces dried tomatoes packed in oil, cut into julienne

Make the dried tomato cream sauce: In a heavy saucepan over medium heat, bring the cream and thyme sprig to a boil. Reduce the heat to low, and simmer gently until the cream is reduced by one third, about 10 minutes. Remove and discard the thyme, add the stock, and simmer for 5 minutes more. Stir in the pureed dried tomatoes and the thyme leaves, season with salt and pepper, and keep the sauce warm until ready to use.

Bring a large pot of salted water to a boil. Cook the fettucine until it is al dente. Drain the pasta, and transfer it to a large bowl. Add the sauce, and toss well to coat. Add the olives and chicken, toss again, and transfer to a serving platter or individual plates. Garnish with the thyme sprigs and the julienned dried tomatoes, and serve immediately.

BACON, CHÈVRE, AND DRIED TOMATO PASTA

•••••••••••••••••••••••••••••

ried tomatoes are best in dishes where they are highlighted for their own flavor. When they are combined with other intense flavors, they frequently clash with the others. They are ideal when fresh tomatoes are not in season.

¼ pound bacon or pancetta

6 garlic cloves, slivered

3 cups (from about 1 bunch) arugula leaves, cut into strips

¼ cup minced dried tomatoes packed in oil

1 pound fresh linguine or tagliarini or ¾ pound dried spaghettini

5 ounces young (not aged) chèvre, crumbled

Kosher salt

Black pepper in a mill

8 pieces dried tomatoes packed in oil, cut lengthwise into strips

In a skillet over medium heat, fry the bacon until it is just crisp. Transfer it to absorbent paper. Remove the skillet from the heat, and let the bacon drippings cool slightly, 3 to 4 minutes. Return the skillet to the heat, add the garlic, and sauté it in the drippings until it is golden. Add the arugula, toss quickly, cover the pan, and let the arugula wilt, about 2 minutes. Add the minced dried tomatoes, stir, and keep the sauce warm until ready to use. Chop or crumble the bacon, and set it aside.

Bring a large pot of salted water to a boil. Cook the pasta until it is just al dente, 2 to 3 minutes for fresh pasta, 8 to 10 minutes for dried. Drain the pasta, transfer it to a large serving bowl, and top with the arugula mixture. Toss quickly, add the chèvre, season with salt and pepper, and toss again. Top with the strips of dried tomatoes and the crumbled bacon, and serve immediately.

MACARONI AND CHEESE

*I*n the 1980s, in California as else-where, we imagined we had mi-nuscule appetites that could be satisfied by pristine portions of prettified food. And, for a time, we had quite a phobia about cheese. Could a yuppie of the era have admitted to a secret lust for grandma's macaroni and cheese? I think not, yet I'll bet that almost everyone, including accomplished cooks, had, and still has, a passion for true macaroni and cheese—rich, thick, and bubbly, and fragrant with the aroma of melted cheddar. Many of us were raised on it, whether it came from grandma's kitchen or, as it often did, from a box. Here is a pre-Kraft version, the kind my grandmother—and quite possibly yours—made before anyone knew how to transform cheese into powder.

4 ounces bacon

1 tablespoon dry mustard, such as Colman's

1 tablespoon Tabasco sauce, Bustelo's Hot Sauce, or other hot sauce

2 cans (24 ounces total) evaporated milk, or 2 cups milk combined with 1 cup heavy cream

3 eggs, beaten

2 teaspoons fresh-ground black pepper

2 pounds sharp cheddar cheese, grated

1 pound dried ditalini or elbow
  macaroni
1 cup fresh bread crumbs (see page
  46)

In a heavy skillet over medium heat, fry the bacon until it is barely crisp. Transfer it to absorbent paper.

In a small bowl, stir together the dry mustard and the hot sauce to make a paste. In a large bowl, mix together the milk, eggs, and pepper. Stir in the mustard paste and two thirds of the cheese. Set the bowl aside.

Preheat the oven to 350°F.

Bring a large pot of salted water to a boil. Cook the pasta until it is just short of done. Drain the pasta, and rinse it under cold running water. Fold the pasta into the cheese-and-milk mixture. Crumble the bacon, and fold it in with the remaining cheese.

Butter or oil a 4-quart baking dish. Fill the dish with the macaroni and cheese, and spread the bread crumbs over the top. Cover tightly with foil, bake for 20 minutes, remove the foil, and bake for 10 minutes more. Remove the dish from the oven and let it for rest for 5 minutes before serving.

Ten Ways to Use Condiment Olive Oil

Confused by all the olive oils on your grocer's shelf? With the popularity of the Mediterranean Diet and all the good news about the health benefits of olive oil, new oils keep appearing. There are just two things to remember. First, you get health benefits from any olive oil, refined or extra virgin, cooked or not. Second, olive oil is the only vegetable fat that contributes significant flavor to a dish. So, use an inexpensive olive oil for cooking and save premium condiment oils for finishing a dish after cooking it, or for one of the following ten uses:

❖ With fresh bread, in place of butter

❖ Drizzled over toasted or grilled bread

❖ As a simple dressing for artichokes

❖ Drizzled over a salad of sliced oranges, sliced red onions, and shaved dry jack

❖ Drizzled over a salad of sliced tomatoes, fresh mozzarella, and fresh basil

❖ Drizzled over creamy polenta that is topped with gorgonzola and toasted walnuts

❖ Drizzled over steamed or grilled fish

❖ Drizzled over beef or tuna carpaccio

❖ Tossed with grilled or roasted vegetables

❖ Tossed with pasta, along with grated nutmeg and plenty of fresh-ground black pepper

Variations:

In the summer, add 2 cups peeled, seeded, and chopped tomatoes to the cheese-and-milk mixture with the cooked pasta.

In the spring, sauté 1 pound young mustard greens, chopped, and 3 garlic cloves, minced, in some of the bacon drippings and fold them into the mixture with the pasta.

BASIC STEAMED RICE

The most important thing to remember when cooking rice is to leave it alone. Or, to paraphrase cookbook author and Zen priest Edward Brown, when you steam the rice, steam the rice. In *Tomato Blessings and Radish Teachings*, Ed writes about taking a new job as head cook at the Zen Mountain Center at Tassajara Hot Springs in Monterey County. He asked his Zen teacher, Suzuki Roshi, for advice, and Roshi said, "When you wash the rice, wash the rice; when you cut the carrots, cut the carrots; when you stir the soup, stir the soup." Being attentive, but not overly attentive, is the key. Steaming rice does not mean lifting the lid every few minutes to see how the rice is doing. It means completing the tasks necessary to letting the rice steam and then letting it do so. The advice to leave the pot undisturbed is as crucial as the instructions to bring the water to a boil or to add salt. Ed also gives the best clue I've heard for determining when brown rice is done and should be removed from the heat. "The rice is done when the bubbling subsides," he tells his readers, "little steam continues to escape, and the aroma has blossomed. If you listen carefully to the pot, you can hear the distinct crackling or popping sound of the rice toasting on the bottom of the pot."

As other grains do, rice absorbs different amounts of liquid depending upon its age; fresher rice absorbs less than older rice. Make adjustments in the amount of water and the cooking time based on a particular supply of rice. In most cases, the variations will be minor.

MAKES ABOUT 3 CUPS COOKED RICE

1 cup long-grain white rice
1⅔ cups water
Generous pinch of salt

Combine the rice, water, and salt in a small (1-quart) heavy saucepan over high heat. Bring to a rolling boil, reduce the heat to low, and simmer, covered, for 15 minutes. Remove the pan from the heat, and let the rice steam, covered and undisturbed, for 15 minutes. Fluff with a fork, and serve immediately or use in another recipe.

Variations:

SHORT-GRAIN WHITE RICE, INCLUDING STICKY RICE: For about 3 cups cooked rice, put 1 cup rice in a strainer or colander and rinse it under cold running water until the water runs clear. Combine the rice, 1½ cups of water, and a pinch of salt in a small (1-quart) heavy saucepan over high heat. Bring to a rolling boil, reduce the heat to low, and simmer, covered, for 15 minutes. Remove the pan from the heat, and let the rice steam, covered and undisturbed, for 15 minutes. Serve immediately or use in another recipe.

LONG- OR SHORT-GRAIN BROWN RICE: For about 4 cups cooked rice, put 1 cup rice in a colander or strainer, and rinse it under cold running water until the water runs clear. Combine the rice, 2 cups of water, and a generous pinch of salt in a medium (1½- to 2-quart) heavy saucepan over high heat. Bring to a rolling boil, reduce the heat to low, and simmer, covered, for 40 to 50 minutes, until the rice is fragrant. Remove the pan from the heat, and let the rice steam, covered and undisturbed, for 15 minutes. Serve immediately or use in another recipe.

WILD RICE: For a scant 4 cups cooked rice, put 1 cup wild rice in a colander or strainer, and rinse it under cold running water until the water runs clear. Bring 4 cups of salted water, vegetable stock, or chicken stock to a boil in a medium (1½- to 2-quart) heavy saucepan over high heat. Add the rice, reduce the heat, and simmer, covered, for 40 to 45 minutes, until the rice has puffed up and most of the liquid

has been absorbed. Drain off any excess liquid, fluff with a fork, cover, and let the rice steam, covered and undisturbed, for 10 minutes before serving.

JASMINE RICE

*R*ice is the center of most Asian meals, in California as elsewhere. Fragrant jasmine rice, much of which is imported from Thailand, is the rice of choice in many home kitchens. As Asian markets become more common throughout the country, jasmine rice is increasingly easy to find. It is inexpensive, particularly if you buy it in 25- or 50-pound sacks. If a bag says "new crop," the rice is from a recent harvest and will retain more moisture than older rice; in such cases, reduce the water to 2¾ cups, so that the rice won't be mushy.

MAKES ABOUT 3½ CUPS COOKED RICE

2 cups jasmine rice

Put the rice in a strainer or colander and rinse it under cold running water until the water runs clear. Or place the rice in a bowl or saucepan and rinse it several times, agitating it in the pan during each rinse. Drain the rice thoroughly.

Place the rice in a 3- or 4-quart saucepan with 3 cups of cold water, and bring to a rolling boil over high heat. Reduce the heat to low, cover the pan with a tight-

Delicious Little Planets

• •

"Think of a typical home-style Thai meal as an edible solar system, with lots of delicious little planets revolving around the sun. The latter, for our purposes, is an abundance of naturally fragrant unseasoned jasmine rice. The planets must not only nourish us and taste good, they must also delight us in their variety, orbiting in a harmonious . . . dance, which we are free to choreograph in a number of ways."

Nancie McDermott, *Real Vegetarian Thai*

fitting lid, and cook for 20 minutes. Do not lift the lid during this time. Remove the pan from the heat, and let the rice steam, covered and undisturbed, for 10 minutes. Fluff the rice with a fork before serving.

JOOK

• •

Jook is a savory porridge served for breakfast, as a late-night snack, or as a restorative meal when you're feeling poorly. From Korea to Thailand, where it is considered the ideal cure for hangovers, you find variations of this savory rice gruel, more reminiscent of Italy's creamy polenta than porridges such as oatmeal. It is comfort food at its finest, and there are endless variations.

Some recipes begin with raw rice, others with cooked. (This recipe begins with raw rice; to use cooked rice, see the Variation.) Some call for water, others a mixture of water and chicken stock. I've seen jooks that incorporate fish into the porridge itself, and others that top it with raw fish, sautéed greens, chicken, or pork. Yet there are certain elements that do not change— the fish sauce, sesame oil, scallions, and pepper.

SERVES 4 TO 6

⅓ cup long-grain white rice
1 tablespoon peanut oil
2 teaspoons kosher salt (omit or reduce if the stock is salty)
3 cups chicken stock
2 tablespoons fish sauce or soy sauce
1 teaspoon white pepper, preferably fresh-ground
2 teaspoons toasted sesame oil
5 scallions, cut into very thin rounds
3 tablespoons cilantro leaves, torn
Toppings (follow recipe)

Put the rice in a strainer or colander and rinse it under cold running water until the water runs clear. Drain the rice thoroughly. Heat the peanut oil in a large heavy saucepan over high heat, and add the rice, salt, stock, and 3 cups of water. Bring to a boil, reduce the heat slightly, stir, and let boil, uncovered, for 4 minutes. Reduce the heat, and simmer, covered, for 1½ hours, stirring now and then, until the rice has the consistency of soft porridge. Remove the pan from the heat, and stir in

Another Thing Entirely

One of the best breakfasts I have ever had was at the home of a Chinese friend, who lived in a beautiful place nestled in the Santa Cruz Mountains. A remarkable buffet of fragrant foods covered the kitchen table. The array couldn't have been more unlike a typical American breakfast—there wasn't an egg, a potato, a rasher of bacon, or a box of cereal in sight. Instead of coffee, there was a pot of hot, aromatic tea. There was a soup with greens, little bits of pork, noodles, and a number of things I did not recognize. There was also the classic Chinese porridge, jook, with a selection of appetizing toppings. I did not have the opportunity that day to learn how the various dishes were made; so, since then, I've had to make my way back to those wonderfully savory moments by instinct, helped along by local Asian markets and the best Chinese cookbooks I can find. Learning a new cuisine is much like learning a new language. Knowing a few common phrases will help you through a vacation, just as knowing a handful of authentic recipes will get you through an occasional meal. But it is another thing entirely to become fluent, or even conversant. To make a language or a cuisine your own, you must learn its grammar, its vocabulary, and its unique idioms and nuances.

the fish sauce or soy sauce and the pepper. Ladle the jook into individual serving bowls, top with a drizzle of sesame oil and a sprinkling of scallions and cilantro, and add a topping or toppings. Serve immediately.

Variation:

To make jook with cooked rice, stir 2 cups cooked long-grain white rice into 5 cups chicken stock in a heavy saucepan over high heat, and bring it to a boil. Reduce the heat, and simmer until the rice is soft and porridgelike, 15 to 20 minutes. Remove from the heat, stir in the fish sauce and pepper, and continue according to the instructions.

Toppings:

GRILLED SALMON FILLET: Marinate and grill the salmon according to the recipe on page 298. Break the salmon into chunks, and top the jook with the fish and a handful of fried shallots (see page 395).

PORK AND GREENS: Top the jook with 1 cup minced or shredded cooked pork, 3 cups greens, such as spinach or mustard greens, sautéed until just wilted, and some Fried Leeks (page 394).

CHICKEN: Top the jook with 1 cup sliced or chopped cooked chicken, such as Lemon-scented Thai Chicken (page 314), some fried shallots (see page 395), and bottled Thai chile sauce.

PRAWNS OR SHRIMP: Top the jook with 8 to 10 ounces cooked prawns or bay shrimp tossed with ¾ cup Thai Lime Chile Sauce (page 149).

POACHED EGGS: Lightly poach 1 egg for each serving, and top the jook with the eggs, fried shallots (see page 395), and bottled Thai chile sauce.

ELEANOR'S RICE WITH DULSE

John and Eleanor Lewallen founded the Mendocino Sea Vegetable Company in 1980. With their three children, the Lewallens harvest sea vegetables, or edible seaweeds, from off the northern California coast near Mendocino. They gather the wild seaweed, rinse it in spring water, and dry it in the sun. It is then sold throughout the world. Nori, used to wrap sushi rolls, is the most familiar sea vegetable to American home cooks, but in California other kinds, like wakame, kombu, sea palm, fucus, grapestone, and dulse, all of which the Lewallens also harvest, are gaining in popularity. In 1996, the Lewallens published the *Sea Vegetable Gourmet Cookbook and Wildcrafter's Guide*, full of Eleanor's recipes, from one of which this recipe is adapted. The dish makes an excellent accompaniment to grilled seafood or poultry.

SERVES 4

2 tablespoons toasted sesame oil, or more to coat the pan

18 to 20 (about 2 bunches) scallions, white and green parts, cut into thin rounds
2 garlic cloves, minced
4 cups cooked long-grain white rice
½ ounce dried dulse, snipped into small pieces
Juice of 1 lime or 1 lemon
2 tablespoons fish sauce or soy sauce
½ teaspoon crushed red pepper

Heat the sesame oil in a large sauté pan over medium heat. Add the scallions, and sauté them until they wilt, 5 to 7 minutes. Add the garlic, and sauté for 2 minutes more. Add the rice and dulse, and toss thoroughly. Add the lime juice or lemon juice, fish sauce or soy sauce, and red pepper, toss well, and cook until heated through. Serve immediately.

SPANISH RICE

Old California cookbooks always include a recipe for "Spanish rice" or "Mexican rice." The simplest recipes have just rice, onions, tomatoes, and stock. The more complex add anything from garlic, green peppers, and olives to chicken and peas; the most elaborate come close to a classic Spanish paella. Some versions are cooked entirely on top of the stove, while others are finished in the oven. In California's Mexican restaurants today, simple Spanish rice is ubiquitous; in the health food restaurants that were common in the 1970s and 1980s, the dish was made with brown rice. Nearly all recipes agree that the rice must be fried before it is simmered in stock. Although it is not traditional, I like Spanish rice with lemon or lime juice squeezed over it.

SERVES 4 TO 6

¼ cup olive oil
½ yellow onion, minced
1 poblano chile, seeded and minced
3 garlic cloves, minced
1½ cups long-grain white rice
3 cups chicken stock or vegetable
   stock, boiling hot
1 cup Tomato Concassé (page 98) or
   1 cup canned crushed tomatoes
2 tablespoons minced Italian parsley
Kosher salt
Black pepper in a mill
2 cups shelled peas, optional
1 lime or 1 lemon, cut into wedges

Heat the olive oil in a large saucepan over medium heat. Add the onion and poblano, and sauté them until they are soft and fragrant, about 8 minutes. Add the garlic, and sauté for 2 minutes more. Add the rice, and sauté, stirring constantly, until it begins to turn golden, 7 to 8 minutes. Add the stock, tomato concassé, and parsley. Season with salt and pepper, reduce the heat, and simmer, covered, until the rice is tender and all of the liquid is absorbed, about 15 minutes. If you like, add the peas to the rice about 5 minutes after the rice begins cooking. Remove the pan from the heat, and let the rice steam, covered and undisturbed, for 10 minutes. Fluff the rice with a fork, adjust the seasonings, and serve immediately, with lemon or lime wedges alongside.

Variations:

For a Mexican version, add 1 teaspoon chipotle powder or other ground dried chile with the rice. Omit the parsley, and add 2 tablespoons minced cilantro leaves just before serving.

To make with brown rice, use brown instead of white rice, increase the amount of stock to 4 cups, and cook the rice until it is tender, about 45 minutes.

ARMENIAN PILAF

Armenians first came to California in the 1880s. Many settled in the Central Valley near Fresno, farming melons, figs, and raisins and practicing viticulture. Some typically Armenian ingredients, such as grape leaves and lamb, and dishes, such as pilafs, became popular in the state, but in general Armenian food in California has remained within ethnic communities, much as Greek cuisine has. This Armenian-style pilaf, which combines rice and pasta, might remind anyone who grew up during the 1950s or later of Rice-A-Roni, but it is lighter and more delicate than the commercial dish.

¼ cup clarified butter (see page 288)

1 cup (about 3 ounces) dried cappellini or other thin pasta, broken into ¾-inch pieces

1½ cups uncooked long-grain white rice, such as basmati

2 cups chicken stock, hot

3 cups boiling water

Kosher salt

Black pepper in a mill

Heat 3 tablespoons of the clarified butter in a heavy sauté pan over medium heat. Add the pasta, and sauté, stirring constantly, until it is lightly browned, 5 to 7 minutes. Transfer the pasta to a bowl, return the pan to the heat, and melt the remaining 1 tablespoon butter. Add the rice, and sauté, stirring constantly, until it is lightly browned, 7 to 8 minutes. Add the stock and 1 cup of the boiling water, reduce the heat to low, and simmer, uncovered, for 10 minutes. Stir in the pasta, add the remaining 2 cups of boiling water, and simmer, covered, for 5 minutes. Remove the pan from the heat, and let the pilaf steam, covered and undisturbed, for 10 minutes. Fluff with a fork and season with salt and pepper. Serve immediately.

ASPARAGUS RISOTTO WITH LEMON

I buy asparagus almost exclusively at farmers' markets, where what you buy has been harvested shortly before dawn that day. In mid-spring, I often find small and tender fresh fava beans on the same day. On those happy occasions, I shell a cup or so of the beans, sauté them briefly, and fold them into the risotto when it is nearly finished.

1 pound asparagus, trimmed of tough ends and cut into 1½-inch pieces

¼ cup olive oil

Kosher salt

Black pepper in a mill

1 small yellow onion, diced

1 shallot, minced

1¼ cups Arborio or Carnaroli rice

4 to 5 cups chicken stock, hot

2 tablespoons fresh lemon juice

1 tablespoon minced lemon zest

½ cup (2 ounces) grated Parmigiano-Reggiano or dry jack

1 tablespoon julienned lemon zest

1 tablespoon minced Italian parsley

Preheat the oven to 500°F. Toss the asparagus with 1 tablespoon of the olive oil in a medium bowl until each piece is coated. Spread the asparagus evenly on a baking sheet, season with salt and pepper, and roast until just tender, 7 to 10 minutes, depending on the width of the asparagus.

Heat the remaining olive oil in a large saucepan. Add the onion, and sauté it until it is soft and fragrant, about 8 minutes. Add the shallot, and sauté for 5 minutes more. Add the rice, and stir with a wooden spoon until each grain begins to turn milky white, about 2 minutes. Keeping the stock hot over low heat, add the stock, ½ cup at a time, stirring constantly after each addition until nearly all the liquid is absorbed. Continue to add stock and stir until the rice is tender but not mushy, a total of 18 to 20 minutes. Stir in the lemon juice, minced lemon zest, and cheese. Fold in the asparagus, and remove from the heat. Taste, and season with salt and pepper. Transfer the risotto to a serving bowl or individual plates, garnish with julienned lemon zest and parsley, and serve immediately.

CARROT RISOTTO WITH GARLIC AND CUMIN

California produces about a quarter of the domestic rice crop. Some of the state's rice farmers recently have begun planting Arborio rice. For risottos, however, I prefer Italian Arborio or Carnaroli. California Arborio rice absorbs liquid differently from the imported varieties and makes for a less creamy risotto. California rice does, however, have the advantage of freshness, and our farmers are working to improve their seed stock; it is an industry to watch. In this recipe, a creamy rice is essential because the dish does not include cheese. Risottos traditionally include cheese, but in this one the flavors of carrots, cumin, garlic, and cilantro stand on their own.

SERVES 4

6 tablespoons olive oil
¾ pound carrots, diced
5 to 6 cups chicken stock, hot
1 small yellow onion, diced
1 tablespoon minced fresh garlic
2 teaspoons ground cumin
1¼ cups Arborio or Carnaroli rice
2 tablespoons fresh lemon juice
Kosher salt
Black pepper in a mill
1 teaspoon cumin seeds, toasted
1 tablespoon minced cilantro leaves

Heat 2 tablespoons of the olive oil in a small skillet over low heat. Add the carrots, and sauté them until they are tender, about 15 minutes. Add 1 cup of the stock, increase the heat to medium-high, and simmer the carrots until the stock is reduced by three quarters. Set aside.

Heat the remaining olive oil in a large saucepan over medium heat. Add the onion, and sauté it until it is soft and fragrant, about 8 minutes. Add the garlic and ground cumin, and sauté for 2 minutes more. Add the rice, and stir with a wooden spoon until each grain begins to turn milky white, about 2 minutes. Keeping the stock hot over low heat, add the stock, ½ cup at a time, stirring after each addition until nearly all the liquid is absorbed. Continue to add stock and stir until the rice is tender but not mushy, a total of 18 to 20 minutes. Stir in the carrots and lemon juice. Taste, and season with salt and pepper. Transfer the risotto to a serving bowl or individual plates, garnish with cumin seeds and minced cilantro, and serve immediately.

MONTEREY ARTICHOKE RISOTTO

Fresh artichokes are most often enjoyed whole with a sauce or dip, but they also contribute appealing flavors when they are incorporated into more complex recipes, such as this risotto. Artichokes can be expensive, and sometimes they are hard to find fresh. You can use canned or frozen artichokes in this recipe, although you will get different results. Be sure to rinse canned artichokes thoroughly to remove their brine.

SERVES 4

4 large artichokes, boiled until just tender (see page 381)
¼ cup olive oil
1 small yellow onion, diced
1 tablespoon minced garlic
1¼ cups Arborio or Carnaroli rice

4 to 5 cups chicken stock, hot
2 teaspoons minced lemon zest
¾ cup (3 ounces) grated Italian fontina cheese
½ cup (2 ounces) grated romano cheese
1 tablespoon minced Italian parsley
Kosher salt
Black pepper in a mill
1 cup Tomato Concassé (page 98)

Separate the leaves of the artichokes from the hearts, and scoop out and discard the thistle-like choke. Cut the hearts crosswise into thin slices; if they are particularly large, cut the slices in half. Cut the meat from the base of each artichoke leaf into thin julienne.

Heat the olive oil in a large saucepan over medium heat. Add the onion, and sauté it until it is soft and fragrant, about 8 minutes. Add the garlic, and sauté for 2 minutes more. Add the rice, and stir with a wooden spoon until each grain begins to turn milky white, about 2 minutes. Keeping the stock hot over low heat, add the stock, ½ cup at a time, stirring after each addition until nearly all the liquid is absorbed. After the third addition of stock, add the sliced artichoke hearts, and stir for 2 minutes. Continue to add stock and stir until the rice is tender but not mushy, a total of 18 to 20 minutes. Stir in the lemon zest, fontina, romano, and half of the julienned artichoke. Taste, and season with salt and pepper. To serve, divide the tomato concassé among individual plates and spoon risotto next to the sauce. Top the portions with the remaining julienned artichoke and the parsley, season with pepper, and serve immediately.

LEEK
RISOTTO

Among the cheeses produced by Laura Chénel Chèvre is tome, a hard aged goat cheese that is perfect for grating. If you have some tome (see Resources), this risotto is a perfect showcase for its delicate flavor and texture. Another California cheese company, Bellwether Farms in Petaluma, makes outstanding Italian-style sheep's milk cheeses, the only sheep's milk cheeses produced in the state and among very few in the country. Any of their aged pecorino-style cheeses would be excellent in this dish.

SERVES 4

2 tablespoons unsalted butter
¼ cup olive oil
4 leeks, white and pale green parts, cut into thin rounds
1¼ cups Arborio or Carnaroli rice
4 to 5 cups chicken stock or duck stock, hot
1 cup (4 ounces) grated Laura Chenel tome or aged asiago
Kosher salt
Black pepper in a mill
8 ounces haricots verts or young green beans, blanched

Heat the butter and 3 tablespoons of the olive oil together in a large saucepan over medium heat until the butter is melted. Add the leeks, and sauté them until they are completely wilted, about 10 minutes. Add the rice, and stir with a wooden spoon until each grain begins to turn milky white, about 2 minutes. Keeping the stock hot over low heat, add the stock, ½ cup at a time, stirring after each addition until nearly all the liquid is absorbed. Continue to add stock and stir until the rice is tender but not mushy, a total of 18 to 20 minutes; when the risotto has been cooking for 15 minutes, stir in the tome or asiago, taste, and season with salt and pepper.

When the rice is nearly done, heat the remaining 1 tablespoon of olive oil in a skillet over medium heat. Add the blanched beans, and sauté to heat through.

Divide the risotto among indidivual plates or bowls, and top each serving with some of the beans. Season with pepper, and serve immediately.

Variation:

Make the Mushroom Ragout (page 255), omitting the polenta. After sautéing the rice for the risotto, add ⅓ of the ragout with the first addition of stock. When the risotto is served, top each serving with a portion of the remaining ragout, season with pepper, and serve immediately.

CORN RISOTTO

*I*n this dish, sweet, rich corn replaces the traditional cheese for an American twist on a classic Italian dish. The fresher the corn, the more pleased you will be with this voluptuous risotto. If you do not have chipotle powder, substitute another ground dried chile or omit it entirely.

SERVES 4 TO 6

4 ears of corn
3 tablespoons unsalted butter
1 small yellow onion, diced
3 ounces pancetta or bacon, diced
1½ cups Arborio or Carnaroli rice
1 teaspoon chipotle powder, optional
5 to 6 cups chicken stock, hot
2 tablespoons snipped chives
Kosher salt
Black pepper in a mill

Hold an ear of corn over a bowl, and rub the point of a sharp knife down the center of each row of kernels to release the juices. Run the knife through a second time, this time close to the cob, to remove the kernels. Repeat with the remaining ears. You should have about 2 cups of kernels. Set the bowl aside.

Melt the butter in a large saucepan over medium heat.

Add the onion, and sauté it until it is soft and fragrant, about 8 minutes. Add the pancetta or bacon, and sauté for 5 minutes more. Add the rice, and stir with a wooden spoon until each grain begins to turn milky white, about 2 minutes. Stir in the chipotle powder, if you like. Keeping the stock hot over low heat, add the stock, ½ cup at a time, stirring after each addition until nearly all the liquid is absorbed. Continue to add stock and stir until the rice is almost tender, about 15 minutes. Add the corn and its juices and cook, stirring, for 2 minutes. Add more stock, and stir until the rice is tender but not mushy, 1 to 2 minutes more. Stir in the chives, and remove the pan from the heat. Taste, season with salt and pepper, and serve immediately.

Variation:

For a vegetarian version of this dish, omit the pancetta or bacon. Replace the chicken stock with a simple corn stock, made by simmering the stripped corn cobs in 4 to 5 cups of water for 15 minutes. Strain, and add additional water if necessary to make 5 to 6 cups.

OLIVE RISOTTO WITH BASIL

*U*nlike European olives, California olives are mildly flavored, the result of a quick processing in lye that strips them of their bitterness and of some of their subtle flavors. Harvested olives are bitter and must go through some sort of processing to be palatable, but all processing methods except soaking in lye require considerable time. It was Freda Ehmann, a California housewife with an olive orchard near Oroville, who in the late nineteenth century developed the quick-processing technique used to produce virtually all table olives in the state today. With competition from inexpensive olive oils from Europe, the California olive oil industry was in decline, and Freda found herself with nearly three hundred gallons of olives on hand. After consulting a University of California professor, she processed the olives in lye on her back porch. Her success spawned the California table olive industry and hastened the demise of the fledgling olive oil industry. Hundreds of olive trees with varieties of fruit undesirable for table olives were ripped out or neglected. In this risotto, California black olives and green olives are combined with more intensely flavored kalamata olives. Use just one or two kinds of olive if you like.

SERVES 4 TO 6

1 bay leaf
2 sprigs of thyme
1 sprig of Italian parsley
1 sprig of basil
4 to 5 cups chicken stock, hot
1 pint small cherry tomatoes, cut in half
2 garlic cloves, minced
2 tablespoons extra virgin olive oil
Kosher salt
Black pepper in a mill
¼ cup olive oil
1 small yellow onion, diced
1 shallot, minced
1 tablespoon minced garlic
1½ cups Arborio or Carnaroli rice
3 ounces California black olives, pitted and minced
3 ounces California green olives, pitted and minced
2 ounces kalamata or niçoise olives, pitted and minced
¾ cup (3 ounces) grated dry jack or Parmigiano-Reggiano
2 tablespoons minced basil
2 tablespoons minced Italian parsley
Sprigs of basil or parsley, for garnish

Add the bay leaf and the sprigs of thyme, parsley, and basil to the stock. Toss together the cherry tomatoes, minced garlic cloves, and extra virgin olive oil in a small bowl, and season with salt and pepper. Set the bowl aside.

Heat the ¼ cup olive oil in a large saucepan over medium heat. Add the onion, and sauté it until it is soft and fragrant, about 8 minutes. Add the shallot, and sauté for 5 minutes more. Add the 1 tablespoon of garlic, and sauté for 2 minutes more. Add the rice, and stir with a wooden spoon until each grain begins to turn milky white, about 2 minutes. Keeping the stock hot over low heat, add the stock, ½ cup at a time, stirring after each addition until nearly all the liquid is absorbed. Continue to add stock and stir until the rice is almost tender, about 15 minutes. Stir in the olives and the cheese, and continue adding stock and stirring until the rice is tender but not mushy, 3 to 5 minutes more. Add the minced basil and parsley, and remove the pan from the heat. Taste, and season with salt and pepper. Divide the risotto among individual plates, top each portion with reserved cherry tomatoes, garnish with herb sprigs, and serve immediately.

THE SENATOR'S GRANDMA'S CABERNET RISOTTO

Because of the long history of Italian immigration, risottos are a staple in many California home kitchens. State Senator Mike Thompson grew up in St. Helena, near the northern end of the Napa Valley. His grandparents lived nearby, and once a week during his childhood he went to their house for dinner. Sometimes he would help his grandmother prepare his favorite dish, a red-wine risotto flavored with sun-dried tomatoes—decades before they were trendy. Mike learned to make this dish by watching his grandmother cook it in a cast-iron Dutch oven; she never wrote down a formal recipe. She used a ladle to add stock, not a measuring cup, and she judged when the risotto was done by how it tasted. His advice on how to achieve the perfect consistency is, simply, "practice makes perfect." Mike strongly recommends that the red wine be cabernet sauvignon, but he says you can substitute a good zinfandel, if you insist.

SERVES 4 TO 6

3 tablespoons unsalted butter
1 tablespoon olive oil
½ yellow onion, diced
3 garlic cloves, crushed
1½ cups Arborio or Carnaroli rice
1 cup cabernet sauvignon
5 to 6 cups chicken stock, hot
¼ cup dried tomatoes packed in oil, drained and minced
1 cup (4 ounces) grated Parmigiano-Reggiano, or more to taste
Kosher salt
Black pepper in a mill

Heat the butter and olive oil together in a large saucepan over low heat. When the butter is melted, add the onion and garlic, and sauté until transparent, 7 to 8 minutes. Add the rice, and stir with a wooden spoon until each grain begins to turn milky white, about 2 minutes. Add the wine, and continue to stir until it is completely absorbed by the rice. Keeping the stock hot over low heat, add the stock, ½ cup at a time, stirring after each addition until nearly all the liquid is absorbed. Continue to add stock and stir until the rice is tender but not mushy, a total of 18 to 20 minutes. Stir in the tomatoes and cheese, taste again, and season with salt, pepper, and, if you like, more cheese. Serve immediately.

PUMPKIN RISOTTO WITH SPINACH AND GARLIC

Pumpkin adds a sweet element to a savory risotto, and garlicky spinach, served alongside, provides an inviting contrast in taste and texture. Serve this risotto with a simple fall-harvest soup for a festive meal on a fall or winter holiday, from Halloween and Dia de los Muertos to Christmas and Twelfth Night.

SERVES 6 TO 8

3 tablespoons unsalted butter
3 leeks, white part only, sliced thin
3 tablespoons olive oil
1 small yellow onion, diced
2 cups Arborio or Carnaroli rice
7 to 8 cups chicken stock, duck stock, or vegetable stock, hot
1 cup pumpkin or winter squash puree (see Note)

2 tablespoons fresh lemon juice
8 garlic cloves, minced
½ cup (2 ounces) grated Parmigiano-Reggiano or dry jack
2 large bunches (about 1 pound each) of fresh spinach
Kosher salt
Black pepper in a mill

Heat 2 tablespoons of the butter in a small heavy skillet over medium heat. When the butter begins to foam, add the leeks, lower the heat, and cook the leeks until they are tender and completely wilted, 6 to 8 minutes. Set the leeks aside.

Heat the remaining 1 tablespoon of the butter and 1 tablespoon of the olive oil in a large saucepan over medium heat. Add the onion, and sauté it until it is soft and fragrant, about 8 minutes. Add the rice, and stir with a wooden spoon until each grain begins to turn milky white, about 2 minutes. Keeping the stock hot over low heat, add the stock, ½ cup at a time, stirring after each addition until nearly all the liquid is absorbed. Continue to add stock and stir until the rice is tender but not mushy, a total of 18 to 20 minutes. Before the final addition of stock, stir in the reserved leeks, the pumpkin or squash puree, and 1 tablespoon of the lemon juice.

Working quickly, heat the remaining 2 tablespoons of olive oil in a skillet or wok over medium heat, add the garlic, and sauté for 2 minutes.

When the rice is cooked, stir in the cheese. Add the spinach to the sautéed garlic, and cook, covered, for 2 to 3 minutes, until the spinach is just wilted. Taste the risotto, and season with salt and pepper. Transfer the risotto to a serving platter or individual plates. Add the remaining 2 tablespoons of the lemon juice to the spinach, toss the spinach to coat it with the olive oil, garlic, and lemon juice, and serve it alongside the risotto.

NOTE: To make pumpkin puree, preheat the oven to 325°F. Cut a small sugar pumpkin into large chunks. Remove the seeds and strings, and place the pumpkin on a lightly oiled baking sheet. Bake for 40 to 60 minutes, until the squash is tender. Or peel the pumpkin, cut it into 2-inch cubes, and steam it. Let the baked or steamed pumpkin cool, peel it, and mash the flesh with a fork. (You will have more than the 1 cup puree you need, even with the smallest sugar pumpkin you can find.) If a sugar pumpkin is not available, substitute Kabocha, Golden Nugget, or Calabaza squash.

CALIFORNIA CHRISTMAS RISOTTO

Domestic teleme cheese was first made, as Monterey jack was, in California in the early 1920s. Teleme is a cow's milk cheese that is similar to jack, but with a higher moisture content. It is coated with rice flour, has a very thin rind, and is sold fresh, not aged. It melts beautifully and contributes a creamy texture to a dish, as in this risotto. When it is not available, use brie rather than jack in its place.

I call this a Christmas risotto as a tribute to my friends John and Jim, with whom I enjoyed the dish one year at Christmas. John had wanted to learn to make risotto, and he chose this recipe from among several I gave him. As Jim cooked chicken sausages outside on the grill—you can grill in December in California, at least in the warmer areas along the coast—John stirred up a stunning rendition of this recipe. The use of dried rather than fresh tomatoes is also appropriate to the winter months.

SERVES 4 TO 6

¾ cup dry white wine
¼ cup dried tomato bits
2 tablespoons unsalted butter
1 tablespoon olive oil
1 small yellow onion, minced
1 shallot, minced
3 garlic cloves, minced

1½ cups Arborio or Carnaroli rice

5 to 6 cups stock, hot

½ cup heavy cream

3 ounces California teleme cheese or
   3 ounces brie, cut into small pieces

Kosher salt

Black pepper in a mill

½ cup pine nuts, toasted

3 tablespoons minced Italian parsley
   or snipped chives

6 pieces dried tomatoes packed in oil,
   cut into thin strips

Bring the wine and the tomato bits to a boil in a nonreactive saucepan. Reduce the heat, and simmer until the wine is reduced by one third. Set the pan aside.

Heat the butter and the olive oil together in a large saucepan over medium heat. When the butter is melted, add the onion, and sauté it until it is soft and fragrant, about 8 minutes. Add the shallot, and sauté for 5 minutes more. Add the garlic, and sauté for 2 minutes more. Add the rice, and stir with a wooden spoon until each grain begins to turn milky white, about 2 minutes. Keeping the stock hot over low heat, add the stock, ½ cup at a time, stirring after each addition until nearly all the liquid is absorbed. Continue to add stock and stir until the rice is tender, a total of 18 to 20 minutes. After the last addition of stock, stir in the reserved tomato bits and wine, and remove the pan from the heat. Stir in the cream and the cheese. Taste, season with salt and pepper, and stir in the pine nuts and half of the parsley or chives. Transfer the risotto to a serving platter or individual plates, garnish with the remaining parsley or chives and the tomato strips, and serve immediately.

California Christmas

"**A**n old man said his boys and him had caught them a mess of carp and the women folk could cook them up for Christmas dinner. Another man said his family had some extra beans and Daddy said we had coffee to share. Other folks said they could fry some pan bread and boil some syrup.... That [Christmas] morning we had us a real back home worship service for baby Jesus and we all said a special thanks for being so blessed. We ate carp and beans, and drank coffee. Then we had us some pan bread with syrup for dessert. Lord, was I stuffed. Everyone gathered round the fire after we ate and told stories about home and other Christmases. It seemed like all the folks were smiling at each other, and pretty soon Momma and Daddy stood right there with their arms around each other, us kids giggling and pointing. California didn't seem half bad."

Gerald Haslam, "California Christmas," in *Okies: Selected Stories* (Peregrine Smith, 1975)

JOHN'S JEWISH BARLEY "RISOTTO"

My friend John Harris, a writer who lives in Berkeley, created this recipe as he was working on a book about the history of the Jewish delicatessen in America. "It's basically the classic mushroom barley soup so popular in Jewish homes and delis," he says of his creation, "but because the liquid is reduced, the focus is on the barley. To replace the Parmigiano cheese—not Kosher!—you'd find in Italian risotto, I sprinkle gremolata over the final dish."

SERVES 4 TO 6

3 tablespoons olive oil
2 yellow onions, diced
4 carrots, sliced
4 garlic cloves, minced
1 pound beef chuck, cut into 1-inch cubes
1 pound mushrooms (of any variety you like), sliced
2 cups pearl barley
1 tablespoon minced Italian parsley
5 cups boiling water
Kosher salt
Black pepper in a mill
⅓ cup Gremolata (recipe follows)

Heat the olive oil in a large sauté pan over medium heat. Add the onions, and sauté them until they are soft and fragrant, about 8 minutes. Add the carrots, and sauté for 5 minutes more. Add the garlic, and sauté for 2 minutes more. Add the beef, and cook it, stirring frequently, until it is browned. Add the mushrooms, and cook them until they are limp, 7 to 8 minutes. Stir in the barley and parsley, add the water, and bring to a boil. Skimming off any foam that forms, simmer, covered, until the barley is tender, about 1 hour. Season with salt and pepper. Ladle into warmed bowls, sprinkle with gremolata, and serve immediately.

Gremolata

MAKES ABOUT ⅓ CUP

Minced zest of 2 lemons
4 garlic cloves, minced
4 tablespoons minced Italian parsley
1 teaspoon kosher salt

Combine all of the ingredients in a small bowl, taste, and correct the seasoning.

GREEN RICE TORTA

This recipe comes to us from a San Francisco firehouse cook named Frank Rey, who was with Engine Company Number 27 in the 1960s. The dish was served hot and topped with butter at the firehouse, as an accompaniment to roast meats; at home, we are told by Georgia Sackett, Frank made the torta for family picnics, where it was served cold. I have adapted this recipe from Frank's original one.

SERVES 6 TO 8

2 tablespoons olive oil
1 pound Swiss chard, trimmed of stems and tough ribs and sliced thin crosswise
3½ cups cooked long-grain white rice
¾ cup (3 ounces) grated Parmigiano-Reggiano
½ cup minced Italian parsley
5 garlic cloves, minced
3 eggs, beaten
1 teaspoon kosher salt
1 teaspoon fresh-ground black pepper
¼ cup fine dry bread crumbs

Preheat the oven to 325°F.

Heat the olive oil in a sauté pan over medium heat. Add the chard, and sauté it until it is just limp, 3 to 4 minutes. In a medium bowl, toss together the chard, rice, cheese, and parsley. Mix together the garlic and eggs and fold them into the rice mixture. Add the salt and pepper, and toss again.

Brush an 8-inch square baking dish with olive oil and scatter the bread crumbs over the bottom and sides. Spread the rice mixture evenly in the pan. Bake for 30 minutes, until the eggs are set and the top lightly golden. Remove the torta from the oven, let it rest for 10 minutes, and cut it into squares. Serve it hot or at room temperature, or refrigerate it and serve it cold.

The Hotter the Fire, the Better the Cooking

Stories abound of the great cooking to be found in firehouses throughout America. Because hours or even days may pass without an emergency, there are opportunities to make complex recipes and elaborate meals. But it's not always the least busy firehouses where the best cooking gets done. In a charming collection of recipes called *San Francisco Firehouse Favorites* (Bobbs-Merrill, 1965), Georgia Sackett writes that "the busiest companies almost always boast the most outstanding cooks, who are often instrumental in a fireman's putting in for a transfer to a certain company." Or, as several firefighters said to Sackett, "The hotter the fire, the better the cooking."

BASIC BEANS

California grows dozens of varieties of dried beans and peas, including most of the world's crop of lima beans. In the Central Valley, commercial production is dominated by light red kidney, dark red kidney, pink, lima, and small white beans; white kidney, pinto, small red, small black, and several other varieties are also grown. Heirloom varieties of beans are grown by a number of small commercial farmers throughout the state. Phipps Country Store and Farm harvests several dozen common and heirloom varieties of beans each year, which are sold at the farm outside of Pescadero, near the coast south of San Francisco, and by mail order. Flageolet, cannellini, cranberry, and scarlet runner beans are among the more familiar varieties offered; among the more interestingly named heirloom beans are prairie appaloosa, wren's egg cranberry, rattlesnake, tongues of fire, and Jacob's cattle. A bean is called an heirloom or heritage variety simply when it has not been grown commercially for a long time.

Both common and heirloom beans are stored and prepared in the same ways. All dried beans should be stored in an airtight container in a cool, dark pantry or cupboard. To store cooked beans, drain the liquid, place beans and liquid in separate containers, and refrigerate, covered, for up to 5 days. Cooked beans also can be frozen, for up to 1 year. Add the cooking liquid back when serving the beans or preparing another recipe that uses them.

One pound dried beans measures about 2 cups and produces about 5 cups cooked beans, enough for 6 to 8 people. For seasoning possibilities, see the Variations.

MAKES ABOUT 5 CUPS,
FOR 6 TO 8 SERVINGS

1 pound dried beans

Rinse the beans in cool water and sort through them to remove any small rocks or other debris, along with any renegade varieties of beans. Put the beans in a large pot, and add water to cover the beans by 2 inches. Soak the beans at room temperature for at least 8 hours or overnight. For a quick soak, bring the beans and water to a boil over high heat, reduce the heat, and simmer, covered, for 10 minutes; remove the pot from the heat, and let the beans soak for 1 hour.

Drain and rinse the beans, return them to the pot, and add water to cover the beans by 2 inches. Bring to a boil over high heat. Skim off any foam that forms, reduce the heat, and simmer gently, partially covered, until the beans are tender. Begin tasting the beans after about 40 minutes; the cooking time will be 45 minutes to 2 hours, depending on the variety of bean. Add water as necessary to keep the beans from burning. When the beans are done, remove the pot from the heat, and use or serve the beans immediately, or refrigerate until ready to use.

The Golden State

"Early California food wasn't Mexican, nor was it pure Spanish. Those first early settlers, Spanish descendants, tried ... to duplicate home dishes but their cooking had to be done with the food at hand.... These first settlers carried with them a limited supply of beans, corn, and dried meal to which were added wild greens, seeds and roots, and the edible fruits of the region. They found an abundance of watercress, wild onions, wild oats, grasses, herbs, and wild grapes. And to cultivate these they recruited their Indian converts into a land army to work the soil with crude implements."

Clementine Paddleford, *How America Eats* (Scribner's, 1960)

Variations:

SEASONED BASIC BEANS: After soaking and draining the beans, add 1 large yellow onion, quartered, 1 large shallot, cut in half, several garlic cloves, 1 celery rib, cut in half, and 1 to 2 sprigs of Italian parsley. Cook as directed. When the beans are done, use tongs to remove and discard the onion, shallot, celery, and parsley. Sometimes the onion and shallot will have nearly dissolved into the beans, which is fine. Season with salt and pepper. Serve, or use in another recipe.

SPICY BASIC BEANS: After soaking and draining the beans, add 1 large yellow onion, quartered, 1 large shallot, cut in half, several garlic cloves, 1 celery rib, cut in half, 1 to 2 sprigs of epazote or parsley, 1 teaspoon cumin seeds, and 1 to 2 serrano chiles, jalapeños, or dried chipotles. Cook as directed. When the beans are done, use tongs to remove and discard the onion, shallot, celery, epazote or parsley, and chiles. Sometimes the onion and shallot will have nearly dissolved into the beans, which is fine. Season with salt and pepper. Serve, or use in another recipe.

BEAN RAGOUT

This ragout can be made with any dried beans, whether common ones sold in supermarkets or heirloom varieties available at specialty food stores and by mail order. If you're pinched for time, it can be made quickly using canned beans. You can use one variety of bean or several; if you use more than one, soak and cook each variety of bean separately before assembling the ragout. Serve the ragout with Steamed Rice (page 217), or topped with grilled fish, such as Grilled Swordfish Steaks (page 295).

SERVES 6 TO 8

1 pound dried beans, soaked and drained
1 sprig of oregano
1 sprig of thyme

1 sprig of marjoram

1 sprig of Italian parsley

1 bay leaf

3 tablespoons olive oil or corn oil

1 yellow onion, diced

1 portobello mushroom (about 8 ounces) or 8 ounces cremini mushrooms, diced

6 garlic cloves, minced

1 teaspoon ground cumin

1 teaspoon chipotle powder or other ground dried chile

¾ teaspoon ground coriander seed

2 cups chicken stock or vegetable stock

Kosher salt

Black pepper in a mill

8 to 10 scallions, white and green parts, sliced thin

Simmer the beans, in separate pots if you are using more than one variety, until they are just barely tender, 45 minutes to 2 hours, depending on the type of bean. Add water as necessary to keep the beans from burning. Drain the beans, and reserve the cooking liquid. (The beans may be cooked the day before and refrigerated.)

Tie together the herb sprigs and bay leaf to make a bouquet garni. Heat the oil in a large sauté pan over medium heat. Add the onion, and sauté it until it is very soft and fragrant, about 15 minutes. Reduce the heat, add the mushrooms, and sauté them, stirring frequently, until they are soft, 8 to 10 minutes. Add the garlic, and sauté for 2 minutes more. Stir in the cooked beans, cumin, chipotle or other

The Harvest Gypsies' Dinner

"The maximum a worker can make is $400 a year, while the average is around $300, and the ... minimum is $150 a year. This amount must feed, clothe and transport whole families.... Observed diets run something like this when the family is making money:

❖ Family of seven—Beans, baking-powder biscuits, jam, coffee.

❖ Family of five—Biscuits, fried potatoes, dandelion greens, pears.

"These are dinners. It is to be noticed that even in these flush times there is no milk, no butter. The major part of the diet is starch. In slack times the diet becomes all starch, this being the cheapest way to fill up. Dinners during lay-offs are as follows:

❖ Family of seven—Beans, fried dough.

❖ Family of five—Oatmeal mush."

John Steinbeck, *The Harvest Gypsies* (Heyday Books, 1936)

dried chile, coriander, stock, and 2 cups of the beans' cooking liquid or water. Add the herb sprigs, bring to a boil, reduce the heat, and simmer, covered, for 40 minutes, until the beans are completely tender and the flavors have come together. Remove and discard the herbs, taste, and season with salt and pepper. Transfer the ragout to a serving bowl, scatter the scallions over the top, and serve immediately.

LIMA BEANS BAKED WITH JACK CHEESE AND CHILES

Lima beans got their name in the late nineteenth century when Robert McAllister acquired some beans from the crew of a Peruvian ship that was anchored near his Santa Barbara home. He'd been a dinner guest on the ship and loved the beans he'd been served, so he planted them on his farm. The beans are named after Lima, Peru, and today are one of the most important crops of the state. This recipe is adapted from an early California recipe.

SERVES 6 TO 8

1 sprig of thyme
1 sprig of oregano
1 sprig of Italian parsley
1 pound dried lima beans, soaked and drained
2 tablespoons olive oil
1 yellow onion, diced
6 garlic cloves, minced
4 Anaheim chiles, roasted, peeled, seeded, and chopped
1 to 2 poblano chiles, roasted, peeled, seeded, and chopped
2 teaspoons kosher salt
1 teaspoon fresh-ground black pepper
2 cups (8 ounces) grated Monterey jack
1 cup chicken stock or vegetable stock
½ cup sour cream
1 cup fresh bread crumbs, toasted (see page 46)
2 tablespoons minced herbs, such as thyme, oregano, Italian parsley, or a combination

Tie together the sprigs of thyme, oregano, and parsley to make a small bouquet garni. Put the beans in a large pot, and add water to cover the beans by 2 inches. Add the bouquet garni, bring to a boil, reduce the heat, and simmer, partially

The First Canned Chile

Today fresh chiles are available throughout the country, but it wasn't always so. In 1898, while he was sheriff of Ventura County in southern California, Emile Ortega founded the first chile-canning plant in the U.S. Until recently, Ortega brand chiles, which are whole or chopped fire-roasted Anaheim peppers, were the only chiles available outside of Latin and Hispanic markets.

covered, until the beans are very tender, about 45 minutes. Remove the pot from the heat, and let the beans cool in their liquid. Remove and discard the bouquet garni, drain the beans, and set them aside in a large bowl.

Preheat the oven to 325°F. Heat the olive oil in a small skillet over medium heat. Add the onion, and sauté it until it is very soft and fragrant, about 15 minutes. Add the garlic, and sauté for 2 minutes more.

Add the onions, garlic, chiles (use 2 poblanos for more heat), salt, and pepper to the beans, and toss to combine. Place one third of the mixture in a 3-quart baking dish. Spread one third of the cheese over the beans, and repeat twice more to use all of the bean mixture and all of the cheese. Pour the stock over the beans and distribute the sour cream evenly on top. Toss together the bread crumbs and minced herbs and sprinkle them evenly over the top. Bake for 30 minutes. Remove from the oven and let cool for 10 minutes before serving.

RED BEANS AND RICE

There are probably as many variations of red beans and rice as there are cooks who make the dish, which is so widely familiar it scarcely needs a recipe. But, if you don't know where you're goin', you need somebody to tell you how to get there. This is the version I've always cooked, although its ingredient list is a lot longer than Johnny

Otis's recipe. "Nothing but beans, ham-hocks, garlic, bay, salt, and pepper," Johnny insists, "and no onions, definitely no onions." Whatever route you choose, make sure there's enough water so the beans don't burn, and have plenty of Tabasco alongside.

SERVES 6 TO 8

2 to 3 hamhocks
4 to 5 celery ribs, diced fine
1 large or 2 medium green bell peppers, diced fine
1 large or 2 medium white or yellow onions, diced
2 bay leaves
1 teaspoon garlic powder
1 teaspoon onion powder
1 teaspoon dried thyme leaves (not ground)
1 teaspoon dried oregano leaves (not ground)
1 teaspoon fresh-ground black pepper
1 teaspoon white pepper, preferably fresh-ground
¼ teaspoon cayenne
Tabasco sauce
1 pound dried red beans, soaked and drained
2 cups uncooked long-grain white rice
Kosher salt

Combine 8 cups of water with the hamhocks, celery, bell peppers, onions, bay leaves, garlic powder, onion powder, thyme, oregano, black pepper, white pepper, cayenne, and 2 teaspoons Tabasco in a large stockpot over high heat. Bring to a boil, reduce the heat, and simmer, uncovered, for about 1 hour, or until the meat is very tender.

Rinse the beans, add them to the pot, and continue to simmer, uncovered, until the beans begin to fall apart, 1 to 1½ hours. Stir frequently and add water as necessary to keep the mixture from becoming too thick and to keep the beans from burning.

Meanwhile, about 20 minutes before the beans will be done, begin cooking the rice.

When the beans are done, remove them from the heat, and use tongs to remove and discard the hamhock bones; use a fork to break up any meat that has remained in large chunks. Taste the beans, and, if you like, add salt.

To serve, place a generous scoop of rice in the center of individual plates and ladle the beans over the rice. Serve with Tabasco on the side.

Variation:

Cut 1½ pounds spicy sausage, such as smoked andouille, kielbasa, or linguica, into diagonal slices. Fry the sausage, and scatter the slices over the individual servings of beans and rice.

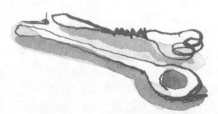

Red Beans and Jive

Johnny Otis has many claims to fame—he's a member of the Rock & Roll Hall of Fame and producer of hundreds of classic rhythm and blues records. He wrote and recorded "Willie and the Hand Jive" in the 1950s. He's a musician, a painter, a writer, and a farmer, a man of Greek ancestry who has spent his entire life in the world of black music and culture. Johnny Otis is a rare classic. In the mid-1980s, he launched the first Johnny Otis Red Beans & Rice Festival in an old armory in Los Angeles. The first day it drew seven hundred people, and it's been growing ever since. Johnny since has turned over the festival to the County of Los Angeles, which values it as an exuberant, down-home family event, now held in the late summer or early fall at Bonelli Park in the town of San Dimas.

Eventually, Johnny moved north, where he hosts a weekly radio show on KPFA-FM in Berkeley. He also grows organic apples and other produce, and he recently founded a nondenominational church. He has launched a second Red Beans & Rice Festival, this one in Santa Rosa. Both festivals feature his version of the classic dish, with plenty of music served up alongside. In the summer of 1997, *Johnny Otis's Cook Book: Red Beans & Rice & Other Rock & Roll Recipes* was published.

BLACK BEAN TAMALES

Because of the lard in the tamale dough, these bean tamales are not vegetarian. You can substitute vegetable shortening, but the tamales will not be as light and flavorful as they are with lard.

MAKES 24 TO 30
MEDIUM TAMALES

2½ cups Spicy Basic Beans (page 236), made with black beans
1 package dried corn husks, soaked in water overnight and drained
6 cups Tamale Dough (page 366)
¼ cup minced cilantro leaves
3 cups (12 ounces) grated Monterey jack
Sour cream, Avocado Sauce (page 63), or Guacamole (page 65)

Taste the beans, and adjust the seasonings, if you like.

Make the tamales: You will want tamales that start with corn husks that measure about 5 inches wide by 6 inches long; for some of the tamales, you will start with husks that are that size, but for others you will need to overlap 2 or 3 smaller husks. Place 1 large corn husk (or 2 to 3 smaller husks) on a work surface. Put a generous 3 tablespoons tamale dough in the center, and use your fingers to pat it out to about a ⅜-inch thickness. Put about 1½

tablespoons beans in the center of the dough, sprinkle minced cilantro over them, and top with a generous tablespoon of cheese. Fold up the long edges of the tamale so that they form a barrier that will keep the dough from squeezing out, and carefully roll the tamale into a cylinder. Tie the ends very tightly with string or with narrow strips of husk. Continue making tamales in the same manner until you have used all of the tamale dough; you will have some corn husks left over.

When all of the tamales are made, line a steamer basket with leftover husks. Place the tamales, standing on end, in the basket in a single layer; do not stack them on top of each other. Steam the tamales, covered, over simmering water for 50 minutes. Remove the tamales from the heat, let them cool for 5 minutes, and serve immediately, with sour cream, Avocado Sauce, or Guacamole on the side.

SONOMA CASSOULET WITH LAMB AND DUCK

This is a simpler cassoulet than French versions, in which preserved meats such as goose and duck confit contribute essential flavors. In this recipe, depth of flavor is provided by a stock made from smoked duck. Although it is not an essential ingredient—you may substitute chicken stock—the cassoulet is transformed when it is used.

¼ cup duck fat or olive oil
1 medium yellow onion, diced
1 head of garlic, cloves separated and
    minced
1 pound dried cannellini beans, Great
    Northern beans, or navy beans,
    soaked and drained
½ pound duck meat, preferably
    smoked, diced
1½ pounds lamb meat, cut into 1-inch
    cubes, or 6 small lamb chops,
    bone-in, trimmed of fat
1½ cups fresh bread crumbs (see page
    46)
1½ cups (6 ounces) grated dry jack
6 cups smoked duck stock (see
    Note) or other duck stock,
    preferably, or chicken stock

Melt the duck fat or olive oil in a heavy skillet over medium heat. Add the onion, and sauté it until it is very soft and fragrant, about 15 minutes. Add the garlic, and sauté for 2 minutes more.

Preheat the oven to 325°F.

Rinse the beans, place them in a large bowl, and toss them with the onions, garlic, and duck. Spread the cubed lamb, or distribute the lamb chops, on the bottom of a baking dish or pan, and top the lamb with the bean mixture. Toss together the bread crumbs and cheese, and spread them over the beans. Pour in the stock, being sure to moisten all the bread crumbs. Bake, covered, for 2½ hours, until the beans are plump and tender, removing the cover of the baking dish for the final 20 minutes of cooking. Remove the cassoulet from the oven, and let it rest for 10 minutes before serving.

NOTE: To make a simple smoked duck stock, simmer 2 smoked duck carcasses, in water to cover, in a large covered stockpot for 3 hours. Strain the stock, chill it, and skim any fat from the surface. Simmer the stock again until it is reduced by one third, and strain it through a fine sieve.

Chapter 8

MAIN COURSES WITH VEGETABLES

MAIN COURSES WITH VEGETABLES

Vegetables

"I heard a trout jump in the river, a late jumper. The trout made a narrow doorlike splash. There was a statue nearby. The statue was of a gigantic bean. That's right, a bean.

"Somebody a long time ago liked vegetables and there are twenty or thirty statues of vegetables scattered here and there in watermelon sugar.

"There is the statue of an artichoke near the shingle factory and a ten-food carrot near the trout hatchery at iDEATH and a head of lettuce near the school and a bunch of onions near the entrance to the Forgotten Works and there are other vegetable statues near people's shacks and a rutabaga by the ball park.

"A little ways from my shack there is the statue of a potato. I don't particularly care for it, but a long time ago somebody loved vegetables."

Richard Brautigan, *In Watermelon Sugar* (Delta, 1968)

GRAND AÏOLI

Aïoli refers to two things, a garlicky mayonnaise-like sauce and an abundant harvest feast in which vegetables, eggs, poached salt cod, and, sometimes, stewed octopus are served with the powerful sauce. It is a traditional Provençal meal ideally suited to California's climate and agriculture. A Grand Aïoli is best in the summer, when there is an abundance of fresh vegetables, including beautiful tomatoes and garlic that is juicy, fresh, and hot. To serve salt cod as part of the feast, you must begin at least a day in advance to soak the fish. Serve the aïoli sauce in the mortar in which it was made, and serve a chilled dry rosé or a Rhone-style red wine alongside.

SERVES 8 TO 10

1 fillet (1¼ to 1½ pounds) salt cod
10 small tomatoes, peeled
8 ounces haricots verts or other
    young green beans, parboiled until
    just tender
6 medium golden beets, cooked,
    peeled, and cut into quarters
18 small new potatoes, roasted in
    olive oil until tender
18 small artichokes, parboiled until
    tender, trimmed, and cut in half
8 to 10 hard-boiled eggs, cut in half
Kosher salt
Black pepper in a mill
1½ cups Aïoli sauce (page 417)
Country-style bread, sliced or cut
    into chunks

One or 2 days before serving, begin soaking the salt cold in cold water, changing the bath several times. The fish will double in size and become more tender as it soaks.

To begin making the recipe: Drain the cod, place it in a shallow pan, cover it with water, and bring it to a simmer. Cover the pan, remove it from the heat, and let the cod sit in the hot water for 15 minutes. Drain and set aside to cool.

Arrange all of the vegetables, grouped by type, and the eggs on a large platter, leaving room in the center for the aïoli sauce. Season the eggs with salt and pepper. Tear the salt cod into chunks and add it to the platter. Set the aïoli sauce, in a mortar or a bowl, in the center of the platter or alongside, place the bread in a basket, and serve immediately.

Summer Harvest Grilled Vegetables

Grilled vegetables are easy to prepare and utterly delicious. Even confirmed carnivores take to the meaty flavor and steaklike texture of grilled portobello mushrooms. Leftover grilled vegetables can be used on sandwiches—bell peppers, eggplant, and portobellos are particularly good—and on pizza, or diced and tossed with hot pasta. They also can be sliced, tossed with a vinaigrette, and served as a warm salad.

SERVES 4 TO 6

6 ears of corn in their husks
2 cups cherry tomatoes
8 bamboo skewers, soaked in water
    for 1 hour
3 red onions

Olive oil
Kosher salt or coarse sea salt
Black pepper in a mill
3 large eggplants, cut into
    ½-inch-thick slices
6 medium zucchini, cut in half
    lengthwise
2 teaspoons ground cumin
3 large portobello mushrooms
6 bell peppers, preferably a mix of
    colors such as red, green, purple, or
    golden
¾ cup Honey Pepper Vinaigrette
    (page 157)
¾ cup White Wine Vinaigrette
    (page 151)
½ cup Jalapeño Butter (page 415),
    optional

Prepare a medium fire in an outdoor grill.

Prepare the vegetables: Carefully pull back the husks of the corn, leaving them attached to the corn. Pull out and discard the corn silks, and cover the ears again with the husks. Thread the cherry tomatoes onto skewers, putting 4 or 5 onto each skewer. Cut the onions in half but do not peel them, and place them cut side up on a plate. Brush them with olive oil, and season them with salt and pepper. Put the eggplant slices on a large platter that will hold them in a single layer. Brush them on both sides with olive oil, and season them with salt and pepper. Put the zucchini in a large bowl, drizzle with enough olive oil to coat them lightly, sprinkle the cumin over them, season them with salt and pepper, and toss lightly. Put the mushrooms on a plate, brush them on both sides with olive oil, and season them with salt and pepper.

Put the peppers and the onions, cut side up, on the grill. Using tongs, turn the peppers frequently so the skins blacken evenly. When the peppers are charred on all sides but not burned, transfer them to a dish and cover them with a tea towel. When the skins of the onions are slightly charred, turn them over and grill them cut side down. Continue to grill them until they are tender, a total of 20 to 30 minutes, turning them as necessary to keep them from burning. When the onions have been on the grill for 10 minutes (or up to 15 minutes if the onions are large or if the fire is not very hot), add the mushrooms and eggplant slices to the grill. Turn the mushrooms and eggplant after about 7 minutes. After turning the mushrooms and eggplant, add the zucchini, corn, and skewered tomatoes to the grill. Grill the zucchini, corn, and tomatoes, turning them 1 or more times so that they cook evenly and do not burn, for a total of 6 to 8 minutes, or until they are tender and cooked through.

While the other vegetables grill, remove the skins, stems, and seeds of the peppers. Cut each pepper lengthwise into 2 to 4 strips, transfer them to a serving bowl, and season them with salt and pepper.

Cut the grilled mushrooms into slices about ⅜ inch thick, put them on a platter with the onions, and spoon some of the Honey Pepper Vinaigrette over the mushrooms and onions. Place the eggplant and zucchini on a separate platter, and spoon some of the White Wine Vinaigrette over

them. If you like, tuck jalapeño butter inside the corn husks. Put the corn and tomatoes on another platter. Serve the vegetables immediately, with the remaining vinaigrettes and, if you are using it, the remaining jalapeño butter, on the side.

BRAISED ARTICHOKES AND ONIONS

*F*resh artichokes are readily available much of the year in California. Ways to cook them, such as braising—traditional in the Mediterranean, where artichokes are also abundant—are familiar to most home cooks. Although you can use canned or frozen artichokes in dishes in which artichokes play a minor role, you should not use them in recipes like this one, where they are more important. Serve these artichokes with creamy polenta (page 347), oven polenta (Variation, page 347), or rice.

SERVES 4

4 large artichokes
¼ cup fresh lemon juice
¼ cup olive oil
8 garlic cloves
1 cup pearl onions, peeled
½ cup dry white wine
Kosher salt

Black pepper in a mill
1 lemon, cut into wedges

Trim away any tough outer leaves of the artichokes, and cut the stems to a length of ½ inch. Using kitchen shears, snip off the sharp tips on the remaining leaves. Cut each artichoke lengthwise into 6 pieces, and remove the thistle-like choke in each section, using a paring knife to cut it

from the heart. Immediately place the artichokes in a large bowl of cold water, and add half of the lemon juice.

In a frying pan large enough to hold the artichokes in a single layer, heat the olive oil over medium heat. Add the garlic and onions, and sauté them, stirring frequently, for 5 minutes; do not let the garlic burn. Using a slotted spoon, remove the garlic and onions from the pan and set them

Yum, Yum, Yum

Filmmaker Les Blank, a native of Florida who came to California to attend college and, like so many others, stayed, has produced remarkable documentaries for nearly three decades. Perhaps best known for *Burden of Dreams*, which documents the making of Werner Herzog's *Fitzcarraldo*, Blank's footage of food contains some of the most delicious images ever filmed. Among Blank's films in which this footage appears are:

A Blank Buffet (1988): A sampler of some of Blank's most memorable scenes of music, people, and food.

Chicken Real (1970): A surrealistic look at a chicken farm that produces 156 million chickens a year. Lots of chicken songs, too.

Garlic Is as Good as Ten Mothers (1980): Blank's zesty ode to the glories of garlic, its history, cultivation, consumption, and curative powers. Introduces a young Alice Waters and documents the first Chez Panisse Garlic Festival. Excellent footage

of legendary North Beach restaurateur Rose Pistola cooking and chatting about her father.

In Heaven There Is No Beer? (1984): The polka is celebrated in a joyful romp that, yes, includes food.

A Well-Spent Life (1971): This documentary of Mance Lipscomb, one of the greatest blues guitarists of all time, includes lengthy scenes of Lipscomb's wife frying chicken. "I was really interested in the chicken, and it becomes more than just someone cooking fried chicken—it's a feeling that comes out of it," Blank says.

Werner Herzog Eats His Shoe (1979): Not only does the German filmmaker really eat his shoe, he cooks it in duck fat and garlic at Chez Panisse, and offers a heady course of philosophy and inspiration, as well.

Yum, Yum, Yum! (1989): A truly mouthwatering exploration of the down-home cooking of French-speaking Louisiana.

aside. Drain the artichokes, pat them dry, and add them to the pan. Sauté them for 3 minutes, turn them, and sauté for 3 minutes more. Return the onions and garlic to the pan, add the wine and the remaining lemon juice, cover tightly, reduce the heat to low, and simmer until the artichoke hearts are tender when pierced with a fork, 25 to 30 minutes. Remove the lid, increase the heat to medium-high, and reduce the cooking liquid by half. Remove the pan from the heat.

To serve, place the artichokes, garlic, and onions on a platter, season with salt and pepper, pour the cooking juices over, and garnish with lemon wedges. Serve immediately.

CALIFORNIA QUESADILLAS

A quesadilla can be simple or complex, a snack or a full meal. These days, you find them everywhere—in airport cafés and fancy restaurants, in neighborhood Mexican cantinas and your best friend's kitchen. They come filled with virtually anything, from traditional cheese and salsa to beans, seafood, and fruit. This basic recipe is the one you'll find in most California kitchens.

SERVES 4

8 large flour tortillas
3 cups (about 12 ounces) shredded or
    crumbled cheese, such as Monterey
    jack, queso fresco, or queso cotija
2 tablespoons torn cilantro leaves
Mexican-style hot sauce or salsa
Guacamole (page 65), optional

Heat a griddle or large frying pan; if the surface is not well seasoned, brush it with olive oil. Warm the tortillas over medium heat, 1 at a time, on both sides. Return 1 of the tortillas to the pan, distribute one quarter of the cheese evenly over the surface, scatter a quarter of the cilantro leaves on top, and top with another tortilla. Cook until the cheese is almost completely melted, about 4 minutes, turn, and cook for 1 to 2 minutes more, until the cheese is completely melted. Transfer the quesadilla to a work surface, and cook the remaining quesadillas in the same manner. Cut each quesadilla into 6 triangles, and serve immediately, with hot sauce or salsa and, if you like, guacamole.

Feral Bees

Honeybees are not native to the Americas; they came with European settlers in the seventeenth century and were called "the white man's fly" by indigenous peoples. Honeybees are particularly vulnerable to disease. Two pests that arrived in the United States in the early 1990s have decimated feral honeybee colonies throughout the country, including in California. Managed colonies have also been hurt.

The loss of feral bees will hurt backyard crops. Bees fly within a two-and-a-half-mile radius of their hives to forage for food, and without foraging bees, backyard gardeners will have an increasingly difficult time, with less pollination bringing lower yields. The effects are less dramatic in larger-scale agriculture, which uses managed colonies.

If you've ever been near a beehive in the summer, you have probably heard the buzzing of the hive. This is the sound of thousands of worker bees fanning their wings to keep the temperature of the hive at 85°F, a temperature that is maintained year-round, regardless of the temperature outside.

Variations:

WITH SCALLIONS AND GARLIC: Cut 12 scallions, white and green parts, into small rounds, and mince 3 to 4 garlic cloves and 2 serrano chiles. Heat 2 tablespoons olive oil in a small sauté pan, and sauté the scallions, garlic, and serranos until they are soft, about 5 minutes. Add one quarter of the mixture to each quesadilla, spreading it on top of the cheese.

WITH AVOCADO: Top the cheese with sliced avocado. Serve the quesadillas with Salsa Cruda (page 57).

WITH NOPALES: Scatter diced roasted or grilled nopales (see box, opposite page) over the cheese.

CHEESE ENCHILADAS VERDE

When I was in college, a little restaurant called Rosie's Cantina was popular with the students. The fare was more traditional Los Angeles than traditional Mexican—the owner, Matthew Freeman, came from Los Angeles—and it was, for the most part, very, very bland, except for a tangy green enchilada stuffed with melted cheese. Rosie's served it topped with sour cream but I always asked for guacamole instead; its rich flavor is a perfect foil for the spicy green sauce. Eventually, Rosie's closed, and

Matthew, abandoning his hopes of escaping family tradition, became an attorney, as all of his brothers and his father had before him. Serve these enchiladas with Hibiscus Flower Sun Tea (page 471), Agua Fresca (page 472), margaritas, or Mexican beer. The salsa verde can be used with all types of enchiladas and tamales, or with grilled fish. Try to find fresh tomatillos; if they are not available, you can substitute canned ones.

SERVES 4

SALSA VERDE
2 pounds tomatillos, husks removed
1 large or 2 medium potatoes, sliced thin
3 tablespoons corn oil, safflower oil, or peanut oil
3 medium yellow onions, cut into ¼-inch slices
8 garlic cloves, minced
5 to 6 serrano chiles, minced
3 tablespoons torn cilantro leaves
Kosher salt

8 corn tortillas
2 pounds Monterey jack, grated
1½ cups Guacamole (page 65)
4 sprigs of cilantro, for garnish
1 lime, cut into wedges
Tortilla chips

Make the Salsa Verde: Wash the tomatillos thoroughly, chop them coarse, and place them in a heavy saucepan with 1 cup water or chicken stock. Bring to a boil, re-

Cactus Cuisine

At the Pasadena farmers' market, founded in 1980, piles of flat cactus paddles—*nopales*—are snapped up by the market's Latino customers. In northern California, one is most likely to find nopales at the Alemany farmers' market in San Francisco or at one of the area's Latino markets, which also carry pickled versions. Nopales ooze slime (as okra does), but when they are grilled the thick liquid evaporates quickly. They can also be roasted. Nopales must be handled carefully, preferably with gloves. Trim around the edges of each paddle, cut off the tough portion where the paddle was attached to the plant, and use a small knife to pare away the spines on the face of the cactus. Cut the nopales crosswise into ½-inch-wide strips, toss with olive oil, season with salt, and either grill them, for about 5 minutes on each side, or roast them, in a 350°F oven for 20 minutes. Dice them and serve them with hot corn tortillas or sliced roasted potatoes (which complement their tangy flavor), and a favorite sauce or salsa, such as Cilantro Sauce (page 285) or Avocado Salsa (page 64). Nopales are also used in traditional Mexican soups and salads.

duce the heat, and simmer, covered, until the tomatillos are soft and tender, 8 to 10 minutes. Remove the tomatillos from the heat and puree them in a food processor or by passing them through a food mill; if you are using a food processor, do not over-process. Cook the sliced potatoes in boiling water until they are tender. Drain them thoroughly.

Meanwhile, heat the oil in a heavy frying pan over medium heat. Add the onions, and sauté them until they are limp, about 8 minutes. Add the garlic and serranos, and sauté for 2 minutes more. Add the tomatillo puree, reduce the heat to low, and simmer for 10 minutes. Add the potatoes and cilantro, season with salt, and remove the pan from the heat. Use the salsa immediately, or refrigerate it, covered, until ready to use.

Thirty minutes or more before making the enchiladas, remove the tortillas from the refrigerator and let them come up to room temperature.

Preheat the oven to 325°F. Warm the salsa, if necessary, and dip a tortilla in it, turning to coat both sides. Set the tortilla on a work surface, place one eighth of the cheese down the center of the tortilla, and fold both sides to the middle to form a cylinder shape. Transfer the tortilla, seam down, to a glass or porcelain baking dish. Continue until all of the enchiladas have been formed. Spoon the remaining salsa over the enchiladas. Bake until the cheese is fully melted and the salsa and cheese are bubbly, about 25 minutes. Remove the enchiladas from the oven, and let them rest for 10 minutes.

Using a long spatula, transfer 2 enchiladas to each of 4 serving plates. Top each portion with a spoonful of guacamole, garnish with a sprig of cilantro and a wedge of lime, and serve immediately,

with the remaining guacamole and tortilla chips on the side.

WILD MUSHROOM STRUDEL

A version of this recipe appeared in my first book, *A Cook's Tour of Sonoma*. When my younger daughter, Nicolle, went off to graduate school she took a copy of the book with her. There, she says, she's made this strudel on numerous occasions, always dazzling her fellow graduate students and even impressing members of the faculty.

SERVES 6 TO 8

DOUGH
1 cup unsalted butter, at room temperature
1 cup cream cheese, at room temperature
2½ cups all-purpose flour
1 teaspoon kosher salt
¼ cup heavy cream

FILLING
2 tablespoons clarified butter (see page 288)
3 shallots, minced
4 garlic cloves, minced
1 teaspoon grated fresh ginger
6 ounces small shiitake mushrooms, stems removed
4 ounces chanterelle mushrooms, or 4 ounces additional shiitakes

Kosher salt

Black pepper in a mill

4 ounces cheese, such as doux de montagne, gruyère, fontina, or Monterey jack, sliced thin

3 scallions, white and green parts, sliced thin

1 egg white mixed with 1 tablespoon water

1 tablespoon sesame seeds, toasted

Make the dough: Using an electric mixer or a wooden spoon, combine the butter and cream cheese in a large mixing bowl until smooth and creamy. Sift the flour and salt together, and gradually add them to the cheese mixture. Add the cream, and refrigerate, covered, for 1 hour.

Make the filling: Heat the clarified butter in a heavy skillet over medium heat. Add the shallots, and sauté them until they are soft and fragrant, 7 to 8 minutes. Add the garlic and ginger, and sauté for 2 minutes more. Reduce the heat to low, add the shiitakes (including the additional 4 ounces, if you do not have chanterelles), and cook them, covered, until they are soft, about 15 minutes. If you have chanterelles, uncover the skillet, and sauté them until they have released their liquid and it has evaporated, about 10 minutes. Remove the filling from the heat, season with salt and pepper, and set aside to cool.

Preheat the oven to 400°F. Lightly oil a baking sheet.

To assemble the strudel, dust a work surface with flour and roll out the dough to form a 10-by-12-inch rectangle. Arrange

the cheese slices lengthwise down the center of the dough, and top the cheese with the mushroom mixture. Scatter the scallions over the mushrooms. Fold the edges of the pastry over to form a long cylinder, brush the edges with the egg white, and press with a fork to seal tightly. Brush the top of the pastry with egg white, sprinkle the sesame seeds over the top, and slash the pastry crosswise every 2 inches, being careful not to cut too deep. Transfer the strudel to the baking sheet. Bake for 20 to 25 minutes, or until the pastry is a light golden brown. Remove from the oven, let rest 10 minutes, slice all the way through crosswise where the slashes are, and serve immediately.

MUSHROOM RAGOUT WITH OVEN POLENTA

*M*ake this ragout using whatever fresh mushrooms are available. One of my favorite California purveyors of specialty mushrooms is Gourmet Mushrooms (see box, page 257), which sells to restaurant chefs, specialty food stores, and some supermarkets, and by mail order. Other purveyors are becoming more common throughout the country.

Cooking polenta in the oven is an excellent method if you are pressed for time. The cornmeal develops a rich depth of flavor, and nothing could be easier—you stir the polenta just once. Keep in mind, however, that polenta cooked in this manner firms up very quickly as it cools.

SERVES 4

POLENTA

1 cup coarse-ground cornmeal
1 tablespoon kosher salt
½ to 1 teaspoon fresh-ground black
   pepper
1 tablespoon butter, cut into pieces
½ cup (2 ounces) grated aged asiago
   or dry jack

RAGOUT

½ cup (about ½ ounce) dried porcini
   mushrooms
2 tablespoons unsalted butter
1 large shallot, minced
1 garlic clove, minced
1 pound assorted fresh mushrooms,
   such as chanterelles, oysters,
   shiitakes, or cremini, cut or broken
   into medium pieces
½ cup minced Italian parsley
Kosher salt
Black pepper in a mill

Make the polenta: Preheat the oven to 350°F. Combine the cornmeal with 4 cups of water in a 1½-quart baking dish. Add the salt, pepper, and butter. Bake, uncovered, for 40 minutes. Stir the polenta, add the cheese, and bake for 10 minutes more, until the cornmeal is tender and all of the liquid is absorbed. Let rest 5 minutes before serving.

Meanwhile, soak the porcini in 1½ cups hot water until they are soft, about 15 minutes. While the porcini soak, melt the butter in a large skillet over medium heat. Add the shallot, and sauté it until it is soft and fragrant, about 7 minutes. Add the garlic, and sauté for 2 minutes more. Add the fresh mushrooms, and sauté them for 4 to 5 minutes, or until they soften.

Strain the porcini, reserving the soaking liquid, and chop them. Add the porcini and the liquid to the fresh mushroom mixture, cover the pan, reduce the heat to low, and cook until the mushrooms are completely limp, 8 to 15 minutes, depending on the varieties of mushrooms. Uncover the skillet, increase the heat to high, and cook until the liquid is almost completely reduced, 7 to 8 minutes. Stir in the parsley, and season with salt and pepper.

Spoon the polenta onto individual plates, spoon the ragout over it, and serve immediately.

Gourmet Mushrooms

In 1977, Canadian biologist Malcolm Clark, who had perfected a technique for growing outstanding shiitake mushrooms quickly, was searching for a location for his fledgling mushroom company. After learning that shiitakes flourish in the same conditions as Gravenstein apples, he moved to the Sonoma County town of Sebastopol, where Russian settlers had planted Gravensteins in the early nineteenth century. Clark established Gourmet Mushrooms, Inc., north of the town, in an area that also produces outstanding pinot noir and chardonnay grapes.

Although best known for its shiitakes, Gourmet Mushrooms grows over two dozen types of fungi. Six delicious varieties they developed themselves. The first was the Pom Pom Blanc, a round white fungus the size of a tennis ball, with a shaggy outer layer that resembles a sheepdog's mane. Next came the Cinnamon Cap, the Blue Oyster, the Golden Oyster, the Clam Shell, and, most recently, the ghostly Trumpet Royale, with its white stem and pale tan cap. The company also gathers wild mushrooms throughout the northwest.

These mushrooms have been heralded by the press but until recently were available almost exclusively to chefs. In 1995, Gourmet Mushrooms began offering a retail basket filled with their signature mushrooms and seasonal wild mushrooms. They ship the basket, which arrives with cooking suggestions for each mushroom, anywhere in the world by overnight delivery.

GARDEN RATATOUILLE

The best airline meal I have ever had was on Air France, when I was fortunate enough to be flying from San Francisco to Paris. After a salad of butter lettuce with a delicate vinaigrette, the main course arrived: a flavorful ratatouille, served chilled and topped with a poached egg, the center of which was perfectly cooked. California, with its abundant produce, lends itself to many wonderful versions of this Provençal stew. In this one, two techniques create a rich and evoca-tive dish. Some of the vegetables are roasted together so that their flavors mingle from the start; others are cooked separately so that they retain their unique flavors and don't overpower the other ingredients. Then they are mixed together and allowed to rest for an hour, their juices mingling and enriching each other but not to an overwhelming degree.

SERVES 6 TO 8

8 ounces (from about 6 heads) garlic cloves
8 ounces whole cremini or white button mushrooms

2 eggplants, peeled and cut into
   1-inch cubes
3 medium or 4 small yellow onions,
   quartered
¾ cup olive oil
2 sprigs of thyme
1 sprig of oregano
2 pounds ripe tomatoes, peeled (see
   page 60)
3 red bell peppers, cut into medium
   julienne
4 zucchini, cut into medium julienne
¼ cup minced Italian parsley
2 tablespoons minced basil
Kosher salt
Black pepper in a mill

Preheat the oven to 350°F.

Toss the garlic, mushrooms, eggplant, and onions together in a bowl, and transfer them to a heavy roasting pan. Pour ½ cup of the olive oil over the vegetables, add the sprigs of thyme and oregano, and cover the pan with aluminum foil. Roast the vegetables until they are tender, 1 to 1¼ hours.

Once the mixed vegetables are in the oven, cut the tomatoes in half and gently squeeze out the seeds and gel. Coat the bottom of another roasting pan with 2 tablespoons of the remaining olive oil, and add the tomatoes, cut side down, in a single layer. Roast the tomatoes in the oven until they begin to darken and caramelize, 40 to 60 minutes.

Heat the remaining 2 tablespoons of olive oil in a heavy skillet over medium heat. Add the bell peppers, and sauté them until they are limp and fragrant, about 10 minutes. Transfer the peppers to a large bowl. Add the zucchini to the skillet, and sauté it until it begins to turn golden brown, about 8 minutes. Add the zucchini to the bowl with the peppers.

Remove the herb sprigs from the roasted mixed vegetables, and discard the sprigs. Break up the roasted tomatoes with a fork and add them to the peppers and zucchini, and add the roasted vegetables to the bowl. Gently toss together all of the vegetables with the parsley and basil. Let the vegetables rest together for at least 1 hour so that their flavors can mingle. Taste the ratatouille, and season with salt and pepper.

Ratatouille may be served at room temperature, chilled, or heated. To heat it, transfer it to a large ovenproof dish and place it in a 325°F degree oven for 20 minutes.

Variation:

For a chilled ratatouille with poached eggs, refrigerate the ratatouille for at least 2 hours. Poach one egg for each guest, cooking the eggs until the whites are set but the yolks still runny. Transfer the eggs to a lightly oiled muffin tin, and refrigerate them until ready to serve. Divide the ratatouille among chilled serving plates, top each portion with a poached egg, season with salt and pepper, and serve.

CHANNA DAL WITH YOGURT AND CHUTNEY

*D*al is the name used by most Indians to refer to all kinds of legumes. It also refers to the finished dish, which might be thin and watery, or thick, or somewhere between the two. You can make this dish with red lentils, *mansoor dal*, which I learned to do when I spent time in southern India in the 1970s, or with yellow split peas, either the supermarket kind or the imported Indian variety, *channa dal*, an adjustment I had to make when I returned to California and couldn't find red lentils. Today, there are thousands of Indian immigrants in the state, many in the Santa Clara Valley, where the computer industry has drawn many newcomers. Consequently, traditional Indian products, including both red lentils and imported channa dal, have become easy to get.

SERVES 4

1 cup yellow split peas or channa dal, or 1 cup red lentils
3 tablespoons peanut oil
1 yellow onion, minced
4 garlic cloves, minced
1 1-inch piece of fresh ginger, peeled and grated
2 teaspoons cumin seeds, toasted and coarsely ground
1 teaspoon turmeric
¼ teaspoon ground cardamom
¼ teaspoon cayenne
2 medium russet potatoes, peeled and cut into 1-inch cubes
Kosher salt
Black pepper in a mill
3 cups steamed basmati rice (see page 217)
¾ cup plain yogurt
1 cup Apricot Chutney (page 424) or bottled chutney
¼ cup cilantro leaves

Pick through the peas or lentils and discard any stones or darkened legumes. Place the peas or lentils in a heavy pot, add 6 cups of water, and bring to a boil over high heat. Reduce the heat to medium, cook for 5 minutes, and skim off any foam that forms on top.

Heat the peanut oil in a small sauté pan over medium-low heat. Add the onion, and sauté it until it is very soft and fragrant, about 15 minutes. Add the garlic, and sauté for 2 minutes more. Stir in the ginger, cumin, turmeric, cardamom, and cayenne.

Stir the onion-spice mixture into the peas or lentils, and add the potatoes. Bring to a boil, reduce the heat, and simmer, partially covered, until the peas or lentils fall apart and the mixture thickens, 40 to 60 minutes, depending on the age of the legumes. Add more water if necessary to keep the dal from burning or drying out. Taste the dal, and season with salt and pepper.

Divide the rice among warmed serving

bowls, ladle the dal over the rice, and garnish with a spoonful each of yogurt and chutney. Scatter cilantro leaves over the dal. Serve immediately, with the remaining yogurt and chutney alongside.

FARMERS' MARKET COUSCOUS

*V*ary the ingredients of this stew according to what's fresh in the garden or at the farmers' market on the day you are going to make it. The stew improves for several days after it is first made, so do not be alarmed at the quantity; it makes great leftovers.

SERVES 6 TO 8

3 tablespoons olive oil
1 large yellow onion, diced
1 head of garlic, cloves separated and sliced thin
1 1-inch piece of fresh ginger, peeled and slivered
1 teaspoon ground dried ginger
1 tablespoon ground cumin
1 teaspoon ground clove
1 teaspoon ground cinnamon
1 teaspoon turmeric
1 teaspoon ground coriander seed
3 tomatoes, peeled (see page 60) and chopped
1 sweet potato, peeled and cut into medium julienne
6 to 8 baby turnips, halved, or 1 large turnip, diced

8 small red new potatoes, halved
10 cups chicken stock or vegetable stock
4 ounces green beans
4 ounces yellow wax beans
1 medium zucchini, cut into medium julienne
4 to 5 jalapeños
1 cup cooked or canned chickpeas
Kosher salt
3 cups instant couscous
½ cup golden raisins, soaked in warm water for 15 minutes and drained
½ cup black raisins, soaked in warm water for 15 minutes and drained
Several sprigs of mint
8 ounces plain yogurt
2 cups Harissa Sauce (recipe follows; make the sauce while the couscous soaks, at * in the instructions)

Heat the olive oil in a heavy skillet over medium heat. Add the onion, and sauté it until it is very soft and fragrant, about 15 minutes. Add the garlic, and sauté for 2 minutes more. Stir in the fresh and dried ginger and the cumin, clove, cinnamon, turmeric, and coriander. Add the tomatoes, sweet potato, turnips, potatoes, and stock. Bring to a boil, lower the heat, and simmer for 15 minutes. Add the green beans, wax beans, zucchini, jalapeños, and chickpeas, and simmer for 15 minutes more. The vegetables should be tender but not mushy. Remove the skillet from the heat and season with salt.

Put the couscous in a large bowl or pot, ladle about 3 cups of the broth from the vegetables over it, cover, and let stand for

15 minutes. Add the raisins, and toss with a fork.

* While the couscous soaks, make the Harissa Sauce (recipe follows).

Place the couscous in the center of a large serving platter and surround it with the vegetables. Ladle some of the broth over all, garnish with sprigs of mint, and serve with the yogurt, the remaining broth, and Harissa Sauce on the side.

Harissa Sauce

MAKES ABOUT 2 CUPS

3 ounces serrano or Thai chiles, minced
6 garlic cloves, minced
2 tablespoons ground cumin
Kosher salt
½ cup extra virgin olive oil
1½ cups cooking broth from the vegetables
2 tablespoons fresh lemon juice
1 teaspoon kosher salt
½ cup torn or chopped cilantro leaves

Combine the chiles, garlic, cumin, salt, and olive oil in a small saucepan. Add the broth and lemon juice, bring the mixture to a boil, and remove the pan from the heat. Add salt to taste, and stir in the cilantro. Serve hot.

Banana Flowers

When Alison and Bill Werts bought some acreage in the foothills of Carpinteria in 1990, they didn't intend to become farmers. But because four of the acres had been newly planted with banana trees that yielded thousands of bananas each year, they try to make the beautiful grove pay for itself by selling the fruit at the nearby Santa Barbara Farmers' Market. Of the varieties of bananas they grow—Mysore, Brazilian, Ice Cream, Cardaba, Mansano, Jamaica Red, and Enano—Mysore, a small, intensely flavored fruit, is their most popular; the Wertses recently replaced a number of the Ice Cream banana trees with Mysores. They also discovered that the local Asian community loves the big banana blossoms; the Wertses sell about a dozen a week to cooks who take them home and sauté them in butter and garlic. Why bananas in California, you might reasonably ask. There are thousands of microclimates throughout the state, and in Carpinteria both avocados and flowers had failed to thrive. When the previous owners of the property planted bananas, they found the ideal match.

PIZZA DOUGH

omemade pizza dough is superior to anything you can buy in a supermarket, and it takes little effort to make. Remember to plan ahead to allow for the rising of the dough.

MAKES 1 12-INCH SHELL

2 teaspoons (about 1 package)
  active dry yeast
⅓ cup warm water
2½ cups all-purpose flour
¾ teaspoon salt
4 teaspoons extra virgin olive oil

Combine the yeast and water in a large mixing bowl, and set the bowl aside for 10 minutes. Stir in ½ cup of the flour, followed by the salt and olive oil. Stir in more flour, ½ cup at a time, until you have ½ cup left. Stir in ¼ cup of the remaining flour, and reserve the remaining ¼ cup.

Turn the dough out onto a floured surface, and knead it until it is smooth and velvety, about 7 minutes, working in as much of the remaining flour as the dough will take. Oil a large mixing bowl, and place the dough in it. Cover with a damp towel, set in a warm place, and let rise for 2 hours, until the dough has doubled. Punch the dough down, and let it rest for 5 minutes. Turn the dough out onto a lightly floured work surface, and, using the heel of your hand, press it into a flat circle. Use a rolling pin to roll it into a 12-inch

circle about ⅜ inch thick. Top the dough and bake it as directed in a specific recipe.

AVOCADO-ZUCCHINI PIZZA

here is no tomato sauce on this bright, spicy pizza. The delicate flavors of the olive oil, zucchini, garlic, chiles, citrus, and avocado shine through like California sunshine.

SERVES 4

Cornmeal
3 cups grated zucchini or crookneck
  squash
2 serrano chiles, minced
5 garlic cloves, minced
1 tablespoon fresh lime juice
Kosher salt
Black pepper in a mill
1 12-inch pizza shell (recipe above)
¼ cup extra virgin olive oil
2 cups (8 ounces) grated or shredded
  cheese, such as Monterey jack, St.
  George (see page 71), fontina, or
  mozzarella
2 tablespoons minced Italian parsley
  or cilantro
1 ripe avocado
Crushed red pepper
1 lime, cut into wedges

Preheat the oven to 475°F. Place a baking stone in the oven or sprinkle a baking sheet or pizza pan with cornmeal.

Toss together the zucchini, chiles, garlic, and lime juice in a small bowl. Taste, and season with salt and pepper. Dust a work surface with cornmeal, and place the pizza shell on it. Drizzle the olive oil over the shell, then spread the zucchini mixture on top. Top with the cheese, spreading it evenly over the zucchini. Scatter the parsley or cilantro over the cheese.

If you are using a baking stone, sprinkle it with cornmeal. Transfer the pizza to the baking sheet, pizza pan, or baking stone. Bake the pizza until the crust is lightly golden and the cheese bubbly, 15 to 20 minutes.

Meanwhile, cut the avocado in half, pit and peel it, and cut it lengthwise into thin slices.

Remove the pizza from the oven, and let it rest for 5 minutes. Cut it into 8 slices, and top each one with avocado slices. Sprinkle salt, pepper, and crushed red pepper over the pizza, and serve immediately, with lime wedges alongside.

SUMMER MARGHERITA PIZZA

*I*n pizzas laden with heavy tomato sauce, the other flavors get muddy or disappear altogether. I make this classic Italian pizza, named after Queen Margherita, the way Neapolitans make their pizzas—with no tomato sauce, and instead with a light brush of olive oil on the crust. Then, flavors such as these summer tomatoes are accented rather than eclipsed. The traditional version highlights the colors of the Italian flag—red (tomatoes), green (basil), and white (cheese). When tomatoes are at their peak, I add orange and yellow cherry tomatoes for even more color.

SERVES 4

Cornmeal
1 12-inch pizza shell (page 262)
3 tablespoons olive oil
20 small or 12 large basil leaves
2 teaspoons minced garlic
2½ cups small cherry tomatoes,
    preferably a mix of red, orange, and
    yellow, cut in half
Kosher salt or coarse sea salt
6 ounces fresh mozzarella, sliced thin,
    or teleme cheese, rind removed,
    sliced thin
Crushed red pepper

Preheat the oven to 500°F. Place a baking stone in the oven or sprinkle a baking sheet or pizza pan with cornmeal. Dust a work surface with cornmeal, and place the pizza shell on it. Spread with the olive oil, arrange the basil leaves on the top, and sprinkle garlic over the leaves. Scatter 1½ cups of the cherry tomatoes over the pizza, distributing them evenly. Season with salt. Arrange the cheese over the top.

If you are using a baking stone, sprinkle it with cornmeal. Transfer the pizza to the baking sheet, pizza pan, or baking stone. Bake the pizza for 18 minutes, or until the edge of the crust is lightly browned. Remove the pizza from the oven, let it rest for 5 minutes, scatter the remaining tomatoes over the surface, sprinkle with salt, and cut into wedges. Serve immediately, with the red pepper on the side.

STRAWBERRY- CHÈVRE PIZZA

This sweet and tangy pizza is excellent for breakfast or brunch. Be sure to use the best strawberries you can find. If you don't care for goat cheese, substitute old-fashioned cream cheese, which is made without gum and other additives; the more common commercial kinds, with gum, have the wrong texture for this dish.

SERVES 4 TO 6

1 teaspoon fresh-grated ginger
1 pint strawberries, sliced
1 tablespoon sugar
Cornmeal
1 12-inch pizza shell (page 262)
1 tablespoon hazelnut oil or walnut oil
5 ounces young (not aged) chèvre, such as chabis, or 5 ounces old-fashioned (without gum) cream cheese
1 tablespoon julienned mint leaves

Pass the ginger through a garlic press to extract the juice. Toss the strawberries with the sugar and ginger in a medium bowl, and refrigerate them, covered, for 1 hour.

Preheat the oven to 500°F. Place a baking stone in the oven or sprinkle a baking sheet or pizza pan with cornmeal.

Dust a work surface with cornmeal, and place the pizza shell on it. Brush the shell with the oil, and crumble the cheese on top. Arrange the strawberries over the cheese.

If you are using a baking stone, sprinkle it with cornmeal. Transfer the pizza to the baking sheet, pizza pan, or baking stone. Bake the pizza for about 18 minutes, or until the edges of the crust begin to brown. Remove the pizza from the oven, let it rest for 5 minutes, and cut it into wedges. Sprinkle mint on each slice, and serve immediately.

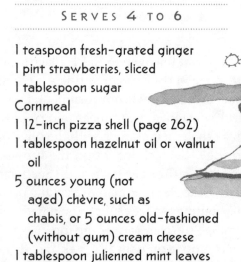

CREAMY GARLIC CALZONE

*U*pscale restarants with wood-fired ovens introduced calzones, filled with anything from traditional pizza toppings to spicy black beans to mélanges of seasonal fruits, to the California diet in the early 1980s. They are easy to make in a conventional oven, too, and the best are not complicated. They do depend upon excellent fresh ingredients.

MAKES 2 CALZONES, TO SERVE 4

Cornmeal
2 12-inch pizza shells (page 262)
10 ounces young (not aged) chèvre, such as chabis, crumbled
2 cups (8 ounces) grated Monterey jack or Italian fontina
½ cup (2 ounces) grated dry jack or romano
10 garlic cloves, minced
3 tablespoons minced herbs, such as chives, basil, thyme, oregano, or a combination
2 tablespoons chopped Italian parsley
1 teaspoon fresh-ground black pepper
Olive oil
1 teaspoon kosher salt

Preheat the oven to 500°F. If you have a pizza stone, place it in the oven.

Sprinkle cornmeal on a work surface,

and place the 2 pizza shells on it. Mix together the 3 cheeses in a bowl, and add two thirds of the garlic, the minced herbs, the parsley, and the pepper. Stir to blend well. Place half of the cheese mixture in the center of 1 shell. Fold the dough over and seal the edges tight, either by folding and pinching or by crimping with a fork. Brush the outside of the calzone with olive oil, scatter half the remaining garlic over the top, and sprinkle with salt. Repeat to make the second calzone.

If you are using a baking stone, sprinkle it with cornmeal, and transfer the calzones to the stone. Otherwise, sprinkle a baking sheet with cornmeal or polenta, place the calzones on it, and put it in the oven. Bake the calzones until the crusts turn golden, about 20 minutes. Remove the calzones from the oven, let them rest for 5 minutes, and serve immediately.

POTATO AND WALNUT PIROSHKI

*P*iroshki are Russian savory turnovers. They are always offered in Russian bakeries, a number of which we are lucky to have in California, especially in the northern part of the state, where Russians first established themselves in the nineteenth century. Although you must get the dough started early, piroshki are not difficult to make at home. Piroshki filled with ground beef or cabbage and sausage are most common, but this potato and walnut filling is an excellent meatless version.

DOUGH

3 cups all-purpose flour

1 teaspoon kosher salt

¾ cup unsalted butter, chilled and diced

6 tablespoons lard, chilled and diced

½ cup ice water

FILLING

3 medium russet potatoes

¼ cup unsalted butter or olive oil

3 tablespoons minced yellow onion

¾ cup walnuts, toasted and chopped

1 tablespoon minced dill or Italian parsley

Kosher salt

Black pepper in a mill

3 egg yolks, beaten

1 egg white

1 tablespoon white sesame seeds, toasted

Make the dough: Combine the flour and salt in a medium bowl. Add the butter and lard, and, using a pastry cutter or your fingers, quickly work the ingredients together until the mixture has the texture of coarse cornmeal. Make a well in the center, pour in the ice water, and use your fingers to incorporate the water into the flour mixture. Gather up the dough into a ball, wrap the ball in plastic wrap, and refrigerate it for 1 hour.

Roll out the dough on a lightly floured work surface into a rectangle about 20 inches by 6 inches. Fold the dough into thirds, creating a rectangle about 7 inches by 6 inches. Rotate the rectangle 90 degrees, roll it out again to 20 inches by 6 inches, and fold it again. Repeat the process 3 more times, ending with a folded rectangle of dough about 7 inches long by 6 inches wide by 1 inch thick. Wrap the dough in plastic wrap and refrigerate it for at least 1 hour and up to 3 hours.

While the dough chills, make the filling: Bring a pot of salted water to a boil. Using the large holes of a cheese grater, grate the potatoes, working quickly so that the potatoes do not discolor. Plunge the grated potatoes into the boiling water, return to a boil, and cook for 3 minutes. Drain thoroughly in a colander or strainer, pressing the potatoes to remove as much water as possible.

Heat the butter or olive oil in a heavy skillet over medium heat. Add the onions, and sauté them for 8 minutes. Add the potatoes, toss to combine, and sauté for 7 to 8 minutes more, until the potatoes are tender. Stir in the walnuts and the dill or parsley, and remove the skillet from the heat. Taste, and season with salt and pepper. Set aside to cool to room temperature. When cool, stir in the beaten yolks. Fill the piroshki immediately, or refrigerate the filling until ready to use.

Make the piroshki: Preheat the oven to 400°F, and butter a baking sheet. Put the chilled dough on a floured work surface, and roll out the dough to a ⅛-inch thickness. Cut circles 3½ inches in diameter. Gather up the leftover dough, roll it out, and cut additional circles. You should have about 30 circles.

Place about 2 tablespoons of filling in the center of each circle of dough, pull the edges of the dough up over the top, and pinch the edges securely together. Place the piroshki, seam side down, on the bak-

ing sheet.

When all of the piroshki have been filled, mix the egg white with 1 tablespoon cold water and brush the piroshki with the mixture. Scatter the sesame seeds over the piroshki. Bake until the pastry is just golden, about 30 minutes. Remove the piroshki from the oven, let them cool slightly on a rack, and serve them warm.

Slide Ranch

Slide Ranch occupies the site of an old Basque dairy farm, atop a rolling green ridge that overlooks the Pacific Ocean near Mill Valley. The ranch is a working farm that provides environmental education to children who live in nearby areas. Today, ask a kid where milk comes from and you are likely to be told, "the supermarket." Pizza comes from the telephone, not from the field where wheat is grown or the garden where tomatoes ripen on the vine. Slide Ranch is all about correcting those impressions with enriching hands-on activities. Children—and, on weekends, entire families—harvest vegetables, collect eggs, milk goats, make cheese, spin wool, and taste honey as it oozes from its natural comb of beeswax. Rather than being told how nature works, they become part of the process. Nearly six thousand children a year participate in the on-site programs of Slide Ranch. The ranch is part of the Golden Gate National Recreation Area. In the mid-1990s the ranch started the process of restoring the buildings that remain from the original dairy farm.

Chapter 9

MAIN COURSES WITH SEAFOOD

MAIN COURSES WITH SEAFOOD

CLAMS WITH GARLIC, LEMON, AND THYME

For this recipe, use whatever clams are available. I use small Manila clams when I can find them; sometimes I use Pacific or Atlantic little-necks, and occasionally steamers. Cockles, which are not clams but are similar and very good, may also be used; I like their small size. This is an adaptable recipe that will work with any small bivalve, even mussels. It is impossible to say exactly how long it will take for all of the clams to open—the time varies according to the variety of clam, the size of the pot, and the intensity of the heat—so you must look at the clams now and then as they cook. Be sure to serve plenty of bread, such as sourdough, with this dish for sopping up the delicious juices.

SERVES 4

2 tablespoons butter
8 garlic cloves, minced
1 shallot, minced
1 cup dry white wine
Juice of 1 lemon
2 tablespoons minced Italian parsley
Several sprigs of fresh thyme
5 pounds small clams in the shell, rinsed

Heat the butter over medium heat in a large heavy pot. When the butter is foamy, add the garlic and shallot, and sauté for 3 minutes. Add the wine, lemon juice, parsley, and thyme. Bring to a boil, reduce the heat, and simmer for 2 minutes. Add the clams to the pot, cover, and cook until the clams open, from 5 to 15 minutes. Remove the pot from the heat, and transfer the clams to a large serving bowl, removing and discarding any clams that did not open. Pour the broth over the clams, and serve immediately.

FIREHOUSE CLAMS AND RICE

The 1965 book *San Francisco Firehouse Favorites* contains both recipes and a glimpse into life at a firehouse, where appetites run high and, on quiet days, there is enough time to cook elaborate meals. When I read the recipe for Cockles and Rice, contributed by fireman Art Treganza of Airport Rescue Company Number 3, I couldn't wait to try it, it looked so good. It was, and after adding a few personal touches, including serrano chiles and cilantro, and making a few adjustments, I now make it frequently. Art offered some good advice in his recipe: "Before rinsing them in fresh water, squeeze cockles together, two by two. If loaded with sand, a cockle will open; discard it."

SERVES 4

2 tablespoons olive oil
1 small white onion, minced

273

1 shallot, minced

1 to 2 serrano chiles, minced

3 to 4 garlic cloves, minced

¼ cup minced Italian parsley

¾ cup basmati or other long-grain white rice

1 cup dry white wine

2 cups fish stock or chicken stock

2 pounds small clams or cockles in the shell, rinsed

2 tablespoons minced cilantro leaves

½ cup (2 ounces) grated dry jack or Parmigiano-Reggiano, optional

Kosher salt

Black pepper in a mill

Heat the olive oil in a heavy stockpot over medium heat. Add the onion and shallot, and sauté them until they are fragrant, about 10 minutes. Add the serranos, using 2 for more heat, garlic, and parsley, and sauté for 2 minutes. Add the rice, and stir with a wooden spoon until all the grains are coated with oil, about 2 minutes. Add the wine, stock, and 3 cups of water. Bring to a boil, reduce the heat, and simmer, covered, for 12 minutes, or until the rice is barely tender. Add the clams, stir, and cook over medium heat until the clams open, 10 to 15 minutes. Add more water if necessary for a souplike, but not too thin, consistency. Stir in the cilantro, and, if you like, the cheese. Remove from the heat, taste, and season with salt and pepper. Ladle into warmed soup bowls, and serve immediately.

CANTONESE SAUTÉED CLAMS IN GARLIC SAUCE

*M*ost recipes for fresh clams call for scrubbing each clam with a small brush. I usually find this unnecessary; the clams I buy are very clean and rarely need more than a good rinse. Check your clams before cooking them, in any case, and if they are gritty or muddy, scrub them clean, rinsing them afterwards in cool water. This version of a traditional Cantonese dish is adapted from *Jang Food: An Inherited Taste*, a collection of family recipes given to me by my friend Lisa Jang, whose family settled in the Los Angeles area. Home computers have made collections of family recipes, such as the Jang collection, easier to produce than in the past, and they provide an invaluable glimpse into authentic home cooking. I often serve these clams on a bed of steamed spinach, chard, or beet greens.

SERVES 4 TO 6

5 garlic cloves, crushed

1 1½-inch piece of fresh ginger, peeled and minced

Pinch of sugar

4 drops toasted sesame oil

Black pepper in a mill

3 pounds small clams in the shell, rinsed

2 teaspoons peanut oil

2 scallions, green and white parts,
   sliced into thin rounds
1 teaspoon diced fresh red chile or ½
   teaspoon crushed dried red pepper

Place the garlic, ginger, and sugar in a mortar and crush them into a paste. Add the sesame oil and several turns of pepper, and mix together briefly. Set aside.

Place the clams in a large heavy pot, add 1 cup of water, and bring to a boil. Reduce the heat, and simmer, covered, until the clams just begin to open, 30 seconds to 2 minutes. Strain the clams, reserving the liquid and setting the clams aside to cool slightly. When they are cool enough to handle, remove the clams from their shells.

Heat the peanut oil, garlic paste, and ½ cup of the reserved cooking liquid in a wok over high heat. When the mixture comes to a boil, add the clams and cook them for about 15 seconds, or until the clams are heated through. Add the scallions and chile, toss briefly, and transfer to a serving platter. Serve immediately.

HANGTOWN FRY

*I*t wasn't called the Wild West for nothing, and one of its characteristics was its occasionally swift and brutal justice, which earned one town—now Placerville, in the Sierra Nevada foothills near Sacramento—the moniker "Hangtown." There are several stories of how Hangtown's most famous culinary legacy developed, the most reliable one involving a gold miner who had struck it rich and devised the most expensive dish imaginable at the time. Eggs in particular were rare and expensive. Gold was plentiful for a time, but food and other commodities were often scarce; an indulgent celebration was not easy to come by.

SERVES 4 TO 6

4 ounces bacon
2 tablespoons unsalted butter
24 small oysters, shucked
¼ cup all-purpose flour
1 egg, beaten
¼ cup fine-ground cornmeal
6 eggs
Kosher salt
Black pepper in a mill
4 cups salad greens, such as mesclun

Fry the bacon in a large heavy skillet over medium heat until it is just crisp. Transfer it to absorbent paper. When the bacon is cool enough to handle, crumble it, and set it aside.

Drain the bacon fat from the skillet,

return the skillet to the stove, and add the butter. Dredge each oyster in the flour, then in the beaten egg, and finally in the corn-meal. Over medium-high heat, fry the oysters until they are just crisp on each side, a total of 4 to 6 minutes. Using a slotted spoon, transfer the oysters to absorbent paper. Quickly beat the 6 eggs, season them with salt and pepper, and pour them into the hot pan. Using a fork to scramble the eggs, cook them until they are just set.

Divide the salad greens among individual plates, and top the greens with eggs. Top each serving with oysters and bacon, grind black pepper over all, and serve immediately.

Ever Think of Sleeping?

"During the limbo hours of Sunday morning when it is too late for bed and too early for tennis, when bars and churches alike are closed, San Francisco revelers sometimes repair to Fisherman's Wharf for Hangtown Fry. Viewed objectively, this gastronomic nightmare hardly beckons weary head or jaded stomach, and had it been called Fourteen-Karat Omelette or Eggs and Oysters Jake, it would probably have faded into oblivion long ago."

Junior League of Pasadena, *California Heritage Cookbook* (1976)

ABALONE STEAKS

Along Highway 1, the Pacific Coast Highway that parallels the California coast, abalone shells are a common sight. Sometimes scores of them are nailed to a picket fence; occasionally the fence itself is made of large shells—up to ten inches across—cemented together in rows, their mother-of-pearl interiors glistening in the sun. These are the trophies of divers who use crowbars to pry the prized univalves from their underwater homes. An abalone is mostly a strong muscle, or foot, which clings with tremendous strength to rocks. Although difficult to harvest, abalone has been overfarmed and now is strictly regulated. Divers taking more than their limit are fined and sometimes arrested. Diving for abalone can be dangerous. Especially along the northern California coast, there are strong currents and sleeper waves, and every year several divers drown while hunting abalone. Great white sharks can be common in these waters, too. Commercial abalone, when it is available, is expensive. In California, we feel lucky when a brave friend shows up at our door with a fresh harvest. Then, there's a spontaneous feast as the cleaning, slicing, and pounding of the abalone meat begins and the air fills with the aroma of garlic sizzling in butter.

SERVES 4 TO 6

1 to 1½ pounds fresh abalone

½ cup all-purpose flour
1 teaspoon kosher salt
½ teaspoon white pepper
Pinch of cayenne
4 to 6 tablespoons butter
1 tablespoon minced garlic
Juice of ½ lemon
1 tablespoon minced Italian parsley
1 lemon, cut into wedges

Cut the abalone lengthwise into very thin slices. Place each slice between 2 sheets of wax paper, and pound with a mallet to tenderize it. Mix together the flour, salt, pepper, and cayenne in a shallow bowl.

Heat 4 tablespoons of the butter in a heavy skillet over medium heat. When the butter is foamy, add the garlic, and sauté it for 1 minute; do not let it brown. Dredge the abalone in the flour mixture, and place, without crowding them, 2 or 3 slices in the skillet. Sauté for 1 or 2 minutes, turn, and sauté until just golden brown, about 2 minutes more. Transfer the abalone to a warmed serving platter. Repeat until all of the abalone has been cooked, adding more butter if necessary. Add the lemon juice to the skillet, and whisk together the cooking juices and the lemon juice. Pour the juices over the abalone, and sprinkle with parsley. Garnish with lemon wedges, and serve immediately.

A Famous Oyster Pirate

As popular as oysters may be today, demand for them is nothing like what it was in the nineteenth century. In California, from the Gold Rush through the early twentieth century, oysters were devoured in great numbers, both raw and in a wealth of recipes, many created by chefs in San Francisco's grand hotels. Among the most celebrated dishes of the time were the oyster omelet, filled with a hundred Olympia oysters, that was served at the Ladies' Grill at the Palace Hotel; Oyster Loaf (page 176); and, of course, Hangtown Fry.

In that era, San Francisco Bay teemed with Olympia oysters, the only oyster native to the eastern Pacific. By the middle of the twentieth century, pollution and overharvesting had forced oyster farming to other sites, to Morro Bay and Tomales Bay in California and to Oregon, Washington, and British Columbia. Today, oysters from Tomales Bay in Marin County are among the best West Coast oysters.

Back when oysters flourished in San Francisco Bay, pirating them could earn you a lucrative living. For a time, one of the pirates was the young Jack London, who at fifteen borrowed money, bought a sloop, and raided oyster beds under cover of night. He sold the pilfered bivalves to saloonkeepers in Oakland, earning more from one night's bounty than he did in three months at his job at a local cannery.

PRAWNS WITH HONEYED WALNUTS

These prawns are often among the eight savory dishes that are prepared for the traditional Chinese wedding banquet. They're easy to make at home, too, even if there's no wedding on the horizon.

SERVES 4

8 ounces walnuts

2 cups sugar

Peanut oil or corn oil, for deep-frying

2 tablespoons white sesame seeds

10 ounces prawns or large shrimps, shelled and deveined

1 egg white

1 tablespoon cornstarch

1 tablespoon mayonnaise

1 tablespoon sweetened condensed milk

Juice of ½ lemon

Bring a small saucepan of water to a boil, add the walnuts, and boil them until the skins have loosened enough to be rubbed off, 2 to 3 minutes. Drain the nuts, and spread them on tea towels to dry. When they are dry, fold the towel over them and rub vigorously to remove the skin.

Place 1 cup of water in a small skillet, bring it to a boil, reduce the heat to medium, and slowly stir in the sugar, stirring in one direction only. Continue stirring until the sugar forms a thick paste. Reduce the heat to low, add the walnuts, and stir to coat them completely with sugar.

Heat about 2 inches of oil in a wok or deep-fryer to 300°F. Fry the walnuts, a few at a time, until they are golden brown, about 3 minutes. Using a slotted spoon, remove them from the oil, place them in a medium bowl, and toss them with the sesame seeds. Separate the walnuts, and set them aside in a single layer on a lightly greased cookie sheet or baking sheet.

Cook the prawns in a pot of rapidly boiling water until they just turn opaque, about 2 minutes. Using a slotted spoon, remove them from the water and let them drain on absorbent paper. Mix together the egg white and cornstarch until smooth, and dip each prawn in the mixture.

Fill a wok or deep-fryer half full with oil, and heat the oil to 300°F. Fry the prawns for 30 to 45 seconds, separating them with a pair of long chopsticks or a long-handled wooden spoon, until they are golden. Remove them from the oil with a slotted spoon and drain them on absorbent paper.

Mix together the mayonnaise, condensed milk, and lemon juice in a small bowl. Coat each prawn with the mixture. To serve, heap the prawns in the middle of a serving platter and surround them with the walnuts.

SHRIMP TACOS WITH AVOCADO SAUCE

Tacos are easy to make at home if you adhere to the basic concept. A taco consists of two small corn tortillas—hot and moist, but not at all greasy—topped with tender, flavorful meat shaved or chopped into bite-size pieces, hot sauce, chopped onion, and cilantro. Salsa should be nearby. Traditional tacos are flat, not folded or wrapped, and are not topped with shredded lettuce, cheese, sour cream, or guacamole.

SERVES 4

1½ pounds medium shrimp (about 50 total), peeled and deveined
¼ cup fresh lime juice
2 teaspoons kosher salt
16 corn tortillas

A Chinese Wedding Banquet

When immigrants settle in a new land, they give up many customs, but foods—and ways of marking special occasions with certain foods—are among the last elements to be lost. Among Chinese immigrants in California, elaborate wedding banquets are an enduring tradition. For the parents of a Chinese bride, Deborah Kwan of San Francisco told me, the wedding banquet is an opportunity to show guests the high regard in which they are held by serving them opulent dishes prepared with rare and expensive ingredients. Some elements of the meal are said to have auspicious meanings, such as peanuts, whose name in Cantonese sounds like "fast birth," and chopsticks, whose name sounds like "fast birth of a son"; and the menu always features eight savory items, because the word for eight sounds like the word for success. Deborah's marriage to Erik Cosselmon, in May of 1996, was celebrated in traditional Cantonese style.

DEBORAH AND ERIK'S WEDDING BANQUET

❖ Oyster Tumble with Lettuce Shell

❖ Sea Cucumber and Abalone over Greens

❖ Sautéed Squab with Mushroom and Vegetables

❖ Shark's Fin Soup with Dried Scallops

❖ Golden Fried Crispy Skin Chicken

❖ Prawns with Honeyed Walnuts

❖ Braised Stuffed Whole Duck

❖ Steamed Whole Gray Sole

❖ "Posterity and Prosperity" Sweet Consomme

❖ Wedding Cake

1 cup Avocado Sauce (page 63)
¼ cup minced white onion
2 tablespoons minced cilantro leaves
2 limes, cut into quarters

Toss the shrimp with the lime juice and salt in a medium bowl, cover, and refrigerate for 1 hour.

Prepare an outdoor or stovetop grill. Grill the shrimp for 2 to 3 minutes per side, until they are opaque. Transfer to a platter, and keep warm.

Warm the tortillas either on the grill or wrapped in a tea towel in a vegetable steamer. Put the avocado sauce, onion, cilantro, and lime wedges in individual bowls. Wrap the hot tortillas, place them in a basket, and arrange everything on a table. Let guests assemble their own tacos, using 2 tortillas for each taco, and topping the tortillas first with shrimp, then with a generous spoonful of avocado sauce, followed by onion, cilantro, and a squeeze of lime.

CRACKED DUNGENESS CRAB, SAN FRANCISCO STYLE

*D*ungeness crab, like other seafood, is best eaten as soon as possible after it is caught. In California, it is typically sold cooked, but you can find it for sale live in San Francisco, Bodega Bay, Fort Bragg, and other cities and towns with fishing fleets and good fish markets. The best way to cook it is to plunge the live crab head first into a large pot of boiling water. It is done when its shell turns red, which takes 10 to 15 minutes. Cracked crab is served both hot and chilled. Some say it tastes best hot and is served chilled primarily because it is sold already cooked; others, including me, disagree and believe it is better cold. To serve a fresh-cooked crab chilled, use tongs to transfer the crab from the pot to an ice water bath, and leave it in the bath for up to 30 minutes before cleaning it (see Note).

SERVES 4

2 medium to large Dungeness crabs, cooked, chilled, and cleaned
¾ cup mayonnaise, preferably homemade (see page 416)
3 tablespoons Dijon mustard
1 teaspoon prepared horseradish
½ teaspoon Worcestershire sauce
¼ teaspoon Tabasco sauce
1 lemon, cut into wedges
Prepared cocktail sauce, optional

Place the crab on a large platter or divide it among 4 individual plates. In a small bowl, mix together the mayonnaise, mustard, horseradish, Worcestershire sauce, and Tabasco. Serve this sauce, along with lemon wedges and, if you like, cocktail sauce, alongside the crab. Dip morsels of crabmeat into one of the sauces or squeeze a little lemon juice over the meat.

NOTE: Although you may, as I often do, ask the fishmonger to do it for you, cleaning a cooked Dungeness crab is easy once you get the hang of it. Set the crab, top shell up, on a work surface. While you hold the legs down with one hand, pull up on the shell with the other. Use your finger to pull out the yellow fat and edible organs, and set them aside to use in a sauce or discard with the shell. Turn the crab over and unfold the apron, or tail, on the underside of the crab; twist it off and discard it. Pull off and discard the gills attached to the shell above the legs. Carefully twist off the legs at the body and set them aside. Rinse the body under plenty of cool water and, if necessary, pull out the white intestine and small mouth (these will sometimes be dislodged as you rinse the crab). Using both hands, break the body in half; if it resists, set it on your work surface and use a cleaver or chef's knife to cut it in two. Crack the claws and legs with a nutcracker or small mallet. Serve the body, claws, and legs in the shell, as in this recipe, or pick out the meat for use in another recipe.

BODEGA BAY CRAB CAKES

Founded as a supply port for the early Russian settlement at Fort Ross, the small town of Bodega Bay became famous in the 1960s as the location for Alfred Hitchcock's *The Birds*.

Although the town has changed, it is recognizable to anyone who has seen the film; even the gas station is still there.

While the birds haven't bothered anyone in a long time, the population of Dungeness crabs, in most years, is thriving. Each year on November 30—the eve of northern California's crab season, which opens on December 1—Bodega Bay fishermen head to sea to sink their crab pots. When they check the pots several hours later, the size of the catch will predict how the season will progress. In some years the crabs are big and plentiful; in others they are small and scarce. Although the official season lasts until July 15, in a good year crab is most plentiful, least expensive, and best-tasting from the start of the season until about mid-February, when the catch begins to taper off. In a poor year, the price of the crab stays high, there is never enough of it, and it seems to disappear by the end of January. These crab cakes have become something of a New Year's ritual in my family.

SERVES 4 TO 6

¼ cup unsalted butter
1 medium yellow onion, minced
2 serrano chiles, minced
1 cup minced celery (from 3 to 4 ribs)
3 eggs, beaten well
½ cup heavy cream
1 tablespoon Dijon mustard
3 tablespoons fresh lime juice (from 1 or 2 limes)
3 tablespoons chopped Italian parsley

1½ cups coarse bread crumbs, lightly
   toasted
4 cups fresh crabmeat
All-purpose flour, for dredging
3½ cups Black Bean Puree (recipe
   follows)
¼ cup minced cilantro leaves
2 limes, cut into wedges
Sprigs of cilantro, for garnish

Melt 3 tablespoons of the butter in a small frying pan over medium heat. Add the onion, and sauté it until it is limp and fragrant, about 8 minutes. Add the serranos and celery, and sauté for 5 minutes more, stirring frequently. Do not let the vegetables brown. Remove the pan from the heat, and let the mixture cool to room temperature.

In a medium bowl, mix together the onion mixture, eggs, cream, mustard, lime juice, and parsley. In a separate bowl, toss together the crabmeat and 1¼ cups of the bread crumbs. Combine the two mixtures, adding more bread crumbs if necessary to form a proper consistency for cakes.

Spread some of the flour on a plate. Melt the remaining 1 tablespoon of butter in a heavy skillet over medium heat. Gently form some of the crab mixture into a cake about 2½ inches wide and ¾ inch thick; the cake will be somewhat loose. When the butter is foamy, dredge the cake in flour, place it in the hot butter, and sauté until golden, about 4 minutes on each side. Repeat until all of the crab cakes have been cooked.

To serve, divide the bean puree among individual plates. Shake and tip the plates so that the beans form a pool over the sur-face. Set 2 to 3 crab cakes on each plate, sprinkle with minced cilantro, garnish with lime wedges and a sprig of cilantro, and serve immediately.

Black Bean Puree

MAKES ABOUT 3½ CUPS

1½ cups black beans, soaked and
   drained
1 yellow onion, quartered
8 garlic cloves
2 serrano chiles or 2 dried chipotles
1 celery rib
¾ teaspoon ground cumin
Kosher salt
Black pepper in a mill

Rinse the beans, place them in a heavy pot, and add water to cover them by 2 inches. Add the onion, garlic, chiles, and celery, and bring to a boil over high heat. Reduce the heat, and simmer, partially covered, until the beans are completely tender and begin to fall apart, 1½ to 2 hours. Using tongs, remove and discard the onions, chiles, and celery. Using an immersion blender or a food mill or food processor, puree the beans. Return to the heat, add the cumin, and simmer for 10 minutes, stirring frequently to prevent sticking. Taste the beans, season with salt and pepper, and set aside until ready to use.

CIOPPINO

here are probably as many versions of cioppino, the San Francisco fish stew, as there are cooks in California. Some cioppinos are thick and concentrated, with lots of tomato paste and heavy tomato sauce; others are leaner, with a restrained amount of fresh tomatoes. Most call for red wine, a few for white, some for no wine at all. I like the lighter versions that do not call for tomato paste,

The Stew Pot

A s early as the California Gold Rush of 1849, Italians lived in virtually every region of the state. Many worked as cooks or owned their own restaurants, and hotels throughout the gold country featured menus with tomatoey sauces and pasta. Around this time, the story goes, Giuseppe Buzzaro, a sailor from Genoa in northern Italy, concocted *cioppino*, a dish that has become a San Francisco classic. Some claim the name comes from the way in which fishermen would *chip in* from their catch as a huge stew simmered on the boat as it headed back into the bay. But Evan Jones, in *American Food*, suggests the savory stew might be a version of *ciupin*, a Ligurian fish soup found on menus in Genoa. California cioppino can include any type of fish and shellfish available in local waters, along with onions, garlic, fresh herbs, and tomatoes.

which I think imparts a sweet and, if the paste is canned, slightly metallic flavor to the stew.

SERVES 6 TO 8

⅓ cup olive oil
2 yellow onions, diced
2 celery ribs, minced
10 garlic cloves, minced
1½ cups minced Italian parsley
¼ cup mixed minced herbs, such as marjoram, thyme, and oregano
1 teaspoon minced rosemary
1 teaspoon minced basil
1 bay leaf
1 teaspoon crushed red pepper
1 teaspoon fresh-ground black pepper
2 cups dry white wine
1 28-ounce can diced tomatoes with their juice
Kosher salt
2 large or 3 small Dungeness crabs, cooked and cleaned (see Note, page 281)
3 pounds small clams or cockles in the shell, rinsed
1 pound medium shrimp, peeled and deveined
2 pounds fish fillets, such as snapper
Garlic bread or other hot crusty bread

Heat the olive oil in a large heavy pot over medium heat. Add the onions and celery, and sauté them until they are soft and fragrant, about 10 minutes. Add the garlic, and sauté for 2 minutes more. Add 1 cup of the parsley, the mixed herbs, and the rosemary, basil, bay leaf, red pepper, black pepper, wine, and tomatoes, and bring to a boil over high heat. Reduce the heat, and simmer, uncovered, for 15 minutes. Season with salt.

Croatian Cioppino

George Bonacich is an apricot farmer in Santa Clara County, as his father and uncles were before him. His relatives came here from an island off the coast of Croatia, where they were fishermen. When they arrived, they wanted to settle down and not spend so much time at sea, and so turned to farming. As George was growing up, family meals consisted of the hearty fare of his parents' homeland, dishes such as spare ribs and sauerkraut. His mother prepared cioppino, too, but different from Italian versions. There was no red wine, George says, but plenty of vinegar. It was a tangy stew with plenty of red pepper. Large amounts of onion, garlic, tomato, and fresh herbs went into the water—there was no stock. If there were fish heads, they were boiled first. There was always ling cod or red snapper, and his mother was very upset if the heads had been chopped off before she got the fish. There were often mussels, because they were cheap, and crab when it was in season. Sometimes, a big slice of fresh bread was placed in the bowl and the stew was ladled on top of it.

Break apart the crab by separating the legs from the body and breaking the body into 3 or 4 pieces. Add the crab to the pot, followed by the clams, shrimp, and fish fillets. Cover the pot tightly, and simmer for about 8 minutes, until the clams have opened and the fish is cooked through.

To serve, divide the seafood among serving bowls, ladle sauce over each portion, and garnish with the remaining ½ cup of parsley. Serve immediately, with hot bread on the side.

MEXICAN SEAFOOD STEW

Achiote, a paste of ground annatto seed, cumin, garlic, vinegar, and oregano, provides depth of flavor in this seafood and pasta stew, a festive dish for special occasions. Vary the seafood according to what is available, and omit the shellfish entirely if you don't want to be bothered. Do make the effort to find achiote, which is sold in Mexican and Latin markets and in specialty food stores.

SERVES 4 TO 6

¼ cup olive oil
1 cup sliced leeks, white part only
2 to 3 serrano chiles, seeded and diced
8 garlic cloves, minced
2 tablespoons achiote

4 cups chicken stock

3 medium zucchini, diced

3 cups Tomato Concassé (page 98)

Kosher salt

Black pepper in a mill

8 ounces small dried pasta, such as
    tripolini, farfalline, or small shells

1 cup Cilantro Sauce (recipe follows)

1 pound medium shrimp, peeled and
    deveined

1 pound fish fillets, such as snapper,
    cut into 1-inch cubes

1 pound fresh mussels or 2 pounds
    manila clams or cockles in the shell,
    scrubbed

1 lime, cut into wedges

Heat the olive oil in a large heavy pot over medium heat. Add the leeks and serranos, using 3 serranos for more heat, and sauté them until they are soft and fragrant, about 15 minutes. Add the garlic, and sauté for 2 minutes more. Break up the achiote with your fingers, and place it in a small bowl. Stir in enough stock to make a paste. Add the achiote paste and the rest of the stock to the leek mixture. Add the zucchini and tomato concassé, and simmer for 10 minutes. Season with salt and pepper.

While the vegetables are cooking, cook the pasta separately until it is just barely done. Drain and rinse the pasta, toss it with 2 tablespoons of the cilantro sauce, and set it aside.

Add the seafood to the vegetables, cover the pot, and simmer for 5 minutes. Remove the pot from the heat. Divide the pasta among heated soup bowls and then ladle the stew over it, being sure that each

serving gets each type of seafood. Top each portion with a spoonful of cilantro sauce. Serve immediately, with a lime wedge and with the remaining cilantro sauce on the side.

Cilantro Sauce

Use this sauce as a dip for chips; on tacos, quesadillas, and omelets; and as a garnish on soups such as Tomato-Cilantro Soup (page 85).

MAKES ABOUT 1½ CUPS

6 garlic cloves

1 serrano or jalapeño chile

2 cups (about 2 bunches) cilantro
    leaves

1 teaspoon kosher salt

¼ cup fresh lime juice (from 3 to 4
    limes)

⅓ cup extra virgin olive oil

Combine the garlic, chile, cilantro, salt, and lime juice in a blender or food processor. Blend or process until the mixture forms a smooth puree. Transfer to a small bowl, stir in the olive oil, taste, and adjust the seasonings.

PORTUGUESE SHELLFISH STEW WITH SAUSAGES

M y friend John Kramer is a wonderful and enthusiastic cook. One day as I was writing this book, he called and invited me to join the other members of the M.F.K. Fisher Democratic Club and Travel Society, a loosely organized group of friends who gather monthly to eat, drink, and dream of

When the Hogs Are Killed

"Chorizo was a delicacy prepared in winter months when hogs were killed, and hung in a cool place for months. [To make chorizo, take] 4 pounds lean ground pork, 1 pound dry red chiles, 1 tablespoon salt, 1 teaspoon black pepper, 1 teaspoon oregano, ½ cup vinegar, 2 garlic cloves, mashed, and ½ cup toasted bread crumbs. Clean chiles, remove seeds, pour boiling water (1 cup) over and steam until soft. Drain, run through a sieve; add the pulp to the meat, knead together with the other ingredients; mold into patties and fry or stuff into sausage casings and hang in cool place."

Ana Bégué de Packman, *Early California Hospitality: The Cookery Customs of Spanish California* (1938)

their next visits to Provence. I had to decline, but asked if I could come at the last minute should I feel satisfied with my day's work. "Of course," he replied. About 8 p.m., I turned off the computer and joined the party. Had I not, I would have missed this wonderful dish.

SERVES 6

1 pound Mexican chorizo
8 ounces kielbasa or linguica, cut into small chunks
2 tablespoons olive oil
2 yellow onions, sliced
2 serrano chiles, minced
8 garlic cloves, minced
8 ounces prosciutto, diced
1 cup Tomato Concassé (page 98) or 1 cup canned diced tomatoes
½ teaspoon crushed red pepper
¼ cup minced Italian parsley
1 cup white wine
2 pounds mussels in the shell, scrubbed
3 pounds manila or cherrystone clams in the shell, rinsed

In a large heavy skillet or stew pot with a lid, fry the chorizo over medium heat, crumbling the meat with a fork, until it is just done, about 7 minutes. Using a slotted spoon, transfer the chorizo to a plate. Pour off and discard the fat, return the pan to the heat, and fry the kielbasa or linguica until it releases most of its fat, about 7 minutes. Transfer the sausage to the plate with the chorizo, and pour off and discard the fat.

Return the pan to the heat, and heat the

China Camp

"**F**rank Quan is a gourmet cook," park ranger Patrick Robards tells me one hot spring evening.

"Each Chinese New Year he has a celebration for friends and family—that includes me—and there are thirteen, maybe fourteen courses. His favorite meat is lamb, which he barbecues, rolled with jelly. I love everything he does with seafood—he makes a sort of cioppino, using all of the local catch plus mussels and abalone. He makes great soups, too."

Frank Quan, born in 1925, grew up in what is the last remaining Chinese fishing village in the Bay Area. At the beginning of the twentieth century, the San Francisco–San Pablo Bay Area was ringed by these villages. When work on the railroads was no longer available, some Chinese immigrants returned to their homeland, some found work in the gold fields, and others got jobs in vineyards and wineries. Those who had come from the fishing villages of Canton, where they had fished the waters of the Pearl and Yangtze Rivers, became fishermen, applying their skills in the fertile bays and deltas, in the process setting up dozens of small villages. No records exist as to when the first village was formed, but we know that as early as the late 1860s and early 1870s several were established.

Today, only China Camp remains, now a museum and a state park, the only such site in the state devoted to a fishery and one of only two that focus on the history of Chinese immigrants. Frank Quan's grandfather, Quan Yick Yuen (also called Quan Hung Quock), operated a store here, and his father, Henry Quan, began the shrimp business that Frank continues today, selling most of his daily catch to Bay Area bait shops but occasionally cooking up a batch of the shrimp for the park's visitors. The 1,560-acre park welcomes about a quarter million visitors a year. China Camp Museum and State Park in San Rafael is open year-round; the telephone number is 415-456-0766.

olive oil over medium heat. Add the onions, and sauté them until they are limp, about 8 minutes. Add the serranos and the garlic, and sauté for 2 minutes more. Stir in the prosciutto, tomatoes, red pepper, parsley, and wine, and bring to a boil. Reduce the heat to a simmer. Arrange the mussels and clams, hinge side down, over the surface of the stew, cover the pan, and cook until the shellfish just open, 6 to 10 minutes. Remove the stew from the heat, and serve immediately.

SAN FRANCISCO SANDDABS

"Nowhere else in the country," Paul Johnson of Monterey Fish commented on my radio show one day, "do people enjoy sanddabs like they do in San Francisco. It's really a local thing." So local and so common that I'd never given them much thought; I've eaten them with unselfconscious pleasure from the time I was a child, taking them entirely for granted. Sanddabs range from Baja California north to the Bering Sea, but they are most abundant in central and northern California, where they are generally harvested with trawl nets, though occasionally a happy sport fisherman hooks one on his line. The fish are small, with a mild flavor and delicate flesh; they need little more than a quick sauté in butter.

SERVES 4

½ cup all-purpose flour
Kosher salt
Black pepper in a mill
¼ cup clarified butter (see box)
3 to 4 pounds whole sanddabs,
    cleaned and heads removed
1 lemon, cut in half
1 tablespoon minced Italian parsley

Season the flour with salt and pepper, and place it in a shallow bowl or on a plate. Heat half the butter in a heavy skillet over medium heat. Dredge the sanddabs in the flour, then sauté them in batches, being sure not to crowd the skillet. Turn them once. They will cook quickly, about 2 to 3 minutes on each side, and are done when flesh around the bone at the head end of the fish is easy to penetrate with a toothpick or skewer. As each batch is done, remove it from the pan, and keep it hot as you cook the remaining batches. When all of the sanddabs have been cooked, transfer them to a serving platter. Melt the remaining butter in the pan, squeeze in the juice of ½ lemon, swirl the pan to pick up any juices, and pour the sauce over the sanddabs. Cut the remaining ½ lemon into wedges, and add the wedges to the platter of sanddabs. Scatter the parsley over the fish, and serve immediately.

To Clarify Butter

Clarifying butter separates the butter fat from the milk solids and whey that reduce its smoke point. This allows you to fry with butter at higher temperatures. Place any amount of butter in a small heavy saucepan over medium heat. When the butter is fully melted, use a spoon to scoop off and discard any whey or other particles that collect on top of the butter. Slowly and carefully pour the butter into a container, leaving the milk solids in the bottom of the pan. Let cool and store, tightly covered, in the refrigerator until needed.

BROOK TROUT MEUNIÈRE

The mountain streams and lakes of northeastern and north central California are filled with trout, but this has not always been the case. Over the last century, the building of California's vast system of dams and waterways, and the growth of industries such as logging and ranching, had caused severe damage to the bodies of water in which trout lived. Populations declined or disappeared altogether. In 1971, sports fishermen and conservationists formed California Trout, an organization dedicated to the preservation of wild trout and the renewal of their habitats. Because of the group's efforts, trout populations have returned to such important areas as the Upper Sacramento River, the Smith River, the East Walker River, and the Mono Lake Tributaries. Certainly, the best way to enjoy trout is when it is grilled on the spot along the banks of a beautiful lake or river and served with nothing more than a squeeze of lemon. This classic recipe is a little more involved, but not much.

SERVES 4

4 brook or lake trout, about 10 to 12
   ounces each, cleaned
¼ cup all-purpose flour
½ teaspoon kosher salt
Black pepper in a mill
3 tablespoons clarified butter (see
   opposite page)
2 to 3 garlic cloves, cut in half
   lengthwise
1 lemon, cut in half
3 tablespoons unsalted butter
2 tablespoons minced Italian parsley
Sprigs of Italian parsley, for garnish

Rinse the fish and dry them on tea towels. In a shallow container long enough to hold a trout, combine the flour, salt, and several turns of black pepper. Dredge each trout in the flour, and pat lightly to shake off the excess flour.

Heat the clarified butter in a heavy skillet over medium heat. Add the garlic, and sauté for 2 to 3 minutes. Remove and discard the garlic. Reduce the heat to medium-low, add the 4 trout, and cook for 4 minutes. Turn the trout, and continue to cook until the skin is brown and crispy and the trout is cooked through, 4 to 5 minutes more, depending on the size of the fish. Transfer to absorbent paper.

Pour off the clarified butter, squeeze half the lemon into the pan, and add the unsalted butter. Swirl the pan until the butter is completely melted and begins to foam. Transfer the trout to warmed serving plates or a warmed platter, pour the butter sauce over the trout, and sprinkle the minced parsley on top. Cut the remaining half lemon into wedges, place the wedges alongside the trout, and garnish with sprigs of parsley. Serve immediately.

GRILLED TROUT WITH BARIANI'S LEMON SAUCE

*T*he Bariani family of Sacramento uses this sauce over grilled trout. It is also excellent with grilled salmon or chicken, or as a sauce for clams and pasta. Emanuele Bariani was kind enough to share this recipe with me.

SERVES 4

1 lemon
¼ cup fresh lemon juice
2 tablespoons white wine vinegar
½ cup extra virgin olive oil
2 small shallots, diced
1 cup minced Italian parsley
Kosher salt
Black pepper in a mill
4 brook or lake trout, about 10 to 12
  ounces each, cleaned

Prepare a medium fire on an outdoor grill.

Make the lemon sauce: Remove the zest from the unsqueezed lemon, and mince the zest fine. Stir together the lemon zest, lemon juice, vinegar, olive oil, shallots, and parsley in a small bowl. Season with salt and pepper. Let the sauce stand for at least 30 minutes and up to 2 hours before serving.

Cut the unsqueezed lemon into very thin slices, and place the slices in the cavity of each trout. Season the trout, inside and out, with salt and pepper. Grill the fish, turning it once, about 4 inches above the heat for 7 to 10 minutes on each side, depending on the size of the trout. When the trout is done, its flesh will pull away from the central bone but still offer some resistance. Do not overcook.

Transfer the trout to a serving platter, spoon the sauce over it, and serve immediately.

CRESCENT CITY TACOS WITH SMOKY PINEAPPLE SALSA

*C*rescent City, the northernmost city on the California coast, is named for its arc-shaped beach. It's home to an active commercial fishing fleet. Rockfish are important commercial fishes along the California coast. There are close to sixty species of rockfish, all members of the scorpionfish family; the most common variety in markets is called Pacific red snapper, but one also sees Pacific snapper, black snapper, and rockcod. For cooking purposes, one species is interchangeable with another. All have a delicate flavor and firm texture, and they are available year-round. In this recipe, snapper is dredged in flour spiked with cayenne, then sautéed and folded into soft corn tortillas. Instead of Grilled Pineapple-Chipotle Salsa, you can use Salsa Cruda (page 57), Smoky Corn

Salsa (page 62), or Avocado Sauce (page 63), if you like. Or dispense with the tortillas, if you wish, and serve the sautéed snapper with Bean Ragout (page 236).

SERVES 4

½ cup all-purpose flour
2 tablespoons cayenne
2 teaspoons kosher salt
Black pepper in a mill
1½ pounds snapper fillets
3 to 4 tablespoons unsalted butter
2 tablespoons minced garlic
Juice of 2 limes
16 corn tortillas
½ cup minced cilantro leaves
¼ cup minced yellow onion
2 limes, cut into quarters
1 cup Grilled Pineapple–Chipotle
   Salsa (page 70)

Combine the flour, cayenne, and salt in a medium bowl, and season with black pepper. If the snapper fillets are large, cut them into 4-inch sections. Dredge the fillets in the flour mixture.

Melt 2 tablespoons of the butter in a heavy skillet over medium heat. Add the garlic, and sauté for 30 seconds. Add several snapper fillets, and sauté for 3 to 4 minutes, or until they begin to turn opaque. Turn the fillets, and cook for 3 to 4 minutes more, until the fish flakes with a fork. Transfer the fillets to a serving platter, and keep them warm. Cook the remaining fillets, adding more butter as necessary.

When the fillets are done, increase the heat to high, add the lime juice, and swirl the pan to deglaze it. If there is any remaining butter, swirl it in the pan until it melts. Pour the pan juices over the snapper.

Heat the tortillas on a hot griddle until they are very soft, then wrap them in a towel. Place the cilantro and onion in small serving bowls. Add the lime wedges to the platter of snapper, and place everything on the table. Guests assemble their own tacos by topping two corn tortillas with a piece of snapper, squeezing lime juice over it, and topping all with cilantro, onion, and salsa.

Grilled Red Snapper

Mix together 2 tablespoons kosher salt, 1 teaspoon black pepper, and ½ teaspoon cayenne, and sprinkle the mixture over 4 red snapper (or other rockfish) fillets. Let the fillets rest for 10 to 15 minutes, brush them lightly with olive oil or peanut oil, and grill them over a medium-hot fire until just done, 4 to 5 minutes on each side. Transfer the fillets to a serving platter, spoon some Salvador's Smoked Tomatillo Salsa (page 61) or Zucchini Salsa (page 67) over them, and let them marinate in the salsa for 10 to 15 minutes. Serve with additional salsa and with hot corn tortillas and lime wedges.

Cannery Row

"Cannery Row in Monterey in California is a poem, a stink, a grating noise, a quality of light, a tone, a habit, a nostalgia, a dream."

John Steinbeck, *Cannery Row* (1945)

To echo the phrasing of its most famous chronicler, Cannery Row is a street, a history, a tourist destination, an underwater vision, a novel, and an image in a song—Bob Dylan's "Sad-Eyed Lady of the Lowlands."

At the heart of Cannery Row today is the Monterey Bay Aquarium, an international tourist attraction that draws close to two million visitors a year. It is housed in the old Hovden Food Products cannery, which was opened in 1916 by the Norwegian canning genius Knut Hovden, christened "King of Cannery Row" for innovations that advanced the industry. The aquarium borders the spectacular Monterey Bay, now a federal marine sanctuary, and is one of the most important ocean research centers in the world. Nearby, restaurants, cafes, and tourist shops line the street that once bustled with the rough-and-tumble characters of Steinbeck's novel—fishermen and vagrants, cannery workers, and the women of the night who worked at the street's once-thriving bordellos.

The area that would become Cannery Row grew out of the ashes of China Point, a Chinese fishing village established in the 1850s and destroyed by fire on May 16, 1906. After the fire, displaced Chinese families leased land to the north at McAbee Beach, an abandoned Portuguese whaling station established in the 1860s. There, the Chinese continued to fish, drying the catch for their own use and to ship to their homeland. They were joined in the 1890s by Japanese immigrants, who fished primarily for abalone and salmon but also for the sardines that soon would be so important. The Japanese delivered most of their catch to Monterey's fledgling canneries; for a time, the canning of abalone and salmon was more common than the canning of sardines. Italian immigrants, who began arriving in the 1880s, also fished, but sold their catch fresh in nearby San Francisco.

Despite the success of the Asian fishermen—the Chinese technique for drying fish was crucial to the canning industry's early success—both Chinese and Japanese immigrants soon became targets of prejudice. It wasn't long before Europeans dominated the region and its vast fishing and canning industry.

The canning of salmon, practiced as

early as 1896, didn't last long. Soon after Harry Malpas opened the first sardine cannery, on Ocean View Avenue in 1908, sardines came to dominate the industry. Preparation was slow. The fish were opened and cleaned, and their heads and tails were removed, by hand. Then they were dried on wooden slats, cooked in boiling peanut oil, drained, and packed by hand into cans that required hand soldering. Only a third of the sardines were processed in this time-consuming manner, however. The bulk of the catch went to the reduction industry, which turned the sardines into fishmeal and oil and was largely responsible for the notorious stench of Cannery Row.

Knut Hovden increased production capacity tremendously when he developed a mechanical technique for sealing cans. Shortly thereafter, Pietro Ferrante, a Sicilian fisherman, revolutionized fishing with a net that could capture huge numbers of schooled sardines. Soon, the catch surpassed the canneries' improved capacity and the boom was on. New canneries, more mechanized and efficient, opened, the fleet expanded, and the sardines cooperated. The catch increased from under eight thousand tons in 1916 to a high of over a quarter million tons in 1941. In 1945, the year Steinbeck's *Cannery Row* was published, 237,246 tons of sardines were processed in Monterey.

Although a few cautious souls warned against overfishing, no one thought the abundance would end. But end it did. In the late 1940s and early 1950s, the catch averaged only about fifteen percent of what it had been a decade earlier. The industry and the region were devastated. Fires, many of them arson, destroyed a number of the canneries, others closed, and the area was virtually abandoned. In 1957, the city of Monterey changed the name of Ocean View Avenue to Cannery Row, as it had been known for so long. The last of the canneries hung on until 1973.

Today, there's an antechamber in the aquarium's new wing, opened in 1996. Overhead, silvery sardines swim in a circular ceiling tank that rings the room, spinning in a dizzying display above the heads of the tourists who pass through on their way to an exhibit of fluorescent jellyfish. It is an exuberant tribute to the canneries that once flourished along Monterey Bay. And beyond the walls of the aquarium the sardines have returned, too, their numbers increasing throughout the 1990s. It is now thought that their disappearance may have been due to the natural ebb and flow of sea life, with its cycles of abundance and scarcity, and not the result of overfishing after all.

STEAMED WHOLE GRAY SOLE

The selection of seafood in markets in San Francisco's Chinatown, and in similar markets in other California cities with large Asian populations, is different from what is available in supermarkets. Much of the fish is sold live or fresh-killed, and there are unfamiliar varieties, too, including gray sole. Gray sole is not a Pacific fish, but it is popular in Chinese communities in California in recipes such as this one, a classic component in a wedding feast (see page 279).

SERVES 4

1 whole gray sole or flounder, cleaned
    and scaled with the head on, about
    4 to 5 pounds
4 teaspoons soy sauce
1 teaspoon sugar
1 teaspoon corn oil or peanut oil
Dash of toasted sesame oil
Pinch of fresh-ground black pepper
1 1¾-inch piece fresh ginger, peeled
    and cut into thin julienne
6 scallions, white and green parts, cut
    into 2-inch-long thin julienne
Additional ginger and scallions, cut
    into thin julienne, for garnish

Rinse the fish and use a tea towel to pat it dry. Place it on a heatproof serving dish with slightly raised sides that will fit into a wok or steamer. If the wok or steamer is too small, cut the fish in half.

In a small bowl, mix together the soy sauce, sugar, corn or peanut oil, sesame oil, pepper, ginger, and scallions. Pour the mixture over the fish.

Steam the fish for 10 to 12 minutes, or until it flakes with a fork. Remove from the steamer, garnish with scallions and ginger, and serve immediately.

SAUTÉED HALIBUT WITH MUSTARD

Two species of halibut, the Pacific halibut and the smaller California halibut, are found in California waters. The flesh of both is firm, but less so than Atlantic species, and the taste is milder. Smaller halibut are often sold in fillets, while larger fish are cut into steaks. In this recipe, mustard forms a light glaze as the fish is cooked. Serve with Carrot Fritters (page 15) and Steamed Rice (page 217).

SERVES 4 TO 6

2 to 3 pounds halibut fillets or steaks,
    cut into 6- to 8-ounce portions
Kosher salt
Black pepper in a mill
¾ cup Honey-Ginger Mustard (page
    421)
3 tablespoons unsalted butter

Season the fish with salt and pepper, and brush it on both sides with honey-ginger mustard. Melt half the butter in a large skillet over medium heat. When it is foamy, add half of the fish in a single layer. Cook for 3 to 4 minutes, until the fish begins to turn opaque. Turn the fish, and cook on the other side for 3 to 5 minutes more, or until the fish flakes with a fork. Transfer to a serving platter and keep warm. Melt the remaining butter, and cook the remaining fish in the same manner.

To serve, brush the top side of the halibut with additional mustard. Serve immediately, with the remaining mustard on the side.

GRILLED SWORDFISH STEAKS

In this recipe, swordfish steaks are rubbed with a mixture of spices before cooking, a technique that has become popular in California in recent years. Spice rubs contribute a lot of flavor without adding fat or calories. You can use this rub with just about any fish, including salmon, snapper, and shark. Serve the fish neat, with only a squeeze of fresh lime juice, or add a sauce or salsa, such as Smoky Corn Salsa (page 62), Roasted Pepper Salsa (page 65), or Grilled Pineapple–Chipotle Salsa (page 70).

SERVES 4

¼ cup chipotle powder or other ground dried chile

1 tablespoon ground cumin
1 teaspoon kosher salt
4 swordfish steaks, about 6 to 8 ounces each
3 tablespoons minced Italian parsley or cilantro leaves
1 lime, cut into wedges

Combine the chile, cumin, and salt in a small bowl. Set the swordfish on a plate and sprinkle a generous teaspoon of the spice mixture over each steak. Spread the rub evenly over the surface, and rub it in gently. Turn the steaks over, and repeat. Each steak should be entirely covered with a thin coating of the spice mixture. Cover with a tea towel and let rest for 20 to 30 minutes.

Prepare a medium fire on an outdoor or stovetop grill. Grill the swordfish, rotating the steaks 90° once on each side to mark them, until it is just cooked through and flakes with a fork, about 5 minutes on each side for 1-inch-thick steaks.

Transfer the steaks to a platter or individual plates. Sprinkle with parsley or cilantro, garnish with lime wedges, and serve immediately.

POACHED SALMON

*P*oached salmon is traditionally served chilled with a mayonnaise-style sauce. In this recipe, it is paired with a fruit salsa. Salmon, with its sweet-tasting flesh, goes well with sweet sauces. You can also serve this salmon with Aïoli (page 417) or with Chipotle Mayonnaise (page 418). Marinated Onions (page 428) make an excellent accompaniment when the salmon is served with Raspberry Mayonnaise (page 418).

Although this recipe is for salmon steaks or fillets, you can poach whole salmon using the same method; a small salmon—7 to 9 pounds—will serve 6 to 8 people.

SERVES 4 TO 6

8 cups Court Bouillon (recipe
  follows), at room temperature
4 to 6 salmon steaks or fillets, 6 to
  8 ounces each
1 cup Strawberry Salsa (page 68),
  Bing Cherry Salsa (page 68), or
  Mango Salsa (page 69)

Pour the court bouillon into a large nonreactive pan or fish poacher. Add the salmon in a single layer, and set the pan, uncovered, over medium-low heat. Using an instant-read thermometer, allow the temperature of the liquid to rise slowly to about 160°F. Maintain the temperature for 10 minutes, adjusting the heat if necessary. Remove the pan from the heat, cover it,

and let the salmon poach for 20 minutes.

Using a slotted spoon, transfer the salmon to individual plates. Top each portion with a generous spoonful of salsa, and serve immediately, with the remaining salsa on the side.

Court Bouillon for Poaching Fish

Poaching fish is best approached casually. When time is limited, you can poach any fish in nothing more than salted water to which you have added a squeeze of lemon or a splash of vinegar. You can add sprigs of herbs, a sliced onion, a shallot or two, and, if you keep it up, pretty soon you'll have a court bouillon.

The most important thing to remember when poaching fish is not to let the temperature of the liquid rise too quickly, and to keep it at a simmer rather than a boil. Fish can be poached in any vessel that will hold the fish in a single layer. For large whole fish, however, a poacher that stretches over two burners is essential. I have developed the habit of poaching fish directly in the liquid, with the vegetables tucked under the poaching rack, a practice that might horrify a more formal cook. The technique works just fine, but feel free to strain the bouillon and discard the herbs and vegetables before using it.

Poaching times vary with different fish, of course, but the Canadian Department of Fisheries recommendation of 10 minutes cooking time per inch of thickness (measured at the thickest point of the fish) is a reliable guideline to follow. Keep in mind that nothing replaces knowing how a cooked fillet, steak, or whole fish looks and feels, knowledge which comes only with experience. Letting fish cool to room temperature in the poaching liquid results in very tender fish.

MAKES ABOUT 8 CUPS

6 cups water
2 cups dry white wine
½ cup white wine vinegar
1 lemon, cut into quarters
1 carrot, chopped
2 yellow onions, quartered
1 medium leek, white and green parts, chopped
3 sprigs of Italian parsley
1 bay leaf
2 tablespoons kosher salt

Combine all of the ingredients in a stockpot, and bring to a boil over high heat. Reduce the heat and simmer, uncovered, for 20 to 30 minutes, skimming off any foam that forms on the surface.

To reuse the court bouillon after the first use, strain it and store it in the refrigerator for up to 3 days. Add additional water or wine, if necessary, to get the volume you need when you reuse it.

The Fragrant Trains of Fort Bragg

· ·

The northwestern part of California, the land of the legendary redwood forests, was once primarily a logging region until you reached the coast, where fishing, too, was an important industry. A logging railroad opened in 1885, and by 1904 passenger service on the line began. In 1925, little single-car gas engines were introduced, prompting the nickname "Skunk cars" because "you could smell 'em before you could see 'em." In addition to providing transportation, the cars delivered mail and groceries to inaccessible areas. Today, California Western Railroad's Skunk Trains follow the same spectacular route through the redwoods, carrying tourists—and the occasional local family, for whom the train may stop in the middle of a bridge, trestle, or forest so that they can jump off and hike home—to and from the historic town of Fort Bragg. At Fort Bragg, tourists can visit Noyo Harbor, home of a fishing fleet and long the center of the region's fishing industry. From November through March, whale-watching tours are offered, and sports fishing continues year-round. Immigrants from Finland and Sweden were the first to settle here, followed soon by Germans and by the Italians who would come to dominate the fishing industry. Truck gardens as well as poultry and dairy farming have been essential from the region's earliest years.

GRILLED SALMON WITH THAI CHILE SAUCE

I came across a version of this Thai chile sauce in a wonderful book called *Real Thai* by Nancie Mc-Dermott, who lives in southern California and teaches Thai cooking around the country. The book is a collection of traditional recipes from Thailand, interpreted with skill and finesse. I've taken some liberties with the sauce, adding a few slices of ginger because it goes so well with king salmon from Pacific waters. The sauce is good on any rich fish, such as tuna, eel, or mackerel. Serve the salmon with several side dishes, such as rice, cucumber salad, cabbage salad, and an assortment of pickled vegetables.

SERVES 4

CHILE SAUCE
½ cup fish sauce
¼ cup palm sugar or brown sugar
¼ cup fresh lime juice (from 3 to 4 limes)
3 to 4 slices of fresh ginger, each about the size of a quarter
1 tablespoon minced garlic
4 to 5 scallions, green and white parts, cut into thin rounds
2 to 3 teaspoons ground dried red chile or crushed red pepper

4 salmon fillets, about 8 ounces each

2 tablespoons peanut oil

Make the chile sauce: Combine the fish sauce, ¼ cup water, sugar, lime juice, ginger, garlic, scallions, and chile in a small saucepan over medium-high heat. Bring to a boil, reduce the heat, and simmer, stirring constantly, until the sugar is dissolved and the sauce begins to thicken slightly. Remove the pan from the heat, and let the sauce cool to room temperature.

At least 30 minutes and up to 2 hours before cooking, arrange the salmon fillets in a shallow dish. Brush the fillets generously with the sauce, turning them so that they are completely coated.

Prepare an outdoor or stovetop grill. When the grill is very hot, remove the salmon from the marinade and brush off any excess sauce; the fillets should be fairly dry. Lightly brush both the grill surface and the salmon with peanut oil, set the fillets on the grill, and cook for 3 to 5 minutes, depending on the thickness of the fillets. Carefully turn the fillets, and cook them until just done, 3 to 5 minutes more. Do not overcook.

Transfer to a warm platter, and serve immediately, with the remaining chile sauce.

ROASTED SALMON WITH ASPARAGUS RISOTTO

oasting salmon in a hot oven is a hands-off technique that is ideal when you want to serve it with another dish, such as a risotto, that requires more attention. This dish is best in the spring, when asparagus is available; in the summer, try the Variation, with Corn Risotto.

SERVES 4 TO 6

Extra virgin olive oil
4 to 6 salmon fillets, about 5 to 6
   ounces each
Kosher salt
Black pepper in a mill
1 tablespoon minced lemon zest
1 recipe Asparagus Risotto with
   Lemon (page 223)
1 lemon, cut into wedges

Preheat the oven to 375°F.

Lightly brush a baking sheet with olive oil. Place the fillets on the sheet, and season them with salt and pepper. Scatter the lemon zest over the fillets, and lightly brush each fillet with olive oil. Cover loosely and set aside for 10 minutes.

Roast the salmon until it is just done, 7 to 10 minutes, depending on the thickness of the fillets. Divide the risotto among individual plates, and add a salmon fillet so that it partially overlaps the risotto. Serve immediately, with lemon wedges.

Variation:

To make the salmon with Corn Risotto (page 227), prepare the Corn Risotto with minced cilantro in place of chives. Replace the olive oil–lemon zest salmon marinade with a rub: Mix together 1 tablespoon chipotle powder or other ground dried chile, 1 teaspoon cumin, and 1 teaspoon salt, and rub some of the mixture into each fillet. Proceed as directed. To serve, garnish with minced cilantro.

SEARED TUNA WITH POTATOES AND BLACKBERRY SAUCE

lackberries grow wild throughout much of California. In their season, June through September, families picking berries along the roadside are a common sight. The berry vines are remarkably resilient, in many areas even a nuisance, thrusting themselves up in the middle of gardens and choking out other plants. You can tell the difference between native and introduced blackberries by their leaves; natives have three leaves, non-natives five. Nothing beats a good berry right off the vine, but with such an abundance of them it's good to have plenty of recipes. In this dish, blackberries and red wine are reduced to make an intensely flavored sauce. The sauce is good with pork, chicken, and grilled duck breast, too.

SERVES 4

3 cups blackberries
1 cup red wine, such as zinfandel, merlot, or sangiovese
¼ cup honey, warmed

The Original 27 Counties

San Diego County shares its southern border with Mexico. The city of San Diego has been important since the state's earliest days; the Mision de San Diego de Alcalá was the first settlement of the Sacred Expedition. Today, development stretches north virtually all the way to Los Angeles, encompassing the once distinct communities of La Jolla, Del Mar, Oceanside, Linda Vista, and others in its northward sweep. Inland from the crowded coastal areas, agriculture still thrives, with dairy farming, tomatoes, and twenty-seven thousand acres of avocados. Here, you'll find fabulous guacamole and other avocado preparations in everything from omelets and tacos to hamburgers and ice cream. Residents of the county take their fish and seafood seriously, too; the fish tacos sold at San Diego's sports arena, for example, are about as good as you'll find anywhere.

2 tablespoons soy sauce
2 tablespoons raspberry vinegar, preferably low-acid black raspberry vinegar
5 sprigs of basil
Kosher salt
Black pepper in a mill
1 pound fingerling or Yellow Finn potatoes, sliced thin and cooked until tender
2 tablespoons extra virgin olive oil
1 tablespoon minced basil
4 tuna steaks, preferably ahi, about 6 to 8 ounces each

Prepare a hot fire on an outdoor or stovetop grill.

Puree 2 cups of the blackberries in a food processor or blender, and pass the puree through a fine sieve to strain out the seeds. Bring the pureed berries and the wine to a boil in a small nonreactive saucepan over medium-high heat. Reduce the heat slightly, and simmer until the volume is reduced by half. Stir in the honey, soy sauce, and 1 tablespoon of the vinegar, add one basil sprig, and simmer, uncovered, for 10 minutes. Taste, and season with salt and pepper. Remove the sauce from the heat, and set aside.

Put the potatoes in a medium bowl, add the remaining 1 tablespoon of vinegar, the olive oil, and the minced basil, and toss to combine. Taste, and season with salt and pepper.

Season the tuna steaks on both sides with salt and pepper. Grill the steaks for 2 to 3 minutes on each side, until they are seared on the outside but rare on the inside.

Divide the potatoes among 4 individual plates, and place the tuna on top. Drizzle sauce over the tuna and potatoes, and garnish with the remaining 1 cup of blackberries and the remaining 4 basil sprigs. Serve immediately, with the remaining sauce on the side.

SEARED TUNA WITH PASTA AND CILANTRO RELISH

Californians eat a lot of ahi or yellowfin tuna. They grill it, broil it, or cut it into cubes and cook it in a wok. Whatever the method, tuna should always be served rare. This spicy cilantro relish can be used as a condiment with any grilled fish; it is also excellent with corn on the cob or simply spread over hot corn tortillas. When corn is in season, add it to this recipe: grill it, cut the kernels from the cob, and toss them with the pasta when you add the relish.

SERVES 4

2 dried chipotles or 2 teaspoons chipotle powder or other ground dried chile

5 garlic cloves, minced

2 cups cilantro leaves

4 ounces (about 1 cup) queso cajito, crumbled, or aged asiago, grated

The Original 27 Counties

Until 1856, the original **San Francisco County** included the land that would become San Mateo County, but today San Francisco County consists only of the city of San Francisco and the Farallon Islands. Once the home of Costanoan tribes, San Francisco was originally called Yerba Buena. The Gold Rush transformed the new settlement into a cosmopolitan center. In less than fifteen years, from 1845 to 1860, the population swelled from only three hundred to nearly sixty thousand; the growth was so rapid that for years thousands of people lived in tents within the city. San Francisco's history is colorful, intriguing, controversial, and delicious. Since its earliest days, newcomers, both overseas and domestic, have sought to throw off the shackles of the more conservative places from which they've come. Bohemians at the turn of the century, beatniks in the 1950s, hippies in the 1960s, and gays and lesbians in the 1970s and 1980s have all contributed colorful chapters to San Francisco's history. A pervasive sense of adventure, rebelliousness, and sensual indulgence, combined with access to the state's abundant resources, has led to innovative cooking among home cooks and restaurant chefs alike.

Juice of 2 limes
½ cup extra virgin olive oil
Kosher salt
6 ounces seed pasta, such as seme di
    melone, orzo, or rosamarina
Black pepper in a mill
4 tuna steaks, preferably ahi, about
    6 to 8 ounces each

Prepare a medium-hot fire on an outdoor or stovetop grill.

If you have whole dried chipotles, put them in a small bowl and cover them with boiling water. Soak them until they are soft, about 30 minutes. Drain and mince them.

Make a cilantro relish: Using a molcajete or a mortar and pestle, grind the chipotles and garlic nearly to a pulp. Add the cilantro leaves, a handful at a time, and grind until you have a coarse paste. (Or put the garlic, chipotles, and cilantro in a food processor, and pulse until they are ground fine.) Transfer to a small bowl, and stir in the cheese thoroughly. Stir in the lime juice and olive oil, taste, and season with salt. Cover the bowl, and set it aside.

Cook the pasta in boiling salted water until it is al dente. Drain it thoroughly, and toss it with 3 tablespoons of the cilantro relish. Keep the pasta warm as you grill the tuna.

Season the tuna steaks on both sides with salt and pepper. Grill the steaks for 2 to 3 minutes on each side, until they are seared on the outside but rare on the inside.

Divide the pasta among 4 individual plates and place the tuna on top. Top each steak with a spoonful of relish, and serve immediately, with the remaining relish on the side.

Chapter 10

MAIN
COURSES
WITH
POULTRY

MAIN COURSES WITH POULTRY

CHICKEN QUESADILLAS

There are several brands of chipotle-based hot sauces available these days; one very good one is Bustelo's, made in northern California. It is not necessary to seek out a specific brand for this dish; it is the smoky flavor of the chipotle itself that you are looking for.

SERVES 4

8 large flour tortillas
3 cups (about 12 ounces) grated mild cheddar or St. George (see page 71) cheese
12 ounces cooked or smoked chicken meat, shredded
1 tablespoon chipotle hot sauce, or 1 tablespoon hot sauce combined with ½ canned chipotle in adobo, minced
1 cup Smoky Corn Salsa (page 62)

Heat a griddle or a large frying pan; if you are using a frying pan, brush the surface with olive oil. Warm the tortillas, 1 at a time, on both sides. Return 1 tortilla to the pan, spread a quarter of the cheese over it, and scatter a quarter of the chicken over the cheese. Add a dash of hot sauce, and top with another tortilla. Cook until the cheese is nearly completely melted, about 4 minutes, turn, and cook for 2 minutes more. Transfer to a work surface, and cook the remaining quesadillas in the same

The Original 27 Counties

Los Angeles County is the most ethnically diverse in California, although you might not know it from the images in the media, which concentrate on the lithe, tanned bodies of the beach communities and the glamour of Hollywood. But within the county you'll find a delicious variety of home-style cooking, from handmade corn tortillas and succulent *carnitas* (pork simmered slowly in its own fat and flavored with everything from orange juice to Coca-Cola) to savory Hungarian beef-and-paprika stews to Korean barbecued beef and *kimchi* pickles. M.F.K. Fisher grew up in the county, in Whittier, with a string of notoriously colorful cooks, such as the flighty Anita, whose repertoire included just two dishes—vanilla flan and very elegant chicken enchiladas. Parts of the original county became Kern County and Orange County, the latter named for the orchards that once dominated the landscape. Although freeways and housing tracts have displaced much farmland, there still are pockets of agriculture in Los Angeles County, including six hundred acres of avocados.

manner. Cut each quesadilla into 6 triangles, transfer them to individual plates, and add a generous spoonful of the salsa to each portion. Serve immediately, with the remaining salsa on the side.

Variation:

Use thin-sliced brie in place of the grated cheese, and top it with strips of smoked duck meat instead of the chicken.

CHILLED CHICKEN BREAST WITH STRAWBERRY SALSA

*T*raditionally, whole chicken is poached in stock on top of the stove. The chicken is wrapped in parchment before it is submerged in the stock and simmered very slowly. In this recipe, marinated chicken breasts are poached in the oven, a gentle method ideal for smaller pieces of chicken. This dish is particularly refreshing in hot weather, served with a well-chilled dry rosé such as Le Petit Faux from Preston Vineyards of Dry Creek Valley.

SERVES 4

4 skinless and boneless chicken
    breast halves, 6 to 8 ounces each
Kosher salt
Black pepper in a mill
8 sprigs of cilantro
½ cup extra virgin olive oil

1 garlic clove, crushed
2 tablespoons strawberry vinegar or
    red raspberry vinegar
2 cups chicken stock
1½ cups Strawberry Salsa (page 68)
1 pint fresh strawberries

Place the chicken breasts in a shallow bowl and season them with salt and several turns of pepper. Add 4 of the cilantro sprigs. Mix together the olive oil, garlic, and vinegar, and pour the mixture over the chicken breasts. Marinate the chicken, refrigerated, for at least 2 hours or up to 4 hours.

About 30 minutes before cooking, remove the chicken from the refrigerator. Preheat the oven to 375°F.

Bring the stock to a boil in a small saucepan. Place the chicken in a baking dish, and pour the stock over the chicken. Bake the chicken, uncovered, for 12 minutes, or until it is just barely done. Remove from the oven, and let the chicken cool in the stock. Transfer the chicken to a plate, cover, and refrigerate for one hour.

To serve, place the chicken on individual plates. Spoon salsa over each portion, garnish with a sprig of cilantro and some strawberries, and serve immediately.

Variation:

Use any classic salsa, such as Salsa Cruda (page 57), in place of the strawberry salsa for a more traditional dish. Use lemon juice in place of the vinegar in the marinade.

PHONY ABALONE

One often comes across a version of this recipe in old California cookbooks and magazines. The chicken breasts bear only a slight resemblance to the real thing, which is expensive and often entirely unavailable—the reason, presumably, for so many recipes that call for chicken instead. California abalone have been overharvested and now are strictly regulated by the state.

SERVES 4

2 boneless and skinless chicken
    breasts, cut in half
3 garlic cloves, sliced
2 cups bottled clam juice
3 tablespoons butter
Kosher salt
Black pepper in a mill
1 lemon, cut in half

Place a chicken breast half between 2 pieces of wax paper. Using a mallet, pound the breast until it is very thin, about ⅛ inch. Repeat with the remaining halves. Place the chicken in a single layer in a glass or porcelain dish. Scatter the garlic over the chicken, pour the clam juice over, and turn the chicken to coat it thoroughly. Refrigerate, covered, for at least 24 hours or up to 36 hours, turning occasionally.

Heat the butter in a heavy skillet over medium heat. Remove the chicken from the marinade, pat it dry, season it with salt and pepper, and sauté it, turning once,

until just done, about 3 minutes on each side. Transfer to a warmed serving platter. With the pan still over medium heat, squeeze the juice of half of the lemon into the pan, swirl 2 or 3 times, and pour over the chicken. Cut the remaining half lemon into quarters, and add them to the platter. Season with salt and pepper, and serve immediately.

GINGER CHICKEN STIR-FRY

Be sure to serve any stir-fry with plenty of steamed rice (see page 217). And remember, the ingredients are not set in stone. If you don't have red bell pepper, use green, or omit it altogether; if all you have is white button mushrooms, those are just fine. It is the technique of cutting all the foods into similar sizes and cooking them quickly that is important.

SERVES 4

1 tablespoon toasted sesame oil
1 tablespoon minced fresh ginger
1 tablespoon minced garlic
1 red bell pepper, cut into thin julienne
1 pound boneless chicken meat
    (breast or thigh), cut into bite-size
    pieces
8 ounces shiitake or cremini
    mushrooms, sliced
8 scallions, white and green parts,
    sliced into rounds

½ teaspoon crushed red pepper
1 tablespoon oyster sauce
¼ cup chicken stock
2 tablespoons fish sauce or 1
    tablespoon soy sauce mixed with
    1 tablespoon water

Heat the sesame oil in a wok over medium-high heat. Add the ginger and garlic, and cook them, tossing and stirring constantly so they do not burn, until they are fragrant, about 2 minutes. Add the bell pepper, and cook it, tossing and stirring, until it is limp, 3 to 4 minutes. Add the chicken and mushrooms, and cook, tossing and stirring, until they are cooked through and tender, about 5 minutes. Add the scallions and red pepper, and cook for 2 minutes more. Add the oyster sauce, stock, and fish sauce or soy sauce, toss quickly, and remove from the heat. Serve immediately, with steamed rice.

GOLDEN CHICKEN CURRY

Curries of all types are popular in California and have been for decades. In the forties and fifties, they formed the theme for dinner parties known as "curries." Today, the approach is less kitschy and more traditional, as ingredients for South Asian, Southeast Asian, and Caribbean curries have become readily available in most areas. Curries should be served with condiments that offer contrasts in taste and texture. Include a sweet chutney, such as Apricot Chutney (page 424), along with yogurt, raisins, and roasted peanuts, if you like. Serve with Steamed Rice (page 217) or Jasmine Rice (page 218).

SERVES 4 TO 6

2 tablespoons curry powder
2 teaspoons ground cumin
1 teaspoon turmeric
¼ to ½ teaspoon cayenne
Pinch of ground cardamom
1 tablespoon all-purpose flour
2 boneless and skinless chicken
    breasts, cut in half
3 to 4 boneless and skinless chicken
    thighs
3 tablespoons clarified butter (see
    page 288)
1 large yellow onion, diced
4 garlic cloves, minced
2 serrano or jalapeño chiles, stemmed
    and minced
¾ cup chicken stock
1 cup coconut milk
Kosher salt

Mix together in a small bowl the curry powder, cumin, turmeric, cayenne, and cardamom. Place half of the mixture and the flour in a plastic or brown paper bag and shake to blend well. Cut the chicken into bite-size pieces and add the chicken, in 2 batches, to the bag of spices, shaking each time to coat the chicken thoroughly. Place the chicken in a shallow bowl and

Curry and the Social Whirl

"In recent years [the late 1940s] in the Hollywoods, and no doubt elsewhere, there has been an increasing popularity of curry dishes in informal entertaining.

"So popular have curry dishes become that a hostess will say, 'I think I'll invite them to a *curry*,' the word having come to designate a special kind of sociable.

"In some regions, at a time in the past, the word beefsteak came into similar use. A *beefsteak* was not an item of food, but a social event.

"In southern California you will, sooner or later, be invited to *a curry*.

"A curry is a party featuring a buffet supper built around one or more curry dishes, and presented on a table with a dis-play of accompanying dishes that in variety compares with the smorgasbord.

"Hostesses try to outdo each other in the extent and variety of the edibles set out.... An expert giver of curries is Marguerite Churchill, an actress of experience, but still young and charming and vivacious. She sets out as wonderful an East Indian curry as anybody we know. On her sideboard is a huge sterling silver bowl big enough to wash a collie in—it's filled with cracked ice—and nestling in it are bottles of cold beer, a most suitable potable for a curry."

Neill and Fred Beck, *Farmers Market Cook Book* (Holt and Company, 1951)

refrigerate for at least 1 hour or up to 3 hours before cooking.

Heat the clarified butter in a large heavy skillet over medium heat. Add the onion, and cook it until it is very soft and fragrant, about 15 minutes. Add the garlic and chiles, and cook for 2 minutes more. Stir in the remaining spice mixture, and add the chicken. Increase the heat to medium-high, and cook the chicken, stirring occasionally, until it begins to turn opaque. Add the stock, reduce the heat to low, and simmer, covered, for about 20 minutes, until the chicken is fully cooked. Stir in the coconut milk, and season with salt. Remove from the heat, and serve immediately.

GRILLED CHICKEN IN HALF-MOURNING

The irresistible name of this recipe caught my eye as I looked through *Elena's Favorite Foods California Style* (1967). It's a peasant rendition, author Elena Zelayeta writes, of a French dish in which sliced fresh truffles are tucked under the skin of a chicken. I have reworked Elena's recipe but left the name as it is, mysterious and pleasing.

SERVES 4 TO 6

3 boneless chicken breasts, skin on, cut in half
Olive Butter (page 416), cut into thin slices
Olive oil
Kosher salt
Black pepper in a mill
¾ cup oil-cured black olives, pitted
2 teaspoons grated lemon zest
Sprigs of Italian parsley

Prepare a medium-hot fire on an outdoor or stovetop grill.

Place the chicken breasts, one at a time, on a work surface. Using your fingers, carefully loosen the skin of the breast and tuck several slices of olive butter between the skin and the meat. Repeat with all of the breasts. Brush both sides of each breast with olive oil, season them with salt and pepper, and set them, skin side down, on

A California Cook

I came across *Elena's Favorite Foods California Style* (1967) in a used bookstore, my eye drawn to James Beard's name on the cover, which also showed a toqued chef turned away from the camera and surrounded by ingredients: fresh garlic and artichokes, smooth-skinned avocados, whole shallots, dried beans, white corn tortillas, red peppers, and a *molcajete* filled with something I could not discern. Intrigued by the author's use of foods not widely available in 1967 in California, I bought the book and thoroughly enjoyed it, even gleaning a few ideas for recipes. Then I began to wonder: Who was Elena? Beard's introduction referred to her as a talented and distinguished cook, and says that she became close friends with another California cookbook author of the time, Helen Evans Brown. The brief biography on the back cover revealed a little more: "Born in Mexico ... her family moved to California and Elena's eyesight failed. She raised herself from the hopelessness of her life by turning to what she knew best—cooking. Today she is a leading authority in the field of cooking, teaches the blind, gives cookery lessons and spreads her inspiring enthusiasm for life in lectures to women's clubs."

the work surface. In a small bowl, toss together the olives and the lemon zest. Divide the mixture among the chicken breasts, placing it in the center of each breast. Shape a breast into a roll, tucking the pointed end inside, and secure it with a metal skewer. Repeat with all of the chicken breasts.

Grill the chicken breasts, turning them frequently, until they are thoroughly cooked, 12 to 18 minutes, depending on their size. Line a platter with parsley, and place the chicken rolls on top. Serve immediately.

THAI-STYLE GRILLED CHICKEN BREAST

Chicken satay—strips of chicken marinated in a savory sauce, threaded on skewers, and quickly grilled—is so common on eclectic California cafe and pub menus that it is easy to forget its Thai origins. In this adaptation, I've borrowed the flavors to create a main course very similar to the original appetizer.

SERVES 4

5 garlic cloves, minced
2 serrano chiles, minced
1 tablespoon fish sauce
1 tablespoon sugar
2 teaspoons curry powder
1 teaspoon turmeric
¼ teaspoon ground cumin
¼ teaspoon ground coriander seed
3 to 4 cardamom seeds, crushed

¾ cup coconut milk
2 boneless and skinless chicken breasts, cut in half
Sprigs of cilantro
1 recipe Asian Cucumber Salad (page 128)
1¼ cups Coconut-Peanut Sauce (page 48)

Combine the garlic, serranos, fish sauce, sugar, curry powder, turmeric, cumin, coriander, cardamom, and coconut milk in a medium bowl. Place the chicken breasts in a glass or porcelain container just big enough to hold them in a single layer. Pour the marinade over, and turn the breasts so that they are fully coated. Refrigerate, covered, for at least 30 minutes or up to 2 hours.

Prepare a medium fire in an outdoor or stovetop grill. Remove the chicken from the marinade, wipe off any excess, and grill for about 7 minutes. Turn the chicken, and grill it on the second side until it is just done, 4 to 7 minutes, depending on the thickness of the meat.

Divide the cilantro among 4 individual plates, and place a cooked breast on each plate. Add cucumber salad to each portion, and serve immediately, with coconut-peanut sauce alongside.

Variation:

To serve as the more traditional chicken satay, soak about 2 dozen bamboo skewers in water for 1 hour. Cut each chicken breast crosswise against the grain into 1-inch-wide strips, and marinate them in the refrigerator for just 30 minutes. Thread a strip of chicken lengthwise onto each skewer, and grill for about 3 minutes on each side. Serve the satay on a bed of cilantro, with the coconut-peanut sauce alongside.

LEMON-SCENTED THAI CHICKEN

In this recipe, the marinade contributes substantial flavor to the chicken, creating a versatile dish that can be served as it is or used in other recipes, such as Fresh Spring Rolls (page 37) or any other recipe where cooked chicken is called for. I am partial to both the texture and flavor of chicken thighs, but if you prefer breasts, use them instead, substituting one breast half for each two thighs. Asparagus with Shiitakes, Shallots, and Almonds (page 385), grilled asparagus, or grilled eggplant make ideal accompaniments to this aromatic dish.

SERVES 4

1 stalk of lemon grass
Juice of 1 lemon
2 tablespoons soy sauce
1 tablespoon fish sauce
3 tablespoons coconut cream or
    2 tablespoons sugar
1 tablespoon minced garlic
2 teaspoons minced fresh ginger
2 serrano chiles, minced

8 boneless and skinless chicken thighs,
    cut in half
2 tablespoons peanut oil
3½ cups cooked long-grain white rice
Lemon wedges

Trim and discard the dry outer leaves of the lemon grass. Using the blade of a large knife, crush the bulb and mince it. Combine the minced lemon grass with the lemon juice, soy sauce, fish sauce, coconut cream or sugar, garlic, ginger, and serranos in a small bowl. Place the chicken pieces in a glass or porcelain container just big enough to hold them in a single layer. Pour the marinade over, and turn the chicken so that it is completely coated. Marinate the chicken, covered, in the refrigerator for at least 1 hour or overnight. Remove the chicken from the refrigerator and let it come to room temperature before cooking.

Heat the peanut oil in a heavy sauté pan over medium heat. Add the chicken, and sauté it until it is cooked through, about 7 minutes on each side. To serve, divide the rice among 4 serving plates, add 4 pieces of chicken to each portion, and serve immediately, garnished with lemon wedges.

CHICKEN WITH 100 GARLIC CLOVES

• •

*C*alifornia produces nearly all of the nation's commercial garlic crop, most of which is a single variety, California Late, grown in the area around Gilroy, home of the famous Gilroy Garlic Festival. In this dish, garlic plays a dominant role, functioning more as a vegetable than as a seasoning. Don't be alarmed; as it cooks, garlic becomes tender, mild, and nutty tasting. This is a good dish for using, when you can find one, a variety other than the standard garlic (see page 20).

SERVES 4

8 to 10 heads of garlic
4 chicken leg-thigh pieces
Kosher salt
Black pepper in a mill
1 lemon, cut into thin rounds
¼ cup extra virgin olive oil
2 tablespoons minced herbs, such as
   Italian parsley, thyme, rosemary,
   chives, or a combination

Preheat the oven to 375°F.

Separate the cloves of each head of garlic and peel each clove. Spread the garlic in the bottom of a 9-by-12-inch baking dish and arrange the chicken pieces on top. Season with salt and several turns of pepper, place the lemon slices on top of the chicken, and drizzle olive oil over all. Bake the chicken for about 40 minutes, or until it is cooked. Remove from the oven, let cool for 5 minutes, and transfer the chicken to a serving platter. Using a slotted spoon, transfer the garlic from the baking dish to the platter. Scatter the herbs over all, and serve immediately.

The Original 27 Counties

• •

The area around Gilroy, near the southern end of **Santa Clara County**, is the country's leading producer of garlic. "There's no such thing as too much garlic" is the motto of the day. Home cooks from all over the country come here every year for a cooking contest that features recipes like chicken with 100 garlic cloves, garlic popcorn balls, garlic pancakes, and chocolate-dipped garlic. Apricots are also a prized crop in the county, and at farm stands you'll find wonderful dried apricots, apricot jams, and apricot pies. Agriculture once dominated the fertile Santa Clara Valley, and for a time the valley grew almost a third of the world's prune crop. Now it has become the heavily populated Silicon Valley, but there's still room for small farms and orchards. Before Prohibition there were more than two dozen wineries; few survived, but viticulture has been rebounding in recent years with the success of such wineries as Mount Eden, David Bruce, Ridge, and Cinnabar.

CHICKEN WITH WHOLE GARLICS AND JALAPEÑOS

Perhaps because garlic is grown in California, it is immensely popular. This was not always the case. *The Book of Garlic*, by John Harris, published in 1974, helped bring it to center stage, as did the Chez Panisse garlic festivals (inspired by Harris and his book), and the Gilroy Garlic Festival, which introduced the stinking rose to thousands of revelers. Before about 1970, most of the state's garlic was processed for garlic powder, garlic salt, and other commercial products. Fresh garlic was sold in little cardboard boxes wrapped in plastic, and it was frequently shriveled and tasteless. If recipes called for fresh garlic at all, it was rarely for more than a single clove. Now, fresh garlic is available everywhere, most of it is pretty good, and it is rarely used with restraint. In this recipe, heads of garlic, their skins intact, are cut in half, with the cloves remaining connected. The cut surface is browned and the half heads are braised. (Occasionally, some of the outer cloves will fall off the head, but don't worry; simply add them to the pan with the rest of the garlic. If the heads are large and firm, they are less likely to fall apart. For smaller heads, do not cut in half, but instead cut about ¼ inch off the stem end;

this will give you a surface to sauté, and will keep the head intact.)

SERVES 4

4 large heads of garlic
2 tablespoons olive oil
2 tablespoons butter
1 chicken (about 4½ pounds), cut up
1 cup chicken stock, preferably homemade (see Appendix 1)
1 cup dry white wine
3 to 4 jalapeños
Kosher salt
Black pepper in a mill
½ cup cilantro leaves

Cut the heads of garlic crosswise in half. Heat the oil and butter in a large saucepan over medium heat. Add the garlic, and sauté it, cut side down, until it begins to brown. Remove the garlic from the pan and set it aside.

Add the chicken pieces to the pan, and brown them for 4 to 5 minutes on each side. Return the garlic to pan. Add the stock, wine, and jalapeños. Reduce the heat to low, cover the pan with a tight lid, and braise until the liquid is reduced and thickened, the garlic cloves are soft when pierced with a knife, and the chicken is cooked, 45 to 50 minutes.

To serve, arrange the half heads of garlic, cut side up, on a platter with the pieces of chicken. Spoon the sauce over, season with salt and pepper, and garnish with the jalapeños and cilantro. Eat the garlic as you would an artichoke, using your teeth to pull the puree out of the skins.

How to Kill a Chicken

Betty Fussell, author of wonderful cookbooks and of scholarly books on food in America, grew up in southern California, a child of the Great Depression. No matter where they lived, she writes in an essay entitled "A Depression Christmas," her grandparents kept chickens. On holidays—Easter, Fourth of July, birthdays, and Christmas—her grandfather would kill one of the chickens; the story reveals a California, and a time, that is all but forgotten:

"Killing a chicken for Christ was an act of contrition and atonement. Pater [her grandfather] would sharpen his ax on a grinding stone by the wooden board he set on a trestle well away from the sheets drying on lines in the yard. Next he would haul a large bucket of hot water from the basement sink. Only then would he look over the flock of Rhode Island Reds, clucking and scratching for worms, to find the fattest, choicest hen.... As my grandfather lunged, the bird squawked and scrabbled for cover. My job was to shoo the bird back toward Grandfather. Once he had it cornered, he would grab the bird by the neck, swing it a couple of times in the air like a lasso, thunk it down on the board, and chop off its head. The head would lie still enough, but the body rose like a feathered Lazarus, blood spouting, wings flapping, clawed feet rushing to and fro, with my grandfather running after it to keep the laundry pure as Ivory Snow. When my grandmother, on one occasion or another, would tell me to stop running around like a chicken with its head cut off, I was fairly warned.

"Pater made short work of the feathers, plunging the body into the bucket to bring forth a dripping corpse half its former size and to pluck its feathers as deftly as my grandmother tatted lace. He would then singe the pinfeathers over a gas burner next to the sink. I liked the smell of burnt skin, like the smell of snuffed candles, and I liked to watch the way he cleaned the bird by cutting out the crop from its neck, then slitting the vent and removing the entrails to disentangle the gall bladder, liver, heart, and gizzard, as if he were some divining prophet. I got to look for eggs. If we were lucky, I might find half a dozen embryonic eggs the size of my thumb, all yellow yolk, and if we were really lucky, a double-yolked one. That was an augury as propitious as a free Fudgsicle stick."

Betty Fussell, "A Depression Christmas," in *Christmas Memories with Recipes* (1988)

TERIYAKI CHICKEN

*T*here was a time in California when you could find teriyaki chicken, a dish introduced from Hawaii, almost everywhere: on restaurant menus, certainly, but also at friends' homes, at wedding dinners, virtually everywhere food was eaten, including the state fair. When I worked as a line cook in a small restaurant near the college I attended, I prepared hundreds of teriyaki half-chickens a week. Only bacon cheeseburgers were more popular.

SERVES 4 TO 6

1 cup soy sauce

½ cup dry sherry

1 cup fresh orange juice

3 tablespoons brown sugar

1 tablespoon minced garlic

2 tablespoons minced fresh ginger

½ teaspoon crushed red pepper

2 tablespoons julienned orange zest

2 medium chickens, cut up, or 12
   chicken pieces of your choosing

1 tablespoon butter

2 oranges, cut into wedges

In a small saucean, combine the soy sauce, sherry, orange juice, brown sugar, garlic, ginger, red pepper, and 1 tablespoon of the orange zest. Bring to a boil over high heat, reduce the heat, and simmer for 5 minutes. Remove from the heat and let cool.

Place the chicken pieces in 2 heavy plastic freezer bags and pour one third of the marinade into each bag. Squeeze out the air, close the bags securely, and massage the chicken so that each piece is thoroughly coated with the marinade. Set in a large pan and refrigerate for at least 4 hours or overnight. Refrigerate the remaining one third of the marinade in a lidded container.

Preheat the broiler.

Transfer the chicken, skin side down, from the bags to a rack; discard the marinade in the bags. Broil the chicken, 6 to 8 inches from the heat, for 15 to 20 minutes. Brush with some of the reserved marinade, turn, and broil, skin side up, for 8 to 10 minutes more, until the skin is crispy and the chicken is cooked through. Near the end of the cooking time, brush again with a little of the marinade. Heat the remaining marinade in a small saucepan; when it comes to a boil, swirl in the butter, remove from the heat, and transfer to a serving bowl.

Arrange the chicken on a large serving platter, sprinkle with the remaining orange zest, garnish with orange wedges, and serve immediately, with the sauce alongside.

GRILLED CHICKEN WITH MAI-WAH'S BARBECUE SAUCE

*L*isa Jang, who with her husband, Jorge Rebagliati, farms oysters in Tomales Bay (see Bay Bottom Beds in Resources), says she uses this sauce, a recipe from her mother, with duck, turkey, steak, and pork. Her mother, whose Chinese name, Mai-Wah, means "beautiful flower," and who was rarely called by her Christian name of Alycia, used it most often on spareribs. You can't be prissy about the technique in this recipe—you must get your hands into the sauce and other ingredients and rub them into the chicken.

SERVES 4

⅔ cup light soy sauce

⅓ cup mirin (rice wine)

4 garlic cloves, smashed

3 slices of fresh ginger, each about the size of a quarter

2 chicken breasts, cut in half, or 4 leg-thigh pieces

3 tablespoons kosher salt

3 tablespoons dark brown sugar

3 tablespoons bottled chile sauce

2 tablespoons hoisin sauce diluted with 2 tablespoons warm water

Combine the soy sauce, mirin, garlic, and ginger in a glass jar. Cover tightly, and refrigerate overnight.

Hoffman Game Birds

*B*ud Hoffman has been raising game birds and chicken at his farm in Manteca, between Stockton and Modesto, for forty years. He has sold the plump, succulent birds commercially for the last fifteen of those years, directly to chefs and at one farmers' market, the Ferry Plaza Market in San Francisco. "If only we could find another day in the week," Bud Hoffman says with a sigh when asked if he plans to expand his business. He sells about thirty-five hundred birds a week, the majority to restaurants.

Bud's poultry wins instant converts, and return customers offer exuberant praise. "Once I had your chicken," they say, "I couldn't buy poultry in a regular market ever again." What accounts for the difference? The feed is basically the same, with one important exception: The Hoffmans don't add filler, as most larger producers do. "It's simple," Bud says, "we can take better care of our birds than someone who farms on a large scale." Hoffman Game Birds—currently, pheasant, quail, partridge, wild turkey, and squab, as well as chicken—are sold within two days of harvesting. Birds are not treated with steroids or antibiotics, and although they are not called "free range," they surpass the guidelines for that designation, with more space per bird than is required and with a substantial amount of time outside.

About 1 hour before cooking the chicken, rub each piece liberally with salt, shaking off any excess. Rub the pieces thoroughly with the soy sauce marinade, then rub them with brown sugar. Using a pastry brush, brush the chicken with the chile sauce, then with the hoisin sauce. Set on a platter, cover loosely, and refrigerate for about 1 hour.

Prepare a hot fire on an outdoor or stovetop grill. (Or preheat the broiler.) Grill the chicken, turning it several times to insure even cooking and to prevent the sugar from burning, until it is tender but still juicy, about 15 minutes on each side. (Or broil the chicken, turning it several times, until it is done, about 20 minutes.) Transfer to a serving platter, and serve immediately.

SPICY RANCH CHICKEN WITH CHORIZO STUFFING

A traditional ranch chicken includes ingredients, such as olives, almonds, and ground chiles, common at the early Spanish ranchos. Although it is not part of the traditional recipe, I add chorizo, another important ingredient at that time. The spicy pork sausage was made at the end of harvest when the hogs were killed, before winter set in.

SERVES 4

1½ pounds chorizo, casings removed
3 serrano chiles, minced
8 garlic cloves, minced
1 cup pitted green olives
2 tablespoons minced cilantro
4 chicken leg–thigh pieces or 2 large chicken breasts, cut in half
1 yellow onion, minced
1 teaspoon ground coriander seeds
½ teaspoon ground cumin
2 tablespoons chili powder

Almonds

California is the only place in North America where almonds are grown commercially. Nearly half a million acres are devoted to their production. The almond industry helps support the honeybee industry—because almonds are not self-pollinating, growers must hire beekeepers, who bring in thousands of hives during the three-week bloom in February when the nut trees must be pollinated. An almond is actually a stone fruit, a distant relative of nectarines, peaches, apricots, plums, and cherries. The tough, fuzzy, gray-green fruit is very bitter; at the center of its hull is the sweet meat we call an almond. Almonds are wonderful eaten fresh and raw before the fruit matures, while the nut itself is still pale green, delicate, and almost milky. The fruit bursts open at maturity, revealing the almond shell inside.

1 cup dry white wine
1 cup chicken stock
¾ cup almonds, blanched and
   toasted

Cook the chorizo, breaking it up with a fork, in a large heavy sauté pan over medium heat. When it is nearly done, remove the pan from the heat, drain and discard all but 2 tablespoons of the fat, and return the pan to the heat. Add the chiles and garlic, and sauté for 5 minutes. Meanwhile, mince half of the green olives, and add them to the chorizo mixture. Remove the pan from the heat, and stir in 1 tablespoon of the cilantro. Let the chorizo mixture cool.

Using your finger, carefully loosen the skin from the chicken, leaving it attached at the edges. When the chorizo mixture is cool enough to handle, stuff some under the skin of each piece of chicken. Set the chicken pieces aside.

Return the pan to the heat and sauté the onion in the pan drippings until it is very soft and fragrant, about 15 minutes. Stir in the coriander, cumin, and chili powder. Cut the remaining olives in half

Before Hotels

From 1769, when Franciscan padres first crossed from Baja California to Alta, or Upper, California, until the Gold Rush of 1849, California resembled a medieval fiefdom, with self-sufficient missions giving way to vast ranchos presided over by the great barons who had been given land by the Spanish governors. The land grants have long since been divided and sold, but stories, recipes, and an adobe building or two survive here and there. Jacqueline Higuera McMahan, a food writer who lives in Oxnard in southern California, is an eighth generation Californian whose great-great-great grandfather José Higuera was granted nearly five thousand acres in the Santa Clara Valley by the region's last Spanish governor, Pablo Vicente de Sola.

McMahan's book, *California Rancho Cooking* (The Olive Press, 1983), tells the story of her family's thriving rancho and recalls the day-to-day life of the early Californios, as the residents of the ranchos were called. There are stories of bears forced to fight with bulls, of aunts competing with aunts to make the most tender tortillas, of feasts that would continue for days. Barbecues were common; special occasions would bring a bull's head barbecue, which required a huge amount of time, equipment, and labor.

"Food was bountiful," McMahan writes, "and there was never a concern if a few more guests would arrive unexpectedly." There were no hotels or inns in those days, and presiding over a rancho meant welcoming unexpected travelers to your table. Guests who arrived at mealtime often would repeat an old Spanish proverb, "It is better to arrive on time than to be invited." It was considered rude, however, to travel without your own knife to cut your meat.

and add them, then pour in the wine and stock. Add the chicken, reduce the heat to low, and simmer, covered, until the chicken is cooked through, about 35 minutes. Transfer the chicken to a serving platter, increase the heat in the pan to medium-high, and reduce the cooking liquid by one third.

Spoon the sauce over the chicken, scatter the remaining 1 tablespoon of the cilantro and the toasted almonds on top, and serve immediately.

CHINESE FIVE-SPICE CHICKEN

I have read advice recommending that you not rinse a chicken before cooking it. Rinsing does nothing to remove dangerous bacteria, the advice goes, and it could contaminate other foods, such as salad greens in the sink where the chicken is washed. But rinsing a chicken is important, to remove any liquids that may have collected in the cavity and that could dilute the flavors of the dish. It should be done, of course, when the sink has been cleared of other foods.

SERVES 4

1 whole chicken, 3½ to 4 pounds
1 large shallot, sliced
4 garlic cloves, sliced
2 teaspoons fish sauce
2 teaspoons hoisin sauce
2 tablespoons Chinese five-spice powder

3 tablespoons butter, at room temperature
1 teaspoon kosher salt
Black pepper in a mill
1 lime, cut in half
1 lime, cut into wedges
Sprigs of cilantro, for garnish

Rinse the chicken, inside and out, in cool water. Pat it dry with a tea towel. Using a mortar and pestle, pound together the shallot and garlic into a paste. Mix in the fish sauce, hoisin sauce, and half of the five-spice powder. Set the mixture aside.

In a small bowl, combine the butter with the remaining five-spice powder, the salt, and several turns of pepper. Set the chicken, breast side up, on a work surface, and use your fingers to loosen the skin from the breast. Place the seasoned butter, in small pieces, under the skin of the chicken, pushing with your finger to distribute the butter as evenly as possible over the meat. Place the lime halves inside the cavity of the chicken. Rub the shallot-garlic mixture thoroughly into the entire surface of the skin. Truss the chicken, place it on a rack set in a roasting pan, cover loosely, and refrigerate for at least 1 hour or up to 2 hours.

Remove the chicken from the refrigerator 30 minutes before cooking. Preheat the oven to 400°F.

Roast the chicken, uncovered, until the internal temperature reaches 160°F and the thigh juices run clear when pricked with a fork, about 1 hour. Remove the chicken from the oven and let it rest for at least 10 minutes. Pour the pan juices into a small bowl. Carve the chicken, transfer it to a platter, and garnish it with the lime wedges and cilantro sprigs. Serve immediately, with the pan juices on the side.

ROAST CHICKEN WITH WILD RICE DRESSING

In California, the designation of "range" chicken is, as the term "organic" is, controlled by the state, which has specific requirements—some costly, some time-consuming—for producers who wish to use it. There are poultry farms, such as Hoffman Game Birds (see page 319), that surpass the requirements for range chickens but do not apply for the bureaucratic blessing and cannot use the term. Look for the best poultry at farmers' markets, or talk to chefs in your area about farmers who may be raising excellent birds. Once you have tasted the difference, you will want to make the effort.

SERVES 4 TO 6

1 cup uncooked wild rice
2½ cups chicken stock or water
5 tablespoons olive oil
1 head of garlic, cloves separated
¾ cup pine nuts
1 teaspoon summer savory leaves
1 teaspoon thyme leaves

1 tablespoon minced Italian parsley
Kosher salt
Black pepper in a mill
1 whole chicken, 4 to 5 pounds, preferably range
Sprigs of summer savory and thyme, for garnish

Wash the wild rice under cool running water and place it in a medium heavy pot over high heat. Pour the stock or water over the wild rice. Bring to a boil, reduce the heat, and simmer, covered, for 35 to 40 minutes, or until all the liquid has been absorbed.

Heat 3 tablespoons of the olive oil in a heavy skillet over medium heat. Add the garlic cloves, and sauté them for 3 minutes, stirring frequently so they do not burn. Add the pine nuts, sauté for 1 minute more, and remove from the heat.

Toss the garlic, pine nuts, savory, thyme, and parsley with the cooked wild rice. Season with salt and pepper.

Preheat the oven to 400°F. Rinse the chicken, inside and out, in cool water. Pat it dry with a tea towel. Season the cavity of the chicken with salt and pepper and fill it with the wild rice mixture. (If there is any dressing left over, place it in a baking dish, and bake it, covered, in the oven during the last 25 minutes of the cooking time.) Truss the chicken, and place it on a rack set in a roasting pan. Rub the remaining olive oil into the chicken skin, season with salt and pepper, and roast for 15 minutes. Reduce the heat to 375°F, and roast until the chicken is cooked through but moist, about 20 minutes per pound.

Remove the chicken from the oven and let it rest for at least 10 minutes. Transfer the dressing to a serving platter, carve the chicken, and arrange it on the platter. Garnish with herb sprigs, and serve immediately.

CORNISH HENS POACHED IN RED WINE WITH FIGS

My mother served Cornish hens as a special treat, an elegant meal finer than our standard fare. The simple roasted birds were usually accompanied by Rice-A-Roni and canned French-style green beans, seasoned with a few pieces of diced bacon if it was a really important occasion. My recipe bears little resemblance to hers, and features both wine and figs from California. The state produces nearly all of the nation's figs; most are grown in the great Central Valley. Some of the best figs I've had, however, have been gathered from abandoned orchards wedged between new housing developments in Sonoma Valley, where fig production was once greater than it is now.

SERVES 4

4 Cornish hens, about 1 pound each
Kosher salt
Black pepper in a mill
4 ripe figs
1 yellow onion, cut into quarters

1 bottle (750 ml) medium-bodied red wine, such as pinot noir, merlot, or a Rhône-style California blend
½ cup sugar
1 1-inch cinnamon stick
2 allspice berries, preferably, or
⅓ teaspoon ground allspice
1 teaspoon whole black peppercorns
2 dried red chiles, such as chile de árbol
1 tablespoon butter

Rinse the hens, inside and out, in cool water. Pat them dry with a tea towel. Season the cavities with salt and pepper. Tuck a fig inside each hen, and tie the legs closed. In a large heavy pot that will hold the hens snugly, combine the onion, wine, sugar, cinnamon, allspice, peppercorns, chiles, and 2 teaspoons salt. Bring the mixture to a boil. Reduce the heat and simmer, stirring until the sugar is dissolved. Remove from the heat and let cool to room temperature.

Place the hens in the poaching liquid and add enough water to fully submerge

Cooking Wines

"Various recipes in this book call for the use of wine. The wine referred to is a salted cooking wine sold at most well stocked grocery stores. The sale of the same is made under approval of the federal prohibition authorities."

Five Hundred Ways to Prepare California Sea Foods (State Fish Exchange, 1930)

the birds. Return the pot to the heat and bring the liquid to a boil. Reduce the heat, and simmer, uncovered, until the hens are fully cooked and tender, about 1 hour. Using tongs or a slotted spoon, transfer the hens to an ovenproof platter, cover, and keep warm in a low oven. Increase the heat to high, reduce the liquid by half, and strain it. Return it to the pan, and reduce the sauce by two thirds.

Place each of the hens on an individual serving plate, untie the legs, carefully remove the fig, and set it next to the hen. Just before serving, swirl the butter into the sauce until it is just melted. Spoon some of the sauce over each portion, and serve immediately.

SMOKED DUCK PIZZA WITH CARAMELIZED ONIONS

Cook onions long enough at a low enough heat and their sugar will begin to caramelize, creating an intensely sweet flavor. For this pizza, the onions are paired with smoky duck and the sweet-hot flavors of a chutney.

SERVES 4

2 tablespoons unsalted butter
2 tablespoons olive oil

1 pound yellow onions, sliced very thin
¼ cup red wine vinegar
2 anchovy fillets, minced
Cornmeal
1 12-inch pizza shell (page 262)
4 ounces smoked duck, cut into julienne
Kosher salt
Black pepper in a mill
2 tablespoons minced Italian parsley
¼ cup Fig Chutney (page 423) or Peach Chutney (page 425)

Heat the butter and olive oil in a heavy skillet over medium-low heat. Add the onions, and sauté them until they are transparent, completely wilted, and slightly sweet, about 25 minutes. Add the vinegar and anchovies, and continue to cook for 30 minutes more. Remove from the heat and set aside to cool.

Preheat the oven to 500°F. Place a baking stone in the oven or sprinkle a baking sheet or pizza pan with cornmeal.

Dust a work surface with cornmeal and place the pizza shell on it. Spread the onion mixture across the top, scatter the smoked duck on top of the onion mixture, season with salt and pepper, and sprinkle the parsley over all. If you are using a baking stone, sprinkle it with cornmeal. Transfer the pizza to the baking stone, pizza pan, or baking sheet. Bake the pizza for 15 to 20 minutes, or until the crust is lightly browned. Remove the pizza from the oven and let it rest for 5 minutes. Cut the pizza into 8 wedges, and top each wedge with ½ tablespoon of chutney. Serve immediately.

GRILLED DUCK BREAST WITH BLUEBERRIES AND LAVENDER

A good duck breast, thick, richly colored, and tender, is as good if not better than a prime steak. Sonoma Foie Gras produces huge, plump duck breasts from the ducks that they raise for foie gras. The duck breast is wonderful simply prepared, either grilled or pan-roasted and seasoned generously with salt and pepper, but during blueberry season I sometimes prepare it more elaborately, in this very aromatic dish.

SERVES 6 TO 8

1 whole breast of Muscovy duck, about 2 pounds
2 teaspoons ground allspice
2 tablespoons minced orange zest
2 teaspoons kosher salt
2 teaspoons fresh-ground black pepper
2 cups light-bodied red wine, such as Beaujolais
½ cup honey
2 tablespoons dried lavender flowers
4 1-inch-long strips of orange zest
1 1-inch cinnamon stick
1 teaspoon whole black peppercorns
3 to 4 whole allspice berries, preferably, or ½ teaspoon ground allspice
1 pint fresh blueberries

1 large handful of dried lavender stems
Lavender flowers and orange wedges, for garnish

Prepare a medium fire in a charcoal grill.

Set the duck breast on a work surface and remove and discard the skin. Mix together the ground allspice, minced orange zest, salt, and pepper in a small bowl. Rub some of the mixture onto the duck breasts, covering all exposed surfaces with a small amount. Set aside for 30 minutes or until the coals are ready.

Meanwhile, prepare the sauce: Combine the wine, honey, lavender flowers, orange zest, cinnamon, peppercorns, and allspice berries in a nonreactive saucepan. Bring to a boil, and reduce the liquid by half. Remove the mixture from the heat and let it steep for 30 minutes. Strain the mixture, discarding the spices, and return the sauce to the pan. Add the blueberries, and cook them over medium heat until they are tender, about 10 minutes. Taste the sauce, and correct the flavors, if you like, with honey, salt, or pepper. For a more refined sauce, puree in a blender and strain.

To grill the duck breast, scatter the lavender stems over the coals and, when they begin to smoke, place the breast on the rack. Grill it until it is just rare, 7 to 10 minutes on each side. Transfer it to a cutting board and let it rest for 5 minutes.

Slice the duck crosswise into thin slices, and arrange on individual serving plates. Garnish with lavender flowers and orange wedges, and serve immediately.

The Original 27 Counties

• •

The first European settlers in **Sonoma County** were Russians, who arrived in 1809. In 1846, the Bear Flag Revolt, in the town of Sonoma, established the short-lived California Republic. The terrain and topography of the county are diverse and beautiful. Sonoma Valley, known as the Valley of the Moon, is breathtaking, and has served as both home and inspiration to such writers as Jack London and M.F.K. Fisher. In Sebastopol, Luther Burbank conducted the experiments that led to the Burbank russet potato, the Santa Rosa plum, and hundreds of other plant varieties. The Russian River winds through the northwestern part of the county, meeting the Pacific at the tiny town of Jenner. The Alexander Valley, in the northeast, remains rustic and largely undeveloped; in the same area is one of the largest systems of geysers and hot springs in the world. Agriculture is the most important industry; home cooks make abundant use of local young lamb, range chickens, and the plump ducks that thrive in the mild climate. At harvest time, Gravenstein apples are turned into applesauce, pies, juice, and apple butter. Beginning in the late 1980s, the wines of Sonoma County started getting the recognition they deserve as among the world's finest.

ROAST DUCK LEGS WITH HONEY TERIYAKI SAUCE

• •

Although duck breasts are best served very rare, duck legs need lengthy cooking to become tender. For this reason, it is often a good idea to cook and serve the breasts and legs separately. Duck legs are much less expensive than breasts, too, making them a good choice for a casual meal. This recipe calls for leg-thigh pieces, but you can also use just the legs. Duck meat is dark and flavorful and holds up to intensely flavored sauces, such as this version of teriyaki that has honey rather than brown sugar.

SERVES 4 TO 6

1½ cups honey, warm
1½ cups soy sauce
1½ cups mirin (rice wine)
10 garlic cloves, minced
1 2-inch piece of fresh ginger, peeled
  and grated
2 teaspoons crushed red pepper
1 tablespoon sesame seeds, toasted
6 duck thigh-leg pieces, preferably,
  or 12 duck legs
6 to 8 scallions, green and white
  parts, cut into thin rounds

Combine the honey, soy sauce, mirin, garlic, ginger, red pepper, and sesame seeds in a medium bowl. Place the duck pieces in a single layer in a glass or ceramic baking dish and pour half of the marinade over, turning the pieces so that they are fully coated. Refrigerate for 1 day, turning the legs in the marinade every few hours. Store the remaining marinade, covered, in the refrigerator; let it come to room temperature before you roast the duck.

Preheat the oven to 350°F. Roast the duck pieces, basting several times with the reserved marinade, until they are very tender, about 45 minutes. Remove them from the oven and let them rest for 10 minutes. Place the remaining marinade in a small saucepan over medium-high heat, and reduce the liquid by half.

To serve, arrange the duck legs on a platter, and scatter the scallions over the top. Serve with the reduced marinade alongside and, if you like, with steamed rice.

BRAISED DUCK WITH OLIVES AND ORANGES

Ducks are raised in many areas of the country, and you'll probably find the best birds by asking local chefs what they use. If that fails, ask your butcher to direct you to a nearby supplier. In California, there are several excellent duck farms, such as Jim Reichardt's Sonoma County Poultry, which produces premium ducks. Reichardt's family founded Reichardt Duck Farm in Petaluma in 1901 and has been raising Imperial Pekin ducks ever since. Most are sold in San Francisco's Chinatown, but some are distributed as far away as New Orleans. For anyone who has been reluctant to cook duck, this recipe is a good place to start. Roasting the duck briefly at a high temperature releases much of its fat, which is discarded before the duck is slowly braised until it is completely tender.

SERVES 3 TO 4

1 medium whole duck, 4 to 5 pounds
1 sprig of thyme
1 sprig of oregano
1 sprig of Italian parsley
1 cup red wine
1 cup duck stock or chicken stock
1 tablespoon minced orange zest
½ cup fresh orange juice
2 large slices of fresh ginger
3 whole cloves
1 1-inch cinnamon stick
Kosher salt
Black pepper in a mill
8 ounces oil-cured or salt-cured black olives
1 orange, sliced thin

Preheat the oven to 375°F.

Rinse the duck, inside and out, in cool water, pat it dry with a tea towel, and prick the skin with a fork in several places, taking care not to puncture the meat itself. Set the duck on a roasting rack in a shallow roasting pan, and roast it for 30 minutes, basting after 10 and 20 minutes with any fat that has been rendered. Remove the duck from the oven, discard the fat, and reduce the temperature of the oven to 325°F.

Tie together the thyme, oregano, and parsley for a bouquet garni. Combine the wine, stock, orange zest, orange juice, ginger, cloves, cinnamon, and bouquet garni in a heavy, nonreactive, ovenproof pot over high heat. Bring the mixture to a boil, and remove it from the heat. Season the duck inside and out with salt and pepper, and place it in the pot with the wine mixture. Add the olives, cover the pot, place it in the oven, and cook until the duck is very tender, 1 to 1¼ hours.

Transfer the duck and the olives to a platter, and keep them warm. Remove and discard the bouquet garni, pour the sauce into a narrow, clear container, and allow the juices to settle to the bottom. Remove the fat with a small ladle or spoon and discard it. Return the sauce to the pot, and reduce it over medium-high heat to about ¾ cup. Taste, correct the seasoning with salt and pepper, and pour the sauce into a small serving bowl.

To serve, carve the duck, place it on a serving platter, and scatter the olives over. Serve at once, with the sauce on the side and, if you like, Creamy Polenta (page 347).

Roast Turkey with Sausage and Sourdough Stuffing

•••••••••••••••••••••••••••••••••

The best part of roast turkey is the dressing. In this recipe, sourdough bread soaks up the turkey juices as well as the flavors of sausage and sage. Sometimes I use simple Italian sausage, at other times I might use a spicy Louisiana andouille sausage or a Mexican or Spanish chorizo. Use whatever sausage you like. California sausage king Bruce Aidells, founder of Aidells Sausage Company and author of several cookbooks, has developed dozens of traditional and innovative sausages, including a turkey-cranberry sausage perfectly suited to holiday recipes such as this one. Aidells sausage is distributed throughout the country.

You will need a clean, white, all-cotton tea towel to cover the breast of the turkey as it roasts.

SERVES 10 TO 12

6 to 8 cups cubed country-style
   sourdough bread
1 medium whole turkey, 18 to 20
   pounds
1½ cups unsalted butter
2 large yellow onions, diced
5 to 6 celery ribs, cut into small dice
1½ pounds sausage

1 large or 2 small bunches of Italian
   parsley, large stems removed,
   minced
3 tablespoons minced sage leaves
1 tablespoon kosher salt
1 tablespoon fresh-ground black pepper

The night before cooking the turkey, cut the bread cubes, spread them out on baking sheets, and let them sit at room temperature overnight so that they dry out.

Place the turkey on a work surface, remove the neck and the innards from the cavity, and set them aside for gravy or stock. Cover the turkey with 1 or 2 tea towels while you make the stuffing, but do not let the turkey sit unrefrigerated for longer than 30 minutes.

Melt 1 cup of the butter in a large sauté pan over medium heat. When the butter is melted, add the onions and celery and sauté them until they are very soft and fragrant, about 15 minutes. Meanwhile, fry the sausages in a skillet over medium heat until they give up most of their fat and are nearly done. Remove them from the skillet and drain them on absorbent paper. When they are cool enough to handle, cut them lengthwise in half and then into ¼-inch-thick slices. (Some types of sausage are best removed from their casings and broken up with a fork as they cook; in this case, simply drain away the fat given off by the sausage.)

Place the bread cubes in a bowl large enough to hold all of the stuffing ingredients. When the onions and celery are tender, stir in the parsley and sage. Pour the contents of the pan over the bread crumbs. Add the sausage, salt, and pepper, let cool slightly, and use your hands to toss the stuffing together.

Season both cavities of the turkey with salt and pepper, and fill loosely with stuffing; do not pack tightly. Truss the turkey, and set it, breast side up, on a rack in a roasting pan.

Preheat the oven to 450°F.

Melt the remaining ½ cup of butter in a medium saucepan. Soak the clean white tea towel in the butter until all of the butter has been absorbed and the towel is thoroughly moistened. Cover the entire breast area of the turkey with the tea towel, folding the towel in half if necessary. Be sure that the turkey breast is covered thoroughly and that the legs are exposed.

Place the turkey in the oven, and immediately reduce the heat to 325°F. Roast for about 20 minutes per pound, until the internal temperature of the turkey reaches 160°F. About 1½ hours before the turkey is done, carefully pull off the tea towel so that the breast skin can brown.

When the turkey is done, remove it from the oven and let it rest for 15 to 30 minutes before carving. Make gravy using the pan drippings.

If you have leftover dressing to cook separately, place it in a baking dish. Use a turkey baster to draw off some of the pan drippings, mix them with a little water, and pour over the dressing. Cover, and bake with the turkey for the last 45 minutes.

Carve the turkey, and place it on a platter. Remove the dressing from the turkey, place it in a serving bowl, and serve alongside the turkey and gravy.

You Are What You Eat

"**G**et your turkey six weeks before you need it," *Los Angeles Cookery*, published in 1881, tells us, "and put him in a coop just large enough to let him walk, or in a small yard; give him walnuts—one the first day, and increase every day by one until he has nine; then go back to one and up to nine until you kill him, stuffing him twice with corn meal each day, in which you put a little chopped onion and celery, if you have it." This technique foreshadows the practice of flavoring the main course from the inside out, so to speak, that became a controversial element of the first Chez Panisse Garlic Festival. For that now famous event, suckling pigs were nursed by mothers who were fed a diet high in fresh garlic. Garlic passes into mother's milk—as any nursing human mother knows—and the little piglets were, in effect, marinated from the inside out, their tender flesh perfumed with garlic. Filmmaker Les Blank documented it all in his film *Garlic Is as Good as Ten Mothers*, which was met at its showings in England and Germany with protests by vegetarians and animal rights activists.

ROAST TURKEY WITH AUNTIE ELLEN'S RICE STUFFING

Home cooking often defies the geographical boundaries of traditional cuisines. In this recipe, American and Cantonese techniques and ingredients intersect in an unusual homespun dressing for Thanksgiving turkey, from Auntie Ellen of the Jang family of southern California.

SERVES 6 TO 8

2 cups uncooked glutinous rice
1 cup uncooked long-grain white rice
1 small whole turkey, 8 to 10 pounds
2 tablespoons peanut oil
1 cup thin-sliced scallions, white and
    green parts
½ cup minced shallots
½ cup Chinese rice wine
1 pound pork sausage, preferably
    Chinese-style, cut into ¼-inch dice
½ cup dried shrimp, optional
3 cups chicken stock
1 teaspoon kosher salt
Black pepper in a mill
2 cups fresh water chestnuts, peeled
    and chopped, or 2 cups water-
    packed water chestnuts, chopped
1½ teaspoons tarragon leaves
1 teaspoon thyme leaves
¼ cup snipped chives

Wild Turkey Chili

Sometimes a great recipe is like an old folktale, or a good joke: It's passed on by word of mouth, and when you try to capture it in another form, such as a written recipe, its spirit becomes elusive or vanishes altogether. Some of the best California home cooking thrives in this way, details passed at a party, a barbecue, around a campfire, over a bottle of wine, by phone, or, these days, by fax or e-mail. The best home cooks are intuitive, with little formal training and often with a better feel for food than those who have gone to a culinary school.

George Snyder is a writer who lives near my home. He arrived in California from Louisiana, by way of a long, slow ruote through the Midwest and Canada, in the mid-1960s. George is a fine, fine cook. When he talks about food, you know he loves to eat well; you can hear the pleasure in his voice. One day we were talking about hunting, and he launched into a description how he makes his wild turkey chili. I grabbed a pen and took down every word.

"Pork is really good in this, too," he began. "Heat a little olive oil in a large heavy skillet, add about a tablespoon of Chimayó chile powder. If it isn't available, use hot New Mexico chile powder. You can get Chimayó in the town of the same name on Highway 79 between Taos and Sante Fe, a place well-known for its rugs. Before the chile powder smokes, add the green part of a bunch of scallions, finely minced; sauté for several minutes until the aroma is very good, then add chopped wild turkey breast, and maybe some vegetables such as yellow crookneck squash. Add a pinch or two of cumin, some fresh oregano, and several grinds of black pepper. If you're using venison instead of turkey, you'll need to add water. Cook it down, until it is thick and tender, and then serve it with rice or rolled corn tortillas. Sometimes I cook black beans for a long, long time until they are very soft; then when the flavor is really concentrated, I add them to the chili and simmer it until little beads of olive oil rise to the surface. The longer it cooks, the better it gets, but keep in mind that if you refrigerate it and reheat it the next day, the chiles will be hotter."

Combine the glutinous rice and long-grain white rice in a large bowl, and add enough water to cover them completely. Soak the rice overnight. Drain it thoroughly.

Place the turkey on a work surface, remove the neck and the innards from the cavity, and set them aside for gravy or stock. Cover the turkey with 1 or 2 tea towels while you make the stuffing, but do not let the turkey sit unrefrigerated for longer than 30 minutes.

Make the stuffing: Heat the peanut oil in a large wok over medium-high heat. Add the scallions and shallots, and stir-fry for 30 seconds. Add the wine, and simmer until it is nearly evaporated. Add the sausage, fry for 1 minute, and add the shrimp, if you are using it, the stock, and the rice. Bring to a boil, reduce the heat, and simmer, uncovered, for about 8 minutes, stirring occasionally to prevent sticking, until all of the stock is absorbed. Add the salt, several turns of pepper, the water chestnuts, and the tarragon, thyme, and chives, and toss together quickly. Remove the mixture from the heat and let it cool to room temperature.

Preheat the oven to 350°F. When the stuffing is cool enough to handle, fill the large cavity of the turkey with 4 cups of the stuffing, being sure not to pack it too tightly. Fill the neck cavity with some of the remaining stuffing. Truss the turkey, set it on a roasting rack over a roasting pan, and roast it for about 20 minutes per pound. Place any remaining stuffing in a buttered baking dish, and bake it in the oven with the turkey during the last 45 minutes of roasting.

Let the turkey rest for 15 to 30 minutes before carving. Carve the turkey, and transfer it to a serving platter. Remove the

Selections from a 1914 Thanksgiving Menu, Beverly Hills Hotel

❖ Strawberries on Stem

❖ California Oyster Cocktails

❖ Salted Jordan Almonds, Mission Olives, Hearts of Celery

❖ Green Sea Turtle, Amontillado

❖ Essence of Chicken, Bellevue

❖ Bread Sticks

❖ Roast Young Calabasas Turkey with Chestnut Dressing

❖ California Cluster Raisins and Nuts

❖ Los Angeles Brewing Co. East Side Ale, 40 cents

❖ California Zinfandel, $1 a quart

❖ Absinthe, $3 a quart

dressing from the turkey, place it in a serving bowl, and serve alongside the turkey.

A Big Sur Thanksgiving

"Until about ten years ago, this little ranch was sixteen miles by trail to the nearest wagon road, and then, having gained the road, there were forty of the stiffest mountain miles anyone can imagine still making a barricade between your hunger and the grocery store. As winter rains made both trail and road impassable by Thanksgiving, the 1890 folk gave thanks for what they had on the ranch.

"Allowing for all these handicaps, I looked about and decided on a Thanksgiving menu without benefit of grocery or town. This is what we had: abalone chowder; roast quail with cornbread and mushroom dressing made savory with wild spices; vegetables—mashed potatoes, beets with mock Hollandaise sauce, zucchini sautéed; cornbread (homeground meal) with fresh butter and sage honey; yerba buena tea or milk; Indian pudding (same homeground cornmeal sweetened with wild honey); pioneer carrot pie.

"This carrot pie was made according to the Boston Cooking School cookbook, only substituting well-mashed carrots for the pumpkin. It was a pie to end all pumpkin pies."

Lillian Bos Ross, from *Carmel Pine Cone* (1939), quoted in *Recipes for Living in Big Sur* (Big Sur Historical Society, 1981)

FORESTVILLE QUAIL WITH APPLE CIDER SAUCE

The land surrounding the small town of Forestville in Sonoma County is covered with gnarled old apple trees that still, in a good year, produce a wonderful crop. In April, the trees send out their pale pink blossoms, and everywhere it looks as if someone had unfurled bolts of lace over the landscape. It is one of the most breathtaking sights in California. Quail dart here and there, the young chicks following their mothers. Not far from Forestville, in the small town of Graton, is a company that makes apple juice and apple cider vinegar, both of which I use in this sauce. But the quails continue to run free; I use farm-raised quail in this recipe. I particularly enjoy this dish with broiled polenta triangles, but you can serve it with soft polenta instead, or omit polenta entirely and serve it with Armenian Pilaf (page 222).

SERVES 4

1 recipe Creamy Polenta (page 347)
Olive oil
2½ cups filtered apple juice
½ cup apple cider vinegar
1 teaspoon fresh-ground pepper
8 boned quails, about 4 ounces each
Kosher salt
Black pepper in a mill

2 tablespoons unsalted butter
2 apples, peeled, cored, and quartered

Prepare the creamy polenta. When it is done, pour it into a small buttered sheet pan and spread it out evenly with a rubber spatula. Brush a sheet of wax paper or parchment paper with olive oil and set it, oiled side down, on top of the polenta. Let the polenta cool to room temperature, then refrigerate it for 1 hour.

Make the sauce: Pour 1 cup of the apple juice into a small saucepan. Bring to a boil, reduce the heat, and simmer, uncovered, until the juice has nearly completely evaporated. Add the remaining apple juice, the vinegar, and the 1 teaspoon of pepper, and reduce the liquid by two thirds. Remove the pan from the heat and set aside.

Season the quails, inside and out, with salt and pepper. Melt 1 tablespoon of the butter in a large heavy skillet over medium heat. When the butter is foamy, add 4 of the quails, and brown them evenly on all sides. Remove them from the skillet, and brown the remaining 4 quails. Remove them from the skillet, add the apples, and brown them evenly. Return the quails to the skillet, add the sauce, and bring to a boil. Reduce the heat, and simmer, covered, until the quails are tender, 15 to 20 minutes, depending on the size of the birds.

Meanwhile, preheat the broiler to high or the oven to 450°F. Brush a baking sheet with olive oil. Cut the chilled polenta into 3-inch triangles, and transfer them to the baking sheet. Broil or bake until the tops just begin to turn golden brown. Turn and

cook on the other side.

Transfer the apples and quails to a serving platter, and keep them warm. Taste the sauce, and adjust the seasoning. Increase the heat under the sauce to medium-high, swirl in the remaining 1 tablespoon of butter, and, as soon as it melts, pour the sauce over the quails and apples. Place the polenta triangles around the edge of the platter, and serve immediately.

ROBERT'S LAVENDER QUAIL

Robert Kourik, a friend and colleague, is a landscape architect who specializes in edible landscapes. He is the author of several books on gardening, many of which include recipes, and he is an expert on growing lavender and cooking with it. On several occasions, he has joined me in cooking classes to demonstrate this technique, for which he uses chicken rather than quail, which you can do, too, if you prefer.

SERVES 4

8 boned quails, about 4 ounces each
Olive oil
Kosher salt
Black pepper in a mill
Several bundles of lavender clippings, stems, and flowers
Fresh or dried lavender flowers, for garnish

Prepare a hot fire on an outdoor grill. Have a griddle or a very large cast-iron pan ready. You will also need 2 heavy bricks.

Brush the quails with olive oil, and season them inside and out with salt and pepper. When the grill is very hot, set the griddle or pan on the rack and wait until it gets hot. Arrange half of the lavender stems on the griddle or in the pan, breaking the stems, if necessary, to fit. Place the quails in a single layer on top of the stems, top with the remaining lavender, and set the bricks on top so that they weight down the quails. Cook for 8 to 10 minutes, or until the lavender produces quite a bit of smoke. Carefully remove the bricks and use 2 large spatulas to turn over the quails, clippings and all. Weight again with the bricks, and cook for 10 minutes more, or until the quails are thoroughly cooked. Carefully remove the bricks, and use tongs to remove and discard the top layer of lavender. Lift out the quails, set them on a serving platter, garnish with lavender flowers, and serve at once.

The Original 27 Counties

The Sacramento River runs along the western edge of **Butte County**, an important agricultural region at the northern end of the great Central Valley. Here you'll find the university town of Chico, home of Sierra Nevada Brewery, maker of a pale ale that was among the first beers of the microbrewery renaissance and still one of the most popular. Chico is surrounded by orchards of pomegranate, persimmon, and almond trees. There are orchards of loquat and kumquat trees as well, the fruits of which have never taken off commercially but are popular among backyard gardeners and home cooks in California. Kiwifruit, introduced in 1904 and immensely popular from the 1960s on, is an important crop in the county; the trees bear fresh fruit from October through May, when most other fruits are out of season. Twenty miles east of Chico is Richvale, where the Lundberg family, originally from Sweden, has been growing rice since 1937. They began by specializing in brown rice, but today they are major growers of basmati, red wehani, black japonica, sticky rice for sushi, and wild rice (a grass rather than a true rice). In the mid-1990s, the Lundbergs began experimenting with arborio and jasmine rices.

ROAST GOOSE WITH WILD RICE STUFFING

California produces nearly all the pomegranates grown commercially in the United States. Most are sold fresh, but some are used to make a thick pomegranate concentrate, occasionally called pomegranate molasses. Its sweet tangy flavor goes remarkably well with dark poultry such as quail, duck, and goose. If you have a hard time finding goose, ask your butcher to direct you to a good source.

SERVES 6 TO 8

1 whole goose, wild or domestic, about 7 to 9 pounds
Olive oil
Wild Rice Stuffing (recipe follows)
6 small white onions, peeled
1 teaspoon ground allspice
4 celery ribs
⅓ cup pomegranate concentrate
Kosher salt
Black pepper in a mill
Seeds from 1 pomegranate

Rinse the goose and pat it dry with a tea towel. Brush it, inside and out, with olive oil. Fill the cavity loosely with the stuffing, and then push the onions into the cavity. Truss the goose, sprinkle the allspice over the skin, and cover the breast with a clean cheesecloth that has been soaked in olive oil.

Preheat the oven to 450°F.

Place the goose on a rack in a roasting pan and surround it with the celery. Add hot water to the pan to a depth of 1 inch. Place the goose in the oven, and immediately reduce the heat to 350°F. After the goose has cooked for 30 minutes, baste the skin with pan drippings and with some of the pomegranate concentrate. Prick the skin with a fork to release the fat. After another 30 minutes, baste again, and then roast until the juices run clear when the thigh is pierced with a fork. The internal temperature of the thigh should reach about 185°F and the stuffing 160°F. The total roasting time will be about 17 minutes per pound for a wild goose and 20 minutes per pound for a domestic goose. Remove the cheesecloth during the final 20 minutes of cooking, and baste frequently during that time with pomegranate concentrate and pan drippings.

Remove the goose from the oven and let it rest for 15 minutes. Spoon the stuffing into a serving dish, and keep it warm. Pour off the fat from the pan drippings, taste, and season with salt and pepper. Carve the goose, arrange it on a platter, scatter pomegranate seeds over the goose and the stuffing, and serve with the stuffing and pan drippings.

Variation:

Omit the stuffing and the pomegranate concentrate. Fill the cavity of the goose with a large sprig of thyme, about 10 heads of garlic, papery outer skins removed, and

1 orange, cut into wedges. Before serving, remove the garlic, place it in a serving bowl, and serve it alongside the goose.

Wild Rice Stuffing

MAKES ABOUT 4 CUPS

3 tablespoons olive oil
1 cup uncooked wild rice
8 to 10 scallions, green and white
    parts, cut into thin rounds
1 cup fresh cranberries, chopped
½ cup pine nuts, toasted
Kosher salt
Black pepper in a mill

Bring 3½ cups of water to a boil in a large heavy pot. Add 1 tablespoon of the olive oil and the wild rice, reduce the heat, and simmer, covered, for 40 minutes. About 35 minutes after the rice is started, heat the remaining olive oil in a sauté pan. Add the scallions, and sauté them for 3 minutes, just until they are limp. Remove the pan from the heat, and stir in the cranberries and pine nuts. Stir the scallion mixture into the rice, and continue to cook the rice until all of the water is absorbed, about 10 minutes more. Remove the pan from the heat, season with salt and pepper, and let the stuffing cool until it is easy to handle.

Chapter 11

MAIN
COURSES
WITH
MEAT

MAIN COURSES WITH MEAT

SOUVLAKI

*S*ome ethnic cuisines, particularly Italian, Spanish, and Mexican, have become so much a part of the wider context of California cooking that their original boundaries have blurred. Others, like Greek cooking, have stayed closer to their roots. Souvlaki, skewers of marinated lamb grilled quickly so the meat remains juicy, is one of the few Greek dishes to be familiar to many of us. Souvlaki goes remarkably well with a Middle Eastern tabbouleh or a South Asian cucumber raita, the latter of which is similar to the Greek mixture of cucumbers, garlic, and yogurt known as *tzatziki*. If you have a rosemary bush with branches to spare, make skewers of them by shaving off the needles with your fingertips and threading the lamb onto the naked branch.

SERVES 4

3 pounds lamb shoulder or leg, cut into bite-size pieces
24 bamboo skewers, soaked in water for at least 30 minutes
Juice of 3 lemons
⅔ cup extra virgin olive oil
8 garlic cloves, minced
2 teaspoons minced rosemary
2 teaspoons minced oregano
Kosher salt
Black pepper in a mill
Sprigs of rosemary, for garnish

Thread the lamb onto skewers and set the skewers in a large shallow baking dish.

Greek Easter

"*M*y earliest memories of Greek Easter revolve around my horror of the whole roasted lamb. While singing the Greek national anthem, my relatives would bring out what looked like a skinned greyhound strung to a pole. You would think that watching this animal being roasted on a spit—along with various relatives bickering over who would eat the eyeballs—would have made me a vegan for life. Yet, as the years passed, I started to eat the lamb and began to realize how wonderful it was, slathered continuously with olive oil, lemon, garlic, and oregano as it was cooked. I got over my aversion, and even started turning the lamb at the spit. I continued to pass on the eyeballs.

"The sunny Sunday afternoons in the San Francisco backyard of my Aunt Christine and Uncle Jerry's house were festive and wonderful, with bouzouki music blaring, the aroma of roasted lamb, and tables loaded with olives, *tzatziki*, Greek salad, circular loaves of *kouloures*, moussaka, and all those amazing phyllo dishes: cheese-filled *tiropetes*, spinach spanakopeta, and, of course, the desserts. Little did we realize at the time that it would be a dress rehearsal for a restaurant they eventually opened in the wine country."

Nick Topolos, San Francisco

Mix together the lemon juice, olive oil, garlic, rosemary, and oregano in a small bowl, and season to taste with kosher salt and pepper. Spoon half of the marinade over the lamb and refrigerate, covered, for at least 2 hours, turning the skewers occasionally to keep the lamb coated in marinade. Reserve the remaining marinade.

Prepare a hot fire in an outdoor or stovetop grill. Grill the lamb, turning the skewers several times, for about 8 minutes, depending on the size of the pieces of lamb. Baste the lamb frequently with its marinade (do not use the reserved marinade) as it cooks. When the lamb is done, transfer the skewers to a platter, garnish with rosemary sprigs, and serve immediately, with the reserved marinade, reheated, on the side.

LEMONY LAMB CHOPS

A lamb chop seasoned with garlic and salt was one of my favorite things to eat when I was a child. Today, I often eat them just that way, but sometimes I do more, as in this recipe, which has a marinade reminiscent of the Greek style of seasoning lamb. Use the same marinade for grilled leg of lamb. Serve with the garlic or black pepper variation of Fresh Pasta (page 203), if you like, or with Armenian Pilaf (page 222).

SERVES 4

8 lamb loin chops or 4 lamb shoulder chops

Kosher salt
Black pepper in a mill
6 garlic cloves, crushed
1 tablespoon minced rosemary
1 tablespoon minced sage leaves
1 tablespoon minced Italian parsley
1 tablespoon minced lemon zest
¼ cup fresh lemon juice
⅓ cup extra virgin olive oil
Sprigs of fresh rosemary, for garnish

Place the lamb chops in a shallow nonreactive dish large enough to hold them in a single layer, and season them with salt and pepper. Mix together the garlic, rosemary, sage, parsley, lemon zest, lemon juice, and olive oil in a small bowl. Pour the marinade over the chops and turn to coat them thoroughly. Refrigerate, covered, for at least 2 hours, turning the chops occasionally to keep them coated in marinade.

Prepare a stovetop grill or preheat the broiler. Remove the chops from the marinade, and brush off the herbs and excess liquid. Grill or broil the chops for 4 to 5 minutes, turn them, and cook them until they are done, 3 to 4 minutes more for rare, depending on the thickness of the chops. Transfer to individual plates, garnish with rosemary sprigs, and serve immediately.

LAMB CHOPS WITH FLAGEOLETS

The little pale-green dried beans known as flageolets have long been common in France, where a classic bistro dish pairs them with roasted leg of lamb. Although the flageolet is not a major bean crop today in California, some smaller farms, such as Phipps Country Store and Farm in Pescadero, grow the beans, and they are becoming more widely available in California and elsewhere. In this recipe, lamb chops take the place of leg of lamb. The dish goes quite well with green beans, especially haricots verts, either blanched or blanched and sautéed, as in Haricots Verts with Shallots (page 394).

SERVES 4

1 cup flageolets, soaked overnight
  and drained
½ yellow onion, cut into wedges
3 garlic cloves
1 sprig of oregano
1 sprig of thyme
4 lamb shoulder chops
Kosher salt
Black pepper in a mill
3 to 4 ounces pancetta, diced
1 shallot, minced

Place the flageolets in a heavy pot and cover them with water by 2 inches. Add the onion, garlic, oregano, and thyme, and bring to a boil over high heat. Reduce the heat, and simmer, partially covered, until the beans are tender, 1 to 1½ hours. Remove and discard the herb sprigs and any large pieces of onion that have not dissolved.

Season the lamb chops with salt and pepper. Heat a large skillet over medium-high heat (add a small amount of mild olive oil if your skillet is not well seasoned);

The Original 27 Counties

In **Solano County**, the pretty little town of Benicia, named for General Mariano Vallejo's wife—a popular hostess and renowned home cook—was the state capital for a brief period in 1853. The first settlers of the county raised cattle and farmed sugar beets, tomatoes, fruits, nuts, and field crops. The town of Vallejo has long been an ethnically diverse city, with substantial populations of Southeast Asian and Hispanic immigrants. Today, Vallejo is home to Marine World USA, where Burma, an Indonesian fruit bat, charms visitors with her remarkably playful personality. Near the northern end of the county is the town of Dixon, known as Lambtown USA because of the sheep raised there for more than a century. At the annual lamb festival, you'll find more home cooks than celebrity chefs, and dishes such as Uncle Ernie's Stuffed Leg of Lamb; lamb ribs marinated in teriyaki sauce, pineapple, and rosemary; and rack of lamb stuffed with bacon, basil, and almonds.

when the skillet is hot, add the chops. Fry them for about 6 minutes, turn them, and fry them until they are done, about 4 minutes more for rare meat. Transfer the chops to a platter and keep them warm. Reduce the heat to medium, add the pancetta to the skillet, and fry it until it is almost crisp. Add the shallot, and cook it until it is soft and fragrant, 7 to 8 minutes.

Drain the flageolets, reserving the cooking liquid. Add the beans to the skillet and toss them with the pancetta and shallots, adding enough cooking liquid to keep them very moist. Taste, and season with salt and pepper.

Divide the beans among individual plates, top each portion with a lamb chop, and serve immediately.

LAMB SHANKS WITH CREAMY POLENTA

*L*amb, beef, and veal shanks are economical cuts of meat long popular with home cooks. It's only recently that restaurant chefs have rediscovered them, lending a new cachet to dishes that are very easy to prepare at home. There is no secret to success; just cook the shanks until the meat falls off the bone. Serve with Gina's Chard (page 390) or Wilted Spinach (page 405) and a robust zinfandel.

SERVES 4 TO 6

6 lamb shanks, about ¾ pound each
Olive oil
10 garlic cloves, unpeeled
3 leeks, white and pale green parts, cut into ¼-inch rounds
2 cups red wine, such as zinfandel or syrah
3 cups beef stock
1 sprig each of Italian parsley, oregano, thyme, summer savory, and rosemary, tied together to make a bouquet garni
Kosher salt
Black pepper in a mill
1 recipe Creamy Polenta (recipe follows)

Preheat the oven to 350°F. Trim the lamb shanks, removing the fell (the thin outer covering), if any is there.

Over medium heat, heat a small amount of olive oil in a heavy ovenproof skillet large enough to hold the shanks in a single layer. Add the garlic, and sauté, stirring constantly, until the cloves just begin to color; do not let them brown. Remove the cloves from the skillet and set them aside. Add the shanks to the skillet, and brown them on all sides. Remove the shanks and set them aside, and drain off all but 2 tablespoons of fat. Add the leeks, and sauté them until they are wilted, about 7 minutes. Return the garlic and the shanks to the skillet, and add the wine, stock, and bouquet garni. Season with salt and pepper.

Cover the skillet, and bake the shanks for 2½ hours. Uncover them, and bake for 30 minutes more. Remove the shanks from the oven, let them rest for 10 minutes, then transfer them to a serving platter. Spoon the skillet juices over the shanks, add several turns of black pepper, and serve immediately, with the polenta alongside.

Creamy Polenta

Polenta is the name given to coarse-ground cornmeal cooked in the savory tradition of Italy. It is simple, hearty fare, especially delicious when made with fresh stoneground cornmeal. Polenta should be stored in a sealed container in the refrigerator; otherwise, the germ present in the stoneground meal will go rancid. If you are pressed for time, make the easy oven Variation.

SERVES 4 TO 6

1 tablespoon kosher salt
1½ cups coarse-ground cornmeal
½ to 1 teaspoon fresh-ground black
   pepper
3 tablespoons butter
¾ cups (3 ounces) grated dry jack or
   Parmigiano-Reggiano

Bring 3 cups of water to a rolling boil in a heavy pot over high heat. Bring another 3 cups of water to a simmer in a separate saucepan. Add the salt to the boiling water, and, using a whisk, stir rapidly in one direction to create a vortex. Pour the cornmeal into the center of the vortex in a thin, steady stream, stirring constantly in the same direction to prevent the formation of lumps. When all the cornmeal has been added, lower the heat, and simmer gently, continuing to stir, until the polenta begins to thicken. Once it does so, switch from the whisk to a long-handled wooden spoon. Add 1 cup of the simmering water, continuing to stir. Use the back of the spoon to break up any lumps against the sides of the pot. Continue to stir the polenta, being sure to reach down to the bottom of the pot, until it is thick and pulls away from the sides of the pot. Taste the polenta to see if it is tender, and add more simmering water if necessary. The polenta will be done in 15 to 60 minutes; the upper end of the range is for certain types of cornmeal that do not become tender quickly.

During the last 5 minutes of cooking, stir in the pepper, butter, and cheese. Remove from the heat. Pour onto a large platter or into a large bowl or individual bowls, and serve immediately.

Variation:

To make easy oven polenta, preheat the oven to 350°F. Stir together 4 cups cold water, 1 tablespoon kosher salt, ½ teaspoon fresh-ground black pepper, 1 cup coarse-ground cormeal, and 1 tablespoon butter, cut into pieces, in a 1½-quart baking dish. Bake, uncovered, in the center of the top rack of the oven for 40 minutes. Open the oven door, pull out the rack, and stir the polenta. Bake 10 minutes more. Let rest for 5 minutes, and serve. To season oven polenta, if you like, stir in ½ cup grated dry jack cheese, 1 tablespoon minced Italian parsley, and 2 teaspoons lemon zest when you stir the polenta after 40 minutes.

OLIVE HARVEST LAMB

Plump, succulent quails hot from the grill are piled high on a platter. Bottles of fresh olive oil, pressed the day before, adorn the table, ready to anoint chunks of crusty bread. Wine glasses, filled with zinfandel from a nearby winery, gleam like big, bold rubies in the soft winter light. This is olive harvest in northern California at Dry Creek Valley's Olive Ridge Ranch, home of DaVero olive oil. Around the table are several dozen friends who have been picking olives since early morning; when the picking is done, we are rewarded by this sumptuous fall feast. I look forward to this day all year. One year the olives were ready earlier than I anticipated. I had already scheduled a dinner party for the evening of harvest, so I had to rush home from the feast to prepare my own. I served this lamb in celebration of California's best olive oil. Although zinfandel is excellent with lamb, I serve this dish with J. Rochioli pinot noir, grown, made, and bottled not far from my home in the Russian River Valley appellation.

SERVES 6 TO 8

1 leg of lamb, boned, about 5 pounds
Kosher salt
Black pepper in a mill
1 recipe Olive Tapenade (page 422)
10 sprigs of rosemary, 6 to 8 inches long
2 pounds new potatoes, such as Yellow Finn, Rose Fir, fingerling, or Yukon Gold, scrubbed
½ pound carrots, cut into 2-inch pieces
6 to 8 shallots
15 garlic cloves, unpeeled
⅓ cup extra virgin olive oil

Preheat the oven to 450°F.

Place the leg of lamb, fat side up, on a work surface. Remove the fell (the thin outer covering), if any is there, and as much fat as possible. Season with salt and pepper, turn the leg over, and spread the tapenade over the inner surface of the leg. Roll up the leg lengthwise around the tapenade, pressing the roll tightly together as you do so, and tie up the roll with twine. Tuck 6 of the rosemary sprigs under the twine around the outside of the lamb.

Place the potatoes, carrots, shallots, and garlic in a roasting pan, season them with salt and pepper, and drizzle with half of the olive oil. Position a rack over the vegetables, moving them if necessary to make the rack fit. Set the lamb on the rack, and drizzle the remaining olive oil over the meat. Transfer to the oven, immediately reduce the heat to 350°F, and roast for 1¼ to 1½ hours (15 to 20 minutes per pound for rare lamb), or to an internal temperature of 125°F.

Remove the lamb and vegetables from the oven and let them rest for 15 minutes. Using a slotted spoon, transfer the vegetables to a serving bowl. Remove the rosemary sprigs and twine from the lamb, cut the lamb into ¼-inch-thick slices, and arrange the slices on a serving platter. Some of the tapenade will probably fall out as you slice the lamb; place it in the center of the platter. Season with several turns of pepper, garnish with the remaining rosemary sprigs, and serve immediately, with the vegetables alongside.

The Garlic Meat Lady from

We're cooking dinner tonight.
I'm making a kind of Stonehenge
stroganoff.
Marcia is helping me. You
already know the legend
of her beauty.
I've asked her to rub garlic
on the meat. She takes
each piece of meat like a lover
and rubs it gently with garlic.
I've never seen anything like this
before. Every orifice
of the meat is explored, caressed
relentlessly with garlic.
There is a passion here that would
drive a deaf saint to learn
the violin and play Beethoven at
Stonehenge.

Richard Brautigan, *The Pill versus the Springhill Mine Disaster* (Delta, 1968)

OVEN-ROASTED LEG OF LAMB WITH SAUSAGE STUFFING AND MUSTARD GLAZE

This has always been one of my favorite recipes, in part because it was the first I ever published, years ago in a small-town newspaper where I was a columnist. Serve it for Easter, I suggested then and still do, and serve it with a fine California merlot, such as Matanzas Creek or Duckhorn, or a French Rhône or California Rhône-style red wine.

SERVES 6 TO 8

1 leg of lamb, boned, about 5 pounds
2 tablespoons olive oil
1 yellow onion, minced
8 garlic cloves, minced
1 pound Italian sausage or other sausage, casings removed
2 tablespoons Dijon mustard
1 teaspoon thyme leaves
1 tablespoon minced Italian parsley
1 cup fresh bread crumbs (see page 46)
1 tablespoon butter, cold

MUSTARD GLAZE
1 cup Dijon mustard
½ cup olive oil
2 teaspoons soy sauce
1 teaspoon thyme leaves

2 teaspoons fresh-ground black
   pepper
3 garlic cloves, pressed

Preheat the oven to 325°F.

Place the leg of lamb on a work surface. Remove the fell (the thin outer covering), if any is there, and as much fat as possible. Set the meat aside.

Make the stuffing: Heat the olive oil in a heavy skillet over medium heat. Add the onion, and sauté it until it is soft and fragrant, about 8 minutes. Add the garlic, and sauté for 2 minutes more. Add the sausage, and cook it, crumbling it with a fork, until it is about half done, about 7 minutes. Stir in the mustard, thyme, and parsley. Toss with the bread crumbs, remove the mixture from the heat, and set it aside.

Make the glaze: Whisk all of the ingredients together in a small bowl until the mixture is smooth.

Place the leg of lamb, outside down, on a work surface. Brush the inside of the leg with the glaze, and spread the sausage mixture on top. Roll up the leg lengthwise, pressing the roll tightly together as you do so, and tie up the roll with twine. Brush the outside surface of the leg with the glaze, and place the lamb on the rack of a roasting pan. Roast the lamb for about 1¼ hours (15 minutes per pound for rare).

When the lamb reaches an internal temperature of 130° to 135°F, remove it from the oven and let it rest for 15 minutes. Place the roasting pan over a stovetop burner on low heat. Add ½ cup water and scrape the pan to loosen the drippings.

Add any remaining mustard glaze, stir well, and simmer for about 5 minutes. Add the butter, a bit at a time, stirring after each addition. When all the butter is melted, pour the sauce into a warm bowl. Cut the lamb into ¼-inch-thick slices, arrange the slices on a serving platter, and top with half the sauce. Pass the remaining sauce on the side.

WINE COUNTRY BEEF FAJITAS

*T*hese sweet and savory fajitas deviate from traditional Mexican fare, as Cal-Mex foods often do, with apple juice and red wine contributing sweet and fruity elements.

SERVES 6

1½ cups fruity red wine, such as
   zinfandel
1 cup apple juice
Juice of 1 lemon
¼ cup sugar
4 garlic cloves, crushed
Pinch of fresh-grated nutmeg
Pinch of crushed red pepper
2 medium yellow onions, cut lengthwise in half

1½ pounds skirt steak
12 corn tortillas
1 recipe Smoky Corn Salsa (page 62)
6 sprigs of cilantro
1 lime, cut into wedges

Combine the wine, apple juice, lemon juice, sugar, garlic, nutmeg, red pepper, and onions in a saucepan over medium heat. Stir until the sugar is dissolved. Remove from the heat and let cool. Cut the skirt steak into 4-inch-wide pieces, place them in a shallow dish, and pour the marinade with the onions over them. Refrigerate, covered, for several hours or overnight.

About 1 hour before serving, remove the skirt steak from the refrigerator. Prepare and have ready a very hot fire in an outdoor grill or heat a stovetop grill.

Using tongs, remove the onions from the marinade and grill them for 10 minutes. Turn them, and grill for 10 minutes more. Meanwhile, remove the steak from the marinade, place it on the grill, grill for 3 to 4 minutes, turn, and grill for 3 to 4 minutes more for rare meat, longer for well-done meat.

Transfer the onions and steak strips to a platter and keep them warm. Grill the tortillas quickly, until they are soft and warm but not crisp. Place 2 tortillas on each of 6 serving plates, quickly cut the onions into thin wedges and the steak into thin strips, and place some of each in the center of each tortilla. Top with salsa, garnish with lime wedges and a sprig of cilantro, and serve immediately.

The Original 27 Counties

• •

Few California counties have as distinct a sense of themselves as **Napa County**, the most famous of all of America's wine-growing regions, known for its suave chardonnays, elegant cabernet sauvignons, and robust zinfandels. Though its eastern and western edges include wild, mountainous terrain, including the magnificent Pope Valley and the Mayacamas Range, its heart is the long, narrow Napa Valley, which stretches north–south for nearly the length of the county. A single artery, Highway 29, runs along the center of valley, with a second thoroughfare, the Silverado Trail, forming a parallel route on the eastern edge. Tourists, more than the number that visit Disneyland each year, flock to the valley to visit the scores of wineries that cover the landscape. In 1846, the Bale Grist Mill was established near Calistoga; it survives today as a working mill within a state park, and you can have your dried corn ground into polenta on the spot. Although viticulture dominates now, some remnants of the early years can be found in the sheep that graze in Los Carneros, in the southwestern corner, and in small farms and cheese factories tucked among the vineyards. Because of the influence of the area's winery and restaurant chefs, home cooking tends to be well-heeled and sophisticated.

GINGER BEEF STIR-FRY

There are few rules when it comes to this recipe and its ingredients. The technique is what is important: For a successful stir-fry, all the ingredients must be cut into sizes that will be finished cooking at the same time. Once you are comfortable with the method and the seasonings, vary the ingredients according to the seasons and your personal tastes. If you are pressed for time, you can omit the marinade for the steak.

SERVES 4

1 to 1½ pounds flank steak or rib-eye steak
1 tablespoon minced fresh ginger
1 tablespoon minced garlic
1 tablespoon minced serrano or Thai chile
1 tablespoon fish sauce
Juice of ½ lime
2 teaspoons sugar
2 tablespoons oyster sauce
1 tablespoon hoisin sauce
1 teaspoon Thai-style red curry paste
3 tablespoons hot water
2 tablespoons peanut oil
1 small red onion, cut lengthwise in half and cut into thin slices
1 small red bell pepper, cut into thin julienne
5 ounces shiitake mushrooms, sliced thin
6 ounces fresh asparagus tips, cut into 1-inch lengths, blanched

4 ounces snow peas
Steamed Rice (page 217)
2 teaspoons sesame seeds, toasted

Cut the steak crosswise into ⅛-inch-thick slices and place them in a small bowl. Mix together 1 teaspoon each of the ginger, garlic, and chile, along with all of the fish sauce, lime juice, and sugar, and pour the mixture over the steak. Let the steak marinate, covered, in the refrigerator for at least 30 minutes or up to several hours. Remove the steak from the refrigerator and let it come up to room temperature before cooking.

Mix together the oyster sauce, hoisin sauce, red curry paste, and hot water in a small bowl. Stir well until the mixture is smooth, and set it aside.

Heat the peanut oil in a wok over high heat. Add the remaining ginger, garlic, and chile, and let them sizzle for about 30 seconds. Add the onion, bell pepper, and mushrooms, and cook, stirring constantly, for 4 to 5 minutes, or until the vegetables begin to wilt. Add the beef, asparagus, and snow peas, pour the oyster sauce mixture over, and cook, continuing to stir, until the meat just begins to lose its color and most but not all of the liquid has evaporated, about 3 minutes.

Place the rice on a serving platter or on individual plates, and place the stir-fry on top. Sprinkle the sesame seeds over all, and serve immediately.

KOREAN-STYLE GRILLED BEEFSTEAKS

oth Los Angeles and San Francisco have thriving communities of Korean immigrants, with many Korean restaurants and markets. This recipe is an adaptation of *bulgogi*, the famous Korean barbecue dish that features thin strips of beef; in this recipe, I call for whole steaks. Squid, octopus, and chicken are also marinated and grilled in a similar fashion. To lend a traditional flair to the meal, serve the steaks with several accompaniments,

The Grill

There is perhaps no cooking technique more quintessentially Californian than grilling. In the vast new housing tracts of post–World War II California, nearly every new home had a patio, and patio living, centered around the grill, became an important part of everyday life. If you were transferred from, say, New Jersey or Chicago to California, one of your rewards was the opportunity to enjoy your patio and your grill nearly year-round.

Grilling's history in North America stretches back beyond California's earliest years. When Spanish explorers arrived in Haiti and found the native people cooking meat over an outdoor fire, they borrowed an indigenous word and called the process *barbacoa*; eventually they brought the term with them to California. In her classic *West Coast Cook Book*, Helen Evans Brown writes that grilled meat was a part of every festive occasion in early California. A fresh-killed steer would hang in the shade of a tree while a fire roared nearby. The *"vaqueros* and their ladies would cut off pieces whenever hunger called, and cook it over the waiting fire," Brown reports. In the state's early years, William Dun-

phy, a wealthy cattle rancher with land in Monterey and Humboldt counties, hosted barbecues at which the steer was spit-roasted whole over large charcoal pits. Some of these early barbecues also featured spit-roasted *cabrito* (suckling goat) and baby lamb.

Today, grilling is as popular as ever in California. After work, it's a simple matter to heat up the grill, toss on a couple of steaks, and make a salad for a quick and typical California dinner. In recent years, Californians' grilling repertoire has expanded to include salmon, jumbo prawns, oysters, eggplant, onions, zucchini, pizza, and even burritos. To most Californians, grilling is second nature; to many, it is an obsession. Some spend thousands of dollars on elaborate gas grills, shiny stainless-steel contraptions that are today's answer to the brick-and-stone towers of a 1950s patio. For those who insist on charcoal or wood fires, nothing replaces their mesquite charcoal, hickory chips, and fragrant dried grapevines; their shelves are lined with grilling books, and everyone gets out of their way when they get out their tongs and mitt.

including *samjan* sauce (see Note), rice, Asian Cucumber Salad (page 128), and an assortment of pickled vegetables.

SERVES 4

---

2 tablespoons mirin (rice wine)
¼ cup soy sauce
2 tablespoons sugar
10 garlic cloves, minced
6 scallions, green and white parts, cut into very thin rounds
½ teaspoon crushed red pepper
2 teaspoons toasted sesame oil
4 steaks, rib-eye or other premium cut, 8 to 10 ounces each

Combine the mirin, soy sauce, sugar, garlic, scallions, red pepper, and sesame oil in a small bowl. Arrange the steaks in a

glass baking dish or other nonreactive container large enough to hold them in a single layer. Pour the marinade over the steaks, turn them until they are fully coated, and refrigerate, covered, for at least 1 hour or up to 4 to 5 hours (the longer the better). Remove from the refrigerator 1 hour before cooking.

Prepare a hot fire in an outdoor grill, preferably, or a stovetop grill. Grill the steaks until they are just rare, 4 to 6 minutes per side. Transfer the steaks to a warm serving platter, and let them rest for 5 minutes before serving.

NOTE: To make *samjan* sauce, mix 2 parts *dhwen-jang*, or Korean bean paste, with 1 part *gochujang*, or Korean barbecue sauce. Both dhwen-jang and gochujang are available in Asian markets. The more commonly available miso may be substituted for dhwen-jang, and *sambal ulek* may be substituted for gochujang.

STEAK FRITES

·······························

The French have brought a lot of excellent ideas to the table, and this one—pan-grilled steak with french fries—is among the best, a classic bistro dish that lends itself to the home kitchen. It's about as informal as food gets and relies upon the quality of the ingredients themselves for its real character. If you or your family has a craving for a simple steak, you needn't look any further than here. If there's no time to make the accompanying french fries, you can take a more American route with a baked potato, or a California route, with roasted vegetables (see chapter 12 for recipes). In the early spring, replace the *frites* with a mound of Roasted Asparagus (page 383).

SERVES 4

1 recipe Perfect French Fries (page 397), prepared through the first frying but not the second
4 steaks, such as New York strip, rib-eye, or other premium cut
Kosher salt
Black pepper in a mill
Olive oil
¼ cup Flavored Butter, such as Olive Butter or Dried Tomato Butter (page 415)

Have the french fries ready for their second frying. Season both sides of each steak with salt and pepper, and brush the steaks with olive oil.

Prepare the oil for the second frying of the *frites*, and heat a ribbed cast-iron skillet or a stovetop grill until it is very hot. Place the steaks in the skillet or on the grill. Cook them, about 4 minutes on each side for rare steaks. Meanwhile, fry the potatoes their second time, then drain them and season them with salt and pepper.

Set the steaks on warmed serving plates and add some of the *frites* to each plate. Top each steak with a spoonful of flavored butter, and serve immediately.

The Original 27 Counties

San Simeon's legendary Hearst Castle presides over the northern part of **San Luis Obispo County**, which stretches from just below Big Sur south to Santa Barbara County. When the first Europeans arrived, by land in 1587 and by sea in 1605, in what would become San Luis Obispo County, they found Native American Chumash tribes. Much of the coastline is isolated by steep cliffs and the sharp rise of the Santa Lucia Mountains. The economy of San Luis Obispo County has been driven as much by oil as by agriculture, which includes large cattle ranches and poultry farms. Before industrial pollution forced it to move north, California oyster farming was centered in Morro Bay. Today, the Central Coast appellation is coming into its own with successful wineries such as Maison Deutz, Adalaida Cellars, Edna Valley Vineyard, Baron Vineyards, Twin Hills Ranch, Hope Farms, Wild Horse, Creston Manor, and Eberle Winery.

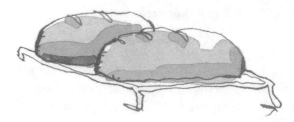

BEEF TENDERLOIN WITH GORGONZOLA BUTTER

Because it is both elegant and easy to prepare, this dish is ideal for a dinner party. The sauce and butter can be made a day in advance, and you should keep accompaniments simple. Serve with Haricots Verts with Shallots (page 394), Roasted Asparagus (page 383), or Grilled Fennel (page 393). Although it is considered traditional to serve a husky cabernet sauvignon with beef, I recommend a full-bodied California pinot noir, such as Mount Eden, Calera, or Williams-Selyem.

SERVES 4 TO 6

1 beef tenderloin, about 2½ pounds
5 garlic cloves, minced
1 tablespoon minced lemon zest
Kosher salt
Black pepper in a mill
1 tablespoon minced rosemary
1 cup hearty red wine
2 2-by-½-inch strips of lemon zest
5 to 7 sprigs of rosemary
2 cups beef stock
¼ cup Gorgonzola Butter (page 415)

Set the tenderloin on a work surface. Mix together the garlic, minced lemon zest, 1 teaspoon of salt, 1 tablespoon of fresh-ground pepper, and minced rosemary in a small bowl. Rub the mixture into the surface of the beef. Refrigerate, covered, overnight.

Preheat the oven to 450°F. Bring the beef to room temperature, and place it on a rack in a roasting pan. Place the meat in the oven, and immediately lower the heat to 350°F. Roast the beef to an internal temperature of 130°F for rare, about 15 minutes per pound. Cook longer for medium-rare.

While the beef cooks, make the sauce: Combine the wine, 1 rosemary sprig, and the strips of lemon zest in a saucepan. Bring to a simmer, and simmer until the wine is reduced by two thirds. Add the stock, and reduce by two thirds again. Remove and discard the rosemary sprig and lemon zest, taste the sauce, and season with salt and pepper. Set the sauce aside.

When the beef is done, remove it from the oven and let it rest for 10 minutes. Carve it into ⅜-inch-thick slices. Divide the slices among warmed serving plates, and top each serving with sauce and a coin of Gorgonzola Butter. Garnish with a sprig of rosemary, and serve immediately.

CALIFORNIA POT ROAST

This is a dish I make every year for the birthday of a friend, artist Ginny Stanford. The zinfandel in the recipe provides a perfect opportunity to serve a great California zinfandel, such

The Farmers' Market and
Los Angeles "Home Cooking"

"A lady later identified as a Miss Birdie Groaner came into the [Los Angeles] Farmers Market about noontime one day and she stood looking hungrily at the appetizing cases at Magee's, Magee being a smart operation in what the trade knows as 'the wet bulk game' ... dill pickles *en barrel*, hoop cheese in bulk, good long-shred kraut bought by the barrel and retailed in paper buckets, and such things as big, black oily Greek olives imported in casks and purveyed, wet, by the pint.... Mr. Magee is a smart one ... he knows that some women sit around all afternoon gabbing and asking whose deal it is, and then they hurry frantically to get home ahead of their husbands to look as if they had been slaving over a hot stove all day. So ... Magee took to baking hams and tossing salads and baking meat loaves that a woman could take home and serve as her very own.

"[Birdie Groaner] bought a thick slab of ham which weighed out at 8 cents' worth. (This was some time back—in 1936, in fact.) ... Miss Groaner besat herself on an upturned melon crate that Martin Melton the Melon Man had left lying in the aisle. She opened her little package and had her baked ham. This seemingly small occurrence made history of a sort. It established the Farmers Market in the restaurant business because other good, uninhibited people followed Miss Groaner's example. Some of them bought rolls ... others bought potato salad and maybe a pickle.

"Thus it was that Magee began to present his good things on paper picnic plates. He supplied little wooden spoons. The manager of the market had to hire girls to gather up crumbs and to snaffle fluttering paper napkins. People began to say that the Farmers Market was more fun than a picnic. Soon there were many places purveying food to be eaten on the premises and today you will find such celebrated specialty kitchens as Consuelo Castillo's, a source of authentic California cookery frequently miscalled 'Mexican food.'"

Neill and Fred Beck, *Farmers Market Cook Book* (Holt and Company, 1951)

as Ravenswood or A. Rafanelli, or, if you prefer a wine with more restrained tannins, Preston.

SERVES 4 TO 6

3 tablepoons olive oil
1 thick chuck roast, 3 to 4 pounds

3 medium yellow onions, cut into
⅜-inch-thick rounds
6 medium leeks, white and pale
green parts, sliced
6 shallots
1 head of garlic, cloves separated
2 cups zinfandel or other hearty red
wine

2 cups beef stock or duck stock
1½ cups (12 ounces) whole or diced
   canned tomatoes
1 sprig each of oregano, thyme,
   rosemary, and Italian parsley, and
   1 bay leaf, tied together to make a
   bouquet garni
1 teaspoon whole black peppercorns
4 medium carrots, cut into 2-inch
   pieces
8 small Yellow Finn or red new
   potatoes

Preheat the oven to 325°F.

Heat the olive oil in a Dutch oven or other ovenproof pot over medium-high heat. When the oil is hot, add the meat and brown it on all sides. Transfer the meat to a plate and set it aside. Add the onions, leeks, shallots, and garlic cloves to the pan and sauté, stirring constantly, until all are lightly browned, 6 to 7 minutes. Return the meat to the pot, and add the wine, stock, tomatoes, bouquet garni, and peppercorns. Bring to a boil, then cover the pot, remove it from the heat, and place it in the oven. Bake for 1½ hours. Add the carrots and potatoes and continue to bake, covered, until the meat falls apart, 1 to 1½ hours more.

Using a slotted spoon, transfer the meat and vegetables to a serving platter. Remove and discard the bouquet garni. Let the roast rest for 10 minutes before serving. Pour the pan drippings into a bowl, and serve them alongside the meat and vegetables.

MARY'S PORTUGUESE BEEF STEW

M ary Rosa Grul grew up in a large Portuguese family in Stockton, east of San Francisco near the Sacramento Delta. She's a great cook who lets the look, feel, and aroma of the ingredients guide her through the preparation of a dish. She never writes down a recipe, and if she forgets an ingredient or a technique, she simply calls her mother or her aunt, the family's best cooks.

SERVES 4 TO 6

1 teaspoon whole cloves
½ teaspoon cumin seeds
3 bay leaves
1 cinnamon stick
3 pounds lean beef, cut into chunks
Kosher salt
Black pepper in a mill
¾ cup canned or homemade tomato
   sauce
¼ cup minced onion
1 garlic clove, minced
1 cup white wine
½ teaspoon ground cinnamon
⅛ teaspoon cayenne
1 teaspoon kosher salt
¼ teaspoon fresh-ground black
   pepper
½ head green cabbage, cored and
   shredded
1 loaf of country-style bread

Preheat the oven to 325°F.

Place the cloves, cumin, bay leaves, and cinnamon stick in a cheesecloth bag, tie it closed, and set it aside.

Season the beef with salt and pepper and place it in a heavy roasting pan. In a small bowl, mix together the tomato sauce, onion, garlic, wine, ground cinnamon, cayenne, 1 teaspoon salt, and ¼ teaspoon black pepper. Pour the mixture over the meat. Add the spice bag, and cover the roasting pan tightly with aluminum foil. Bake for 2¼ hours. Add the cabbage, cover tightly again, and continue to cook until the meat is completely fork tender, about 45 minutes more.

Remove the stew from the oven and remove and discard the spice bag. Cut the bread into ¾-inch slices, place a slice or two in individual serving dishes, and top the bread with stew. Serve immediately.

BEEF CHILI COLORADO

If you're feeling feisty and ready for a friendly fight, declare that you have a recipe for the world's best chili. Put a handful of people together anywhere, including in California, and there's sure to be at least one chili aficionado eager to defend his or her version. Many California communities hold chili contests, a few of which I've been lucky enough to judge. This recipe was passed on to me by word of mouth years ago, by a bartender

Tamale Pie

As I spoke with friends and colleagues while writing this book, no recipe was more controversial than tamale pie. It seemed to be the culinary equivalent of white zinfandel: Wine lovers look askance when white zin is mentioned, and foodies of every stripe cringe when asked about tamale pie. One friend simply refused to ask his Mexican mother-in-law for a recipe, not wanting to appear a foolish gringo. Yet tamale pie has a certain authenticity, or at least historical roots, as I discovered in Jacqueline Higuera McMahan's *California Rancho Cooking*. Her Great-Grandma Silva's Chileña Pie could easily be the source for what by the 1950s had become a ubiquitous and bland California dish. Her version, with garlic, cumin, and chile powder, and with steak rather than ground beef, was anything but bland. I now make tamale pie when I have leftover Beef Chili Colorado. I put the chili in a heavy baking dish, add pitted California black olives and a cup or two of corn cut fresh from the cob, top with grated cheddar cheese, and then top it all with tamale dough (page 366). I bake the pie, covered tightly with aluminum foil, in a 350°F oven for about 50 minutes.

who worked at a dive in a small northern California town. By now, it bears only passing resemblance to his version. He used beef ground for chili; I prefer to cut sirloin by hand into small cubes. He insisted on

Gebhardt's Chili Powder; I like to grind my own dried chiles. Neither of us adds beans, but they're an option in this recipe, if you want them. I serve beans alongside, not in the chili itself. In California, chili almost always comes with condiments like minced white onion, minced cilantro, grated cheddar cheese, and chopped olives. I prefer it simply with sliced scallions. The beverage of choice is cold beer.

SERVES 6 TO 8

2 tablespoons olive oil
2 large yellow onions, diced
2 to 3 jalapeños, minced
6 garlic cloves, minced
2 pounds beef sirloin or chuck, cut into small cubes
3 tablespoons all-purpose flour
3 to 4 tablespoons medium-hot red chili powder, store-bought or homemade (see Note)
1 to 2 tablespoons chipotle powder or other dried ground chile
2 teaspoons ground cumin
2 teaspoons dried oregano
¼ cup white wine vinegar
3 cans (10 ounces each) red chile sauce, preferably Las Palmas brand
2 cups beef stock or water
Kosher salt
Black pepper in a mill
3 cups cooked pinto beans (see Note), optional
2 bunches (about 20) of scallions, green and white parts, cut into thin rounds

Heat the olive oil in a large heavy skillet over medium heat. Add the onions, and sauté them until they are very soft and fragrant, about 15 minutes. Add the jalapeños, using 3 for more heat, and garlic, and sauté for 2 minutes more. Increase the heat to high, add the beef, and, stirring constantly, brown it thoroughly. Reduce the heat to medium. Sprinkle the flour over the meat, stir, and add the chili powder and chipotle powder or other dried chile. Cook, stirring, for 2 minutes. Add the cumin, oregano, and vinegar, and stir thoroughly. Stir in the red chile sauce and stock or water. Increase the heat to medium-high, bring to a boil, reduce the heat, and simmer, partially covered, until the meat is very tender and the sauce has thickened, about 2 hours. Stir occasionally to prevent sticking, and add water if the chili becomes too dry. If you like, stir in the beans and some of their cooking liquid after 1¾ hours. Taste the chili, and season with salt and pepper. Serve immediately, topped with the scallions, or refrigerate overnight before serving; refrigerated chili improves for several days.

NOTE: To make homemade chili powder, roast several dried chiles of a single type, such as ancho, New Mexico, or chipotle, in a heavy skillet over medium heat for about 3 minutes, turning them once. As soon as the chile releases its fragrance, remove it from the pan and let it cool. Chop it coarse, and grind it in a spice mill, coffee grinder, or molcajete. Use immediately or store, covered, in a cool pantry.

NOTE: Cook pinto beans using the Spicy Basic Beans variation for Basic Beans (page 236).

Chasen's Chili

"**P**lease send me ten quarts of your wonderful chili in dry ice," Elizabeth Taylor wired from Rome, where she was filming *Cleopatra* in 1962. Other devotees of the chili from the Los Angeles restaurant included Jack Benny, J. Edgar Hoover, Richard Nixon, Ronald Reagan, Henry Kissinger, and Bebe Rebozo. Although proprietor Dave Chasen never divulged the recipe during his lifetime, it has since appeared in various publications. The ingredients are unremarkable—pinto beans, canned tomatoes, bell pepper, onions, garlic, parsley, butter, beef chuck, pork shoulder, Gebhardt's Chili Powder, and ground cumin—and certainly not traditional, "a kind of bastard chili" in the words of its maker.

ROASTED GARLIC MEATLOAF

My mother never made meatloaf, and so, as a child, I found it mysterious and exotic. The circumstances under which I made it for the first time insured that it would remain so. I was about thirteen, and I was visiting my friend Josephine DeLaura. I spent as much time as I could at her house, having fallen wildly in love with her brother, Wayne. One day after school, Mrs. DeLaura was making meatloaf. I asked to help, and as I recount the story I can feel the fatty ground beef, stretched with lots of oatmeal, the slippery raw eggs, and the tiny bits of onion squish between my fingers as I knead the ingredients together under Mrs. DeLaura's calm instruction. I remember pressing the meatloaf into its pan and pouring ketchup over the top, and I remember thinking, too, that I would give anything to stay there at Mrs. DeLaura's side, anticipating the arrival of her son, forever. But when Wayne burst through the door minutes later, he just glanced into the kitchen and said, "You!," and went straight into his room, slamming the door behind him. Today, my meatloaf bears little resemblance to Mrs. DeLaura's version, but I still think of her and of Wayne whenever I make it. In this recipe, roasted garlic puree helps keep the meat moist and the cheese contributes a creaminess as well. Dried tomato bits and halves replace ketchup, as they often do in California now.

SERVES 6 TO 8

2 tablespoons olive oil
1 yellow onion, minced
1 shallot, minced
4 garlic cloves, minced
1½ pounds ground chuck
¾ pound ground pork
½ cup dried tomato bits or ¼ cup dried tomatoes packed in oil, drained and pureed
1 cup (4 ounces) grated dry jack
⅓ cup Roasted Garlic Puree (page 45)

2 eggs, beaten
1 cup fresh bread crumbs (see page 46)
2 tablespoons minced Italian parsley
1 teaspoon minced thyme
1 teaspoon minced oregano
2 teaspoons kosher salt

The Original 27 Counties

Mariposa County—*mariposa* is Spanish for butterfly—originally encompassed one fifth of California, but it has gradually decreased in size as new counties have been formed. Although the region enjoyed a boom during the Gold Rush, today it is a peaceful area of unspoiled rivers and valleys and of giant sequoia trees. The western gate to Yosemite National Park is in the county. Domingo Ghirardelli, father of the California chocolate industry, got his start here in the small town of Hornitos, where he operated a small market during the Gold Rush. Before the county was divided, it included Lindsay, home of the state's olive processing industry, now part of Tulare County. California olives, found in everything from salads and spaghetti sauce to tamale pie and meatloaf, have become a signature ingredient in California home cooking. Many Armenian immigrants settled in the original Mariposa County, near Fresno, and played a leading role in the development of the state's thriving raisin industry.

1 teaspoon fresh-ground pepper
12 dried tomato halves packed in oil

Preheat the oven to 350°F.

Heat the olive oil in a small skillet over medium heat. Add the onion and shallot, and sauté them until they are very soft and fragrant, about 15 minutes. Add the garlic, and sauté for 2 minutes more. Transfer the onion mixture to a medium mixing bowl, add the ground chuck and ground pork, and mix well. Add the dried tomato bits, dry jack, and garlic puree, and mix well. Add the eggs, mix well, and add the bread crumbs, parsley, thyme, oregano, salt, and pepper. Mix well until all the ingredients are evenly distributed.

Pack the meatloaf mixture firmly into an 8-inch loaf pan. Arrange the dried tomato halves over the top. Bake the meatloaf until it is cooked through, about 1 hour. Let the meatloaf rest for at least 10 minutes before serving.

JOE'S SPECIAL

In California one hears of many Joes who have taken credit over the years for inventing this dish. Scores of San Francisco restaurants have served one version or another of the classic for decades, and it remains popular. To make an authentic version at home, ask your butcher for beef ground for chili, which is a coarser grind than regular ground beef. If you can't get it, use the regular variety. Restaurant versions typically omit cheese; you can include it, if you like, as I sometimes do.

3 tablespoons olive oil
1 yellow onion, diced
6 garlic cloves, minced
1 pound ground beef, preferably
    ground for chili
4 eggs, beaten
Kosher salt
Black pepper in a mill
1 teaspoon Tabasco sauce or other
    hot pepper sauce
1 pound fresh spinach, stems trimmed,
    leaves torn into pieces
¾ cup (3 ounces) grated or sliced
    jack, cheddar, or fresh asiago
    cheese, optional

Heat the olive oil in a medium heavy skillet over medium heat. Add the onion, and sauté it until it is soft and fragrant, about 8 minutes. Add the garlic, and sauté for 2 minutes more. Add the ground beef, and cook it until it has lost most of its color, using a fork to break it up as it cooks; do not overcook. Season the eggs with salt, pepper, and Tabasco, and pour them over the meat. Cook, stirring gently all the while, until the eggs are almost but not quite set, then top the mixture with the spinach, cover the pan, and cook until the spinach wilts, about 2 minutes. Gently fold the wilted spinach into the egg mixture, top with the cheese, if you like, and season with salt and pepper. Transfer to a serving bowl or individual plates. Serve immediately, perhaps with toasted sourdough bread on the side.

CHORIZO AND NOPALES PIZZA

For a more traditional dish, you can use corn tortillas, fried in a little oil until they are crisp, in place of the pizza dough. Instead of pizza you'll have something closer to a tostada, though without the beans that are usually spread over the tortilla before other ingredients are added. I prefer the chewy texture of the pizza dough, even if it isn't a classic combination with these ingredients.

Cornmeal
1 12-inch pizza shell (page 262)
1 tablespoon extra virgin olive oil
1 teaspoon pureed canned chipotles in
    adobo sauce
½ pound chorizo, sautéed and
    crumbled
3 ounces pitted California black
    olives, cut lengthwise in half
¾ cup diced nopales, pan-fried
    until their liquid is released and
    evaporated
¾ cup (3 ounces) grated cheddar
    cheese
½ cup fresh corn cut from the cob
    (from about 1 ear)
2 tablespoons minced cilantro leaves

Preheat the oven to 500°F. Place a baking stone in the oven or sprinkle a baking sheet or pizza pan with cornmeal.

Dust a work surface with cornmeal, and place the pizza shell on it. Combine the olive oil with the chipotle puree and brush the mixture over the dough. Distribute the chorizo over the shell and scatter the olives and nopales over the meat. Distribute the cheese over the top, followed by the corn and the cilantro.

If you are using a baking stone, sprinkle it with cornmeal. Transfer the pizza to the baking sheet, pizza pan, or baking stone. Bake the pizza until the edges of the crust are lightly browned, about 18 minutes. Let rest 5 minutes, cut into wedges, and serve immediately.

PORK AND GREEN CHILE TAMALES

Whenever I ask my friend Rachel Cisneros what her mom or aunt fills tamales with, she looks bemused and stares at me as if I just don't get it. Finally she says something like, "Well, they'd probably just use whatever was in the refrigerator," implying that tamales are no big deal and that they are a good thing to do with leftovers. Tamales do become a bigger deal at Christmas, when Rachel's family gets together to make hundreds of them (see opposite page). In this recipe, pork is simmered with onions, garlic, and serranos for a very tender filling. I usually serve a spicy bottled hot sauce with these, but they are also excellent with fresh salsa.

MAKES 24 TO 30 MEDIUM TAMALES

2 pounds pork loin or shoulder, cubed
1 small yellow onion, quartered
6 garlic cloves
3 serrano chiles
2 tablespoons lard or olive oil
2 serrano chiles, minced
4 poblano chiles, roasted, peeled, and diced
Kosher salt
1 package dried corn husks, soaked in water overnight and drained
5 cups Tamale Dough (recipe follows)
2 limes, cut into wedges

Put the pork, onion, garlic, and whole serranos in a heavy pot and cover them with water. Bring to a boil over medium-high heat, reduce the heat, and simmer, partially covered, until the meat is very tender, about 45 minutes. Drain the meat and reserve the cooking liquid.

Melt the lard or heat the olive oil in a large heavy skillet over medium heat. Add the minced serranos, and sauté them until they are soft, 4 to 5 minutes. Add the poblanos and the pork, and sauté, stirring constantly, for 3 minutes more. Strain 1½ cups of the cooking liquid into the skillet. Bring to a boil, reduce the heat, and simmer until the liquid is reduced by half, about 10 minutes. Season with salt, and set aside to cool.

Make the tamales: You will want tamales that start with corn husks that measure about 5 inches wide by 6 inches long; for some of the tamales, you will have husks that are that size, but for others you will need to overlap 2 or 3 smaller husks. Place 1 large corn husk (or 2 to 3 smaller husks) on a work surface. Put a generous 3 tablespoons of tamale dough in the center and use your fingers to pat it out to about a ⅜-inch thickness. Put about 2 tablespoons of the pork filling in the center of the dough. Fold up the long edges of the tamale so that they form a barrier that will keep the dough from squeezing out, and carefully roll the tamale into a cylinder. Tie the ends very tightly with string or with narrow strips of husk. Continue making tamales in the same

Christmas Tamales

"One year we ran short of corn husks," Rachel Cisneros, who lives in the Santa Clara Valley, told me. "We had to hurry up with dinner—some of the freshly made tamales, of course—so we could wash our used corn husks and recycle them for the rest of the filling."

Rachel and her family have been making tamales at Christmas for decades, as her parents' families did before she was born. Her mother, Juanita, said, "My family made them on New Year's Eve, and my husband's tradition was to make them on Christmas Eve. We have done it ever since I can remember."

"The kids loved to knead the dough," Juanita continued, "and they would be covered in masa up to their elbows. The dough must be kneaded until it floats in water, and that's when we are ready to fill the tamales. We have a few drinks, and the more we have, the bigger the tamales get, because we want to finish. Sometimes we start as early as noon and the last batch might not be done until nine at night. But we always have our guacamole and chips and we have a good time."

Techniques for wrapping tamales vary. "My grandmother tied her tamales, but we don't. We fold them." Rachel said. "But she added other things—sliced tomato, bell pepper, onion, and olives. Now, we just use pork and chile sauce, like my father's family. And we keep some of the masa separate to make sweet tamales, with raisins, walnuts, and *piloncillo* [raw cone-shaped sugar], which we serve with coffee or milk."

For years, the Cisneros family made their tamales on Christmas Eve, trimming the tree at the same time. The bathtub was full of soaking corn husks, and everyone had a role in the tamale assembly line. They have made changes as the family has grown; now they make tamales in early December and freeze them until the big Christmas feast. Instead of a single location where everyone gathers, the branches of the extended family of seventy make tamales separately, to have for dinner that same night and to contribute to the Christmas table.

manner until you have used all of the tamale dough or all of the pork filling; you will have some corn husks left over.

When all of the tamales are made, line a steamer basket with leftover husks. Place the tamales, standing on end, in the basket in a single layer; do not stack them on top of each other. Steam the tamales, covered, over simmering water for 50 minutes. Let cool for 5 minutes, and serve immediately, with wedges of lime to squeeze over the tamales.

Tamale Dough

MAKES ABOUT 6 CUPS

8 ounces (about I cup) lard
I tablespoon kosher salt
I pound masa harina for tamales
2½ cups chicken stock
½ teaspoon baking powder

Beat the lard in a heavy-duty mixer (or by hand in a large bowl, using a heavy whisk) until it is white and fluffy. Mix in the salt and masa harina. Add the stock and the baking powder, and mix vigorously. The dough is ready when a spoonful floats in a bowl of water.

Variation:

For beef tamales, use Beef Chili Colorado (page 359) made with chuck or sirloin in place of the pork. After topping a husk with chili, top the chili with 1 tablespoon grated cheddar cheese and 1 teaspoon sliced scallion. Proceed as directed.

PERRY'S PORK CHOPS

In 1968, Tony Kozlowski planted his first raspberry canes in Forestville, in western Sonoma County. The Kozlowski Farms retail store opened the next summer, in time for the first crop of berries. Today, it thrives as a destination for local customers and tourists alike, along with such food luminaries as Julia Child, who has stopped by on several occasions. Tony and his wife, Carmen, operated the farm for years. When their three children, Carol, Cindy, and Perry, were old enough, they became involved with the family business, too. In 1980, Kozlowski Farms introduced the first of their fruit vinegars. I use their red raspberry vinegar when I make this dish, based on a recipe created by Perry.

SERVES 4

2 tablespoons flour
½ teaspoon kosher salt
¼ teaspoon white pepper
1½ teaspoons minced rosemary
4 large center-cut pork chops
2 tablespoons olive oil
3 garlic cloves, minced
½ cup beef stock
½ cup dry vermouth
4 small sprigs of rosemary
¼ cup red raspberry vinegar, preferably low-acid
¼ cup half-and-half

Porcelain Pigs

"Here the Livermore region ends, in a sunlit world of ravines, white sycamores, and smooth hills that are dark-straw, the tint of the Coast Range. You climb west over them into 'Mission country,' old and drowsier, on a flat that runs down into Santa Clara Valley.... This tawny, green-splotched country has the look of Spain. It is farming land, with a scattering of small towns.... Warm Springs, which has a pool of hot water, where the Spanish-Californian women scrubbed clothes in the 1840s, had suddenly grown fashionable, and San Franciscans bowled down to it in coaches for a week end of bathing and croquet. It was a spa, a little Saratoga, until the earthquake of 1868 destroyed all of it but two adobes, of which one still remains, a relic of the Spanish days, and therefore precious, its upper story protected by a casing of wood, though even that was warped by the temblor.

"That was the adobe of José Noriega, one of the great cattle ranchers hereabouts, who so liked company that he waylaid travelers, and once detained a party of them for half a year. He grew figs, the plump Largo Negro, to be preserved in wine—and this is still good fig country. He raised pigeons for squabs baked in pastry, and even pigs, roasted at the suckling age, and anointed not with their own fat, but with olive oil, which embrittles the skins and gives them the crackle of porcelain."

Idwal Jones, *Vines in the Sun* (Morrow, 1949)

Mix together the flour, salt, pepper, and ½ teaspoon of the minced rosemary in a medium bowl. Dredge the pork chops in the mixture, and set them aside.

Heat the olive oil over medium heat in a large heavy frying pan. Add the garlic, and sauté for 2 minutes. Add the pork chops, and brown them on both sides. Drain off any excess fat, return the pan to the heat, and add the stock, vermouth, and 2 of the rosemary sprigs. Bring to a boil, reduce the heat to low, and simmer, covered, for 1 hour.

Transfer the pork chops to a warm plate. Remove and discard the rosemary sprigs. Add the vinegar to the cooking liquid, increase the heat to high, and reduce the liquid by one half. Stir in the half-and-half, and reduce again until the sauce has thickened and coats the back of a spoon. Taste the sauce, and adjust the seasonings. Pour the sauce over the pork chops, and sprinkle with the remaining minced rosemary. Garnish with the remaining rosemary sprigs, and serve immediately.

GRILLED PORK CHOPS WITH SALVADOR'S SALSA

We Americans have a tendency to cook pork until it is over-done, which results in dry, tough meat. For juicy, tender pork, buy thick chops, set the grill rack as far above the heat as possible, and remove the chops from the grill the moment the juices run clear. A wooden skewer is ideal for piercing the meat.

SERVES 6

6 thick center-cut pork chops
Kosher salt
Black pepper in a mill
1½ cups Salvador's Smoked Tomatillo
   Salsa (page 61)

Prepare a medium-high fire in an out-door grill. Season the pork chops with salt and pepper and let them come to room temperature.

Grill the chops for about 8 minutes, turn them, and grill for 7 to 8 minutes on the other side, or until the juices run clear when the meat near the bone is pierced with a fork or a skewer.

Place the chops on a serving platter and spoon half of the salsa over them. Let the chops marinate in the salsa for 10 to 15 minutes before serving, with the remaining salsa alongside.

Gold Rush Prices

"When we arrived [in San Francisco] the first of June there was but very few storehouses, all kinds of provisions were lying in every direction in the streets, carts running over bags of flour, and rice, and hard bread, pork selling at six dollars per barrel, now flour is selling at forty dollars per barrel, pork at sixty five. [S]ugar we paid three cents a pound, when we came, is now fifty.... The land is very rich, would yield an abundance if it was cultivated, but no one can wait for vegetables to grow to realize a fortune, potatoes are twenty cents a pound, beets one dollar and seventy five cents a piece, tomatoes, dollar a pound but we have them for dinner notwithstanding, we have made more money since we have been here than we should make in Winthrop [Maine] in twenty years.... [T]he Dr bought a half barrel of pickle in salt, after soaking them, I put up fourteen quart bottles, sold them for six dollars more than we gave for the whole.... The seat of government is established at San Hosea [San Jose], about 60 miles from this, in a most delightful spot where they have plenty of fruit and vegetables."

Mary Jane Megquier, letter to a friend, November 11, 1849, from *Apron Full of Gold: The Letters of Mary Jane Megquier*, edited by Polly Welts Kaufman (University of New Mexico Press, 1994)

PATTERSON PORK LOIN

Only five percent of the apricots grown in California are sold fresh. More than half the crop is canned, about a quarter is dried, and the remainder is frozen. I've named this recipe, which uses three forms of apricots—fresh, dried, and cooked into jam—after the town of Patterson in Stanislaus County, where apricot orchards have thrived for decades. Make Mary's Easy Apricot Jam (page 431) if you have the time; if not, use bottled jam. When apricots are not in season, omit the fresh apricots.

SERVES 6 TO 8

¼ cup olive oil

2 yellow onions, diced

12 garlic cloves, minced

1½ cups white wine

1 1-inch cinnamon stick

4 whole cloves, crushed

½ teaspoon cumin seeds

½ teaspoon ground cumin

Pinch of fresh-ground nutmeg

8 ounces apricot jam, homemade (page 431) or bottled

1½ pounds chicken-apple sausage, casings removed

½ cup dried apricots, minced

½ cup pine nuts

1 center-cut pork loin, 3½ to 4 pounds, boned

¾ cup fresh bread crumbs (see page 46)

1 to 1½ pounds (about 8 to 10) fresh apricots

Make an apricot sauce: Heat 2 tablespoons of the olive oil in a large heavy skillet over medium heat. Add half of the onions, and sauté them until they are very soft and fragrant, about 15 minutes. Add half of the garlic, and sauté for 2 minutes more. Add the wine, cinnamon, cloves, cumin seeds, ground cumin, and nutmeg, and stir in the apricot jam. Increase the heat to high, bring to a boil, reduce the heat to low, and simmer for 15 minutes. Transfer to a medium saucepan and set aside.

Heat the remaining 2 tablespoons olive oil in the skillet and return it to medium heat. Add the remaining onions, and sauté until soft and fragrant, about 8 minutes. Add the remaining garlic, and sauté for 2 minutes more. Add the sausage and cook it, using a fork to break it up, until it just loses its color, 5 to 6 minutes. Add the dried apricots and the pine nuts. Stir in 2 tablespoons of the sauce and set aside to cool.

Preheat the oven to 325°F.

Using a thin, sharp knife, cut a pocket from each end of the loin toward the center; you are not slicing the surface of the loin, but instead are opening up a narrow tunnel. When the sausage mixture has cooled, transfer it to a pastry bag fitted with a large round tip. Insert the bag as far as it will go into the pocket at one end and squeeze in about half the mixture. Repeat at the other end of the loin.

Place the pork loin on a rack in a roasting pan and brush it with some of the apricot sauce. Bake the loin, brushing it several times with more apricot sauce, for 20 to 25 minutes per pound, until it reaches an internal temperature of about 160°F. About 15 minutes before it is done, cut the fresh apricots in half, place them on the rack with the loin, and brush them with apricot sauce.

Remove the pork loin from the oven and let it rest for 15 minutes. While it rests, bring the remaining apricot sauce to a boil for 3 minutes, then remove it from the heat and let it cool slightly. Cut the pork into ¼-inch-thick slices, arrange the slices on a serving platter, and surround them with the roasted apricots. Spoon sauce over all, and serve immediately, with the remaining sauce on the side.

FRESNO PORK ROAST WITH HOT SPICED RAISINS

In a normal year, more than half of the world's raisin crop comes from California, mainly from a single variety of grape, the pale green Thompson seedless. Before this popular table grape became widely available in the late nineteenth century, raisin production was limited and difficult, hampered by the inconvenience of a small fruit filled with big seeds. Today, raisins are made similarly the world around. The grapes are hand-picked and spread in rows between the vines to dry in the sun. Their bloom—the coating of natural yeast that clings to all

grapes—remains intact and the dried grapes turn almost black. A small percentage of the annual crop is processed differently: The ripe grapes are dipped into olive oil or another vegetable oil before they are dried, a process that removes the blooms, hastens dehydration, and results in the pale fruit sold as golden raisins. Recently, other seedless varieties of grapes, such as Red Flame, have been used to produce raisins; look for them at farmers' markets and specialty food stores.

SERVES 4 TO 6

2 pork tenderloins, about 1¼ pounds each
1 tablespoon minced lemon zest
2 teaspoons kosher salt
1 teaspoon fresh-ground black pepper
1 cup (packed) brown sugar
⅓ cup white wine vinegar
1 1-inch cinnamon stick
3 thin lemon slices
1½ cups raisins

Several hours before serving, remove the pork from the refrigerator and set it on a work surface. Combine the lemon zest, salt, and pepper in a small bowl, and rub the mixture into the tenderloins. Set them on a platter or baking sheet, cover lightly, and return to the refrigerator.

Combine the brown sugar, vinegar, cinnamon stick, and ⅔ cup water in a small saucepan. Bring to a boil, reduce the heat, and simmer for 5 minutes, stirring constantly. Add the lemon slices and raisins, and simmer for 10 minutes more, stirring frequently. Remove from the heat, and let rest at room temperature for at least 30 minutes.

Central Valley Swedes

The town of Kingsburg, population 7,205, lies in the center of the great San Joaquin Valley about ten miles south of Fresno, the region's biggest city. Kingsburg began as a railroad town in 1875. Swedish immigrants first settled in the area in 1886, motivated, like the Danes who founded Solvang (see page 372), by reports of California's mild winters. Frank Rosendahl and C.A. Johnson were the first native Swedes to settle here. Shortly thereafter, Andrew Ericson, on hearing about the fertile, sunny valley with its abundant water, brought, from Michigan, the largest Swedish colony. By the 1920s, some 94 percent of Kingsburg's population was Swedish. Wheat farms once thrived in the area, but with better irrigation came other crops, the principal ones today being table grapes, stone fruit, watermelons, and cotton. Kingsburg is also the headquarters for Sun-Maid Raisin Growers, the largest dried-fruit processing plant in the world. Thousands of tourists come each year to downtown Kingsburg, which has been remodeled to evoke the town's Swedish history, celebrated each May with a huge festival that includes a traditional maypole dance.

Preheat the oven to 350°F.

Remove the tenderloins from the refrigerator 30 minutes before cooking. Place the tenderloins on a roasting rack set over a roasting pan, and brush them generously with the liquid from the raisins. Roast the tenderloins for 20 to 25 minutes, brushing them 2 or 3 times with the liquid from the raisins, until the meat reaches an internal temperature of 160°F.

Remove the tenderloins from the oven and let them rest for 10 minutes. While they rest, bring the raisins in their liquid to a boil for 3 minutes, then remove the mixture from the heat and let it cool slightly. Cut the tenderloins into ¼-inch-thick slices. Arrange the slices on a serving platter, spoon the spiced raisins over them, and serve immediately.

SOLVANG ROAST PORK WITH PRUNES AND APPLES

"My mom is the best cook in the world," Rikka Ann Rasmussen of Solvang says, and she offers this recipe as proof. A roast such as this one always formed the centerpiece of a huge Christmas smorgasbord, and Rikka, who today assists farmers and farmers' markets with marketing, says it is the one dish that guarantees she will never become a vegetarian. Rikka insists that her mother always let the pork sit at room temperature for several hours after she rubbed the marinade into it, and swears that was what made it so good.

SERVES 4 TO 6

1 pork loin or pork roast, about 5 pounds
2 tablespoons minced sage
2 tablespoons minced garlic
2 teaspoons kosher salt
2 teaspoons fresh-ground black pepper
1 teaspoon ground cloves
2 cups prunes, pitted
3 to 4 apples, preferably a mix of tart and sweet, peeled, cored, and sliced thin
3 tablespoons all-purpose flour

At least 30 minutes before cooking, set the pork on a work surface. Mix together the sage, garlic, salt, pepper, and cloves in a small bowl. Rub the mixture into the meat, covering its surface completely. Cover the pork with a tea towel and let it sit at room temperature until ready to cook.

Preheat the oven to 450°F.

Set the pork on a rack in a roasting pan and place it in the oven. After 10 minutes, reduce the heat to 325°F. Roast the pork until it is completely tender, 3 to 3½ hours (40 to 45 minutes per pound); the long, slow cooking will result in the meat being so tender that it falls apart. After 1½ hours, add the prunes and apples to the pan, and continue to cook. When the roast is done, remove it from the oven and transfer it to a serving platter. Using a slotted spoon,

add the fruit to the platter.

Discard as much of the fat as you can skim or pour off, then set the roasting pan on a stovetop burner over medium heat. Add the flour, and stir constantly until it is golden brown. Slowly add 1 cup of water, whisking constantly. Simmer, stirring from time to time, for 3 to 4 minutes, or until the gravy thickens; if it is too thick, add more

The Gas Crisis

Solvang, near the coast in southern California north of Santa Barbara, began in 1911 as an intentional community formed by a group of Danes who came from back East. Here, the weather was better and they could farm. They purchased land, and established Atterdag College (since closed and torn down), a general store, restaurants, and a hotel. More Danes moved into the community, and soon their relatives followed them. They farmed, especially field crops, and life continued as they had planned it for decades, until the 1970s. Then the first of the nation's gas shortages hit, and it wasn't long before people from Los Angeles—a lot of them—realized that a journey to Solvang was the kind of day trip they could make without straining the gas budget. Solvang became a typical tourist destination. Today, the buildings still sport their Danish architecture and restaurants still serve Danish fare, but now it's a commercial version of what was authentic not very long ago.

water. Correct the seasoning with salt and pepper to taste, and pour the gravy into a sauce boat. Slice the pork, and serve it immediately, with the gravy alongside.

BORDER TOWN CHIPOTLE PORK

*M*any years ago I returned to my birthplace of San Diego for a visit, and there, in a small and now forgotten cantina, I tasted chipotles for the first time. I was young and inexperienced, with a palate to match; I tasted little beyond their searing heat, and was barely aware of their subtle flavors filtering through a prism of smoke. In this recipe, pork is slowly baked in a puree of chipotles until it falls apart. The result is a boldly flavored rustic dish. Chipotles are smoked ripe chiles, almost always jalapeños. The most common way to find them is canned in a vinegar-tomato sauce called adobo sauce, but recently dried chipotles have become more widely available. This recipe calls for the canned version.

SERVES 6 TO 8

1 can (7 ounces) chipotles in adobo
   sauce
1 cup grapefruit juice
1 large pork loin, 3 to 4 pounds,
   trimmed of fat
2 heads of garlic, cloves separated
   and peeled
12 to 16 corn tortillas

Esther Garcia's Mexican Menu

• •

*A*bout all we know today about Esther Garcia is that she was a famous hostess in San Francisco; in her time, she was one of the few women identified by her own, rather than her husband's, first name. The January 25, 1937, edition of *The San Francisco Shopping News*, an advertising newspaper, featured her Mexican menu and shortcut recipes.

Menudo
Frijoles Refritos
Chiles Rellenos
Enchiladas
Toasted Tortillas
Coffee or Beer

Her enchilada sauce was made by making a roux of oil or grease, three quarters of a pound of chile powder, and one tablespoon of flour, and then adding enough water to create a sauce the consistency of thick gravy. Fill enchiladas, she advised, with chopped onions and ground beef or any icebox leftovers, such as chicken.

2 limes, cut into wedges
1 bunch of cilantro, large stems
   removed, chopped
2 cups (8 ounces) grated cheddar
   cheese

Preheat the oven to 300°F.

Puree the chipotles with their sauce and the grapefruit juice in a blender or food processor. Place the pork loin in a heavy ovenproof pot, add the garlic cloves, and pour the chipotle puree over the pork. Bake, covered, until the pork is completely fork tender, about 3 hours. Remove the pork from the oven and let it rest 15 minutes before serving.

Heat the tortillas over a low flame or on a medium-hot griddle until they are warmed through but still soft. Wrap them in a towel or place them in a tortilla basket to keep them hot.

Place the pork on a work surface and use a large knife or cleaver to hack it into big chunks. Transfer to a large serving platter, arrange the limes and cilantro next to the pork, and add the cooked garlic

cloves. Serve immediately, with the cheese and tortillas alongside. Guests fill their own tortillas with pork, garlic, cheese, a squeeze of lime juice, and several cilantro leaves.

TRINITY VENISON STEW WITH OLIVES AND MUSHROOMS

*B*ig game hunting is strictly regulated in California. Elk, antelope, bear, and bighorn sheep, in addition to deer, are all hunted, but on a very limited basis. The season for deer and most other game varies by region; only wild pigs may be hunted all year. Today, farm-raised game is readily available from many sources, and your butcher should be able to lead you to a reliable supplier. You may substitute beef in recipes that call for venison, but the dish will lack a depth of flavor. Serve the stew with simple roasted red potatoes on the side.

SERVES 4 TO 6

3 to 4 pounds venison meat, cut into
    2-inch cubes
Kosher salt
Black pepper in a mill
¾ cup red wine vinegar
1¾ cups full-bodied red wine

The Original 27 Counties

Outdoor recreation—hunting, fishing, camping, hiking, and skiing—is the one of the most important industries in **Trinity County**, a remote region of northern California that includes the Trinity Alps, Shasta-Trinity National Forest, and portions of Six Rivers National Forest. If you're yearning for fresh brook trout cooked over a campfire, this is the place. There's a good chance that the steaks at your neighbor's barbecue came from cattle raised on one of the county's many large ranches.

1 cup all-purpose flour

2 teaspoons dry mustard, such as Colman's

⅓ cup bacon drippings

1 yellow onion, diced

¼ cup minced Italian parsley

1 teaspoon thyme leaves

1 pound cremini mushrooms, cut in half (see Note)

2 cups pitted black olives

1 cup beef stock, duck stock, or veal stock

Place the venison meat in a glass or ceramic bowl, season the meat with salt and pepper, and pour the vinegar and ¾ cup of the wine over. Refrigerate overnight.

Drain the venison and pat it dry with tea towels. Combine the flour and mustard with 2 teaspoons black pepper and 1 tablespoon salt in a medium-size paper bag. Add about a third of the venison, and shake vigorously to coat the venison with the flour mixture. Use a slotted spoon to remove the venison from the bag, shaking off excess flour. Set the floured meat on a plate. Continue until all the meat is floured.

Heat the bacon drippings in a large heavy skillet with a lid over medium heat. Add the venison, and brown the meat on all sides. Add the onion, and sauté until the onion is very soft and fragrant, about 15 minutes. Stir in the parsley, thyme, mushrooms, and olives. Add the stock and the remaining 1 cup of red wine. Bring the liquid to a boil, reduce the heat, and simmer, covered, until the venison is completely fork tender, about 2 hours. Taste, and season with salt and pepper.

Remove from the heat and let rest 10 minutes. Serve immediately.

NOTE: If you like, substitute wild mushrooms, such as chantarelles or cèpes, for the cremini.

Where the Buffalo Roam

The dazzling island of Santa Catalina shimmers under the Pacific sun just twenty-six miles off the coast of Los Angeles. Tourists have been visiting the seventy-six-square-mile island since the late nineteenth century. There is golf, sport fishing (for marlin, swordfish, yellowtail, barracuda, mackerel, black sea bass, sanddabs, and more), snorkeling, and scuba diving, and there are accommodations from campgrounds to luxury hotels. Yet the interior of the island remains much as the Spanish explorers found it, with its native subspecies of quail and ground squirrel and the native Channel Island fox. In 1924, for the filming of *The Vanishing American*, fourteen American bison were brought ashore. Today, about two hundred of the buffalo roam the interior of the island, along with boar, goat, and deer, which also were introduced. Hunting of turkey, goat, boar, and deer is permitted in season by bow and arrow only. Close to ninety percent of the island is now protected by the Santa Catalina Island Conservancy.

Chapter 12

VEGETABLE SIDE DISHES

VEGETABLE SIDE DISHES

BOILED ARTICHOKES

Artichokes can be boiled, steamed, braised, or grilled. Boiling is the simplest method, particularly for artichokes that are large and meaty. Artichokes keep well once cooked, so you might want to cook more than you need for a given meal and serve the extra ones chilled the next day. Serve artichokes with one of the sauces at the end of this recipe, with Aïoli (page 417), or with a vinaigrette, such as Red Wine Vinaigrette (page 152), Mustard Vinaigrette (page 152), or Lemon Vinaigrette (page 153).

SERVES 4

1 tablespoon salt
4 large artichokes
Dipping sauce (recipes follow)

Fill a large pot two thirds full with water, add the salt, and bring to a boil over high heat.

Using kitchen shears, snip off the tips of the outer leaves. If you have conical artichokes, slice off the top ½ inch with a sharp knife. Round artichokes are flat on top and do not need to be trimmed.

Carefully place the artichokes in the boiling water (they will float), and bring back to a boil. Reduce the heat, and simmer, covered, until you can pull off a leaf easily, 15 to 35 minutes, depending on the size and age of the artichoke. Transfer them to a colander or strainer and drain them. Serve them hot, at room temperature, or chilled.

Dipping Sauces for Artichokes

GARLIC BUTTER: Melt ½ cup butter in a small saucepan. Add 6 garlic cloves, minced or pressed, and simmer for 1 minute. Remove from the heat and serve.

MUSTARD CREAM: Mix together 1 cup sour cream with ¼ cup Dijon mustard, 1 teaspoon kosher salt, and 1 teaspoon fresh-ground black pepper.

How to Eat an Artichoke

Eating an artichoke can be something of a puzzle if you've never seen it done. Set the artichoke on a plate, stem end down. Hold a single leaf by its pointed end and pull it loose. Dip the broad part of the leaf into an accompanying sauce and then place it in your mouth, with the inner side of the leaf down. Bite the leaf firmly but not too hard and pull it between your teeth, scraping the length of the leaf. Discard the leaf and begin again. When all of the outer leaves have been eaten, use a paring knife to separate the thistle-like choke from the heart. Season the heart with a little sauce or salt and pepper, and savor it. Many artichoke lovers consider the heart the finest part.

LEMONY STEAMED ARTICHOKES

*I*t takes a little longer to steam artichokes than to boil them, but the results are excellent. In addition, steaming offers the opportunity to infuse the artichokes with additional flavors, such as garlic and lemon zest. You may also tuck in the leaves (and flowers, if you have them) of fresh herbs, such as thyme, marjoram, or oregano.

SERVES 4

4 large artichokes
6 garlic cloves, sliced thin
Zest of 1 lemon, cut into strips
2 tablespoons extra virgin olive oil
Olive oil, for dipping
Kosher salt or coarse sea salt, optional

Fill the bottom portion of a vegetable steamer half full with water, set it over high heat, and bring to a boil.

Using kitchen shears, snip off the tips of the outer leaves. If you have conical artichokes, slice off the top ½ inch with a sharp knife. Round artichokes are flat on top and do not need to be trimmed. Tuck several slices of garlic and strips of lemon zest into each artichoke at random, then drizzle olive oil over the top of the artichoke, so that it slides down into the interior of the vegetable. Place the artichokes in the top of the vegetable steamer, set over the boiling water, and reduce the heat.

Simmer, covered, until the artichokes are tender and an inner leaf comes out easily when pulled with tongs, 25 to 60 minutes, depending on the size and age of the artichoke.

Remove from the steamer and serve either hot or chilled, with olive oil and, if you like, salt alongside. Dip the leaves and the heart into the olive oil, and sprinkle with a little salt, if you like.

The Original 27 Counties

*W*hen you cook a fresh artichoke or savor a California strawberry, there's a good chance it was grown in **Santa Cruz County**, an area first called Branciforte after the Marqués de Branciforte, viceroy of New Spain. Cabrillo landed at Monterey Bay, the northern part of which is in the county, in 1542. Nearby the pueblo of Branciforte flourished until 1866, when it was absorbed by the town of Santa Cruz. The county's extensive redwood groves gave rise to early sawmills; by 1902, Big Basin Redwoods State Park had been founded to protect the trees. You'll find dedicated surfers, as well as great white sharks, along the coast, but much of the county remains rustic, with many vineyards, apple orchards, and strawberry and artichoke fields. The tiny town of Bonny Doon has one of the state's largest commercial lavender fields.

BRAISED ARTICHOKES AND NEW POTATOES

Artichokes and potatoes make excellent companions; the potatoes soak up the flavorful juices released by the artichokes and, in this recipe, the flavors of the lemon, wine, and herbs.

SERVES 4 TO 6

1 pound very small artichokes,
   trimmed of coarse outer leaves
1 pound small new potatoes
⅓ cup olive oil
Juice of 1 lemon
½ cup dry white wine
Small sprigs of rosemary and thyme
Kosher salt
Black pepper in a mill
1 lemon, cut into wedges

Preheat the oven to 350°F. Place the artichokes and potatoes in an ovenproof dish, add the olive oil, lemon juice, wine, and herb sprigs, season with salt and pepper, and cover tightly. Place in the oven and cook until the artichokes and potatoes are completely tender, 40 to 50 minutes. Remove from the oven and use a slotted spoon to transfer the vegetables to a serving platter or individual plates. Garnish with lemon wedges, and serve immediately.

ROASTED ASPARAGUS

California produces approximately seventy percent of the nation's asparagus crop. There is no better or simpler way to prepare asparagus than by roasting, which intensifies the flavor and creates a pleasing texture as well. Unlike asparagus that is boiled or steamed, roasted asparagus does not need to be peeled. Good asparagus needs no condiments, yet certain sauces provide another element of flavor and interest. After having your fill of simple, unadorned asparagus, serve it with Warm Bacon-Shallot Vinaigrette (page 158) or Raspberry Mayonnaise (page 418).

SERVES 4 TO 6

2 pounds fresh asparagus
2 tablespoons olive oil
Kosher salt
Black pepper in a mill

Preheat the oven to 475°F. Snap off the tough ends of the asparagus spears.

Place the asparagus in a single layer on a baking sheet, drizzle with olive oil, and toss so that each spear is coated lightly with oil. Season with salt and several turns of pepper. Roast the asparagus until it is just tender when pierced with a fork, 8 to 15 minutes, depending on the size of the spears. Remove the asparagus from the oven, transfer it to a serving platter, and serve immediately.

ASPARAGUS WITH SHALLOT VINAIGRETTE AND EGG MIMOSA

*E*gg mimosa refers simply to eggs that are cooked until both the white and yolk are just set and then are sieved or grated fine. It is used frequently as a garnish for salads and certain cooked vegetables. Eggs of excellent quality, such as those found at farmers' markets, are essential for optimum flavor.

SERVES 4 TO 6

2 eggs

1 pound asparagus

2 teaspoons olive oil

Kosher salt

Black pepper in a mill

4 slices of pancetta or strips of
    bacon, diced, optional

⅓ cup extra virgin olive oil

1 medium shallot, minced

1 garlic clove, minced

2 tablespoons white wine vinegar

1 tablespoon minced Italian parsley

Preheat the oven to 475°F.

Bring a small saucepan of water to a boil and, using a strainer or slotted spoon, lower the eggs into the water. Reduce the heat, and simmer for 10 minutes. Remove the eggs from the pan, and set aside for about 10 minutes. Transfer the eggs to a bowl of cool water.

Snap off the tough ends of the asparagus spears. Spread the asparagus in a single layer on a baking sheet, drizzle with the olive oil, and season with salt and pepper. Roast the asparagus until it is just tender when pierced with a fork, 8 to 15 minutes, depending on the size of the spears.

While the asparagus roasts, make the dressing: If you are using pancetta or

The Original 27 Counties

*O*ne of the best places to get a sense of the diverse ethnic cuisines of **Sacramento County** is at Sacramento's flourishing farmers' markets, with their abundance of Asian ingredients. The Sacramento Delta, between the San Joaquin and Sacramento rivers, is one of the most fertile regions in California. Yet the first European explorers declared the area barren, because the terrain was covered not with trees but with low-growing grasses. Today, the area around Isleton is a center of asparagus production, and other crops in the county include tomatoes, corn, sugar beets, pears, prunes, rice, and alfalfa. The vast waterways of the Delta are popular for hunting and fishing; crawdads are celebrated in an annual festival. One of Sacramento's most acclaimed daughters, Joan Didion, made the city and its once-thriving hop industry the subject of her first novel, *Run River*.

bacon, fry it in a small saucepan until it is just crisp, and transfer it to a small bowl. If you are not using the bacon or pancetta, simply begin with this step: Add 1 tablespoon of the extra virgin olive oil to the pan, add the shallot, and sauté it over medium heat until it is fragrant, about 5 minutes. Do not let it brown. Add the garlic, and sauté for 2 minutes more. Add the vinegar, and heat through. Add the remaining extra virgin olive oil, and remove from the heat. Season with salt, pepper, parsley, and, if you are using it, the bacon or pancetta. Taste, and adjust the seasoning if necessary.

Arrange the asparagus on a serving platter, spoon the dressing over, and set aside. Peel the eggs, and press them through a medium sieve or grate them on the smallest blade of a cheese grater. Scatter the eggs over the asparagus, and serve immediately.

ASPARAGUS WITH SHIITAKES, SHALLOTS, AND ALMONDS

*C*alifornia is the leading grower of premium shiitake mushrooms in the United States. The state is also a major producer of asparagus, growing more than two thirds of the U.S. crop, and it is the only state in which almonds are grown commercially in significant amounts. Asparagus and shiitake mushrooms are often combined in stir-fry recipes; in this recipe, asparagus is roasted, a technique that intensifies its flavor, then topped with stir-fried shiitakes and toasted almonds. For added taste and texture, you can garnish the finished dish with fried shallots or fried leeks (page 394).

SERVES 4

1 pound asparagus
2 teaspoons olive oil
Kosher salt
Black pepper in a mill
3 tablespoons toasted sesame oil
2 teaspoons grated fresh ginger
2 teaspoons minced garlic
2 small shallots, sliced thin
8 ounces shiitake mushrooms, stems removed
2 tablespoons fish sauce
2 teaspoons soy sauce
½ cup blanched slivered almonds, toasted

Preheat the oven to 475°F.

Snap off the tough ends of the asparagus spears. Spread the asparagus in a single layer on a baking sheet, drizzle with the olive oil, and season with salt and pepper. Roast the asparagus until it is just tender when pierced with a fork, 8 to 15 minutes, depending on the size of the spears.

While the asparagus roasts, heat the sesame oil in a wok. Add the ginger, garlic, and shallots, and sauté for 2 minutes, stirring constantly. Add the shiitakes, fish sauce, and soy sauce, and cook, stirring frequently, until the mushrooms are limp, 7 to 8 minutes.

Divide the asparagus among small serving plates, top with the mushroom mixture, scatter some of the almonds over each portion, and serve immediately.

ROASTED BEETS WITH WALNUTS AND ROQUEFORT

*N*o blue cheese is currently made in California, but a California purveyor, Ig Vella of Vella Cheese Factory in Sonoma County, makes an excellent version to the north in Oregon.

The Delicious Revolution

Some people go so far as to credit Berkeley's Chez Panisse, mecca to the sophisticated palate and inspiration to hundreds of chefs and farmers, with transforming the way people everywhere eat. There is little doubt that California Cuisine, with its emphasis on locally grown, simply prepared food bursting with freshness and flavor, sprang to life there.

Chez Panisse was born out of Alice Waters's desire to evoke the tastes she discovered in France in the 1960s, a journey that has become a part of American culinary history. Born and raised in New Jersey, Alice was nineteen when she went to France for the first time. There her palate was dazzled by the simple pleasures of a warm baguette, a green bean salad, a raw oyster. It was the entire French approach to eating—the quality of conversation, the outdoor markets, the direct interaction between farmers and shopkeepers—that Waters wanted to recreate. At first ignorant

of the magnitude of what she was taking on, she has been astonishingly successful. A staggering number of modern food trends—from baby vegetables and roasted garlic to goat cheese and free-range chicken—can be traced, at least in part, to Chez Panisse.

"In the beginning," Waters says, "I wanted the food I'd eaten in France, but I didn't really know what it meant to get it. There was a realization over fifteen years that food came from people who really cared about what they were doing, from special varieties that were picked at the right time and eaten that day."

What Waters did was to create a demand and a market for the best quality of food. The restaurant tracked down sources other than the large food-service companies that for years had been supplying restaurants with increasingly generic cheeses, meats, poultry, and produce. Word spread, first through the Bay Area and then

If you find Roquefort cheese too intensely flavored, consider using Oregon blue in its place.

SERVES 4 TO 6

1 pound small beets, preferably
    golden, white, or Chioggia
1 tablespoon olive oil
½ cup walnuts, toasted
2 tablespoons extra virgin olive oil

Black pepper in a mill
2 ounces Roquefort, crumbled

Preheat the oven to 350°F.

Wash and trim the beets but do not peel them. Toss them with the olive oil in a bowl, and transfer them to a baking sheet. Roast them until they are tender when pierced with a fork, 40 to 90 minutes, depending on their size.

Remove the beets from the oven and

beyond, that Chez Panisse was eager to buy ingredients from small-scale producers who had a personal stake in and connection with what they grew or made. Soon a trail of farmers, ranchers, cheesemakers, and other purveyors made its way to the restaurant. New restaurants similar in spirit followed, creating a rapidly expanding market and introducing more and more consumers to the state's seasonal bounty. It wasn't long before home cooks in California began to seek the same variety, quality, and freshness.

The enthusiasm ignited by Chez Panisse reached all the way to the California state legislature, which in the mid-1970s at last passed a law allowing nonstandard-sized produce to be sold to the public, thus giving birth to contemporary farmers' markets. Similar laws were passed around the country, spawning a wealth of outdoor markets where home cooks could buy seasonal produce, handcrafted cheeses, backyard eggs, and free-range poultry from the people who grew it, made it, tended it, or harvested it. In the best of these markets, distributors and whole-

salers are absent, and only farmers and other direct producers are allowed.

In 1995, Waters created the Chez Panisse Foundation, which sponsors such endeavors as the Edible Schoolyard, at Berkeley's Martin Luther King Middle School, which gives city kids a hands-on feel for how foods are grown and tended. Eleanor Coppola, who is filming a documentary about Chez Panisse, says that Waters "believes that if kids can learn to garden, to cook, to eat a fresh tomato, if they can learn to take care of themselves, then they can learn to take care of the planet. It's a very powerful message."

Chez Panisse celebrated its twenty-fifth anniversary in 1996. Alice Waters's vision has not diminished and her passion has not ebbed. She has resisted proposals to license the restaurant's name or to expand to new locations. Instead, she now concentrates on the foundation's work and directs her efforts toward influencing the next generation. The delicious little revolution in Berkeley lives on.

set them aside until they are cool enough to handle. Using your fingers, remove and discard the beet skins. Cut the beets into wedges, and place the wedges in a small serving bowl. Add the walnuts and extra virgin olive oil, toss, add several turns of pepper, and toss again. Scatter the Roquefort over the beets, and serve immediately.

SWEET-AND-SOUR RED CABBAGE

You'll find this sweet and savory dish, called *rodkaal* in Danish, on virtually every holiday table in the Danish town of Solvang (see page 372), near Santa Barbara in southern California.

SERVES 4 TO 6

1 head of red cabbage (about 2 pounds)

2 tablespoons brown sugar, or more to taste

¼ cup apple cider vinegar, or more to taste

1 large or 2 medium tart apples, peeled, cored, and diced

1 teaspoon kosher salt, or more to taste

Core the cabbage and cut it into very thin slices. Place it in a large heavy pan, and add ½ cup water and the brown sugar and vinegar. Bring to a boil over medium-

Earthquake Lights

California is famous for its earthquakes. Less known are its earthquake lights, which Mike Marinacci writes about in his delightful *Mysterious California: Strange Places and Eerie Phenomena in the Golden State*. Hollister, in central California, rests atop the San Andreas Fault system. In 1961, a poultry farmer in the area, Reese Dooley, reported a sequence of bright flashes in the sky that lit up a nearby hillside during an earthquake. The illuminations are thought to be caused by oscillations in the air or by the electricity generated in quartz-bearing rocks by the tremors. These lights have been recognized in Japan—part of the fault system, known as the Ring of Fire, that circles the Pacific Rim—for centuries and have inspired at least one ancient haiku:

> *The earth speaks softly*
> *to the mountain which trembles*
> *and lights up the sky*

high heat, reduce the heat to low, add the apple, and simmer, covered, until the cabbage is completely wilted and tender, about 20 minutes. Remove from the heat, and add the salt. Taste, and adjust the seasoning with more sugar, vinegar, or salt, if you like. Transfer to a bowl or platter, and serve immediately.

HUBERT'S ALGERIAN CARROTS AND ZUCCHINI

A pivotal time in my life as a cook was when I worked in a tiny bistro called A Chez Nous. It was owned by a French-Algerian family, the Saulniers, who had come to California in the 1960s. I was a waitress there while attending college nearby. Hubert, the younger son, was the chef, and I spent as much time as I could with him in the kitchen. This dish was served as a complimentary appetizer. I learned to make it entirely by taste; Hubert never told me what to do, he just had me taste it, and taste it again, and then make it so that my version was just like his. In the process, I developed my skills as an intuitive cook.

SERVES 6 TO 8

1 pound zucchini
1 pound carrots, peeled and cut
    diagonally into ⅛-inch slices
½ cup extra virgin olive oil
3 tablespoons ground cumin
1 teaspoon brown sugar
3 tablespoons minced garlic
Juice of 3 lemons
2 tablespoons minced Italian parsley
Kosher salt
Black pepper in a mill

Cut the zucchini into rounds about ¼ inch thick; if the zucchini are particularly large, first cut them lengthwise in half. Steam them over rapidly boiling water until they are very tender, about 15 minutes. Transfer the zucchini to a strainer or colander and let them drain for 15 minutes. Place the zucchini in a bowl.

Meanwhile, steam the carrots over rapidly boiling water until they are just tender, about 10 minutes. Put them in a bowl and set them aside.

Pour ¼ cup of the olive oil over the carrots, and add 2 teaspoons of the cumin, the brown sugar, 2 teaspoons of the garlic, 1 tablespoon of the lemon juice, and the parsley. Toss together, season with salt and several turns of pepper, and set aside.

Pour the remaining ¼ cup olive oil over the zucchini, and add the remaining cumin, garlic, and lemon juice. Stir with a wooden spoon, add at least 2 teaspoons salt and a few turns of pepper, and stir again. Taste the zucchini and correct the seasoning; it sometimes requires another generous addition of salt.

Place the carrots and zucchini next to each other, but not mixed together, on a large serving platter. Serve at once, or refrigerate, covered, for up to 4 days.

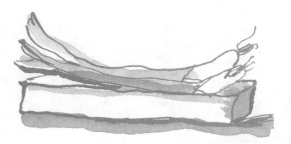

ROASTED CARROTS

Roasting carrots draws out their natural sweetness and deepens their flavor. If you will be preparing these for use in another recipe—a soup, for example—cut them into chunks; for a crowd or if you are pressed for time, cut them into coins. For a side dish, cut diagonal slices.

SERVES 4 TO 6

1 pound carrots, cut diagonally into
   2-inch slices
2 to 3 tablespoons olive oil
Black pepper in a mill
Kosher salt

Preheat the oven to 350°F.

Toss the carrots with just enough olive oil to coat them very lightly, and place them in a heavy roasting pan. Add several turns of pepper. Roast the carrots until they are very tender, about 45 minutes. (Coins will take about 20 minutes, and large chunks up to 1 hour).

Remove the carrots from the oven, transfer them to a serving platter, season with salt, and serve immediately (or use in another recipe).

GINA'S CHARD

In California, Swiss chard is a year-round crop. It is, however, often thought of as a winter crop because there are times when it's one of the only fresh, local vegetables around. This recipe can be made any time of year, and is an excellent accompaniment to poultry, pasta, and, especially, to risotto, where its tart and tangy flavors balance the rich creaminess of the rice. I call the recipe Gina's Chard, after my older daughter, because it was the one that finally convinced her that she could enjoy eating greens.

SERVES 4 TO 6

2 bunches (about 2 pounds) of Swiss
   chard, washed but not dried, tough
   stems removed
¼ cup extra virgin olive oil
1 tablespoon minced garlic
1 tablespoon minced lemon zest
1 teaspoon kosher salt
½ teaspoon crushed red pepper

Cut the wet chard leaves crosswise into ¾-inch slices. Pour the olive oil into a wok or a large sauté pan. Sauté the garlic over medium heat for 1 minute. Add the chard, toss quickly, cover the pan, and cook until the chard is wilted, about 3 minutes.

Add the lemon zest, salt, and red pepper, and toss quickly. Remove from the heat, transfer to a serving dish, and serve immediately.

KASMA'S RED CHARD WITH CORN, SHRIMP, AND GARLIC SAUCE

When my friend and colleague Kasma Loha-Unchit came to California from her native Thailand in 1972, there were many ingredients she couldn't find. She could locate simply curry pastes and a couple of brands of fish sauce, but not much else. There was no Thai basil, for example, so she used Italian basil. In the 1980s, all that began to change. Many foods in California were also new to her. She was particularly inspired by our red chard, which she had never seen before. When I asked Kasma how California's bounty had influenced her traditional cooking, she shared this recipe with me.

SERVES 4

1 bunch (about 1 pound) of red chard
1 ear of corn, shucked
6 ounces medium shrimp, shelled and deveined
2 to 3 tablespoons peanut oil
6 garlic cloves, minced
2 tablespoons oyster sauce, preferably Thai
1 tablespoon fish sauce
2 teaspoons rice vinegar
1 teaspoon sugar
1 to 2 pinches of white pepper

Rinse the chard in cool water and drain it thoroughly. Shred the chard leaves and stems by stacking several leaves and cutting them crosswise into ¼-inch strips. Keep the stems separate from the leaves. Cut the corn kernels off the cob. Cut the shrimp crosswise into small pieces about the size of a peanut.

Gray Soggy Vegetables

By 1847, the first Chinese immigrants had settled in San Francisco. They were soon joined by thousands more, many of whom helped build the transcontinental railways. At that time, many middle-class families hired cooks, and it was often Chinese immigrants who filled the positions. Although their employers rarely allowed them to prepare traditional Asian fare, these early Chinese cooks had a significant impact on California cookery, especially with vegetables. Cookbooks of the era instructed home cooks to boil vegetables for astonishing lengths of time—one and a half hours for green beans, for example—which resulted, of course, in gray, mushy, bland vegetables. Asians cooked vegetables quickly so that they retained their full flavors, crisp textures, and bright colors. "Thus, vegetable cookery on the West Coast," writes Evan Jones in *American Food*, "was never again categorically as bad as in other regions."

Heat a wok over high heat until it is smoking. Add the oil, swirl to coat the wok's surface, and let the oil heat for 15 to 20 seconds. Add the garlic, stir quickly, add the shrimp, and cook for 10 to 15 seconds. Add the chard stems, and stir-fry for about 1 minute. Add the chard leaves and the corn. Stir-fry vigorously until the leaves have wilted. Add the oyster sauce, stir for several seconds, and add the fish sauce. Continue to stir-fry until the chard is tender, 1 or 2 minutes more. Add the vinegar and sugar during the last 30 seconds of cooking, stir, and add the white pepper. Remove from the heat, and serve.

CALIFORNIA SUCCOTASH

Succotash is a Native American recipe traditionally made with corn, beans, and squash. In this recipe, nopales (leaves of prickly pear cactus) and poblano chiles replace the squash and beans for a lighter version with spicy, tart flavors. Southern California farmers' markets almost always have nopales, and they are increasingly common in the north, too; they are showing up in supermarkets around the country as well. This recipe evolved from a recipe for corn that I found in *Elena's Favorite Foods California Style*, by Elena Zelayeta, a remarkable book from 1967 that called for ingredients virtually unknown to the general population at the time. Zelayeta called for chipotles, *queso*

cajeta, polenta, and lamb's tongue as if they were in everyone's pantry. If you come upon the book in a used bookstore, don't pass it by.

SERVES 4 TO 6

4 to 6 ears of corn
1½ cups diced nopales
3 tablespoons butter
1 yellow onion, diced
1 to 2 poblano chiles, seeded and diced
2 garlic cloves, minced
1 teaspoon chipotle powder or 1 canned chipotle in adobo sauce, minced or pureed
Kosher salt
Black pepper in a mill
½ cup (2 ounces) grated Monterey jack

Shuck the corn, cut the kernels from the cob, and set them aside. Place the nopales in a heavy skillet over medium-high heat, and pan-fry them, stirring frequently, for about 15 minutes, until the liquid that oozes from them has evaporated and they are just tender. Remove them from the heat and set them aside.

Heat the butter in a heavy sauté pan over medium-low heat. When the butter is foamy, add the onion and poblanos, using 2 for more heat, and sauté them until they are very soft and fragrant, about 15 minutes. Stir in the garlic, chipotle, corn, nopales, and ¼ cup water, and simmer gently, covered, for 10 minutes. Stir the mixture, season it with salt and pepper, and scatter the cheese over it. Cook, covered, for about 2 minutes more, just until the cheese melts. Transfer to a serving dish, and serve immediately.

GRILLED FENNEL

*T*he outdoor grilling of vegetables— or of any food, for that matter— need not be reserved for summer, even if you don't live in a place that is warm year-round. If you have a fireplace, you can set up a Tuscan grill, available at many cookware shops and hearth stores, over the fire. Many kinds of stovetop grills are available, too.

Grilling fennel successfully is largely a matter of preparation; once the fennel is sliced properly, there isn't much left to do except allow it to cook slowly on the grill.

SERVES 4 TO 6

2 to 3 large fennel bulbs, stalks and
    fronds removed
Olive oil
Kosher salt
Black pepper in a mill
Juice of ½ lemon

Prepare a medium fire in an outdoor or stovetop grill.

Place the fennel bulbs, root ends down, on a work surface. Slice them vertically into ¼- to ⅜-inch-thick slices, making sure each slice remains attached to the root end. Brush both sides of each slice with olive oil, and

season with salt and pepper. Transfer the bulbs to the grill. Rotate the bulbs 90 degrees to mark them, and turn them over once, after about 7 minutes. The fennel is done when it is tender but still juicy, about 7 minutes more. Transfer the bulbs to a serving platter, and season with lemon juice.

BRAISED FENNEL

*F*ennel is one of many vegetables popularized in California by Italian immigrants. Unlike artichokes, also introduced by Italian farmers, it took a while for fennel to catch on, but now you find it everywhere. Fennel is often one part of a more complex dish, such as a stew, soup, or salad, but in this recipe it is highlighted for its own qualities, including the soft buttery texture it develops when cooked slowly.

SERVES 4 TO 6

2 pounds (about 3 large or 6 to 8
    small) fennel bulbs
8 ounces chanterelle mushrooms,
    optional
¼ cup olive oil
6 small shallots
Kosher salt
½ cup dry white wine
Juice of ½ lemon

Remove the stalks and fronds from the fennel bulbs; reserve and chop 1 tablespoon of the fronds for a garnish. Cut away any bruised or discolored spots on the bulbs. Cut the bulbs in half lengthwise. Break any large mushrooms, if you are using them, into medium pieces.

Warm the olive oil in a heavy sauté pan over low heat. Place the fennel bulbs, cut side down, in the pan and tuck the shallots in the spaces between the bulbs. Season with salt, cover the pan, and cook until the cut side of the fennel just begins to turn golden brown, about 15 minutes. Turn the fennel, sprinkle with salt, cover the pan, and continue to cook until the other side of the fennel begins to color, about 10 minutes more. Add the wine and, if you like, the mushrooms, cover the pan, reduce the heat to very low, and braise until the fennel is completely tender and the juices have concentrated, about 1 hour. Remove from the heat, transfer to a serving dish, drizzle with lemon juice, garnish with the chopped fronds, and serve immediately.

HARICOTS VERTS WITH SHALLOTS

The tiny, pencil-thin green beans called haricots verts grow so quickly that they sometimes must be harvested twice a day. Supermarkets sometimes carry them, but farmers' markets, beginning in late spring, are a more reliable source. Another way to serve them is blanched, tossed with a simple vinaigrette and topped with cherry tomato halves. I use them, too, atop summer risot-

tos or alongside roast chicken stuffed with wild rice.

SERVES 4

3 tablespoons clarified butter (see page 288)
2 shallots, minced
8 ounces haricots verts
Kosher salt
Black pepper in a mill

Bring a pot of salted water to a boil. Heat the butter in a medium skillet over low heat, until it begins to take on a little color. Add the shallots, and sauté them until they are limp, 4 to 5 minutes. Drop the haricots verts into the water, and bring back to a boil. Leave the beans in the water for 1 minute, then drain them immediately. Shake off any excess water, add them to the pan with the shallots, and toss quickly. Season with salt and pepper, transfer to a serving dish, and serve immediately.

FRIED LEEKS

Fried leeks, shallots, onions, and garlic are traditional garnishes in many Asian cuisines, but they also make excellent side dishes, in the spirit of American onion rings. Serve them alongside Grilled Salmon with Thai Chile Sauce (page 298) or any grilled seafood, or in salads and sandwiches. Fried leeks make an ideal substitute for bacon in a vegetarian BLT.

SERVES 4

6 to 8 leeks, white and pale green
    parts
2 cups olive oil
Kosher salt
Black pepper in a mill

Wash the leeks thoroughly and set them on a tea towel to dry. Cut them into thin rounds. Pour the olive oil into a medium saucepan over medium-high heat, and bring the oil to about 350°F. Add a handful of leeks to the oil, stir quickly with a wooden spoon or chopstick, and fry until just golden brown and crisp. Use a long-handled strainer to remove the leeks from the oil, and place them on absorbent paper to drain. Continue until all the leeks have been fried. Season with salt and pepper. These leeks are best if served immediately, but they will keep in the refrigerator in an airtight container. To reheat, place them on a baking sheet in a 350°F oven for 12 minutes.

Variation:

Prepare Fried Shallots in the same way. Peel them, trim off the root end, slice them thin, and fry them in hot oil. They make an excellent garnish for Jook (page 219).

GRILLED SPRING ONIONS

• •

Although any type of onion can be grilled over coals or roasted in a hot oven, few are as delicious as spring onions, delicate, sweet onions harvested before they turn into bulbs. In Catalan in northeastern Spain, there is a variety of onion known as *calçot*. During its brief season in February and March, it is featured in numerous restaurants and in outdoor festivals called *calçotadas*, where people consume fifty, a hundred, or more at a time, with a mild Romesco sauce. The spring onions available at California farmers' markets are even sweeter than calçots and so flavorful that condiments of any sort are unnecessary.

SERVES 4 TO 6

40 spring onions
¼ cup olive oil
Kosher salt
Black pepper in a mill

Prepare a medium fire in a grill (or preheat the oven to 475°F).
Wash the onions, trim off the root ends, pull away any blemished outer leaves, and trim the onions to a uniform length. Place the onions in a large bowl, drizzle with olive oil, and toss, using your hands to be sure all the onions are coated. Spread the onions in a single layer on the grill, and turn them every few minutes until they are cooked through and tender, about 15 min-

utes. (Or spread the onions in a single layer on a baking sheet, and bake them until they are tender, about 20 minutes.)

Transfer to a serving platter, season with salt and several turns of pepper, and serve immediately.

RED ONION TART

This is a scrumptious tart that you could serve as a light main course as well as a side dish. It's also a good dish in which to use fresh-cured anchovies, if you have some. If you can't find them, omit them; oil-packed or salt-cured canned anchovies are too strongly flavored for this recipe. The recipe for the pastry makes enough for 2 large tarts; the filling is enough for 1 large tart or 8 small ones. If you make a large tart, freeze the remaining half of the dough to use at another time.

MAKES 1 LARGE OR
8 SMALL TARTS

3 tablespoons olive oil
3 to 4 red onions, sliced
Pastry for Savory Tarts (recipe
  follows)
2 teaspoons minced oregano leaves
Kosher salt
Black pepper in a mill
Anchovy fillets, for garnish, optional

Preheat the oven to 400°F.

Heat the olive oil in a large skillet over medium heat. Add the onions, and sauté them until they are limp, about 8 minutes. Stir in the oregano, and season with salt and pepper.

Remove the dough circles from the refrigerator, leaving them on the parchment-lined baking sheet. If you are making a large tart, transfer the onions to 1 large circle; if you are making small tarts, divide the onions among the smaller circles; in either case, leave a 2-inch margin around the edges. Using your fingers, gently fold the edges up and over so that they extend about 1 inch over the onions. Pleat the edges as you fold them up. If you are using them, drape the anchovies over the onions.

Bake until the pastry is golden brown and the onions very soft and fragrant, 40 to 45 minutes for large tarts, 35 to 40 minutes for individual tarts. Transfer the tarts to a rack to cool. Serve warm or at room temperature.

Pastry for
Savory Tarts

This simple and reliable recipe comes from Kathleen Stewart, who operates the Downtown Bakery and Creamery across from the town square in Healdsburg. Throughout the year, the bakery sells sweet and savory tarts filled with seasonal fruits and vegetables. The dough itself has become so popular with home cooks that the store sells it frozen. It is very easy to make, and you can freeze it, too, if you like. Tarts made with this dough, which is rolled out and then assembled free-form rather than being pressed into a tart pan, traditionally are known as galettes.

MAKES PASTRY FOR
2 LARGE OR
8 SMALL TARTS

2 cups all-purpose flour
¾ teaspoon kosher salt
¾ cup unsalted butter, cold
½ cup ice water

Combine the flour and salt in a medium bowl. Using your fingers or a pastry cutter, cut in the butter, until the mixture resembles coarse cornmeal. Work very quickly so the butter does not become too warm. Add the ice water and gently press the dough together with your hands until it just comes together; do not overmix. Form the dough into a ball, wrap it tightly in plastic wrap, and refrigerate it for at least 30 minutes. (At this point, the dough can be wrapped with a second layer of plastic and stored in the freezer for up to 3 months.)

Line a baking sheet with parchment paper and set it aside. Cut the dough into 2 pieces for large tarts or 8 for individual tarts. Place the pieces on a floured work surface and pat them flat with the palm of your hand. If you are making large tarts, roll the dough pieces out into circles about ⅛ inch thick and 14 inches in diameter; for small tarts, roll the pieces out into circles ⅛ inch thick and about 6 inches in diameter.

Set the dough circles on the baking sheet, cover lightly with a tea towel or aluminum foil, and refrigerate until ready to use. (The dough can be frozen, tightly wrapped, at this point, too.)

Variation:

For pastry for sweet tarts, add 2 teaspoons sugar to the flour and reduce the amount of salt to ¼ teaspoon.

PERFECT FRENCH FRIES

The secret to making perfect french fries is double frying, which results in the ideal texture and color. Although olive oil is not essential, its high smoke point (about the same as other refined vegetable oils) and its healthy fatty acid profile make it a good choice. Do not use an extra virgin olive oil, however, which has a lower smoke point and would be quite expensive in the quantities needed here.

SERVES 4 TO 6

3 pounds russet potatoes
Olive oil
Kosher salt

Wash the potatoes thoroughly, and dry them but do not peel them. Cut them into pieces approximately ⅜ inch wide, ⅜ inch high, and 3 to 4 inches long. Soak the potatoes in cold water for at least 1 hour. Drain them, and dry them on a tea towel; do not use paper towels, small fragments of which might cling to the potatoes.

Pour 3 to 4 inches of oil into a deep-fryer or a deep heavy saucepan over medium heat, and bring the temperature of the oil to about 350°F. Carefully add a handful of cut potatoes to the oil and jiggle the fryer basket or stir a little with a heavy spoon to insure that the potatoes do not stick to each other. Fry for about 4 minutes, or until the potatoes have become slightly crisp but have not taken on color. If you are not using a deep-fryer with a basket, use a wire strainer or a slotted spoon to remove the potatoes and transfer them to absorbent paper to drain. Repeat until all of the potatoes have been fried once. Remove the oil from the heat, and let the fried potatoes rest and cool completely.

Before serving the fries, fry them a second time: Reheat the oil to between 350° and 360°F. Fry the potatoes in batches until they are golden, 3 to 4 minutes. Remove the potatoes, transfer them to absorbent paper to drain briefly, and place them in a

---

Storing Potatoes or Onions

Although they are sold year-round, most mature potatoes are harvested from September through November. Stored properly, away from light and between 45° and 50°F, they will keep well. Onions like the same conditions, but you should never store the two together in the same drawer or cupboard; each gives off a gas that shortens the life of the other.

---

basket or on a platter. Season with salt, and serve immediately.

AVOCADO MASHED POTATOES

Rich and luscious is the best way to describe these potatoes. You might add fragile, as well—they must be served promptly and devoured at a single sitting (it's hard to imagine they wouldn't be), or the avocado will turn gray and its flavor will decline.

SERVES 4 TO 6

2 pounds russet potatoes, peeled and
   cut into chunks
⅓ cup heavy cream
1 tablespoon unsalted butter
1 jalapeño or serrano chile, minced
2 ripe Hass avocados
1 teaspoon fresh lime juice
2 teaspoons kosher salt
Black pepper in a mill

Place the potatoes in a large pot and cover them with water. Bring to a boil, reduce the heat, and simmer, covered, until the potatoes are tender, 15 to 20 minutes, and drain immediately.

Meanwhile, combine the cream, butter, and chile in a small saucepan. Bring to a simmer, remove the pan from the heat, cover, and let steep for 15 to 20 minutes.

Press the hot potatoes through a potato ricer and into a medium bowl. Cut the avocados in half, remove the pits, and scoop out the flesh, placing it in a small bowl. Using a fork, mash the avocado, add the lime juice and 1 teaspoon of the salt, and mix thoroughly. Add the cream mixture to the potatoes and mix well with a wooden spoon. Fold in the avocado, taste, add the remaining salt and several turns of pepper, mix, and serve immediately.

Variation:

Fry several strips of bacon until crisp, drain on absorbent paper, crumble, and scatter over the surface of the potatoes just before serving.

ROASTED ROSEMARY POTATOES

This dish is extremely versatile. You can vary the herbs to go with the rest of the menu, add whole unpeeled garlic cloves or sliced peeled garlic cloves, thin-sliced shallots, or even minced serrano chiles. Use very small, creamy-textured potatoes for the best results.

SERVES 4 TO 6

3 tablespoons butter
3 tablespoons olive oil
1½ pounds small firm potatoes, such as new reds, Yukon Gold, Yellow Finn, or fingerlings

2 teaspoons minced rosemary
2 teaspoons kosher salt
Black pepper in a mill

Preheat the oven to 375°F. Place the butter and olive oil in a heavy roasting pan or ovenproof frying pan, set it over medium heat, and melt the butter. Remove the pan from the heat, add the potatoes, scatter the rosemary over them, and season with salt and pepper. Shake the pan to coat the potatoes in the butter–olive oil mixture, then cover the pan with foil, sealing it very tightly. Bake for 35 minutes. Remove the foil and test the potatoes by piercing one of them with a fork. Return them to the oven, uncovered, and bake until the potatoes can be easily pierced, 10 to 25 minutes more, depending on the size of the potatoes. Serve immediately.

POTATOES IN PARCHMENT

When I was a child, one of my favorite things to eat was canned new potatoes that I sliced, sprinkled with onion powder and garlic salt, wrapped in aluminum foil, and baked in the oven until they sizzled. This version uses fresh ingredients to evoke that early recipe.

SERVES 4

1 pound red new or Yellow Finn potatoes

1 small red onion, sliced very thin
1 tablespoon minced garlic
2 tablespoons extra virgin olive oil
2 tablespoons butter, optional
1 tablespoon minced Italian parsley
Kosher salt
Black pepper in a mill

Wash the potatoes thoroughly and parboil them until they are about half cooked, 8 to 10 minutes. Drain, rinse, and allow to cool slightly. Cut the potatoes into very thin slices.

Preheat the oven to 350°F.

Place four 13-by-10-inch sheets of parchment paper or aluminum foil on a work surface. Make a crease in the center of each sheet parallel to the 10-inch-long edges. Arrange a small layer of onions in the center of 1 side of each sheet. Top with a portion of potatoes and sprinkle with garlic. Drizzle with olive oil and top with a dab of butter, if you like. Sprinkle parsley over the top, and season with salt and pepper.

Close the packets: Brush the 4 outer edges of each sheet with a little melted butter or olive oil. Fold the unfilled side of the sheet over and press so that the edges stick together. If it is not already in this position, orient the sheet so that the fold is the top edge. Make a crease in the upper left corner; the crease should meet the top edge about 1 inch to the right of the corner, and it should meet the left edge about 2 inches down from the corner. Fold the corner toward the center of the packet. Working counterclockwise, make folds, each of which overlaps the previous fold, until you reach, and have folded in, the upper right

corner. The packet will be roughly the shape of a semicircle.

Transfer the packets to a baking sheet, and bake them for 20 minutes. Remove them from the oven, and place them on individual plates, alongside the main course. Guests tear open the packets themselves. Serve immediately.

Variations:

To make on a charcoal grill, use aluminum foil. The potatoes can also be baked in a single foil or parchment packet, which will need to be about twice the size of the smaller packets. Cook larger packets for 35 minutes. To make Potatoes and Zucchini in Parchment, omit the onions, add 1 small zucchini, cut into very thin rounds, to each package, and drizzle with 1 teaspoon lemon juice.

TWEET'S POTATO AND MUSHROOM TART

For a brief time in the early 1990s, there was a tiny cafe called Tweet's in Santa Rosa, next door to the newspaper where I was a columnist. Tweet had been Evelyn Cheatham's nickname since childhood, and she ran the little place as if she were cooking for her friends, with homemade jams, biscuits, and scones, fresh-squeezed orange juice, and the best poached eggs. These splendid potatoes were served daily for breakfast, but they're great at any time. Tweet's closed, but eventually, as I wrote this book, I managed to find Evelyn, in upstate New York, and she graciously shared the recipe with me.

SERVES 6 TO 8

5 to 6 medium Yukon Gold potatoes, peeled and sliced ⅛ inch thick

2 tablespoons unsalted butter, melted

¼ cup fresh bread crumbs, toasted (see page 46)

3 ounces (about 2 cups) sliced white button mushrooms

Kosher salt

Black pepper in a mill

2 cups (8 ounces) grated jack cheese

1 cup sliced scallions, white and green parts

¼ cup heavy cream

Preheat the oven to 350°F. Put the potatoes in a bowl, cover them with cool water, and set the bowl aside.

Brush the inside of a 9- or 10-inch glass pie dish with the melted butter. Scatter the bread crumbs evenly on top. Drain the potatoes thoroughly in a strainer or colander, and distribute one third of them on top of the crumbs. Spread the mushrooms on top, season with salt and pepper, and top with two thirds of the cheese. Top with half of the remaining potatoes, then all but 2 tablespoons of the scallions, then the remaining potatoes. Season again with salt and pepper. Scatter the remaining

Dirty Girl Produce

Fan Tan Farms, a three-and-a-half-acre farm in the mountains above Santa Cruz, is located off Highway 9, a half mile from the busy intersection of Highways 1 and 9 and Interstate 17. Drivers race by the farm, never suspecting the voluptuous beauty that thrives, a fertile secret, so near. Operated by Jane Friedman, who is originally from the East Coast, and Alie Edwards, a native of the area, Fan Tan grows an enormous selection of top-quality produce, from salad greens, spring onions, and broccoli rabe to tomatoes, carrots, and edible flowers. In addition to selling directly to local chefs, Friedman and Edwards sell their goods, under the name Dirty Girl Produce, at several farmers' markets in the area.

cheese and scallions on top, pour the cream over, and season with more salt and pepper. The tart should rise 1 to 1½ inches above the top of the pie dish.

Cover the tart tightly with aluminum foil. Bake the tart until the potatoes are tender but not too soft, 50 to 60 minutes. Let the tart rest for 10 to 15 minutes, cut it into wedges, and serve immediately.

BAKED MINIATURE PUMPKINS

Until the mid-1980s, these miniature pumpkins were used almost exclusively for decoration—indeed, they were often coated with shellac so they would last longer. Then farmers around the state began growing them for food and selling them at farmers' markets and to upscale supermarkets. They are delicious, and they make perfect individual servings. The white ones shimmer like tiny Halloween ghosts, encouraging youngsters to gobble them up. They make an excellent and festive side dish for the holidays. Choose the seasoning, either rosemary or nutmeg, according to what works with the rest of the meal.

SERVES 4

4 miniature pumpkins, orange or white
12 garlic cloves, peeled
4 teaspoons butter or 8 teaspoons extra virgin olive oil
Black pepper in a mill
4 small sprigs of rosemary or 1 teaspoon fresh-grated nutmeg
Boiling water

Cut off the stem ends of the pumpkins, creating a circular opening large enough for inserting a spoon. Reserve the tops intact, to serve as lids. Scoop out the seeds and fibers inside, rinse the pumpkins in cool water, and invert them on absorbent paper to drain.

Preheat the oven to 350°F. Set the pumpkins, open side up, in a baking dish, and place 3 garlic cloves in each cavity. Divide the butter or olive oil among the cavities, and season each with several turns of pepper. Add a rosemary sprig or some nutmeg to each pumpkin. Set the stem lids on top of their pumpkins, pour about ¼ inch of boiling water into the bottom of the baking dish, and place the dish in the center of the oven. Bake for about 40 minutes, test the inside flesh with a fork, and, if it is tender, remove the pumpkins from the oven. If it is still a little resistant, bake for 10 to 15 minutes more, until the flesh pulls away from the sides of the pumpkin.

Remove the pumpkins from the oven and place them on a platter or on individual plates, next to the main course. Serve immediately.

NOTE: If you have a microwave, it is ideal for softening up the pumpkins to make it easier for you to cut off their tops. Cook the pumpkins on high for about 7 minutes, until you can easily slice off the top with a knife. Then continue cooking them in a conventional oven.

WINTER SQUASH PUREE

*U*se any of the dense-fleshed winter squashes, such as Delicata, Kabocha, or sugar pumpkin, for this recipe. If you use a large squash, roast the entire thing and set some aside for soup, muffins, or other dishes.

SERVES 4 TO 6

1 medium or 2 small winter squash (about 2 pounds)
Olive oil
2 heads of garlic, papery outer skins removed
Sprigs of fresh thyme
3 to 4 tablespoons unsalted butter, cut into chunks, at room temperature
1 teaspoon minced thyme
Fresh-grated nutmeg or ½ teaspoon ground nutmeg
Kosher salt
Black pepper in a mill

Preheat the oven to 350°F.

Cut medium squash into quarters, smaller squash in half. Scoop out the strings and seeds. Brush each piece of squash with olive oil and set it, cut side down, on a heavy baking sheet. Rub the garlic with olive oil, and set it alongside. Tuck thyme sprigs under the squash. Bake the squash until it is very tender when pierced with a fork, about 60 minutes.

Remove the squash from the oven and let it cool until it is easy to handle. Scoop the flesh from the squash, and pass it through a food mill into a medium bowl. (Or use a heavy fork to mash it into a puree.) Squeeze out the pulp of the garlic, and add it to the squash. Add the butter, and mix together thoroughly. Add the minced thyme and season to taste with nutmeg, salt, and pepper. Transfer the puree to a heavy ovenproof serving dish, return it to the oven, and bake for 15 minutes. Serve immediately.

BRAISED RADICCHIO

*P*ancetta or bacon simmering in vinegar releases an aroma that transports many people, especially children and grandchildren of European immigrants, to their childhood, calling up memories of braised cabbage, wilted lettuce, and similar dishes. My Russian grandmother often prepared wilted lettuce for my Austrian grandfather and, for me, the scents that filled the house were enchanting. He was an intimidating man, however; I never asked for or got a taste. But I never forgot that aroma. In this modern version, ingredients unknown to my grandmother contribute delicious elements to what remains a rustic dish with a long history.

SERVES 4 TO 6

1½ pounds radicchio, trimmed of
   bruised leaves
2 tablespoons olive oil
3 ounces pancetta, diced
1 shallot, minced
½ cup red wine vinegar or currant
   vinegar
Kosher salt
Black pepper in a mill
1 5-ounce log chèvre, cut into coins,
   optional

If the radicchio heads are small, cut
them in half; if they are large, cut them into
quarters. Heat the olive oil in a heavy
skillet over medium heat. Add the
pancetta, and fry it until it is nearly but not
quite crisp, about 6 minutes. Add the shallot, and cook it until limp, 4 to 5 minutes
more. Add the radicchio, cut side down,
cook for 2 minutes, and add the vinegar.
Cover the pan, and cook until the radicchio
is wilted and tender, about 10 minutes.
Season with salt and pepper, and transfer
the radicchio to a serving platter or individual plates. Top each piece of radicchio
with a coin of chèvre, if you like, spoon the
pan drippings over all, grind black pepper
over, and serve immediately.

ROASTED SHALLOTS

Like roasted garlic, roasted shallots are creamy and nutty-
flavored. Yet unlike garlic,
which is best when cooked moist in olive
oil, shallots can be almost dry-roasted, with
just a little olive oil and, if you like, a splash
of balsamic vinegar. You may roast the
shallots whole and unpeeled, but, if you do
so, select shallots of the same size so that
they cook at the same speed. If your shallots vary in size, peel them and cut them
into chunks of equal size. Serve roasted
shallots as a side dish with meats, including beef stew, game, and chicken.

SERVES 4 TO 6

1 pound firm shallots
2 tablespoons olive oil
2 tablespoons balsamic vinegar
Kosher salt
Black pepper in a mill

Preheat the oven to 350°F.
Place the shallots in single layer in a
heavy baking dish, toss with the olive oil
and balsamic vinegar, and season with salt
and several turns of pepper. Bake the shallots until they are tender when pierced by
a fork, 30 to 45 minutes, depending on their
size. Turn the shallots several times as they
cook. Remove them from the oven, transfer
to a serving dish, and serve immediately.

WILTED SPINACH

Wilted spinach is a pristine and lovely dish, especially when the spinach is picked fresh from the garden or brought home fresh from the farmers' market. Spinach is a cool-weather crop, making it an excellent foil for rich winter foods such as cassoulets and risottos. Recently, baby spinach leaves have begun showing up in farmers' markets and some grocery stores; they are wonderfully delicate and tender.

SERVES 4 TO 6

2 bunches (about 1¾ pounds) of
    fresh spinach, large stems removed
1 lemon, cut into wedges
Kosher salt

Fill a basin with lukewarm water, immerse the spinach in the water, and agitate it with your hands to loosen all the dirt, grit, and sand. Transfer the spinach, shaking off excess water as you lift it up, to a large tea towel to drain.

Place the spinach in a large pot or wok with a lid, set over medium heat, cover, and cook until the spinach is just wilted, 1 to 2 minutes.

Remove the spinach from the heat and transfer to individual plates or a serving bowl. Garnish with lemon wedges, season with salt, and serve immediately.

Variation:

Sauté 4 to 6 garlic cloves, minced, in 1 tablespoon of olive oil. Wilt the spinach, toss it with the sautéed garlic, and serve garnished with the lemon.

Grilled Cherry Tomatoes

When you have an abundance of cherry tomatoes: Soak wooden skewers for 1 hour. Prepare an outdoor grill. Thread 4 or 5 cherry tomatoes onto each skewer, and grill them for about 6 minutes, turning them several times. Transfer them to a platter and season with salt and pepper. They make an excellent accompaniment to any grilled seafood, poultry, or meat.

FRIED TOMATOES WITH CREAM

In California, we often have excellent tomatoes through early November, although sometimes a hard frost will end the season abruptly as early as late September. These tomatoes in a creamy sauce are excellent in the fall, when temperatures are cool. Serve this dish alongside a simple pasta or with plenty of hot bread to sop up the delicious sauce.

SERVES 4 TO 6

4 large tomatoes

2 tablespoons snipped chives
2 tablespoons minced Italian parsley
2 tablespoons minced cilantro
4 garlic cloves, minced
2 serrano chiles, minced
2 tablespoons unsalted butter
½ cup dry white wine
½ cup heavy cream
Kosher salt
Black pepper in a mill
Chives, for garnish
Sprigs of parsley, for garnish

The Original 27 Counties

More than half the tomatoes grown in California come from **Yolo County**, where tomato fields stretch for miles across the flat terrain. Almonds, fruit, and field crops are grown as well. Tucked here and there throughout the county are truck farms, the owners of which sell their harvest at farmers' markets in Sacramento and San Francisco. Originally home to Suisun and Wintun tribes, the area was not explored by Europeans until the 1820s. Wheat was an important early crop. California's first alfalfa was planted here in 1840, and the state's first salmon cannery was established on the banks of the Sacramento River in 1864. Davis, in the southern part of the county, is home to a branch of the University of California that is among the country's top agricultural research centers.

Remove the stem end of each tomato and cut the tomatoes, parallel to the equator, into ⅜-inch slices. Arrange the tomatoes in a single overlapping layer on a large plate, and distribute the chives, parsley, cilantro, garlic, and serranos over them. Cover with a tea towel and let marinate for 2 to 3 hours.

Heat the butter in a large heavy skillet over medium heat. Remove the tomatoes from their marinade (reserving the marinade), and sauté them, in batches so you do not crowd the skillet, until they are completely heated through, about 2 minutes on each side. Transfer the tomatoes to a serving plate, keep them warm, and continue until all are cooked.

Transfer the tomato marinade to the skillet, add the wine, increase the heat to high, and deglaze the pan. When the wine is almost completely evaporated, reduce the heat, add the cream, swirl, and simmer until the liquid is reduced by one third. Season the cream sauce with salt and pepper, pour it over the tomatoes, garnish with chives and parsley, and serve immediately.

BAKED TOMATOES PROVENÇALES

This classic dish from the south of France seems to be on everyone's table during the California tomato season. It often accompanies grilled or roasted meats, but it is also excellent alongside a simple pasta dish.

SERVES 6

6 medium slicing tomatoes, ripe but
    slightly firm
6 garlic cloves, sliced thin
2 tablespoons minced basil or Italian
    parsley
¼ cup extra virgin olive oil
1 cup fresh bread crumbs
Kosher salt
Black pepper in a mill

Preheat the oven to 375°F.

Cut a slice off the stem end of each tomato just above the shoulder, where the tomato begins to widen. Put the tomatoes cut side up in a baking dish and top each one with garlic, basil or parsley, and a teaspoon of olive oil. Toss the bread crumbs with the remaining olive oil and season them with salt and pepper. Top each tomato with bread crumbs.

Bake the tomatoes until they are soft and just begin to brown, about 45 minutes. Let them rest 5 minutes before serving.

Fiddler's Green Farm

From early March well into May, Jim Eldon has beautiful purple asparagus, crisp, plump, and fragrant. His Fiddler's Green Farm, near Davis, offers dozens of crops throughout the year, from sugar snap peas in the spring to thirty varieties of heirloom tomatoes in the summer. Eldon sells his produce at farmers' markets, and during the height of the season has about 130 subscribers in the Sacramento area who receive weekly boxes of produce directly from the farm. Fiddler's Green also makes its own sun-dried tomatoes from several varieties including Yellow Taxi, Early Girl, Oregon Spring, and Black Prince. Production is simple—the tomatoes are cut in half, placed on old prune racks, and set out to dry in the hot Central Valley sun.

GRILLED ZUCCHINI

When I operated a small restaurant in the mid-1980s, these grilled zucchini were the most popular appetizer or side dish on the menu. Vegetarians loved them, and parents found them an easy vegetable to convince kids to eat. They couldn't be simpler to prepare, and they're a quick recipe for the summer when it's hard to keep up with even one prolific zucchini plant.

SERVES 4 TO 6

8 medium zucchini
⅓ cup extra virgin olive oil
Juice of 1 lemon
3 garlic cloves, crushed
1 teaspoon ground cumin
Kosher salt
Black pepper in a mill

Cut the zucchini lengthwise in half. In a shallow bowl or baking dish, combine the olive oil, lemon juice, garlic, and cumin. Add the zucchini, turning until each piece is fully coated. Season with salt and several turns of pepper. Let the zucchini marinate in the dressing for at least 30 minutes or up to 2 hours.

Prepare a medium fire in an outdoor grill or heat a stovetop grill.

Grill the zucchini, cut side down, for 7 to 8 minutes, or until it is clearly marked by the grill and just beginning to become tender. Turn the zucchini, and grill for 4 to 5 minutes more, or until the zucchini is tender but not soft when pierced with a fork. Transfer to a serving platter, add more salt and pepper, and serve.

FALL COLACHE

In her *West Coast Cook Book*, Helen Evans Brown writes that a vegetable stew called colache was one of few vegetable dishes regularly prepared at the great California rancheros. Her recipe is simpler than mine, though the spirit remains the same; the fall harvest is the source of both. Certainly, the rancheros did not have pancetta, used here in place of the lard or bacon they would have had. Use either pancetta or bacon, or, for a completely vegetarian dish, replace the meat with an additional 3 tablespoons of olive oil. The colache makes a substantial accompaniment to roast beef, lamb, or poultry.

SERVES 6 TO 8

3 tablespoons olive oil
8 ounces pancetta, diced
2 yellow onions, diced
3 green poblano chiles, seeded and diced
2 serrano chiles, minced
1 small winter squash, such as Red Kuri, small sugar pumpkin, or Delicata, peeled, seeded, and diced
4 small potatoes, such as Rose Fir or Yellow Finn, peeled and diced
1 pound small green beans, cut into 1½-inch lengths
1 cup Tomato Concassé (page 98) or 1 cup canned diced tomatoes
1 cup fresh corn kernels (from about 2 ears)
Kosher salt
Black pepper in a mill

Heat the olive oil in a large heavy skillet over medium heat. Add the pancetta, and fry it until it is almost but not quite crisp. Add the onions, and sauté them until they are limp, about 8 minutes. Add the poblanos and serranos, stir, and sauté for 4 to 5 minutes, until the chiles are limp. Add the squash and potatoes, and sauté for 5 minutes more. Add the green beans, tomatoes, and 1 cup of water, reduce the heat to medium-low, and simmer, covered, until the squash is tender, 25 to 30 minutes. Stir in the corn kernels, cook for 5 minutes more, and remove the skillet from the heat. Taste, and season with salt and pepper. Serve immediately.

Chapter 13

CONDIMENTS, CHUTNEYS, AND PRESERVES

CONDIMENTS, CHUTNEYS, AND PRESERVES

FLAVORED BUTTERS

lavored butters, also called compound butters, are easy to make and add flavor to a variety of dishes, from simple breads and pastas to grilled seafood and roasted meats. Toss fresh pasta, for example, with the basic recipe here, or with Olive Butter, Gorgonzola Butter, or Dried Tomato Butter, three of the Variations that follow. You can add zest to turkey, lamb, or beef burgers by pressing a coin of the basic flavored butter or of Jalapeño Butter into the center of the meat as you shape the burger. Make flavored butter in a food processor or by hand. After it is made, press it into a decorative mold or roll it into a log, and refrigerate or freeze it. You can use this basic recipe to make any flavored butter.

MAKES A LITTLE MORE THAN ½ CUP

½ cup (1 stick) unsalted butter, at room temperature
1 small shallot, chopped
2 tablespoons minced herbs, such as Italian parsley, chives, or oregano
Kosher salt
White pepper, preferably fresh-ground

Place the butter, shallot, and herbs in a food processor. Pulse, scraping the sides if necessary, until the shallot is minced and the mixture is evenly mixed. Season with salt and white pepper, and pulse again for about 15 seconds. Transfer the mixture to a small bowl. (Or place the ingredients in a small bowl and use a fork to mix them together.)

To shape the butter into a log, spread it in the center of a sheet of plastic wrap, wrap the butter loosely, and use the palm of your hand to roll a log about 1¼ inches in diameter. Wrap the log tight in plastic wrap, and refrigerate it to chill it thoroughly. To freeze, add 1 or 2 additional layers of plastic wrap. Use refrigerated butter with 10 days, frozen butter within 3 months.

To slice coins from the log, unwrap the butter, dip a sharp knife in hot water, and cut ⅛-inch-thick slices.

Variations:

DRIED TOMATO BUTTER: Use 1 shallot, minced, 3 tablespoons minced dried tomatoes packed in oil, and 1 teaspoon thyme leaves along with kosher salt and fresh-ground black pepper. Serve with brie and slices of baguette, with pasta, or with roasted asparagus, steamed green beans or broccoli, or grilled onions.

GORGONZOLA BUTTER: Use 3 ounces Italian gorgonzola cheese, 1 teaspoon minced rosemary, and 2 teaspoons fresh-ground black pepper. Serve with beef and with pasta.

JALAPEÑO BUTTER: Use 2 garlic cloves, crushed, 1 jalapeño, seeded, and 1 tablespoon minced cilantro leaves along with kosher salt and fresh-ground black pepper.

Excellent with grilled pork and with grilled beef burgers.

NASTURTIUM BUTTER: Use 1 small shallot, minced, 1 teaspoon thyme leaves, 1 teaspoon minced Italian parsley, about 20 nasturtium flowers, stems removed, a pinch of sugar, kosher salt, and white pepper. Serve with pasta and with grilled seafood.

OLIVE BUTTER: Use 1 small shallot, minced, 2 tablespoons minced olives, 1 tablespoon minced Italian parsley, and fresh-ground black pepper. Excellent with lamb and with pasta.

PISTACHIO BUTTER: Use 3 tablespoons roasted pistachio nuts, ground fine, along with kosher salt and fresh-ground black pepper. Serve with seafood or turkey, or with pasta, garnishing the finished dish with whole roasted pistachios.

HOMEMADE MAYONNAISE

*I*n a mayonnaise, no single ingredient should dominate, which is why olive oil, especially a deep-flavored extra virgin olive oil, is not the best choice. Yet olive oil is appealing because of its health benefits. You can use up to ¾ cup of olive oil in this recipe if you like, but be sure it is a very mild oil without pronounced olive flavors.

MAKES ABOUT 1½ CUPS

1 whole egg, at room temperature

1 egg yolk, at room temperature
1 teaspoon Dijon mustard
2 teaspoons white wine or Champagne vinegar, preferably medium-acid
½ teaspoon kosher salt, or more to taste
¼ teaspoon white pepper, preferably fresh-ground
1¼ cups corn oil or peanut oil
1 to 2 tablespoons fresh lemon juice

Place the whole egg, egg yolk, mustard, vinegar, salt, and pepper in a blender or food processor. Blend or process for 30 seconds. With the machine running, add the oil slowly in a steady stream until all of it has been incorporated, then add 1 tablespoon of lemon juice. Taste the sauce, and add more salt or lemon juice, if you like.

Transfer the mayonnaise to a medium bowl. If the mayonnaise is too stiff, use a whisk to mix in 1 tablespoon of boiling water. Refrigerate, covered, for at least 2 hours before using. Store, covered, in the refrigerator for up to 7 days.

Variation:

For herb mayonnaise, mix 2 to 3 tablespoons minced fresh herbs, such as Italian parsley, chives, oregano, marjoram, basil, sage, or savory, into the mayonnaise after adding the lemon juice.

AïOLI

*Y*ou can find aïoli—the garlic mayonnaise of Provence— made with a single clove of garlic or with more than a head's worth. Until recently, the American palate favored the milder versions, recoiling from the bold power of a true aïoli. Today, chefs make aïolis with all sorts of ingredients, from roasted garlic and basil pesto to curry spices; this recipe is simpler and more traditional, but it does pack a wallop. The quality and freshness of the garlic is crucial. Cloves should be plump and firm to the touch. Do not use shriveled, dessicated cloves or cloves that have sprouted green shoots. The olive oil, too, should be the best possible, although a really big Tuscan oil may have too strong a flavor. Provençal oils are good, as are the better California ones, such as DaVero or B.R. Cohn Estate. Note that true Provençal aïoli does not include lemon juice; it's often added in American kitchens, however, and you may do so, especially if the aïoli will be served alongside seafood, green vegetables, or other foods that go well with lemon.

MAKES ABOUT 2 CUPS

1 head of garlic (about 12 cloves),
  cloves separated, peeled, and
  crushed
1 teaspoon kosher salt
2 egg yolks, at room temperature
1½ to 1¾ cups extra virgin olive oil
Pinch of cayenne

1 teaspoon fresh lemon juice, or more
  to taste, optional

Place the garlic and salt in a mortar. Grind them with a pestle to a very smooth, nearly liquid paste. Add the egg yolks, one at a time, mixing well after each addition. Set the pestle aside, and use a whisk to add the oil, at first just a few drops at a time, mixing well after each addition. Gradually increase the amount of oil in each addition, but never add more oil than is absorbed quickly. When as much oil as possible has been incorporated, add the cayenne and, if you like, the lemon juice. Taste, and correct the seasonings. If the aïoli is too stiff, use a whisk to mix in 1 tablespoon of boiling water. Refrigerate, covered, for at least 2 hours before using. Store, covered, in the refrigerator for up to 5 days.

Variation:

To make aïoli in a blender or food processor, blend or process 1 whole egg, 2 egg yolks, 1 teaspoon Dijon mustard, 8 to 10 garlic cloves, and 1 teaspoon salt for 30 seconds, until the garlic is nearly completely pureed. With the machine running, slowly drizzle in 2 cups of olive oil. Add a pinch of cayenne and, if you like, 1 to 2 tablespoons fresh lemon juice. Transfer to a small bowl. If the aïoli is too stiff, whisk in 1 to 2 tablespoons of boiling water.

RASPBERRY MAYONNAISE

*B*e sure to use a low-acid vinegar in this recipe. A high-acid vinegar, such as one of the French raspberry vinegars, is too strong. The olive oil should be mildly flavored.

MAKES ABOUT 1½ CUPS

1 whole egg
1 egg yolk
2 teaspoons Dijon mustard
¼ cup low-acid (4.5 percent) raspberry vinegar
1 teaspoon sugar
Kosher salt
¼ teaspoon white pepper, preferably fresh-ground
1¼ cups olive oil

Place the whole egg, egg yolk, mustard, vinegar, sugar, salt, and pepper in a blender or food processor. Blend or process for 30 seconds. With the machine running, add the oil slowly in a steady stream. When all of the oil has been incorporated, transfer the mayonnaise to a small bowl. Taste, and correct the seasoning. Use immediately, or store, covered, in the refrigerator for up to 1 week.

Variation:

Make Blueberry Mayonnaise by using blueberry vinegar in place of the raspberry vinegar, and adding a generous pinch of ground cloves.

CHIPOTLE MAYONNAISE

*U*se this spicy, robust mayonnaise wherever you want an extra jolt of flavor and heat—on burgers and other sandwiches, perhaps, as a condiment with grilled seafood, or in potato salads.

MAKES 1½ CUPS

2 egg yolks, at room temperature
1 tablespoon red wine vinegar
Juice of 1 lime
1 teaspoon kosher salt
¼ teaspoon white pepper, preferably fresh-ground
1 teaspoon Dijon mustard
1 tablespoon pureed chipotles in adobo
1 cup unrefined corn oil or mild olive oil
2 tablespoons minced cilantro leaves

Place the egg yolks, vinegar, lime juice, salt, pepper, mustard, and pureed chipotles in a blender or food processor. Blend or process for 30 seconds. With the machine running, add the oil slowly in a steady stream. If the mayonnaise becomes too stiff, blend in 1 tablespoon of boiling water. Transfer the mayonnaise to a bowl, and fold in the cilantro. Refrigerate, covered, for at least 2 hours before using. Store, covered, in the refrigerator for up to 7 days.

Some California Place Names

Names of towns, cities, rivers, creeks, valleys, and other locations reveal much about a place—its ethnic heritage, its agriculture, its temperament. Here are some revealing California names:

Apple Valley
Agua Caliente ("hot water")
Bachelor Valley
Bass Lake
Bay Farm Island
Bee Rock
Berry Creek
Blossom Valley
Cabbage Patch
Calabasas ("winter squash")
Citrus Heights
Coffee Creek
Dairy
Dairyville
Dutch Flat
El Sobrante ("the leftovers")
Fish Camp
Fish Rock
Forks of Salmon
French Camp
French Corral
French Gulch
Frogtown

Fruitvale
Genoa
Grapevine
Honeydew
Lemoncove
Lemon Grove
Lemon Heights
Lemon Valley
Los Olivos
Manteca ("lard")
New Idaho
Olive
Orange
Panama
Peardale
Potato Slough
Quail Valley
Raisin City
Rice
Strawberry Valley
Sugar Loaf
Vacaville ("cow town")
Vineberg
Walnut Creek
Walnut Grove
Weed
Wheatland
Whiskeytown

Variation:

For a quick chipotle mayonnaise, stir 2 tablespoons of chipotle puree, 2 tablespoons minced cilantro, and 1 tablespoon lime juice into 1 cup store-bought mayonnaise.

CURRY MAYONNAISE

*C*urry powder and the individual spices that go into it need to be cooked briefly to remove their raw taste. Use this mayonnaise to make curried chicken salad, or toss it with shrimp, scallops, lobster, or a combination for a scrumptious seafood salad.

MAKES ABOUT 1¼ CUPS

2 tablespoons olive oil
2 teaspoons minced yellow onion
1 tablespoon curry powder
1 teaspoon grated fresh ginger
1 teaspoon cumin seeds, toasted and
  ground
½ teaspoon turmeric
Pinch of cayenne
Pinch of ground white pepper
1 cup best-quality mayonnaise,
  preferably homemade (page 416)

Heat the olive oil in a small sauté pan over medium-low heat. Add the onion, and sauté it until it is limp and fragrant, about 7 minutes; stir frequently so that it does not brown. Add the curry powder, ginger, cumin, turmeric, cayenne, and white pepper, and stir over the heat for 2 minutes. Remove from the heat and let cool. Stir the mixture into the mayonnaise in a small bowl, cover, and refrigerate until thoroughly chilled, at least 2 hours. Store, covered, in the refrigerator for up to 1 week.

CHÈVRE MAYONNAISE WITH OLIVES

*L*aura Chenel's first book, *Chèvre! The Goat Cheese Cookbook*, includes many casual single-sentence recipes, along with more traditional full recipes, for cooking with goat cheese. One of the short recipes was the inspiration for this mayonnaise, excellent on grilled chicken and grilled portobello mushroom sandwiches.

MAKES ABOUT 1½ CUPS

1 egg yolk, at room temperature
½ cup extra virgin olive oil
8 ounces young (not aged) chèvre,
  such as chabis, broken into small
  pieces, or 8 ounces fromage blanc
2 teaspoons Dijon mustard
1 teaspoon fresh lemon juice
3 garlic cloves, crushed and minced
3 tablespoons minced black olives
1 tablespoon snipped chives
½ teaspoon kosher salt
½ teaspoon fresh-ground black
  pepper

In a medium mixing bowl, whisk together the egg yolk and half of the olive oil. When the mixture is smooth, use a fork to incorporate half of the chèvre. When the mixture is smooth again, add the remaining cheese. Using a whisk, add the remaining olive oil and the mustard and lemon juice. Whisk vigorously until smooth. Fold in the garlic, olives, and chives. Taste, and season with salt and pepper. Use immediately, or refrigerate, covered, for up to 1 week.

Variation:

To make the mayonnaise in a food processor, place the egg, chèvre, mustard, lemon juice, and garlic in the work bowl and process until smooth. With the machine running, drizzle in the olive oil in a steady stream. If necessary, stop to scrape down the mixture from the sides of the bowl. Using a rubber spatula, transfer the mayonnaise to a bowl, fold in the olives and chives, taste, and season with salt and pepper.

HONEY-GINGER MUSTARD

The heat in mustard comes from a chemical reaction between an enzyme and a glucoside present in mustard seed that occurs when the ground seed is mixed with water. It takes twenty minutes for the full reaction to occur and you must wait that long if you want a mustard to develop its full heat and flavor. Of the many flavored mustards I have made over the years, this is the most popular. It is an essential accompani-

ment to Carrot Fritters (page 15).

MAKES ABOUT 1 CUP

2 tablespoons hot dry mustard, such as Colman's
1 tablespoon ice water
¾ cup Dijon mustard
¼ cup honey
¼ cup minced candied ginger
1 teaspoon grated fresh ginger
2 garlic cloves, minced
½ teaspoon fresh-ground black pepper
2 tablespoons minced cilantro leaves

Mix the dry mustard with the ice water in a small bowl to form a smooth paste. Let the paste sit for 20 minutes. Add the Dijon mustard, honey, candied and fresh ginger, garlic, pepper, and cilantro, and stir until the mixture is smooth. Let the mustard rest for at least 30 minutes before using. Store, covered, in a glass jar in the refrigerator.

CHÉVRE

CALIFORNIA OLIVE MUSTARD

This mustard is delightful on tuna sandwiches or in tuna salads. It is also excellent as a condiment on bruschetta or on sandwiches of summer tomatoes, with all types of grilled vegetables, and with roasted potatoes.

MAKES ABOUT ¾ CUP

2 tablespoons minced California
  black olives
2 tablespoons minced green olives
1 tablespoon minced oil-cured olives
1 garlic clove, minced
½ teaspoon thyme leaves
Zest of 1 lemon, minced
¾ cup Dijon mustard

Combine the olives, garlic, thyme, and lemon zest in a small bowl. Fold in the mustard. Store, covered, in the refrigerator for up to 3 months.

OLIVE TAPENADE

Tapenade is best used within a day or two of making it; you can store it, covered, for a little longer in the refrigerator, but the flavors will decline. You can vary the type of olives you use based on what is available and on your preferences. Use several kinds or just one.

If you are not used to strongly flavored olives, have half the olives be California black olives, which are very, very mild.

MAKES ABOUT 2 CUPS

1 cup kalamata olives, pitted
1 cup cracked green olives, pitted
1½ cups niçoise olives, pitted
6 garlic cloves, minced
1 tablespoon minced Italian parsley
2 anchovy fillets, rinsed
⅓ cup extra virgin olive oil
Black pepper in a mill

Using a very sharp knife (do not use a food processor), mince the olives. Place them in a bowl, and toss them with the garlic and parsley. Using a mortar and pestle, pound the anchovies until they form a paste. Add the anchovy paste to the olives, pour in the olive oil, and toss together lightly. Let the tapenade sit for 30 minutes before using.

Variation:

Add 1 tablespoon minced lemon zest and 1 tablespoon minced orange zest to the tapenade.

Russia in California

Life along the coast of northern California in the early nineteenth century was not easy for the Russians who first settled the area. A government report reveals both the necessities of living and the difficulty of obtaining them:

"Everyone has confirmed that there are no ways to help [a settler] live and feed a family on a single salary, with one ration of flour and one pound of meat (with bones) a day. Consequently, there is indeed no way the office can reduce debts; on the contrary they increase year by year. In order to give an idea of the expenses of a Russian [settler] at [Fort] Ross, I add here the debts of one of them, Vasily Permitin, who has a wife and five children. For 1832 he received on his salary's account:

Wheat   *126.4 pounds*
Wheat flour   *152.5 pounds*
Barley   *72.25 pounds*
Dried Meat   *36 pounds*
Fresh Beef   *63 pounds*
Lard   *21.6 pounds*
Cow's Butter   *9.9 pounds*
Tallow Candles   *12.5 pounds*
Salt   *12.6 pounds*

Copper Utensils   *4 pounds*
Millet   *9 pounds*
Circassian Tobacco   *19.8 pounds*
Soap   *24.3 pounds*
Tea   *9.6 pounds*
Sugar   *42.8 pounds*
Treacle   *9.5 pounds*
Wool Felt   *2 bundles*
Cotton Stockings   *1 pair*
Flannel Blankets   *2 bundles*
Cotton Dress   *1*
Soles   *21 pairs*
Uppers   *10*
Cotton Ends   *5 pieces*
Medium Sheepskins   *2*
Flemish Linens   *49 feet*
Calico   *74.6 feet*
Ticking   *39.6 feet*
Trouser Burlap   *49 feet*
Gingham   *46.3 feet*
Soldier's Broadcloth   *4.6 feet*

"All these total 728 rubles, 17 kopecks at existing prices, while Permitin's annual salary is 350 rubles."

Quoted in James R. Gibson, "Russia in California, 1833: Report of Governor Wrangel," *Pacific Northwest Quarterly*, October, 1969

FIG CHUTNEY

In the United States, we usually use the word *chutney* to indicate thick sweet relishes, either homemade or bottled, such as Major Grey's, one of the most common bottled chutneys. In Indian cuisine, the word refers to fresh condiments as diverse as a puree of cilantro and mint or this mixture of figs, lemon juice, and crushed red pepper, as well as the more familiar cooked fruit chutneys. Serve a selection of fresh and cooked chut-

neys when a curry is the main course. Because these figs are unpeeled, you should
try to find pesticide-free organic fruit.

MAKES ABOUT 2½ CUPS

12 unpeeled ripe figs, stemmed and
    coarsely chopped
4 garlic cloves, crushed
2 tablespoons fresh lemon juice
1 teaspoon kosher salt
2 teaspoons cumin seeds, toasted
    and crushed
½ teaspoon crushed red pepper

Combine the figs, garlic, lemon juice,
salt, cumin, and red pepper in a food
processor. Pulse several times until the figs
are chopped fine; scrape down the sides if
necessary. And ½ cup water and pulse
again until the mixture forms a coarse
puree. Transfer to a nonreactive container,
cover, and refrigerate until ready to use.
Store, covered, in the refrigerator for up
to 4 days.

APRICOT CHUTNEY

California produces nearly all of the
nation's apricots, yet a mere five
percent of the state's crop is sold
fresh. The season is short, and today a good
fresh apricot is nearly as difficult to come
by as a tomato with old-fashioned backyard flavor. The best place to find apricots
is at a farmers' market. If you locate a good
source, buy a quantity and make a batch of
this delicious chutney. A chutney such as

this one easily will keep a year; just be sure
to label the jars and store them in a cool,
dark cupboard.

MAKES 8 TO 10 PINTS

5 pounds ripe apricots, halved and
    stoned
3 pounds sugar
1 pound dried currants
½ cup minced garlic (from about
    2½ heads)
6 serrano chiles, seeded and cut into
    thin julienne
6 ounces fresh ginger, peeled and
    grated
½ ounce whole dried chiles, such as
    serranos or chiles de árbol, chopped
    coarse
2 cups apple cider vinegar
1 cup balsamic vinegar
2 tablespoons kosher salt

Combine the apricots and sugar in a
large heavy pot over medium heat, and stir
until the sugar is dissolved. Add the currants, garlic, serranos, ginger, and dried
chiles, and stir well. Stir in the cider vinegar and balsamic vinegar, add the salt, and
bring to a boil. Reduce the heat, and simmer for 1 hour, until the mixture is thick
and has darkened slightly. Pour the chutney into hot sterilized half-pint or pint jars,
leaving ¼ inch of head room at the top. Seal,
and process in a hot-water bath for 15 minutes. Set the jars on tea towels to cool, and
check that each jar is sealed properly. Store
in a cool, dark cupboard for up to 1 year.
Refrigerate after opening.

PEACH CHUTNEY

I make this chutney whenever I have an abundance of ripe yellow peaches. I never make it with white peaches, such as the spectacular Arctic Gems grown by Dry Creek Peach and Produce in Healdsburg, for the simple reason that their season is so short and they are so delicious that I think it is a shame to do anything with them other than eat them neat. Serve this chutney whenever you would serve a traditional mango chutney, with curries of all types, as well as with grilled and roasted meats and poultry.

MAKES 5 TO 6 PINTS

3 pounds ripe peaches, peeled and cut into ⅛-inch-thick slices

3 pounds sugar

1 pound black or golden raisins

2 heads of garlic, cloves separated and chopped

4 ounces fresh ginger, peeled and grated

½ ounce whole dried chiles, such as serranos or chiles de árbol, chopped coarse

2 cups red wine vinegar

1 tablespoon kosher salt

Combine the peaches and sugar in a large heavy pot over medium heat, and stir until the sugar is dissolved. Add the remaining ingredients, stir well, and bring to a simmer. Simmer for 1¼ hours, until the peaches have fallen apart and the raisins are plump and juicy. Pour the chutney into hot sterilized half-pint or pint jars, leaving ¼ inch of head room at the top. Seal, and process in a hot-water bath for 15 minutes. Set the jars on tea towels to cool, and check that each jar is sealed properly. Store in a cool, dark cupboard for up to 1 year. Refrigerate after opening.

The Original 27 Counties

Yuba County, bordered on the west by the Feather River and on the east by the northern part of the Sierra Nevada range, was not settled by Europeans until 1841, when John Sutter leased part of his land to a Prussian immigrant named Theodore Cordua. At the confluence of the Feather and Yuba rivers, Marysville, named for a survivor of the Donner Party, was a busy river port and trade center for the numerous mining towns in the area during the Gold Rush. Hops once dominated the region's agriculture; their production all but vanished from the state and is only now enjoying a renaissance in a few areas. Crops in Yuba County include rice, peaches for canning, and prunes, a favorite ingredient among home cooks here.

RHUBARB–STRAWBERRY CHUTNEY

This chutney is midway between a fresh chutney and a preserved one. It does not have enough sugar or vinegar in it to act as a preservative and should be enjoyed within a few days of making it.

MAKES ABOUT 3 CUPS

1 pound rhubarb, peeled and cut into 1-inch pieces

1 tablespoon minced fresh ginger

1 cup sugar

½ cup apple cider vinegar or sherry vinegar

¾ cup dried currants

1 pint fresh strawberries, chopped coarse

Combine the rhubarb, ginger, sugar, vinegar, and currants in a medium nonreactive saucepan, and bring to a boil. Reduce the heat, and simmer until the rhubarb is tender and the currants are plump, about 25 minutes. Add the strawberries, stir, and taste the chutney. Add more sugar or vinegar to correct the sweet-acid balance, simmer for 5 minutes, and remove from the heat. This chutney maybe be served warm or chilled. Store, covered, in the refrigerator for up to a week.

GREEN TOMATO–PEAR CHUTNEY

Make this chutney at the end of tomato season, when the weather suddenly turns cold and lots of green tomatoes linger on the vine.

MAKES 10 TO 12 PINTS

8 pounds unripe green tomatoes, firm and free of blemishes

2 teaspoons kosher salt

4 pounds firm pears, peeled, cored, and cut into ¼-inch-thick slices

1 head of garlic, cloves separated and minced

1 ½-inch piece of ginger, peeled and sliced thin

1 can (7 ounces) chipotles in adobo sauce, pureed

3 pounds brown sugar

4 cups apple cider vinegar

1½ cups dried currants

2 tablespoons minced orange zest

Core the tomatoes, slice them very thin, and sprinkle them with the salt. Set them aside, covered, in a cool place overnight.

Drain the tomatoes and combine them with the remaining ingredients in a large heavy nonreactive pot. Bring to a boil, reduce the heat to low, and skim off any foam that forms. Simmer the chutney for 3 hours, stirring frequently, until it is very thick and

The Death of the Dancing Raisins

For a time, the California Dancing Raisins were big stars in television commercials and print advertising. Evocative of Motown groups such as the Temptations, the animated raisins with their white gloves boogied to the beat of "I Heard It Through the Grapevine" while singing the praises of one of California's most important crops. The ads were paid for out of fees levied on growers by California's agricultural marketing orders, which had been in effect since 1936. According to the orders, a commodity group was to collect a tax from growers of that commodity, and the tax was used to advertise and market the commodity.

Along came Brian Leighton, attorney for several raisin growers, challenging the legality of the orders. Leighton had earlier represented the state's almond grow-ers, claiming that the marketing orders violated the growers' First Amendment rights, in particular the right *not* to speak—in this case, the right not to be forced to speak in an advertisement. He had succeeded, and so precedent was on his side when he made the challenge, again successful, that quieted the raisins. The raisins became wallflowers.

First Amendment concerns notwithstanding, there have been some unfortunate results of the dissolution of the orders. With the loss of funds, commodity groups cut back sharply on their activities, in the process discarding reams of important material. The archives of the California Apricot Commission, for example, were simply tossed into the dumpster—recipes, history, everything—when the commission's offices closed.

clear. Remove from the heat and ladle into hot sterilized pint jars, leaving ¼ inch of head room at the top. Seal, and process in a hot-water bath for 15 minutes. Set the jars on tea towels to cool, and check that each jar is sealed properly. Store in a cool, dark cupboard for up to 1 year. Refrigerate after opening.

MARINATED GRAPES

In the late 1960s, Cesar Chavez organized grape pickers in the San Joaquin, Imperial, and Coachella valleys of California to strike against the major growers for recognition of their union and for improvement in their appalling working and living conditions. The strike led, statewide and ultimately nationwide, to a boycott of table grapes. Even today, though the strike is long over, many

Californians resist buying commercial table grapes.

Grape growers use a lot of pesticides; if you can, make these grapes with organic fruit. You can store these grapes for several weeks in the refrigerator, serving them for snacks, as a garnish on salads, alongside seafood, or sliced into a refreshing salsa.

MAKES 3 PINTS

2 pounds seedless grapes, such as Red Flame
2 cups red wine
2 cups black raspberry or red wine vinegar
1 cup sugar
6 whole cloves
6 allspice berries
6 cardamom seeds, crushed
1 tablespoon whole black peppercorns
3 1-inch cinnamon sticks

Rinse the grapes well under cool running water, discarding any bruised or de-

cayed grapes, and drain them thoroughly. Divide the grapes among 3 pint jars. Combine the wine, vinegar, sugar, cloves, allspice, cardamom, and peppercorns in a heavy saucepan over medium heat, and stir constantly until the sugar is dissolved. Remove from the heat and let cool. Add a cinnamon stick to each jar, pour the wine mixture over the grapes, close the jars with their lids, and refrigerate for at least 3 days. The grapes will keep for several weeks in the refrigerator.

MARINATED ONIONS

Onions soaked in a spiced wine marinade make an excellent accompaniment to all types of seafood and to grilled meats and poultry.

MAKES ABOUT 4 PINTS

3 pounds medium red onions, peeled and sliced very thin
2 cups red wine
2 cups raspberry vinegar or red wine vinegar
1 cup sugar
Several gratings of nutmeg
8 allspice berries, crushed
5 whole cloves, crushed
1 1-inch cinnamon stick
5 cardamom seeds, crushed
1 tablespoon whole black peppercorns

How to Make Red Grapes

Maybe you thought they grew that way. But the August 29, 1941, issue of *Family Circle* tells housewives of the day that they can make red grapes by simmering Thompson green seedless grapes in sugar, water, and plenty of red food coloring.

Divide the onion slices among 4 pint jars; do not pack the jars too tight. Combine the wine, vinegar, sugar, and spices in a heavy saucepan over medium heat, and stir constantly until the sugar is dissolved. Remove the pan from the heat and let cool. Pour the marinade over the onions, distributing the spices as evenly as possible among the jars and discarding the cinnamon stick. Close the jars with their lids. Marinate the onions in the refrigerator for at least 24 hours before using. Store, covered, in the refrigerator for up to 3 weeks.

PRESERVED LEMONS

Once found mainly in North African cuisines, preserved lemons recently have become popular in the United States. I began making them when my friend Anna Cherney (see page 140) invited me to pick fruit from her remarkably fecund Meyer lemon tree, an enormous decades-old tree that would bear a thousand lemons at a time. This recipe is for a smaller amount, in case you aren't blessed with the same abundance. Because the entire lemon, skin and all, is used in this recipe, use organic lemons that have not been sprayed with pesticides or herbicides.

MAKES 1 QUART

12 organic lemons, preferably Meyer lemons
¾ cup kosher salt
2 tablespoons sugar
¾ cup fresh lemon juice
Olive oil

Wash the lemons well and dry them thoroughly. Slice them lengthwise into sixths or eighths, depending on their size, and pick out any visible seeds. Mix together the salt and sugar in a large nonreactive bowl, add the lemon slices, and toss the mixture to coat the lemons. Place

California's Own Lemon

In 1908, Frank Meyer, an "agricultural explorer" employed by the U.S. government, brought a lemon tree to California from Beijing. Its fruit was mildly sweet as well as tart, its skin thin, its pulp abundantly juicy. Because its Chinese name was not recorded, botanists called it the Meyer lemon. Meyer lemon trees proved hardy and resistant to cold, but, because they were vulnerable to a virulent form of the virus tristeza, they were labeled a public nuisance and scores were ripped out and destroyed. Several counties made planting the tree illegal, a restriction that remains today in a few areas, even though the University of California at Riverside has developed a variety that is immune to the disease. Recently, the fruit, in season for most of the year, has been enjoying a renaissance among California chefs and home cooks.

the lemons in a quart jar, and add the lemon juice. Cover the jar tight with plastic wrap and then with its lid (the lid will corrode without the plastic wrap), and store in a cool, dark cupboard for 7 days, turning it upside down each morning and righting it at night, so that all of the lemons spend time in the liquid. On the seventh day, top off the jar with olive oil.

If you will use the preserved lemons within the month, there is no need to refrigerate them. You can hold them longer, but their flavor decreases with refrigeration.

The Original 27 Counties

El Dorado County, which stretches from Folsom Lake in the west to Lake Tahoe in the east, got its name because it was at John Sutter's mill, in Coloma, that the Gold Rush began. An enormous influx of treasure seekers swarmed into the area, and neither the county nor California would ever be the same. Towns sprung up overnight like winter mushrooms, and many disappeared as quickly; the names of some of the towns linger on in tales of the era— Murderer's Bar, Loafer's Hollow, and Spanish Hill, for example. Today, the old ghost towns draw tourists to the area. Fruit farming is the primary agriculture, with a thriving industry in secondary products like preserves, jams, jellies, and applesauces.

ZINFANDEL APPLESAUCE

California's idyllic weather works against its apple crop; still, the state ranks fourth in the country in apple production. Apple trees prefer colder winters than typically occur in the state's main apple-growing regions, around Sebastopol in western Sonoma County, where orchards were planted by Russian settlers in the nineteenth century, and Watsonville in Monterey County. The Central Valley has large plantings now, too, though the hot summers can hurt the quality of the fruit; to the east, in El Dorado County in the Sierra Nevadas, there are successful orchards that benefit from cooler weather. When the weather cooperates, however, California apples are outstanding. In Sebastopol, old apple orchards border new vineyards, a union mirrored in this mildly spicy apple sauce.

MAKES ABOUT 2 QUARTS

5 pounds apples, preferably Gravensteins
2 cups zinfandel
5 whole cloves
3 allspice berries
1 ½–inch cinnamon stick
½ to 1 cup sugar
Several gratings of nutmeg

Peel and core the apples and cut them into chunks. As you work, drop the chunks into a bowl of cool water with a squeeze of lemon juice in it to prevent browning. Drain the apples, and place them in a large nonreactive saucepan over medium heat. Add the zinfandel, cloves, allspice, and cinnamon, and cook, stirring every few minutes, until the apples are tender, 15 to 20 minutes. Using a slotted spoon, transfer the apples to a bowl. Strain the cooking liquid, discarding the spices, and return the liquid to the pan. Increase the heat to high and reduce by one half. Press the apples through a potato ricer, add them to the reduced wine, stir in ½ cup sugar, taste, and add more sugar, if you like. Add the nutmeg, reduce the heat to low, and simmer for 5 minutes. Remove from the heat, and serve the applesauce warm or refrigerate it until it is chilled.

MARY'S EASY APRICOT JAM

Mary Duryee has lived in northern California her entire life, first in Sebastopol, where she was born, then in Marin County for a number of years. She returned to Sebastopol in the 1980s. In 1988, I moved into a house she and her husband, Guy,

own, a redwood-shingle cottage overlooking a small valley with the Atascadero Creek beyond. I happened to move in on my birthday; awaiting me were one of Mary's beautiful cakes, a blackberry pie, and several jars of her homemade jams, including this apricot jam. The secret to this simple jam is to use really good apricots that are very ripe. It is not necessary to process fruit jams in a water bath, but be sure to sterilize the canning jars and to follow the manufacturer's instructions for the lids.

MAKES ABOUT 3 PINTS

3 pounds apricots, pitted
3 cups sugar

Place the apricots in a large heavy pot over high heat. Cook for 6 to 8 minutes, stirring constantly, to reduce the juices released by the apricots. When the liquid is thick, stir in the sugar and bring to a vigorous boil. Cook, stirring, for 3 to 4 minutes, or until the mixture coats the back of a spoon with a sheet of syrup.

Remove from the heat and ladle the jam into hot sterilized canning jars. Seal the jars according to the manufacturer's instructions. Store in a cool, dark cupboard for up to 4 months.

DESSERTS

DESSERTS

SUMMERTIME APPLE CRUMBLE

The Gravenstein is the first apple of the year to come into season, ripening in California a full month or more before varieties such as Jonathan, McIntosh, and Golden Delicious are ready for harvest. Late-ripening apples are built to last, and some keep, stored in a cool pantry or root cellar, for weeks or even months. But, like other summer fruits, the Gravenstein demands immediate attention; it does not store well and becomes unpleasantly mushy as it ages. Eaten soon after harvest, however, it is one of the best apples in the world. This recipe comes from my friend Mary Duryee, who grew up in Sebastopol, where the first commercial Gravenstein orchard in California was planted in the late 1880s. You can make this simple dessert using another apple variety, if you like. Serve with fresh-whipped cream or with ice cream.

SERVES 6 TO 8

8 to 12 apples, preferably Gravensteins, peeled, cored, and sliced
1 cup sugar
¼ teaspoon fresh-grated nutmeg
Juice of ½ lemon
2 teaspoons ground cinnamon
3 tablespoons cornstarch
4 thick slices country-style bread
1 tablespoon powdered sugar
2 tablespoons unsalted butter

Place the apple slices in a large pot with the sugar, nutmeg, lemon juice, 1 teaspoon of the cinnamon, and 1 cup of water. Bring to a boil over medium-high heat, reduce the heat, and simmer until the apples are just tender, 7 to 10 minutes. Dissolve the cornstarch in ¼ cup water, add it to the apples, and shake the pot (do not stir) to distribute it. Bring to a boil again and cook until the mixture thickens slightly.

Meanwhile, toast the bread twice, break it into chunks, and place the chunks in a food processor with the remaining 1 teaspoon of cinnamon, the powdered sugar, and the butter. Pulse until the mixture has been reduced to crumbs.

Transfer the apples to a serving bowl, spread the seasoned crumbs on top, and serve immediately.

GRILLED APRICOTS WITH FROMAGE BLANC

Nothing finishes a backyard barbecue better than fruit grilled over the dying embers. (If you have a gas grill, hence no embers, grilled fruit is still great.) The best fruits for grilling, in my opinion, are apricots, peaches, and nectarines (see the Variations for the latter two), but when they are not in season other good choices are firm-ripe bananas, pear halves, or thick slices of pineapple. For a more elaborate dessert, top any grilled fruit with Spicy Chocolate Sauce (see the Variations).

8 ounces fromage blanc
1 teaspoon minced lemon zest
1 tablespoon fresh lemon juice
1 teaspoon vanilla extract
1 to 2 tablespoons superfine sugar, preferably, or granulated sugar
10 ripe apricots, cut in half and pitted

Prepare a fire in an outdoor grill.

Mix together the fromage blanc, lemon zest, lemon juice, vanilla extract, and 1 tablespoon of the sugar in a small bowl. Taste, and add more sugar if you like. If you have a pastry bag, spoon the mixture into a pastry bag fitted with a large star tip.

Place the apricots, skin side down, on the grill. Grill them until they just begin to soften and brown, 3 to 5 minutes. Arrange them, skin side down, on a serving tray. If you have a pastry bag, pipe a star of the fromage blanc mixture into the center of each apricot half; if not, spoon some of the mixture into the center. Serve immediately.

Variations:

TO GRILL PEACHES AND NECTARINES: Omit the fromage blanc mixture. Cut 10 peaches, nectarines, or a combination in half, pit them, and grill them, skin side down, for 3 minutes. Squeeze lemon juice over them and turn them over. Grill, cut side down, until they are soft and tender,

about 3 minutes more, and transfer them to a serving plate. Sprinkle with sugar and serve immediately, with lemon wedges alongside.

WITH SPICY CHOCOLATE SAUCE: Combine 4 ounces bittersweet chocolate, chopped, and 2 tablespoons milk or half-and-half in the top of a doubler boiler. Set over very hot but not boiling water for about 2 minutes, stirring until smooth. Remove from the heat, and add ¼ teaspoon vanilla extract and ¼ teaspoon cayenne. If the sauce is too thick, stir in 1 or 2 tablespoons more of warm milk or half-and-half. Fill the apricots with the fromage blanc mixture, drizzle the chocolate sauce over them, and serve immediately.

BERRY COBBLER

This traditional cobbler, topped with a biscuit crust, is a perfect showcase for your best summer berries, of whatever variety you have.

SERVES 6 TO 8

1 quart berries, such as blackberries, raspberries, olallieberries, or blue-berries
1 tablespoon fresh lemon juice
⅓ to ½ cup sugar
2 tablespoons brandy or 1 teaspoon vanilla extract
2 tablespoons instant tapioca

BISCUIT TOPPING
¾ cup all-purpose flour

1 teaspoon kosher salt
½ teaspoon baking powder
1 tablespoon sugar
2 tablespoons unsalted butter, chilled,
   cut into small pieces
½ cup heavy cream

Preheat the oven to 350°F.

Toss together the berries, lemon juice, and ⅓ cup of the sugar in a bowl. Taste, and add more sugar if you like. Mix together the brandy or vanilla and the tapioca in a small bowl. Transfer the berries to a deep baking dish, top them with the tapioca mixture, and toss to combine.

Make the topping: Combine the flour, salt, baking powder, and sugar in a medium mixing bowl. Add the butter and, using a pastry cutter or a fork, quickly mix it in until the mixture forms crumbs the size of small peas. Form a well in the center, pour in the cream, and, using your fingers, quickly mix the dough until it comes together. Knead once or twice, place on a floured work surface, and roll out to ½ inch thick. Cut shapes, such as stars, hearts, or circles, about 2 inches across. Cover the berries with the pastry shapes.

Bake the cobbler until the pastry turns golden brown on top and the berries are thick and bubbly, about 40 minutes. Remove from the oven and let cool slightly. Serve warm.

Variations:

Use a combination of strawberries, blueberries, and sliced peaches. Or combine golden and red raspberries.

California Berries

The loganberry was developed in 1881 by James Logan, a botanist, who crossed a California wild blackberry with a red raspberry. The hardy hybrid, with its abundant yield, survived and thrived. But forty years after its creation, the boysenberry, developed by Rudolph Boysen, surpassed the loganberry's yield, producing about five tons of berries to the acre. It was Walter Knott who in 1933 harnessed the commercial potential of the boysenberry. His successful berry fields went on to become Knott's Berry Farm, a favorite southern California tourist destination today.

BING CHERRY COMPOTE

Bing cherries come into and out of season quickly, especially if the weather is hot. California has an early cherry season, beginning sometime in May. By the middle of June the cherries have vanished until the next year. In the Midwest, the cherry season begins as California's ends.

SERVES 4

3 cups ripe Bing cherries, pitted
1 cup sugar

1 cup red wine, such as gamay
   beaujolais or a Rhône-style blend
1 2-inch-long piece of vanilla bean
2 2-inch-long strips of lemon zest
2 tablespoons brandy
1 quart White Chocolate Ice Cream
   (page 463) or French vanilla ice
   cream

Combine the cherries, sugar, wine, vanilla bean, and lemon zest in a non-reactive saucepan over medium-high heat. Bring to a boil, reduce the heat, and simmer until the cherries are just soft, 10 to 15 minutes. Remove from the heat, stir in the brandy, and let sit, covered, for 30 minutes.

Remove and discard the vanilla bean and lemon zest. Serve the compote warm over the ice cream. Or refrigerate and serve chilled with the ice cream.

The Original 27 Counties

Before large portions of it were carved off to form new counties, **San Joaquin County** stretched from the San Francisco Bay east all the way to the Sierra Nevada range. The county is named for the river that flows through it. French immigrants were the first Europeans to settle here. The coming of the Southern Pacific Railroad had a tremendous impact. Lodi, in the northern part of the county, became a thriving center for food processing and shipping, allowing the region's agriculture to expand greatly. Food processing remains important today, as is agriculture, especially in cherries, apricots, grapes, sugar beets, and fresh vegetable crops. Stockton is an important inland port, with a 75-mile-long deep-water channel to the San Francisco Bay.

MEDJHOOL DATE MOUSSE

The Coachella Valley, roughly a hundred miles east of Los Angeles, is the center of the leading date-producing region of the United States. Summers in the low desert valleys of south central and southeastern California are long, hot, and, of course, dry, all of which conditions are necessary for a successful date harvest. Deglet Noor, a fairly dry variety of date originally from Algeria, accounts for most of the production, but the Medjhool date, succulent and soft, with a velvety texture, has been growing more popular in the last couple of decades.

SERVES 4 TO 6

1 cup whole Medjhool dates, pitted
¼ cup brandy
¼ cup unsalted butter, at room
   temperature
¾ teaspoon vanilla extract
1 tablespoon fresh lemon juice
3 eggs, separated
¼ cup powdered sugar, sifted
1 cup heavy cream

Whole Medjhool dates, for garnish

Combine the pitted dates, brandy, and ¼ cup of water in a small saucepan over medium-high heat. Bring to a boil, reduce the heat, and simmer gently, covered, for 10 minutes. Remove from the heat, stir in the butter, and let cool slightly. Add the vanilla extract and lemon juice, and puree the mixture in a blender or food processor. Set the date puree aside.

Beat the egg yolks and powdered sugar until the mixture forms a ribbon when the beaters are lifted. Place the mixture in the top of a double boiler over simmering water and cook, whisking constantly, until it thickens, 3 to 4 minutes. Transfer to a large mixing bowl, whisk in the date puree, and stir until the mixture is smooth and has cooled slightly.

Beat the cream until it forms soft peaks. In a separate bowl, beat the egg whites until they form stiff but not dry peaks. Fold the egg whites into the date mixture, then fold in the whipped cream. Transfer to individual serving dishes or a serving bowl and refrigerate, covered, for at least 4 hours, or until the mousse is set and chilled through.

Serve chilled, garnished with whole dates. Biscotti make a good accompaniment.

Variation:

Place the chilled mousse in a pastry bag fitted with a star tip. Pipe stars of mousse onto California dried apricots halves, top each with a roasted pistachio, and serve with other small desserts.

Papaya with Lime

To serve 4, cut 2 papayas in half, scoop out the seeds, and place a papaya half on each of 4 serving plates. Cut 2 limes in half, place a lime half next to each papaya half, and serve immediately.

FIGS POACHED IN HONEY AND LAVENDER

Apples, pears, and figs take beautifully to poaching. The flavors of the poaching liquid infuse the fruit, which becomes very tender. The poaching liquid itself takes on the flavor of the fruit, which is intensified when the liquid is boiled down into a rich syrup. Culinary lavender flowers can be found in herb shops and some natural foods stores, but if you can't locate them, don't worry; simply omit them.

SERVES 4 TO 6

1 bottle (750 ml) red wine, such as
    zinfandel, Sangiovese, or gamay
    beaujolais
¼ cup dark honey
1 tablespoon lavender flowers
18 ripe figs

Combine 1 cup of the red wine with the honey and lavender flowers in a heavy nonreactive saucepan over medium heat, and stir until the honey is dissolved. Add the figs and enough wine to cover them. Bring to a boil, reduce the heat, and simmer, uncovered, poaching the figs until they are plump and tender, 30 to 40 minutes. Using a slotted spoon, transfer the figs to a serving bowl. Strain the poaching liquid, discard the lavender, and return the liquid to the pan. Increase the heat to high, and reduce the liquid by about three quarters, or until it forms a syrup. Pour the sauce over the figs, and serve immediately.

Variation:

Place 2 tablespoons mascarpone next to the figs in each serving.

Oranges with Vanilla Sugar

For a refreshing winter dessert, peel oranges (2 per person), preferably blood oranges, taking care to remove all of the white rind, and cut them crosswise into ¼-inch-thick slices. Arrange the slices on a platter and sprinkle them with Vanilla Sugar (page 458), about ¾ teaspoon sugar per orange. Refrigerate until chilled, at least 1 hour. For a more elaborate dessert, divide the oranges among individual plates and add a scoop of vanilla ice cream or orange sherbet and 2 or 3 gingersnaps or sugar cookies to each serving.

PEACHES AND BLACKBERRIES WITH VANILLA BRANDY

More than two hundred varieties of peaches and nectarines are grown in California, where the harvest begins as early as late April and continues into October. The best-tasting fruit is found in June, July, and sometimes August. Most of the state's peach crop is sold in the West, while nectarines, actually a type of peach, are shipped throughout the country. Given the number of family farms in California, it is not uncommon to find peaches and nectarines for sale along a country road, where handwritten signs alert passing drivers; because peaches, especially, do not travel particularly well, buying them right at the farm often means you'll get better fruit than you usually have. In late June or early July, white peaches come into season, with the Arctic Gem variety ripening near the end of the month-long season. It is worth whatever effort it takes to find them; you won't find a better peach.

Although this recipe is very easy to make, you will need to plan ahead by 2 weeks, in order to have the flavored brandy ready.

SERVES 4

4 white peaches, peeled, pitted, and sliced

Saucer Peaches

"There were many plants growing then in Whittier which are now curiosities, and hard to procure from fancy nurseries. There were guava bushes, brought by the Mexicans I suppose, and loquats and kumquats brought by the Chinese.... On our corner ... there were peaches and apricots, and I think a couple of almonds ... and on the northeast corner ... were handsome date palms and, in the Moorheads' yard in the back, a beautiful tree of saucer peaches, which are almost unknown to most Americans today.... I suspect they were Chinese. They were without doubt the most delicate fruit I ever ate, and I am told that they are impossible to ship from one country or state, or even one village, to another.... When they were ripe, Mrs. Moorhead would lay some on a tray and hurry across the street to our house with them, and we would eat them at the next meal. The best way would have been to peel them at the table, so quickly did they turn brown and bruised, but fruit was always skinned and cut up and heavily sugared in little dishes in our basically Midwestern cuisine. Almost surely we poured cream over the peaches, a deserved treat. What we liked best, though, was to stand under the tree when the Moorheads were picking [and] eat whatever fell to the ground.... The fruits were perhaps a fat inch wide and half an inch deep, of a tender green, and with a wee seed as big as a baby pea in the middle."

M.F.K. Fisher, *Among Friends* (Knopf, 1971)

---

1 pint fresh blackberries
1 to 2 teaspoons sugar
¼ cup vanilla-infused brandy (see Note)

Place the peaches in a medium bowl. Add the blackberries and 1 teaspoon of the sugar, and toss lightly. Pour the brandy over the fruit and refrigerate, covered, for 30 minutes. Taste, and add more sugar, if you like. To serve, divide the fruit and the liquid among 4 chilled dessert plates. Serve immediately.

NOTE: To flavor brandy with vanilla, split 1 whole vanilla bean lengthwise and add it to a pint of premium brandy. Age in a cool, dark cupboard for at least 2 weeks before using. As you use the infused brandy, you can replenish the bottle with fresh brandy. The vanilla bean will continue to flavor the brandy for about 3 months.

PEACH PIE

When I asked my friend Mary Duryee, who makes magnificent pies, for her recipe for peach pie, she said, "Yikes! I never thought of following a recipe, and, as you know, I've never made just one pie in my life." After a little experimenting, we came up with this recipe, which couldn't be easier. The fruit is the main event, Mary emphasizes, and for that reason she likes a thin crust as well as fruit picked at the peak of their season. Sometimes Mary adds a dash of grated nutmeg; occasionally I add about ¼ teaspoon of vanilla extract.

SERVES 4 TO 6

8 to 10 peaches, peeled, pitted, and
    cut into ¼-inch-thick slices
Juice of 1 lemon
½ cup sugar
2 tablespoons cornstarch
1 9-inch pie shell (recipe follows)

Preheat the oven to 375°F. Combine the peaches, lemon juice, sugar, and cornstarch in a large bowl, and toss together lightly. Transfer the mixture to a 9-inch pie pan lined with the pie shell. Bake the pie for 35 to 40 minutes, or until the edges of the crust are lightly browned. Let the pie rest for 15 minutes before serving.

Pastry Dough for Pies

The secret to making a good pie crust is to handle the ingredients as little as possible, working quickly so that you do not develop the gluten in the flour, which makes the pastry tougher. Some people swear that lard makes the lightest and flakiest pie crust; I agree, although I sometimes prefer the taste of a crust made with butter. This dough can be used both for pie crusts and tart crusts.

MAKES 1 9-INCH PIE SHELL

1 cup all-purpose white flour
½ teaspoon kosher salt
½ cup unsalted butter, chilled, cut
    into pieces, or 4 ounces lard,
    chilled
3 to 4 tablespoons ice water

Combine the flour and salt in a medium mixing bowl. Using your fingers or a pastry cutter, cut in the butter, working very quickly so that it does not become too warm, until the mixture resembles coarse cornmeal. Make a well in the center of the flour and pour in 3 tablespoons of the water. Use your fingers to mix the dough together quickly; add more water if necessary for the dough to come together. Press the dough into a ball, wrap it in plastic wrap, and refrigerate it for at least 30 minutes or up to 2 hours. Roll out the dough to a diameter of about 12 inches, and press it into a 9-inch pie pan. Refrigerate, covered, until ready to bake or fill, but not much longer than overnight.

PEARS POACHED IN RED WINE

The pristine flavor of a poached fruit dessert does not eclipse the meal itself, as heavier desserts do, and the clean texture of the fruit cleanses the palate, leaving you feeling refreshed rather than overfed. As is true in some other places as well, there is never a time when pears are not in season in California, so this dish can be made at any time of the year. Use whatever variety of pear is at its peak.

SERVES 4

1 bottle (750 ml) red wine, such as gamay beaujolais, zinfandel, or a Rhône-style blend
1 cup sugar
2 2-inch cinnamon sticks
4 whole cloves
½ teaspoon whole black peppercorns
3 cardamom seeds
2 whole allspice berries
4 ripe pears, peeled, stems and cores intact

Combine the wine, sugar, cinnamon, cloves, peppercorns, cardamom, and allspice in a nonreactive saucepan that will hold the pears snugly. Bring to a boil over medium heat, and stir until the sugar is dissolved. Reduce the heat to low, lower the pears carefully into the liquid until they are fully submerged, and simmer, uncovered, poaching the pears until they are tender but not mushy, 15 to 30 minutes, depend-

ing on the ripeness of the pears and on their variety. Remove the pan from the heat and allow the pears to cool slightly in the liquid.

Transfer the pears to 4 warmed serving plates. Return the cooking liquid to high heat, and reduce the liquid by about three quarters, or until it forms a thin syrup, 15

The Original 27 Counties

Mendocino County stretches along the Pacific Coast from Sonoma County north to Humboldt County. The Eel and the Russian, its major rivers, run parallel to each other, north–south, most of the length of the county. The first European settlers came from Finland and Sweden; they were followed by Germans and Italians. Around Boonville, in the southern part of the county, an unusual dialect known as Boontling is still heard. Hopland is named for the hops that once grew in profusion here. Today, there is a booming wine industry, particularly in the Anderson Valley, where chardonnay and pinot noir grapes, both used in sparkling and still wines, thrive in the coastal fog. Mendocino County, with its dramatic coastline and lush forests, is a popular tourist area, with abundant hunting and fishing as well. There are numerous pear orchards, small-scale farms, and artisan food producers. Café Beaujolais in the village of Mendocino attracts visitors from all over the country.

to 20 minutes. Strain the sauce and discard the spices. Spoon sauce over the pears, and serve immediately.

Variations:

Before cooking them, cut the pears in half and core them. Serve with White Chocolate Ice Cream (page 463).

Before cooking them, cut the pears in half, core them, and cut them into 1-inch chunks. (This will reduce their cooking time considerably.) Garnish with toasted almonds and sprigs of fresh mint, and serve with biscotti.

PEAR GINGERBREAD

Who doesn't love gingerbread? Its aroma as it cooks is nearly enough to drive one mad with hunger. Serve it warm, at room temperature, or chilled, and be sure, after removing it from its baking pan, to use your finger to scrape up any of the gooey residue left in the pan—it is delicious.

SERVES 6 TO 8

½ cup unsalted butter, melted
½ cup (packed) brown sugar
1 egg
1 tablespoon grated fresh ginger
2 teaspoons grated orange zest
2½ cups sifted all-purpose flour

1½ teaspoons baking soda
1 tablespoon dry mustard
1 teaspoon ground ginger
1 teaspoon ground cinnamon
½ teaspoon kosher salt
½ cup light molasses
½ cup honey

The Original 27 Counties

Tuolumne County is one of the most strikingly beautiful regions of the state, with numerous lakes as well as a large portion of Yosemite National Park within its borders. In 1923, the Tuolumne River was dammed and the spectacular Hetch Hetchy Valley in the northwestern part of the park was flooded in order to create the reservoir that provides water to San Francisco and the Bay Area. The valley's acorns were among the native ingredients gathered by the Miwok and Yokuts people who originally lived here. The acorns were an important staple that was ground into flour, cooked into a porridge much as polenta is cooked today, and baked in the sun into dense breads. Every now and then you hear rumors that Hetch Hetchy may be allowed to return to its natural state, but, with California's ongoing water shortages, it is unlikely to happen soon. Cattle ranches—beef is one of California's most important agricultural products—dominate the area's agriculture.

½ cup boiling water
½ cup fresh orange juice
2 ripe pears, peeled, cored, and cut
   into large dice

Preheat the oven to 350°F. Butter a 9-inch round cake pan.

Pour the butter into a large mixing bowl, add the brown sugar, and mix well. Stir in the egg, fresh ginger, and orange zest. Set the mixture aside. In a separate bowl, sift together the flour, baking soda, mustard, ground ginger, cinnamon, and salt. In a third bowl, mix together the molasses, honey, boiling water, and orange juice. Fold in the pears.

Add one third of the dry ingredients to the butter mixture, stir well, then add one third of the molasses mixture, and stir well again. Add another one third of each, then the final third of each, stirring well after each addition. Pour the batter into the pan. Bake for about 1 hour, or until the center springs back when lightly touched. Remove the gingerbread from the oven, let it cool on a rack for at least 10 minutes, and remove it from the pan. Serve warm.

California's Black Gold

Louis Pellier, a French horticulturist, was about to settle in Chile when he got word of the discovery of gold at Sutter's Mill. He was lured north, and for a time he was successful mining for gold. Yet the harsh winters of the mountains sent him to the milder climates of San Francisco and San Jose, where he returned to his horticultural background and began planting fruit trees. It was when he returned home to marry his French sweetheart that he changed California agricultural history. Before Pellier, there were no prunes in California. When he returned with his bride, he brought with him cuttings of *prune d'agen*, a variety of plum ideal for drying. These cuttings, planted in the fertile Santa Clara Valley, gave California's prune industry its start. By 1880, there were fifty-four hundred acres planted with the fruit, and Pellier died—more or less of a broken heart, the story goes, over his failed marriage—just as the industry was on the brink of enormous growth. His younger brother took over the orchards and went on to found Mirassou Vineyards in San Jose. For years, the name of Louis Pellier and his role in the prune industry was lost, and his brother received all of the credit. But today, the site of his first garden is commemorated as Pellier Park in San Jose, and he is regarded as the father of the state's prune industry. There now are about a hundred thousand acres of prune orchards in California, most north of Sacramento, though there is significant acreage in the Central Valley, too.

THIRTY-SIX LADY PRUNE CAKE

The exact details have been lost, but some thirty years ago the California Prune Board held a recipe contest. Thirty-six of the entries were identical, each from a farmer's wife who said this cake was her favorite way to use prunes.

SERVES 12

PRUNE CAKE
2 cups prunes, pitted
1 cup olive oil
1½ cups sugar
3 eggs, lightly beaten
1 teaspoon ground cinnamon
1 teaspoon ground allspice
1 teaspoon ground nutmeg
1 teaspoon baking soda
1 teaspoon kosher salt
1 teaspoon vanilla extract
1 cup buttermilk
2 cups all-purpose flour, sifted
1 cup walnut pieces

BUTTERMILK GLAZE
1 cup sugar
½ cup buttermilk
½ teaspoon baking soda
1 tablespoon light corn syrup
½ cup butter

Place the prunes in a medium saucepan and cover them with 1 cup of water. Bring to a boil, reduce the heat to low, and simmer them until they are tender, about 10 minutes. Remove from the heat, drain, and mash with a fork. Set aside.

Preheat the oven to 350°F. Butter a 13-by-9-inch baking pan.

Beat together the oil and sugar in a large mixing bowl until smooth. Stir in the eggs, spices, baking soda, salt, and vanilla. Add the buttermilk, flour, and walnuts, and mix quickly until fairly smooth. Fold in the prunes. Pour the batter into the baking pan. Bake for about 45 minutes, or until a toothpick inserted into the center of the cake comes out clean. Remove from the oven, and, using a fork, prick the cake evenly over its entire surface. Set it aside to cool for 5 minutes, remove it from the pan, and place it on a cooling rack.

While the cake is baking, make the glaze: Place the sugar, buttermilk, baking

Martin Seely's Prune Monkeys

In 1905, Martin Seely thought he had found the answer to the rising cost of labor in his Santa Clara Valley prune orchard. Seely imported five hundred monkeys from Panama, divided them into gangs of fifty, and assigned a human foreman to oversee each gang. Off they went, scurrying to the orchard and up the trees to gather Seely's prunes, which they did, promptly and efficiently. They also ate the fruit, every bit of it, as fast as they could pick it, leaving nothing behind for Seely.

soda, corn syrup, and butter in a large saucepan over medium heat, and stir constantly until the butter is melted. Continue to cook, stirring occasionally, for about 45 minutes, until the mixture turns a darkish brown and forms a soft ball when a little of it is dropped into ice water.

While the cake is still warm, set it on a plate and pour the glaze over it. Serve immediately, or refrigerate in an airtight container for up to 1 week.

QUINCE POACHED IN WHITE WINE AND HONEY

Quince is a fascinating fruit. Its pale yellow flesh is astringent when eaten raw. When it is cooked it turns pink and it becomes seductively sweet. It is excellent peeled, sliced, and sautéed in butter for use in pies, tarts, and strudels. Yet perhaps because it is best when it is cooked, quince has never become particularly popular, and it can be difficult to find. I am fortunate enough to be able to get mine fresh off the tree outside my living-room window.

SERVES 4

1 cup honey
3 cups dry white wine, such as
   sauvignon blanc or chardonnay
½ vanilla bean, split lengthwise
4 whole cloves
3 1-inch-long strips of lemon zest
4 to 6 quince, peeled

Combine the honey and wine in a nonreactive saucepan over medium heat and stir until the honey is dissolved. Add the vanilla bean, cloves, and lemon zest. Carefully submerge the quince in the liquid, and simmer them until they are tender, 30 to 40 minutes, depending on their size. Remove the pan from the heat and let the quince cool slightly in the liquid.

Using a slotted spoon, transfer the quince to a serving platter. Return the pan to the heat, and simmer until the liquid is reduced by two thirds, about 20 minutes. Strain the sauce, discarding the vanilla, cloves, and lemon zest. Serve the quince at room temperature, with the hot poaching liquid spooned over them.

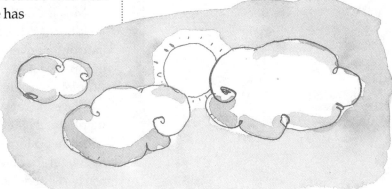

The Original 27 Counties

The area that is now **Santa Barbara County** was once the homeland of Chumash Indians. Today the city of Santa Barbara reveals its Spanish influences in its architecture, street names, and cuisine. An hour north you'll find the planned settlement of Solvang, where traditional Danish architecture and authentic Danish cooking can be found. The state's first walnut groves were planted in the area around 1770; in the early twentieth century the walnut industry shifted north, where the climate is more suitable. A small amount of olive oil is still produced from trees planted by the first Spanish settlers. The county is home to citrus and apple orchards, strawberry fields, and avocado groves, and it is the only place in the state where bananas are grown commercially. Other agriculture includes ranching, poultry farming, and seed production. In the last decade or so, the region's viticulture has flourished. With wineries such as Zaca Mesa, Byron, Sanford, and Mosby, and vineyards such as the highly acclaimed Bien Nacido Vineyard, one of the state's best sources for pinot noir and chardonnay, Santa Barbara County has established itself as an important viticultural area.

BRIE WITH STRAWBERRIES, CHOCOLATE, AND GARLIC

The idea of pairing garlic with chocolate might shock some, but in fact the combination is quite good when the garlic is mellowed by slow cooking and sweetened with a little butter and sugar.

SERVES 6 TO 8

2 tablespoons unsalted butter
1 head of garlic, cloves separated, peeled, and cut into slivers
2 tablespoons sugar
4 ounces bittersweet chocolate, chopped or broken into pieces
2 8-ounce rounds ripe brie, at room temperature
2 pints strawberries
1 baguette, sliced thin

Preheat the oven to 275°F.

Melt the butter in a small ovenproof pan or skillet. Add the garlic, shake the pan to distribute it evenly, and sprinkle the sugar on top. Roast in the oven until the garlic is completely tender, about 20 minutes.

Place the rounds of brie on a large serving platter. Heat the chocolate in the top of a double boiler over simmering, not boiling, water for about 2 minutes, or until it is nearly melted. Remove from the heat, and fold in the garlic. Pour the mixture over both rounds of brie. Arrange the straw-berries and baguette slices on the platter, and serve immediately.

STRAWBERRY-RHUBARB TART

Strawberries and rhubarb are har-vested early in the spring and are often the first splash of color after the pale pears and apples of winter. As other fruits come into harvest, make this tart with sliced nectarines, apricots, peaches, plums, or even passionfruit. The recipe for Pastry for Savory Tarts makes enough for 2 large tarts, while the filling in this recipe is enough for 1 large tart or 8 small ones. If you make a large one, freeze the remaining dough to use at another time.

MAKES 1 LARGE TART OR 8 SMALL TARTS

1½ pounds fresh rhubarb, peeled
1 pint strawberries, sliced
3 tablespoons all-purpose flour
1 to 1¼ cups sugar
Pastry for Savory Tarts (page 396), sweet Variation
2 tablespoons unsalted butter, melted
1 tablespoon sugar

Preheat the oven to 400°F.

Cut the rhubarb into 1-inch-long pieces. If any rhubarb is wider than 1 inch, cut it lengthwise in half. You should have about 5 cups. Place the rhubarb in a large

bowl, add the strawberries, and sprinkle with the flour and 1 cup of the sugar. Toss gently until all of the rhubarb and straw-berries are coated with sugar and flour. Taste, and add the remaining ¼ cup sugar if you prefer a sweeter mixture. Let the mixture rest for at least 10 minutes.

Remove the dough circles from the re-frigerator, leaving them on the parchment-lined baking sheet. If you are making a large tart, transfer the fruit mixture to 1 large circle; if you are making small tarts, divide the fruit mixture among the smaller circles; in either case, leave a 2-inch margin around the edges. Using your fingers, gen-tly fold the edges up and over so that they extend about 1 inch over the fruit. Pleat the edges as you fold them up. Brush the edges with the melted butter, and sprinkle with the 1 tablespoon sugar.

Bake until the pastry is golden brown and the fruit soft and bubbly, 40 to 45 minutes for large tarts, 35 to 40 minutes for individual tarts. Transfer the tart or tarts to a rack to cool. Serve warm or at room temperature.

Strawberries in Their Own Juice

Rinse as many strawberries as you would like, drain them thoroughly, and place them in a bowl. Sprinkle with 1 tablespoon of granulated sugar for each pint of strawberries, toss gently, and refrigerate for at least 1 hour. The berries will make their own juice.

GINGER-CHÈVRE TART

*H*ere is cheesecake taken to the next level, a thin, elegant tart that is perfumed with plenty of fresh and candied ginger. I often serve the tart with Rhubarb-Strawberry Chutney (page 426) or Green Tomato–Pear Chutney (page 426) alongside.

MAKES 1 9- OR 10-INCH TART

CRUST
½ cup unsalted butter, at room temperature
¼ cup powdered sugar
1 teaspoon vanilla extract
1¼ cups all-purpose flour
¾ cup toasted walnuts

FILLING
10 ounces chèvre
½ cup sugar
1 egg
1 egg yolk
¾ cup heavy cream
2 tablespoons grated fresh ginger
⅔ cup coarse-chopped candied ginger

Make the crust: Place the butter and powdered sugar in a food processor and process until they are well blended.

Add the vanilla and flour, and process again until the flour is incorporated into the butter. Add the walnuts, and pulse the processor several times to work the walnuts in. Transfer the dough to a bowl, cover, and refrigerate for 1 hour. Clean the processor's work bowl.

Preheat the oven to 400°F.

Press the chilled dough into a 9- or 10-inch tart pan with a removable bottom. Bake for 15 to 20 minutes, or until the crust is lightly browned. Remove from the oven and let cool thoroughly before filling.

When ready to bake, preheat the oven to 350°F.

Make the filling: Place the chèvre, sugar, egg, and egg yolk in the food processor and pulse until smooth. Add the cream and fresh ginger, and process again until smooth; do not overprocess. Spread the candied ginger over the baked pie crust, and pour the chèvre custard over the candied ginger. Bake the tart for about 25 minutes, or until the custard is firm and the top pale golden; do not overbake. Remove from the oven and let cool slightly. Cut into wedges, and serve.

GOLDEN CHEESECAKE

*T*his is an unusual cheesecake I first encountered at a cheese tasting conducted by the California Milk Advisory Board. It is nothing like other cheesecakes, and its sweet and savory flavors are remarkably good. Try to find old-fashioned cream cheese—without gum or other additives—to use in this recipe; its texture is superior to other types of cream cheese.

SERVES 10 TO 12

1 tablespoon unsalted butter, at room temperature

FIRST LAYER

1 pound cream cheese, preferably old-fashioned, at room temperature
½ cup (4 ounces) ricotta cheese
¾ cup sugar
2 teaspoons vanilla extract
¼ teaspoon kosher salt
4 egg whites, beaten to soft peaks

SECOND LAYER

2 cups (8 ounces) grated sharp cheddar cheese
8 ounces cream cheese, preferably old-fashioned, at room temperature
1 cup sugar
¼ teaspoon kosher salt
4 egg yolks, lightly beaten
¼ cup dessert wine, such as Muscat

Preheat the oven to 350°F. Rub the inside of an 8-inch springform pan, or a deep tart pan with a removable bottom, with the butter.

Make the first layer: In the bowl of an electric mixer fitted with the paddle, combine the cream cheese and ricotta until smooth. Add the sugar, vanilla, and salt, and mix until well blended. Fold in the egg whites, and pour the mixture into the pan, using a rubber spatula to spread the mixture evenly. Set aside, and clean the bowl of the mixer.

Make the second layer: In the bowl of the mixer, combine the cheddar and cream cheese, mixing until they form a smooth paste. In a small bowl, whisk together the sugar, salt, and egg yolks until smooth and creamy. Add the wine, and mix well. Add the egg mixture to the cheddar mixture and mix well until fully incorporated. Spread this mixture over the white mixture in the pan. Draw a knife blade through the two several times to create a marbling effect, but do not actually mix together.

Bring a tea kettle filled with water to a boil. Place the pan with the cheesecake in a larger pan and set both pans in the oven. Pour boiling water into the larger pan so that it comes about half-way up the sides of the cheesecake pan. Bake until the top of the cake is golden and is almost firmly set, 1 to 1¼ hours. Carefully remove the pans from the oven, lift the cheesecake pan out of the water, and set it on a cooling rack. Let it cool until it is just warm to the touch, about 1½ hours. Release the sides if you have used a springform pan, or, if you have used a tart pan, lift out the tart. Wrap

California's Parade of Foods

"In times like these every woman knows the importance of giving her family foods that build health and energy. She knows also that penny-wise economy is very much in order. California's golden sunshine and good earth produce a perennial parade of incomparable foodstuffs marching toward your table. It behooves every one of us to get in step with the parade of home-grown foods, building our State and encouraging our growers by making use of California-grown oranges, lemons, raisins, apples, peaches, pears, prunes, olives, walnuts, almonds, meats—and California-Grown Sugar! There's nothing finer anywhere. Use it in preparing wartime energy-building foods, from daily desserts to your season's canning.

"For your family's enjoyment and well-being, I give you these tested and timely recipes. By the way, my motto for the duration is: 'Measure Sugar Carefully.'"

Katherine Kerry, *California's Parade of Foods*, a World War II–era recipe pamphlet

CRANBERRY-WALNUT PIE

Walnuts were introduced to California by Spanish missionaries around 1770, but it wasn't until trees were imported from Chile in 1867 that the commercial industry was launched. Today, walnuts grow in several regions of the state, including along the north coast, in the Sierra Nevada foothills, and in the Central Valley. Some of the best walnuts in the state can be found at farmers' markets in October. The cranberries add a tangy flavor and a rosy hue to traditional walnut pie. For a more classic version, see the Variation.

SERVES 6 TO 8

1 recipe Pastry Dough for Pies (page 444)
3 eggs
½ cup (packed) brown sugar
1 cup light corn syrup
½ cup unsalted butter, melted
1 teaspoon vanilla extract
1 tablespoon brandy
1 tablespoon fresh orange juice
2 teaspoons minced orange zest
1 teaspoon ground cinnamon
¼ teaspoon kosher salt
¾ cup fresh cranberries, minced
1 cup (4 ounces) walnuts, toasted and chopped coarse

the cheesecake with plastic wrap, and refrigerate for at least 5 hours or overnight before serving.

Roll out the dough and press it into a

9- or 10-inch pie dish or tart pan with a removable bottom. Cover, and refrigerate for at least 30 minutes.

Preheat the oven to 350°F. Beat the eggs in a medium bowl until they are frothy. Whisk in the brown sugar and the corn syrup. Whisk in the butter, vanilla, brandy, orange juice, orange zest, cinnamon, and salt. Fold in the cranberries and walnuts, and pour the filling over the dough. Bake for 40 to 45 minutes, or until the the edges of the crust are golden and the pie is set. Let the pie rest for at least 2 hours before serving. If you have used a tart pan, remove the pie from the pan when serving.

Variation:

To make a classic walnut pie, omit the orange juice, orange zest, and cranberries, and increase the brandy to 2 tablespoons and the walnuts to 1½ cups.

SODA SPRINGS MUD PIES

From late November through the early spring, thousands of skiers head to the Sierras in northeastern California to indulge in their favorite sport. When skiers return to the lodge, chilly and pleasantly exhausted, they indulge in big meals, warm alcoholic potions,

The Original 27 Counties

Monterey County, the land of lettuce, artichokes, strawberries, sardines, and jack cheese, was once home to Costanoan and Esselen Native Americans. Between 1771 and 1791, three missions were established along Monterey Bay. The county stretches along the coast for a hundred miles, from the Pajara River in the north down through Big Sur, one of the most breathtakingly beautiful coastlines in the world. The eastern boundaries include the Coast Range and Diablo Range mountains. Inland, Salinas and King City are important agribusiness centers; the county produces more lettuce than any other area its size in the world. Home cooking in the county makes abundant use of local artichokes. Look for them deep-fried; in quiches, frittatas, gratins, pies, and casseroles; and in sweet artichoke cakes with walnuts and raisins. An eastern portion of the original Monterey County was separated off to form San Benito County, one of the best places in the state to forage for authentic Mexican food—and a wonderful place to get invited home for dinner.

and rich desserts, such as this pie, which came to me from some friends who are avid skiers in Soda Springs.

MAKES 2 9-INCH PIES, TO SERVE 8 TO 12

PIE DOUGH

2 cups all-purpose flour

2 egg yolks

2 tablespoons sugar

1 cup unsalted butter, chilled, cut into
   pieces

FILLING

1 cup unsalted butter, chilled, cut into
   pieces

8 ounces unsweetened chocolate

8 eggs

3 cups sugar

1 tablespoon vanilla extract

Make the pie dough: Sift the flour into a large bowl. Make a well in the center, and add the egg yolks and sugar. Using your fingers, mix the ingredients together. Quickly work the butter into the flour mixture. Press into a ball, wrap in plastic wrap, and chill for 1 hour.

Remove the dough from the refrigerator, divide it in half, and roll out each piece to fit a 9-inch pie dish. Transfer each piece to a pie dish, trim the edges, and refrigerate for at least 1 hour.

Preheat the oven to 325°F.

Make the filling: Melt the butter and chocolate in the top of a double boiler over simmering water. When both are melted, stir them together. Set aside to cool just slightly. Beat the eggs in a medium bowl until they are thick and pale yellow, mix in the sugar and vanilla, and add the chocolate mixture. Pour half of the filling into each pie crust. Bake the pies for 30 minutes. Remove from the oven and let cool to room temperature before serving.

The Original 27 Counties

• •

Shasta County, once home to Native American Modoc peoples, encompasses the northernmost portion of the Sacramento Valley. Gold mining here was brief, and it wasn't long before lumber, poultry farming, cattle ranching, and field crops became the most important industries. More than half of the land is within national forests. Lassen Volcanic National Park contains Lassen Peak, one of very few active volcanoes in the continental United States. The extensive Shasta Lake, a major recreation area, was created when the 602-foot Shasta Dam was built as part of the Central Valley Project. Just north of the county line in Siskiyou County is the majestic Mount Shasta, a 14,162-foot solitary volcanic peak that has been the subject of mysterious tales and legends since the days of the Modocs. The Lost Continent of Lemuria, with a network of cities inhabited by white-robed prophets and a big cache of gold, is said to lie under the mountain. Some explorers claim to have spotted large reptilian creatures, members of a supposed race of humanoids called Lizard People. Stories of a race of giants that lie buried near the mountain, and countless sightings of ghosts, elves, and space aliens, continue to intrigue visitors to the area.

KIMBERLY'S TRUFFLES

K imberly Every, whose family founded Kozlowski Farms in Healdsburg, created these luscious truffles when she was eleven years old. She won first place in a berry-cooking contest for her efforts.

MAKES ABOUT 5 DOZEN TRUFFLES

1 pound bittersweet chocolate, broken into pieces

½ cup raspberry liqueur, such as framboise
10 egg yolks
1 cup butter, cut into pieces, at room temperature
3 cups powdered sugar, sifted
¾ cup unsweetened cocoa powder
60 perfect raspberries, optional

Combine the chocolate and the liqueur in the top of a double boiler over simmering water. When the chocolate has melted, remove the mixture from the heat. Whisk in the egg yolks, 1 at a time. Add the butter, a piece or two at a time, stirring well after each addition. Add the powdered sugar,

Father Chocolate

On June 18, 1852, Ghirardely & Girard opened in San Francisco near what is now Fisherman's Wharf. By 1855 the company was processing chocolate and manufacturing syrups, liquors, and coffee, which they peddled in the streets of the city. Eventually Girard was dropped from the name, and the spelling was changed to Ghirardelli, possibly to make pronunciation easier.

In the 1860s, an employee—records do not indicate who—of Domingo Ghirardelli's chocolate factory made a discovery that was to secure the company's success and its founder's renown. Someone noticed that if you hung a cloth bag of processed chocolate in a warm room, the cocoa butter would drip out and leave behind a residue that could be ground into

chocolate powder. The powder initially was called "Broma," and in its first year on the market, 1867, the company sold 571 pounds. Eventually it was renamed ground chocolate, and, within a few years, Ghirardelli was selling a million pounds a year. Domingo Ghirardelli died on January 17, 1894, in Rapallo, Italy, while visiting his daughter and her husband.

On April 18, 1906, much of San Francisco was destroyed by earthquake and fire. Ten days later, the chocolate company ran an advertisement in the *San Francisco Chronicle* announcing that their stock was uninjured and that they would resume manufacturing within a few days. Today, Ghirardelli Square is a major tourist attraction for visitors to Fisherman's Wharf.

¾ cup at a time, mixing very thoroughly with a wooden spoon after each addition. When all of the sugar has been incorporated and the mixture is smooth, refrigerate it, covered, until it is chilled through, at least 2 hours.

To form the truffles, remove the chilled chocolate mixture from the refrigerator and place the cocoa powder in a medium bowl. Coat your hands with a little of the cocoa, place about 1½ teaspoons of the truffle mixture in the palm of one hand, and roll between both palms until it forms a ball. Drop it into the bowl of cocoa, shake the bowl until the truffle is fully coated with cocoa, and set the truffle on a tray. If you like, make a slight indentation in the top and set a raspberry in it, pressing it so that it stays in place. When all of the truffles have been rolled, refrigerate them until ready to serve.

Vanilla Sugar

Place 4 cups of sugar and 1 whole vanilla bean, split lengthwise in half, in an airtight container. Cover tightly, and store in a cool, dark cupboard for at least 3 weeks before using. You can replace what you use with fresh sugar until you notice that the aroma of vanilla is beginning to decline; I would not add more than an additional 4 cups of sugar over 3 to 4 months. Serve with sliced oranges (see page 442), sliced grapefruit, or blackberries; in fruit salads; in toppings for cobblers; or to sweeten tea.

ANGEL'S WINGS

When George Bonacich, an apricot farmer in the Santa Clara Valley, was in the Korean War, his Croatian-born mother made these incredibly delicate cookies, called *hrustules*, and sent them to him. Many would be broken, of course, but some survived intact, gossamer talismans of home.

MAKES ABOUT 100 COOKIES

6 eggs, beaten, at room temperature
1 cup unsalted butter, at room temperature
1 cup whiskey, or more as necessary
Pinch of sugar
6 cups all-purpose flour, or more
Corn oil or peanut oil, for deep-frying
1 cup powdered sugar, for dusting

Beat together the eggs and butter in a medium bowl until smooth. Add the whiskey and sugar, and stir in the flour to make a smooth dough. Add more whiskey or more flour until the dough is the proper consistency to roll out. Break off a piece of dough about the size of an orange and roll it out on a floured surface until it is very, very thin. Using a pastry wheel or pizza cutter, cut the dough into 6-by-1-inch strips.

Pour 1 inch of oil into a heavy skillet over medium-high heat. Heat the oil until it is hot but not smoking, about 350°F. Place the powdered sugar in a medium strainer.

Fry the strips, being sure not to crowd the pan, until they just begin to color. Using a slotted spoon, transfer the strips to absorbent paper and drain briefly. Dust liberally with powdered sugar. Continue until all of the dough has been fried.

More Greek Easter Memories

"While the most of the action and dancing took place in the backyard, I would retreat to the living room where the desserts were. There would be the festive Easter breads with traditional red eggs baked into them; baklava; the phyllo-and-custard dish *galato bouriko*; and my favorites, *kourabiedes*, shortbread-type cookies often shaped like stars and always covered with powdered sugar.

"As the lamb turned and the dancers circled outside, I would slyly take a kourabiede or two—there were ample quantities, so I figured no one would be the wiser. One year I grew quite bold and ate fourteen. I thought I would go undiscovered until my aunt asked me if I had been at the dessert table; though my mouth said no, I had neglected to examine my navy sweater vest. I had so much powdered sugar covering me, I looked like someone auditioning for a part as a drug lord on 'Miami Vice.'

"For a number of years, my aunt kept the desserts in the basement, not so much to keep me from them but to share a laugh at my pilfering."

Nick Topolos, San Francisco

NICK'S EASTER COOKIES

The recipe for these little Greek cookies, called *kourabiedes*, came to me from my friend Nick Topolos's mother. Although not herself Greek, Nick's mother has a great appreciation for the food and has developed the ability to decipher Greek cookbooks. Nick tells me that he and his mother believe that Greek women conspire to keep their recipes secret, leaving out key ingredients and steps. "What we learned over time," he says, "was to buy a number of Greek cookbooks and compare recipes to divine what was missing." When serving, Nick says to be sure to make all nearby children wear dark clothing (see box, at left).

MAKES ABOUT 36 TO 48 COOKIES

2 cups unsalted butter, at room temperature
½ cup powdered sugar
1 egg yolk
2 teaspoons vanilla extract
5 to 6 cups cake flour
Powdered sugar, for dusting

Preheat the oven to 350°F. Line a baking sheet with parchment paper.

Using a heavy-duty mixer, beat the butter until it is light, fluffy, and nearly white, about 10 minutes. Add the sugar, and beat thoroughly. Add the egg yolk, beat thoroughly, then add the vanilla, and beat thoroughly again. Add the flour, ½ cup at a time, until a soft dough that can be handled easily is formed. Form the dough into walnut-size balls. Flatten each ball in your

hand and pinch it while turning it to form a star or crescent shape. Place the cookies on the baking sheet, and bake for about 15 minutes, until their color has changed a little.

Dust a sheet of aluminum foil with sifted powdered sugar. Transfer the hot cookies to the foil, and sift more powdered sugar on top of them. Place the cookies in individual muffin papers and store them in an airtight tin.

Life in Solvang

When Rikki Rasmussen left her home town of Solvang at the age of seventeen, she was stunned, she says, by how the rest of America ate. Until then, everything she had ever had had been made from scratch; she knew nothing of packaged mixes for brownies, cakes, and cornbread. She had never eaten a doughnut. The town didn't even have a pizzeria, so, when she and her friends got their driver's licences, they would drive an hour south to Santa Barbara for pizza.

Solvang is a planned Danish community, and Danes, Rikka says, love a party and love to drink, especially *aquavit*. Rikki's family and their neighbors cooked and ate lots of seafood, meat, and potatoes. Solvang had wonderful delicatessens full of pickled herring and Danish sausages, and bakeries that used real butter in everything.

"I still miss my grandmother's butter cookies," she says. When her paternal grandfather asked her maternal grandmother for a cookie recipe, Rikki reports, Grandma Martina ticked off the ingredients quickly.

"What about flour? Isn't there any flour in the cookies?" Grandpa asked.

"Any damn fool knows you put flour in," Martina responded.

WALNUT–BLACK PEPPER BISCOTTI

Biscotti have become so prevalent these days, with so many bakeries and purveyors selling them commercially, that people seem to have forgotten how easy they are to make at home.

MAKES 36 TO 40 BISCOTTI

3 tablespoons walnut oil or olive oil
2 eggs
1 cup (packed) dark brown sugar
1 to 2 teaspoons coarse-ground black pepper
2 cups all-purpose flour
1 teaspoon baking soda
½ teaspoon kosher salt
¼ teaspoon ground nutmeg
Pinch of ground cardamom
1 cup coarse-chopped walnuts, lightly toasted

Preheat the oven to 375°F. Butter and flour a baking sheet.

Whisk together the oil, eggs, brown sugar, and pepper (use 2 teaspoons pepper if you want a stronger flavor) in a medium mixing bowl until the mixture is smooth and creamy. In a separate bowl, combine the flour, baking soda, salt, nutmeg, and cardamom. Slowly stir the dry ingredients and the walnuts into the egg mixture. The dough will be stiff and sticky.

Sprinkle flour over a work surface. Divide the dough into 3 pieces. Form each piece into a rope about 10 inches long and 2½ inches in diameter. Set the ropes on the baking sheet, and use your fingertips to flatten the top of each rope just slightly. Bake for 25 minutes.

Remove the loaves from the oven and cool them on racks for about 5 minutes. Transfer to a clean work surface and cut each loaf into diagonal slices ½ inch wide. Place the slices, cut side down, on a clean, dry baking sheet, and bake them for 10 minutes. Turn them, so that the opposite cut side is down, and bake for 10 minutes more, until they are lightly toasted.

Let the biscotti cool. Store them in airtight jars or tins.

MANGO GELATO

Mangos do not grow in California, but they are popular and widely available. Mangos served with sticky rice sweetened with coconut cream and coconut milk is a popular dessert in many of the state's Thai restaurants. Mango gelato is common, too, and easy to make at home. Serve it, if you like, atop a bed of fresh raspberries, blackberries, or olallieberries.

MAKES ABOUT 3 CUPS

1 cup sugar
2 cups mango puree (see Note)
Juice of 1 to 2 limes

Combine the sugar and 1 cup of water in a heavy saucepan over high heat. Stir until the sugar is completely dissolved. Remove from the heat and let cool to room temperature.

Place the mango puree, the juice of 1 lime, and the sugar syrup in a blender. Blend until the mixture is smooth. Taste, and add more lime juice for a tarter mixture. Refrigerate for at least 2 hours or overnight.

Freeze the mango mixture in an ice cream maker according to the manufacturer's instructions. Store, tightly covered, in the freezer overnight before serving.

NOTE: To make 2 cups mango puree, peel 2 large or 3 medium-to-large mangos, cut the flesh from the seeds, and place the flesh in a food processor. Pulse until you have a puree. Or make the puree by mashing the flesh with a fork.

GINGER ICE CREAM

Ginger ice cream is a common and welcome dessert throughout California in Chinese restaurants and homes.

MAKES ABOUT 2 QUARTS

6 cups half-and-half
4 ounces fresh ginger, peeled and
   grated or minced
6 egg yolks
½ cup sugar
½ cup (packed) dark brown sugar
½ teaspoon kosher salt
2 teaspoons vanilla extract
½ cup candied ginger, minced

Scald the half-and-half in a medium saucepan over medium heat. Remove it from the heat, stir in the fresh ginger, and let steep for 30 minutes.

Strain the half-and-half, discard the ginger, wipe the saucepan clean, and return the half-and-half to it. Whisk together the egg yolks, sugar, brown sugar, and salt in a medium bowl until they are thoroughly mixed and very creamy. Slowly pour the mixture into the scalded cream, whisking all the while. Set the saucepan over medium heat, and stir with a whisk until the mixture thickens. Remove from the heat immediately, whisk in the vanilla, and continue to whisk quickly as the mixture cools slightly. Cover the custard, and refrigerate it for several hours or overnight.

Freeze in an ice cream maker according to the manufacturer's instructions. Toward the end of the freezing time, fold in the candied ginger. Store, tightly covered, in the freezer until ready to serve.

Mrs. Hoover's California Persimmon Ice Cream

"Peel 6 large well-ripe California persimmons; mash well with two cups sugar; add juice of two oranges and one lemon, a pinch of soda between fingers, a few drops of vanilla. Beat all well together; add to that 4 quarts of cream. Freeze at once, turning slowly."

Recipe from Mrs. Herbert Hoover, contributed to *The Pals Club Cook Book*, published by the Lodi, California, Women's Club in 1941. Proceeds from the sale of the booklet benefited the war effort.

LAVENDER ICE CREAM

Surrounding the town of Grasse, in the hills above Nice in the south of France, vast fields of lavender saturate the air with their perfume in June, when the flowers are in bloom. The utterly intoxicating aroma can be enjoyed in California now, too. Matanzas Creek Winery in southeastern Santa Rosa, in Sonoma County, and the Bonny Doon Lavender Farm in the tiny town of Bonny Doon, in Santa Cruz County, both have vast lavender fields that bloom in the late spring and early summer. Boony Doon Lavender Farm is not open to the public, but Matanzas Creek is open daily, and celebrates its lavender with a festival each year in June. The winery sells a variety of lavender products, including culinary-grade lavender, lavender spice mixtures, and lavender tea.

MAKES ABOUT 2 QUARTS

6 cups half-and-half
¾ cup culinary lavender flowers, available in health food stores and natural foods markets, and by mail order (see Resources)
½ teaspoon minced rosemary
Zest of 1 lemon
6 egg yolks
¾ cup dark honey, such as lavender honey
½ teaspoon kosher salt

Scald the half-and-half in a medium saucepan over medium heat. Remove it from the heat, stir in the lavender flowers, rosemary, and lemon zest, and let steep until cool. Cover the mixture, and refrigerate it for several hours or overnight.

Strain the half-and-half into a saucepan, and heat through. Whisk together the egg yolks, honey, and salt in a small bowl until the mixture is thoroughly combined. Slowly pour the mixture into the half-and-half, whisking all the while. Set the saucepan over medium heat, and stir the mixture with a whisk until it begins to thicken. Remove the pan from the heat immediately, and continue to whisk quickly as the mixture cools slightly. Cover the custard, and refrigerate it for several hours or overnight.

Freeze in an ice cream maker according to the manufacturer's instructions. Store, tightly covered, in the freezer until ready to serve.

WHITE CHOCOLATE ICE CREAM

Although Ghirardelli is the best-known of California's chocolate purveyors, Guittard Chocolate Company, founded in San Francisco in 1868, is nearly as old. The company still thrives today in Burlingame, south of the city. Guittard makes a fine white chocolate. White chocolate, which true chocolate lovers consider a travesty, is all about silky texture and the darkly seductive flavor of vanilla. Until recently, white chocolate referred not only to true white chocolate, made with cocoa butter, but also to mixtures, made with other vegetable fats, that were totally unlike the real thing. New regulations from the federal government now require white chocolate to be made exclusively with cocoa butter.

MAKES ABOUT 2 QUARTS

6 cups half-and-half
2 vanilla beans, split open lengthwise
6 egg yolks
¼ cup sugar
Pinch of salt
4 ounces white chocolate, chopped

Scald the half-and-half in a medium saucepan over medium heat. Remove the half-and-half from the heat, add the vanilla beans, and let steep for 1 hour.

Remove and discard the vanilla beans. Whisk together the egg yolks, sugar, and salt in a medium bowl until they are thoroughly mixed and very creamy. Slowly pour the mixture into the scalded half-and-half, whisking all the while. Set the saucepan over medium heat, and stir with a whisk until the mixture thickens. Remove the pan from the heat immediately, add the white chocolate, and stir gently with a wooden spoon until the chocolate is melted. Cover the custard, and refrigerate it for several hours or overnight.

Freeze in an ice cream maker according to the manufacturer's instructions. Store, tightly covered, in the freezer until ready to serve.

Chapter 15

BEVERAGES

BEVERAGES

CALIFORNIA LEMONADE

There's little reason to try to improve on simple fresh-made lemonade. But this version rounds out the lemons' flavor in an interesting way, with lemon grass and lemon basil. This lemonade is particularly good with Meyer lemons (see page 429), but they are not always easy to locate and you will be fine without them.

SERVES 4

2 stalks of lemon grass, bruised
2 sprigs of lemon basil
1 cup Simple Syrup (recipe follows)
1½ to 2 cups fresh lemon juice,
    preferably from Meyer lemons
3 cups spring water, cold
Ice cubes

Combine the lemon grass, lemon basil, and simple syrup in a small saucepan over medium heat. Bring to a boil, remove the mixture from the heat, and set aside to steep until cool. Strain into a pitcher, add the lemon juice and water, stir, and refrigerate, covered, until thoroughly chilled. Serve over ice.

Simple Syrup

Simple syrup is the ideal sweetener for cold beverages such as lemonade and agua fresca.

MAKES ABOUT 3 CUPS

4 cups sugar
2 cups water

Combine the sugar and water in a heavy saucepan over high heat. Bring to a boil, reduce the heat, and simmer, without stirring, for 4 to 5 minutes, or until the sugar is completely dissolved and the syrup is completely transparent. Remove from the heat, cover, and let cool. Store, covered, in the refrigerator, and use as needed.

RASPBERRY LEMONADE

This recipe comes very close to my memory of a fragrant, tangy juice I had many years ago at a farm stand near San Diego. I don't know how that wonderful elixir was made, but this recipe comes very close to my recollection of it.

SERVES 4 TO 6

2 cups fresh lemon juice
1 pint fresh raspberries, pureed and
    strained
¾ cup honey or Simple Syrup (recipe
    above), or more to taste
4 cups sparkling water, cold
Ice cubes

Combine the lemon juice, raspberry puree, and honey or simple syrup in a large glass jar, and stir well. Refrigerate until thoroughly chilled. To serve, fill tall glasses with ice, fill them two thirds full with sparkling water, and fill to the top with the raspberry mixture. Stir well, and serve immediately.

The Original 27 Counties

Contra Costa County, with impressive Mt. Diablo as its most prominent feature, once was home to Native American Bolbone peoples. Coal was mined here briefly in the mid-nineteenth century, and Port Costa, on the Carquinez Strait, where the Sacramento Delta opens into San Pablo Bay, was an early shipping port for the state's wheat industry. The nearby town of Crockett was the site of a major sugar refinery. Today, much of the county is fully part of the San Francisco–Oakland metropolitan area and is dominated by sprawling subdivisions, business parks, and shopping malls. Still, farming thrives in rural pockets here and there. There is a farm that specializes in heirloom dried beans, there are a few still-productive olive trees left from the nineteenth century, and even vineyards linger on. Up the delta from the major population centers of Concord and Walnut Creek you'll find the little town of Pittsburg, where if you're lucky you'll run into some townsfolk fishing for crawdads. The mud bugs are feted with their own annual festival, but the delta no longer can meet the demand—crawfish are flown in from Louisiana for the event.

STRAWBERRY LEMON COOLER

*U*se the sweetest, best-tasting strawberries you can find. Supermarket berries have gotten better in recent years, but many remain a pale imitation of a really good berry grown with care and harvested when fully ripe. Look for the best berries at local farmers' markets, or make the drink when you have an abundance of berries from your garden.

SERVES 4 TO 6

1 pint strawberries, pureed
½ cup Simple Syrup (page 469)
1 cup fresh lemon juice
Sparkling water, spring water, or
   Champagne, chilled
Sprigs of mint

Combine the the strawberry puree, simple syrup, and lemon juice in a large pitcher. Stir well, and refrigerate until thoroughly chilled. Add enough sparkling water, spring water, or Champagne to make about 6 cups, and stir again. Pour into chilled glasses and garnish each with a small sprig of mint.

THAI LIMEADE

Thai-style limeade is salty, often without any sugar at all. I find the sugarless versions irresistible, but this sweeter version, still with a hint of saltiness, is closer to what we Americans expect in a limeade. Try this tangy drink during hot weather; in California, we drink it with spicy Asian food or fiery Mexican fare.

SERVES 4 TO 6

Zest of 6 limes, minced
1 to 2 teaspoons kosher salt, or less to taste
½ cup boiling water
1 cup fresh lime juice (from 8 to 10 limes)
1½ cups Simple Syrup (page 469)
3 cups spring water
Ice cubes

Place the lime zest and salt in a small bowl, pour the boiling water over, and let steep for about 20 minutes. Pour the water through a strainer into a large pitcher or glass jar, and discard the zest. Stir in the lime juice, simple syrup, and spring water, and refrigerate until thoroughly chilled. To serve, fill tall glasses with ice cubes and pour the limeade over. Serve immediately.

HIBISCUS FLOWER SUN TEA

When the weather cooperates, you can make sun tea using almost any herb or tea you like. Tea made in this way is more delicate, less biting than tea made with boiling water. Iced hibiscus tea is common in Mexican restaurants throughout California. The dried flowers are sold in bulk in herb shops and health food stores, and in packages in Latin markets.

MAKES 4 QUARTS

2 ounces dried hibiscus flowers
¾ cup honey, or more to taste
Ice cubes
Slices of orange or lemon

Tie the hibiscus flowers in a cheesecloth bag or put them in a large tea ball, leaving plenty of room for them to expand. Place the bag or ball in a large glass (not plastic) jar, add 4 quarts of water, secure the lid, and set the jar outside in the sun. Leave it until the water takes on a deep ruby hue, at least 2 hours and up to 6 hours; the timing will depend on the time of year and the warmth of the day. Bring the jar into the kitchen, remove and discard the hibiscus flowers, and stir in the honey until the tea is as sweet as you like. Refrigerate until thoroughly chilled. Serve over ice, garnished with a slice of lemon or orange. The tea will keep, covered in the refrgerator, for up to a week.

AGUA FRESCA

Agua fresca is the colorful drink served at taquerias and Mexican cafés throughout California. Two, three, or more kinds sit enticingly on the counter in huge glass jars, waiting to be ladled into tall paper cups. Each taqueria is likely to have its own unique selection, though most have several flavors in common, especially horchata (made with rice and cinnamon), cantaloupe, and pineapple. An agua fresca is the perfect foil to the heat of a fiery salsa and taco, and it is utterly refreshing in hot weather. My two favorite flavors, both easy to duplicate at home, are melon and pineapple:

SERVES 4 TO 8

Melon Agua Fresca

4 cups chunks of melon, such as
    watermelon, cantaloupe, or Casaba
1 cup Simple Syrup (page 469)
3 cups spring water
Ice cubes

Using a conventional blender or an immersion blender, puree the fruit briefly, leaving it just slightly chunky and not completely liquefied. Pour the puree into a large glass jar or pitcher, add the syrup and water, and stir. Refrigerate, covered, for at least 1 hour. To serve, pour over ice in a tall glass. Serve the same day you make it.

Pineapple Agua Fresca

1 pineapple
½ to 1 cup Simple Syrup (page 469)
3 cups spring water
Ice cubes

Peel the pineapple, cut out the eyes, remove the core, and cut the flesh into chunks. Puree the pineapple in a conventional blender (an immersion blender will not work) in two batches, until it is nearly but not completely liquefied. Pour the puree into a glass jar or pitcher, stir in ½ cup of the syrup, taste, and add more syrup, if you like, for a sweeter drink. Add the water, and refrigerate for at least 1 hour. To serve, pour over ice in a tall glass. Store, refrigerated, for up to 2 days.

BIG SUR BREW

I came across this aromatic brew in a charming little 1981 book, *Recipes for Living in Big Sur*. Credited to Claire Chappellet, who helped put together the book, it is called "Cup of Happiness—A Yogi's Big Sur Brew," and readers are told to savor it when there's a big storm brewing outside. Big Sur is one of California's most spectacular natural features, a stretch of coastline, creeks, mountains, and redwood trees south of Monterey. Parts of Big Sur are nearly as pristine today as they were five thousand years ago, when the Esselen Indians lived

The Watermelon Sun

"We have an interesting thing with the sun here. It shines a different color every day. No one knows why this is, not even Charley. We grow the watermelons in different colors the best we can.

"This is how we do it: Seeds gathered from a gray watermelon picked on a gray day and then planted on a gray day will make more gray watermelons.

"It is really very simple. The colors of the days and the watermelons go like this—

Monday: red watermelons.

Tuesday: golden watermelons.

Wednesday: gray watermelons.

Thursday: black, soundless watermelons.

Friday: white watermelons.

Saturday: blue watermelons.

Sunday: brown watermelons.

"... I like best tomorrow: the black, soundless watermelon days. When you cut them they make no noise, and taste very sweet. They are very good for making things that have no sound. I remember there was a man who used to make clocks from the black, soundless watermelons and his clocks were silent."

Richard Brautigan, *In Watermelon Sugar* (Delta, 1968)

---

their simple, nomadic life as hunter-gatherers, gleaning from the land, air, and sea a harvest of wild mushrooms, greens, seeds, berries, roots, bulbs, game, birds, fish, and shellfish that changed with the seasons. This simple tea of fragrant spices is indeed comforting during a storm, yet welcome nearly any other time as well.

MAKES 2 QUARTS

12 whole black peppercorns
4 cinnamon sticks
1 1-inch piece of fresh ginger
2 tablespoons whole cardamom
   seeds
12 whole cloves
8 coriander seeds
8 cups spring water

Milk
Honey

Combine all of the spices and the water in a large nonreactive saucepan over high heat. Bring to a boil, reduce the heat, and simmer for about 20 minutes, or until the mixture is fragrant and deeply colored, like black tea. Remove the brew from the heat, strain, pour into mugs, add milk and honey, and serve.

CHAI

*C*hai is a spicy Indian tea that has become tremendously popular in California. In the mid-1990s chai began appearing on market shelves in boxes, ready to be reheated, and on blackboard menus in virtually every coffeehouse in the state. There are lowfat, nonfat, and sugarfree versions, all of which violate the simplicity of traditional Indian chai, a sweetened black tea rich with milk and redolent with spices. The commercial versions are not nearly as delicious as fresh-made chai, which is both easy and inexpensive to make at home.

SERVES 4

3 cups milk
3 cups spring water
⅓ cup sugar
2 tablespoons black tea, such as
   orange pekoe, keemun, or assam
1 2-inch cinnamon stick
8 whole black peppercorns
2 whole cloves
3 to 4 cardamom seeds
¼ teaspoon cumin seeds
1 to 2 whole allspice berries
⅛ teaspoon fresh-grated nutmeg

Bring the milk, water, sugar, and tea to a boil in a heavy saucepan. Remove the pan from the heat, add the spices, cover, and let steep for 15 minutes. Return the mixture to high heat, and, just when the mixture boils, strain it into a teapot or individual teacups. Serve immediately. Or store, covered, in the refrigerator, and reheat to serve.

MEXICAN HOT CHOCOLATE

*B*oth chocolate and vanilla are gifts the New World gave to the Old. In North America, drinks that combine chocolate and vanilla have an ancient history, dating back at least to the Aztecs. Look for Ibarra brand Mexican chocolate in Latin markets and specialty food stores; if you cannot find any Mexican chocolate, another bittersweet chocolate will do fine.

SERVES 4

4 cups whole milk
⅓ to ½ cup sugar
1 vanilla bean, split
1 2-inch cinnamon stick
Pinch of cayenne
Pinch of finely crushed black pepper
3 ounces Mexican chocolate or other
   bittersweet chocolate, chopped
Grated chocolate, for garnish
Fresh-grated nutmeg, or ½ teaspoon
   ground nutmeg, for garnish
Cinnamon sticks, for garnish, optional

Combine the milk, sugar, vanilla bean, cinnamon stick, cayenne, and black pepper in a heavy saucepan over medium heat. Bring to a boil, stirring all the while, and remove the pan from the heat. Cover the pan and let steep for 15 minutes. Strain the milk, discard the vanilla and cinnamon, and return the milk to the pan. Over medium-low heat, add the chopped chocolate, and stir until it is melted and fully incorporated into the milk. Taste, and stir in more sugar, if you like. Pour into mugs, grate chocolate and nutmeg over each serving, and serve immediately, garnished with a stick of cinnamon, if you like.

LARRY'S JAILHOUSE SANGRITA

*L*arry Watson, founder of Bustelo's Backyard, a California company that makes hot pepper sauces, named his version of sangrita for a friend who found himself in a Mexican jail. A traditional Mexican sangrita is made with a combination of tomato and citrus juices. In this particular Mexican jail, however, there were no tomatoes or tomato juice, and inmates developed this version to accompany tequila—which apparently was available. Larry recommends following a sip of sangrita with a shot of premium tequila and suggests that tossing both into a blender with a little ice makes an outstanding if unusual margarita.

SERVES 6 TO 12

The Original 27 Counties

Yuba City is the county seat of **Sutter County**, a topographically and geologically dramatic area in which low-lying farmlands give way to the Sutter Buttes volcanic mountain range. Cycles of floods plague the area, one of which in 1862 destroyed the estate of John Sutter, who had retired to his vineyards and orchards here after his mill was overrun by Gold Rush fortune hunters. Extensive floods in the 1990s provided dramatic images on the evening news; the scene of a dog sitting on the roof of a house as the waters rise all around gave millions of people their first, and perhaps only, view of Yuba City. (The dog eventually was rescued by helicopter.) The agriculture is diverse, with numerous fruit and nut orchards, vegetable farms, poultry farms, and cattle ranches. Marshlands in the county support rice farming. Away from the sophistication of the coast, this is a different California, where home cooking is rustic and robust—roast pork with a rice, prune, and walnut casserole, for example—and where you'll probably never encounter a baby vegetable that isn't still growing.

4 cups fresh orange juice
2 cups fresh lime juice (from 16 to 20 limes)
¼ cup grenadine
2½ teaspoons kosher salt

1 medium yellow onion, chopped
¼ cup Bustelo's Very Hot Pepper
   Sauce or other hot sauce
12 ounces premium tequila, optional

Set aside 2 cups of the orange juice. Place all of the remaining ingredients, except the tequila, in a blender. Blend well, then pour the mixture into a large pitcher. Stir in the reserved orange juice, and refrigerate until thoroughly chilled.

To serve, chill small glasses and pour 2 to 3 ounces sangrita into each. If you like, fill shot glasses with tequila, and serve the two side by side.

The Shirley Temple

That ubiquitous child's drink of ginger ale, grenadine, an orange slice, and a maraschino cherry was invented at Chasen's, the famous Los Angeles restaurant that catered to the elite of the movie world for nearly fifty years. Apparently, the child star threw a tantrum one night, jealous of her parents' before-dinner cocktails. She wanted her own. The first Shirley Temple cocktail was quickly concocted to quiet her down.

GINGER BEER

A little restaurant in Healdsburg called Samba Java served a refreshing, intensely gingery ginger beer, one of the many things I missed when the restaurant closed. A few years later my daughter Gina took a job at Kitchen, a new restaurant owned by Jan Salisbury, Samba Java's last chef. One day after work, Gina presented me with the handwritten recipe. Though you must start the day before, it is very easy to make and just the thing to have on hand in the summer. It keeps for a few days, so make a big batch, as in this recipe.

MAKES ABOUT 10 CUPS

2½ pounds ginger, peeled and
   chopped
1¼ pounds sugar
Juice of 1 pound of limes
8 cups boiling water
2 teaspoons (about 1 package)
   active dry yeast
Bottled ginger ale
Ice cubes

Put one third of the ginger in a food processor and pulse until reduced to a very fine pulp. Transfer the pulp to a heavy nonreactive container. Process the remaining ginger in 2 batches, and add the pulp to the container. Add the sugar and lime juice to the ginger, pour the boiling water over, and stir to mix well. Let stand, covered with a tea towel, at room temperature for 6 hours.

Add the yeast, stir, and let the mixture sit, covered with a tea towel, at room temperature overnight. It will begin to ferment.

Strain the beer through cheesecloth, then squeeze the pulp by hand to extract as much liquid as possible. Refrigerate until thoroughly chilled. Serve over ice, in chilled glasses if you like, with 4 parts bottled ginger ale to 1 part ginger beer. Store, covered, in the refrigerator for up to 4 days.

KIR ROYALE

Kir originated in Dijon, France, where the mayor, for whom the drink is named, devised the combination of white wine and cassis as a way to encourage more people to drink the wines of the region. It was a Californian who took the concept a step further and added drops of the sweet liqueur to Champagne, christening the combination *Kir Royale*.

SERVES 5

1 bottle good Champagne, preferably, or sparkling wine
2½ teaspoons crème de cassis

Fill champagne flutes with Champagne, add ½ teaspoon cassis to each glass, and serve immediately.

California Cocktails

Cocktails go in and out of fashion, in California as elsewhere. During their heyday, which coincided with Hollywood's most glamorous decades—from the 1930s through the early 1960s—many emerged as classics from legendary California establishments like Chasen's and The Players in southern California and the Buena Vista Bar and Trader Vic's in the Bay Area. Among California's claims to cocktail fame:

❖ Flame of Love Martini (sherry, orange peel, vodka or gin)

❖ Jack Rose (applejack brandy, grenadine, lemon)

❖ Rob Roy (vermouth, scotch, bitters)

❖ Side Car (cognac, lemon juice, Cointreau)

❖ Moscow Mule (vodka, ginger beer, lime)

❖ Irish Coffee (coffee, Irish whiskey)

❖ Mai Tai (dark rum, curaçao, grenadine, lime juice, sugar syrup)

❖ Temple Bell Tiger (tangerine juice, vodka, curaçao)

FOUR PERFECT MARGARITAS

*R*egardless of who really made the very first margarita—will we ever know?—few dispute the technique for making the best. Forget the snowcone versions that freeze your sinuses and ignore those concoctions that add anything from pureed canned strawberries to neon-blue liqueurs. Here's the simple classic.

SERVES 4

4 lime wedges
Kosher salt in a shallow dish
Cracked ice cubes (not crushed ice)
6 ounces of 100-percent-agave
    silver tequila, such as Patron,
    Herradura, or Cuervo Tradicional
½ cup fresh lime juice, preferably from
    Mexican limes
3 ounces Cointreau

Rub the rim of each glass with a wedge of lime, dip the rim in the salt, and shake off excess salt so that there is a delicate ring of salt around the edge of the glass.

Fill a cocktail shaker with cracked ice, add the tequila, lime juice, and Cointreau, cover, and shake gently for 10 to 15 seconds, until the container becomes frosty. Strain into each of the glasses. (If you have only a small cocktail shaker, you will have to make the 4 margaritas in 2 batches. If you have no cocktail shaker, fill a pitcher with cracked ice, add the tequila, lime juice, and Cointreau, stir for 15 seconds with a long metal spoon, and strain into glasses.)

Green Walnuts in the Sun

*R*idgely Evers, a software executive, and Colleen McGlynn, a chef, live in Sonoma County on the edge of Dry Creek Valley. There they produce DaVero Extra Virgin Olive Oil from four thousand Italian variety olive trees Ridgely imported in 1990. They also make—for themselves, not commercially—nocino, the luscious green walnut liqueur originally from Italy. Each summer on the Feast of San Giovanni, which coincides with the summer solstice, they pick green walnuts, choosing an odd number—twenty-one, they say—of medium-size nuts. They clean and quarter the walnuts and place them in a clear glass jar with a few whole cloves, the peel of one orange, a cinnamon stick, and a quart of 100-proof vodka. They seal the jar and place it outside in the sun for at least forty days, shaking it now and then when they think about it. Then they filter the mixture, add a simple syrup made with 2 cups sugar and 1½ cups water, return it to a clean container, cover it tightly, and keep it in a cool pantry until Christmas, when they filter the nocino again, transfer it to individual bottles, close them with a cork, and age them for one year.

FLAVORED VODKA

Commercial flavored vodkas have been all the rage in the 1990s, but they are nothing new. Russian cookbooks published in the U.S., from the 1950s and earlier, offer homemade versions, which have never really been uncommon as Christmas gifts. I make flavored vodkas in small batches of just one cup, and I frequently make three or four different types at a time. Since we drink vodka in small amounts—an ounce or two over ice is typical—there is no sense in making large quantities, unless for gifts. Vodka is, of course, a traditional accompaniment to caviar. It is also excellent served with gravlax.

MAKES 1 CUP

1 cup best-quality vodka, such as
   Stolichnaya
1 flavoring agent (list follows)

Combine the vodka and the flavoring agent in a small jar, cover, and leave in the freezer for at least 1 week. To serve, strain the vodka into a shot glass and serve neat, or pour it over ice in a small glass. To make larger quantities, simply increase the amounts of both ingredients, then strain into bottles instead of glasses.

Flavoring Agents

* 4 to 5 whole allspice berries
* 10 dried apricot halves
* 1 teaspoon whole black peppercorns
* 1 fresh chile, such as jalapeño, serrano, or Thai
* 1 dried chipotle pepper
* 1 1-inch cinnamon stick
* 10 whole dark-roasted coffee beans
* 2 tablespoons whole fresh cranberries
* 2 teaspoons Earl Grey tea leaves
* 1 2-inch strip of lemon zest
* 1 vanilla bean

PEACH DAIQUIRIS

Daiquiris are practically the official drink at summer backyard barbecues in California, especially when temperatures soar to the nineties and higher. I make them when white peaches are in season, but if white peaches are not available, any good ripe peach or nectarine will do. You can also make daiquiris using strawberries, plums, mango, pineapple, or a dense melon such as cantaloupe. Adjust the simple syrup and the lime juice to balance the flavors and sweetness of the particular fruit.

SERVES 4

½ cup light rum
2 ounces triple sec
4 ripe peaches, peeled, pitted, and
   sliced

Juice of 2 limes
1 to 2 tablespoons Simple Syrup
  (page 469)
Crushed Ice

Blend the rum, triple sec, peaches, and lime juice in a blender until smooth. Taste, and add as much simple syrup as necessary for the sweetness you like; the amount will vary depending on the sweetness of the peaches. Fill individual glasses with crushed ice, pour the daiquiris over, and serve immediately.

APPENDIX 1: STOCKS

RICH VEGETABLE STOCK

Vegetarians can use this vegetable stock wherever beef stock or poultry stock is called for in this book, although the flavor and texture will not be quite the same, of course. Vegetable stocks lack the gelatin of meat and poultry stocks.

MAKES 6 TO 8 CUPS

3 large yellow onions, skins on, quartered

1 bunch of celery, ribs separated and trimmed of outer leaves

3 tomatoes

2 heads of garlic, cut crosswise in half

1 bunch (about 1 pound) of Swiss chard

3 large leeks, cut lengthwise in half

3 carrots, chopped coarse

3 zucchini, cut into chunks

1 small bunch (about 12 sprigs) of Italian parsley

3 sprigs of thyme

3 sprigs of oregano

½ cup olive oil

Preheat the oven to 350°F.

Place the vegetables and herbs in a large roasting pan, drizzle the olive oil over them, and roast them for 40 minutes. Transfer the vegetables, herbs, and pan drippings to a large heavy stockpot, and add water to cover. Bring to a boil, reduce the heat, and simmer, uncovered, for 1½ hours, adding more water if necessary. Strain the stock, return it to the heat, and simmer, uncovered, until reduced by one third, about 40 minutes.

Use immediately, or let cool and refrigerate, covered, for up to 7 days. To freeze the stock, heat it, transfer it to airtight containers, and label them. Let cool thoroughly, and freeze for up to 3 months.

CHICKEN STOCK

Chicken stock is the best all-purpose stock for home cooking; it contributes flavor and structure to soups, stews, sauces, and other dishes. It is easy and inexpensive to make, but keep in mind that for a flavorful stock you must begin with flavorful chicken. Make your stock from range, or free-range, chickens if possible. If duck is readily available where you live, use it, for it makes an even better basic stock. Ask your butcher to direct you to a source for duck and then ask for parts, such as wings, that are inexpensive and make excellent stock.

MAKES ABOUT 10 CUPS

1 yellow onion, skin on, quartered

1 medium carrot, cut into chunks

1 celery rib, trimmed of outer leaves

1 leek, cut into chunks

3 tablespoons olive oil

5 pounds chicken parts, such as backs, necks, feet, meaty carcasses, and wings

Preheat the oven to 325°F.

Place the vegetables on a baking sheet, toss them with the olive oil, and roast them for 45 minutes, or until they are tender and beginning to color.

Place the chicken parts and 5 quarts of water in a large heavy stockpot. Transfer the vegetables and pan drippings to the pot. Bring to a boil, reduce the heat, and simmer, partially covered, for 3 hours. Remove the stock from the heat, let it cool slightly, and strain it. Return the stock to the pot, bring to a boil, reduce the heat, and simmer, uncovered, until reduced by one third.

Use immediately, or let cool and refrigerate, covered, for up to 5 days. To freeze the stock, heat it, transfer it to airtight containers, and label them. Let cool thoroughly, and freeze for up to 3 months.

Variation:

For Duck Stock, use duck parts in place of chicken parts and proceed as directed. For Smoked Duck Stock, use smoked duck parts.

BEEF STOCK

A good stock is one of the best gifts you can give a soup, sauce, or stew. I suggest taking one weekend every few months to prepare stocks for the coming season. You will need more during the fall and winter months, of course, when soups are heartier and often require a full-bodied meat stock. Freeze your stocks in quantities of 1 to 2 cups.

MAKES 6 TO 8 CUPS

3 pounds lean beef, trimmed of fat and cut into large chunks

2 to 3 pounds beef marrow bones

1 medium yellow onion, skin on, cut in half

1 medium carrot, cut into chunks

1 celery rib, cut into chunks

1 leek, cut into chunks

3 large tomatoes, cut into chunks

Olive oil

Kosher salt

Black pepper in a mill

Several sprigs of Italian parsley

1 tablespoon black peppercorns

Preheat the oven to 325°F.

In a large heavy stockpot over medium heat, brown the beef evenly on all sides. Add the marrow bones and 12 cups of water, and bring to a boil over high heat. Reduce the heat, skim off any foam that forms, and simmer, uncovered, for 45 minutes.

Meanwhile, place the vegetables in a

roasting pan, toss with enough olive oil just to coat them lightly, and season with salt and pepper. Roast the vegetables for 45 minutes, or until they are tender and beginning to color.

Transfer the vegetables and any pan drippings to the stockpot, and add the parsley and peppercorns. Simmer, partially covered, for 2 hours. Remove the stock from the heat, let it cool slightly, and strain it.

Use immediately, or let cool and refrigerate, covered, for up to 7 days. When the stock is thoroughly chilled, remove any fat that coagulates on the top. To freeze the stock, heat it, transfer it to airtight containers, and label them. Let cool thoroughly, and freeze for up to 3 months.

FISH STOCK

Sometimes you can get fish carcasses from your butcher or fishmonger; at other times you'll need to buy whole fish to make stock. Whatever its source, the fish should be fresh and not smell stale or fishy. When you can find it, use monkfish, which makes excellent stock. You do not, however, need to buy expensive fish, or fish of a specific kind, to make stock.

MAKES 6 TO 8 CUPS

4 to 5 pounds fish carcasses, heads on, skinned
1 large yellow onion, skin on, quartered
1 lemon, cut in half
3 sprigs of Italian parsley
1 bay leaf
1 teaspoon black peppercorns
1 cup dry white wine

Using a cleaver, chop the fish carcasses into chunks. Rinse the chunks thoroughly in cool running water to remove any specks of blood.

Place the fish, onion, lemon, parsley, bay leaf, peppercorns, and wine in a large stockpot, and add water to cover. Bring to a boil, reduce the heat, skim off any foam that forms, and simmer, partially covered, for 25 minutes. Remove from the heat, let cool slightly, and strain. Return the stock to the pot, bring to a boil, reduce the heat, and simmer, uncovered, until reduced by two thirds.

Use immediately, or let cool and refrigerate, covered, for up to 3 days. To freeze the stock, heat it, transfer it to airtight containers, and label them. Let cool thoroughly, and freeze for up to 3 months.

APPENDIX 2: RESOURCES

ABALONE ACRES
20190 Highway 1
Marshall, California 94940
415-663-1384
Fax 415-663-9246
Farm-raised abalone.

THE ABALONE FARM
P.O. Box 136
Cayucos, California 93430
805-995-2495
Fax 805-995-0236
Farm-raised abalone.

ADAMSON'S HAPPY HAVEN RANCH
1480 Sperring Road
Sonoma, California 95476
707-996-4260
Fax 707-996-5121
Hot pepper jams, chutneys, and preserves. Mail order.

BAY BOTTOM BEDS
Santa Rosa, California
707-578-6049
Farmers and purveyors of Preston Point oysters.

BELLWETHER FARMS
9999 Valley Ford Road
Petaluma, California 94952
888-527-8606 / 707-763-0993
Fax 707-763-2443
Sheep's milk cheese; organic cow's milk cheeses. Mail order.

BRISTOL FARMS
Fine grocer and cookware store. Cooking classes held regularly at Manhattan Beach store and intermittently at other locations. Six locations, all in southern California: Long Beach (562-430-4134); Manhattan Beach (310-643-5229); Rolling Hills Estates (310-541-9157); Westlake Village (805-370-9197); and Woodland Hills (818-227-8400).

BUSTELO'S BACKYARD
P.O. Box 231
Occidental, California 95465
888-287-8356 / 707-874-1663
Fax 707-874-1692
Oak-aged hot pepper sauces.

CALIFORNIA ARTICHOKE ADVISORY BOARD
P.O. Box 747
Castroville, California 95012
408-633-4411
Fax 408-633-0215
Marketing organization for California artichokes; provides consumer brochures and recipes.

CALIFORNIA AVOCADO COMMISSION
1251 East Dyer Road, Suite 200
Santa Ana, California 92705
714-558-6761
Fax 714-641-7024
Represents California's sixty-five hundred avocado growers; provides consumer brochures, recipes, and information on the state's two

avocado festivals, in Fallbrook in the spring and in Carpinteria in the early fall.

CALIFORNIA OLIVE OIL COUNCIL
14301 Arnold Drive, #29
Glen Ellen, California 95442
707-939-9609
Fax 707-939-8999
Organization of California's olive oil producers. Located at The Olive Mill, a cooperative olive oil mill and retail shop.

CALIFORNIA OLIVE OIL FESTIVAL
15140 Sonoma Highway
Glen Ellen, California 95442
888-654-8350
Each May, producers of California extra virgin olive oils gather on the grounds of B.R. Cohn Winery in the Valley of the Moon; all oils available for tasting and purchase.

CASTROVILLE ARTICHOKE FESTIVAL
P.O. Box 1041
Castroville, California 95012
408-633-2465
Fax 408-633-0485
Two-day tribute, founded in 1960, held annually in the last week of September.

LAURA CHENEL CHÈVRE
4310 Fremont Drive
Sonoma, California 95476
707-996-4477
Fresh and aged chèvre.

THE CHILE SHOP
109 East Water Street
Sante Fe, New Mexico 87501
505-983-6080
Fax 505-984-0737
Chiles, ristras, blue corn products, and more. Catalog; mail order.

C.K. LAMB
11100 Los Amigos Road
Healdsburg, California 95448
707-431-8161
Fax 707-431-8100
Lamb and lamb products, including corned lamb and fresh tongue.

THE COOK'S LIBRARY
8373 West Third Street
Los Angeles, California 90048
213-655-3141
Fax 213-655-9530
Wide selection of cookbooks, including many on California cooking.

CORTI BROTHERS
5810 Folsom Boulevard
Sacramento, California 95819
916-736-3800
Fax 916-736-3807
Olive oils, balsamic vinegars, Japanese sea salt, California caviar, and more. Newsletter; will ship.

COYOTE CAFE GENERAL STORE
132 West Water Street
Santa Fe, New Mexico 87501
505-982-2454
Fax 505-989-9026
Chiles, beans, nuts, chocolate, masa harina, hot sauces. Catalog; mail order.

CULINARY KITCHEN
Food for Thought Natural Market & Deli
1181 Yulupa Avenue
Santa Rosa, California 95405
707-575-7915
Fax 707-575-8074
Cooking classes with a local as well as a vegetarian emphasis.

CYPRESS GROVE CHÈVRE
4600 Dows Prairie Road
McKinleyville, California 95519
707-839-3168
Fax 707-839-2322
Goat cheeses.

D'ARTAGNAN, INC.
280 Wilson Avenue
Newark, New Jersey 07105
800-327-8246
Sausages, foie gras, quail, and game. Catalog; mail order.

DAVERO EXTRA VIRGIN OLIVE OIL
1195 Westside Road
Healdsburg, California 95448
707-431-8000
Fax 707-431-5780
Dry Creek Valley olive oil from Italian varieties of olive trees.

DRAEGER'S CULINARY CENTERS
222 East Fourth Avenue
San Mateo / 415-685-3700
1010 University Drive
Menlo Park / 415-688-0688
One of the largest upscale food and cookware markets in the world. Wide selection of cookbooks. Cooking classes.

FAMILY WINEMAKERS OF CALIFORNIA
1400 K Street, Suite 304
Sacramento, California 95814
916-498-7500
Fax 916-498-7505
Association of three hundred table wine producers. Hosts a wine tasting open to the public in the fall in San Francisco.

GERHARD'S NAPA VALLEY SAUSAGE
901 Enterprise Way, Suite B
Napa, California 94559
707-252-4116
Fax 707-252-0879
Specialty sausages.

GILROY GARLIC FESTIVAL ASSOCIATION
P.O. Box 2311
Gilroy, California 95021-2311
408-842-1625
Fax 408-842-7337
One of the largest and best known of California's food festivals; garlic, garlic braids, garlic cookbooks, and all manner of garlic paraphernalia available for sale.

GOAT'S LEAP CHEESE
3321 St. Helena Highway North
St. Helena, California 94574
707-963-2337
Fresh and aged chèvre. Limited mail order.

GRAND AÏOLI GARLIC FESTIVAL
P.O. Box 1552
Sebastopol, California 95473
707-576-1124
Intimate festival in the French tradition featuring California produce, garlic, and olive oil; garlic braids, bulk heirloom garlic, and dozens of varieties of seed garlic available for sale. Late September.

HOG ISLAND SHELLFISH COMPANY
P.O. Box 829
Marshall, California 94940
415-663-9218
Fax 415-663-9246
Farmers and purveyors of Tomales Bay oysters, Manila clams, mussels, and abalone.

HOMECHEF KITCHEN STORE AND
  COOKING SCHOOL
*Cookware, cookbooks, and demonstration and
participation cooking classes. Five locations:
Corte Madera (415-927-3191); Palo Alto (415-
326-3191); Sacramento (916-487-3191); San
Francisco (415-668-3191); and San Jose (408-
374-3191).*

JOSIE'S BEST
P.O. Box 5525
Santa Fe, New Mexico 87502
505-473-3437
Fax 505-473-5808
*Posole, frozen chiles, and chili powder. Price
list; mail order.*

JUST TOMATOES CO.
P.O. Box 807
Westley, California 95387
800-537-1985
Fax 800-537-1986
Dried tomatoes. Catalog; mail order.

KASMA'S COOKING SCHOOL
105 Echo Avenue
Oakland, California 94611
510-655-8900
*Thai and other Southeast Asian cooking classes
in the home of Kasma Loha-Unchit, author of
It Rains Fishes.*

LOLETA CHEESE FACTORY
P.O. Box 607
252 Loleta Drive
Loleta, California 95551
800-995-0453 / 707-733-5470
Fax 707-733-1872
*Cheddar, jack, havarti, and fontina. Catalog;
mail order.*

KERMIT LYNCH WINE MERCHANT
1605 San Pablo Avenue
Berkeley, California 94702
510-524-1524
Fax 510-528-7026
*Mustard, anchovies, olive oil, olives, lavender
honey, and extra virgin olive oils from Provence,
Tuscany, and Liguria. Newsletter; mail order.*

MARIANI ORCHARD FARM STAND
1615 Half Road
Morgan Hill, California 95037
408-779-5467
Fax 408-776-1575
*Fresh apricots that taste like they should; lim-
ited mail order.*

MARIN FRENCH CHEESE COMPANY
7500 Red Hill Road
Petaluma, California 94952
707-762-6001
Fax 707-762-0430
*Breakfast cheese, schloss, camembert, and brie
under the Rouge et Noir label.*

JOE MATOS CHEESE FACTORY
3669 Llano Road
Santa Rosa, California 95407
707-584-5283
St. George cheese. Will ship.

MENDOCINO WINEGROWERS ALLIANCE
P.O. Box 1409
Ukiah, California 95482
707-744-1363
Fax 707-744-1364
*Grape growers and the county's 37 wineries
together promote the industry. Information
on annual auction and barbecue as well as the
area's wines and wineries.*

NAPA VALLEY VINTNERS ASSOCIATION
P.O. Box 141
St. Helena, California 94574
707-942-9775
Fax 707-942-0171
Information on the valley's wine and wineries. Holds the Napa Valley Wine Auction, the largest and most spectacular of all wine auctions; sells out months in advance of the June gala.

NATURE'S PANTRY
P.O. Box 1913
Sonoma, California 95476-1913
707-938-5174
Heirloom dried beans, chiles, California olive oil, and other handcrafted California food products, nearly all organic. Catalog; mail order.

O OLIVE OIL
P.O. Box 590939
San Francisco, California 94159
415-460-6598
Fax 415-460-6599
Condiment olive oil made by crushing ripe organic mission olives with organic Meyer lemons.

OAKVILLE GROCERY MAIL ORDER
   COMPANY
101 South Coombs, Suite Y-3
Napa, California 94559
800-455-2305
Fax 707-254-1846
California products, including Katz & Co. preserves and one of the best selections of California olive oils in the country. Catalog; mail order.

OLIVE HILL OIL COMPANY
15140 Sonoma Highway
Glen Ellen, California 95442
707-938-4064
Producers of B.R. Cohn Estate Olive Oil and other products, including premium vinegars.

PHIPPS RANCH
P.O. Box 349
Pescadero, California 94060
800-279-0889 / 415-879-0787
Fax 415-879-1622
Common and heirloom dried beans. Catalog; mail order.

G.B. RATTO, INTERNATIONAL GROCERS
821 Washington Street
Oakland, California 94607
510-836-2250
Grains, beans, flours, vinegars, olive oils, French butter, spices, and more.

REDWOOD HILL FARMS GRADE-A GOAT
   DAIRY
10855 Occidental Road
Sebastopol, California 95472
707-823-8250
Fax 707-823-6976
Fresh and aged chèvre, goat's milk, and yogurt.

RUMIANO CHEESE COMPANY
P.O. Box 305
Crescent City, California 95531
707-465-1535
Jack, dry jack, and cheddar cheeses. Mail order.

SEA STARS GOAT CHEESE
5407 Coast Road
Santa Cruz, California 95060
408-423-7200
Fax 408-454-0838
Fresh chèvre and goat ricotta.

SLIDE RANCH
2025 Shoreline Highway
Muir Beach, California 94965
415-381-6155
Fax 415-381-5762
Operational teaching farm within the Golden Gate Recreational Area. Call for reservation.

SONOMA CHEESE FACTORY
2 Spain Street
Sonoma, California 95476
800-535-2855 / 707-996-1000
Sonoma jack, cheddar, and teleme cheeses. Catalog; mail order.

SONOMA COUNTY WINERIES ASSOCIATION
California Welcome Center
5000 Roberts Lake Road
Rohnert Park, California 94928
800-939-7666 / 707-586-3795
Fax 707-586-1383
Information on the Sonoma County Showcase and Wine Auction, held in July, as well as on member wineries.

SONOMA FOIE GRAS
P.O. Box 2007
Sonoma, California 95476
800-427-4559
Foie gras, duck magret, and duck fat. Mail order.

SOUTHLAND FARMERS' MARKET
  ASSOCIATION
1308 Factory Place, Box 68
Los Angeles, California 90013
213-244-9190, ext. 10
Fax 213-244-9180
Provides listings of farmers' markets throughout California.

SPECTRUM NATURALS
133 Copeland Street
Petaluma, California 94952
800-995-2705
Fax 707-765-1026
Manufacturers of specialty oils, including unrefined vegetable oils like corn oil and olive oil.

SPRINGVILLE APPLE FESTIVAL
P.O. Box 414
Springville, California 93265
209-539-0619
Held in the fall in spectacular setting in the foothills of the Sierra Nevadas; many varieties of apples available for sale.

SUR LA TABLE
Cookware, cookbooks, and cooking classes. Three locations in California: Berkeley (510-849-2252); Pasadena (626-744-9987); and San Francisco (415-732-7900).

TANTE MARIE'S COOKING SCHOOL
271 Francisco Street
San Francisco, California 94133
415-788-6699
Fax 415-788-8924
One of the state's longest-running private cooking schools; classes at all levels.

TIERRA VEGETABLES
13684 Chalk Hill Road
Healdsburg, California 95448
707-837-8366
Fax 707-433-5666
Dried and smoked chiles, including chipotles and chipotle powder. Catalog; mail order.

TIMBER CREST FARMS
4791 Dry Creek Road
Healdsburg, California 95448
707-433-8251
Fax 707-433-8255
Organic nuts, dried fruits, and dried tomatoes, including dried-tomato products. Catalog; mail order.

TOMATO FESTIVAL
California Coast Wine Center
5007 Fulton Road
Fulton, California 95439
Sponsored by Kendall-Jackson Winery, held the second weekend of September at the winery's demonstration gardens, where over 120 varieties of heirloom tomatoes are grown; tomatoes available for tasting and sale.

VELLA CHEESE COMPANY OF CALIFORNIA
315 East Second Street
Sonoma, California 95476
800-848-0505 / 707-938-3232
Fax 707-938-4307
Jack, dry jack, and cheddar cheeses. Catalog; mail order.

VIVANDE PORTA VIA
2125 Fillmore Street
San Francisco, California 94115
415-346-4430
Fax 415-346-2877
Italian olive oils, olives, vinegars, cheeses, and more. Catalog; mail order.

THE WINE INSTITUTE
425 Market Street, Suite 1000
San Francisco, California 94105
415-512-0151
Fax 415-442-0742
Information, research, and advocacy for the wine industry. Website—wineinstitute.org—provides excellent information and links to other California wine sites.

YERBA SANTA GOAT DAIRY
P.O. Box 1048
Lakeport, California 95453
707-263-8131
Fresh and aged chèvre under the Alpine label. Brochure; mail order.

ZAP (ZINFANDEL ADVOCATES AND
   PRODUCERS)
118 Hillside Drive
Woodside, California 94062
415-851-2319
Fax 415-851-5579
Nonprofit group dedicated to spreading the word about zinfandel. Sponsors an annual zinfandel tasting in San Francisco in January; sells out well in advance.

APPENDIX 3: BIBLIOGRAPHY

AGRICULTURE

Chan, Sucheng. *This Bittersweet Soil: The Chinese in California Agriculture, 1860–1910*. Berkeley, 1986.

Leung, Peter C.Y. *One Day, One Dollar: The Chinese Farming Experience in the Sacramento River Delta, California*. Taipei, 1995.

Marti, Donald B. *Historical Directory of American Agricultural Fairs*. New York, 1986.

Scheuring, Ann Foley, editor. *A Guidebook to California Agriculture*. Berkeley, 1983.

CALIFORNIA COOKERY

Addleman, Pat, Judith Goodman, and Mary Harrington, editors. *Recipes for Living in Big Sur*. Big Sur, Calif., 1981.

Anderson, Electra Lynn. *The Beverly Hills Hotel Cookbook, 1912–1928*. Beverly Hills, 1985.

Ash, John. *From the Earth to the Table*. New York, 1995.

Beck, Neill, and Fred Beck. *Farmers Market Cook Book*. New York, 1951.

Benet, Jane. *The San Francisco Cookbook*. San Francisco, 1958.

Berger, Frances de Talavera. *Sumptuous Dining in Gaslight San Francisco, 1875–1915*. New York, 1985.

Bergeron, Victor J. *Trader Vic's Book of Food & Drink*. New York, 1946.

Brown, Helen Evans. *West Coast Cook Book*. New York, 1991.

Burns, Jim, and Betty Ann Brown. *Women Chefs: A Collection of Portraits and Recipes from California's Culinary Pioneers*. Berkeley, 1987.

Callahan, Genevieve. *The New California Cook Book*. New York, 1955.

Calvello, Tony, Bruce Harlow, Georgia Sackett, and Shirley Sarvis. *San Francisco Firehouse Favorites*. New York, 1965.

Carroll, John Phillip, and Virginia Rainey. *California the Beautiful Cookbook*. San Francisco, 1991.

Carter, Mark, and Christi Carter. *Carter House Cookbook*. Berkeley, 1991.

Cerwin, Herbert, editor. *Famous Recipes by Famous People*. San Francisco, 1940.

Chenel, Laura, and Linda Siegfried. *Chèvre! The Goat Cheese Cookbook*. Santa Rosa, Calif., 1983.

Ferrary, Jeannette, and Louise Fiszer. *The California-American Cookbook*. New York, 1985.

Frantz, Gilda, editor. *Cooking: The Art of Innocent Alchemy*. Los Angeles, 1975.

Giannini, Yelva. *The Giorgi Sisters Cookbook*. Leawood, Kans., 1968.

Glozer, William K., and Liselotte F. Glozer, *California in the Kitchen*. Privately printed, 1960.

Goodwin, Betty. *Chasen's*. Santa Monica, 1996.

Goodwin, Betty. *Hollywood du Jour*. Santa Monica, 1993.

Harris, Lloyd J. *The Book of Garlic*. Berkeley, 1974.

Hoffman, Mable, and Gar Hoffman. *California Cooking*. Tucson, Ariz., 1983.

Johnson, Mrs. Charles G., editor. *The Pals Club Cook Book*. Sacramento, 1945.

Jordan, Michele Anna. *A Cook's Tour of Sonoma*. Boston, 1990.

Junior Alliance of Lincoln Child Center. *The Best Parties Ever and More . . .* Oakland, 1977.

Junior League of San Francisco. *San Francisco à La Carte*. Garden City, N.Y., 1979.

Junior League of San Francisco. *San Francisco Encore.* Garden City, N.Y., 1986.

Ladies of San Rafael. *San Rafael Cook Book.* San Rafael, Calif., 1906.

Landmark's Club, The. *The Landmark's Club Cook Book.* Los Angeles, 1903.

Lewallen, Eleanor, and John Lewallen. *Sea Vegetable Gourmet Cookbook and Wildcrafter's Guide.* Mendocino, Calif., 1996.

Lorenzo, Henry R. *The Farm Fresh Fruit Cookbook.* San Francisco, 1987.

Marks, Rowena. *California Cooks.* Los Angeles, 1970.

McMahan, Jacqueline Higuera. *California Rancho Cooking.* Lake Hughes, Calif., 1983.

McMahan, Jacqueline Higuera. *Chipotle Chile Cook Book.* Lake Hughes, Calif., 1994.

Mondavi, Robert, Margrit Biever Mondavi, and Carolyn Dille. *Seasons in the Vineyard.* New York, 1996.

Morse, Kitty. *The California Farm Cookbook.* Gretna, Louisiana, 1994.

Ortiz, Joe. *The Village Baker.* Berkeley, 1993.

Patent, Greg. *New Cooking from the Old West.* Berkeley, 1996.

Preston, Mark. *California Mission Cookery.* Albuquerque, N.M., 1994.

Prokupek, Milan, Sr. *Manka's Czech Cookbook & Memories.* Inverness, Calif., 1979.

Rain, Patricia. *The Artichoke Cookbook.* Berkeley, 1985.

Robertson, Roxana D. *Golden Gate Gourmet.* San Carlos, Calif., 1958.

Sebastiani, Sylvia. *The Sebastiani Family Cookbook.* Secaucus, N.J., 1970.

State Fish Exchange. *Five Hundred Ways to Prepare California Sea Foods.* Sacramento, 1930.

Sunset Magazine. *Sunset's Favorite Company Dinners.* San Francisco, 1933.

Valley Guild, The. *The Steinbeck House Cookbook.* Salinas, Calif., 1984.

Voltz, Jeanne. *The California Cookbook.* New York, 1970.

Waters, Alice. *The Chez Panisse Menu Cookbook.* New York, 1982.

Waters, Alice. *Chez Panisse Vegetables.* New York, 1996.

Wine Advisory Board. *Favorite Recipes of California Winemakers.* San Francisco, 1981.

Worthington, Diane Rossen. *The California Cook.* New York, 1994.

Worthington, Diane Rossen. *The Cuisine of California.* Los Angeles, 1983.

Zelayeta, Elena. *Elena's Favorite Foods California Style.* Englewood Cliffs, N.J., 1967.

GENERAL AND ETHNIC COOKERY

Brown, Edward Espe. *Tomato Blessings and Radish Teachings.* New York, 1997.

Doshi, Malvi. *A Surti Touch: Adventures in Indian Cooking.* San Francisco, 1980.

Field, Carol. *The Italian Baker.* New York, 1985.

Gilbert, Fabiola. *Historic Cookery.* Las Vegas, N.M., 1970.

Jones, Evan. *American Food.* Woodstock, N.Y., 1990.

Kirlin, Katherine S., and Thomas M. Kirlin. *Smithsonian Folklife Cookbook.* Washington, D.C., 1991.

Kitchen Arts and Letters. *Christmas Memories with Recipes.* New York, 1988.

La Place, Viana. *Unplugged Kitchen.* New York, 1996.

Loha-Unchit, Kasma. *It Rains Fishes: Legends, Traditions, and the Joys of Thai Cooking.* San Francisco, 1994.

McDermott, Nancie. *Real Thai: The Best of Thailand's Regional Cooking.* San Francisco, 1992.

Southworth, May E. *The Motorists Luncheon Book.* New York, 1923.

Wood, Ed. *World Sourdoughs from Antiquity.* Berkeley, 1996.

CALIFORNIA HISTORY AND CULTURE
Brautigan, Richard. *In Watermelon Sugar.* New York, 1968.

Brautigan, Richard. *The Pill Versus the Springhill Mine Disaster.* New York, 1968.

Brautigan, Richard. *Revenge of the Lawn; The Abortion; So the Wind Won't Blow It All Away.* Boston, 1982.

Cortes, Carlos. *Portuguese Americans and Spanish Americans.* New York, 1981.

Dary, David. *Seeking Pleasure in the Old West.* New York, 1995.

Didion, Joan. *Run River.* New York, 1963.

Didion, Joan. *The White Album.* New York, 1979.

Edwords, Clarence E. *Bohemian San Francisco.* San Francisco, 1914.

Fisher, M.F.K. *Among Friends.* New York, 1971.

Fisher, M.F.K. *The Art of Eating.* New York, 1954.

Gillenkirk, Jeff, and James Motlow. *Bitter Melon: Stories from the Last Rural Chinese Town in America.* Seattle, 1987.

Hart, James D. *A Companion to California.* Berkeley, 1987.

Haslam, Gerald. *Coming of Age in California.* Walnut Creek, Calif., 1990.

Haslam, Gerald. *Okies: Selected Stories.* Layton, Utah, 1975.

Hemp, Michael Kenneth. *Cannery Row.* Pacific Grove, Calif., 1986.

Kaufman, Polly Welts, editor. *Apron Full of Gold: The Letters of Mary Jane Megquier, 1849–1856.* Albuquerque, N.M., 1994.

Loftis, Anne. *California: Where the Twain Did Meet.* New York, 1973.

Mangelsdorf, Tom. *History of Steinbeck's Cannery Row.* Santa Cruz, Calif., 1986.

McCunn, Ruthanne Lum. *Chinese American Portraits.* San Francisco, 1988.

Paquette, Mary G. *Lest We Forget: The History of the French in Kern County.* Fresno, 1978.

Sokolov, Raymond. *Why We Eat What We Eat.* New York, 1991.

Steinbeck, John. *Cannery Row.* New York, 1945.

Steinbeck, John. *The Harvest Gypsies.* Berkeley, 1936.

GUIDEBOOKS
Carter, Bob. *Food Festivals of Northern California.* Helena, Mont., 1997.

Carter, Bob. *Food Festivals of Southern California.* Helena, Mont., 1997.

Fish, Tim, and Peg Melnik. *The Napa and Sonoma Book.* Stockbridge, Mass., 1992.

Landau, Carol, and Katie Landau. *California Festivals.* San Francisco, 1993.

Marinacci, Mike. *Mysterious California: Strange Places and Eerie Phenomena in the Golden State.* Los Angeles, 1988.

Unterman, Patricia. *Food Lover's Guide to San Francisco.* San Francisco, 1995.

WINE AND SPIRITS
Balzer, Robert Lawrence. *California's Best Wines.* Los Angeles, 1948.

Conrad, Barnaby, III. *Absinthe: History in a Bottle.* San Francisco, 1988.

Conrad, Barnaby, III. *The Martini.* San Francisco, 1995.

de Villiers, Marq. *The Heartbreak Grape: A California Winemaker's Search for the Perfect Pinot Noir.* New York, 1994.

Fisher, M.F.K. *The Story of Wine in California.* Berkeley, 1962.

Jones, Idwal. *Vines in the Sun.* New York, 1949.

Laube, James. *California Wine.* New York, 1995.

Ray, Eleanor, with Barbara Marinacci. *Vineyards in the Sky.* Stockton, Calif., 1993.

Robinson, Jancis, editor. *The Oxford Companion to Wine.* Oxford, England, 1994.

Roby, Norman S., and Charles E. Olken. *The New Connoisseurs' Handbook of California Wines.* New York, 1992.

Thompson, Bob. *The Wine Atlas of California and the Pacific Northwest.* New York, 1993.

INDEX

Honey-Ginger Mustard, 421
Mustard Cream, 381
Mustard Glaze, 349
Mustard Vinaigrette, 152

N

Nachos, California, 70
Nectarines, Grilled, 438
Noodle Salad, Glass, 144
Noodle Soup, Asian, 96
Nopales, 253
California Quesadillas with
Nopales, 252
California Succotash, 392
Chorizo and Nopales Pizza, 363

O

O Olive Oil, 125
Oceanside Seafood Salad, 142
oils, storing, 153
Olive, Green, Chicken Salad, 145
Olive Harvest Lamb, 348
Olive Mustard, California, 422
Olive Oil
about, 12–13
uses for, 216
Olive Risotto with Basil, 228
Olive Tapenade, 422
Olive-Basil Pasta, 204
Olympia Oyster Cocktail, 30
omelets, 193–94
Onions
Braised Artichokes and Onions,
249
Grilled Spring Onions, 395
Marinated Onions, 428
Onion Pie with Pancetta, 197
Red Onion Tart, 396
storing, 398
Orange Salad, Antonio's, 136
Orange Zest Pasta, 81
Oranges with Vanilla Sugar, 442
Ortega, Emile, 238
Ortiz, Joe and Gayle, 170
Otis, Johnny, 239, 240
Oysters, 31, 277
Hangtown Fry, 275
Olympia Oyster Cocktail, 30
Oyster Chowder, 103
Oyster Loaf, 176
Oysters on the Half Shell, 29
Spicy Grilled Oysters, 32
varieties of, 31

P

Paddleford, Clementine, 236
Pancetta, Onion Pie with, 197
Papaya with Lime, 441

Pappardelle with Walnuts and Dry
Jack, 204
Parsley Salad, 119
Pasta, 204
Armenian Pilaf, 222
Bacon, Chèvre, and Dried
Tomato Pasta, 214
Beet Pasta, 204
Black Pepper Pasta, 204
Bustelo's Pasta al Zinfandel, 210
Carrot-Cumin Pasta, 204
Chester's Garlic Pasta, 205
Chicken Pasta with Rosemary,
212
Fresh Pasta, 203
Garlic Pasta, 204
Linguine with Artichokes and
Clams, 211
Linguine with Chèvre, Herbs,
and Tomatoes, 208
Linguine with Dungeness Crab,
210
Macaroni and Cheese, 215
Nicolle's Pasta Salad, 135
Olive-Basil Pasta, 204
Orange Zest Pasta, 81
Pappardelle with Walnuts and
Dry Jack, 204
Pasta with Blackeye Peas, 209
Pasta with Chicken, Olives, and
Dried Tomato Cream Sauce,
214
Pumpkin-Rosemary Pasta, 204
Seared Tuna with Pasta and
Cilantro Relish, 301
Seed Pasta Salad with Golden
Tomatoes, 133
Spaghetti with Tapenade, Basil,
and Tomatoes, 207
Spaghettini al Pesto, 206
Summer Pasta Salad, 134
Pastry (See also Dough)
Pastry Dough for Pies, 444
Pastry for Savory Tarts, 396
Pastry for Savory Turnovers, 17
Pastry for Sweet Tarts, 397
Peaches
Grilled Peaches, 438
Peach Chutney, 425
Peach Daiquiris, 479
Peach Pie, 444
Peach Soup, 78
Peaches and Blackberries with
Vanilla Brandy, 442
Peanut, Coconut-, Sauce, 48
Pears
Avocado and Pear Salad with
Smoked Chicken, 147

Brie, Pear, and Prosciutto Pizza,
28
Green Tomato–Pear Chutney,
426
Pear Gingerbread, 446
Pears Poached in Red Wine, 445
Peas, Blackeye, Pasta with, 209
Pellier, Louis, 447
Pepper Salsa, Roasted, 65
Peppers, Red, Roasted, 7
Persimmon Bread, 167
Persimmon Ice Cream, Mrs.
Hoover's California, 462
Pesto, Spaghettini al, 206
Phony Abalone, 309
Pies (See also Tarts)
Cranberry-Walnut Pie, 454
Onion Pie with Pancetta, 197
Pastry Dough for Pies, 444
Peach Pie, 444
Soda Springs Mud Pies, 455
Tamale Pie, 359
Walnut Pie, 455
Pilaf, Armenian, 222
Pineapple Agua Fresca, 472
Pineapple Vinaigrette, 156
Pineapple-Chipotle Salsa, Grilled,
70
Piroshki, Potato and Walnut, 265
Pizza
Avocado-Zucchini Pizza, 262
Brie, Pear, and Prosciutto Pizza,
28
Chorizo and Nopales Pizza, 363
Pizza Dough, 262
Smoked Duck Pizza with
Caramelized Onions, 325
Strawberry-Chèvre Pizza, 264
Summer Margherita Pizza, 263
Plum Sauce, Sweet-and-Sour, 36
Plum Soup, 77
Polenta, Creamy, 347
Polenta, Oven, 256, 347
pomegranate seeds, about, 132
Pork (See also Sausages)
Border Town Chipotle Pork, 373
Brie, Pear, and Prosciutto Pizza,
28
California Eggs Benedict, 192
Cloverdale Meatball Soup, 109
Fresno Roast Pork with Hot
Spiced Raisins, 370
Grilled Pork Chops with
Salvador's Salsa, 368
Hamhock and White Bean Soup,
99
Jook with Pork and Greens, 220
Patterson Pork Loin, 369

Perry's Pork Chops, 366
Pork and Green Chile Tamales, 364
Roasted Garlic Meatballs, 45
Roasted Garlic Meatloaf, 361
Solvang Roast Pork with Prunes and Apples, 371
Thai Meatballs with Coconut-Peanut Sauce, 47
Portobello Mushroom Sandwiches, 175
Portuguese Kale Soup, 108
Portuguese Shellfish Stew with Sausages, 286
Pot Roast, California, 356
Potatoes
  Avocado Mashed Potatoes, 398
  Braised Artichokes and New Potatoes, 383
  Marshall House Potato Salad, 150
  New Potatoes with Golden Caviar, 37
  Perfect French Fries, 397
  Potato and Walnut Piroshki, 265
  Potato Salad with Chèvre Mayonnaise, 130
  Potato Salad with Grilled Steak, 149
  Potato-Cheddar Soup, 93
  Potatoes and Zucchini in Parchment, 400
  Potatoes in Parchment, 399
  Roasted Rosemary Potatoes, 399
  storing, 398
  Tweet's Potato and Mushroom Tart, 400
Prawns (See also Shrimp)
  Caesar Salad with Grilled Prawns, 121
  Fresh Tomato Aspic with Prawns and Aïoli, 220
  Grilled Prawns with Strawberries and Fennel, 34
  Jook with Prawns, 220
  Prawns with Honeyed Walnuts, 278
Preserved Lemons, 429
Preston, Lou, 170–73
Preston, Mark, 354
Prune Cake, Thirty-six Lady, 448
Pumpkin
  Baked Miniature Pumpkins, 402
  Pumpkin and Roasted Garlic Soup, 91
  Pumpkin Empanadas, 17
  Pumpkin Risotto with Spinach and Garlic, 230

Pumpkin-Rosemary Pasta, 204
puree, to make, 231

Q
Quail, Robert's Lavender, 335
Quail with Apple Cider Sauce, Forestville, 334
Quan, Frank, 287
Quesadillas, California, 251
Quesadillas, Chicken, 307
Quince Poached in White Wine and Honey, 449

R
Radicchio, Braised, 403
Radishes with Butter and Coarse Salt, 5
Ragout, Bean, 236
Ragout, Mushroom, with Oven Polenta, 255
raisins, about, 371, 427
Rasmussen, Rikka Ann, 163, 371, 460
Raspberry Coleslaw, 127
Raspberry Lemonade, 469
Raspberry Mayonnaise, 418
Raspberry Mignonette, 30
Ratatouille, Garden, 257
Rebagliati, Jorge, 90, 319
Red Beans and Rice, 239
Red Chard with Corn, Shrimp, and Garlic Sauce, Kasma's, 391
Red Gazpacho, 84
Red Onion Tart, 396
Red Raspberry Vinaigrette, 155
Red Snapper, Grilled, 291
Red Wine Vinaigrette, 152
Reichardt, Jim, 328
resources, for California products, 484–90
Rey, Frank, 233–34
Rhubarb-Strawberry Chutney, 426
Rhubarb-Strawberry Tart, 451
Rice (See also Risottos; Wild Rice)
  Armenian Pilaf, 222
  Basic Steamed Rice, 217
  Eleanor's Rice with Dulse, 221
  Firehouse Clams and Rice, 273
  Green Rice Torta, 233
  Jasmine Rice, 218
  Jook, 219
  Mexican Rice, 222
  Mexican Rice and Bean Salad, 133
  Persephone's Salad, 132
  Red Beans and Rice, 239
  Roast Turkey with Auntie Ellen's Rice Stuffing, 331

Spanish Rice, 221
Spicy Beef Strips and Rice Balls, 44
Steamed Brown Rice, 218
Thai Chicken and Rice Soup, 106
Rick, Charles, 180
risottos, 223–33
Rochioli, Joe, xxii, xxiii
Roelz, Axel, 150
Rosemary, Chicken Pasta with, 212
Rosemary Potatoes, Roasted, 399
Rosemary-Lemon Marinade, 213
Roshi, Suzuki, 217
Russian River Valley viticultural area, xxii–xxiv

S
Sackett, Georgia, 233–34
Sage and Dry Jack Scones, 164
salads, 113–58
Salami Sandwiches, Italian, 179
Salmon
  Grilled Salmon with Thai Chile Sauce, 298
  Jook with Grilled Salmon Fillet, 220
  Poached Salmon, 296
  Roasted Salmon with Asparagus Risotto, 299
  Roasted Salmon with Corn Risotto, 299
  Salmon Chowder with Ginger and Lemon Grass, 104
Salsa Cruda, 57
Salsa Mexicana, 57
Salsa Verde, 253
salsas, 53–71
salt, about, 5
Salvador's Smoked Tomatillo Salsa, 61
samjan sauce, 354
Sanddabs, San Francisco, 288
sandwiches, 174–80
Sangrita, Larry's Jailhouse, 475
Santa Catalina island, 375
Sardines, 33, 292–93
  Grilled Sardines, 32
  Sardines in Garlic Butter, 33
Satan's Lily Soup, 89
Sauces
  Avocado Sauce, 63
  Basic Tomato Sauce, 26
  blackberry sauce, 299
  Cilantro Sauce, 285
  Coconut-Peanut Sauce, 48
  garlic mojo sauce, 354
  Golden Tomato Concassé, 98
  Golden Tomato Sauce, 27